Richard B. Peiser and David Hamilton | **THIRD EDITION**

PROFESSIONAL REAL ESTATE
DEVELOPMENT | THE ULI GUIDE
TO THE BUSINESS

Copyright 2012 by the Urban Land Institute

Printed in the United States of America. All rights reserved. No part of this book may be reproduced in any form or by any means, electronic or mechanical, including photocopying and recording, or by any information storage and retrieval system, without written permission of the publisher.

Urban Land Institute
1025 Thomas Jefferson Street, NW
Suite 500 West
Washington, DC 20007-5201

Recommended bibliographic listing:
Peiser, Richard B., and David Hamilton. *Professional Real Estate Development: The ULI Guide to the Business*. Third Edition. Washington, D.C.: Urban Land Institute, 2012.

Library of Congress Cataloging-in-Publication Data

Peiser, Richard B.
Professional real estate development : the ULI guide to the business / Richard B. Peiser and David Hamilton. -- 3rd ed.
   p. cm.
ISBN 978-0-87420-163-5
1. Real estate development. I. Hamilton, David. II. Title.
HD1390.P45 2012
333.3068--dc23
                            2012016521

ULI Catalog Number: P101

About the Urban Land Institute

The Urban Land Institute is a non-profit research and education organization whose mission is to provide leadership in the responsible use of land and in creating and sustaining thriving communities worldwide.

The Institute maintains a membership representing a broad spectrum of interests and sponsors a wide variety of educational programs and forums to encourage an open exchange of ideas and sharing of experience. ULI initiates research that anticipates emerging land use trends and issues, provides advisory services, and publishes a wide variety of materials to disseminate information on land use development.

Established in 1936, the Institute today has nearly 30,000 members and associates from some 92 countries, representing the entire spectrum of the land use and development disciplines. Professionals represented include developers, builders, property owners, investors, architects, public officials, planners, real estate brokers, appraisers, attorneys, engineers, financiers, academics, students, and librarians.

ULI relies heavily on the experience of its members. It is through member involvement and information resources that ULI has been able to set standards of excellence in development practice. The Institute is recognized internationally as one of America's most respected and widely quoted sources of objective information on urban planning, growth, and development.

Project Staff

Gayle Berens
Senior Vice President
Education and Advisory Group

Adrienne Schmitz
Project Director and Editor
Senior Director, Publications

James Mulligan
Managing Editor

Joanne Platt
Publications Professionals LLC
Manuscript Editor

Betsy VanBuskirk
Creative Director

John Hall Design Group
Book and Cover Designer
www.johnhalldesign.com

Craig Chapman
Senior Director, Publishing Operations

About the Authors

RICHARD B. PEISER

Richard B. Peiser, PhD, is the first Michael D. Spear Professor of Real Estate Development in the Department of Urban Planning and Design at the Harvard Graduate School of Design (GSD) and director of the university-wide Real Estate Academic Initiative. Before coming to Harvard in 1998, he was associate professor of urban planning and development at the University of Southern California where he founded and directed the Lusk Center for Real Estate Development, and the Master of Real Estate Development Program.

At Harvard, he founded and directs the Advanced Management Development Program and coordinates the other executive education programs in real estate at GSD, as well as joint real estate programs with Harvard Business School. He directs the Master of Urban Planning Concentration in Real Estate and cochairs the Master of Design Studies Program in Real Estate and Project Management at GSD.

Peiser has published over 100 articles in academic and professional journals. His primary research focuses on developing an understanding of the response of real estate developers to the marketplace and to the institutional environment in which they operate, particularly in the areas of urban redevelopment, affordable housing, and suburban sprawl. His current research is on urban modeling using Los Angeles as a test case, and nonperforming loan resolution. His other books in progress are on high-end luxury retail development and on the economics of new towns around the world. He teaches real

estate development and finance as well as field studies on complex urban development problems.

Professionally, he has developed affordable housing in Texas and California as well as land and industrial properties. From 2004 to 2007, he served as a founding partner of the China Real Estate Investment Company and its Shanghai-based subsidiary KaiLong REI Project Investment, investing institutional capital in real estate projects in China's major cities. He is also a valuation and economic-damage expert for litigation with respect to apartments, land, office, and retail development projects and portfolios.

Peiser was born in Houston and grew up in Dallas. He received his BA from Yale University, his MBA from Harvard University, and his PhD in land economy from Cambridge University. His first teaching appointment was at Southern Methodist University in Dallas. He has held visiting appointments at Stanford and Cambridge universities, Seoul National University, the University of Ulster, and the University of Regensburg. He is a former trustee of the Urban Land Institute and former coeditor of the *Journal of Real Estate Portfolio Management* and currently serves on the board of Berkshire Income Realty, Inc., a publicly traded company based in Boston, and on the Board of Overseers for the New England Wildflower Society.

DAVID HAMILTON

Trained as an architect, David Hamilton has managed innovative real estate development projects on a variety of scales, ranging from medical and university campuses to award-winning high-tech office and R&D spaces. As a codirector of the Cambridge Innovation Center, he managed the design and construction of a widely acclaimed private sector incubator for technology-related business. As a principal of Qroe Farm Preservation Development, Hamilton led project design, entitlement, and construction efforts for Bundoran Farm in Charlottesville, Virginia, widely regarded as a model for sustainable development. He speaks and writes on the role of private sector development in the management and preservation of large-scale working landscapes, and the implications of exurban development on agricultural land uses. As chief operating officer of Qroe's affiliate Geobarns, he has been recognized as a leader in the development of new models of sustainable, affordable homebuilding and light commercial construction.

Hamilton has contributed to various ULI publications on topics ranging from inner-ring suburban regeneration to conservation development strategies. He teaches introductory real estate finance and development courses and advises design students on project economics at Harvard University's Graduate School of Design. He is a graduate of Middlebury College and Harvard University, where he cowrote *The Harvard Project on the City: Lagos*. Hamilton lives in Middlebury, Vermont.

Authors

PRIMARY AUTHORS

Richard B. Peiser
Michael D. Spear Professor of Real
  Estate Development
Harvard University Graduate School
  of Design
Cambridge, Massachusetts

David Hamilton
Principal
Qroe Farm Preservation Development
Boston, Massachusetts

CONTRIBUTING AUTHORS

Sofia Dermisi
Professor of Real Estate and Pasquinelli
  Family Distinguished Chair
Walter E. Heller College of Business
Roosevelt University
Chicago, Illinois

Alex Duval
Director
Portman Holdings
Atlanta, Georgia

Nick A. Egelanian
Founder and President
SiteWorks Retail Real Estate
Annapolis, Maryland

PRIMARY CONTRIBUTING AUTHORS, PREVIOUS EDITIONS

Ken Beck
Senior Vice President
ASW Realty Partners
Woodland Hills, California

Anne B. Frej
Real Estate and International
  Development Consultant
Santa Fe, New Mexico

Dean Schwanke
Senior Vice President
Urban Land Institute
Washington, D.C.

Frank Spink
Principal
Spink Consultancy
Annandale, Virginia

ADDITIONAL CONTRIBUTORS

James McCandless
Vice President
Streetsense
Bethesda, Maryland

William Shewalter
Principal
Vistacor Development Company
Boca Raton, Florida

Paul Vogel
Executive Vice President
RDR/SiteWorks
Chicago, Illinois

ULI STAFF CONTRIBUTORS

Adrienne Schmitz
Senior Director, Publications

Ronnie Hutchinson
Intern

REVIEWERS

Heather Arnold
Director of Market Analysis
Streetsense
Bethesda, Maryland

Ryan Beible
Senior Construction Manager
First Potomac Realty Trust
Bethesda, Maryland

David Falk
Senior Fellow
School of Public Policy
University of Maryland
College Park, Maryland

David Farmer
Managing Principal
Keystone LLC
Naples, Florida

Roy Higgs
Chairman Emeritus
Development Design Group, Inc.
Baltimore, Maryland

Nick Javaris
Cofounder
Terranomics Retail Services
San Francisco, California

Jeff Kingsbury
Managing Principal
Greenstreet, Ltd.
Indianapolis, Indiana

Steven LaPosa
Assistant Professor, Finance and
  Real Estate
Colorado State University
Fort Collins, Colorado

Tom Moriarty
Principal
The Eisen Group
Washington, D.C.

H. Pike Oliver
Senior Lecturer in City and Regional
  Planning
College of Architecture, Art and
  Planning
Cornell University
Ithaca, New York

Yaromir Steiner
Chief Executive Officer
Steiner + Associates
Columbus, Ohio

STUDENT REVIEWERS

Jeremy Hoffman
J. Matthew Ritz
John Sheff
Carolina Uechi
Graduate School of Architecture,
  Planning & Preservation
University of Maryland

Contents

Contents | CONTINUED

FOR SUPPLEMENTAL MATERIALS, SEE WWW.ULI.ORG/PRED.

Preface

Real estate developers face an awesome responsibility. The communities and buildings they create become the fabric of our civilization. They influence people's lives in a multitude of ways. What they build affects how near or how far people come to realizing the lifestyle of their dreams. Developers play a key role in determining the financial health of cities and the everyday experiences of their inhabitants. Where people play, work, and shop; how long it takes them to get there; and the quality of the amenities and environment that they find all depend to a large extent on the work of developers.

Developers face a much more complex world than they did even 20 years ago. Everyone has a stake in their activities. The days are past when a developer could unilaterally decide what he wanted to build and then build it without consulting community leaders, neighbors, and others affected by the development. The political, environmental, and financial context is changing just as rapidly as the market itself. In the 1990s, the development industry went through the most wrenching adjustment since the Great Depression as a result of overbuilding in virtually all segments of the industry combined with the collapse of the S&L industry. In the wake of the global financial crisis of 2008–2009, the real estate industry once again endured wrenching changes as commercial mortgage–backed securities (CMBSs) and other securitized financing vehicles collapsed, 8 million homes went through foreclosure, unemployment rates soared, and burgeoning debt forced enormous cutbacks in government spending and private debt. The latest cycle has

had very different impacts from those of the S&L crisis, with more regional differences depending on the extent of overbuilding.

Three major changes have occurred over the last ten to 20 years that have affected the development industry dramatically: globalization and institutionalization of ownership, securitization in the financial markets (notwithstanding the CMBS collapse), and the technological revolution. These changes create both opportunities and obstacles for beginning developers. Entrepreneurial development is harder today than it was 30 years ago—it requires more capital to get started and more time to get projects off the ground.

At a time when the development industry is undergoing such rapid change, why do we need a book on how to develop real estate? First, if sound development principles had been practiced by all the developers of real estate who lost their buildings in the recent down-cycles, much of what was built would have never been conceived, let alone financed. Second, the recovery phase of the real estate cycle is the best time for newcomers to enter the development business.

Third, qualified developers will always be necessary, and they should have the best possible training. The incredible pace of development in emerging markets such as Brazil, China, and India creates an enormous need for people with development skills. Development is not for amateurs. When projects go bankrupt or are poorly designed, the whole community loses, not just the developer and his financiers. Why should tenants have to put up with poorly designed spaces? Why should

communities have to suffer the tax losses of ill-conceived projects and unoccupied buildings?

Successful development requires understanding not only how to develop good real estate projects but also how to determine their impacts on neighborhoods and cities. Long-term real estate values are directly tied to the quality of the urban areas where they are situated. Developers must take an active role in protecting and enhancing the long-term economic health of the cities in which they build.

Although this book was conceived as a practical guide for developing five major real estate types—land, residential, office, industrial, and retail—it is intended to do much more. Successful developers must have a thorough understanding of urban dynamics, of how and why cities grow. They must be informed critics of architecture; they must be knowledgeable about construction, law, public approvals, and public finance; and they must have the fundamental real estate skills in finance, market analysis, leasing and sales, and property management. Real estate development is the art—and, increasingly, the science—of building real estate value by managing development risk. Development expertise can be applied to much more than building new buildings and subdivisions. Development talents are essential for such activities as buying empty office buildings and leasing them, renovating older warehouses, repositioning shopping centers by changing the tenant mix, securing development entitlements for raw land, and buying distressed debt and workout properties from banks and turning them around.

Development is exciting because it is dynamic. The conditions that enabled developers to be successful in the latter part of the 20th century are different from the ones that will govern in the 21st century. As the conditions change, so will the skills that developers require to be successful. This book presents the collective wisdom of developers in both successful and unsuccessful projects, acquired throughout their careers. It is organized by property type to emphasize the different risks and concerns of particular products. The overall steps, however, are the same.

The challenge of building more livable cities can only be met by qualified developers working together with other real estate professionals, public officials, and neighborhood representatives. Perhaps the greatest challenge is to evolve a fairer and more efficient development process—one that reflects the needs and aspirations of all groups while eliminating the many hurdles that raise the costs of development without providing commensurate benefits. Of one thing we can be certain: the expertise that developers require will be different tomorrow from what it is today. Let us hope that tomorrow's developers are equipped to meet the challenge.

Acknowledgments

The third edition of *Professional Real Estate Development: The ULI Guide to the Business* is the culmination of four years of work begun in 2008. As did the previous two, this third edition benefits from over 100 new interviews, all new case studies, and new spreadsheets reflecting current rents, costs, and taxation.

Since the new edition's inception, the world has gone through the global financial crisis and the United States has experienced the deepest recession since the Great Depression. Interestingly, the book's first publication in 1992 dealt extensively with the S&L crisis of the late 1980s. A constant theme emphasized by many of the contributors to the new edition is how they have dealt with the enormous consequences for real estate from the economic cycles.

In every sense of the word, this book is a cooperative effort. I have been blessed with wonderful students over the years at Harvard and previously at the University of Southern California. This edition is the collaboration of three of my best former students at Harvard: David Hamilton, Sofia Dermisi, and Alex Duval. David Hamilton is fully my coauthor. Indeed, he has taken the lead on updating a majority of the chapters. Each of the product chapters has been revised by a single author. David Hamilton revised chapter 3 on land development, a chapter to which he contributed significantly in the previous edition. I focused on multifamily residential development in chapter 4. Sofia Dermisi revised chapter 5 on office development. And Alex Duval revised chapter 6 on industrial development. Nick Egelanian, a retail consultant, revised chapter 7 on retail development. Each chapter has entirely new case studies,

updated exhibits, financial information, and spreadsheets. I would also like to acknowledge Wynne Mun's work on the spreadsheets in chapter 4. He brought his extraordinary talents to bear on both the programming and the presentation of the five stages of analysis.

David and I are forever grateful to Adrienne Schmitz, who not only is the official ULI editor of the book but also has guided the book's development at every step of the way. The current edition stands on the shoulders of the two previous editions. The handiwork of my previous ULI editors and coauthors—Anne Frej and Dean Schwanke—is evident throughout the new book. They bear no responsibility for errors or omissions in the latest edition, but the new edition would not be what it is without their enormous contributions.

David and I have relied on the help of a series of research assistants from among my best students at Harvard Graduate School of Design. Sara Lu, Corey Zehngebot, and Lily Gray did admirable work on interviews with developers, preparation of the apartment case study, and follow-up of editorial questions. GSD doctoral candidate Kristen Hunter did a superlative job of conducting and compiling numerous interviews for chapter 4, and with Arianna Sacks updated the industry-wide survey presented throughout chapter 1.

David also wishes to thank a number of industry leaders and young professionals who answered his question "what's happening now in real estate?" when it seemed every potential answer might be proved wrong by the next week's unprecedented events. Zvi Barzilay, Steve Kellenberg, and Elizabeth

Plater-Zyberk shared their insights on new residential communities. David Goldberg, Stewart Fahmy, and Matt Kiefer contributed on regulatory and entitlement issues. Chris Lewis updated our compensation survey. Judi Schweitzer and Joel Kotkin educated the authors on demographic and market trends; Toni Alexander and Chad Rowe updated our thinking on sales and marketing. Rob Bowman and John Fullmer of Charter Homes and Kevin Wronske of the Heyday Partnership contributed their excellent professional projects to the financial analysis and development case studies in chapter 3. John Knott, Buzz McCoy, and Don Killoren each offered a depth of insight commensurate with their reputations and too broadly influential on the text to cite here. Finally, David wishes to thank his wife Hillary for her support and forbearance during this project, which has been as stimulating as it was daunting. After two years of interviews, David wishes to report that the leadership in our field is strong and intellectually engaged with the issues of the day, and is looking forward to the opportunities of the coming decade.

Sofia Dermisi wishes to thank Dan Schuetz for the Denver case study and Debbie Moore, Jess Arnold, and Natasha Dasher for the Houston case study in the office chapter. Alex Duval would like to acknowledge the outstanding help of Thomas Gibson and Allen Arender of Holladay Properties for the case study in the industrial chapter and the input of Jay Puckhaber on many other issues in the chapter. Nick Egelanian is grateful to Roy Higgs, Nick Jaravis, James McCandless, William Shewalter, Yaromir Steiner, and Paul Vogel for pulling together information and offering their guidance and expertise.

As in previous editions, I owe a tremendous debt to friends and mentors from ULI. Some of them are no longer with us—Charlie Shaw, Harry Newman, Bob Baldwin, and Charlie Grossman in particular. This book reflects the wisdom of a number of industry giants whom I have been privileged to know—Gerald Hines, Joe O'Connor, Jim Chaffin, Stan Ross, and Buzz McCoy—as well close friends from academia—Bill Poorvu, John McMahan, and Alex Garvin. I am especially grateful to my colleague and coteacher of the field studies classes at Harvard, Bing Wang, who has pushed forward the boundaries connecting real estate and design. I am grateful to my colleagues at Harvard and USC who have helped to forge my views about urban development over the years—Alan Altshuler, Alex Krieger, Arthur Segel, Peter Gordon, Rahul Mehrotra, Jerold Kayden, Carl Steinitz, and Tony Gomez-Ibanez, as well as colleagues from other schools—Richard Arnott, Alex Anas, Jim Berry, Alastair Adair, Karl Werner-Schulte, and Glenn Mueller.

All these people deserve credit for helping make this third edition as good as possible. They are absolved of any mistakes, the full responsibility for which is our own.

Last but not least, my wife Beverly has endured the absences and preoccupation to get the book finished. I cannot thank her enough for all that she does for me. It is to my children and my students that this book is dedicated in the hope that the knowledge and practice of real estate development, in its fullest meaning, will be better tomorrow than they are today.

Richard B. Peiser

PROFESSIONAL REAL ESTATE
DEVELOPMENT | THE ULI GUIDE
TO THE BUSINESS

1

Introduction

What Is a Developer?

Few job descriptions are as varied as that of real estate developer. Development is a multifaceted business that encompasses activities ranging from the acquisition, renovation, and re-lease of existing buildings to the purchase of raw land and the sale of improved parcels to others. Developers initiate and coordinate those activities, convert ideas on paper into real property, and transform real property into urban fabric. They create, imagine, finance, and orchestrate the process of development from beginning to end. Developers often take the greatest risks in the creation or renovation of real estate—and they can receive the greatest rewards.

Developers must think big, but development is a detail business. Successful developers know that they must double- and triple-check everything. The clause overlooked in a title policy or the poorly done soils test can have serious consequences. Developers are ultimately responsible for their projects, and even if someone else is negligent, developers must deal with the consequences of an error or omission. A good developer is flexible, ready for the unexpected, and adaptable to rapidly changing conditions. During the approval process, for example, a developer must often negotiate with neighborhood groups that seek major changes to a proposed project. If the developer is unwilling to compromise or if the project has been conceived in a way that does not allow flexibility, the group could have the power to kill the project altogether. A developer must be able to address all stakeholders' concerns without compromising the project's economic viability.

Managing the development process requires special talents—not the least of which is common sense. Developers must have a clear vision of what they want to do; they must also demonstrate leadership to communicate and deliver that vision. Successful developers by nature often have strong opinions, but they must be good listeners and collaborators. They cannot possibly be authorities on the myriad fields of expertise involved in a project, so their success depends on their ability to coordinate the performance of many other parties—and on their judgment and skill in putting those inputs together in a coherent way.

Developers work with a variety of people and groups: most obviously, building professionals, including surveyors, planners, architects, and other designers; specialized consultants, contractors, and tradespeople; and tenants and customers hailing from many different businesses—sometimes with divergent goals. Developers must work closely with attorneys; bankers and investors; planners; elected and appointed officials at the city, regional, and state levels; and an increasingly complex network of regulators and inspectors. In addition to professionals, the developer must communicate effectively with citizens groups, homeowners associations, and community organizers with varying degrees of sophistication. Success comes from knowing the questions to ask and whom to ask, having a familiarity with best practices and rules of

In La Quinta, California, Wolff Waters Place provides rental housing for low-income families. The project is certified LEED Silver and Gold.

thumb, and being able to sift and evaluate conflicting advice and information.

The spark of creativity—in designing, financing, and marketing—can distinguish successful developers from their competitors. Management of an innovative project team is a balancing act. Too much guidance may stifle creativity; too little may lead to a chaotic process and unmanageable results. Obtaining creative, cutting-edge work from the team without exceeding the budget is one of the fundamental challenges of managing the development process, and it requires the combination of a rigorous overall process along with room for flexible exploratory work within this regimen.

Real estate development is an organic, evolutionary process. No two developments are exactly alike, and circumstances in a project change constantly. For beginners, development often appears easier than it is. Most beginning developers have to work harder than seasoned professionals to keep a project moving in the right direction.

Solving problems as they occur is the essence of day-to-day development, but anticipating the unexpected and managing the risks are the keys to a satisfying career. Laying the necessary groundwork before an important meeting, arranging an introduction to the best prospective lender, creating the best possible setting for negotiations, and knowing as much as possible about the prospective tenant's or lender's needs and concerns before meeting with them will help ensure success.

Many developers say that it is better to be *lucky* than *good*. According to Phil Hughes, president of Hughes Investments, Inc., "In this business you'd better be lucky *and* good. Luck may be where opportunity meets preparation, but in our business the developer makes his own preparations and his own opportunities, and it is up to the developer to introduce the two."[1]

The Book's Approach and Objectives

This book is directed to beginning developers and other professionals who work in or around the real estate industry. Readers are assumed to be familiar with at least one or two segments of this industry, through their daily activities, academic training, or personal investment. Even seasoned professionals may gain a better understanding of the role they play in the development process: What are the rules of thumb concerning the way developers do business with them? What are the critical elements affecting the success of the development? Why does the developer, for example, care about the concrete contractor's slump test? What type of certification enables a developer to close a permanent mortgage? In short, how does the detailed business of development make great places?

This book addresses in detail five major types of development that beginning developers are most likely to undertake: land subdivision, multifamily residential, office, industrial, and retail. Single-family housing is not addressed except insofar as land developers sell subdivided lots to homebuilders. Each of the five product types is described from start to finish: selecting sites; performing feasibility studies; evaluating alternative approaches; identifying markets and tailoring products to them; financing the project; working with

Understanding the Real Estate Industry

The real estate industry is divided into five main product types: residential, office, commercial, industrial, and land. The market for each product type can differ dramatically by region and by location relative to employment centers, transit stops, or other location factors. Interestingly, such historic correlations of value and location no longer necessarily hold across the board. Some suburban nodes, for example, boast office rents higher than their center cities, and examples abound of formerly blighted neighborhoods rapidly gentrifying as they become appealing to changing residential preferences. These kinds of shifting parameters illustrate the successful developer's need for intellectual curiosity and openness to continuing improvement and education.

Building design and site density represent two other primary dimensions for categorizing different segments of the property market. Each combination represents a different building type, cost structure, and end-user profile. For example, high-rise apartments with structured parking cost much more to build and operate than do garden apartments. Rents must be higher, and to be successful, the market study must demonstrate sufficient unmet demand for units from higher-income people who want high-rise rental apartments in a given location. Choices made in development must continually balance market demands with project economics.

contractors; and marketing, managing, and selling the completed project.

The development process, although similar for each product, is different in detail and emphasis. For example, preleasing is not necessary for apartment development and has no meaning for land development, yet it is critical for office and retail development. Likewise, market analysis for industrial buildings is highly specialized, versus residential or other commercial uses.

The book contains three main parts: an introduction to the development process, discussions of individual product types, and a look at trends in the industry. Chapters 1 and 2 contain an overview of the development process, paths of entry into the business, and strategies for selecting and managing the development team. Chapters 3 through 7 describe development of the five main product types. Chapters 3 and 4 also provide detailed step-by-step summaries of the core processes for development analysis and will serve as references for the other product types. Because many steps are the same for all income property types, chapter 4 describes in detail certain steps common to all product types, such as how to calculate financial returns for the overall project and for individual joint venture partners. After reading chapters 3 and 4, readers should then turn to the sections of the book that concern the particular product type in which they are interested. A final chapter discusses industry trends, emerging issues, and the developer's social responsibility. Case studies at the ends of chapters 4, 5, 6, and 7 show how the principles discussed in the chapters are used to develop actual projects.

The breadth and detail of this book should not be considered a substitute for remaining up-to-date with market and regulatory conditions. No two communities, and no two projects, are alike, and despite the long history of real estate development, nearly everything is subject to change. New regulatory approaches, construction innovation, even Supreme Court cases can upend longstanding best practices and standards presented in this book. Although this book is intended to be a primer covering all aspects of development, it is no substitute for expert local advice from experienced developers and professionals involved in the process.

A wealth of information is available online to facilitate every step of development—from real-time market analysis and local demographics to government approvals and financing. Indeed, one of the most important trends today is the impact of technology on the conduct of the development process.

Requirements for Success

Developers take risks. At the low extreme of the risk spectrum, developers may work for a fee, managing the development process for other owners or investors. In this role, they might incur a small degree of risk from investing some of their own money in the venture or having an incentive fee that depends on their bringing the project in under budget or with faster leasing at higher rents. At the other extreme, developers can undertake all the risk, investing the first money in the project, taking the last money out, and accepting full personal liability. Failure could mean bankruptcy.

Developers also manage risk. They minimize, share, hedge, or eliminate risk at each phase of the development process before moving forward. They attempt to minimize the risk at an early stage to make sure that the risk of investment for upfront costs—when a project's prospects are most uncertain—is balanced with the likelihood of success. Beginning developers must usually accept greater risk than experienced developers do, because beginners lack a strong bargaining position to transfer risk to others. They must often begin with projects that experienced developers have passed over. Beyond this basic truism, though, Phil Hughes argues that beginning developers often take on more risk than they have to. They need to look harder to find the right opportunity, but every project includes opportunities to reduce risk.

Many people are attracted to development because of the perceived wealth and glamour associated with the most successful developers. To be sure, development can offer enormous rewards, tangible and intangible. Besides the economic considerations, many developers relish the role of creating lasting contributions to the built environment. The feeling of accomplishment that comes from seeing the result of several years of effort is, for this type of person, worth the trouble and sleepless nights along the way.

Development's risks, however, require a certain kind of personality. Individuals must be able to wait a relatively long time for rewards. Three or more years often pass before the developer sees the initial risk money again, not to mention profit. Generally, this delay is growing as projects and approvals become more complicated. Developers risk losing everything they have invested at least once, and sometimes several times during the course of a project. Events almost never go exactly as planned, especially for beginners or those moving into new product types or markets. Developers must be able to live with some level of constant risk.

Development can be extremely frustrating. Developers depend on a variety of people outside their own organization to get things done, and many events, such as public approvals, are not under the developer's control. One developer recalls that when he started developing single-family houses, he often became frustrated when work crews failed to show up as promised. Only after he learned to expect them not to show up and was pleasantly surprised when they did, did building become fun. The public approval process has become much more time-consuming and costly over the last two decades, greatly reducing the developer's control over the process and adding considerably to risk, especially in the early stages when risk is already highest.

The impact of local politics on real estate development cannot be overstated, especially for a beginner. A project's feasibility is a function not just of market demand but also of what the local jurisdiction demands. A project might work financially but if local officials, or neighborhood activists, don't agree, approvals will not be granted, and the project will not go forward. It is crucial for the developer to build a good relationship with local officials and the community and to understand their interests.

Until beginners develop sufficient skill and self-confidence, they should probably work for another developer and learn about the process without incurring the risk. Even with experience, developers often start with a financial partner who bears most of the financial risk. One way to limit risk is to start on projects that involve leasing or construction risk but do not involve all the risks in a completely new development: an apartment renovation, for example. In any event, one should start on projects where the at-risk investment can be lost in its entirety without causing undue stress.

Even the smallest projects today typically require $50,000 to $100,000 cash up front, or "pursuit capital," to advance it to the point where equity and debt funding can be raised. A developer should never begin a project without having at least twice as much cash on hand as seems necessary to get the project to the point where other funding is available. The upfront cash is only part of the total cash equity that a developer will need to complete a project. Most lenders today require a developer to invest cash equity to cover 25 to 40 percent of total project cost. Total cash equity need not be in hand or even sufficient to purchase the land, but it should carry the project through to a point where the developer can raise other funds from investors or lenders or has cash flow from operations.

Developers can limit risk substantially by taking care in their acquisition (see chapter 3). For example, closing on land should take place as late in the process as possible. If 60-day or 90-day closings are typical in a community, beginning developers should look first for a land seller who is willing to allow 180 days. The land might cost more, but the added time may be worth the difference. If public approvals such as zoning changes are necessary, developers can often make the necessary approvals a condition of purchasing the land. Doing so will allow developers to shift some of the risk of approval to the seller, and it will align seller and buyer interests in the approval process. If public approvals or financing falls through, the developer will avoid spending precious capital on sites that cannot be developed profitably. Purchase options on property that provide control over a site without having to purchase it immediately are one of the greatest tools for developers. They reflect the developer's ability to negotiate and to satisfy the seller's needs at the same time.

Raising equity for one's first deal is perhaps the biggest hurdle for beginning developers. In general, developers want equity that is available immediately. If they have to raise it before they can close on a property, sellers become nervous about their ability to close and are less willing to let them tie up the property in the first place. Options may overcome many financial obstacles with creatively constructed purchase agreements, but sellers must have confidence that financing is available.

Beginning developers often do not have established sources of equity unless they have sufficient funds out of their own pocket or from family or business connections. Even if the equity funds are not guaranteed, one must have them at least tentatively lined up before entering into a purchase contract. In most cases, investors want to see what they are investing in before they commit funds. They should, however, be precommitted to the extent possible. The developer secures such commitments by speaking to potential investors in advance and soliciting their interest in investing in the type of property, location, and size that the developer plans to find. Investors are more eager to invest when it is clear that the developer has done the homework, that is, investigated the local market carefully to demonstrate in advance that demand for a certain product exists, and that costs and regulations will enable the developer to meet this demand. The message for prospective investors is straightforward and may even be formalized with a strategic partnership or memorandum of understanding: if the developer can find a property that meets certain already-identified specifications, then investors would be interested in supplying equity for the deal. Equity requirements and rules of thumb on terms for outside equity are discussed in detail in chapter 3, but this area is particularly prone to change. In particularly hot markets, developers may find a sense of urgency among potential equity partners, desiring to get in on a prospective deal. In a downturn, equity retreats, and equity terms will become dearer, or investment may not be available under any terms. Investor intent, even written intent, is never a guarantee.

Although problems are inevitable, they almost always have solutions. Fortunately, the development process becomes easier as developers gain experience and undertake successive projects. Beginners spend lots of time pursuing capital for projects, but once a track record is established, they may discover that lenders are calling them to offer to do business.

The most difficult project is the first one, and if it is not successful, a beginning developer may not get another chance. Thus, selecting a project that will not cause bankruptcy if it fails is imperative. Because of increasing difficulty in obtaining public approvals and financing, a developer should not be surprised if he has to attempt five or more projects before one gets underway.

Paths for Entering the Development Field

No single path leads automatically to success in real estate development. Developers come from a variety of disciplines—real estate brokerage, mortgage banking, consulting, homebuilding, commercial construction, lending, architecture, planning, and legal services, among others. Academic programs that award master's degrees in real estate development typically look for students who are already experienced in one field but who want to become developers.[2]

FIGURE 1-1 | The Partnership Continuum

	ADVISORY	PARTNERSHIPS			ACQUISITION
	Developer is hired by owner as consultant to provide advice and project management services	Owner retains possession of land with developer managing process and sharing in profits	Property is transferred to a new entity jointly owned by developer and owner	Owner gives developer option to acquire property, which closes following completion of planning and permitting	Developer acquires property from owner "as is" at agreed-on fixed price
ROLES/CONTROL					
Owner	Planning direction and approval of all aspects	Planning direction and approval of major project components	Early planning direction and share of major decision making	Early planning direction	Very limited role
Developer	Management of process subject to owner approval	Management of process subject to owner approval of plan, budget, and major decisions	Management of process provided certain benchmarks are being met	Management of process if meeting milestones; complete responsibility after acquisition	Complete responsibility for development process
CONTRIBUTION					
Owner	Land and all project costs, including developer fees	Land and project costs	Land and share of project costs	Seller note to finance portion of acquisition cost	None
Developer	Expertise and experience	Partial deferral of fees	Share of development costs	All project costs, land deposits, and required acquisition equity	All acquisition and project costs
COMPENSATION					
Owner	All sales revenue (including "profit")	Most profits from project	Land value; priority return on land value and capital contribution; split of profits	Land value	Land value, discounted for entitlement risk
Developer	Fees for time, paid current	Fees for time, partially paid current; percentage-based incentive fee	Agreed-on fee for management role; priority return on capital contribution; split of profits	Development fees and project profits	Development fees and project profits

Most people learn the business by working for another developer. Jobs with developers, however, are very competitive. Moreover, many jobs that are available with developers do not provide the broad range of experience needed. Although larger developers usually hire people for a specialized area, like property management, leasing, sales, or construction, the ideal entry-level job is to work as a project manager with full responsibility for one or more small projects, or to work for a small firm that provides the opportunity to see and do everything.

Some positions in the real estate industry make it easier to move into development. Many developers start as homebuilders, then move vertically into land subdivision or expand laterally into apartment or commercial development. Others begin by constructing projects for other developers. Developers might start as commercial brokers, using a major tenant-client as an anchor to develop a new office building or finding a site to develop for a build-to-suit tenant. Developers might also start as mortgage brokers; by controlling a source of funding, a mortgage broker could make the transition to development by overseeing the financial side of a joint venture with an experienced developer. Many experienced developers are willing to undertake joint ventures with a new partner if the partner brings a deal to the developer that strategically expands his current business.

Finding the First Deal

One of the most famous teachers of development, James Graaskamp, emphasized that to start, beginning developers must control at least one of four assets—land, knowledge, tenants, or capital. If they control more than one, the task becomes easier. If developers control land, then the task is driven by supply—a site looking for a use. If developers control knowledge or tenants, then the task is driven by demand—a use looking for a site. If they have capital, they have a choice.

Thin Flats, an infill condominium project in north Philadelphia, was developed by Onion Flats, LLC, a small, family-run firm. The eight-unit development is certified LEED Platinum, in part for its green roof, solar water heating, and rainwater harvesting that reduce energy and water consumption by an estimated 50 percent.

TIM MCDONALD

MARIKO REED

A USE LOOKING FOR A SITE

All development is ultimately driven by demand. Determining who needs space—potential buyers or tenants—and what type of space they need is the starting point for all development projects. The initial market analysis should define the gaps in the market and the product or products that will fill them.

Knowledge can take several forms. Many developers capitalize on their familiarity with a particular local market gained from their previous experience in the field. Knowledge of the marketplace can give beginning developers the competitive edge they need—where space is in short supply and which tenants are looking for space, for example. The ability to convince potential lenders and investors that the market exists with supporting evidence in the form of market research data or letters of intent from prospective tenants is an invaluable asset for beginning developers, as they do not have a long track record to prove their capabilities.

For commercial developers, whether they are beginners or seasoned, finding the tenant/user is the most important task. Quality tenants can help draw lenders or investors and can overcome resistance from neighboring homeowners or government agencies. Their creditworthiness is the key to financing new development because it is the tenant that makes the property valuable, not the building itself.

Many developers enter the business through contacts with potential tenants, perhaps by developing a new building for a family business or for the company for which they work. Knowing a particular tenant's needs and controlling its decision about location might enable the beginning developer who works for a firm to participate as a principal in the deal. Knowledge about sources of financing is another way to break into the business. Assisting an established developer who needs money or a friend who has control over a tenant to find a lender or investor can enable one to become a principal in his or her first deal. All these cases start with a use looking for a site, and the use defines requirements for the site. The developer's task is to find the site that best fits the demand.

A SITE LOOKING FOR A USE

Another possible starting point is controlling a well-located piece of property. Many developers start by developing family-owned or company-owned land. Others begin by convincing a landowner to contribute the land to a joint venture in which the developer manages the development. In both cases, development is driven by supply.

The first question developers must answer is, "What is the highest and best use of the land?" Developers must not only consider what offers the highest return (office buildings, for example), but they must also study demand for that product. Unless demand is sufficient, the site will not produce an attractive return.

At a given point in time, every site has a highest and best use that will maximize its value. Every potential buyer analyzes a property's highest and best use (and diligently compares it with other potential uses) before presenting an offer for a property, hoping to turn a profit. In fact, a property's selling price is determined by many buyers deciding what the highest and best use is and bidding accordingly. The owner's valuation of the site developed to its highest and best use at that time determines whether to go ahead with development or to wait.

Whether to develop immediately or to wait depends on an assessment of changes in use or density in the future. This calculation involves an understanding not only of market demand but also of town planning, infrastructure development, and the political and regulatory process. A tract at the corner of two highways on the edge of town, for example, might eventually make a good site for a shopping center; but if current demand for retail space does not justify a shopping center, the most profitable current use may be single-family lots. Waiting five years, however, would offer a higher profit because the shopping center could then be justified, but of course carrying costs, price changes, and regulatory risk might mitigate this differential. The apparently simple "highest and best use" analysis can quickly become dizzyingly complex, bearing on assumptions about timing, future value, and opportunity cost.

When the developer already owns the site, the market study should indicate what to build, how much to build, the expected sale price or rental rate, and the amount of time that sales or leasing will likely require. While the market study is underway, the developer should investigate site conditions (the area of land that is buildable, the percentage that contains slopes, environmental factors, flood and other safety issues, and so forth) and find out what public approvals are necessary.

The development strategy should be created once the developer has acquired information about the market, engineering, and environmental and public approvals needed. A large site does not necessarily need to be developed all at once. Financing capacity is usually limited by the combined net worth of the developer and his partners, including the unencumbered value of the land (land value net of loans).

Who Becomes Developers? How Do They Start?

ULI members who were identified as development professionals were surveyed about their experiences as beginning developers in August 2010. The following summary, based on the 239 completed surveys, gives an idea of the background of people in the development industry who are active in community development.

A PROFILE OF DEVELOPERS

All respondents are actively engaged in real estate development. Figure A shows the breakdown of the types of firms represented.

Figure B breaks down respondents' developments over the previous ten years by property type.

In addition to development activities, respondents had also been involved in the purchase of land and completed residential, office, retail, and industrial projects (figure C).

CAREER PATH TO DEVELOPMENT

Those surveyed identified their previous three positions. Respondents represented a broad range of experiences, including accounting, brokerage, construction, lending, real estate consulting, and law, among others (figure D). Other than development, project management was the most common step on the development career path. First jobs showed a wide range, indicating that brokerage and construction, among others, offer good entry points to development. Many respondents had spent time furthering their education, with 15 percent identifying it as a first step. Approximately 7 percent of respondents have held only one job on the way to their career, as indicated by the drop in responses as one moved from the first to the second job on the table.

The most popular product type for respondents' initial project was residential development (figure E). Their second and third projects were more evenly split among land development, residential, retail, and office development. The most popular product type for the developer's third project was evenly split between residential and office development. The increase in office development involvement likely occurred in part because by their third project, respondents had gained the greater experience required for office development.

In running their businesses, respondents devoted their primary attention to the front end of the development process: site acquisition, procurement of regulatory approvals, market analysis, and design (figure F). Site acquisition, the regulatory and approval process, and design and planning were most identified as the development phases developers had concentrated on.

LESSONS LEARNED

If they had the opportunity to redo their projects, most respondents would have done certain things differently. Many respondents highlighted mistakes made at the front end of their projects that came back to haunt them, such as team selection, due diligence, and the entitlement process. During planning and construction, the majority cited the importance of selecting competent, experienced team members and of effectively coordinating them. As James Ellison, cofounder of Mode Development, LLC, wrote: "Projects are very complex and are comprised of a very eclectic cast of characters. Your job as the developer is essentially the same as the director of a movie. You have to make the best of your location, get the best out of your actors, and stay within the budget of the studio all in a short period of time. Organization, accounting, relationships are all key." Having partners that understand your operations and vision is essential, and many respondents highlighted the importance of thoroughly vetting team members and joint venture partners.

Another major concern was being skilled at the intricate details of the approval process to avoid resource-draining delays. Many spoke of the importance of forming strong relationships with local regulatory bodies and bringing in the community early in the process. Brian McCarl, vice president of acquisitions for Newland Communities, echoed this sentiment: "Real estate is a unique endeavor that often engages community and political structures in decision making about how to deploy private capital for private ownership. All real estate is in essence a public/private partnership. Failure to factor in the public decision-making process and values into decision making is a good recipe for failure. Do your homework at the neighborhood, city, and state level before you invest and start spending money."

Another dominant concern was thorough due diligence in acquisitions. Many agreed that a bad acquisition is almost impossible to rectify, although many successful deals made their profits in the acquisition and entitlement phases. Land value comes through entitlements so developers should ensure that their acquisitions have approval strings attached. Understanding the market through extensive preliminary study will alleviate the risk of getting stuck with an unworkable project. As Michael Brodsky, CEO of Hamlet Companies, summed it up, "Time spent planning lessens time spent fixing." Many highlighted that developers should use the market to shape their decisions, think about the end user, and not seek to impose a use on a site. "Focus on what the market is and wants, not what you want or what zoning allows," wrote George Casey, president of Stockbridge Associates.

It is crucial to recognize which obstacles are immediate, short term, and temporary, and which ones are deal breakers. Many respondents addressed the importance of maintaining a critical distance from the project and allowing research and a conservative pro forma to generate a commitment to the deal—not an emotional excitement for building or site.

As Chris Squier, vice president of mixed-use development for Crosland Development, LLC, wrote, "Don't fall into the trap of entering into a project with a 'best case' pro forma that only gets worse as time goes on."

Many discussed the importance of knowing when to walk away. Although it is difficult to let go of a project, knowing when to cut losses differentiates successful developers. Stephen Arms, managing member of Marthasville Development, LLC, gave the following advice: "Don't be afraid to walk away from a project if conditions change. Believe in 'sunk cost' accounting (also known as the more common phrase 'don't throw good money after bad')."

Looking forward, a number of those surveyed commented on the increased importance of urban, mixed-use, and infill projects, as well as sustainable development. "Sustainable development practices are not optional. A balance between economic, environmental, and social objectives must be planned into every 21st-century project," advised Elias Deeb, president and owner of Cedrus, LLC.

FIGURE C | Projects Purchased by Respondents, Past Ten Years

	# Firms	%
Residential	460	34
Land development	449	33
Office	215	16
Retail	174	13
Industrial	67	5
Total projects purchased	1,365	100

FIGURE A | Firm Characterization

	# Firms	%
Small regional developer/owner	130	52
Large regional developer/owner	46	19
National or global developer/owner	32	13
REIT	10	4
Private equity/investment management firm engaged in development	10	4
Public or nonprofit developer/owner	9	4
Other	11	4

FIGURE D | Most Typical Career Paths to Development

	JOBS HELD (%)		
	First	Second	Third
Brokerage	14	6	4
Construction	12	6	6
Development	3	12	47
Project management	7	25	13
Real estate consulting	6	11	5
Student	15	10	8

FIGURE B | Projects Built by Respondents, Past Ten Years

	# Firms	%
Residential	1,874	48
Land development	742	19
Office	654	17
Industrial	374	10
Retail	292	7
Total projects built	3,936	100

FIGURE E | First Three Projects (%)

	First	Second	Third
Land development	31	23	18
Residential	36	33	27
Retail	10	19	19
Office	14	18	26
Industrial	9	7	10

FIGURE F | Primary Areas of Focus (%)

Focus	PRODUCT TYPE						Total
	Land	Residential	Retail	Office	Industrial	All	
Site acquisition	23	22	22	20	24	15	15
Regulatory approvals	20	17	15	10	3	21	17
Market analysis	10	10	8	10	9	7	9
Design and planning	11	13	13	17	6	13	13
Construction/development financing	5	11	10	10	9	11	9
Permanent financing	3	5	8	6	9	5	5
Joint ventures	8	7	7	10	6	9	8
Construction	5	9	6	9	12	8	8
Marketing/leasing	4	8	9	8	6	5	7
Operations/maintenance	4	4	6	7	9	3	5
General advice	5	5	5	5	9	4	5

FIGURE 1-2 | You Must Control One of These to Get Started

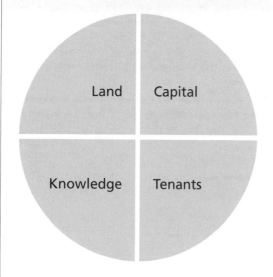

Land

Capital

Knowledge

Tenants

IMPROVING THE CHANCES OF SUCCESSFUL DEVELOPMENT

Selecting the location and type of the first development project should not be left to serendipity, nor should beginners necessarily grab the first opportunity they see. Failure will make it that much harder to obtain backing for another opportunity. The first deal (1) establishes the developer's track record; (2) sets the tone for the quality of future developments; (3) establishes an image in the marketplace; (4) creates a network of consultants, brokerages, and other business relationships for future deals; and (5) builds relationships with bankers and investors. Still, every beginning developer makes mistakes. One should get the best advice possible but not be afraid to make a decision and move on.

A maxim of development is that it takes just as long and is just as difficult to undertake a small deal as it is to undertake a large one. By this logic, developers should look for the largest deal they can confidently execute. Although the maxim is true to a degree for experienced developers and for large companies with overhead to amortize, it is not true for beginning developers.

A principal objective of the developer's first deal is to establish a track record, the absence of which is perhaps the beginning developer's greatest handicap, so the right size project is critical. A rule of thumb is to look for a project that can be put together in about

six months; one that is within the developer's financial capabilities—personal resources plus those that can be raised through family, friends, or other currently identifiable partners. A general rule of thumb is that the combined financial net worths of the partners must be at least as large as the project's total cost. In times of tight money, net worth requirements may be even greater.

Most projects today require substantial cash equity, which is often the determinant of a "doable" project: If lenders require 40 percent equity, for example, raising $400,000 equity for a $1 million project is much easier than raising $4 million equity for a $10 million project. If the developer has created value over and above the project cost, it may be possible to reduce the amount of cash equity required by the bank. *Value* is a function of signed leases and market rental rates. If the appraised value for a project costing $10 million to build were, say, $12 million, then a 70 percent loan would provide $8.4 million, leaving only $1.6 million of required cash equity.

In addition to preferring *smaller* deals, beginning developers should search for *simple* deals—deals that require fewer steps and a shorter time to bring to fruition.[3] Although small buildings can be just as complex as larger ones, the criteria for selection should emphasize projects that do not require a lengthy and uncertain process of public approvals.

One exception is that smaller "problem" deals may offer an opportunity that experienced developers have passed over. For example, larger developers may decide that a site requiring special attention to curing problems with easements, boundaries, or flooding is not worth the necessary time and effort. A beginner, however, might be able to tie up the property at little cost while working out the problems. Another opportunity can be found with sites owned by local and state governments and redevelopment agencies, because large developers may prefer to avoid government red tape. Unless the site is simply put up for auction, however, the beginner might need to demonstrate a track record to convince government officials to work with him. Nonetheless, keeping officials aware of continuing interest in a project as the government works through various procedures and public hearings can give the beginner an edge when the agency finally issues a request for proposals or advertises the property for sale.

In most cases, beginning developers must give personal guarantees to secure financing. Banks typically look at the net worth of the developers and partners in the deal before granting a construction loan. In some instances, however, the tenant's credit on a long-term lease or letter of intent may take the place of the developer's credit.

One advantage of developing a small part of a larger tract of land is that the rest of the land can be used as collateral for financing the first project. Defaulting on the loan, however, might entail loss of the entire site: once the land is pledged as collateral, the bank can foreclose on it after default to collect any balance owed.

Development projects that begin with a site looking for a use provide an attractive way for beginning developers to start, because they will not be required to locate and tie up land until a deal can be put together. Although such projects are perhaps the easiest way to get into development, the parcel in question may not be the best site to develop at a given time. Nevertheless, many properties can be developed profitably. Skillful developers can identify the most marketable use, determine a development strategy, and then implement it.

When money is more readily available, it becomes much easier for beginning developers to find financing. In such times, there is often more money available than there are "good deals." Another successful strategy for beginning developers who have extensive local relationships, especially brokers, is to meet in advance with potential financial partners (especially local private investors) to determine what kinds of deals they are looking for. Armed with this information, developers

The Concept of Present Value

An understanding of present value is essential for developers.[a] Present value analysis equalizes the *time value* of money. Because one can earn interest on money, $100 today will be worth $110 in one year at 10 percent interest and $121 in two years with annual compounding. Ten percent interest represents the *opportunity cost* if one receives the money in, say, two years rather than now, and meaningful comparison of sums accruing at different times requires discounting each to comparable present values.

The present value of $121, received in two years, is $100. That is, the *discounted value* of $121 at a 10 percent discount rate, received in two years, is $100 today. If the discount rate (opportunity cost rate) is 10 percent, then it makes no difference whether one receives $100 today or $121 in two years.

The formula for calculating present value is as follows:

$$PV = FV \left[\frac{1}{(1+r)} \right]^n$$

where *PV* is present value; *FV* is future value; *r* is the discount rate; and *n* is the number of years. Thus, the present value of $121 received in two years at a 10 percent discount rate is

$$PV = \$121 \left[\frac{1}{(1+0.10)} \right]^2 = \$100$$

The landowner's dilemma about developing the land immediately into single-family lots or waiting for five years to develop a shopping center is solved by applying present value analysis. Suppose, for example, that land for single-family development today is worth $100,000 per acre ($1,076,400/ha), whereas land for a shopping center would be worth $200,000 per acre ($2,152,800/ha) in five years. If the personal discount rate is 10 percent, then $200,000 to be received in five years is worth $124,184 today—clearly more than the value of the land if it is developed for single-family houses. The best option is to wait. In this example, if the discount rate is 20 percent rather than 10 percent, then the present value of $200,000 is only $80,375. At the higher discount rate, the best decision is to develop the land for single-family lots today.

Which discount rate—10 percent or 20 percent—is appropriate? The answer depends on risk. Generally, land development (except for single-family houses) is considered the riskiest form of development because of uncertainties about entitlements and market absorption, which are exacerbated by the length of the approval process. Development risk for buildings depends on local market conditions. Office development is considered riskier than industrial or apartment development because the lead time is longer and space has been oversupplied in many markets.

Because of the high rates of return and high risk associated with development, most developers have personal discount rates of at least 20 percent.[b] That is, they expect to earn at least 20 percent per year on their investment.

Discount rates consist of three components:

Real return rate + Inflation + Risk = Discount rate premium

or 3% + 5% + 12% = 20%

If inflation increases to 10 percent, then a developer's required return increases to 25 percent. The risk premium depends on the particular property and might range from as low as 4 percent for a completed office building to 15 to 20 percent for a recreational land development.

[a]For further discussion of present value, see Mike E. Miles, et al., *Real Estate Development: Principles and Process*, 4th Ed., Washington, D.C.: Urban Land Institute, 2007, pp. 207–209.

[b]Technically, the target discount rate is the rate for which the net present value of a project is greater than or equal to zero. When the NPV => 0, then it delivers a rate of return on equity that is => the discount rate. This discount rate is also known as the target internal rate of return.

can look for deals that meet the investor's preferences. If a suitable property is found, the developer can tie it up and present it to the financial partner quickly for a "go" decision. Time is critical: often the developer must "go hard" on the land purchase within 30 to 60 days, so having the financial partner ready and waiting to look at deals quickly is very important. When money is widely available, the market is likely to be hot, with lots of activity. In such times, sellers are more likely to demand shorter closing times and shorter free-look periods during which the buyer does feasibility studies before putting up a nonrefundable deposit ("going hard"). The customary amount of deposit, or terms of diligence, may increase in severity as well.

In the final analysis, a developer's strongest assets are a reputation for integrity and an ability to deal in good faith with a multitude of players. A large developer may be able to outlast the opposition in a contentious deal, but the best advice for a beginning developer is to avoid such situations altogether.

Managing the Development Process

Development is distinct from investment in *income-producing properties*, because it involves much more risk. Many firms and individuals invest in operating properties, buying existing properties and managing them for investment purposes. Investors often incur some risk in leasing and may make minor renovations that entail some construction risk. Developers, on the other hand, take on a set of additional development risks. Most developers also hold on to properties, at least until liquidity is required, after they are developed—that is, during the operating phase—thus incurring the ongoing risks associated with operations.

Developers may take on different degrees of ownership and risk depending on their ownership structure and the complexity of the project. Developers who operate alone and invest only their own money are said to be *100 percent owner/developers*. They furnish all the cash equity, accept all the risk and liability, and receive all the benefits. The concept of a 100 percent owner/developer is useful for quickly analyzing development opportunities, because if a project does not make economic sense in its entirety (as viewed by someone who has all the risks and rewards), it will make even less sense as a joint venture or other form of partnership.

No generally accepted definition exists to determine who is a developer and who is not, but a developer can be defined as the person or firm that is actively involved in the development process and takes the risks and receives the rewards of development.[4]

Many people involved in a development project incur risk. Those who design, build, and lease a building for a fee are agents of the owner and are developers insofar as they are engaged in the processes of development, but they incur no risk if the fee is fixed. If, however, the fee depends on the project's success, the individual accepts some performance risk associated with development. Development risk is associated with delivery of the entire project and thus may be distinguished from performance risk associated with individual tasks (such as contractors who accept construction risk when they have a fixed-price contract). Most rewards in development are proportional to the risk one takes on. Experienced developers are able to transfer some or most of the risk to others by using other people's money or by finding a lender who will give them nonrecourse financing (lending without personal liability). They still carry the burden of delivering a successful project, however. In almost all cases, developers will have something at risk, such as front money for feasibility studies, investment in preliminary designs, earnest money, or personal liability on construction financing.

Development companies increasingly serve as development managers for major institutions. In this role, they perform all the normal functions of developers except that they bear little or no risk. The institution—a bank, an investment group, an insurance company, a foreign corporation, or a major landowner—bears the risk. The developer works for a management fee and usually a percentage of the profits (10 to 20 percent) if the project is successful.

Historically, developers have preferred to own real estate rather than to manage it for others, because ownership has enabled them to leverage completed projects into new deals as they amass wealth. Nevertheless, major developers have increasingly accepted roles as managers, either to keep their staffs busy during slow periods or to enter new markets with minimal risk. Firms that succeeded in finding these scarce roles in the Great Recession of 2007–2009[5] have benefited from steady, though modest, cash flow.

Property management, brokerage, tenant representation, construction management, and other tasks in the skill set of developers can become, at any time, valuable, or at least sustainable, as service businesses. Developers building an organization should know, however, that in times of distress, competition for these service contracts increases dramatically, and banks and other property owners will find themselves in excellent bargaining positions for these services.

Truly outstanding or niche businesses stand a better chance of providing cash flow in these periods.

REAL ESTATE CYCLES

The adage "timing is everything" is especially applicable to real estate development. The importance of real estate cycles cannot be overemphasized. Like other large, capital-intensive purchases, real estate is highly sensitive to changes in interest rates and macroeconomic conditions like employment and migration. Income properties provide insufficient cash flow to be financed when interest rates move above certain levels. For-sale developments, such as housing subdivisions, office buildings, or residential condominiums, suffer from higher financing costs and from the effect of rising interest rates on the amount of money that potential purchasers can borrow. When rates are high, buyers tend to wait for them to come back down before buying a property. The development industry is further affected by high interest rates because development firms typically are smaller than most corporate bank customers. When money is scarce, lenders tend to prefer their non–real estate customers. Even very sound projects can be difficult to finance because lenders fear the unknown development risks.

The supply as well as the demand side moves up and down. Lenders often appear to exhibit a herd mentality, all seeming to prefer the same type of product or geographic area at the same time. Supply of investment capital follows product types through cycles. Successful residential subdivisions will draw additional investment, as they did in the Sunbelt in 2002 through 2005, until the moment when demand indicators, such as median home prices, begin to falter. Sensing, correctly or not, that the sector is overbuilt, lenders tighten underwriting standards for these projects. The resulting "credit crunch" can be sudden and, to the developer, overly drastic. Larger and multiphase projects, in particular, may find that tightening credit can affect even their performing loans, which may have been in place for many years.

One unintended consequence of the widespread availability of market data and business news seems to be that such turns in opinion can happen faster than ever before, with the shift from robust growth to pullback turning on a few indicators or opinion leaders, and on timescales that may not align with project funding needs.

Selecting the right time to enter development is crucial. Most beginning developers plunge ahead, regardless of the general economic climate, and often their success in financing the first project depends on their timing with respect to the cycle. Ironically, financing a project toward the end of a positive market cycle (when many lenders are enthusiastic about a particular geographic area and product type) is often easier. Toward the end of the positive cycle, however, risk increases as the competition for tenants or buyers intensifies. If supply becomes excessive, those who were the last to enter the market are usually the first to get in trouble, because their costs are higher and competition is fierce for tenants.

Even in a period of relatively stable overall economic growth, real estate markets are cyclical, as a result of the lagged relationship between demand and supply for physical space. Glenn Mueller, professor of real estate at the University of Denver, divides the market cycle into four distinct phases: recovery, expansion, hypersupply, and recession (see figure 1-4). Each phase is characterized by different changes in vacancy and new construction, as well as changes in rent. The position of property in the market cycle differs by property type and location. This type of analysis is helpful for understanding market timing—when the market is most favorable for new development.

A project launched early in the positive cycle means less competition for the developer, but it also means financing is likely to be scarcer. Long lead times required for finding the right site, designing the project, and receiving zoning and other public approvals mean that developers must be able to perceive new market opportunities before others do—often before they have become popular among lenders. The developer, then, will often have to convince lenders of an opportunity that is not obvious to all market players.

During the early stage of the development cycle, land is cheaper, terms are softer, and there is less entitlement and market risk. During later stages, landowners push more risk onto the developer. Developers may be required to take land down outright, with increased entitlement and market risk, as well as carrying costs. Closing times are shorter, and free-look periods are shorter or even unavailable for due diligence before contingencies are removed on purchase contracts.

How does a developer determine where a city is with respect to the economic cycle? General economic indicators, such as unemployment rates and business failures, provide information on general economic conditions. Although national conditions determine

Starting in Phase I—Recovery at the bottom of a cycle, the marketplace is in a state of oversupply from previous new construction or negative demand growth. At this bottom point, occupancy is at its trough. As excess space is absorbed, vacancy rates fall and rental rates stabilize and even begin to increase. Eventually, the market reaches its long-term occupancy average where rental growth is equal to inflation.

In Phase II—Expansion, demand growth continues at increasing levels, creating a need for additional space. As vacancy rates fall, rents begin to rise rapidly, pushing rents to cost-feasible levels. At this stage, demand is still rising faster than supply, and there is a lag in the provision of new space. Demand and supply are in equilibrium at the peak occupancy point of the cycle.

Phase III—Hypersupply commences after the peak/equilibrium point when supply is growing faster than demand. When more space is delivered than is demanded, rental growth slows and eventually construction slows or stops. Once the long-term occupancy average is passed, the market falls into Phase IV.

Phase IV—Recession begins as the market moves past the long-term occupancy average with high supply growth and low or negative demand growth. The extent of the down cycle is determined by the difference between supply growth and demand growth. The cycle eventually reaches bottom as new construction and completions slow or as demand begins to grow faster than new supply added to the marketplace.

FIGURE 1-3 | Physical Real Estate Cycle Characteristics

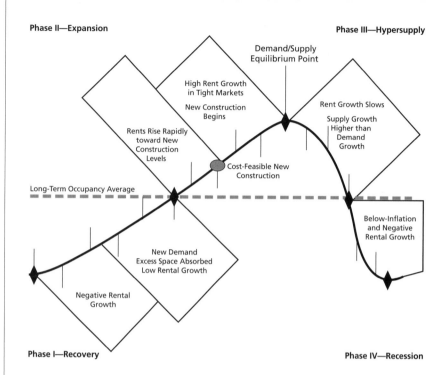

Source: Glenn Mueller, Legg Mason Real Estate, Baltimore, Maryland.

FIGURE 1-4 | National Property Type Cycle Locations

Phase II—Expansion

Phase III—Hypersupply

Retail—Factory Outlet +3
Senior Housing

Apartment +1
Office—Downtown

Long-Term Average Occupancy

Health Facility

Phase I—Recovery

Phase IV—Recession

Hotel—Full Service +1
Hotel—Limited Service +1
Industrial—R&D Flex
Industrial—Warehouse
Office—Suburban
Retail—1st Tier Regional Malls +1
Retail—Power Center +1
Retail—Neighborhood, Community +1

1st Quarter 2010

Source: Glenn Mueller, Franklin L. Burns School of Real Estate and Construction Management, University of Denver, Denver, Colorado.

fluctuations in interest rates and credit availability, local data are more relevant. As the local market starts to approach the top of the economic cycle, rent increases slowly, if at all, and the supply of new space increases faster than absorption of that space. The peak of the cycle passes when new supply exceeds absorption, causing vacancy rates to increase.

Real estate cycles create windows of opportunity for financing and strong market demand in advance of a large supply. If developers can synchronize their development efforts with the cycle, they can greatly improve their chances for success. The odds against beginners increase if they try to develop against the cycle. The biggest problem that beginners face is completing a suitable project within the window of time for which the market is favorable. The favorable window (Phases I and II in figure 1-4) may extend two to three years, but the chances for success decline significantly in Phase III, and financing may be almost impossible in Phase IV.

GETTING STARTED

The first step in the development process for beginning developers who do not already own land is to select a target market, in terms of both geographic area and type of product. Staying close to the area where a developer has done business for a number of years is a major advantage, for success often depends as much on personal relationships as on skill. All real estate is local, and knowing the market is critical to getting started. On the other hand, having a specific tenant or ultimate buyer is a powerful way to begin—anywhere. Except for major projects (high-rise office buildings, shopping malls, major business parks) for which nationally recognized developers compete, local players have major advantages over outsiders. They understand the dynamics of the local area. They know the direction in which the area is growing and how buyers, tenants, and lenders feel about various neighborhoods. They know a good price and where prices have been changing rapidly. They know whom to call when they need information or need something done. It may take a year or longer for a newcomer to begin to understand these factors.

Newcomers can *become* insiders, however, even if they are recent arrivals. The best way is to bring in a local partner who is well connected in the community—an especially important move if public approvals are required. Another way is to use banking connections from home to open doors in the new community. Whatever the approach, newcomers have to work harder to overcome the natural suspicion of

outsiders and to equalize the competitive advantage of local developers who have better information and more contacts.

After deciding *where* to do business, the next question is *what* to develop. For beginning developers, the answer is simple: develop a product with which you are familiar—provided that lenders will make the money available. Even developers with no experience can sell potential investors and lenders on their knowledge of the product type if they study the local market to determine rents, competition, the regulatory environment, local tastes, local construction methods, and the types of units or buildings in greatest demand. Although beginners can successfully branch out into a new product type, they lack the background to fine-tune information about design and construction costs or to predict potential pitfalls. Beginners who do branch out cannot work alone; they will probably have to bring in an experienced partner to get financing.

Identifying a product that the market lacks can make a project successful: finding that niche is the developer's challenge. Market niches are defined geographically and by product type. They can be as narrowly defined as, say, an apartment complex that has more two- and three-bedroom units than do other projects in the area or a multitenant warehouse building with front-loaded garages.

Designing for a specific market is how developers create a competitive advantage. Finding that special market, however, usually requires more than a good market study. It requires a perception of the market that other developers do not have, because if a market opportunity is obvious, another developer is probably already building to satisfy the demand. Thus, the beginner must understand the market well enough not just to act, but to do so before other developers see the opportunity.

STAGES OF DEVELOPMENT

The six main stages of development—feasibility and acquisition, design, financing, construction, marketing and leasing, and operations and management—are described for each major product type—land, apartments, offices, industrial space, and retail space—in chapters 3 through 7.

Figure 1-5 shows the timeline of development for an apartment building or small office building. The *development period* runs from the signing of the purchase contract for the land through lease-up of the building (Month 36). The development period covers

How Four Developers Got Started

CHICKIE GRAYSON

Chickie Grayson is the president and CEO of Enterprise Homes, Inc., where she has been for 23 years. Her interests in problem solving and "seeing something happen" originally attracted her to the profession. She says, "Seeing 'sticks and bricks' and knowing you're providing people with a great place to live, but also seeing homeowners and renters and how meaningful the development or new home is to them," are all very rewarding aspects to her job. She describes developments as "one big puzzle" and relates the need to have a lot of balls in the air; she enjoys keeping them moving in the right direction. Developers are the ones who coordinate all the players and really make the communities happen, she notes. She defines a good developer as someone who knows "a little about everything, not a lot about anything, but knows where to get it." Her secret to success is to constantly move things forward and not let any problems stop her.

Grayson's first development was four communities in Baltimore City, Maryland, for a total of 176 for-sale homes. The development and construction schedule was aggressive. The interest level was so high that the company was able to presell all the homes. The homes were modular and constructed in a factory, which helped with the fast-paced construction timeline. The funding for the development was a mix of federal (one of the last Urban Development Action Grants), state, city, and other resources. This mix remains typical of Enterprise's approach to financing developments today. Grayson has received many compliments from homebuyers. "I didn't buy a home; I bought a community," said one resident, reflecting the pride felt by both owners and renters, and the energy and hard work that the residents contributed to making a great place to live. Grayson feels that this is a sign of a successful partnership: "Enterprise provides the material; the community provides the pride. Enterprise works hard with the community beforehand to make sure they're providing the right product, then follows up afterward to learn about what the residents liked and what could be improved for the next project."

Typically, Enterprise's projects come in under budget. The staff works hard in the beginning to make sure that they have the numbers right; 50 percent of the work they do is up front, before they even close on a property. Grayson keeps a list of lessons learned and opportunities for future projects and shares advice from this experience. She says that utility companies can be challenging to coordinate but are essential to the project, so building good relationships with them is key for future developments. Soil problems can also slow projects down—they had significant problems in the Baltimore City development—and she recommends performing as many advance soils tests as possible.

Grayson offers advice for those starting out: "You don't need a lot of expertise; that will come on the job. You do need to be really curious and always learning." She identifies the challenge of always having enough capital as the most difficult part of getting started. "It typically takes two to four years to see revenue; meanwhile, you need to make money to stay in business, which requires capacity and expertise." Her approach to developing housing is twofold: "To develop, you need land, money, will, and perseverance. For success, you need a great product at a very competitive price."

TARA HERNANDEZ

Tara Hernandez is president of New Orleans–based JCH Development where she specializes in adaptive use of historic buildings for mixed-income and mixed-use projects. Public/private partnerships and complex financial structures are part of her expertise and competitive advantage.

After earning her master of science in real estate development from MIT in 1992, she returned home to New Orleans and began her own real estate development and consulting firm. She assisted the community development departments of several financial institutions and local nonprofits with their redevelopment efforts. Their primary mission was to redevelop blighted housing and restore neighborhoods in many historic districts in the city, through homeownership initiatives. Many of these efforts focused on Community Reinvestment Act goals. Additionally, she developed her own projects, with a similar strategy of restoring blighted housing into homeownership opportunities for market-rate households. She redeveloped in several neighborhoods throughout the city. The strategy was based on the results of her graduate thesis work on redeveloping neighborhoods. She was hired by a financial institution whose strategy included the redevelopment of a historic neighborhood adjacent to a credit union it had recently acquired. They targeted a 16-square-block area and acquired all the vacant and blighted residential buildings for redevelopment as single-family homes for first-time homebuyers. A pool of people were waiting to move in, she recalls, so the homeowners were actually able to participate in certain decisions, such as color selections for their units. These buildings were laid out in a "double-shotgun style" with one room adjacent to another and little privacy. She converted the old layout into single-family dwellings and created privacy for the future owners.

Hernandez looked for ways to collaborate with HRI Properties, whose owners she met while in school. On breaks from MIT, she would return to New Orleans and meet with members of the real estate community—from all aspects of the profession, including development, finance, and consulting. In this way, she began building relationships within the

New Orleans real estate community that still continue today. The principals at HRI continued to reach out to her for an opportunity to work together. Timing worked out well with an opportunity to redevelop a project in Shreveport that HRI was starting. That was a transitional time for her as she was expecting her first child and had an increasing desire to work on larger projects. She went on to redevelop several large conversions of historic industrial buildings into mixed-income lofts in Shreveport and New Orleans, Louisiana, as well as in St. Louis, Missouri. She also became a member of the executive team and worked at the firm for almost eight years.

After Hurricane Katrina, Hernandez decided to capitalize on opportunities for creative redevelopment. Creativity is one of the top traits that a developer must possess, she asserts, along with patience, persistence, and attention to detail. Above all, she believes the two keys to successful development are teamwork and communication. Her strategy has been to involve all team members early in the process (including investors, architects, and contractors) and to take a collaborative approach. Often, this approach manages time, minimizes errors, and provides an outlook of potential obstacles or challenges that the team may face.

As a result, all her projects have been completed on or ahead of schedule and on or under budget. On one project, a particularly effective aspect of this collaborative approach involved bringing in a facilitator every three months to mediate with key people on the team (including subcontractors) and to keep clear, honest communication. This process raised issues that may have otherwise gone unmentioned. "The culture and environment are better if you lay the cards on the table and keep everyone's interests aligned," she explains.

Another key element to her success is being proactive. She tries to anticipate as many unforeseen conditions as pos-

sible, and historic buildings often have many. "You're not going to think of everything," she cautions, "but if there's anything you're uncomfortable about, look into it and minimize the risk as soon as possible. You will never cover everything, but trying will help."

The most difficult part of starting a development company is the uncertainty. Funding predevelopment for an uncertain amount of time can be challenging, and nothing ever goes as anticipated. "There are usually one to two years of predevelopment; then you break ground and need time to lease it up," she explains. These prolonged periods can add up before one realizes any revenue. Often a new developer is required to pay out of pocket for all aspects of the predevelopment process, including funding approvals.

JCH Development has incorporated many sustainable aspects into its practice. The focus on historic adaptive reuse is a major element, since no demolition is required. One current example is the redevelopment of a former mayonnaise-manufacturing facility into Blue Plate Artist Lofts, comprising 72 mixed-income residences. The lofts will offer a preference for artists and will be built with sustainability in mind. JCH is also working with the local university to provide faculty housing close to campus, to place a priority on energy efficiency, and to sponsor a central recycling program for all its properties, helping to minimize waste, reuse materials, and recycle materials, such as extra wood and mulch. Through these commitments, JCH is able to implement some component of sustainability into every property. In addition, it is working on several retail projects that will help create urban mixed-use districts that employ innovative aspects of the urban environment. From the beginning, the team considers everything. "We build to a standard: would I want to live there and shop there myself?" Hernandez notes. Beyond that, they consider what might make

each property a unique experience and a standout from other developments. She concludes, "Historic buildings create opportunities to take advantage of things that are already in place. . . . You have to think through the future."

DON KILLOREN

A founding principal of Celebration Associates, based in Virginia, Don Killoren has been involved in the development of master-planned communities since 1979. He has served as general manager of award-winning communities throughout the Southeast and has been chair of ULI's Community Development Council.

After graduating from Georgia State University in 1972, Killoren began as an assistant property manager for John Portman in Atlanta and transitioned to the company's development team, focusing for four years on the development of Atlanta's Peachtree Center. Killoren counsels those entering development to work first for someone else, seeking out a capable and inspiring individual, and to worry about the specific job later. "Find a leader, someone who is nurturing and who lights a fire under people. It helps if the organization is small . . . allowing the beginner exposure to all aspects of the business, rather than to a limited administrative, analytical, or marketing role."

Having gained property and project management skills, Killoren left to work with Thomas E. Lewis, former legal counsel of Portman Properties, managing a 2,500-acre (1,012 ha) community in Florida and broadening his expertise to residential land development and homebuilding. As president of Lewis-Killoren Properties, Killoren says he began to discover his real talent for process management, organization, and coordination of the entitlement, development, and construction process. "Many people in the real estate business misdiagnose their skills," says Killoren. He counsels beginning developers to consider their strengths and weaknesses, as the diversity of project types and job descriptions in real estate means there are lots of opportunities for individuals to do jobs they are only mediocre at. He advises young developers to focus on the parts of development where they excel and to find partners, staff, and consultants to do an equally good job on the tasks outside your "sweet spot."

Joining community developer Erling Speer, Killoren helped develop the ULI-award-winning Mariner Sands golf course community and country club, where he began to understand the increasing importance of "software," or community organizations and programming. Increasingly integrated and sophisticated structures for clubs, community governance, and educational functions have grown from their beginnings in golf course development to become a part of most master-planned communities, and Killoren foresees the trend continuing. "Education, health care, and community-based volunteerism are all becoming a more integrated part of the community development toolkit, and real estate project managers must manage these entities with the same intensity they apply to physical planning and construction. We're moving from building stuff to building community."

Following his tenure at E. Speer & Associates, Killoren joined the Walt Disney Company as director of community development. As part of Disney's expansion from core entertainment and hospitality businesses into community development, Killoren was tapped for a leading role in the development of large retail and mixed-use residential projects, including the new town of Celebration, Crossroads Shopping Center, and the Magnolia Creek community. Celebration, particularly, served as a laboratory for refinement of new urbanist ideas, and the architectural precedents and controls there have informed Killoren's efforts to shape identity in subse-

quent projects. Lessons learned on these Florida projects were exported, as Killoren assisted in the shaping of residential development strategy for EuroDisney, near Paris.

In addition to development projects, Killoren spearheaded a company-wide environmental strategy, culminating in the creation of the Disney Wilderness Preserve. This 12,000-acre (4,856 ha) preserve is essentially a giant wetland mitigation project, offsetting impacts from Disney's and other entities' development activities, which has been managed according to state-of-the-art resource management plans. The result is a national model for ecological restoration and sustainable land management and a crown jewel in the Florida Nature Conservancy.

With several major projects under their belt, Don Killoren and Charles Adams left Disney in 1997 to found Celebration Associates (CA), a development and advisory firm. The decision to strike out on their own was difficult, but Killoren recalls, "Development at Celebration was winding down, several of the key players in the division had left, and we found ourselves knowing a lot about building the types of projects others wanted to build, and wanted to see built in their communities." CA's first client was its former employer, the Walt Disney Company.

Assembling a partnership, CA assessed its strengths and divided tasks into financial (primarily Adams), planning and development (primarily Killoren), and sales and marketing (shared responsibility). Building a team, the partners looked for "smart, energetic, and intelligent utility players" who could manage many different kinds of activities. In the early years of the partnership, they focused on consulting, requiring less capital investment, and structured deals to work toward sweat equity positions. To maintain a lean structure, they depended on consultants for virtually all nonexecutive functions. They still prefer to staff projects, rather than the central

office, but have expanded to a group of partners that oversees particular areas of expertise, such as sales and marketing or design, in all CA projects, even as these individuals may take a particular role within one or more project teams.

The firm has built strategic alliances with a major landowner-investor and developed several linked communities in Clear Springs, South Carolina, as well as the Governor's Club community in Chapel Hill, North Carolina. It has also partnered with Crosland, Inc., a diversified development and construction firm in Charlotte, to develop the award-winning Homestead Preserve and Bundoran Farm communities in Virginia, and more recently the redevelopment of the Mount Washington Resort in New Hampshire.

As the extended recession has slowed development projects across the Southeast, Killoren has come to appreciate the lessons learned in prior downturns over his career. CA's early and necessary emphasis on consulting, which the partners have maintained over the years as a means of "keeping sharp," has become an essential strategy of survival for firms like Celebration Associates. The company's relatively lean corporate structure and dependence on consultants and strategic partners have enabled it to adapt more nimbly than most, and its facility with financial reporting and investor communication, honed in a large organization, has preserved its reputation in a time when all developers are having unpleasant conversations with lenders and investors.

Reflecting on his nearly 40-year career, Killoren says his most important lesson has been that for an individual to succeed in development over the long haul, his interest cannot be solely financial. "It has to be about more than money. A good developer is giving an enduring gift to the community. Find something you like, do it well, and make that amount of money adequate."

JAIR LYNCH

Jair Lynch is the president and CEO of JAIR LYNCH Development Partners, "an urban regeneration company that specializes in the responsible transformation of urban markets." His career inspiration began at Stanford during his undergraduate years, where he studied urban design and civil engineering. He started there two months before a significant earthquake shook San Francisco. Lynch recalls that this event turned the city "into a laboratory for urban designers and civil engineers. Questions arose, such as what happens when you remove a highway from a city? Highways had been dividing the community for years, and it was fascinating to watch the city rebuild." Travel also influenced Lynch's passion for urban environments. As a world-class athlete (his impressive résumé includes winning a silver medal on the parallel bars as captain of the U.S. Olympic gymnastics team in 1996), he has enjoyed traveling to many cities across the globe. What fascinates him most? "How cities and places have evolved over time, and how things work," he shares.

After graduation from Stanford, Lynch's first job in the development world was for Silicon Graphics, Inc., as a project engineer/manager in its Real Estate and Development Department. The company was a manufacturer of high-performance computing solutions, and its business strategy was to attract the best talent by providing new amenities and developing facilities around the country and the world. Because the company was accustomed to young people in positions of leadership, Lynch was allowed much more responsibility than he might have had elsewhere as a 24-year-old without much experience. As he says, "They gave me a tremendous amount of latitude and allowed me to make decisions beyond my level of experience. On the other hand, I had a 24-year-old's perspective and knew what kinds of things young programmers would want

in their work environment." Lynch assisted in creating innovative workplaces with amenities such as juice bars and yoga studios that are now considered standard in the high-tech industry. The Mountain View Campus was later sold to Google for its headquarters.

He worked at Silicon Graphics for only four years, but gained an extraordinary amount of experience since development in the Silicon Valley moves so quickly. He says that the most critical aspects of his first experiences were the latitude and responsibility that he was given, the speed of the decision-making process in Silicon Valley, and his desire to learn.

The next stage that significantly influenced Lynch's career path occurred at Harvard University, where he focused on his ideas about development and created a hierarchy approach to urban regeneration. His framework blossomed into a structure that he calls "The Five Stages of Development." The five-stage progression is categorized as "1: Neglect; 2: Hope; 3: Rebirth; 4: Awareness; 5: They're there" and represents a perspective that is central to the way he approaches projects today.

In 1998, Lynch moved back home to Washington, D.C., but not many developers there were convinced that opportunities existed in the urban neighborhoods. He opened his own firm out of necessity and a drive to have a positive effect on neighborhoods. His company's first project was the Thurgood Marshall Center—a rehabilitation of the first African American YMCA, repurposed as a mixed-use complex of offices, a conference center, and a school. The project had financing and construction issues, but the most challenging part was making the deal bankable. "It languished for a long time with the grand idea of being one use—a museum. It needed to be mixed-use, but getting people used to that idea was challenging." In addition, the zoning had to change in order for mixed use to even be an option,

and many minds had to be convinced for that to happen. Lynch finally knew that the project would materialize when the financing was secure. Bringing in an anchor tenant was key to obtaining the financing; until that point, it could have not happened. As part of the financing structure, the firm received federal funding through a Community Development Block Grant.

This project set the stage for Lynch's business model and led to a more robust thesis on the reimagining of places. His firm focuses on places, not just buildings. It is committed to taking care of endangered places so they don't get swept away by market swings. Regeneration typically takes 10 to 20 years for the whole process; as a young firm, the partners have not been able to follow one neighborhood from Stage 1 through Stage 5 yet, but that is the goal. Lynch asserts that defining these stages and positioning themselves to follow a neighborhood through each are one way to hurdle the high barrier of entry in the field of development. He elaborates, "Often, complex financing is involved. If we can provide a visioning and a master plan, later come back with a library, and later with a hotel, we can build a longstanding relationship with the neighborhood and develop a level of trust that it would take other developers longer to earn."

Lynch attributes his success to his ability to evolve and not to get stuck in particular formats. "Being someone who creates new environments, you have to be willing to change dramatically. This involves recognizing new definitions of urban conditions." His desire to be part of that change is one of the reasons he is so resilient. His primary advice for emerging developers is to recognize the value of getting access to processes and systems very early and learning the basics. "There is a lot of leakage in real estate, and trying to do things on your own too early can cause inefficiencies."

all the major development risks, including financial, construction, and marketing. The *operating period* technically runs from the certificate of occupancy (when the building is ready for occupancy) until the building is sold. The *stabilized operating period* runs from the time the building is fully leased until it is sold. The stabilized operating period is the time frame used for standard appraisals of the building's value.

The stages can overlap considerably. In the timeline, *predevelopment* covers the period from first identification of the development site to the start of construction. In figure 1-5, predevelopment is shown as the first 12 months. Ideally, this period would be reduced to four to six months, allowing the developer to start construction at the same time the land deal is closed. Reducing the predevelopment period is difficult to achieve, but the shorter the period, the lower the cost and risk.

Four of the six stages of development occur during predevelopment: feasibility studies, design, financing, and marketing. In fact, a developer should be reasonably confident about the prospects for success on a project before he even signs the initial purchase contract. Developers rarely "go hard" (remove contingencies) on the purchase contract until they are very confident that they can obtain all necessary public approvals to build what they want and can raise all necessary financing for it. The primary purpose of predevelopment is to give the developer the necessary confidence to move forward. Before closing on a new project, a developer should be almost absolutely certain that the proposed project can be developed profitably according to his plans and objectives.

Figure 1-6 summarizes the steps common to developing most types of property—determining a project's feasibility, design, financing, construction, marketing, operation, and management. It illustrates a fundamental principle of development: that development is an iterative process in which the developer obtains more and more precise information in each iteration until he has enough confidence in the information to make a go/no-go decision. As figure 1-5 shows, certain steps can be taken simultaneously, whereas others must be taken sequentially. For example, active preleasing for an office building begins as soon as preliminary design drawings are ready to show to prospective tenants. Preleasing occurs throughout the development period, from financing through construction.

In Seattle, Washington, Rainier Vista Community is a transit-oriented development with access to light rail and major bus lines.

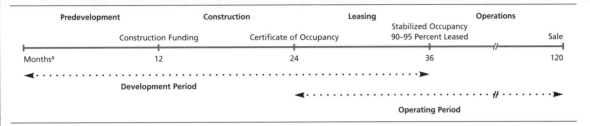

*Time varies widely according to a project's size, complexity, and location. Predevelopment may take two to four years or more in California but require only 90 days in some other parts of the country.

Analysis of the numbers becomes more detailed and more sophisticated at each step. The initial contract for earnest money may require only a simple capitalization analysis to see whether or not land cost yields the desired overall return (net operating income divided by total project cost). Before the earnest money contract becomes final, however, an annual cash flow pro forma is necessary, at least for the operating period. It should reflect the actual square footage planned, projected rents (based on the market analysis), and estimated construction costs. For the next iteration, a monthly cash flow projection during the construction period is necessary to convince the lender that enough cash will be available to complete the project. It will be based on still more accurate information about costs (from detailed design drawings) and revenues (including rent concessions and tenant improvement allowances). Finally, for a joint venture or equity syndication, a cash flow statement is necessary that combines both construction and operating periods and illustrates the timing of equity requirements, distributions of cash, tax benefits, and proceeds of sales (see chapter 4). The level of detail should correspond to the quality of information available at each stage. For example, preparing a monthly spreadsheet for 60 months before reasonably accurate construction costs and market data have been assembled is a waste of time and money, yet developers need enough information to make a good decision at each stage. The information should be comparable in quality for all the different parameters, and it should be as comprehensive as possible for a given level of risk money.[6]

At each stage, certain items must be completed before moving to the next stage. For example, before

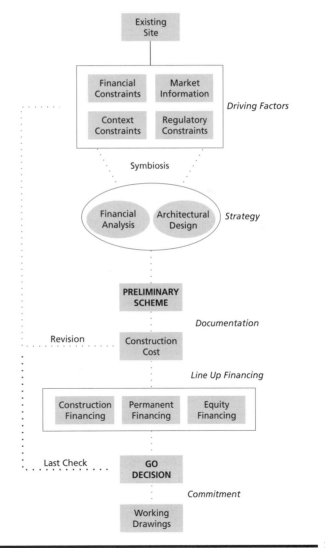

FIGURE 1-6 | The Go Decision

FIGURE 1-7 | The Development Process for a Corporate User

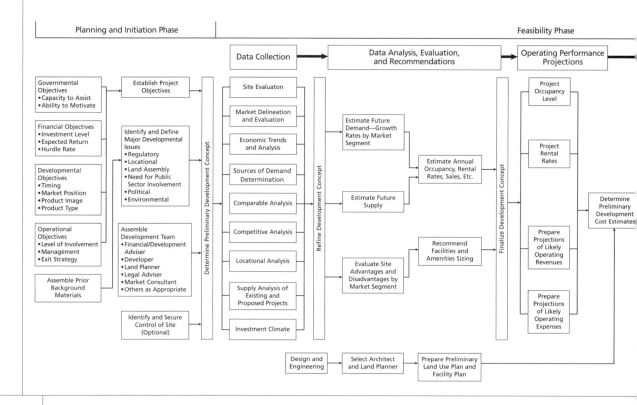

lenders consider a mortgage application, the developer usually must provide conceptual drawings, a boundary survey, title information, information about the site's feasibility, market surveys, personal financial information, and an appraisal. (Because different lenders have different requirements for appraisals, however, it may be wise not to order an appraisal until a promising lender has been identified. Otherwise, another appraisal might be necessary.) The sequence of steps to be taken and even the steps themselves change frequently in development. The rate of change in the development world is one of its major sources of excitement. It also gives beginning developers a better chance to compete with experienced developers, because all developers must adapt to, and keep up with, changing conditions or they will fail.

Financial markets in the late 1990s and early 2000s were highly liquid and stable. Large developers, particularly, found a wide variety of financing alternatives available, thanks primarily to the institutionalization of credit markets. Large developers frequently have credit lines from banks that provide capital for site acquisition and even construction financing. This credit line can

take the place of development and construction loans on individual properties. These relatively liquid credit markets seized up completely in response to escalating subprime mortgage defaults in 2008, and the subsequent crash and macroeconomic woes of 2008 to 2010 make the future shape of institutional finance difficult to discern. It should be explained here that this Great Recession was different from normal real estate cycles. First, rather than supply overtaking demand, there was a cataclysmic drop in demand because of the financial freeze, followed by a drop in gross domestic product and a large jump in unemployment. Further, although other cycles tended to be regional in nature, the Great Recession was nationwide, albeit with varying degrees of severity. The sequence of events in this downturn and thoughts on the future shape of real estate finance are discussed in detail in chapter 8.

The development process resembles the construction of a building. The foundation must be level if the walls are to be straight. Each step in the process depends on the quality of previous steps. Badly negotiated or written agreements with lenders, contractors, tenants, or professionals will be costly to correct. At

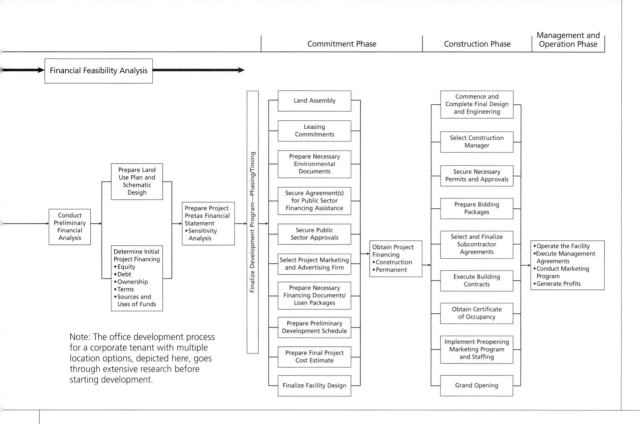

	Commitment Phase	Construction Phase	Management and Operation Phase

Financial Feasibility Analysis

Conduct Preliminary Financial Analysis

Prepare Land Use Plan and Schematic Desigh

Determine Initial Project Financing
• Equity
• Debt
• Ownership
• Terms
• Sources and Uses of Funds

Prepare Project Pretax Financial Statement
• Sensitivity Analysis

Finalize Development Program—Phasing/Timing

Land Assembly

Leasing Commitments

Prepare Necessary Environmental Documents

Secure Agreement(s) for Public Sector Financing Assistance

Secure Public Sector Approvals

Select Project Marketing and Advertising Firm

Prepare Necessary Financing Documents/ Loan Packages

Prepare Preliminary Development Schedule

Prepare Final Project Cost Estimate

Finalize Facility Design

Obtain Project Financing
• Construction
• Permanent

Commence and Complete Final Design and Engineering

Select Construction Manager

Secure Necessary Permits and Approvals

Prepare Bidding Packages

Select and Finalize Subcontractor Agreements

Execute Building Contracts

Obtain Certificate of Occupancy

Implement Preopening Marketing Program and Staffing

Grand Opening

• Operate the Facility
• Execute Management Agreements
• Conduct Marketing Program
• Generate Profits

Note: The office development process for a corporate tenant with multiple location options, depicted here, goes through extensive research before starting development.

worst, they might halt completion or occupancy of the project. In the typical real estate development, where interest costs and promised returns tick away with time, lawsuits and their associated delays are losers for everyone involved. When disputes involve government agencies or the interpretation of public approvals, "you can't beat city hall" is true in most cases. Developers must understand that a "victory" obtained by litigation is often a pyrrhic and value-destroying win.

Because each stage depends on the preceding one and because the developer must depend on other people to do much of the work, an adequate monitoring system is essential. A critical path chart can be assembled for each development, showing not only the events that must occur before others can be accomplished but also the amount of time each step should take. It also shows which events are on the critical path (those requiring the shortest time) and which events have some slack time. Critical path analysis makes it possible to calculate how much extra it will cost to shorten the path by paying workers overtime or paying extra freight charges to receive materials more quickly. The monitoring system provides the best

way to reinforce the written documents. For example, when an issue arises and three or four written confirmations of the contract are available (which are part of the monitoring system), the parties can more easily find a solution to the issue.

The early stages of development are especially important and involve many iterations of planning and analysis before the architectural plans and other arrangements are finalized. A common mistake is to go into too much detail too soon. For example, obtaining detailed working drawings before a market feasibility study has been completed is a waste of money. The market study should influence the design. And if the market is not as healthy as it appeared, the developer may want to abandon the project before sinking additional costs into it.

Projects go through several stages of risk. Developers' *at-risk capital* is the total amount of money that can be lost at a given moment. During the period in which the developer makes preliminary assessments of the market and the site, the risk money is typically limited to what is spent on feasibility studies and conceptual design. As soon as the developer goes hard on the land

Advice for Beginning Developers

Three themes emerge from the advice given by members of ULI's Small-Scale Development Council: (1) be well prepared at all times; (2) work with experienced people, even if they are more expensive; and (3) anticipate delays throughout the development process.

SITE ACQUISITION

- Correctly analyze the purchase price of a site to include usable, not total, square footage.
- Anticipate problems with sellers who are not familiar with real estate and delays while a disputed estate is being settled.
- Analyze the site's physical constraints, including the availability of utilities.
- Conduct a soils test and check for hazardous waste.
- Identify the site's legal and political constraints, such as the availability of the required zoning or the existence of a moratorium on building.
- Research the market before purchasing the site.

REGULATORY PROCESS, OBTAINING APPROVALS

- Be prepared to work with the community to resolve concerns and challenges to the project.
- Take time to understand the local political climate.
- Prepare for the local regulatory process and public hearings.
- Use qualified and experienced consultants, lawyers, and architects to give your project added credibility.
- Anticipate and do not underestimate delays in the approval process.

PRODUCT SELECTION, MARKET, AND ECONOMIC FEASIBILITY

- Remember that when an opportunity is obvious, it is obvious to everyone—resulting in a great deal of competition.
- Develop toward the higher end of the market for your product type, where there is more margin for error. Low-end projects typically have slimmer profit margins.
- Choose a respected market consultant with a strong reputation in the city where your project is located.
- Decide how much time to allocate for the feasibility study. Some developers consider this step to be vital and maintain that the study should be thorough; others feel it should not be belabored.
- Make sure that extensive primary research accurately identifies all competition, whether under construction or still on the drawing boards.

DESIGN, SITE PLANNING, ENGINEERING, AND CONSTRUCTION

- Do not complete the design without paying attention to the market study.
- Work closely with the architect and the contractor.
- Be careful not to ignore important information, even if it requires redesign or additional approvals.
- Use a flexible design that can be easily adapted to different tenants' needs.
- Accept the design and recognize that it will never be perfect.
- Spend sufficient time and money to check all references before retaining contractors and subcontractors.

CONSTRUCTION AND DEVELOPMENT FINANCING

- Establish relationships with several lenders to eliminate lengthy delays.
- Deal with experienced lenders.
- Make adequate allowances for contingencies.
- Remember that it could take three to four months to process a $10 million loan—even if the lender says that it will take only six weeks.
- If the market softens, be able to cover interest out of your own pocket until the market comes back.

PERMANENT FINANCING

- Establish good communications with the lender.
- Prepare a detailed, professional presentation package for the lender.
- Secure the permanent loan before beginning construction. (Beginning developers might be forced to do so, even if they would prefer to wait until after the project is built and leased.)
- Be aware of trends in interest rates.

EQUITY FINANCING

- Investigate the financial records of sources of equity.
- Find two or three compatible partners who can provide or raise equity for the project.
- Do not give away too much equity position to secure funds, because nothing may be left to give if you come up short.

JOINT VENTURES AND PARTNERSHIPS

- Structure a fair deal so that no partner is burdened with excessive risk and meager profits.

- Make clear who is in charge of the project.

- Avoid establishing goals that conflict with those pursued by other partners.

- Have agreements ready to cover dissolution of the partnership.

- Monitor changes in tax legislation that could affect returns.

- Establish a record of regular, honest communications with partners.

MARKETING AND LEASING

- Be prepared for unanticipated changes or a weakening market.

- Find a broker you trust and can work with.

- Understand the importance of marketing the project yourself.

- Create a suitable tenant mix for commercial projects.

- Be specific about tenant improvements and tenants' responsibilities in the lease, and include escape clauses for your own protection.

- Be creative about concessions. Consider buying stock in a tenant's startup company, paying moving expenses, or providing furnishings.

- Understand the implications of leasing versus sales on tenants' earnings and balance sheets.

- Advertise that you have made a deal or signed a lease.

- Recognize brokers with incentives, such as dinners and awards.

OPERATIONS, MANAGEMENT, AND MAINTENANCE

- Pay close attention to building management and operations. Find a first-rate building manager.

- Budget properly for postconstruction maintenance.

IN GENERAL

- Stick to geographic areas and product types with which you are familiar.

- Think small. Find a first project that is within your financial capabilities and can be developed in a reasonable amount of time.

- Never begin a project just because you have financing available.

- During the feasibility stage, keep investment in the project low to maximize your flexibility.

- Do your homework. Know what the holes in the market are and how to plug them—quickly.

- Never enter a negotiation that you are not prepared to leave.

- Attend to details. Whether you are designing a building or negotiating a lease, you personally must be on top of every detail. You must rely on your professional consultants, but if you do not understand the details, you should arrange for someone else to help you.

- Do not be afraid to make a nuisance of yourself. The people you are dealing with are usually very busy and hard to reach. You may have to make several telephone calls or personal visits before you talk to them. Learn to be tenacious—nicely.

- Do not deceive yourself by ignoring facts and warning signs as they are presented to you. Be aware that self-deception occurs most often with evaluation of the market.

- Increase the time you think you need to develop a project—perhaps by twice as much. Do not promise cash payments to investors by a certain date. Be neither overly optimistic nor overly conservative in your assumptions.

- Be able to turn on a dime and switch your strategy instantly.

- Follow up on *everything*. Never assume that something has been done just because you ordered it.

- If you promise something to a lender, a professional consultant, a tenant, or a purchaser, deliver.

- Communicate honestly and often with your lenders and investors. Avoid deals that show early signs of being contentious.

- Recognize that the buck stops with you. A million excuses can be found for things that go wrong in a development project, but you have the ultimate responsibility for ensuring that they go right.

FIGURE 1-8 | Developer Exposure over Time

The money that a developer can lose if a project fails is illustrated here for a 160-unit, bond-financed apartment project. Exposure is greatest just before bond closing when the developer has invested $270,000 in a project that could still fall apart if the bonds fail to close.

Month	Activity	Cost	Total Investment to Date	Current Value to Date	Exposure
1	Land optioned	$15,000	$15,000	$0	$15,000
	Extensions	21,000			
	Architecture	10,000			
	Inducement	10,000			
7	Inducement received		56,000	0[a]	56,000
9	Land closing	388,000	444,000	403,000[b]	41,000[c]
	Architecture	10,000			
	Appraisal and market study	10,000			
10	Fannie Mae commitment	24,000	488,000[d]	403,000	85,000
	Architecture	15,000			
	Engineering	20,000			
	Equity syndication	50,000			
	Bond costs	100,000			
15	Bond rate secured		673,000[e]	403,000	270,000
16	Bonds closed	338,000	1,011,000[f]	0	

Source: Stages of investment for August Park Apartments, Dallas, Texas, developed by Peiser Corporation and Jerome Frank Investments.

[a]The inducement is transferable but has a one-year limit.

[b]The land value had increased by an amount sufficient to cover sales commission costs if it had to be resold.

[c]At the time of closing on the land, the earnest money ($15,000) is recovered.

[d]The Fannie Mae commitment adds value only if bonds can be sold.

[e]Most legal costs have no value if the bonds are not closed.

[f]At bond closing, the risks are substantially eliminated, as all financing parameters are fixed.

purchase contract, the nonrefundable earnest money is also at risk. The money at risk escalates dramatically when the developer closes on the land, pays for financing commitments, or authorizes working drawings and on-site analysis. These events should be delayed as long as possible, until the developer can answer as many questions as possible or obtain the best information to use to decide whether or not to proceed with the project. Developers' most precious asset is their risk capital—the money they have to spend on projects up front to obtain control of property and to determine project feasibility. The last thing a developer wants is to tie up risk capital in land that cannot be developed as planned. Experienced developers know that it is worth paying a little more up front to have the option to extend the closing on the land until they are certain they can proceed with development.

Because each deal has its own distinctive characteristics, limiting risk as much as the developer would like is not always possible. In very hot markets, for example, a free look may not be possible and earnest money may be forfeitable from the first day, or the developer might have to close on the land in 60 days, before securing a firm commitment for financing the future development. Two general principles apply:

- Recognize that development is an iterative process in which each iteration brings more accurate information and puts a greater amount of money at risk.

- Spend enough money to get the quality of information needed, but do not risk more than is necessary for each level of commitment.

Conclusion

Real estate development requires many different talents and skills for managing people and managing risk. Development is fundamentally a creative process, and managing creative people and motivating them to do their best work are one of the elements necessary for success. Development involves solving numerous problems. No matter how well planned a project is, unexpected events arise and must be overcome.

Beginning developers may come from all facets of the real estate industry. They face a much harder road than experienced developers do, not only because they are going through the steps of development for the first time but also because they must establish many new relationships with advisers, consultants, professionals, financiers, and others involved in the process. For these reasons, a simple, more straightforward project is preferred. The first project should not

FIGURE 1-9 | Typical Months Elapsed for Development of a Small Office or Apartment Building

Stage of Development	Area with Few Regulations	Area with Many Regulations
1. Earnest Money Contract Signed	0	0
2. Earnest Money Committed	1	1
3. Market Study	2	2
4. Preliminary Design	3	3
5. Engineering Studies	5	6
6. Approvals[a]	6	24[b]
7. Financing Commitment	7	26
8. Working Drawings and Building Permits	9	36[c]
9. Land Purchase and Construction Loan Closed[d]	9	36

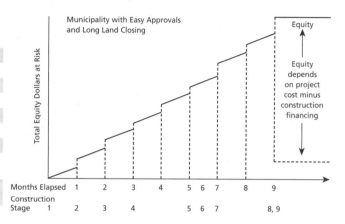

[a]Assuming no zoning changes are necessary.

[b]Environmental, political, design review, and other approvals can take two to five years.

[c]Building permits can take six to nine months after working drawings are finalized.

[d]Most sellers require closing on the land sooner than nine months, but the deal should not be finalized without tentative financing commitments and approvals in place.

---

set a new precedent or require difficult public approvals or new forms of financing.

Jerry Rappaport offers the following advice to beginning developers:[7]

- Use your competitive advantage, whatever it is, to *source* deals. If you find them, the money will come.
- Control over your life is a complete myth. The deal grabs you by both ankles and pulls you down.
- Take a long view of the business. You won't make it all happen in one transaction.

The key to successful development is serving the needs of a particular segment of the market in a particular location. In almost every instance, it also means serving the needs of a particular individual (whether a mayor, corporate president, business owner, landowner, or homebuyer), who must have his or her needs met in a particular manner. Above all, it requires an understanding of what the local market is missing. No one—not even the most experienced developer—has a monopoly on this knowledge. Beginning developers succeed by identifying an opportunity and pressing ahead. They will face obstacles that they cannot envision in advance, but perseverance, hard work, and integrity will enable them to succeed.

NOTES

1. Phil Hughes, president of Hughes Investments, Inc., Greenville, South Carolina, reviewed this chapter and many of his comments were integrated into the text.

2. See ULI's *Directory of Real Estate Development and Related Education Programs* (10th ed.) for a list of more than 60 undergraduate and advanced degree programs.

3. Operating risk may be higher for smaller projects than for larger projects, however, because the loss of one tenant can jeopardize the project's cash flow. Further, a small apartment or small office project costs more to operate per dwelling unit or per square foot. Nevertheless, total development risk is lower for a smaller project.

4. Phil Hughes adds that the definition of a developer ought to include the ability to control the process. He distinguishes between a full developer and a fee developer, who faces many of the same risks and rewards but does not control the project because he works for somebody else. "This is also true for 'corporate developers,' who are not satisfying themselves personally but satisfying committees and others. The whole of the corporate committee and the development manager make up the 'developer.' A developer has risk/reward and control. Otherwise, he is someone's employee."

5. See www.nber.org/cycles/sept2010.html for information regarding the periods referred to throughout this book as the Great Recession and the financial crisis.

6. Accuracy is measured by how narrow the range is around an estimate. Statistically, it is defined by the standard deviation of the estimate. For example, a construction cost estimate of $100,000 with a standard deviation of $10,000 means that 68 percent of the time the actual costs should range from $90,000 to $110,000. A standard deviation of $20,000 means that 68 percent of the time the costs should range from $80,000 to $120,000.

7. "Under the Radar Screen: Success Strategies for Small-Scale Developers," ULI Spring Meeting, May 11, 2000, Miami, Florida.

2

Organizing for Development

Aside from the location and configuration of the site, the keys to success for small developers are the quality of their development team and their access to capital. Small developers can often use the same professional consultants as larger firms, buying not just expertise but credibility in the marketplace by affiliation. Even experienced developers, moving into new markets or product types, will often find that appropriate local consultants, or firms experienced with the particular product, can mitigate their risk in pursuing innovative projects.

More fundamentally, the cyclical history of real estate development has proved repeatedly that a lean central organization is a key to surviving downturns. One way to maintain a small, lean organization is to use consultants for noncore and project-related tasks. To select a consultant who will enhance the team, find the best person or company available, even if it costs a little more (when price must drive the decision, spend first on the knowledge areas furthest from your own internal expertise); be certain that the person or company has direct experience with the particular type of product under consideration; consider the prospective consultant's strategic value beyond the project at hand; look for people and firms that add value beyond their core competence: an engineer, for example, who might have productive relationships with planning staff; beware of firms that depend completely on one, or a few, clients; select people who are familiar with local conditions, who have worked constructively with the anticipated approval authorities; and solicit other developers' opinions on consultants in the area.

Finding the best team for the job can take time. From the day they start in business, beginners should assemble names of prospective consultants and interview them. Development often follows a "hurry up and wait" pattern, and slow times between tasks are a great time to periodically extend the developer's network. Assembling a team from scratch is difficult; more experienced developers have already established a network of consultants, contractors, and professionals, and building a permanent team takes more than one project. Nonetheless, the time and effort spent in finding the best possible team are a good investment. Developers can spend as much time in search of relationships as they do in seeking investment capital.

Forming Partnerships

Even more important than the assembly of the team is the structuring of the development or operating partnership. The result of a hastily assembled partnership can be heartache and financial risk. The safest partnerships are those in which the partners have come to know each other through a long history of working together. Over time, the partners can understand each other's strengths and develop confidence in their associates' integrity. Beginning developers, of course, seldom have such historical relationships, though they may have some. The beginner must remedy this limitation by making good strategic partnership choices and

In Chicago, Bethel Commercial Center includes retail space, offices, a bank, and a daycare center.

being diligent in the legal structuring of the development entity.

Partnerships are frequently formed around specific projects, and developers might have different sets of partners for each of several projects. Partnership arrangement can evolve over time. Early deals might involve several partners, each filling a major function, like financing or construction. In subsequent deals, the number of partners might diminish as the developer learns how to obtain the needed expertise without sharing project equity.

Landowners are often partners in a beginner's early projects. Even if the landowner is not able to contribute critical analytical or management skills, his or her involvement can be very valuable. Landowners may contribute their property as equity—always scarce for the beginning developer—but they might also supply debt, via seller financing, at terms unavailable through financial institutions. Even if they do not materially participate, landowners can tie up land while financing and approvals are obtained. In income property, key tenants might also be offered partnerships to induce them to lease space in the project, particularly if the project can be designed around the tenant's specific needs. Both landowners and tenants, however, generally view real estate as a noncore activity, for which they will tolerate little risk.

A common mistake in forming partnerships is to choose partners with similar rather than complementary skills. Typical complementary pairings include capital and development experience or construction and management experience. Whatever the match, partnerships work best when everyone shares equitably in risks and returns and is equally able to cover potential losses. In most partnerships, however, one person is wealthier than the others and will understandably be concerned about ending up with greater risk, even if the partnership agreement allocates this burden equally. This concern may be overcome in

Hudson Green, a 48-story mixed-use complex in Jersey City, New Jersey, was developed by a partnership between Equity Residential and K. Hovnanian.

several ways, beginning with the concerned partner's selection of an appropriate liability-limiting structure, before entering the partnership. Within the partnership agreement, the capital partner may also specify that a partner who is unable to advance the necessary share of capital will lose his or her interest, and from the beginning the wealthier partner can be given more of the return, or less of the management workload, to compensate for greater potential liability.

A major source of problems in partnerships, especially general partnerships in which everyone has equal interests, is uneven distribution of the workload, or inadequate compensation for partners handling the day-to-day work of creating and implementing a project or projects. Successful developers think of compensation primarily in terms of incentive, rather than fairness. Key areas of responsibility must be determined in advance, and types of compensation should be defined appropriately to incentivize each. For example, one partner might receive a greater share of the development fee, with another receiving more of the leasing fee. To save cash, it might be preferable to accrue fees rather than to pay them as earned, so long as funding is adequate to meet expenses and provide a "living wage" and tax distributions to the working partners.

Even if accrued compensation is not part of the initial deal, variation in cash flow may require timing adjustments. Accounting for partners' interests in a "capital account" is good practice, offering an ongoing check on the appropriate equity investment of each partner and allowing management to address imbalances at distributions or capital calls.

Partnerships can last for years, so the choice of partners is critical. Large developers that bring in less experienced partners for specific deals generally enjoy a rather one-sided partnership, ensuring them management control; beginning developers, however, do not have the same negotiating power and must carefully weigh each additional partner who dilutes their potential equity interest and management flexibility.

Working out the partnership arrangement in advance, with legal advice, is essential for anticipating and avoiding conflict. A written agreement that defines each partner's role, responsibilities, cash contributions, tax needs, and share of liabilities and that sets out criteria for the dissolution or modification of the partnership is an essential document. Many members of general partnerships formed casually and on the basis of verbal assurances have been shocked to discover that they are liable for their partners' debts unrelated to the partnership's purposes. In fact, those types of liabilities are often the default condition of a general partnership constructed without good legal advice.

The most basic approach to a partnership combines someone with extensive development experience and someone whose credit is sufficient to obtain financing. The financial partner should have net worth at least equal to the total cost of the project under consideration, and preferably twice that amount. Some banks might require a higher multiple or specific collateralization of the loan. If the partnership does not include someone with sufficient credit, then the partners will have to find someone to play that role before they can proceed. Other developers, high-net-worth individuals or syndicates of these investors, or family and friends may be promising candidates for beginners without access to institutional capital.

Bringing in any financial partner before the full requirements for cash equity and the amount of net worth are known is a mistake. If, for example, the financial partner is to provide the necessary financial statement and, say, $800,000 cash equity for 50 percent of the deal, the developer may be required to give up an unnecessarily high portion of ownership if he later finds that an additional $100,000 cash equity is needed. On the other hand, with no financial partner waiting in the wings, a prospective lender could lose interest while the developer is locating one. The ideal situation is to line up one or more prospects in advance, with a general understanding of the types of projects being pursued and a commitment to invest if certain criteria can be met by a deal, in a particular time frame.

The Firm's Organization and Management

Development is always a team effort. A development team can be assembled in one of several ways. At one extreme, a large company might include many services, from architecture to construction management and leasing. The advantages of a robust organization are obvious: at each phase of development, critical services are performed in house, presumably with better quality control and coordination than outside vendors would offer. Additionally, each ancillary business can become a profit center for the firm, as principals find themselves asking, "Why give the broker that 6 percent?"

Developers must, however, be careful of "mission creep" into activities too far from the core competence of the principals. More common is the other end of the spectrum: a development company might consist of one or two principals and a few staff members who hire or contract with other companies and professionals for each service as needed. Although requiring more contract management and external communication, the advantages of a lean organization are substantial. This lesson is learned at every market downturn, when firms that are able to shed overhead quickly can extend their viability with low or no operating income. Limiting the "burn rate" of the development firm is good practice in a strong market, and it becomes an essential survival skill in a serious downturn.

From the perspective of organization, development can be a low-cost business that is relatively easy to enter, assuming one has the credibility and relationships needed to access investment capital. A development company can be started by just one person, with little investment in equipment or supplies beyond an office. Small developers are often able to compete effectively against larger organizations, using technology and consultants to leverage the capabilities of the principals. Although larger developers might obtain better prices in some areas and will certainly have easier access to money, they also tend to have higher overhead expenses and are usually slow to respond to market changes.

ORGANIZATIONAL LIFE CYCLES

Like most enterprises, development firms typically pass through three stages—startup, growth, and maturity—and each stage is characterized by distinct risks and opportunities.

STARTUP. Startup is characterized by work toward two short-term goals—successfully completing the first few projects and establishing consistent sources of revenue to cover overhead. During this stage, firms are more likely to be *merchant builders*, selling their projects after they have been completed and leased, rather than *investment builders*, holding them for long-term investment. "During the startup period, the developer's entrepreneurial skills are the critical ingredient. The developer has to develop contacts—with investors, lenders, political leaders and staff, investment bankers, major tenants, architects, engineers, and other consultants. Eternal optimism and the ability to withstand rejection are essential."[1]

A common startup pitfall is overexpansion before the company has developed the staff and procedures to handle greater activity and new types of business. When tenants or buyers sense that a developer is not responding to their needs quickly enough, that developer's reputation is likely to suffer. The growing developer must build staff and establish procedures for accounting, payable and receivable processing, leasing, tenant complaints, reporting functions to investors and lenders, construction administration, property management, and project control. Successful developers know that accountability is just as important for functions handled by consultants as it is for in-house services. A related mistake is hiring too many people too quickly. A startup business seldom has enough cash to pursue every line of business, and those that watch the overhead closely during startup tend to fare better than those whose first priority is projecting a high-profile image. Some of the most successful developers have built thousands of apartment units and millions of square feet of industrial and office space with a professional staff of only three or four, contracting with consultants for virtually everything. Although homebuilders operating this way can suffer a reputation as a "briefcase contractor," the developer role is already one of entrepreneurial coordination, and limited in-house capabilities are seldom marks against the firm's reputation, if the principals' standards of integrity and professionalism are consistently upheld.

GROWTH. A firm in the growth stage has achieved a measure of success. It has instituted procedures for running the business and has assembled a team of players to cover all the major development tasks. It is beyond the point at which a single mistake on a single project can lead to bankruptcy. This firm is in a position to make strategic decisions about its future: what kinds of projects will be pursued, in what markets, with what sort of capital structure?

Maintaining the mission and entrepreneurial energy of the founders and inculcating that spirit into new team members are always challenges for growing firms. The firm must implement controls and procedures, without bureaucratic sclerosis. Development at any scale requires quick decisions. The key is to maintain direct involvement of the firm's principals through this growth phase. Adding capacity and processes must always be considered as a way to leverage principals' time, rather than as a replacement for their judgment and expertise.

Employees who are used to the freewheeling atmosphere of a startup organization sometimes resist the increased level of oversight by senior management; thus, in the growth phase, a firm may find itself with a new problem: retention of key players. The firm must maintain an entrepreneurial environment that motivates qualified, aggressive people. A one-person firm succeeds because that one person accepts risk and controls every aspect of the process. But when staff becomes necessary to handle the workload, the transition from one-person leadership to greater hierarchy can be difficult. Not only must the right staff be in place, but the founders must also be able to delegate.[2]

The right staff for a startup organization is not necessarily right for an organization in the growth phase. Many development firms are, at least at the beginning, family businesses. The difficult transition in this case is often generational. Family dynamics can complicate the transfer of management control, and, even after the transfer, the founding parent may remain in the background, giving directions that may not match the firm's current model. Many firms never make it through this transition.

Conflict can also arise in family firms when the second generation is eager to take risks and try new projects at a time when the founding generation is becoming more risk averse. If the founding generation cannot find a way to let the second generation pursue its goals or have a chance to fail, the younger generation may leave the firm, at least for a time. Recognizing this dynamic, some developer-parents insist that their children work elsewhere before they join the family firm. This strategy offers the additional benefit of making principals in the firm aware of benchmarks and best practices in other organizations. Often, family-controlled development companies skip a generation; the second generation leaves the business to work elsewhere while the third generation enters the business. Wise managers plan ahead for problems, recognizing their children's needs to achieve success on their own and understanding their forebears' needs as stakeholders.

MATURITY. Firms reach maturity after they have established a track record of successful projects and have built an organization to handle them. Mature development companies have built a network of relations with financial, political, and professional players and have cash flow and assets that confer staying power, the so-called deep pockets. These firms tend to focus on larger, more sophisticated projects that tend to be more profitable and that require fewer manag-

ers than multiple smaller, less predictable projects. With higher barriers to entry, they usually face less competition.

Mature firms are more averse to risk, and their managers want to fully comprehend and mitigate the risks that they take. They have often built up a large net worth that the owners want to protect. They do not need to assume as much risk as they did previously, as lenders and equity investors are eager to participate with them. Developers can often reduce or avoid personal liability on notes, and financial partners are willing to assume more financial risk in return for an equity position in the project.

Several characteristics are typical of mature firms, regardless of their size, organization, and style of management:

- They know how to manage market risk, particularly in overbuilt markets.
- They have distributed authority and responsibility within the firm.
- They can evaluate the firm's effectiveness and efficiency.
- Most important, they can attract, challenge, compensate, and retain good people.

Wolverton Park in Milton Keynes, United Kingdom, is a redevelopment of a former railroad engineering works. Today, the mixed-use development includes office, residential, retail, and more than 400 parking spaces.

PLACES FOR PEOPLE

Organizing for Development

ORGANIZATIONAL STRUCTURE

During startup, organizational structure is less an issue than it is during growth and maturity. In the early years, most developers resist formalized organizations. Everyone reports directly to the owner, who makes all the major decisions. As firms grow, the delegation of authority, especially in financially sensitive areas, becomes essential because the owner's time and availability are limited. Sometimes, an outside consultant or new CEO is needed to instigate necessary change.

In most firms, the principals control the same few decisions: site acquisition, financing arrangements and major leases, and timing and terms of the sale of a project. A common practice among even very large firms is for the principals to retain the responsibility for making deals, initiating and maintaining strategic relationships, hiring and compensation, the activities most reliant on personal contacts, reputation, and understanding of the firm's strategy, while tactical responsibilities may be delegated.

Development firms are organized by function (that is., construction, sales), by project, or by some combination of the two. Smaller firms are more often organized by project, larger ones by function. That is, owners of small firms tend to appoint one individual to be in charge of each project, with the group working on that project responsible for all aspects of it—financing, construction, marketing, leasing, and general management. In large firms, on the other hand, one group is responsible for each key function across all projects.[3] In some organizations, employees report to two different managers, one responsible for function and the other for geographic area or product line. Increasingly, firms use a hybrid model, where partners, who may represent expertise in leasing, construction, or deal structure, each take on direct responsibility for general management of a project, drawing in the other partners on project tasks where their expertise falls short. A firm's organizational structure often reflects how it has grown and evolved over time. Some of the largest firms maintain a project-manager structure because they have grown by giving partners responsibility for specific geographic areas, product types, or both. Regardless of where firms begin, structure should be evaluated periodically as the firm grows, to maintain partners' comfort with the framework as their responsibilities change.

COMPENSATION

Manager compensation is a major issue facing owners who want to align employees with the firm mission. One answer is to give key individuals equity in the firm. According to John O'Donnell, chair of the O'Donnell Group in Newport Beach, California, "The reason you give employees equity is you can't pay them what they would command on the open market. Instead, you give them a stake in the future." For senior executives, this might be true partnership equity, whereas key personnel at the project level might receive phantom equity.

Computed from firm or project profits like a bonus, phantom equity is an incentive for project managers, encouraging them to think like entrepreneur-owners. Unlike real equity, however, the individual does not legally own an interest in the project and is not liable for capital contributions. The project manager's signature is therefore not required for transactions, which is important because junior staff turnover is not uncommon in this cyclical business. Also, if a partnership includes more than one property, phantom equity in the firm avoids the accounting difficulty of project-specific interest, which may complicate operating agreements or joint ventures. O'Donnell's firm measures the performance of each property each year and contributes the appropriate share of the manager's profit to a phantom equity account. If, for example, the property makes $100,000 and the manager has a 5 percent interest in it, the account is credited $5,000. If the property loses $100,000, the employee does not have to cover his share of the loss out of pocket, but paper losses accrue to the account and must be "repaid" before future profits are distributed. In this way, the employee does not have to worry about raising cash to cover potential liabilities but participates materially in both the upside and downside potential of the business.

Many firms provide for a period of five to ten years before an employee's phantom equity becomes vested. O'Donnell's firm, for example, might give an employee 2.5 percent of a project after three to five years of employment. Each year after the employee becomes vested, he or she receives an additional 0.5 percent, up to a limit of 5 percent. If a vested employee leaves the company, O'Donnell retains the right to buy out that person's interest at any time based on a current appraisal of the property and he retains the right to select the appraiser. If someone leaves the company without notice, he might buy out that employee's interest immediately. On the other hand, a longtime secretary who leaves to start a family or a manager who gives advance notice (say, three months) might receive profit distributions for years,

FIGURE 2-1 | National Real Estate Compensation Survey, 2011

Position	BASE SALARY RANGE[a]			BONUS AS % OF SALARY[b]
	High	Median	Low	Average
EXECUTIVE & CORPORATE POSITIONS				
Senior Executive				
Chief executive officer	$622,300	$476,000	$300,000	142.9%
Chief operating officer	405,400	301,800	209,000	90.6
CFO/top financial executive	362,300	275,000	190,000	79.6
Executive				
Top capital markets executive	275,000	225,000	153,000	62.1
General counsel	307,100	256,600	186,200	71.7
Top marketing executive	200,000	145,800	107,100	30.5
Top IT executive/director	183,600	140,000	115,800	24.3
Top human resources executive	175,600	125,000	99,300	32.3
Corporate				
Human resources manager	98,000	80,000	68,100	12.6
Payroll/benefits specialist	62,000	52,800	45,200	7.0
Marketing manager	81,600	68,500	60,000	10.5
IT manager	113,300	96,900	82,100	12.1
IT engineer/analyst	84,500	70,000	58,900	8.3
Office manager	64,200	54,100	44,700	8.3
Administrative assistant	46,100	41,800	36,800	5.2
Finance/Accounting				
Controller	133,400	112,900	92,100	15.8
Assistant controller	99,300	86,600	73,500	11.5
AP/AR manager	71,200	61,100	50,000	9.0
Accounting clerk	45,900	39,300	35,600	5.8
COMMON POSITIONS IN OFFICE/INDUSTRIAL REAL ESTATE				
Property Management				
Vice president, property management	161,600	140,000	119,900	21.5
Regional property manager	142,000	115,000	95,000	20.0
Property manager I (<250,000 ft²)	77,500	67,700	55,300	9.4
Property manager II (250,000–500,000 ft²)	78,000	69,000	59,800	8.0
Assistant property manager	54,800	49,200	43,900	6.7
Building engineer	68,000	57,200	50,100	5.5
Maintenance engineer/technician I	41,600	36,000	32,600	3.9
Leasing				
Senior leasing executive	153,900	120,000	74,000	95.3
Leasing manager	113,800	85,000	60,300	39.0
Typical leasing agent/representative	71,100	53,000	43,500	41.5
Development/Construction				
Development VP/director	191,100	165,100	128,300	38.0
Development manager	129,300	105,700	89,300	19.3
Project manager	97,700	84,900	73,200	13.2
Project administrator	60,900	54,300	48,000	9.3
Construction manager	121,100	102,300	85,700	15.4

Source: CEL & Associates, Inc. / CEL Compensation Advisors, LLC ©2011 National Real Estate Compensation and Benefits Survey - All Rights Reserved.

[a]High = 75th percentile, Median = 50th percentile, Low = 25th percentile.

[b]CEL & Associates, Inc., has intentionally excluded extraordinary salary and/or annual bonus awards from this table in order to not distort the results.

Organizing for Development

thus enjoying the project's potential to the extent that his or her tenure vested these rights.

No formula exists for determining how much equity a developer should give away to attract top managers. Beginning developers may have to pay experienced project managers 25 percent of a project's profits, whereas established developers may need to pay only 1 to 5 percent. Employees' risks are lower with a more established developer, so their shares of the profits are lower. One major developer, for example, has three levels of participation, which are given not as rewards but as career paths. The lowest level is *principal*. Project managers who are star performers are eligible.

They receive up to 10 percent (5 to 7.5 percent is typical) of a project in the form of phantom equity. The next level is *profit and loss (P&L) manager*, someone in charge of a city or county area. P&L managers are responsible for several projects and principals; they receive 15 to 20 percent of the profits from their areas. Their interest is also in the form of phantom equity. The top level is *general partner*, reserved for managers of a region, state, or several states. General partners receive real equity, are authorized to sign documents on the firm's behalf, and incur full risk.

Real estate is a cyclical business; in each downturn, a substantial portion of capable junior and middle

Strategic Planning and Thinking: Planning the Business

EVALUATE THE PRESENT SITUATION.
- What are the company's accomplishments? How do they compare with previous goals?
- Where is the company headed? How should it get there?
- What are the owner's or founder's interests and expectations?
- What is the external environment?
  - Market changes and trends
  - Changes affecting products and services
  - Opportunities from changes
  - New and old risks and rewards
  - Political environment
- Who are key competitors? Where do they excel?

ANALYZE THE COMPANY'S STRENGTHS AND WEAKNESSES.
- What properties has it developed, bought, marketed? How successful have they been?
- How has the firm done in the past?
  - Management capabilities
  - Threats
  - Opportunities
- What past decisions would be changed?

SPECIFY GOALS FOR THE STRATEGIC PLAN.
- What is the financial strategy?
- What is the firm's strategy regarding products?
  - Quality
  - Investor or merchant builder
- Does the company need to diversify its product?
- Does the company need to diversify its location?

- What is the company's strategy regarding land?
  - Land banking versus carrying land in slow times
  - Developed land versus raw land
- What is the marketing strategy?
- What is the strategy regarding production and construction?
- How does the company get the job done?
- What is its management and organizational strategy?

SPECIFY AN ACTION PLAN—PROGRAMS, STEPS, OR TASKS TO BE CARRIED OUT—CONCERNING RISK, REWARD, AND REALITY.
- What activities is the company engaged in now?
- What is the state of financial planning?
- Where do equity and debt come from?
- Are changes expected?
- How strong are financial suppliers?
- What will be its financial needs in the next 24 months, the next 36 months, or longer to meet strategic goals?
- What are the company's objectives? What metrics is it committed to achieve?
- How strong will lines of communication and internal controls be for
  - Financial results
  - Acquisition and development
  - Operations: property management, leasing, tenant improvements, customer relations
  - Controls and measurement
  - Responsibilities and budgets

Source: Sanford Goodkin, president/CEO, Sanford R. Goodkin & Associates, San Diego.

managers leave the industry. As a result, even in relatively weak markets, the most experienced professionals can be in relatively short supply. Firms respond with creative and highly motivating compensation packages to attract and, more importantly, to retain these experienced hires. Compensation for top performers is usually paid through bonuses rather than salary and can range from 10 percent of salary, at the project level, to well over 100 percent for executives.

Personnel costs are typically 60 to 80 percent of most operating budgets, and they are the most critical component of a management or operating company. Benefit costs, especially for health care, continue to rise, and as in every industry, managers are increasingly sharing these increases with employees. Even before the financial crisis of 2008–2009, many firms were also downsizing, and the uncertainty and cash flow disruption of the past few years have made many managers consider the benefits of a lean payroll. The lean organization will use more outside contractors to fill interim needs. "They just can't afford to pay everyone market rates [for high-end people] every day, all the time," says Chris Lee, president of CEL & Associates in California.

STRATEGIC PLANNING

Most beginning developers—and even many large ones—do not have a formal strategic plan. Rather, they may focus on a specific demographic market, or a neighborhood, or a property type, but within these parameters the firm will respond to opportunities as they arise. In this way, developers build expertise and a track record of success, and more opportunities tend to arise within a well-chosen market. Organically, the firm's competence can become its business strategy.

As firms gain maturity, size, and diversity, they may benefit from more formal strategic planning. A strategic plan gives junior team members a sense of the direction of the business and gives them direction on how to contribute at the deal or project level. The effect of a good strategic plan, then, can be counterintuitive: encouraging more decentralization of the day-to-day activity of the firm. The plan should include budgets, a master schedule tied to the budget, and systems for approving and tracking projects. The accompanying feature box summarizes the major issues that strategic planning should address. Just as important is to include the assumptions, identified trends, and external dynamics that underpin elements of the strategy, so that they may be reevaluated in future revisions of the plan.

The strategic plan helps the company achieve its objectives faster, because everyone understands the firm's immediate goals and longer-term objectives. Such plans are most effective when prepared with broad participation and when the resulting strategy flows into clearly defined tasks. Whereas the business plan is strategic, the budget is tactical; that is, the budget lays out the specific approach that will be used to follow the broad strategy of the plan. The strategic plan culminates in an *action plan*, which should establish specific protocols for managers to follow—for example, policies for evaluating the competition and an area's long-term economic outlook, or for evaluating individual deals, contractors, or joint ventures against the criteria of the strategic plan.

Choosing Consultants and Contractors

Assembling a team of professionals to address the economic, physical, and political issues inherent in a complex development project is critical. A developer's success depends on the ability to coordinate the completion of a series of interrelated activities efficiently and at the appropriate time.

The development process requires the skills of many professionals: architects, landscape architects, and site planners to address project design; market consultants and brokers to determine demand and a project's economics; multiple attorneys to handle agreements and government approvals; environmental consultants and soils engineers to analyze a site's physical and regulatory limitations; surveyors and title companies to provide legal descriptions of a property; contractors to supervise construction; and lenders to provide financing.

Even the most seasoned developer finds that staying on top of all of a project's technical details is difficult. For beginners, a key is to find consultants and partners who can help guide the development process, as well as provide technical knowledge. Regardless of experience, most developers can benefit from continuing investment in their own training, and in updated software and communications tools to leverage their personal project management abilities. Developers may find small subcontractors lack technologies and communications tools—even e-mail. Working with these firms may present continuing difficulties.

LOCATING A CONSULTANT

To begin the search for a consultant with particular expertise, developers should first seek the advice of successful local developers who have completed projects similar to the one under consideration. They should ask experienced developers about the consultants they use and their level of satisfaction with the consultants' work. Beginners should also remember, however, that established developers may consider newcomers the competition, and it may take some time to build the trust necessary for a frank exchange of opinions. Beginning developers might take advantage of networking opportunities by joining associations of local developers or national organizations geared toward the real estate product of interest, be it residential, shopping centers, or business parks. The key is to be active in such organizations by serving on committees and participating in events.

Developers should obtain a list of the consultants whose work has impressed public officials and their planning staffs. Staff is often prohibited from recommending professional service firms, but usually at least an informal opinion for or against a specific firm can be obtained. Certain approvals might hinge on the reputations of specific team members; indeed, part of consultants' value could lie in the connections they maintain with the public sector. Because governments have pulled back from some services, relying on certifications of outside professionals, many tasks that were once performed by public servants may now be performed in the private sector by the very same people. A common example is soil evaluation, a function of departments of public health, which is commonly performed by "authorized evaluators," who are typically former department employees who retain both the knowledge of their field and relationships with the approving agency.

Associations of architects, planners, and other development-associated professionals are another source of potential consultants. Such organizations usually maintain rosters of members, which are useful as a screening tool because most professional and technical organizations have defined certain standards for their members. Those standards might include a certain level of education and practical experience, as well as a proficiency examination. Most associations publish trade magazines that provide a wealth of information about the field and are often available online.

SELECTING A CONSULTANT

Strategies for selecting consultants vary according to the type of consultant being sought. The most common approach is a series of personal interviews.

Beginners should not hesitate to reveal their inexperience with the issues being addressed or to ask potential consultants to explain clearly their duties and the process of working together. Consultants will profit by dealing with a developer, so they should be expected to take the time to explain the fundamentals.

A proper interview should address the developer's concerns regarding experience and attitudes. The developer should look for a consultant with experience in developing similar projects. An architect or market consultant who has concentrated on single-family residential development would be inappropriate for a developer interested in an office or retail project.

The developer must be sure to ask for references and then must contact those references personally to learn about the consultant's quality of work and business conduct, ability to deliver on time and within budget, interest in innovation, tolerance for clients' direction, and professional integrity.

The developer may also inspect some of the consultant's work—marketing or environmental reports, plans and drawings, and finished projects. The developer should be comfortable with the design philosophy of a prospective member of the creative team and satisfied with the technological competence of a potential analytical consultant.

The developer must be certain that the chosen firm has the personnel and facilities available to take on the assignment. This balance is difficult to achieve because the developer is likely to be attracted to small firms' personal attention to his needs, while being sensibly wary of involvement with an organization without capacity or staying power. If a consultant appears to be struggling to keep up with current responsibilities, the proposed project is likely to suffer from neglect. A good rule of thumb is that the proposed project should represent no more than a third of the consultant's overall business.

Having ascertained the overall fitness of the consulting group, the developer should establish who will be the project's manager and request a meeting with that person and then examine several projects for which that manager was responsible. Beginning developers are often reluctant to involve themselves in "other people's business," but it is not inappropriate to ask that specific personnel and time allocations be delineated in the professional services agreement. Toward that end, the developer is well advised to find out what subconsultants the firm would be likely to hire, and how the scope of work will make each sub accountable to the project timeline and performance standards. It may be possible to speak with key sub-consultants as well, to map out a plan for completing the assignment together. Successfully accomplishing the assignment will require coordination between the consultant and its subs, and the client who will be dependent on these individuals should know who will be responsible for what.

Hiring a firm is a two-way street. While the developer is sizing up the consultant, a similar process is going on across the table. Displaying a positive attitude about the project and the consultant's potential contributions is important. A beginning developer should not be offended when the consultant asks about his experience and competence to complete a development project, the existence of adequate financial resources and accounting capacity to pay the bills, the feasibility of the proposal, the ability to make timely decisions, and what might happen if the project is delayed or aborted.

Consultants need to be confident about a developer's ability to meet obligations and should know when they are working "at their own risk." This last consideration has become especially important over the last few years, as cash flow difficulties for developers and owners of real estate have trickled down into crises at firms offering development services. An experienced consultant will appreciate an open and honest conversation about when work will be compensated, and some caution in releasing work for future projects.

Finally, the developer should judge whether he has established a rapport with the people being considered during the preliminary interview. The ability to get along with these people is essential for the project's completion, so if problems arise at this point, the developer should consider whether dealing with them daily is possible. Thinking ahead to the long timeline of some development projects, the developer may wish to consider whether the organization has the same rapport at the junior level as is found at the executive level. Compatibility is a key to the project's success—and to preserving the developer's sanity.

If, after checking references, the developer feels uncomfortable with any aspect of the consulting firm, eliminating the firm from further consideration may be the most sensible move. If the developer's responses are favorable about the firm as a whole but not about the particular person being assigned to the project, he should raise these concerns with the firm's principals.

Who Is Involved, and When, in the Development Process?

SITE SELECTION
- Brokers
- Title companies
- Market consultants
- Transactional attorneys

FEASIBILITY STUDY
- Market consultants
- Economic consultants
- Construction estimators
- Surveyors
- Mortgage brokers and bankers
- Land use attorneys
- Engineers

DESIGN
- Architects
- Land planners/landscape architects
- General contractors/construction managers

- Surveyors
- Soils engineers
- Structural engineers
- Environmental consultants

MARKETING
- Brokers
- Public relations firms
- Advertising agencies
- Graphic designers
- Internet service firms

FINANCING
- Mortgage brokers and bankers
- Construction lenders
- Permanent lenders and syndicators
- Title companies
- Appraisers

CONSTRUCTION
- Architects
- General contractors
- Engineers
- Landscape architects
- Surety companies
- Authorized inspectors

OPERATIONS
- Property managers
- Specialty and amenity maintenance teams

SALE
- Brokers
- Appraisers

THROUGHOUT THE PROCESS
- Attorneys (title, transactional, land use, litigation)

A larger firm should have another staff person available, but a smaller firm may not. The developer must be assured that the most qualified people will be assigned to the project, that those people will continue to be available until the project is complete, and that the team will leave behind it a legible paper trail for future phases or operating partners to recover the design logic, legal justification, or operational guidelines for decisions made during development.

RATES

Consultants should willingly quote a fee for their services, presenting a written proposal reflecting the costs for delivery of the desired product. Depending on the particular expertise, this quote may be a simple lump-sum bid, an hourly rate, or a menu of services and associated costs. The developer will benefit from having as much information in writing as possible. Although cost is an important factor, it must be balanced by experience and by the quality of the consultant's past work. Developers should be careful not to choose simply the lowest price. If detailed proposals are available, developers should compare the proposed budgets to see how the money is allocated and to identify the differences in proposals to judge whether the numbers are reasonable. They should also ensure that the prices include the same types of services. For example, a lower fee could possibly exclude services that will later be required, necessitating future additional charges. A lower quotation might also exclude the amount needed to cover unforeseen incidents. The issue of unforeseen costs is a hazard of the development business, and it is often the case that changes to the scope and cost of services ultimately represent a larger range than the differences in initial quotes. It is therefore essential that any professional services agreement spell out clearly the types of events that could trigger additional costs (inadequate base drawings, new regulatory requirements), the process by which the scope may be changed and the notice required to do so, and the specific unit prices for additional work.

Once a firm has been selected, most developers prefer to employ a fixed-price contract, using the figures quoted in the proposal. Payment can be made in several ways, depending on the nature of the product to be delivered. A schedule could be used to establish milestones, such as the delivery of a specified work product that triggers an agreed-on payment, or developers might find that allowing projections of cash flow to establish a monthly schedule is more advantageous. Smaller jobs might require a lump-sum payment up front.

Some consultants, like lawyers, work according to a time-and-materials (T&M) agreement, with the client billed according to staff members' hourly rates and the cost of materials used to complete the task. Materials include reimbursable expenses, such as printing or shipping, which may receive a markup for management time. New clients are an unknown for which many consultants will prefer T&M arrangements. T&M agreements are complicated, however, and require constant monitoring to verify the amounts that are being billed and to understand them in relation to the overall project scope. Less experienced developers lack benchmark information about appropriate costs for handling specific tasks, making these agreements inherently risky. When constructing T&M agreements, the client should be clear on a dollar value that may be billed each period without prior approval, so that a casual approval to "take care of that" does not turn into an unanticipated receivable at the end of the month. One experienced construction manager advises, "Regardless of careful construction and monitoring, T&M agreements require trust and common expectations for the work to be performed. Executing these arrangements with strangers is a recipe for administrative headache and hurt feelings."

Retainer agreements that pay the consultant a flat monthly fee should be avoided because such arrangements can be very costly in the long run. When delays stop work on an aspect of the project for which billing continues apace, not only is cash flow impaired but the incentives of developer and consultant may become warped when 50 percent of the work is completed, but 90 percent of payment has been received. Retainer agreements are usually appropriate only for elements of a project that are truly ongoing, such as public relations management during the lease-up period, or for services that may be thought of more as insurance for eventualities that may occur, such as land use counsel during the development period.

Regardless of the chosen method of compensation, both the developer and the consultant must negotiate a mutually agreeable performance contract. The contract must explicitly list each duty that the consultant is expected to complete. The developer should expect that services not explicitly included in the agreement will probably require future negotiations that will most likely lead to additional costs for the developer. The contract should clearly spell out a schedule for the delivery of services, including a definitive date for delivery of the final product, and expected turnaround for major steps in the process.

WORKING WITH CONSULTANTS

After the parties sign the agreement, the working relationship with the consultant begins. The developer must work closely with the consultant to ensure that everything proceeds according to schedule. The development team is made up of a group of players whose tasks are interrelated, and the tardiness or shoddy work of a single firm could set off a chain reaction and cause costly delays.

As the team leader, the developer must ensure that each consultant is provided with accurate information and that information produced by one consultant is relayed to the others. Any changes in the project's concept should be communicated immediately. The developer must be sensitive to the effect that changes in the project will have on the consultants' collective analysis; sudden change could alter requirements for the design, environmental analyses, and parking, for example. Any alterations could be costly, as consultants might demand extra compensation to address the changing elements of the project. It is advisable that the developer begin due diligence and have some idea of the project's viability before spending significant funds on designers.

A healthy working relationship with consultants is vital. Developers should contribute information and ask questions throughout the process but should also show a willingness to accept consultants' ideas. Good consultants can decrease development costs and improve a project's marketability.

A developer must have the management skill necessary to coordinate consultants' efforts while ensuring that all parties respect the developer's ultimate authority to make decisions. Problems can also occur, however, when a developer's ego gets in the way of good advice. A good developer knows when to listen to and accept the advice of others.

The Design/Construction Team

The design/construction team includes an array of consultants and contractors who perform tasks ranging from site analysis and planning to cost estimating, building design, and construction management. The work that they perform and/or manage represents the bulk of the project's total soft costs, and effectively managing their contributions is critical to the success of the development project.

ARCHITECTS

Both beginning and experienced developers depend on architects for advice and guidance. Some developers appoint the architect to head the design portion of a project, and sometimes the construction period as well. Most developers, however, prefer to be their own team leaders, both to maximize their influence on the design and to expedite time-critical processes. Beyond building and site design expertise, architects usually offer extensive experience with the regulatory and physical constraints placed on development and are a valuable asset in communicating with other consultants and in coordinating design with construction processes.

Jamestown Properties converted Warehouse Row, a redevelopment of 19th-century warehouses in Chattanooga, Tennessee, into an urban, mixed-use project with restaurants, boutiques, offices, and event space.

JAMESTOWN PROPERTIES

The search for an architect must be thorough. Only those firms and individuals whose experience is compatible with the proposed project should be considered. It is crucial that the architect be focused on delivering a workable product at a reasonable cost. Those more used to designing high-end custom homes where cost is not an issue may not be suitable for a development of production homes. Beginning developers especially may lean on the project experience of the architect, and an inexperienced architect is likely a better match for a more seasoned client. The developer should always check a firm's credentials and ensure licensure in the state where the project will be built; building departments require the stamp of a state-admitted architect.

The developer and the architect must share a common philosophy of design, though the developer will often benefit from the broader experience of a design professional, and the developer must feel comfortable with the architect selected. A good architect respects the developer's opinions and can work through disagreements. At the same time, the developer must consider every decision but respect the architect's knowledge and experience. Some developers prefer to hire an architect whose work has withstood the test of time; others look for an architect known for innovative designs that make a distinctive statement and may give the developer a competitive advantage or a benefit in public relations or approvals.

When the developer has found an architect, the next step is to reach a written agreement. A set of standard contracts provided by the American Institute of Architects (AIA) provides the basis for defining the relationship between developer and architect. AIA Document B101, *Standard Form of Agreement between Owner and Architect*, clearly outlines the architect's duties in the development process and is widely used in real estate development. Developers should remember, however, that this agreement was written from architects' perspective and seeks to protect their interests.[4] In some circumstances, modifications to the AIA agreement form are appropriate, although both parties should be aware that a body of opinion and case law exists for interpreting this standard document, and changes may introduce uncertainty in interpretation of additional terms.

Sometimes, architects are given responsibility for all facets of the project's design, as well as selecting and supervising land planners, landscape architects, engineers (except survey, soils, and environmental engineers), and parking and other programmatic con-

sultants, as well as all facets of the project's design. Few experienced developers recommend this practice, however, and some prefer to maintain every subdiscipline in direct contractual relationship with the developer/owner, to maintain long-term accountability to the project and to better understand and manage cost.

The design phase lasts from the creation of the initial concept to the completion of the final drawings. The design is based on a program that outlines the project's general concept, most notably its identified uses and amenities, and initial allocations of floor area or acreage for each. It is increasingly common for planners or architects to participate in the programming phase, particularly in urban, mixed-use locations where this calculation can be very complex.

Initially, the architect prepares schematic drawings that include general floor and site plans and that propose basic materials and physical systems. A construction cost estimator or contractor should review the design and assess its economic implications at least at the conclusion of each design phase. These schematic drawings are an important component in presentations to lenders and should include a basic set of presentation images, such as rendered elevations or a physical or digital 3-D model.

Upon approval of schematic drawings, architects typically move into a "design-development" phase, where the original concept begins to be fleshed out into construction systems and a more precise division of functional spaces. Most major design decisions are made in the schematic and design-development drawing stages, and as each phase proceeds, changes to the design become more difficult and expensive. Even under the inevitable time constraints, it is nearly always better to address design concerns as they arise than to table these issues assuming they can be fixed later. The design team should include not only the contractor or construction manager but also marketing, leasing, and property management representatives. If those team members are not yet named, then the developer should ask potential contractors, brokers, and property managers to review and criticize the preliminary drawings. Beautiful, but unmarketable projects can lead to finger-pointing later.

After approval of the design-development package, the developer typically has the first real handle on the potential cost of the project. At this point, estimates are reviewed against the design drawings, and major budget busts should be resolved before going forward. Upon approval of the design and cost, the architect produces specification drawings, also called

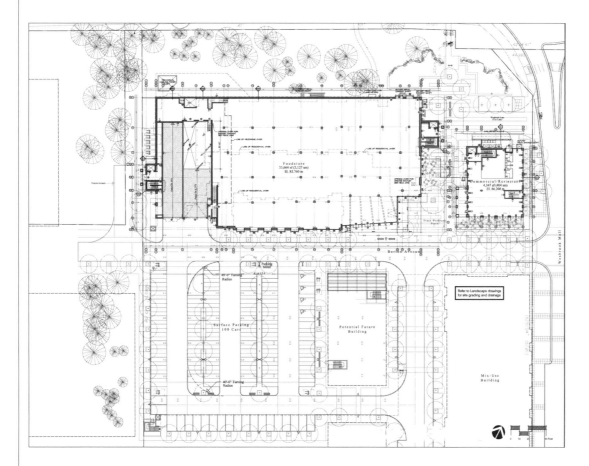

working drawings. Specifications include detailed drawings of the materials to be incorporated with the mechanical, electrical, plumbing, and heating, ventilating, and air-conditioning (HVAC) systems. Generally, drawings pass through several iterations before the final plans and specifications are finished. The developer should review these interim drawings, referred to as 25 percent, 50 percent, 75 percent, or 95 percent complete. After addressing all the developer's concerns, the architect completes final drawings and specifications.

Because most developers are interested in the project's image and feel, they often spend their time reviewing drawings, at the expense of specifications. Doing so is a mistake. The quality, durability, and safety of a structure are as dependent on "the spec" as on the drawings. The spec is typically organized around the Construction Standards Institute's *Master-Format*, which groups construction materials into categories consistent across all types of projects, and a master specification defines not only materials but also precisely how and by whom each material should be installed. It is therefore an incredibly important

Site plans are the result of a team effort. Consultants should be involved early in the development process to ensure that they have a say in important decisions. Site plan for Granite Terrace, Vancouver, Canada.

document for the long-term operation of the building because it governs the warranty of nearly every material in the building. In reviewing partially completed designs, both drawings and specifications, the developer should pay particular attention to the implications for potential users by visualizing how commercial tenants or residents will react to the design, asking brokers, tenants, and other developers to identify the needs of the target groups and soliciting real estate professionals' comments on the design drawings as they progress.

The next phase of the architect's duties involves compiling the construction documents, including the package used to solicit bids from contractors. This package includes the rules for bidding, standard forms detailing the components of the bid, conditions for securing surety bonds, detailed specifications identifying all components of the bid, and detailed working drawings. The developer also relies on the architect's experience to analyze the bids and to help select the best contractor for the job. Although the architect is best suited to understand the components of bids on a design, the developer is the one who will have to live with those bids, and with missing or misunderstood scope or cost during the development phase. For this reason, developers must thoroughly understand the bids, and they may wish to introduce special format requirements so that bids dovetail with the development and operating budgets they will be administering on the project.

Once construction begins, the architect is responsible for monitoring—but not supervising—the work site. The architect is expected to inspect the site periodically to determine whether contract documents are being adequately followed. Constant monitoring is beyond the scope of the architect's responsibility, requires additional compensation, and is more effectively achieved with a fee-compensated construction manager.

The developer also relies on the project architect—or project engineer, in the case of infrastructure development—to confirm that predetermined phases during construction have been satisfactorily completed. The approval involves a *certificate of completion* necessary for disbursement of the contractor's fee. The AIA provides another standard certificate that addresses the architect's liability resulting from confirmation, noting that the architect's inspections are infrequent, that defects could be covered between visits, and that the architect can never be entirely sure that construction has been completed according to the plan.

The relationship between architect and developer commonly follows one of two models. The *design-award-build* contract is most traditional in the United States and breaks the project into two distinct phases, with the architect completing the design phase before the developer submits the project for contractors' bids. The alternative, the *fast-track* approach, involves the contractor during the early stages of design because the contractor's input at this stage could suggest ways to save on costs, making the project more economical and efficient to construct.

The fast-track method is primarily a cost-saving device, as it uses time efficiently to reduce the holding costs incurred during design. The developer is able to demolish existing structures, begin excavation and site preparation, and complete the foundation before the architect completes the final drawings. One risk involved with the fast-track approach, however, is that the project is under construction before costs have been determined, and before necessary approvals are finalized.

Several methods are available for compensating architects for their services, including T&M agreements and fixed-price contracts. The latter specify the amount that the architect will receive for completing the basic services outlined in the performance contract; any duties not listed in the contract are considered supplementary and require additional compensation. Another method calculates architectural fees as a fixed percentage (usually 3 to 6 percent) of a project's hard costs. Architects contend that this method fairly accounts for a project's complexity. The disadvantage of this method is that it provides no incentive to the architect to economize. It is often necessary to engage the architect and other professionals on the basis of either T&M or a short-term retainer during project conceptualization, because the project scope remains unclear, and then shift to a fixed-price arrangement when the project is more defined and subject to better quantification. Hybrid models of compensation are also popular, where a particular milestone will be priced as a "not-to-exceed," with hourly billing against the maximum, and no cost authorized beyond that number. In this way, the architect offers the client protection against overruns but is paid within an established range for work performed.

Regardless of the mode of calculating compensation, the architect is always entitled to additional reimbursable expenses—travel, printing, photocopying, and other out-of-pocket expenses. Beginning developers should be aware that, on a project with even a fairly simple path through public approvals, printing costs for the many dozens of required drawing sets can be well into five figures.

LANDSCAPE ARCHITECTS

Landscape architects do much more than plant trees and flowers. Landscape architects work with existing conditions—topography, soil composition, hydrology, and vegetation on a site—to create a functional setting and a sense of place for the project. They are responsible for working with the architect to produce an external environment that enhances the development, for devising a planting and hardscape plan, and for incorporating components into the project, like plants, trees, furnishings (benches, for instance), walkways, artwork, and signs. Landscape architects can also save energy costs by selecting plants that provide shade and with grading and planting approaches that solve drainage problems.

It is becoming increasingly common for landscape architects to take a leading role in entitling projects. Communities commonly demand open space of new projects, and at any rate expect to have a say on landscaping of public roads and views. In land development projects, in fact, landscape architects may take the lead, because their drawings are often the most instructive to the community and, with emphasis on the green and natural, sometimes the most appealing vision of the project.

Landscape architects first develop preliminary plans and then manage the completion of those plans. They obtain bids, complete working drawings and final specifications, prepare a schedule, and inspect the site to verify that the contractor implements the plan correctly. Expertise in other kinds of construction does not necessarily translate into landscape construction and installation. Many very expensive installation problems in landscapes can be virtually invisible to the untrained eye—inadequate soils testing or preparation, or poor subsurface drainage—so it is advisable to have someone with specific expertise inspect the project at least upon completion, if not periodically through construction.

Hiring the landscape architect can be the architect's responsibility, but developers should inspect the chosen landscape architect's work to determine that they are comfortable with the design philosophy. The American Society of Landscape Architects maintains rosters and certifies its members. Landscape architects typically work through conceptual planning on a T&M basis, then bid a lump sum to complete working drawings and specifications, and, generally, return to working on an hourly basis to supervise completion of the plans. A monthly or weekly retainer may also be used for construction administration.

LAND PLANNERS

With land development projects and larger building projects, land planners allocate the desired uses to maximize the site's total potential and determine the most efficient layout for adjacent uses, densities, and infrastructure. Individual building projects usually rely on the judgment of the architect and market consultants. The land planner's goal is to produce a plan with good internal circulation, well-placed uses and amenities, and adequate open space. Land planners should prepare several schemes that expand on the developer's proposal and discuss the pros and cons of

each with the developer. The developer coordinates the land planner's activities with input from marketing, engineering, economic, and political consultants to ensure that the plan is marketable, efficient, and financially and politically feasible. On land development projects, the land planner is the principal professional consultant. Reputation and past projects are the best indicators of a land planner's ability. A key characteristic to look for in a land planner is the ability to work well with the project engineer and architect. Because the activities of a land planner vary widely, many architects and landscape architects offer "planning" on their menu of services. Although the skill sets certainly overlap, and some architects are definitely capable of high-quality site planning, professional planners often bring more to the table than simply their skills. When evaluating a planner, developers should be aware of the office's relationships with the entities granting approvals, as well as its relationships with infrastructure contractors and landscape construction firms.

ENGINEERS

Engineers play a vital role in the development of a building. Several types of engineers with specific expertise—structural, mechanical, electrical, civil—are required to ensure that the design can accommodate the required physical systems. They are sometimes engaged by the project architect and sometimes contract directly to the owner or developer. Regardless of the relationship, they must maintain a very close relationship with the architectural staff as the project design unfolds. For this reason, the client should seek the architect's input when selecting all the project engineers. Larger architectural firms may have an in-house engineering staff, which can expedite coordination but limit competition; smaller firms prefer to hire individual engineers project by project.

Although the architect may make recommendations or offer a list of candidates, the developer should reserve the right to select engineers after inspecting their qualifications; reviewing previously completed projects of the same scope and property type, including interviewing the project's proponent; and checking their working references with various general contractors and local building inspectors. Contractors may have strong opinions about engineers that they have worked with in the past. Although these opinions should be considered, the developer should also understand that projects often place engineers and contractors on opposite sides of the process, and contractors can resent the oversight of an engineer.

Engineers must be licensed by each state in which they operate, and plans cannot receive approvals unless signed by a licensed professional engineer. Developers should clarify which submittals require stamps from which kinds of engineers.

The architect may hire certain engineers as subcontractors and then must be responsible for subcontract deliverables, schedule, and budget. Engineers are generally required on all substantial construction projects, including new developments, renovations, or additions to existing structures. The engineer's fee schedule is usually included in the architect's budget and generally ranges from 4 to 7 percent of the overall soft cost. When engineers subcontract to architects, evidence of payments to subs should be required in the architectural contract, because nonpayment or default by the architect can sometimes result in a *mechanic's lien*[5] on the property.

During the initial design phase, the architect works with the engineers to develop and modify working drawings to accommodate the project's structural, HVAC, electrical, and plumbing systems. Each engineer then provides a detailed set of drawings showing the physical design of the systems for which the engineer is responsible. The architect is responsible for coordination of each successive drawing set and for instructing the engineers to resolve any conflicts.

Structural engineers assist the architect in designing the building's structural integrity. They work with soils engineers to determine the most appropriate foundation system and to produce a set of drawings for the general contractor explaining that system in detail, especially the structural members' sizing and connections. Structural engineers can range from sole practitioners who produce framing plans for single-family homes to large professional practices that can engineer steel-framed high rises. Developers of specialty buildings for medical offices, labs, and the like should be aware that these building types require specialized expertise beyond the generic professional engineer credential.

Mechanical engineers design the building's HVAC systems, including mechanical plant locations, airflow requirements for climate control and public health, and any special heating or cooling requirements, such as computer rooms in office buildings or isolation wards in hospitals. Many firms offer a combined MEP (mechanical, electrical, plumbing) practice, allowing them to take responsibility for the building's plumbing design, but developers should never feel obligated to lump all engineering specialties together in one firm if specific expertise can be found elsewhere.

Electrical engineers design the electrical power and distribution systems, including lighting, circuitry, and backup power supplies and specifications for inbound site electrical utilities. Civil engineers design the on-site utility systems, sewers, streets, parking lots, and site grading. Wise project managers clearly delineate where each engineer's jurisdiction terminates: for example, "site utilities" may extend to within three feet (0.9 m) of the building envelope, while "building electrical" may be within this boundary.

Effective project coordination relies on upfront communication, and engineers should be included early in the design process. Experienced developers generally facilitate a series of meetings with all architectural and engineering project personnel to define scope and communication channels and to discuss

Terrazzo is a ten-story residential tower located in the Gulch, a LEED-ND neighborhood in Nashville, Tennessee. The tower is certified LEED Silver.

BILL LAFEVOR, COURTESY OF CROSLAND

each discipline's goals and objectives in depth. For example, if the goal is to construct a high-efficiency building with systems that result in lower operating costs—digital thermostats, automated or remotely monitored off-site HVAC system controls, automatic water closets—these project aims need to be spelled out early in the process. It is increasingly common for developments to aim for performance certification, such as LEED (Leadership in Energy and Environmental Design), EarthCraft, or at a minimum EnergyStar, and such goals magnify the importance of early engineering and cost-estimating coordination. Costs of LEED certification, for example, vary widely by product type and by the strategic choices made to get to certification. Increasingly, developers report that the "green premium" for more sustainable construction is falling rapidly, with faster payback as utility costs rise. Developers should be aware of cost tradeoffs between higher development costs and lower ongoing operating expenses and furnish engineers with the criteria they will need to make decisions on their behalf.

Ronald Stenlund, president of Central Consulting Engineers, advises developers and their engineers to insist on two-year warranties on all installed mechanical systems.[6] It is vital that each component, particularly for a building's heating and cooling systems, go through a full season of startup and shutdown to be evaluated. Unfortunately, a one-year guarantee is the industry standard, and this period generally begins on the *shipping* date rather than the *installation* date. Further, maintenance people must be properly trained in the nuances of each system and gain familiarity with their operations.

One concern of all developers is having their soft costs come in over budget. According to Stenlund, "Failure to achieve effective communication among the developer, architect, and engineering staff early in the process is the single most common cause for project delays, redesigns, and cost overruns. Coordinating the team early, defining expectations, and developing a congruent project vision are the three keys to minimizing this risk factor."

SOILS ENGINEERS

Experienced developers recommend completing at least a few basic soils tests on a site before purchasing the property. Soils engineers can conduct an array of tests to determine a site's soil stability, the level of its water table, the presence and concentrations of common toxic materials, and any other conditions that will affect construction. Geotechnical engineering is not

an exact science, but hiring skilled, registered professionals reduces uncertainty and can at the very least indicate whether further testing should be conducted.

A soils engineer first removes a cross section of the soil by boring the surface of the site to a specified depth. That sample is then analyzed. Laboratory tests disclose the characteristics of the soil at various levels, the firmness of each of those levels, and, if requested, the presence of certain toxic materials. On smaller sites with no water or other potential problems, one boring test in the middle may be sufficient. On other sites, boring tests are usually completed in the middle and near the anticipated building corners and critical roadway or bridge locations. If the presence of toxic materials is suspected across the site, more borings may be necessary, but the project engineer should be consulted for a customized test approach. The soils engineer prepares a detailed report on the composition of the underlying soil, complete with an analysis of the characteristics of each layer. Soil composition is classified according to color, grain size, and firmness. The soils engineer also recommends the type of foundation system most appropriate for the site, based on the laboratory findings and tests to determine the soil's strength.

A bearing test determines the soil's ability to support the planned structure at the anticipated depth of the foundation. The soils engineer digs out a portion of the site to the designated level to complete the test. The soils engineer also determines the stability of the site's slope. During excavation, for example, digging straight down may be difficult because the remaining soil might cave in. The engineer is expected to use the results of the test to calculate the excavation angle that will leave the remaining soil intact.

Soils engineers participate with the architect and the structural engineer to design the most effective type of foundation system to support the proposed structure. They generally work on a lump-sum basis. A soils analysis can cost from $1,000 to $100,000, depending on the site's size and the number of test borings and types of tests necessary.

ENVIRONMENTAL CONSULTANTS

Though increasing environmental regulation has resulted in a substantial increase in specialty environmental consulting for real estate, there are two basic types of environmental consultants: one type, engaged during feasibility and approvals, analyzes the project's economic, social, and cultural effects on the surrounding built environment; the second type, engaged in the design phase, determines, in conjunction with soils engineers, mitigation for impacts associated with the development. Impacts can range from intrusion on streams or wetlands to increases in traffic, noise, and emissions. Planning and budgeting for environmental consultants can only follow a solid understanding of the regulatory process. Land use attorneys and planners are good sources of information, and they should be consulted early. Some aspects of on-site evaluation require long lead times, and some can only be accomplished during certain times of year. Emergent or seasonal wetlands, for example, might only be identifiable when wetland-associated plants are visible in the spring. The developer must also understand at what point in the approvals process formal environmental reviews are required.

Environmental reviews are often necessary for development projects of significant size and scope, and they are generally required and administered by state environmental quality agencies. Reviews usually focus on impacts to the immediate surroundings caused by the proposed development, such as increased traffic, reduced air quality, sunshine and shading, and infrastructure requirements.

The environmental approval process varies in rigor based on state and local regulations and attitudes.

These reviews are often sensitive political actions and demand a balancing diplomacy and insistence from the developer. Although no developer wants to be perceived as an environmental threat, it is also important to insist that statutory timelines and requirements are followed, as many developers have found the environmental review process to be abused by project opponents as a way to delay legitimate and low-impact projects.

The financial outlay, time, patience, and perseverance required to successfully navigate an environmental review and secure final building permits must not be underestimated. The process is governed by the appropriate level of government that first determines whether or not a developer is obligated to complete a formal environmental analysis, and which tier of study is indicated by the project. This process is triggered if a project exceeds various size or scale thresholds or affects environmentally sensitive areas, such as wetlands or an endangered species' habitat. Empowered by

Biltmore Park Town Square in Asheville, North Carolina, integrates retail and entertainment uses, offices, a hotel, and a variety of residential types on a 57-acre (23 ha) site. The master plan is LEED-ND certified.

PATRICK SCHNEIDER PHOTOGRAPHY

federal legislation, including the National Environmental Policy Act of 1969, each state and locality has created its own environmental laws to which developers must adhere, and these laws vary widely.

The least stringent type of required analysis is usually an environmental impact statement, which is sometimes referred to as an environmental site assessment. A more stringent environmental impact report (EIR), based on state and local legislation, may be ordered when a project is expected to pose substantial alterations to the built or natural environment. It is advisable to analyze the legislation to understand the various thresholds that trigger a partial or full EIR, as there are times when more thoughtful design can eliminate or limit the scope of an EIR.

A developer should select an environmental consulting firm that is respected for its technical expertise, independence, and impartiality. Because the results of an environmental report can become a political issue, developers must judge the level of complexity and controversy their project is likely to create and select a consulting team that has experience in projects of a similar magnitude. To ensure impartiality, some cities provide a list of acceptable firms from which a developer may choose. In California, the public sector often randomly assigns an environmental consulting firm to the developer and in some cases, the public agencies may reserve the right to select and manage the consultant, while requiring the developer to pay the consultant.

An EIR not only describes the proposed development, the site, the overall design parameters, and the project's effect on the local community but also proposes appropriate mitigation measures to offset negative effects, such as increased traffic congestion, soil runoff, and construction impacts. In the case of traffic impacts, the mitigation measures may include widening certain streets, adding left-turn lanes, adding traffic signals, converting some streets to one-way, or expanding public transit service to the area. Major projects may require significant off-site improvements, even new freeway interchanges.

Once a draft of the EIR has been prepared, it is submitted to various state and local agencies, circulated to concerned parties, and made available to the general public; each is allowed a specific period to submit comments. These comments may lead to significant design changes, but they will at a minimum require some sort of response, usually in writing. At this point, a developer must be extremely careful of making promises and making statements beyond the facts at hand.

Thereafter, the developer's environmental consultant must produce a final EIR that responds to all comments. Any mitigation measure(s) recommended by the consultant must be feasible for the developer to implement. In fact, agencies that regulate environmental impacts typically offer multiple methods of mitigation for those impacts, often allowing cash payment to a state-administered fund in lieu of specific performance. The timing and magnitude of these measures can vary greatly, so the developer must insist on analysis of the potential avenues for mitigation and make an informed decision. Public bodies, usually the planning commission, the city council, or both, generally include mitigation measures in their conditions for project approval, or at least as a condition for the release of completion bonds. These conditions are sometimes referred to as *exactions*, which are burdens placed on the developer to make financial payments or complete on-site and off-site improvements to mitigate the project's environmental effects.

Any change to the development plan requires simultaneous changes to the consultant's analysis and will sometimes require an informal check with regulators to ensure continued compliance with the rules as understood before. A sound development strategy is to secure input from all concerned parties as early as possible, even before the draft submission of the EIR, and to incorporate as many of those changes into the proposed design as possible. Regulators, for the most part, understand this strategy, and many are willing to meet informally, before submittals or review, to answer questions and to outline the process ahead. Developers should take advantage of such an offer, but they should be wary of releasing information in a public process before the design is complete. A balance can be struck by making the conversation about the rules rather than about the development.

The environmental review process can be a moving target and, if not managed effectively, can lead to skyrocketing development costs and delays that wipe out returns. For complex urban projects, it is not unheard of for a developer to have to change the entire project, including use, height, and overall square footage. As this process unfolds, it is important to keep an eye on the market, as the time it takes to secure permits is independent of economic and market cycles and may cause the developer to miss the market or the financing window altogether.

The cost of hiring an environmental consultant varies according to the size and complexity of the project analysis. Most consultants work on a lump-sum basis, with payment schedules tied to performance milestones. Developers should consider that the contract scope of an environmental consultant likely assumes typical regulatory jurisdiction and action, but environmental regulation is a relatively new field. As Matt Kiefer of Goulston & Storrs says, "We are entering a phase of regulatory experimentation. As the public sector has pulled back from direct involvement [in development], the emphasis has moved to performance-based measures."[7] Compliance with these standards can be notoriously difficult to determine. Surprising regulatory interpretations are to be expected, and they will often result in changes to the scope of the consultant.

The consultant's contractual obligations usually end with the production of the final report, although the developer might additionally require the consultant to make presentations and answer questions from municipal staff, or from the public at hearings. Following contract expiration, the consultant's compensation is based on a T&M agreement. The contract with the consultant must be reviewed to determine what is and is not included in the initial scope of responsibilities. It is worth noting that, at the point of completion of the contract, the developer will be deeply bound to the consultant by his prior work on behalf of the project, so T&M rates should, if possible, be negotiated up front, as the developer's leverage typically declines after the initial contract.

Another type of environmental consultant a developer may have to engage specializes in detection, containment, and removal of hazardous materials. Hazardous materials have become a major concern for developers and a significant source of litigation and liability, as well as delays and increased costs for containment and soil removal. Consequently, environmental analysis, including soils analysis, should incorporate tests to determine the presence of toxic materials, particularly heavy metals and known or suspected carcinogens. Ascertaining a property's previous use(s) is important, as particular uses connote the potential presence of different materials. Developers should be aware that brownfield sites with known or perceived contamination are not the only sites that warrant caution. Greenfield sites that, at the time of acquisition, appear the picture of cleanliness and health may, for example, have supported commercial orchards in the 1930s, when the pesticide of choice was powdered lead arsenate. In this example, the appropriate testing might only be ordered if historic aerial photos have been analyzed.

Environmental reports consist of three phases of analysis. Many lenders require a Phase I analysis for almost any kind of project; it simply involves a title search of previous users to determine the likelihood of toxic contamination. If the Phase I report finds potential contamination from, say, a gas station, dry cleaners, or industrial user, a Phase II report is required to determine the extent of any perceived problem. It usually includes analyzing soil samples, and it always includes at least a cursory examination of the property for clues to the location and potential extent of any problems. If the Phase II analysis finds possible off-site contamination or a serious threat of contamination of the water table, a Phase III analysis will be required.

It is vital to inspect every development site for the presence of hazardous materials, because liability for any future cleanup falls to any and all parties named on the chain of title and may result in personal recourse to the developer—even if the contamination predated the developer's acquisition of the site in question. Because hazardous waste contamination can involve millions of dollars in cleanup costs, years of delay, and potentially expensive litigation, prudent developers perform the necessary environmental analyses before they acquire a property.

SURVEYORS

Surveyors determine a property's physical and legal characteristics—existing easements, rights-of-way, and dedications on the site—and prepare a site map plotting these characteristics. This critical information reveals how much of the site can be built out and the allowable square footage and densities. Because of this obvious relation to parcel value, and because of the central role of the survey in the documentation of the purchase and sale transaction, surveyors are typically among the first project consultants to be hired, typically well before money goes hard on a purchase. Developers often attempt to delay soft-cost expenditures as long as possible, but paying for surveys early can avert disaster in the acquisition. Developers should note that some survey services critical to both design and approvals, such as aerial-topographic interpolation, can only be done (or done accurately and economically) during certain times of year in some regions.

Developers commonly use four types of survey services: a *boundary survey*, a *construction survey*, a *construction stakeout*, and an *as-built survey*. The boundary survey determines the boundaries of the site (easements and other legal requirements affect ownership of the property being plotted on a map).

The construction survey plots the location of relevant infrastructure—water, sewers, electricity, gas lines, and roads—to assist in planning connections to utility services and physical characteristics related to development, such as flood zones, watershed areas, and existing improvements. Surveyors also augment the work completed by soils engineers, analyzing a site's topography, likely runoff and slope, and the implications for civil engineering of the building's proposed location. The surveyor will typically return after project design to perform a construction stakeout, which involves the physical setting of annotated stakes that will direct the grading, excavation, and paving crews in construction. Precision of the construction staking directly affects the quality of construction on site. Finally, when all major construction is complete, a surveyor may be brought back to the site for an as-built survey. Approval authorities often require as-built drawings, which precisely indicate building corners, utility locations, public and private roadways, and drainage improvements critical to offsite uses.

A good surveyor also shows all title impingements by making sure everything in the title is found in the survey. One developer suggests walking the site with the surveyor to observe any positive or negative influences on the site that can then be reconciled with the title.[8]

Costs for surveyors vary according to the type of work they perform, the detail required, and the number of surveys requested. The American Land Title Association has defined standard survey types for various kinds of real estate transactions. Developers should find out early which level of survey will be required by their lender and buyers and commit to at least that level of detail. In addition, municipal, state, and federal regulators may require differing levels of survey accuracy, particularly in topographic surveys. Developers should inquire about these requirements and contract for the most stringent that will be required by any agency during the development period.

Surveyors may work on a lump-sum contract or a T&M agreement. As with other consultants, developers should insist on predictable and firm pricing as early as possible, but additional survey work will likely be required at some point in the process. It is thus advisable for clients to negotiate T&M pricing in the context of the initial agreement, so that this work can proceed affordably and quickly when it is needed. As a general rule, someone who has surveyed the property in the past will be less expensive because he has already done a vast majority of the work. A search of existing plats of the property will indicate the name of

the surveyor firm at that time; if it is still in business, the developer would be well advised to solicit a bid. Surveyors can also be important allies because of their involvement with the local regulatory community. In smaller communities, surveyors perform many of the roles more commonly ascribed to land planners and can often represent projects to zoning boards and city councils more effectively than lawyers.

PARKING AND TRAFFIC CONSULTANTS

Parking and traffic capacity are often major limiting factors for real estate development. High land values and restrictive local parking ordinances require a well-devised parking plan. A qualified parking consultant takes into account all the significant factors involved in designing the optimum parking for the site. The parking consultant should be included early in the design process so that the architect can incorporate parking recommendations in the overall design.

Parking consultants may be responsible for many aspects of a project: (1) evaluating the economics of a surface lot versus a parking structure, (2) designing an efficient parking configuration, (3) discovering whether local municipal codes can accommodate the estimated parking demand, (4) determining whether parking should be provided free or at a fee, and (5) deciding where the points of ingress and egress will be.

Parking is an expensive undertaking, costing tens of thousands per space for a structured garage. Consequently, the services of a well-qualified consultant are

At Ballantyne Corporate Place in Charlotte, North Carolina, more than 1,800 parking spaces are accommodated in garages, allowing more open space to be preserved.

BISSELL

Organizing for Development

often essential to project economics. Referrals from the architect and other developers can provide a list of potential consultants. Parking consultants usually work under a lump-sum contract or at an hourly rate.

Traffic consultants are included here because their firms' capabilities often include parking consultation, but the variety of issues they can address is much wider. Traffic studies, for example, are a common requirement of the EIR process detailed earlier. In many jurisdictions, the developer must prove that the proposed development is adequately served by existing roads and transit; inadequate infrastructure is a prime justification for delay and denial by approval authorities.

ASBESTOS ABATEMENT PROFESSIONALS

Renovation or adaptive use of a building constructed between 1920 and 1976 is likely to run the risk of asbestos contamination. Pricing for abatement is competitive in major construction markets. The industry has developed efficient methods of service delivery, and the amount of asbestos requiring removal is declining. Asbestos was commonly used for fireproofing and insulation in the United States until 1973, when federal legislation prohibited its future use for those purposes. Asbestos was sprayed on underlying columns, beams, pipes, and ducts of buildings; above ceilings; and behind walls. It was also used in building materials, such as tiles, exterior siding, and countertops. And in some parts of the country, fibers were mixed directly into wet plaster for interior wall surfaces. Asbestos is hazardous when *friable* (that is, flaky or powdery); if disturbed, its fibers become airborne and are likely to be inhaled. The U.S. Environmental Protection Agency (EPA) regulates activities like renovation and demolition that could release asbestos into the air and outlines appropriate methods of disposal. Even the installation of sprinkler systems, electrical and plumbing repairs, and any interior reconfiguration might require some form of asbestos abatement.

Removing asbestos requires the services of qualified professionals and permits for disposal of the waste; the hazards inherent in the process could lead to legal repercussions if inexperienced firms are hired to carry out the tasks. The firm selected should be bonded by a certifiable surety company. Both the consultant hired to determine the extent of contamination and the contractor responsible for removing it should be licensed by the state, and it is generally a good idea to engage separate individuals for these two tasks. Developers may contact the regional office of the EPA

and the National Asbestos Council for lists of qualified professionals.

Asbestos abatement occurs in two stages: inspection and removal. Consultants charge by the hour or by the square foot. Surveys for a typical 20,000-square-foot (1,860 m²) building, for example, might be around $3,000 for the physical inspection. Consultants collect about 50 samples from the building to determine what material requires removal. These tests cost about $30 per sample.

Estimates for abatement can vary widely, but one important factor is often out of the developer's control. Many jobs must be carried out while other areas of the building or complex are occupied, which can greatly increase the cost of removal as HVAC systems and connecting spaces must be protected while work proceeds.[9]

CONSTRUCTION CONTRACTORS

Construction contractors are required to complete an array of services (both before and during construction) on time and, ideally, on budget. They can provide a reality check on such critical matters as construction materials, structural and architectural design, local construction practices, and pricing information and can help establish a realistic budget when brought in early on a project.

Developers can select a contractor through negotiations with a particular firm or through open bidding. To find a good contractor, developers should solicit a number of contracting firms, asking them to submit proposals or general statements of qualifications. Responses should include descriptions of past projects, references from clients and lenders, résumés outlining the experience of key employees (particularly the proposed project engineer or manager), and, possibly, verification that the company is bondable. Payment histories from business credit-reporting agencies, such as Paydex, and audited financial statements should also be reviewed. These submissions can be used to select a company for direct negotiation.

In open bidding, developers send out a notice requesting bids and statements of qualifications. The problem with this approach is that contractors are reluctant to spend time bidding on a project unless they think that they have a good chance of being selected. As a result, the developer may not attract an adequate number of responses from which to choose, especially if the firm is new to development and proposing a relatively small project in a hot market. Two to four weeks are necessary to allow contractors to return satisfactory responses. A comprehensive bid will take longer, on a complex project, but the time can be accelerated by involving likely bidders as the project goes through construction documents.

The most effective way to limit the number of bidders but still ensure that the targeted firms will respond is a combination of a request for qualifications and competitive bidding. After reviewing several contractors' qualifications, developers may ask the best three, four, or five contractors to prepare a bid for the project. A preference for one contractor could result in direct negotiations with a particular firm. Developers should not feel obligated to conduct protracted bidding if they have already found the best contractor for the job. It is equally important that developers who wish to continue working in a market must respect the time of major contractors. Contractors should not be brought into a bidding process in which they have no chance of success, simply to "keep the other guy honest."

Jonathan Rose, principal of Jonathan Rose Companies, suggests keeping in mind three points when choosing contractors:[10]

1. Find someone who is experienced in the product type being considered for the project. A specialist in assisted living facilities will likely not be an appropriate choice for multifamily housing.
2. Be certain that your project amounts to no more than one-third of the contracting firm's total workload, a good benchmark for organizational and financial stability. That is, if you have a $20 million project, look for a contractor with at least $60 million in total business at the time the contract is signed.
3. Ask for and check references to understand how the contractor has performed for past clients.

During the design stage, a contractor working for fees or a construction price estimator (also called a *quantity surveyor*) should check the architect's drawings and formulate an estimated budget for completing the project. A permanent contractor, once hired, is responsible for completing a construction cost estimate based on the construction drawings completed by the architect. If the developer chooses to put the project on a fast track, the contractor should be a helpful source of creative and cost-effective suggestions during preliminary design.

One of the contractor's tasks is to set up a projected schedule for disbursing loans from the construction lender. The contractor's major responsibility, however, is

Two Constitution Square in Washington, D.C., transforms an obsolete industrial area into a vibrant business and residential district. It is located near transit and has been certified LEED-ND.

the project's physical construction, including soliciting bids from and then hiring all the subcontractors—construction workers, plumbers, painters, and electrical and mechanical contractors. The contractor is legally responsible for building a safe structure and must hire the best-qualified employees and subcontractors.

Two basic methods are used to determine the contractor's compensation: bids or contracts. Bids are requested to be in the form of a lump sum or some derivative of a cost-plus-fee contract. A lump-sum bid is used when the design is already established and all the construction drawings are complete before selecting the contractor. This option is rarely feasible for beginning developers, however, because they are probably not willing or able to underwrite the cost of complete drawings until the decision to construct is finalized.

Contractors' fees are based on the size of the project, the number and amount of anticipated change orders, and so on. On a $10 million project, a contractor should be expected to charge a fee equivalent to 5 percent of total hard costs—in addition to project overhead and on-site supervision costs.

A cost-plus-fee contract is a preferable means of compensating experienced contractors with excellent reputations. Under this option, all costs—labor, salaries of accountants and other such employees, travel, construction materials, supplies, equipment, and fees for all subcontractors—should be explicitly set forth in the contract. The costs should not include overhead and administrative expenses for the contractor's main or branch offices, and they should not include full costs for assets that are used only partially for the job being bid. Costs that cannot be accurately estimated before contract should be negotiated on a unit basis, such as price per cubic yard of fill, leaving only the quantity to be accurately recorded during construction.

The contractor must calculate the time required to complete the project as a basis for a fixed or percentage fee. Most developers avoid a percentage fee because it does not incentivize the contractor to minimize costs, but these concerns can also be addressed with performance bonuses.

Often, the construction lender requires the contractor to guarantee a maximum cost, or gross maximum price, when the cost-plus-fee method is used. In such cases, the architect is responsible for providing drawings with sufficient detail to allow the contractor to solicit quotes from subcontractors to calculate the maximum cost. Guaranteed maximum cost contracts can include an incentive to save costs; perhaps 25 to 50 percent of the developer's savings could be shared with the contractor if total project costs are less than the guaranteed maximum. Another model is to split the contingency fee; that is, the developer and the contractor split every dollar saved under budgeted costs, which could amount to 5 to 10 percent of a project's costs.[11]

The developer must make sure, however, that the contractor does not sacrifice quality to receive the bonus. Maintaining high quality is accomplished by detailed attention to project specifications and construction documents. Other types of incentive bonuses can also save costs. A bonus for early completion pays a defined amount for completing the work by a specific date; some contracts pay a fixed amount for each day that work is completed before the deadline. By the same token, bonus clauses can be used to penalize the contractor for being late. Some contracts include a liquidated damage clause or a penalty clause to cover late completion. Not surprisingly, contractors dislike such clauses, which, they argue, undermine teamwork.

Bonus and incentive clauses are a tool for guaranteeing the contractor's performance. The developer incurs costs, however, most notably in the necessary monitoring of the contractor's performance.

Real Estate Service Firms

A variety of service firms can provide a wide range of real estate services that are critical in the development process. These firms are usually brought into a project to perform specific, short-term tasks.

MARKET CONSULTANTS

Successful real estate decisions hinge on the availability of reliable and accurate information. A market consultant provides the professional assessment of a proposed project's appeal to various quantifiable groups or types of buyers and tenants. Their deliverable, the *market study*, analyzes the proposed project's feasibility based on current and projected market conditions. Lenders, investors, design professionals, and sales staff all use the market study at various points in the development process.

Some developers complete their own market studies, and lenders may accept a well-documented study by a developer, particularly for a small project. But it is always a good idea to get a third-party perspective on the market from a professional market analyst. Which market consultant to hire is one of the most important decisions made during the predevelopment period. Developers may ask other developers for recommendations; however, lenders' recommendations are particularly important because their decisions depend on the market data proving the project's feasibility. Although a few national consulting firms offer real estate market studies, market intelligence is a highly localized business. Developers in a well-documented geographic area, trading in a common product bought, sold, or leased frequently, may be well served by a nationally known firm. For niche products, in secondary markets, local knowledge is irreplaceable.

The databases the market consultant maintains are useful indications of the consultant's approach. Aside from being technically proficient, the consultant must be able to understand the nuances of the market that may not be readily apparent. A good market consultant can identify the proposed competition and thoughtfully analyze the political situation.

Developers should ask to see several market studies that the consultant has produced and make sure that they are comfortable with the assumptions and techniques used. The style of writing and presentation of the report should be carefully examined as well.

The market consultant is responsible for producing a final study that should address all factors affecting the proposed project's feasibility. As a client, the smart developer looks for a comprehensive study that will give independent evidence about the marketability of the development proposal. (The specific features of the process for various property types are discussed in the appropriate sections of chapters 3 through 7.)

The study should include a profile of tenants or buyers to be targeted and the amenities and lease terms to be offered. It is increasingly common for marketing professionals to define these target groups in "psychographic" terms, rather than simply demographic and income criteria. As such, a well-conceived market study may go beyond identifying the buyer and begin to suggest ways of reaching, vetting, and converting leads to sales. The architect should use the market information to help determine the project's design, unit sizes, amenities, and so on so that they appropriately address the market.

After the feasibility and business-planning phase, a good market study provides a foundation for sales and marketing decisions and can be particularly useful when multiple brokers or sales agents must cooperate on a single project. The market study can provide the framework for a sales narrative about the project, its neighborhood, and qualitative aspects of the project's "lifestyle."

A market consultant's fee is based on the level of detail that the developer requests. Preliminary information may be obtained for less than $5,000, while a detailed report may cost from $25,000 to $100,000 or more, depending on the complexity of the study. For a preliminary analysis or a quick inventory of the market, the consultant may work on an hourly basis, but larger, more complex studies require a fixed contract.

APPRAISERS

The appraisal report should state the property's market value and offer supporting evidence. Three methodologies can be used to complete an appraisal: the *income approach*, the *market approach*, and the *cost approach*. The income approach is preferred for all income-producing property (commercial, industrial, office, and rental apartments). Value is determined by dividing the project's net operating income by an appropriate capitalization rate. Income determination of value depends on the definition of net income used, and when comparing multiple properties, developers should know that the terms are the same. The market approach uses recent information about sales of properties similar to the subject property to determine a market value. This approach is used most often with single-family residential properties, condominiums, and land. The cost approach estimates the cost to construct a project similar to the one under consideration. It is used to determine the value of recently completed buildings or of buildings without a deep and liquid market, such as specialized industrial facilities. The appraiser should use standard techniques and professionally accepted forms to produce a credible report. Appraisal costs range from $500 for a single-family house to $10,000 or more for a large office building.

Investors, potential buyers, and lenders require a professional appraisal to arrive at a market value that will set the amount of the loan for the proposed project.

Lending institutions usually employ in-house appraisers or select an independent outside firm. Professional appraiser organizations can supply references; their members must demonstrate certain minimum standards to gain admission and are issued a credential such as MAI (Member of the Appraisal Institute).

ATTORNEYS

Many facets of real estate development—taxes, land use, leases, and joint venture partnerships, for example—require separate legal specialists. No single attorney can be an expert in all these topics. For zoning and other activities involving public hearings, an attorney with a proven success rate in cases involving a particular public body might be the proper choice. The ability to work behind the scenes with the local planning staff and politicians may be an attorney's greatest asset in such cases. Developers of the type of project under consideration can often recommend good land use attorneys.

Attorneys are essential for producing partnership or syndication agreements and contracts for consultants, acquiring property, writing up loan documents and leasing contracts, and negotiating the public approval process. The process of obtaining public approvals can be an intimidating maze for a beginning developer without an experienced attorney and may lead to costly delays or outright rejection. Even when a developer chooses to represent himself in dealings with public authorities, the opinion of a knowledgeable land use attorney is critical. A zoning opinion, for example, provides the owner or developer with a defensible understanding of the development potential and constraints on a particular site, and a seasoned attorney can provide, very early on, a review of a proposed project and an educated opinion on the required steps to approvals and on appropriate time allocations as the developer plans a schedule.

Most developers request that a partner of the law firm or a well-established attorney work on their cases, preferring to pay a little more for the top person to guarantee the best job. For technical work

Wisconsin Place is an infill development in Chevy Chase, Maryland. The project includes retail, office space, underground parking, and luxury residences. It was developed by a partnership of three large developers: New England Development, Archstone, and Boston Properties.

like syndications and contracts, highly recommended junior associates with three or four years of experience may be more cost-effective. Attorneys generally bill clients by the hour, although fixed prices for certain transactions are not uncommon. The developer should obtain an estimate of the total cost for a job before authorizing it and should reach an understanding early on about what constitutes "approval" for work done on the developer's behalf. Developers who are not lawyers themselves must also admit that they do not necessarily know how long certain tasks will take, and they must be open with their attorney about their fee expectations.

Leonard Zax, the retired chair of Latham & Watkins real estate group, gives the following tips for getting the best work from one's attorneys:[12]

- The scope of different attorneys' work may overlap, and important issues and transactions sometimes slip through the cracks. The development firm's general counsel is the best person to ensure legal continuity for a project. In lieu of retaining corpo-

rate counsel, it is prudent to appoint one individual already involved in the project as responsible for patching any gaps in representation.
- Distinguish legal advice from business comment.
- Clients need to understand the greater context in which their legal counsel is operating. Be aware of all matters pending between a firm you have hired and public bodies that have influence over your project.
- The most effective lawyer is not always the tough table pounder, nor is he or she effective by always agreeing with the developer. The most effective lawyers take time to listen and formulate a candid opinion of the legal elements that need to be addressed. And developers should listen to their attorney. Too many developers rush to judgment and do not have the patience to hear their counsel's entire opinion—often on complex issues that are critical to the project's success.
- Do not establish a fee structure that encourages cutting corners.

TITLE COMPANIES

Title companies certify who holds title to a property and guarantee the purchaser and lender that the property is free and clear of unexpected liens that may cloud the title. Title companies will defend any future claims against properties that they insure. The type of title policy determines the extent of the protection. Most policies follow a standard format, but many real estate investors fail to read and understand what protection their title policy provides, and to whom, which can lead to problems if claims are asserted after closing and costly litigation ensues.

When selecting a title company, developers should make sure that the company has the financial strength to back any potential claims—they are rated like other insurance companies—and should research its record to find out how long a company takes to obtain a clean title.

Title companies often provide additional services. They provide, free of charge, both current and potential customers with a profile of a property in which the customer is interested. The profile details ownership, property taxes paid, liens, easements, size of lot and improvements, grant and trust deeds, notes, and most recent sale price. Title companies also provide local data, such as comparable sales information and plat maps.

A preliminary title report specifying current liens against the property can be prepared for a fee. The preliminary title is not an insurance policy, but it is a close reading of the existing title. It highlights any potential problems a future owner may need to clear before title is transferred. Standard title policies do not usually provide insurance protection for taxes or assessments not shown as existing liens; interests, claims, or easements not shown by the public records; conflicts in boundary lines; mining claims and water rights; or liens for services, labor, and material that do not appear in the public records. Of particular interest in some areas are historic but unrecorded easements of access, for example, historic public rights-of-way known as "phantom roads," rights to which can be asserted long after actual use has been discontinued. More common are potentially valid claims, such as family members' interests in property, which have not been claimed or recorded, but which might still be within the statutory time limit for doing so. An ALTA (American Land Title Association) policy offers extended coverage that does cover such unrecorded claims; it requires the kind of in-depth survey that sophisticated purchasers usually demand.

Title fees can be obtained from any representative of the company and are usually applicable statewide. They are commonly quoted on a scale that slides according to the sale price of the property being insured. More often than not, the seller pays for title insurance, though terms of the purchase and sale agreement can address this directly. Costs associated with ALTA title insurance are variable but are nationally competitive and are usually under $1 per $1,000 of asset value.

SURETY COMPANIES

Developers need insurance to guard against a consultant's or contractor's failure to perform an agreed-on task, and municipalities often require similar guarantees for a developer's performance. Such a failure may have serious economic and legal consequences for the development project, and potentially for the community. For instance, a contractor's failure to meet obligations could result in a lien on the developer's property, delaying if not stopping sales altogether. All public works projects must, by law, be bonded for performance because liens cannot be placed on public property. Private projects do not have to be bonded, but in most instances some form of bond is recommended, and bonding of infrastructure can allow developers greater flexibility in constructing improvements at a pace consistent with sales. Contractors are generally required to be *bondable*, meaning that they qualify for surety coverage.

General contractors deal directly with a surety company to obtain performance and payment bonds. The developer is required to inform all contractors that bonds will be required before bids are submitted, and contractors consequently adjust their bids to pass on the cost of bonds to the developer. Bondable contractors generally establish a relationship with one surety company and fix an upper bonding limit of credit, which restricts the amount of bondable work that the contractor can perform. Construction bonds are a specialized product, offered by few insurance companies. A surety bond involves a three-party contract in which a surety company (or, simply, a *surety*) joins with a principal, usually the contractor, in guaranteeing the specific performance of an act to the developer or municipality, also referred to as the *beneficiary*.

Bonding should not be interpreted as a negative comment on the contractor. Rather, it is a validation of the contractor's ability to deliver a finished product. Before issuing a bond, the surety thoroughly analyzes the contractor's firm, including its qualifications and previous experience, its financial stability, and its management structure, and inventories its equipment.

Based on these facts, the surety appraises the contractor's ability to complete the project. If the firm is deemed stable, the surety issues the appropriate bonds and work can proceed. Even if the developer chooses not to require any construction bonds, the surety's seal of approval is an affirmation of the contractor's quality.

The three main types of bonds are performance, payment, and completion.

Performance bonds guarantee the developer that if the contractor fails to complete the agreed-on contract, the surety is responsible for seeing that the work is finished. The agreement allows the surety to compensate the developer with an amount equal to the money needed to complete the project or to hire a contractor to finish the job. Lenders sometimes insist on bond coverage for their own protection. The general contractor, either at the developer's request or on its own, requires subcontractors to purchase performance bonds and may be requested to provide evidence of this bonding to the client.

Payment bonds guarantee that the surety will meet obligations if the contractor defaults on payments to laborers, subcontractors, or suppliers, protecting the property against liens that might be imposed in response to nonpayment. Developers, lenders, or both often require the general contractor to purchase these bonds to protect them against any future claims of nonpayment made by subcontractors or suppliers. Payment bonds are usually issued concurrently with performance bonds; both bonds often appear on the same form.

Completion bonds, often referred to as *developer off-site* or *subdivision bonds*, ensure local municipalities that specified off-site improvements will be completed. Many states require local municipalities to secure the bonds as assurance that the developer will complete the improvements.

The developer may require bid bonds during the solicitation of contractors' bids. A bid bond, issued by a surety, guarantees the developer that winning contractors will honor their accepted bids. If, for example, a winning contractor finds out that its bid was significantly lower than the others submitted, it may be tempted to withdraw the offer. In such instances, the surety pays damages to the developer, in theory to compensate for time and money lost.

A municipality may not require bonding for private on-site improvements, but it may prohibit presales of property dependent on those improvements until they are completed. Such a prohibition can be a major impediment to some kinds of development projects. In some jurisdictions, the developer may post a bond, surety, or cash deposit to the benefit of the municipality, guaranteeing construction of private, on-site improvements, such as roads or utility service, and thereby gain the right to close sales on properties dependent on those services. The benefits to project cash flow of this approach can be considerable. Where on-site infrastructure is bondable, the municipality will make an independent assessment of the cost to complete the approved improvements and will set the bond amount for each major segment of infrastructure. Bonds will be released by application when the work is complete, following an inspection by an agent of the municipality. Some jurisdictions allow for partial release, such as when a particular road within a development is complete. Rates for these bonds are comparable with the others outlined here.

In most states, surety companies must charge uniform rates. For performance and payment bonds, the rate charged is the same regardless of whether 50 or 100 percent of the contract price is guaranteed; therefore, developers should ask for 100 percent coverage. Rates are based on the contract price and are calculated on a graduated payment scale. The rates for completion bonds are generally higher because they involve additional underwriting.

Opinion is divided about the need to secure the various forms of surety bonds. Performance and payment bonds cost roughly 1 percent of the construction costs, so it is up to the developer to decide whether or not bonding is worth the abated risk.

Ventura Lofts in Houston was developed by Sueba USA Corporation on the site of an abandoned office building. It consists of 265 rental apartments.

PAUL DYER PHOTOGRAPHY

FIGURE 2-2 | Typical Real Estate Sales Commissions

Product Type	Percent of Total Price
Raw land	5–10
Single-family houses	3–7
Apartment building	3–6
Office building	3–7
Industrial building	4–6
Shopping center	4–6
Hotels	3–6

BROKERS/LEASING AGENTS

Real estate brokers and leasing agents are hired to sell or lease a project to prospective tenants and buyers. Developers can benefit greatly from the services of a skilled salesperson who is able to quickly and completely lease or sell a project at or near the pro forma pricing. Developers must decide whether to sign an agreement with an outside real estate broker or to place an agent on the payroll. The decision is usually based on the type and magnitude of the project.

The use of in-house agents is most appropriate for large projects and large development firms that can carry the cost. The benefit of an in-house staff is that the developer hires and trains the staff during initial planning, and the agents become very familiar with the project, providing input during design and merchandising. Using in-house sales staff typically results in more complete attention from brokers, who are by nature always on the lookout for the next listing. Direct control over sales on one project also has benefits for other projects of the development firm, as leads, techniques, technological investment (such as website development and mass communications), and advertising can be coordinated and shared. Brokerage can also be a profit center for the project, especially once a project has achieved some operational stability, and general awareness and interest are high.

Small development firms may find it useful to retain outside brokers with local knowledge and who have lower carrying costs. Brokers are usually aware of potential tenants with existing leases that are about to expire; brokers from large brokerage houses may have information about regional or national tenants. In residential and resort sales, a regional or national firm may have relevant experience selling similar products in other markets and may offer creative ways to approach out-of-town relocation buyers.

It is essential to interview representatives from a number of firms to select one with relevant experience. If a perspective broker does not respond positively to the project, another broker should be found, but consistently tepid response from the broker community should concern the developer, especially if elements of the design and marketing plans are still being refined. If a prospective broker currently represents a competitive development, that broker should not be hired because of potential conflicts of interest. Brokers and agents typically have deep roots in their communities and can be early voices in support of the positive economic and neighborhood effects of a project.

The working relationship between developer and broker is defined in a contract referred to as a listing agreement. Under an open *listing agreement*, the developer may recruit several brokers and is responsible for paying a commission only to the one who sells or leases the property. If the developer completes a transaction without the broker's assistance, no commission is necessary. An exclusive listing agreement involves, as its name suggests, a single broker.

The most common form of agreement for developers is an *exclusive right-to-sell listing*. In this instance, the developer selects one broker, who automatically receives the commission no matter who sells the property, including the developer. In the event that another broker brings a buyer to the listing broker's property, it is usually up to the two to negotiate a split of the commission. To prevent conflicts that might scuttle sales, developers may wish to specify the split in the listing agreement. Predictability and fair treatment are essential, as in all dealings with brokers, who must spend substantial and uncompensated time learning about properties, with hopes of someday being compensated by matching a buyer to the product. Respect for the broker's time and business needs will go a long way toward a friendly reception for the beginning developer's project.

Successful projects have been completed with marketing and sales in house, both with outsourced and with a combination of in-house marketing and independent brokerage. Allowing brokers to plan, implement, and pay for the promotional campaign involves them and gives them a sense of responsibility. Since they are compensated only upon sale, the logic goes, they should control the investment of marketing dollars and reap the rewards of success. Developers often prefer to pay for the promotion themselves, however, to retain control over the timing, intensity,

FIGURE 2-3 | Typical Lease Commissions (Percentages by Year)

Property Type	1	2	3	4	5	6–10	10+
Shopping center	6	5	4	4	3	3	3
Office building	6	5	4	4	3	3	3
Industrial building	5	4	3	2	1	1	1

Note: Commissions are calculated as a percentage of undiscounted gross rents for the primary term, typically half paid on full execution of the lease and the balance at opening for business. Commissions are subject to negotiation and vary widely.

and nature of marketing, as well as to maintain the overall image of their project.

In leasing, the broker's responsibility is to negotiate leases with prospects while keeping in mind the developer's goals regarding rates of return and preferred type of tenant. The developer should establish lease guidelines for the broker to follow and should readily accept leases presented by the broker within those guidelines so as to maintain credibility with the brokerage community. Once the project is leased, the developer may retain the broker to lease space as it becomes available.

The developer should negotiate a schedule for commissions that will provide incentives to lease or sell the building as quickly as possible—for example, by providing higher commission rates or bonuses for tours and contracts early in the project to gain momentum.

Real estate brokers work almost exclusively for commission. The broker and the developer negotiate the rate of compensation, which varies according to the type, size, and geographic location of the project, and is typically based on a percentage of the total price for sales (see figure 2-2).

Lease commissions payable to the broker are calculated as an annual percentage of the value of a signed lease for each year of the lease. Over the term of the lease, the percentages paid to the broker are scaled down (see figure 2-3). Half the aggregate commission is typically paid upon execution of the lease and half is paid at move-in.

PUBLIC RELATIONS AND ADVERTISING AGENCIES

Promotion spreads the word about the project to the community and differentiates it from the competition in the minds of potential users. Developers often neglect promotion, hoping instead that the project will sell itself; this approach is almost always a mistake.

Part of the process of selecting a public relations or advertising agency involves attending presentations at which the agencies under consideration offer examples of their previous work, samples relevant to the proposed project, and promotional ideas for the project.

Public relations firms not only produce news releases, press kits, newsletters, and mailings conveying information about the project but also can create situations that will give the project positive exposure in the community. Different projects and product types require different approaches to attract interest from potential consumers, and the agency chooses the tools that are most appropriate for a given project. The agency should also be a source of creative ideas to market the project effectively, and it should be involved as early as possible in the conceptual design phase. Aesthetic and programmatic choices, typically made to satisfy concrete demand illustrated in market studies, may also have implications for the project's branding and identity. Simple and inexpensive choices like street names and amenity locations and types can also be important to advertising strategy, and the input of professionals with these concerns in mind can be invaluable.

Good promotional plans draw attention to the project at strategic moments—groundbreaking and topping-off ceremonies, for example. A good public relations firm can be an invaluable asset when a project is proposed in a contentious political environment. A well-conceived campaign can gain favorable publicity for the project and sell it to the community. Organized community events, complete with well-designed presentations, introduce the company and the project to the neighborhood and local politicians and leave a favorable impression.

A public relations firm can handle advertising, and an advertising agency can often handle public relations. Sometimes, a firm with one or the other strength can be retained for both duties, with support from a stronger player in their secondary skill set. Advertising involves placing ads strategically to promote the project and maximize its exposure vis-à-vis the cost of appearance in media. Many different media and promotional techniques are available, including newspapers, radio and television, and outdoor signs, but most real estate developments receive the majority of inbound traffic now via Internet search and social media websites. A paid Internet search is a cost-effective way of gathering self-directed potential buyers and tenants and depends on a comprehensive strategy developed by experts in the algorithms of search engines. Most advertising firms are well versed in at least the basics of online campaigns, but the developer should not be satisfied with basic knowledge. If a firm's online facility is weak, its efforts should be supplemented by an experienced technology-oriented firm.

Regardless of how many entities make up the team, it is essential to assemble a comprehensive marketing and public relations plan, with the developer's input, early in the project, preferably at least a year before sales or leasing begin. Advertising and public relations firms, as well as associated professionals in digital media, generally work on monthly retainers plus expenses to cover radio, television, online, newspaper, billboard, and magazine advertising.

PROPERTY MANAGEMENT

Following construction and lease-up, the developer's focus becomes operational rather than visionary, with the new focus placed squarely on maximizing value at the time of sale. The two overriding goals are to maintain rental rates and high occupancy rates. As such, this next phase of the project's life calls for sustained property management.

Property management can be handled through an in-house staff or through a skilled outside service provider. This decision rests squarely on the development firm's internal organizational skills, whether property management can be a profit center, the amount of time this activity will command, and the opportunity

costs inherent in this activity as opposed to pursuing other revenue opportunities. Each situation is unique, and the developer should reflect on the overall vision for the company and how it meshes with this activity. Maintaining property management in house provides certain advantages:

- direct property oversight and quality control;
- constant tenant contact;
- a diversified organizational revenue stream; and
- insight into changing tenant operational issues, which can lead to future development opportunities and higher project quality.

But in-house property management also has some disadvantages:

- Time cost may be high compared with other revenue-producing activities.
- Property type organizational skills, staffing, and experience are limiting factors.
- Economies of scale place smaller developers at a competitive disadvantage compared with professional property management firms.
- Property management can end up becoming a cost center as opposed to a profit center.

The manager should provide a comprehensive short-, medium-, and long-range strategic property plan specifying the frequency of physical inspections, maintenance needs, and a replacement schedule. This plan is particularly important for large capital expenditures, such as roof maintenance and replacement, HVAC systems, and other physical and structural issues. In certain projects with repeated units, even very small expenditures like window washing can add up to severely affect cash flow. Budgeting and planning for the year ahead will reduce unforeseen operating costs and diminish the likelihood of emergency repairs. As frontline personnel, property managers address all aspects of the developer's relationship with tenants. Initially, managers should supervise the tenant improvement and move-in processes, making sure everything proceeds smoothly; it is very important for tenant relationships to start off on a high note.

Effective managers maintain communication with tenants, so that any problems can be quickly resolved with a high degree of customer satisfaction. It is important to keep in mind that the developer's reputation is at stake; complaints from tenants directly to the developer are a signal that the property manager is not performing effectively.

FIGURE 2-4 | Developing a Marketing Strategy

Market Analysis
— Before Going Hard
— Before Land Closing

Target Analysis

Marketing Strategy

Leasing
Brochures
Market Analysis
Property Management Personnel
Public Relations
Advertising
Merchandising
Leasing Personnel

Some contracts call for the property manager to also serve as the leasing agent. This arrangement can be beneficial, as the management firm has the most intimate relationship with the property. A large number of vacancies, however, may call for a more aggressive leasing strategy or may require the expertise of a leasing broker with broader market knowledge. Each situation is unique, and the developer must decide who is more capable of filling any vacancies that arise. High turnover rates are a sign that something—physical, managerial, or both—is amiss, and the developer should take action to determine the causes and remedies.

Operations run more smoothly when the management company is given authority to sign contracts, to release budgeted funds for scheduled maintenance, and to implement capital improvements. The agreement between developer and property manager should specify dollar limits on what the manager can spend before the owner's approval is required, with the owner's approval necessitated in all instances of projected capital expenditures.

It is important for tax, audit, and tracking purposes that funds belonging to the property owner and to the management entity be maintained in separate accounts. The management firm should set up a trust account to protect the owner's funds and to prevent any commingling of funds between properties and entities. Audit reports should be prepared regularly (twice a year is recommended) so the developer can verify rental collections, deposits, occupancies, vacancies, management expenses, and capital expenditures.

Property management services are generally priced as a percentage of the property's gross revenue, except for very high-end residential units, where the fee might be a fixed dollar amount per unit). Property managers typically negotiate a fee ranging from 1 to 5 percent of gross revenue.

The fee is predicated on the amount of management activity and degree of difficulty the project presents. When comparing bids from management firms, the developer should be careful to determine which costs are included in the fee and which are additional billable expenses to the property (management and maintenance salaries are most notable). This fee does not include maintenance labor and material costs provided by outside vendors.

Some management firms offer to perform property management at break-even cost or at a loss in exchange for securing the right to all potential leasing or sales fees generated by the project. And some brokerage firms offer management services. Developers should proceed cautiously in this regard, as the skills required to effectively engage in each activity are very different.

Most larger developers manage their own properties through dedicated in-house staff or a wholly owned subsidiary. Beginning developers generally choose to use an outside source because property management represents an enormous commitment of human resources to the project, and many management tasks become profitable only when personnel, equipment, and purchasing can be amortized over multiple properties.

The third-party property management firm should be evaluated based on its experience with the type of project under consideration. Careful evaluation should examine a list of all properties under its management, a client contact list, and the résumés of staff assigned to the project. It is important to visit (preferably unannounced) representative properties currently under management to get a sense of maintenance quality, staffing, and overall tenant satisfaction. An additional selection criterion is the buying power of the management firm, which generally is a function of its size: larger firms can purchase services less expensively by employing economies of scale, which can lead to lower operating costs.

A good source for locating a third-party property management firm is the local chapter of the Institute of Real Estate Management, which is part of the National Association of Realtors.[13] A property manager's job begins in earnest once tenants begin to occupy the property. Daily functions include collecting rents from tenants and paying recurring expenses, maintaining common areas, and ensuring that necessary repairs are carried out by soliciting bids, selecting vendors, and overseeing the quality of workmanship.

Lenders

Lenders have two major concerns: the developer and the project. Lenders first evaluate the developer's experience and credibility. They learn whether the developer has ever defaulted on a note, how much the company is worth, whether the developer will guarantee the note, and whether the developer has the ability to deliver the project on time and within budget. Lenders then analyze the project, assessing location, the pro forma, and whether it is sufficiently preleased if already constructed.

Among the most important qualities that a lender looks for in a developer are honesty and organization. Demonstrating these qualities is especially important for developers without a track record or without a reputation in a given community.

Construction lenders lend money to build and lease a project. Permanent lenders finance the project once it is built through long-term mortgages. For both types of lenders, the developer's potential gain is less important than the lender's potential loss. For instance, can the developer withstand fluctuations in the interest rate during the development period? Does the developer have sufficient equity to cover extra costs if interest rates go up during the construction period or if it takes longer to lease the project?

Relying on their knowledge of the area, lenders weigh the developer's potential for success against their own fees and exposure. For a construction loan, lenders usually require the developer to supply a market feasibility study and an appraisal. Permanent lenders are concerned about a project's long-term potential.

The amount of preleasing that lenders require depends on the type of project and whether the loan is for construction or permanent financing. Apartment buildings require little preleasing for either type of financing. Office projects must be 50 to 75 percent preleased, or more in soft markets or shaky economies. Preleasing requirements for retail and industrial projects fluctuate dramatically with the market.

Lenders study a project's tenant mix carefully. Strong anchor tenants with high credit ratings and a diversity of other tenants are desirable in both retail and office projects. Construction lenders are con-cerned about tenant mix because they depend on the permanent lender to take out the construction note. Thus, determining the criteria for tenant mix before leasing begins is a critical step. Special project types, such as mini-warehouses and auto marts, are harder to finance because they are considered riskier than conventional retail and industrial projects, having a very limited pool of buyers in the event of foreclosure action. Some lenders finance them, but at higher loan rates than for conventional projects.

Even experienced developers need to convince lenders about the economic viability of their projects. Beginning developers, or those lacking a reputation in the community or real estate industry, must sell themselves and their firms as well.

To find a lender, developers can begin by making a list of prospects. They may want to start at the bottom of the list and practice their presentations before introducing the project to a lender with which they really want to work.

To build a reputation, developers need to avoid common mistakes. In addition to understanding the local market and demand for their product, they must have a well-developed, thorough, and realistic budget;

Cosmopolitan on the Canal in Indianapolis is a luxury rental development of 218 apartments. It was developed by Flaherty & Collins Properties as part of a redevelopment of the downtown.

Organizing for Development

set a realistic timeline with milestones; and have money in reserve or access to capital. Additionally, the developer must demonstrate competency in construction, sales, and leasing.

Fees are often based on the size of the deal. For projects under $10 million, lenders typically assess between zero and one point (0 to 1 percent of the total loan amount) for the service of providing the loan.[14]

Each lender receives a fee as well as coverage of certain expenses, such as appraisals. Additionally, if loan brokers are involved in finding a lender, they too will be paid a fee, typically 1 percent of the loan amount. If a project is anticipated to be unusually risky, an additional one to two points may be added. If the project is larger than $10 million, the fee may not increase proportionally; the net fee may actually be less.

The following are factors that lenders consider when evaluating a potential borrower.

FINANCIAL BACKING/EQUITY. Both permanent and construction lenders are interested in the sources of excess capital. Does the developer have enough resources to carry the project or will the lender be expected to do so (unacceptable for lenders)? Many developers fail because they do not plan cash flow and are unable to finance unexpected costs. Lenders want evidence that the developer has cash available, or at least the ability to raise capital if interest rates go up during construction, if leasing is slower than expected, or if extraordinary cost overruns occur. Lenders also want clear evidence that the borrower understands his financing needs. For example, does the borrower want to find the cheapest loan, one with flexibility, or one with the highest loan proceeds?

MANAGERIAL CAPABILITY. Does the developer understand real estate? In particular, does the developer understand how to work with the local government, subcontractors, and leasing agents? The developer must assemble a team that satisfies these concerns. It is helpful if developers show a catalog with the economic results of transactions they have been involved in, such as cash in and cash out, time period, and internal rates of return. They may also want to include a description of both the good and the challenging aspects of their past development projects. An organized, thorough, and internally consistent application with necessary photos, maps, plans, and financial information creates a good first impression and demonstrates a developer's managerial capabilities.

CHARACTER. Is the developer open and honest about the obstacles and challenges associated with the development? Lenders look for developers who share their values regarding development quality, marketing, and management. Does the developer repay debts and keep promises? Is the developer litigious?

Developers should answer all lenders' concerns, recognizing that lenders' greatest fear is that they will be left with an unviable project. Developers must demonstrate their commitment, resolution, and professionalism. It is best if the developer anticipates problems before lenders point them out.

Sources of Financing for Real Estate Projects

Several types of financial institutions are potential sources of real estate loans.

COMMERCIAL BANKS

Commercial banks are a principal source of both construction and miniperm loans. They usually prefer to lend money for a short term—one to three years—through the construction and leasing period, at which time the permanent lender pays off the construction lender. For larger developers, commercial banks may grant miniperm loans up to five years. These loans are especially attractive during periods of high inflation when developers expect permanent mortgage rates to fall. One hundred percent financing is sometimes available on a superior project, although 70 to 80 percent financing is more common today. In tight money markets, 60 to 65 percent loans are often the only financing available. Beginning developers are more likely to find a local bank than a larger national bank to fund their first few projects. Construction loans are usually made by local and regional banks because of their familiarity with local conditions. Moreover, they have the ability to oversee and properly manage the loan during the construction phase and to monitor the process and progression of construction. After a developer has completed three or four successful projects, larger national banks, which tend to lend greater amounts of money, show more interest. Banks are reluctant to participate in joint ventures but will take part in participating mortgages, which offer the developer higher loan-to-value ratios while giving the bank higher yields through participation in project cash flows.

SAVINGS AND LOAN INSTITUTIONS

Although S&Ls were once a prime source of financing for beginning developers, their role today has been greatly diminished. They are no longer allowed to own subsidiary companies, and they cannot participate in real estate joint ventures. Today, they make primarily home and apartment loans.

INSURANCE COMPANIES

Life insurance companies fund large projects with long-term loans, typically ten years, and provide both construction and permanent financing. Loans may have fixed rates, unlike those from most construction lenders. Beginning developers with a limited track record will have difficulty attracting an insurance company to a project. For merchant builders, though, the requirements for insurance companies may be worth investigating, as they can provide a source of funding for institutional buyers of completed and stabilized projects.

PENSION FUNDS

Pension funds have become a major source of financing for real estate as they have sought to diversify their investments. Their large and increasingly diverse portfolio targets have made them attractive financing prospects for developers. They finance both construction loans and longer-term mortgages, usually at fixed rates. Generally, they finance large projects undertaken by experienced developers. Pension funds often employ advisers who perform all the functions that a traditional real estate owner or lender performs on behalf of the pension fund. They evaluate the project's location, market potential, projected cash flow, the developer's reputation, and the project's quality. Pension fund investments can take longer to finance because decisions do not rest with an individual, but are made by a committee in the organization.[15]

FOREIGN INVESTORS

Global money markets, including foreign investors and foreign banks, play a role in real estate, both in the United States and abroad. Both private capital and sovereign funds poured into U.S. markets during the early 2000s' boom. Looking ahead, an increasingly globalized financial system will no doubt continue to attract capital from abroad. Just as important, real estate developers and owner/managers must contend with high-growth foreign economies as competitors for investment capital that once would have been reluctant to accept the risk of overseas investment. Although most foreign investors prefer to buy developed properties, usually employing low rates of financial leverage, they also have been important sources of development capital for larger firms.

MICHAEL ARDEN

Avalon Burbank in Los Angeles County was developed by Avalon Communities, a REIT that specializes in developing, acquiring, and managing rental apartment communities.

SYNDICATIONS AND REAL ESTATE INVESTMENT TRUSTS

Syndications and real estate investment trusts (REITs) provide a way of carving up real estate ownership into small pieces that many people can afford. They have been used for raising equity capital and mortgage financing for development projects. Both vehicles limit investors' liability and provide pass-through tax benefits that flow directly to the investor, thus avoiding the additional layers of taxation associated with corporate ownership. Public syndications are no longer a significant source of capital, although private syndications remain the best source of capital for small developers through limited partnerships and joint ventures with a local or regional investment outlook.

REITs have become an increasingly significant mechanism for raising capital to fund development projects, and they are dominant players in the acquisition of medium to large completed development projects. REITs are entities that combine the capital of many investors to acquire or provide financing for all forms of real estate. A REIT serves much like a mutual fund for real estate, in that retail investors obtain the benefits of a diversified portfolio under professional management. Its shares are freely traded, usually on a major stock exchange, and the REIT's assets are assembled by sector, with an eye toward specific investment goals, such as capital appreciation, current cash flow, or value potential. The acquisition criteria of REITs are important even to developers who never deal directly with them. Their size within the market for debt and equity financing makes their criteria important bench-marks for any real estate investment, and developers must contend with the presence of public REIT stocks as an alternative, diversified vehicle for investing in real estate. In any potential investor's mind since the late 1980s must be the question, "Could I just get the upside, with far less risk, by investing in a REIT?"

PRIVATE EQUITY INVESTORS AND JOINT VENTURES

The most likely financial partner for a beginning developer is a private investor, who can be almost anyone with sufficient net worth and sophistication to invest. Besides putting up the necessary equity, the private investor may be willing to sign a personal guarantee on the construction note—something that beginning developers often require to obtain their first construction loan, or a loan for a project substantially larger than their track record. Occasion-ally, a private investor funds a project's total cost. The profit split with private investors may range from 80/20 (80 percent to the investor) to 50/50, but regardless of the split the return to the investor will be privileged over developer profit.

To align the partners' incentives, the developer should always make some cash investment. On small deals, this investment ranges from 5 to 33 percent of the total equity, but in larger deals it may be as little as 1 or 2 percent. The developer may also be required to take on the first assignment of risk, that is, cover losses up to a certain amount. Because the investor risks a greater percentage of the equity for a lesser percentage of the profit, it is important to have complete confidence in both the project and the developer's reputation before pursuing a deal.

Investment firms also assemble equity capital from multiple investors to fund new development or to buy existing real estate. Many of these firms work with Wall Street to match up investment funds with developers that provide desired program uses or desired markets in particular locales. Beginning developers who work hard to develop the track record to attract Wall Street money are often surprised at the prohibitive cost of this sort of equity capital. It is worth noting that reporting requirements and other administrative costs rise at least as quickly as the amount financed. Having made the jump to institu-tional financing, it is not uncommon for developers to recall fondly the simpler arrangements of small deals with high-net-worth individuals.

THE BOND MARKET AND COMMERCIAL MORTGAGE–BACKED SECURITIES

The issuance of commercial mortgage–backed securi-ties (CMBSs)—the sale of bond-like interests in portfo-lios of mortgage-backed loans backed by commercial real estate and sold through the capital markets to individual and institutional buyers—gained market share in overall holdings of real estate debt, growing from less than 0.5 percent of the value of outstanding commercial real estate mortgages in 1989 to almost 14 percent in 2000. This sector ground to a halt in the 2008–2009 financial crisis and the forced receivership of the government-sponsored entities like Fannie Mae. As of this writing, issuance of CMBSs remains mori-bund. Still, the growth of securitized debt has deeper roots than the early 2000s' run-up in real estate prices, and developers of quality large-scale projects should anticipate a return of these financing sources.

CREDIT COMPANIES

Some large U.S. corporations use their power in financial markets to establish *credit companies*. Some of these companies, such as GE Capital and GMAC, provide construction and redevelopment financing. Compared with banks, credit companies are subject to less federal government regulation. As a result, they are often willing to lend on projects that involve more risk or are more complex than those within the parameters of commercial banks. Often, however, they charge higher interest rates and require stronger recourse measures in the event of default.

MEZZANINE DEBT

Since the 1980s, mezzanine debt has been established as an intermediate funding mechanism that usually supplements the equity investment and first mort-gage. Any of the lenders identified above may use it. Typically, deals with mezzanine debt are structured with a 70 percent mortgage, 5 to 25 percent mez-zanine debt, and the remainder from the developer's equity. Unlike a mortgage, a partnership interest is assigned in case the developer defaults on the loan, making mezzanine a convertible debt-equity instru-ment, whose pricing typically reflects that hybrid position. As such, mezzanine financing must always be compared with preferred equity investment. These loans are typically short term, anticipating takeout by lower-rate debt or sale, and have higher fees: 2 to 3 percent is common. Mezzanine debt loan rates were running 11 to 13 percent in the early 2000s (3 to 5 percent above prime) and like many other sources of project financing, the mezzanine market substantially collapsed during the financial crisis of 2008–2009. Although interest rates are significantly higher than construction and permanent loan rates, these loans take the place of equity, thereby reducing the most expensive money that a developer has to raise.

CONSTRUCTION LENDERS

Several different types of lenders finance construction loans. The specific institution funding a project depends on the development team's level of experience and the type and size of the project. Most construction loans today have interest rates that float with the prime rate. Construction loan interest rates typically run 150 to 300 basis points (1.5 to 3 percent) over prime, depending on the developer's size, experience, and credit rating. Thus, if the prime lending rate (to a bank's best customers) is 6 percent, construction loan rates would be 8 percent, assuming a 200–basis point spread over prime.

Beginning developers should start their search for construction financing with a banker they know. They should ask for referrals and choose half a dozen potential lenders. They may also solicit the advice of other developers in the field.

Once the construction loan is closed and the construction lender begins to fund construction of the building, the developer should be aware of the lender's concerns and try to address them before they become problems. If a project is falling behind schedule or going over budget, the developer should inform the lender quickly and not allow the lender to hear the news from its inspector, or from third parties. All experienced real estate lenders understand the complications that can arise during the development process. They can often advise the developer about financial strategies that can be employed while the obstacles are being overcome. Regardless, it is paramount to keep lenders informed to maintain their confidence and trust in the developer.

Developers must recognize and address the varied concerns of construction lenders:

- **Design**—Lenders are increasingly concerned about a project's design. The general trend is toward better-quality projects, and national trends toward sustainability or preferred project types (rentals versus condominiums, for example) may be built into lending officers' guidelines for approval.

- **Permits**—Developers must prove that all permits and entitlements are either in place or forthcoming so that the project is not subject to delays or moratoriums.

- **Environmental Factors**—Most lenders require a borrower to indemnify and hold them free and harmless of any liability resulting from toxic or hazardous waste located on a site. Lenders typically require at least a "Phase I" assessment before closing.

- **Insurance**—The builder's risk and general liability insurance must be in place; usually, with lenders named as additional insureds, and as new contractors join the project, certificates may be required of each.

- **Developer's Capacity**—Lenders evaluate whether the developer's associates or partners can complete the project if the developer is suddenly injured or they must bring in another individual.

- **Credibility/Integrity/Cash**—Lenders analyze the developer's credibility and integrity and the status of his cash flow—anything that may prevent the completion of the project.

- **Disbursements/Inspections/Lien Releases**—Most lenders inspect the site monthly to verify requests for payments. If a lender has problems with lien releases (suppliers and contractors can file a *mechanic's lien* against the property if they are not paid), the lender may write joint checks to the developer and contractor. A joint check must be endorsed by all payees, and it helps a lender ensure that the contractor and suppliers are paid so that the collateral is unencumbered. The check endorsement by the contractor serves as proof of payment and protects the lender (and the developer) against frivolous mechanic's liens.

- **Standby Commitments**—Construction lenders are not in the permanent mortgage business. They require assurance that their loan will be repaid at or soon after completion. Standby commitments provide assurance to construction lenders when permanent financing has not yet been arranged. Normally, the standby commitment is never exercised because developers find permanent financing before their construction loans expire. Standby commitments are available from certain banks, insurance companies, credit companies, and REITs. Fees for standby commitments run 1 to 2 percent of the total loan amount each year that it is in force but remains unfunded (the developer has not borrowed any funds under the standby commitment). If the standby loan is actually funded, interest rates typically run 5 percent or more over the prime rate. Although standby commitments are expensive, they allow developers to proceed in situations where a construction lender demands some form of takeout commitment before it will fund the construction loan.

Once the loan agreement is operational, the developer must make prompt and punctual payments, maintain the project in good operating order, and keep all insurance and taxes up-to-date. If problems arise, the lender should be informed immediately. By being candid, a developer will retain the lender's confidence and find it easier to obtain financing the next time.

MORTGAGE BANKERS AND BROKERS

Both mortgage bankers and mortgage brokers help developers obtain financing for their projects. In some cases, the broker assists the developer in getting financing but does not have direct access to funds, whereas the banker has direct access to funds and usually services the loan as well.[16] The relationship between the banker or broker and the client differs somewhat. The banker has a fiduciary relationship with the client, whereas a broker acts as an intermediary and merely looks for the best combination of funding for the client. A developer may use a single broker or hire different brokers to help find mortgage financing and equity financing. Brokers assist the

White Provision in Atlanta is an adaptive use of a 1910 meatpacking plant. The project comprises a mix of office space, retail, restaurants, and condominiums.

ROLEN PHOTOGRAPHY

borrower in preparing a summary package for the deal, including underwriting and research, marketing the loan to many lenders using their established relationships, and negotiating, processing, and closing complex deals and transactions.

Some developers believe that using a mortgage broker adds an unnecessary middleman, but others say it is necessary because loans can be very complex and a financial specialist such as a broker can help find more creative solutions to financing. Some developers also believe that it is important to give bankers or brokers exclusive rights to assemble the capital to maintain their full attention, rather than spreading this responsibility to multiple parties. In such cases, the developer may want to require the intermediary to seek other investors and split fees if necessary or to go to other bankers to access their exclusive list of lenders. In some instances, a developer may ask the banker or broker to work with the developer's own established contacts for lenders, which may result in cutting the broker's fee.

Not every banker or broker is suited for every project. Developers should not be afraid to ask brokers and bankers for their credentials and references and should find out which projects they have financed and how well versed they are in the real estate business. Developers must also question how a prospective lender's specific system works: How do the developer and contractor request draws? Will the lender allow a land draw up front? How often will the lender visit the site? How and when are interest, points, and origination fees paid? At the same time, developers can indicate their readiness to use a lender's services again if they prove to be satisfactory this time. Eventually, developers may want to approach lenders with the idea of starting a long-term relationship. Once a relationship with a banker or broker is established, a developer can get the most out of the association by considering the entity as an integral part of the team whose function is to bring expertise about the capital market to the table. It is also important to provide full disclosure of both the strengths and weaknesses of the deal to the banker or broker.

Mortgage brokers' fees vary. The standard fee is 1 percent of the loan amount. The lender also charges fees for the application, the appraisal, and all the other costs of a loan.

PERMANENT LENDERS

The permanent loan provides the takeout (repayment) for the construction loan. Banks, insurance companies, and pension funds make permanent loans.

Increasingly, permanent loans are securitized on Wall Street, where they are sold to investors in the CMBS market.

Traditionally, a developer must have a permanent loan takeout in place to obtain construction financing. Larger, more experienced developers with strong balance sheets may be able to get a construction loan without a permanent loan commitment, but beginning developers most likely will need to have a commitment for a permanent loan before they can begin construction. Permanent financing usually has fixed interest rates, and although the loan is typically amortized over 30 years, the term of the loan is often limited to ten years. At the end of that time, the note is renegotiated or refinanced by a new permanent loan.

Most of the concerns listed previously for construction lenders apply equally to permanent lenders. Permanent lenders look to the property more than to the borrower for assurance that they will not lose their investment. In most cases, developers do not sign personally on permanent loans. Thus, a strong and fully leased property owned by a financially weak party will obtain financing more quickly than an unleased property with a strong owner.

A developer should thoroughly understand the lender's criteria, such as the percentage that must be preleased, and should compare effective borrowing costs on different mortgages—a computation (discussed in chapter 4) that takes into account interest rates, fees, points, prepayment penalties, and other costs, as well as anticipated holding time until the developer sells or refinances the property.

Conclusion

Development is always a team effort. The lenders, contractors, professional consultants, and other specialists described in this chapter represent the major players with whom developers must be familiar, but they are not the only ones. As development becomes increasingly complex, other talents and specialties must be found, and particular regional characteristics sometimes require unusual specialties. For example, environmental and political consultants were only rarely employed as recently as 20 years ago. Today, they are commonly part of the development team.

Successful projects depend on the developer's ability to manage the many participants with divergent experience in a process toward a common goal. As development becomes a more complicated and expensive business, simply gathering and sifting through the relevant information becomes a herculean—and

critical—task. The developer must be able to recognize high-quality work in many disparate disciplines and must know when to ask questions, whom to ask, and what to ask. The developer must strike a delicate balance between trust in the decisions of the players on the team and constant oversight of work on the critical path of the development timeline. If mistakes are made, the developer is ultimately responsible: to investors, to lenders, and to the community.

NOTES

1. Richard Hardy, "Strategic Planning in Development Firms," *Journal of Real Estate Development* (Spring 1986): 29.

2. Interview with Peter Inman, Inman and Associates, Irvine, California, 2010.

3. Small homebuilding firms and industrial developers also tend to be organized by function because the nature of their business is repetition. Repetition, especially in leasing and construction, lends itself to more functional organization, in which activities are more specialized.

4. See www.aia.org for more information.

5. A mechanic's lien gives a contractor the right to retain the property if payment is not made.

6. Interview with Ronald Stenlund, president, Central Consulting Engineers, Green Bay, Wisconsin, November 2010.

7. Interview with Matthew Kiefer, attorney, Goulston & Storrs, Boston, Massachusetts, 2010.

8. Interview with Jonathan Rose, principal, Jonathan Rose Companies, Katonah, New York, May 2002.

9. Interview with Douglas Hahn, senior environmental scientist, URS Corporation, Los Angeles, California, March 2002.

10. Interview with Jonathan Rose, May 2002.

11. Interview with Patrick Kennedy, owner, Panoramic Interests, Berkeley, California, March 2002.

12. Interview with Leonard Zax, Latham & Watkins real estate group, Washington, D.C., December 2001.

13. www.irem.org.

14. *Points* are expressed as percentages (1 or 2 percent), whereas *basis points* are expressed as hundredths of a percent (100 basis points = 1 percent).

15. NAREIM, the National Association of Real Estate Investment Managers (www.nareim.com), is the association to which pension fund real estate advisers belong. Member organizations represent a very important class of financing sources for developers, as well as jobs for real estate students.

16. *Loan servicing* involves collecting loan payments and sending them to the current holder of the loan. The originator often sells loans to another lender. The servicing agent does not necessarily change if the loan is sold.

3

Land Development

Overview

Subdivision of land is the principal mechanism by which communities are developed. Technically, *subdivision* describes the legal and physical steps a developer must take to convert raw land into developed land. This chapter examines those steps, which may apply to tracts of any size, for any use, using the development of small residential subdivisions as an example. Subdivision is a vital part of a community's growth, determining major elements of its appearance, its mix of land uses, structures of governance, and basic infrastructure, including roads, drainage systems, water, sewerage, and public and private utilities. Subdivision regulations have evolved from earlier rules as requirements and preferences have changed for adequate streets, utilities, setbacks, and development densities to create a suitable living environment while protecting valuable ecological and cultural resources.

Developers and planners have often led the way toward better regulation, their projects demonstrating how improved standards can lead to superior development patterns for communities. Developers must be mindful of the impact that their projects may have on local communities. Even when their projects conform to existing zoning requirements, developers must justify their projects to local communities in terms of beneficial (or at least not adverse) effects on the environment, traffic, tax base, schools, parks, and other public facilities. Thus, in the broader sphere of urban development, developers must respect the symbiotic relationships that tie the private and the public sectors together.

SUBDIVIDING LAND

The subdivision process generally takes place in three stages: raw land, semideveloped land (usually divided into 20- to 100-acre [8–40 ha] tracts[1] with roads and utilities extended to the edge of the property), and developed or subdivided land, platted into individual homesites and 1.5- to ten-acre (0.6–4 ha) commercial parcels, ready for building. The latter is typical for large projects on previously undeveloped parcels. Smaller projects and infill and redevelopment sites typically skip the second phase. The process of converting raw land to semideveloped land differs from region to region, depending on the pattern of landownership, the capacity of local developers and financial institutions, legal frameworks of local and state authority, and the institutional mechanisms for providing roads and utilities.

To ease the conversion process, some states, such as California and Texas, rely heavily on special districts created to finance utility services. Where such vehicles do not exist, developers must wait for the community or utility company to furnish utility service, pay for the extension of roads and utility lines themselves, or form consortiums with other landowners to pay for shared road and utility extensions.

Conversion of raw land to semideveloped land tends to be a project for larger, well-capitalized developers. Such developers typically work with 200- to 1,000-acre (81–405 ha) tracts of land, which they subdivide into smaller 20- to 100-acre (8–40 ha) parcels. They provide the major infrastructure, including arterial roads,

A pedestrian bridge links White Provision, a mixed-use development in midtown Atlanta, to an adjacent commercial development.

JOHN CLEMMER PHOTOGRAPHY

utilities, and drainage systems for the smaller parcels so that they can subsequently be subdivided into buildable lots. Figure 3-1 shows the structure of the land conversion industry and the roles of typical players.

In suburban fringe areas, the developer may skip the second stage and convert the raw land directly to subdivided lots. Direct conversion is more common in slower-growth areas and in places where municipal utility companies or cooperatives install the utilities. Land does not become available for development in a smooth pattern. Rather, farmers, timber interests, and other landholders may sell parcels for reasons such as a death or retirement, an impending change of land use law or zoning, or simply in response to an attractive offer. Because large, contiguous tracts of land rarely become available at one time, leapfrog development that pushes farther away from the city center and low-density sprawl often occur.[2] Sprawl results in inefficient use of roads and other infrastructure and the inability to provide municipal services, such as mass transit, emergency services, and utilities, in a cost-effective manner. Leapfrogging, however, may lead to opportunities for small developers. The land parcels that are passed over during the first wave of development can offer opportunities for infill projects. Such sites, while not without difficulties, are often better located and more competitive in terms of market potential than greenfield sites farther from the city. The complexity of developing such parcels can also serve as a barrier to entry, thus reducing competition from regional and national developers who often value repeatable and predictable processes over any particular site or submarket.

Developers must understand the dynamics of market and regulatory forces. They must be politically astute because they serve as the primary agents of physical change in a community. Residents tend to resist change and fight new development unless it offers them a tangible benefit. Developers must gain the support of those who play major roles in determining local land use: elected officials, planning and zoning boards, utility companies, regional air and water quality commissions, traffic commissions, governance boards, press and other opinion leaders, and increasingly well-organized citizens groups and neighbors.

Developers should also be adept in dealing with multiple government jurisdictions because the appropriate jurisdiction for a given use, on a given parcel, may be unclear, particularly in unincorporated areas.

Historically, developers could safely assume a right to develop land as long as they met the zoning and other land use requirements, but this presumption of development rights has largely dissolved. Even when a project conforms to existing zoning, development rights may be subject to reduction, phasing, or outright moratorium, depending on the attitudes of neighboring residents and the political environment. The likelihood of obtaining necessary approvals in a timely fashion is one of the major risks that developers must evaluate before committing themselves to a project. Developers should be well versed in local politics and have an abundance of personal alliances, as even relatively problem-free tracts may require a lengthy approval process before a project can proceed. Successful developers know that the difficulty of the approval process can be as much about sequence and timing as cost. Poor coordination among reviewing agencies can increase timelines substantially. Even a well-conceived project can lose money by taking too long to get to market.

Developers must be involved in the regulatory process and must help educate their communities. Many

FIGURE 3-1 | Types of Land Investors

	Raw Land Buyer	Land Speculator	Predeveloper	Land Developer	Builder/End User
Major function	Begins conversion	Holds; waits for growth to approach	Analyzes market; clears regulatory hurdles	Installs utilities; completes subdivision	Buys lots; builds structures for sale, rent, or own use
Typical financing	Noninstitutional, cash or local banking	Noninstitutional, cash or local banking	May attract institutional investment	May attract construction loans and long-term investors	May attract construction loans and long-term investors
Typically sells to	Land speculator	Other speculator; last in line sells to developer	Land developer or end user	Other (smaller) builders or end users	Other (smaller) builders or end users
Typical length of tenure	10+ years	8–10 years	2–5 years	1+ years	Indeterminate

communities have found that poorly conceived anti-growth measures can have unintended consequences, such as raising housing prices or exacerbating sprawl. In recent years, the concept of "smart growth" has gained support among planners and developers as a way of accommodating inevitable growth while addressing livability, the environment, and the economy by directing growth toward urban centers, transit infrastructure, employment centers, and public amenities (see chapter 8).[3] Where growth occurs in exurban areas, developers have advanced concepts of "conservation development" to minimize the footprint of growth and mitigate impacts on agricultural and environmental assets.

Developers have become advocates for affordable housing, both in the sense of legally defined affordability, with incentives and financing alternatives driving a competitive business toward this mission, and in the sense of market-based innovation in starter homes and more modestly priced, land-conserving housing solutions.

LAND DEVELOPMENT VERSUS BUILDING DEVELOPMENT

This chapter focuses on small-scale land development, typically involving 20 to 100 acres (8–40 ha). Although the techniques described here apply to any form of land development, beginning developers are most likely to become involved with small residential or mixed-use subdivisions, and warehouse or light-industrial development.

Many developers engage in both land development (sometimes called "horizontal development") and building development (vertical building). When they perform both activities on the same tract, they often view the two activities as a single project. They are actually distinct types of development, and each should be analyzed on its own merits. In modeling a project, such analysis amounts to considering oneself the purchaser of finished lots, so that returns can be analyzed on both components of the business independently.

Many considerations arise when a developer is in charge of both land and building development on the same property. For instance, independent homebuilders may be reluctant to buy lots because of the competition from the developer's own building activities, especially in light of the developer's cost advantage and presumed asymmetrical knowledge. The problem of building on some lots and selling others can be alleviated by bringing in builders who will target their product to a different market segment and by coordinating their activities to achieve a harmonious aesthetic and well-tailored mix of product.

Customs vary in different regions when it comes to developing small residential subdivisions. In some areas, it is typical for homebuilders to subdivide the land and build the houses together, using a single construction loan—especially for tract houses in communities that require public hearings on house plans and on lot subdivision.[4] It is also possible that lenders may prefer to underwrite these activities separately, given their different risk profiles and collateralization.

In general, land development is riskier but more profitable than homebuilding because it is dependent on the public sector for approvals and infrastructure and involves a long investment period with no positive cash flow. Assuming this combination of risk and investment must be rewarded by the market.

Project Feasibility

Although opportunities exist for many types of land, beginning land developers are advised to search for comparatively problem-free tracts of land: land that is already served by utilities and is appropriately zoned or requires only administrative public approvals. Although raw land may be available, the resources and the time required to entitle and bring utilities to a tract are beyond the capabilities of beginning developers. Time and money are better spent building a track record of successful small projects.

MARKET ANALYSIS BEFORE SITE SELECTION

Market analysis occurs twice during land development—before site selection and after site selection, as the project is better defined. The objective of market analysis before site selection is to identify which segments of the market are underserved and which sorts of buyers might be lured by a competitively priced and appropriately designed development. Large developers have the luxury of investigating a number of markets, even internationally, to select the most competitive product type and location. Beginners lack the resources required for such an exploration. In addition, they usually want to remain close to home, in familiar territory with personal connections. If possible, their projects should be near enough for them to keep a close watch over on-site progress. Further, local planning bodies and regulatory agencies tend to view local developers less suspiciously than they might view out-of-towners.

This is not to say that more distant opportunities should not be considered, but beginning developers have enough difficulties to overcome without the additional hurdles of distance and unfamiliar markets, officials, and building practices. Moreover, beginning developers' primary concern, aside from developing stable cash flow, should be the cultivation of their reputation, which is easier with multiple projects in one market.

A developer's primary market decisions concern the proposed project's use, location, and size. Use preferences might arise from market conditions, such as a perceived shortage in one type of housing or commercial space or from construction expertise in a particular type or scale, which may offer functional or price advantages versus the market. If a developer has no preference for a specific use, then each segment of the market—residential, industrial, commercial, or mixed-use—should be analyzed. Real estate markets are highly segmented, and a developer cannot infer from the demand for residential development that retail development is also in demand (see chapter 1 for an overview of market cycles by type). Similarly, a developer should not assume that demand for the same product extends across multiple submarkets.

It used to be common practice for a developer to select a use and a target market and then find a suitable parcel of land. Today, with developable sites at a premium in so many metropolitan regions, it is common to select the site first, possibly even "tie it up," and then undertake market analyses to identify potential uses and markets for that parcel. If the developer has already identified the land use for which excess demand exists, the purpose of the market analysis is to identify the particular market segment (for instance, "midpriced, single-family houses for move-up families") and the location where demand is greatest. This formulation simplifies the task, though, because for most developers, mitigating market risk means pursuing multiple potential markets at once, often in the same community.

Major sources of information are brokers, lenders, and, in particular, builders to whom the land develop-

The master-planned Biltmore Park Town Square combines retail and office space, a hotel, and a variety of residential types on a 57-acre (23 ha) site.

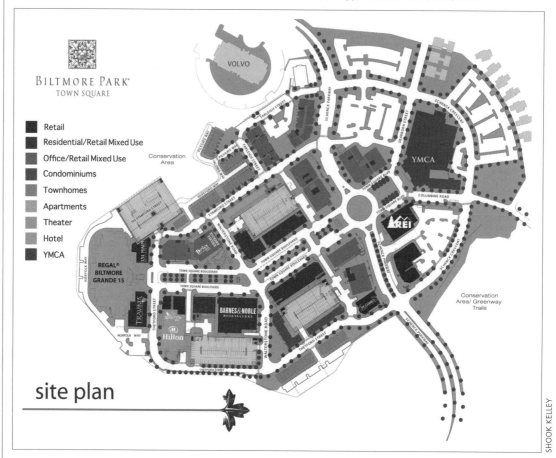

SHOOK KELLEY

er will market the developed sites. Because developers and homebuilders are prospective clients, they are usually eager to provide assistance. Some caution is advised, however, because some of these builder-clients will also be competitors. It is also possible to obtain relevant market information at little cost from other sources. Major lenders, market research firms, and brokers often publish quarterly or annual reports for apartments, office space, single-family houses, and industrial space. A wealth of economic and market information can also be found on the Internet, particularly in the case of for-sale housing, which is served by the Multiple Listing Service and other private market reporting services. Assembling this information and analyzing it can take considerable effort, even at the early stages, so it may be more efficient to hire a market consultant. The most important questions to be answered concern the market for the proposed product type:

- Where are the most desirable areas or parts of town?
- What are the hottest segments of the market?
- Who are the most active buyers? What are their characteristics and preferences?
- Are there competitors other than new subdivisions (that is, renovations, conversions)?
- If a builder owned land in that area, what would he build?
- For what types of building are lenders giving loans?
- For what types of building are lenders not giving loans?
- Where are building permits being issued? What kinds of permits are they?
- What physical features and amenities are especially popular?
- Are amenities built into the sale price or are they fee supported?
- Who are the main builders? Are they producing custom, semicustom, or tract home products?
- Who else is developing in a particular area? What are they building? How many units (or square feet) are planned or in the approvals pipeline for the future?
- How many units are they selling per month, and how long at this pace?
- What are the standard deal terms that builders are using to buy lots?
- Are other developers subordinating lot prices, financing construction, or offering other hidden subsidies?

Major homebuilders project the annual demand for units by price category throughout their metropolitan area. They break down the number of houses sold in each market area of the metropolitan region by $25,000 or $50,000 intervals. For example, suppose it is estimated that 56 percent of all new housing units will be sold in the western part of town and that 75 percent of the units will be priced under $300,000. If the total projected demand for the city is, say, 500 houses in 2012, the demand for houses costing under $300,000 in the western section of town would be 210 units (56 percent × 75 percent × 500).

After estimating demand, developers should ask how much of that demand can be captured by their project. Irrationally exuberant capture rate projections are among the most common pitfalls of even experienced developers. This calculation should be based on extremely conservative assumptions, and the correct answer depends on the number of similar projects selling in the market, and on how competitive the proposed development is likely to be. Developers must consider whether their site is less physically attractive or accessible or features the same level of amenities as the competition. Suppose a given area contains 2,100 lots in 20 subdivisions. If each of four developers has five of the subdivisions, each developer's share of the market captured would be 25 percent, or 525 lots (25 percent × 2,100). Many developers allocate more lots to subdivisions that possess better amenities, terrain, or management. They also look at historical absorption rates by different subdivisions and developers. Depending on the weight given to each factor, the analysis indicates that the developers should capture more or less than their prorated share. If they anticipate selling twice their share, however, then the other developers must theoretically lose market share by the same amount. In the short run, builders can steal market share from other builders, if they have a better design, amenity package, or location. In the long run, however, builders who are losing sales will cut prices or increase marketing, incentives, or amenities until they regain their share.

Land developers must remember that their product is an intermediate good used for an end product. The demand for finished lots depends on the demand for houses—not just for any houses but for houses in the price range that justifies the lot price. If demand for those houses declines, so will the demand for lots.

The ratio of lot price to house price has risen since the 1960s and may vary from about 20 to 50 percent. Higher ratios may be found in areas such as infill sites in high-income cities and suburbs and in high-priced metropolitan areas like Los Angeles, San Francisco, Washington, D.C., and Boston. A general rule of thumb is that builders pay approximately 25 percent of the finished house price for the lot. Thus, if they build houses that sell for $200,000, they can afford to pay $50,000 for the lot. Developers should not, however, rely on rules of thumb but should carefully investigate local market conditions. A rule of thumb can be useful to quickly understand the economics of a particular land purchase. If a particular parcel's price, zoning, and development costs would break even at $75,000 per lot, the developer may conclude that this deal has a low likelihood of success as currently envisioned.[5]

Suppose the absorption rate is ten units per month for $200,000 houses, compared with 15 units per month for $160,000 houses. Builders of the $200,000 houses will pay $50,000 per lot rather than $40,000 per lot for the less costly houses. If developers proceed with their projects under the assumption that they can sell $50,000 lots, they may be in trouble if the market turns out to favor the less expensive houses. Even if they are willing to accept the lower sale price of $40,000 per lot, their lenders may set loan covenants that prevent—or at least delay—the sale.[6]

Market research is a critical first step, not only for selecting a site but also for assembling a list of builders to approach. Another benefit of the preliminary market analysis is that even while looking for sites, the developer can generate interest among builders. One might focus on smaller builders who build five to 50 houses per year, and who are likely to purchase a few lots at a time in a subdivision. The builders will tell the developer where they want to build and what the ideal lot size, configuration, and amenity package are. If the developer can meet their requirements, builders may even precommit to purchasing the lots by a letter of intent. Such commitments, while seldom legally binding, can be the linchpin of the developer's first deal. A firm purchase letter from a creditworthy builder can give the beginner the credibility needed to obtain financing.

SITE SELECTION AND ACQUISITION

In selecting a site, beginning developers face a number of limitations that can be overcome only with diligent research. To overcome the limitations,

- choose a manageable geographic area for the search; a good guideline is "no air travel";
- set an appropriate time frame for investigating market conditions;
- do not depend exclusively on brokers to find sites; and
- do not look for "home runs"; build a reputation on singles and doubles.

Site Evaluation Factors

MARKET AREA AND COMPETITION
- Existing inventory
- Pipeline
- Similar products that may compete
- Meaningful price points

LOCATION AND NEIGHBORHOOD
- Proximity to key metro locations
- Quality of surrounding environment
- Existing housing stock, other buildings
- Schools and churches
- Parks, clubs, and recreational facilities
- Other amenities
- Shopping and entertainment
- Public improvements (existing and planned)

UTILITIES
- Water and sewer/septic
- Electricity (availability and quality)
- Teledata/broadband/cable TV
- Wireless reception

PHYSICAL CONDITIONS
- Visibility and accessibility
- Slopes and required grading
- Vegetation, forestry, and agriculture
- Existing structures
- Soils and hydrology
- Toxic wastes and nuisances
- Wildlife and ecological features

LEGAL CONSTRAINTS
- Utility and private easements
- Covenants and deed restrictions

REGULATORY ENVIRONMENT
- General climate toward development
- Exactions and impact fees
- Future infrastructure work/takings
- Approval process and timeline
- Methods of citizen participation
- Administrative vs. board approvals
- Upcoming elections and rule changes

Because beginners lack reputation and contacts, they are less likely to hear about deals firsthand. But deals that have been "on the street" are not necessarily bad deals. A property may have been passed over for many reasons: the site may be too small or otherwise uneconomical for a large firm but may be suitable for the beginner. In addition to working with a network of brokers, developers should not be afraid to talk to landowners whose land is not currently for sale. Direct contact may generate a deal or lead to a possible joint venture or favorable terms of purchase. Large landowners know one another, and even a "no" may eventually lead to a referral.

SITE EVALUATION. The relative importance of various factors of subdivision development depends on the end user of the lots. The major site evaluation factors are summarized in the accompanying feature box, and greater detail regarding site evaluation for residential development can be found in chapter 4.

Many physical, legal, and other factors must be considered before buying a site. Among the more important items, the developer should

- make sure all easements are plotted on a map and that any easement problems are cleared up and any purchase arrangements for easements made before closing;
- check for drainage problems and ascertain the level of the water table, which affects sewer lines, septic tanks, and building foundations;
- check seismic hazard maps to make sure that faults do not cross the land;
- check flood insurance and Flood Hazard Area maps;
- check Federal Housing Administration (FHA) requirements concerning width of roads, culs-de-sac, and other design requirements;
- investigate whether any parties are likely to delay or stop the sale; pay particular interest to seller's family;
- make sure that utilities such as water, sewer, gas, electricity, and communication lines are available;
- check with planning/zoning and engineering departments about off-site requirements;
- check permit costs, impact fees, and exactions, and consider statutory accelerations or upcoming changes;
- check for appropriate zoning and research actual—not statutory—approval timelines for similar projects;

- determine whether all necessary development approvals will be granted, or make closing contingent on approval;
- make sure that builders will be able to obtain building permits in a timely fashion;
- check for environmental issues—especially if a body of water lies on the land; avoid wetlands, as they usually involve a time-consuming approval process;
- beware of unusual soil chemistry or composition, such as sulfates or high clay levels;
- check for radon, a harmful derivative of uranium that is present in many areas;
- check historical aerial photos that may show evidence of toxic waste, such as storage tanks on the site;

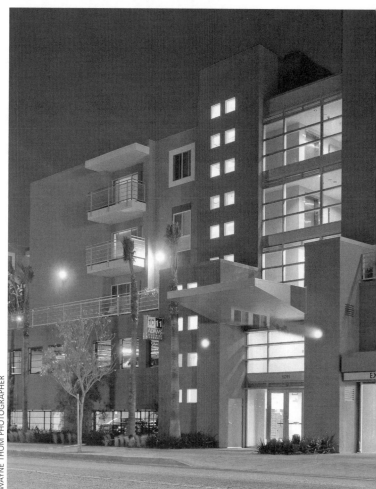

Adams & Central in south Los Angeles combines 80 units of mixed-income housing with a street-level grocery store and other shops, and underground parking.

WAYNE THOM PHOTOGRAPHER

- check construction lenders' requirements for environmental site assessments;
- check for landfills and other nuisance-generating sites close by, including informal or illegal sites;
- look for smoke, fumes, or odors, and check the land at all times of the day; and
- always walk the land.

The developer should also carefully consider the surrounding environment. What is the overall political climate? Will the community object to new development or does it support growth? Is the planned development compatible with the surrounding neighborhood or with approved comprehensive plan goals? If so, is the plan up for review soon? Are shopping, schools, and parks nearby? If schools are an issue for the project, what is their reputation and in what direction is that reputation moving?

SITE ACQUISITION. In land development, as in other forms of development, a three-stage contract is customary: a free-look period, a period during which earnest money is forfeitable, and closing. This point of negotiation is as important as price: purchasers want as much time as they can to close with as little money at risk as possible. Sellers want the reverse: for the closing to occur as quickly as possible with as much forfeitable earnest money at stake as possible. The agreed-on terms depend on the state of the market and can change rapidly.

In slow markets, favorable terms of purchase are more likely. With fewer buyers, sellers are typically more willing to give a potential purchaser more time to investigate the property without requiring hard earnest money. In a hot market, sellers are less afraid of losing any particular deal and are more concerned about tying up their property when another buyer, and possibly a better offer, may be just around the corner. As conditions in the marketplace shift toward seller-dictated terms (requiring cash offers without financing contingencies, short due diligence periods, and high prices), the market is likely nearing its apex, so the beginning developer who is having trouble competing as a buyer may just be better off waiting.

If the site consists of multiple parcels under separate ownership, progress is further complicated by the fact that all the necessary parcels must first be acquired. Land assembly is a tricky business and usually requires sophisticated negotiation and acquisition techniques to ensure that the owner of the last or other key parcels does not insist on an exorbitant price.

The terms of acquisition set the stage for everything else, and an overpriced or complicated takedown of land can doom an otherwise well-conceived project. When buying land, developers are chiefly concerned about whether or not they can build what they want, whether they have time to study all site conditions affecting feasibility, and whether they will be able to assemble market data, obtain financing, and assess project economics in a business plan before the required closing.

Sites with special problems, such as easements or contamination, may prove attractive but must be approached with caution because they may be more difficult than a beginner can handle. Beginning developers are usually thinly capitalized, leaving little room for unanticipated costs or delays. Before deciding to tackle problem sites, beginning developers must determine whether the problem can be solved within a reasonable time frame and cost. If they cannot answer that question affirmatively with a high level of confidence, they should probably look for another site.

Because of possible legal complications, developers generally use an attorney during land acquisition, no matter how straightforward a transaction might appear to be. Each part of the country has its own terminology for the sequence of steps in property acquisition. In Texas, for example, the first step is called *signing the earnest money contract*; in California, it is *going into escrow* on the purchase contract; and in Massachusetts, the initial offer is an *offer to purchase* agreement. In most cases, these actions initiate a free-look period during which various contingencies have to be resolved. This agreement is binding and contains all the contingencies, at least in summary form. It stipulates that on or before a certain date, the parties will enter into a *purchase and sale agreement*, which enumerates and records all aspects of the transaction.[7]

Even before submitting a purchase contract, purchasers may discuss or submit a *letter of intent* or term sheet to sellers that sets out the business terms for purchase of the property. The letter of intent specifies the property to be purchased, its price, payment terms, timing, release provisions (for transfer of lien-free subparcels, in the case of seller financing, to the buyer), and other major business points. Letters of intent are especially helpful when the purchaser or seller plans to use a long, specially written legal purchase agreement rather than a standardized broker's form. The letter of intent saves time and unnecessary legal expense in the beginning because it clarifies the primary aspects of the transaction. If the buyer and seller cannot come to agreement on the major business terms, there is no point in exchanging full legal documents. The letter of intent is nonbinding, but it does call for signatures by both parties to signify agreement on the major transaction points.

The *offer to purchase* must spell out all contingencies and any penalties other than specific performance (compelling the parties to consummate the agreed deal) for failure to close. They typically include physical inspections, environmental assessments, regulatory approvals, title checks, and/or financing approval. A common mistake is for purchasers to assume they can negotiate more contingencies or other issues in the purchase and sale agreement. The latter cannot be more restrictive than the offer to purchase unless both parties agree to the changes. Three items make the offer to purchase binding: (1) specific consideration, enough to entice the seller to take the property off the market for a given period; (2) proper identification of the property; and (3) a time to close or to enter into the purchase and sale agreement. The offer to

Steps for Site Acquisition

BEFORE OFFER

1. Verify that a market for the property type exists.

2. Determine the price you can pay by running preliminary financial pro formas.

3. Determine whether or not the seller can sell the property for the price you want to pay. (Estimate the seller's basis and outstanding mortgages on the property.)

4. Find out why the seller is selling the property. (Is the sale necessary, or can the seller wait for a better price?)

5. Check the market for comparable properties in the area and their prices over a multiyear period.

OFFER

1. Ask for at least 60 days for due diligence. If a broker brought the developer the deal, the developer might expect that the broker also contacted four or five other developers and that 60 days for due diligence may therefore not be acceptable to the seller.

2. Place a refundable deposit, or earnest money. Customary percentages vary widely by region and by deal size.

3. Request specific due diligence that must be provided by the seller, such as surveys, soils reports, hazardous waste clearances and certifications, preliminary design and engineering studies, preapproved plans, development rights determinations, or agency approvals.

4. Negotiate terms and fees for unilateral extension of closing (monthly fee, number of months available).

DUE DILIGENCE

1. If zoning must be changed for the project, ask for closing to be contingent on zoning approvals; if it is not approved, the earnest money is refunded. Be sure to state in the offer exactly what constitutes approval, for example,

   * general plan approval;
   * rezoning approval;
   * conditional use permits (variances or waivers);
   * development agreements;
   * tentative tract or parcel map;
   * final tract or parcel map;
   * grading plan approval;
   * site plan approval;
   * design approval; and
   * building or disturbance permits.

2. Answer other questions:

   * Can a good title be secured?
   * How much of the site is buildable, how soon? What are the existing leases, easements, slopes, soils, floodplain, drainage, and geological conditions?
   * Can you build what you want to? How many units, of what size and at what density, can be built? Can parking and amenities be built?
   * Can financing be obtained not only for land but also for the improvements you envision?

3. Accomplish the following before closing on the land:

   * preliminary design drawings;
   * conceptual estimate of construction costs;
   * mortgage package preparation;
   * commitment from permanent lenders;
   * commitment from construction lenders;
   * receipt of regulatory approvals or assurances that they can be obtained (zoning opinion or development rights determination); and
   * selection of construction manager and property manager (who should assist in designing the project).

4. If more time is needed, ask for it. If the seller refuses, ask for the deposit money back and pull out of the deal.

CLOSING

1. Closing typically occurs 60 days after due diligence is complete, although longer periods can often be negotiated.

2. Closing can be made dependent on a variety of factors, including the availability of financing and the removal of toxic wastes.

purchase should include a provision for return of the purchaser's deposit if a purchase and sale agreement is not signed.[8]

Purchase Contract or Earnest Money Contract. Whether or not a letter of intent is used initially, the purchase contract (also called *purchase and sale agreement* or *earnest money contract*) is the primary legal document for purchase of property. It sets out all terms of purchase, indemnities, responsibilities for delivering title reports (usually the seller) and other documents, performing due diligence, and remedies in the event that the sale does not close. Signing the final purchase agreement may happen immediately in the case of a simple purchase contract for one or several lots, or it may drag on for weeks or even longer if buyers and sellers haggle over individual provisions. Although purchase contracts are almost always negotiated following due diligence, the purchaser may use the time delay in signing to begin to line up financing, to recruit builders, or to advance project design. Until the purchase contract is signed, however, the buyer is at risk of the seller's accepting another offer. Complicated purchase contracts are appropriate in complex transactions of larger properties, but beginning developers should keep it simple. Overly complicated legal paperwork may signal the seller that the buyer is litigious and vice versa.

Contingencies. Contingencies in the purchase contract refer to events that must occur before the purchaser "goes hard" on the earnest money. Beginning developers often make the mistake of including many unnecessary contingency clauses that only complicate the negotiations. The most all-encompassing clause is one that makes the sale "subject to obtaining financing." If, for whatever reason, financing is not available, then earnest money is returned. Another encompassing clause is "subject to buyer's acceptance of feasibility studies." The contract may spell out those studies to include soils, title, marketing, site planning, and economic feasibility. As long as the clause gives the buyer discretion to approve the reports, it effectively gives the buyer a way out of the contract. As soon as the buyer goes hard, though, he is subject to forfeiting the earnest money paid to the seller if the sale is not completed.

Most sellers will not give a blanket contingency for more than 30 to 60 days. Local market conditions determine whether sellers will give buyers a free-look period.

An important contingency in the purchase agreement is that the seller must support the developer in obtaining zoning and other necessary approvals. In areas where extensive public approvals make the allowable building density uncertain, some developers purchase sites on the basis of the number of units approved. In this case, the seller has a strong incentive to assist in the approval process. For example, if the price is $50,000 per unit and permission is given to build 100 units on the site, then the purchase price would be $5 million. If the developer receives approval for only 80 units, the price would be $4 million. Having the seller on the developers' side can be valuable in a tough approvals environment, where developers may have less credibility than longtime landowners.

As a general rule, 3 to 5 percent of the total purchase price or a payment of $25,000 to $50,000 for smaller deals is required as earnest money for a 90- to 120-day closing. Because the earnest money theoretically compensates the seller for holding the property off the market, the earnest money usually bears some relation to the seller's holding cost or the opportunity cost of risk-free interest on the sale price. The amount is negotiable but has to be large enough so that the seller believes that the buyer is viable and serious about closing. Financing land is expensive—usually at least two points (2 percent) over prime. For example, if the prime rate is 10 percent and the land loan is 12 percent, then a four-month closing would incur holding costs of 4 percent ($4/12 \times 12$ percent).

In hot markets, sellers may sometimes try to get out of a sale because they have received a higher offer. Although each state has its own property law, buyers generally control a purchase contract as long as they strictly observe its terms. Most contracts state that a clause is waived if the buyer does not raise concerns in writing before the expiration date of the clause or contingency. If the clause (such as buyer's approval of title reports) is not automatically waived according to the contract, however, the seller may argue that the buyer failed to perform in a timely fashion and that the contract is therefore null and void. If the seller tries to get out of the contract before the expiration date, the threat of litigation is usually sufficient to bring the seller back to the table. Pending litigation makes it very difficult to sell the property to anyone else and can tie up a property; it is a last resort on the part of the buyer.

Release Provisions on Purchase Money Notes. One of the most important areas of negotiation concerns the release provisions on purchase money notes (PMNs)—seller financing used to purchase the property (also called *land notes*). Release provisions refer to the process by which developers remove and unencumber individual parcels in larger tracts from the sellers' land notes. Release provisions are also a major part of the negotiation with the developers' lenders (discussed in "Financing" below).

Lenders require a first lien on the developer's property. Lien priorities are determined strictly by the date that a mortgage is created. Thus, land notes automatically have first lien position, unless sellers specifically subordinate land notes to land development loans, which they almost certainly will not. Developers must release land from the land note before they can obtain development financing from lenders. The unencumbered land constitutes their equity. Even if developers finance development costs out of their own pockets, land must be released from the land note for the developer to deliver clear title to builders or other buyers of the lots. Buyers need clear title (free of liens) before they can obtain their own construction financing. Buyers usually view land note financing favorably during the predevelopment period before they take down the construction loan, as long as they have the option of paying it off at any time.

Land sellers' main economic concern is that they will be left holding a note with inadequate underlying security. As landowners, they also do not wish to have a large property fragmented by a failed development. They therefore want strict release provisions that require the developer to pay down more on the land note than the actual value of the land to be released, leaving more land as security for the unpaid portion of the note. Additionally, they wish to preserve their unreleased parcels in a contiguous piece. The developer's objective, on the other hand, is to achieve maximum flexibility in the location and acreage of land to be released. Ideally, the developer wants to be able to release the maximum amount of land for the minimum amount of money, but this flexibility is particularly important early in the project's life, when costs have exhausted a large proportion of the developer's capital, and positive cash flow is critically important.

Suppose a developer purchases 100 acres (40 ha) for $1 million with an eight-year land note for $800,000, or $8,000 per acre ($20,000/ha). The note is amortized at the rate of $100,000 per year. Suppose the developer also negotiates a partial release provision that calls for a payment of $12,000 per acre ($30,000/ha). If the developer wants to sell 25 acres (10 ha) to a builder, then he must pay the seller $300,000 (25 × $12,000 or 10 × $30,000) to release the land. Without carefully worded language, the developer's $300,000 payment reduces the seller's note from $800,000 to $500,000. Instead of reducing the note principal balance immediately, the special language permits the developer to pay interest only on the note for the next three years. A clause "all prepayments

Tips for Land Acquisition

Conversations with a variety of successful developers have produced a number of useful tips regarding land acquisition.

- Make sure the owner is willing to sell the land. Sellers may use your bids to negotiate with others.

- Do not let the seller dictate the use of the property after the sale.

- Beware of appraisals of sites that have not been physically analyzed for hazardous or other undesirable conditions.

- When rezoning is necessary, attempt to buy the land on a per-unit basis, giving the landowner an incentive to help obtain approvals.

- If a conditional use permit or variance will be needed, ask the current owner to sign a waiver to allow you to act as his or her agent in dealing with the city or county before closing.

- If you obtain seller financing, make sure the seller frees up some of the land immediately so that you can build on it. You need to be able to give the construction lender a first lien on the land.

- In some states, such as California, you should use a *deed of trust* for purchase money mortgages so that the seller cannot claim a deficiency judgment against you if you default.

- Concerning "no-waste" clauses, be sure to read the fine print on the trust deed form because you may not be able to remove trees or buildings on the property until the note is paid off.

- Make sure you select a title company that is strong enough to back you up if you need to defend a lawsuit involving title. Some nationwide title companies enfranchise their local offices separately so that you do not have the backing of the national company.

- Make sure that the seller's warranties survive the close of escrow. Consult your attorney for the current state law on this topic.

- Beware of broker commissions. A broker who casually mentions a property as you drive by it may try to collect a commission if you later buy it.

are credited toward the next principal installments coming due" means that the next three principal installments are paid by the $300,000 payment, but that repayment of the note is not accelerated. The developer will not have to make another principal payment for three years. Without the language in the clause, the seller would probably construe that the $300,000 payment simply shortens the remaining life of the note from eight to five years. The developer, of course, wants the flexibility of the full term, so that it will not be necessary to sell the land prematurely or to find other financing sources to pay off the land note. It is increasingly common for release payments to be negotiated as a simple percentage of net sale price, subject to review against developers' initial representations of lot pricing, but the principle still holds.

Developers never want to release more land from the note than is necessary at any one time, because seller financing is usually their lowest-cost source of money. Thus, they should try to avoid release provisions that call for releasing land in strips or contiguous properties.[9] If releases must occur on contiguous properties, developers would be forced to release the entire property to develop or sell a tract at one end. Sellers will rightfully be concerned if developers can "cherry-pick" the most desirable land and then abandon the rest of the project. To get around this problem, the release provision can assign values to parcels or strips in the property that reflect market values. Thus, prime land may have a release price that is significantly higher than that for less desirable land. Alternatively, the provision may call for the developer to release two acres (0.8 ha) of less desirable land for every acre (0.4 ha) of desirable land, or the release may be spelled out in a predetermined sequence of parcels coinciding with the phasing plan of the development. In short, a variety of structures can be employed to assuage sellers' concerns, but developers must maintain the ability, within reason, to change direction.

KEY POINTS OF A PURCHASE CONTRACT. A variety of clauses and provisions should be included as part of the initial purchase contract to minimize later renegotiations with the seller:[10]

- **Supplementary Note Procedure**—This clause allows the sale of subparcels (parcels within the original tract) to builders and other developers without paying off the underlying first lien. This provision, which must be specifically negotiated, allows the developer to pass on seller financing to builders through a supplementary note, which gives builders more time before they need to pay the full lot cost. Nevertheless, unless the seller is willing to subordinate seller financing, the supplementary note has first lien position, which means that builders who purchase subparcels must pay off the note before they can obtain construction financing, as construction lenders also require a first lien position. In fact, builders usually pay off the supplementary note with the first draw on the construction loan.
- **Out-of-Sequence Releases**—This clause satisfies the developer's need to release certain parcels out of sequence for major utilities or amenities.
- **Joinder and Subordination**—This clause provides for the seller to join within 30 days any applications for government approvals made by the developer. It also provides for the seller's subordination agreements, required by any government authority for the filing of subdivision maps or street dedications.
- **Transferability**—This clause protects the seller from having the deal he has negotiated transferred to another buyer, presumably giving the buyer the benefit of any appreciation added value. Nontransferable contracts may give the seller unreasonable influence if the buyer needs to bring in a partner later.
- **Subordination of Subparcels**—Most sellers are unlikely to allow subordination of their note to development lenders. They may be willing, however, to allow subordination on one or two subparcels. This action can help the developer obtain the development loan without paying off the land note.
- **Seller's "Comfort Language"**—The seller is not required to execute any documents until he or she has approved the purchaser's general land use plan.
- **Ability to Extend Closing**—This clause permits the purchaser to extend the closing by 30 or 60 days by paying additional earnest money.
- **Letters of Credit as Earnest Money**—The developer can greatly reduce upfront cash requirements if the seller will accept letters of credit as earnest money. Letters of credit can be cashed by the seller on a certain date or if certain events occur, such as a purchaser's failure to close. For example, this type of clause might say, "Purchaser may extend the closing for 60 days by depositing an additional $50,000 letter of credit as additional escrow deposit."
- **Property Taxes**—Many municipalities and counties have categories such as *open space* or *agricultural land* that give the owner a reduction in taxes. When the land is developed, the owner must repay the

tax savings for the previous three or five years. This assessment, commonly known as "rollback," can amount to a major unexpected cost to the developer if it is not provided for in the purchase agreement. For example, such a provision might say, "Seller agrees to pay all ad valorem tax assessments or penalties assessed for any period before the closing as a result of any change in ownership or usage of the property." In addition, some areas with agricultural-use taxation will only guarantee these favorable tax rates to landowners who enroll their parcels in voluntary restrictive use agreements. These agreements can run five or ten years, and since they are not easements, they will not necessarily be visible in the recorded history of the parcel deed.

- **Title Insurance**—The seller usually (though not always) pays the title insurance policy. Many title insurance policies have standard exception clauses, however, such as a survey exception.[11] The party responsible for paying the insurance premium for deleting these exceptions is subject to negotiation.
- **Seller's Remedy**—If the purchaser defaults, the seller's sole remedy is to receive the escrow deposit as liquidated damages. This clause prevents the seller from pursuing the purchaser for more money if the sale falls through.

These clauses constitute only a small fraction of all those included in a standard purchase contract. They are highlighted here because they represent items that the purchaser should try to negotiate with the seller. Experienced developers use a specially prepared standard form that includes such clauses. Sophisticated sellers may insist on using their own custom contract, to which these clauses will probably have to be added. An experienced real estate attorney should always assist in the preparation of contracts.

MARKET ANALYSIS AFTER SITE SELECTION

After tying up a site, the developer should reexamine the target market for the proposed project. Special features of the selected site, as well as changes to the overall economic climate, may indicate a different market from the one identified during the preliminary market analysis undertaken before site selection. Land uses change slowly, but markets can change quickly.

At this stage, analysis should concentrate on location, neighborhood, and amenities. For example, suppose a developer's initial target market is buyers of move-up houses selling from $350,000 to $400,000. If sales in that price range are moving steadily, the

developer may want to continue with such a program, even if several other developers are competing at the same price point. But if the developer has found that market to be saturated, with forward indicators such as building permits or presale deposits beginning to soften, he may modify plans and develop a lower-priced community. Alternately, a more upscale product that is not represented in the market may be appropriate if demographics and market prove favorable. Developer Dan Kassel cautions, "When you're selling 'home,' you can't help having your own ideas about that word, a vision of what it might mean, but you must absolutely subordinate your personal vision to what you can learn about your customer."[12]

The market analysis at this stage helps the developer

- advance physical planning: market data help determine the specific target market and therefore the size and configuration of lots, amenities, and other fundamental aspects of the design;
- compile the appropriate documentation (for example, a development appraisal) to obtain a loan and refine a business plan for investors; and
- attract builders and partners: a credible market study and statistical backup will be essential in communicating the value of the proposed community.

Unless a subdivision is very small or the developer has already secured informal commitments from builders, a local market research firm that specializes in subdivision development should be hired. Ideally, the market research firm should already have a database covering all the competing subdivisions. From its analysis, the market research firm should be able to assist the developer in determining the best market for the lots, and the total number of lots that the developer can sell per month, grouped by lot size and price range. The report should document total housing demand and supply for the market area and, from that number, project demand and supply for the specific product type and submarket area the developer's project will serve (see feature box on page 86). The bottom line of the market study should be a projection of the number of units that can be sold each month by product type and the projected sale price. For example, suppose demand for $200,000 to $250,000 townhouses is 200 houses per year (16 per month) in the submarket and two subdivisions are competing for buyers. Expected sales would be approximately five per month, assuming that each subdivision captures its share of total demand. However, this figure should never be assumed to be the pace of sales. Demand is never totally met by product that is actually developed. Many potential buyers will not purchase what is offered because it is too expensive, it is not to their taste, or any number of other reasons. Projections of the pace of sales must always be tempered by observation of market reality. Regardless of what demand statistics show, if other developers of similar projects in the general area are selling only two or three units per month, it is unlikely that anyone—particularly a newcomer—will sell twice as many. Developed lots are an intermediate factor, not the only factor, in the production of housing. Although a shortage of housing may exist, a surplus of lots may also exist. Therefore, the market study should examine demand and supply for both the final housing product and developed lots.

Generally, a homebuilder purchases (*takes down*) more than one lot at a time. A lot sale may include four or five, or as many as 100 lots, depending on the type of project, size of builder, and market conditions. *Rolling options* are a popular method for master developers to control builders' takedown of lots. These options provide for the builder to take down a designated number of lots every quarter or year. The option gives the builder an assured supply of lots, at a predictable wholesale price, while giving the land developer an out from the contract with the builder if he cannot sell as many houses as anticipated. The rolling option typically has a built-in price escalation in the lot price—perhaps a 2 to 4 percent increase per year. Rolling options can be structured to protect the interest of the master developer, the builder, or both.[13] The master developer wants to have some assurance that the builder will meet or exceed the takedown schedule and that he cannot tie up future option increments if he is not performing. The builder wants to ensure continued availability of lots—but does not want to pay before he needs them. He wants to carry as small an inventory of lots as possible and wants the ability to decline future options with as little notice or penalty as possible.

The builder may pay option fees, which are usually based on the value of the unexercised options. Paying option fees is a tradeoff against a reduction in the price escalation: If option fees are paid, the price escalation is lower. Higher option fees are a technique to encourage the builder to take down the option sooner (to avoid paying the option fee). Option fees are paid even if the future increments are not acquired. For example, suppose a master developer has 200 lots. The deal may provide that the builder has an option to purchase annual increments of 50 lots over a four-year period. If the builder fails to take down any scheduled increment, he may lose his option rights to all future increments. The builder can exercise his options more quickly and will pay value escalations and/or option fees on unexercised options. Incentives other than cash may be attractive to builders. If the community is unique, access to custom-home clients through an "approved builder" list may be an attractive incentive, or simply favorable land subordination deals may more effectively address builders' risk than option pricing.

What Makes a Good Market Study

PROPER DELINEATION OF THE MARKET AREA

The geographic area where competing subdivisions are sampled should be large enough to include the entire quadrant of the city where your project is located, but small enough to exclude areas that derive their economic value from proximities the subject site does not share.

PROPER DELINEATION OF THE COMPETING MARKET PRODUCT TYPES

A market should not be defined so narrowly that it omits relevant competition, which leads to underestimated supply. For example, low-cost single-family houses compete with condominiums for buyers.

THE CAPTURE RATE

The capture rate of lots for the subdivision should take into account both the total demand in the marketplace and the number of other subdivisions. In metropolitan areas with populations greater than 1 million, capture rates in excess of 5 percent for *any* project, are suspect. Capture rates greater than 30 percent may be appropriate for very specialized products (which should connote a small overall market as well), or within a severely supply-constrained market. The case for a supply-constrained market must also look at the development pipeline.

EMPLOYMENT AND ABSORPTION RATES

Projections of demand should be based both on employment projections and on historic absorption rates in the area. Large increases relative to historic absorption rates are always suspect.

REGULATORY PROCESS

A project's feasibility is affected by regulations from the local, state, and federal levels. It is important to understand these regulations and be able to navigate the approval process efficiently. The developer's goal should be to reduce risk at every step in the process.

ZONING AND PLATTING. The process of subdividing land is called platting or mapping. Platting usually involves a zoning change, typically from a low-density designation to a density one or two steps up the zoning spectrum. In suburban fringes, land is often zoned *agriculture* or some other nearly nondevelopable designation that must be rezoned to allow lot subdivision and development. Every locality has a different procedure for zoning,[14] though there are common elements. In the Northeast and Mid-Atlantic, zoning is administered at the township level, or by the city in urban areas. In the South and West, the process is driven by county or municipal government. Vast differences in the professionalism of staff and officials exist among jurisdictions. Rezoning applications are formal proposals to the regulatory agency, typically an appointed planning commission, to modify the jurisdiction's zoning map to allow a different use or greater density on specific parcels. The applicant must make the case that the proposed changes, though not consistent with the existing map, are consistent with goals of the jurisdiction's comprehensive plan and are beneficial, or at least not detrimental, to the infrastructural and fiscal environment. In reality, the process is politically fraught, and the topics of discussion are likely to be concerns of abutters, ranging from traffic to property values to noise and other nuisances, as well as larger issues of urban structure and infrastructure.

The process can take from several months to many years, depending on the environmental and political sensitivity of the site. Many sites are also subject to the approval of special agencies or commissions, which adds costs and time. For example, land in California that is located within 1,000 yards (915 m) of the ocean is subject to the California Coastal Commission's jurisdiction. Fulfilling the commission's requirements may add years to the time necessary to secure subdivision approvals. Because even many experienced developers lack the staying power to pilot a site through the commission's process, beginning developers are well advised to avoid situations that involve lengthy and expensive approval processes.

Platting Process. Platting is the official procedure by which land is subdivided into smaller legal entities. It is the means by which cities and counties enforce standards for streets and lots and record new lot descriptions in subdivisions. The legal description of a house lot typically follows this form: "Lot 10 of Block 7143 of Fondren Southwest III Subdivision, Harris County, Texas." The legal description parallels the platting procedure. The developer submits a plat of the property showing individual blocks and lots. In some areas, platting requires a public hearing, even if the intended use conforms to the zoning. In other areas, no public hearing is required as long as the platted lots are consistent with zoning and all other subdivision regulations. Even when platting is legally an administrative process, the developer may find himself drawn into a public process by companion ordinances to the subdivision law, such as water protection or critical slope protections.

The number of units permitted to be built on a given parcel usually depends on a combination of several factors, including minimum lot width and depth, setbacks, alley requirements, and street rights-of-way. The target market determines whether a developer plats the greatest possible number of lots, creates larger lots for more expensive houses, or includes a mix of types. A developer should avoid going for the highest allowable density unless previous experience has shown that the resulting density and smaller lots are consistent with target market demand. With that in mind, it is fairly common for developers to enter the process proposing density near the maximum allowable, knowing that the process will almost always result in a reduction from the initial proposal. In areas with transferable development rights (TDRs), this action can have additional benefits, as the developer may be able to monetize any surplus of rights beyond his business plan by selling them to other developers on the TDR market. Even in areas without formal TDRs, tax-funded conservation can compensate developers for entitled, but unused, developable lots. Both processes are complex legal arrangements, and a land use attorney should be consulted before acquisition to ensure that the development's structure allows these kinds of transactions.

Replatting a previously platted area can present unexpected difficulties, especially if the developer must *abandon* (that is, remove from official maps) old streets or alleys. In Dallas, Peiser Corporation was investigating a site when it unexpectedly found that *all* abutting property owners had to agree to the abandonment of a mapped but never built alley. With 50 homeowners involved, the likelihood of unanimous agreement was almost zero. The developer passed on the site, despite having invested considerable time and money.

In addition to platting requirements, the subdivision may be subject to restrictive covenants imposed by the seller or a previous owner. Restrictive covenants should show up in the initial title search and, even if their enforceability is questionable, they may have a profound influence on the type of development allowable.

Developers should be aware of opportunities and pitfalls caused by multiple, overlapping regulatory jurisdictions. Massachusetts, for example, is a "home rule" state, meaning that local authorities overlay many state approvals with their own, and vice versa. In home rule states, major land use changes can happen quickly, certainly within the timeline of even a modestly scaled development. In "Dillon's Rule"

states, such as Virginia, major regulatory change must often be authorized by state legislators, which usually means a developer will have a one- or two-year warning before such changes are enacted. A land use attorney can advise the developer on such issues. Although the public dissemination of land use information is improving with the advent of geographic information system (GIS) technology, many critical requirements are not available online—or if they are, their amendments are not. Some relevant codes are not even published in the commonwealth's general laws. Developers should invest early in local expertise to

- identify all necessary approvals;
- provide realistic timelines in light of local customs; and
- advise on the likely content (and expense) of conditions or necessary mitigation.

The U.S. Supreme Court and Development Regulations

Although most subdivision regulation follows local and regional bodies, the U.S. Supreme Court plays an important role in the regulation of real estate development by ensuring that state and local regulations do not infringe on constitutionally protected private property rights. Each year, federal and Supreme Court rulings are written that clarify, and sometimes upend completely, commonly encountered land use regulations. Developers must rely on attorneys to keep abreast of changing regulation, but a few key decisions are important to understand. Most land deals cannot economically tolerate a lengthy litigation, so many developers accept regulatory intervention without question. Developers should not assume that regulators are knowledgeable about their legal authority.

- In *Nollan v. California Coastal Commission* (1987), the Court established standards for mitigation that require a "rational nexus," between the impact and the required mitigation or regulated improvement.

- In *Lucas v. South Carolina Coastal Council* (1992), the Court held that if a regulation denies the landowner "all economically beneficial" use of his land, then compensation is required under the takings clause of the Fifth Amendment. The only exception to this rule is when the regulation affects an activity that was already barred under state law principles of property or nuisance law.

- In *Dolan v. City of Tigard* (1994), the Court established standards for regulations that require a landowner to dedicate land for public use as a condition of development approval. The government must be able to show a "rough proportionality" between the impact of the development and the public benefit that is being exacted. To date, the Court has not applied the proportionality rule to impact fees or other monetary exactions.

The Supreme Court also reviews federal regulations that affect development in areas including endangered species and wetlands.

- In *Solid Waste Agency of Northern Cook County v. U.S. Army Corps of Engineers* (2001), the Court found that the corps lacked the authority under the Clean Water Act to regulate a wetland that does not physically abut a navigable waterway. The precise effect of this recent decision, which may affect vernal pools and other isolated wetlands, will likely depend on lower court rulings that address various fact-specific situations.

More recently, the Court has addressed the issue of takings for the purpose of economic development.

- In *Kelo v. City of New London* (2005), the majority opinion clarified the range of "public benefits" for which a taking of land was constitutionally justified. Further clarification based on individual facts is to be expected, and the proliferation of new kinds of land use regulation, such as urban growth boundaries, performance-based rules for stormwater, energy efficiency, and carbon, will likely be sources of continuing confusion over the next decade, as the courts catch up to industry and regulation.

Filing a Subdivision Application. Every jurisdiction has its own procedure for obtaining subdivision approval. Most jurisdictions have at least a two-stage process that requires approval from the planning commission and then the city council or county supervisor. California, for example, has a two-tier process. The first tier is the *general plan*, which defines land use for all parts of the city and is reviewed every five years. Most important for new subdivisions, it defines which areas are encouraged for development and which are not. General plans may also be linked to the capital budget for a city or county. The capital budget designates planned public expenditures for utilities, roads, parks, and other infrastructure improvements. The significance of the general plan is that it is relatively easy to obtain permission for zoning changes that are in accord with the general plan. Changes contrary to it—such as development in an agricultural zone or apartments in an area designated for single-family residences—may be almost impossible to get approved. Land that is designated for agricultural use must be changed to urban use, specifying property type and density, in the general plan before a specific plan (the second tier) can be created to develop the property. This step takes considerable lead time when general plans are revised only every five years.

Specific plans spell out the actual zoning, density, and, in some cases, the footprint, street access, and other details of the proposed development. Specific plans are even more detailed than zoning and, once achieved, may tie the developer to a particular development scheme. Changing a specific plan often requires a new round of public hearings and subjects the developer to the full risks associated with regulatory change. These risks have grown substantially in recent decades as more and more communities have attempted to curtail growth. Any public review can be highly politicized, giving the planning commission and city council the opportunity to impose new restrictions, to require more investment by the developer (exactions), or to lower the allowable density of development.

Phasing. Most subdivisions larger than about 200 lots are divided into phases. Even a much smaller development may be phased if the developer's company is small and has limited resources, or if a portion of the land remains unavailable until later. Each phase typically involves a single filing of the plat and subdivision restrictions. Developers finance and construct utilities, roads, and other improvements necessary to create finished lots for each entire phase. Therefore, phases should not be so large that they cannot be

financed or absorbed by the market in a reasonable time frame—usually within 18 to 24 months, or one economic cycle. Delineation of phases is a balancing act, because developers usually want the critical mass of a substantially complete development project as quickly as possible, to reassure buyers skittish about new communities. At the same time, communities may demand to review every aspect of a multiphase project at once, to assess impacts of the whole. Jo Anne Stubblefield, of Hyatt and Stubblefield, advises not to file more than the first phase of a project at the outset, especially for larger properties. Once plans are recorded, the developer may be held to them for a phase that is years away, limiting the ability to change with market conditions. Moreover, most of the regulatory process makes it advantageous to plat in smaller portions, again to preserve flexibility later if the market changes.[15]

REGULATORY CONCERNS. Land development regulation has become so complicated that it would take an entire book to describe the many different forms of regulation that a developer will encounter. Staying on top of new local ordinances is not enough. A developer must know which regulations are about to come into force, which are still under discussion, and which are only vague proposals. The lead times required to get a development off the ground are often long—and increasing. The more agencies involved, the longer it takes. Projects in California's coastal zone and in environmentally sensitive mountain areas have been known to take ten years or longer to secure approvals. Litigation over public approvals for larger tracts is becoming the rule rather than the exception.

"Political involvement," says Scott Smith of La Plata Investments, "is no longer just a good idea; it's critical. Good relationship building with the city planner, city manager, and water/sewer officials is obviously necessary, but don't forget larger issues. We work hard at developing relationships with state and national political parties—a move that may have seemed unjustified until now—when we face a ballot initiative that could kill development even of existing projects."[16]

"What has changed . . . is really the intensity of competition for land entitlement. As competition for land entitlement (and associated costs) heats up, political involvement is becoming more critical," according to Al Neely, formerly of Charles E. Smith Co. "If you are not a consensus builder, you just won't make it. That means consensus at all levels, not just three or four government agencies, but community activists and advocacy groups as well. You have to engage people and get them on board."[17]

Tim Edmond, former president of St. Joe/Arvida, adds, "Make sure you understand fully the cost and time required for entitlements, and then add 30 percent to your estimate."[18]

Roger Galatas, president and CEO of Roger Galatas Interests in the Woodlands, Texas, advises that credibility with regulatory agencies is built with words *and* actions. "That means, do what you say you'll do. Successful developers engage regulators themselves or send their most senior people. What does it say about you if you send someone junior to make your presentation to the planning board?"[19] Four major regulatory issues affect most land developers today: vesting of development rights, growth controls, environmental issues, and traffic congestion.

Vesting of Development Rights. Historically, if developers could obtain zoning, they had the right to build what the zoning allowed. If they owned or bought a property that was already zoned, they were entitled, without public hearings, to develop the property within the limits established by the zoning. But this situation is no longer true in many parts of the country. If a court decides that the developer's right to develop was not *vested*, despite having spent considerable money on improving the land, he may be denied the right to proceed. Standards for vesting vary widely. In development-friendly areas of the Southeast, vesting may be assumed at the preliminary plat (analogous to a general plan) and is secure at the final plat, subject to administrative renewals. In California, vertical construction may be required to prove vested development rights.

In California, Florida, and Hawaii, development agreements have become a popular solution to the problem of securing vested development rights. Development agreements, which are negotiated between the developer and the municipality, ensure that the ground rules under which a developer builds are the same as those that were in effect at the time the agreement was signed. Development agreements protect the developer's right to build a specified number of residential units (or square feet of nonresidential space) in exchange for providing certain facilities to the community. The validity of development agreements are currently being tested in court, and the outcome will determine whether the obvious advantages of these contracts for both sides can be reliable.

Growth Controls. Growth management programs focus on guiding community development and responding to development proposals comprehensively, rather than piecemeal as applications are submitted. They are used to ensure a level of quality in development, including conservation of open space, and that infrastructure is in place to support new development as it occurs.

Growth management provisions are often incorporated in local zoning ordinances. They typically include

- linkage of zoning approvals to capital budgeting investments in infrastructure;
- establishment of growth boundaries to limit the supply of developable land and direct density to urban centers and transit nodes;
- ceilings on the number of housing units or square feet of space that can be constructed in the jurisdiction, or annual quotas on building permits;
- linkage of development and availability of water supply, sewage capacity, or, conceivably, any limited natural resource; and
- linkage of projects and specific public facilities, such as schools, transit, or road improvements.

Growth management is not a new issue. Communities have been able to limit the number of building permits that they issue annually ever since the *Ramapo*[20] and *Petaluma*[21] decisions in the 1970s. Over time, growth management has become more sophisticated and more widespread.

Communities adopt antigrowth or smart growth measures for two main reasons: first, as a reaction to the changing character of the community; and second, in response to overburdened infrastructure—schools, sewers, parks and open space, and, most important, local roads. Traffic congestion drives many antigrowth measures. The capacity of roads and intersections has become the primary criterion in many communities of when and how much new development will be allowed. Developers are often required to build additional traffic lanes, install new traffic lights, and even build new freeway interchanges for major projects to receive approval. As public sector investment has stagnated, municipalities have ironically become more dependent on these exactions and proffers by private developers.

Well-informed and serious debate over growth and development can lead to positive changes in land use regulations. A growing number of local and state governments provide incentives to developers of environmentally sensitive projects, including density bonuses, waived fees, fast-track reviews, and infrastructure improvements, such as parks, roads, and pedestrian links. The city of Austin's Smart Growth Matrix, for instance, provides developers with a range of incentives, including the waiving of permit fees and assistance with infrastructure, if a project meets the city's objectives for development.

Environmental Issues. Since the late 1970s, developers of larger projects in some jurisdictions have been required to submit environmental impact statements (EISs) and reports (EIRs) to receive project approval from federal and state agencies. Over time, the size of projects that require an EIR steadily decreased, and enforcement has become more rigorous. This trend is expected to continue, and in time, almost all development projects will be required to produce some form of environmental impact analysis. The requirements are increasingly coming from local zoning and companion codes, such as groundwater protection ordinances. Formal EISs cover all potential impacts of new development on a community, including impacts on water, biodiversity, vegetation, animal habitat, archaeology, and public facilities, such as roads, schools, utilities, and community services. In smaller projects, EIRs may address only the external impacts of the project beyond the site boundaries; in projects of 500 acres (200 ha)

or more, the most consequential impacts may be within the site. Some environmental issues requiring extensive due diligence include location in a 100-year floodplain, wetlands, and the presence or potential

The Waterfront at Pitts Bay in Hamilton, Bermuda, turned a four-acre (1.6 ha) brownfield site into a vibrant mixed-use project incorporating residential, office, and retail space and a 45-slip marina.

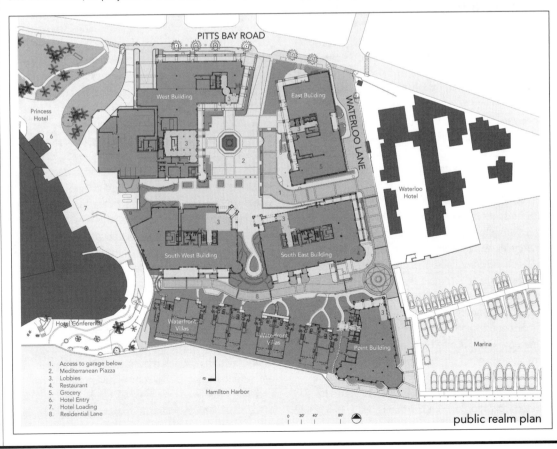

PITTS BAY ROAD

WATERLOO LANE

Princess Hotel

West Building

East Building

Waterloo Hotel

South West Building

South East Building

Hotel Conference

Waterfront Villas

Waterfront Villas

Point Building

Marina

Hamilton Harbor

1. Access to garage below
2. Mediterranean Piazza
3. Lobbies
4. Restaurant
5. Grocery
6. Hotel Entry
7. Hotel Loading
8. Residential Lane

0 20' 40'   80'

public realm plan

presence of endangered species, cultural resources, or toxic waste. Each of these items should show up on an EIS, but the developer should not assume that an EIS protects his investment completely. Financing typically requires a "Phase I" environmental site assessment (ESA), which is a cursory review intended to highlight areas of concern for additional tests. Recommendations in an EIS/ESA for additional study should send a wise developer immediately to an attorney. Responsibility for the results of such investigation is complicated, and prudent developers will be sure they know their responsibilities before moving forward on a Phase II study.

EISs are circulated to interested parties, with comments invited. Reviewers' responses are then appended to the statement, which may be modified as a result of the comments. Federal legislation allows litigation over the adequacy of coverage in an EIS, a step that can cause great delays.[22] Developers should never assume that compliance with federal law translates to compliance with state law. State laws often conflict with similar federal laws, so it is important to consult an attorney to clarify obligations. Although the developer may ultimately be right in a court of law, the time and cost of litigation could break a young or undercapitalized developer.[23]

One of the most sensitive aspects of EIRs concerns hazardous waste. On a project outside Houston, for example, the EIR reported some open pools of oil adjacent to a new subdivision, but no further research was done. More than 300 houses had been built in the subdivision when it was discovered that the oil pools were toxic. The homebuyers sued the builder, the developer, the engineers, the lenders, and almost everyone else remotely connected with the subdivision. The eventual settlement was for hundreds of millions of dollars.

For land developers, sites that encompass brownfields present both constraints and opportunities. The U.S. Environmental Protection Agency (EPA) defines brownfields as "abandoned, idled, or underused industrial and commercial facilities where expansion or redevelopment is complicated by real or perceived environmental contamination." Although many of these sites are problematic because of their industrial locations and the potential cost of cleanup, well-located brownfields may be attractive for development. Amendments to the Superfund law in 1997 hold lenders harmless when financing the redevelopment of brownfield sites, and at least 35 states have enacted legislation to limit cleanup liability. As a result,

insurance companies are writing policies to limit the developer's liability, and financial institutions are making loans for the development of brownfields.

In 1997, the 100-year-old deteriorating Atlantic Steel mill in midtown Atlanta became the focus for brownfield redevelopment. Jacoby Development, Inc. (JDI) partnered with AIG Global Real Estate in a $2 billion project to add over 15 million square feet (1.4 million m²) of retail to midtown Atlanta. Some environmental remediation was required throughout the 138-acre (56 ha) property. By using site-specific risk-based criteria to develop the appropriate environmental remedy, JDI integrated the environmental remediation with the overall master plan. The removal of over 165,000 tons (150,000 t) of soil contaminated by various metals, volatile organic compounds, and free products of oily substances was sequenced to allow for the simultaneous installation of underground infrastructure. Additionally, the steel slag on site was covered with a combination of hard-cap (roads, buildings, and so forth) and soft-cap (two feet [0.6 m] of clean dirt) methods. Remediation was completed in the range of $10 million, instead of the original estimates projected at around $30 million. The reuse of this site will generate about $30 million or more in tax revenue for the city of Atlanta.[24]

State and local agencies are becoming increasingly knowledgeable about cost-effective cleanup methods and are frequently willing to provide grants or tax incentives and cap or reduce liability for cleanups.

Value can be added to a project in the course of solving some of these environmental problems if the developer is flexible enough in acquisition. Roger Galatas notes, "We've had success in these situations by creating land trusts, environmental trusts, conservation easements, and other structures to deal with endangered species, wetlands, and cultural resources, which can then be carefully marketed as amenities for the overall development project. This matter has to be dealt with up front, however, incorporating risk in the acquisition program and acquiring enough land to allow the developer to give up parcels to these kinds of structures without serious damage to the project's economics."[25]

Traffic. Traffic congestion in many suburbs is as bad or worse than congestion in urban centers. As a result, concerns about traffic are often at the root of slow-growth/no-growth movements. Traffic studies are a standard part of environmental impact reviews. Localities often require developers to pay for major off-site road improvements to receive approvals. Legal precedent in these matters requires "rough proportion-ality" and "a reasonable nexus" for exactions, meaning that the required contribution may not be unreasonably large, relative to the economic value of the approval, and that some connection must exist between the exaction and the impact of the approved project.[26]

FINANCING INFRASTRUCTURE. Regulatory uncertainty is integrally tied to the time and cost of providing or obtaining necessary infrastructure facilities, including utilities, roads, and drainage and potentially parks, schools, treatment plants, and fire and police stations.

A variety of methods for financing infrastructure are available:

- **General Taxes**—Historically, street and utility improvements have been financed by bonds that were repaid by general property tax revenues.
- **Federal and State Grants**—Historically, federal and state grants have assisted local communities in building water treatment facilities, sewage treatment plants, highways, and other infrastructure.
- **Impact Fees**—These fees are imposed on the developer at the final plat or building permit and are usually computed per unit, per square foot, or per dollar value of finished construction.
- **User Fees and Charges**—Such fees and charges are a traditional means of obtaining revenues. Monthly fees (water and sewer fees, for example) are pledged as revenue streams to repay bonds issued to finance the facilities and to pay operating and maintenance expenses.
- **Assessment Districts**—These districts can issue bonds and impose a special tax levy on property owners who benefit from specific public improvements in the district.
- **Special Districts**—Special districts are similar to assessment districts, except that their governing bodies are separate from the local government. They can issue bonds and levy taxes on property owners in their jurisdiction.
- **Tax Increment Financing Districts**—Increases in tax revenues that result from new development in a specified area are earmarked for public improvements or services in that area, rather than using the general fund.
- **Developer Exactions**—The developer is required to install or pay directly for community facilities in return for approvals.

Developers must thoroughly understand public and private infrastructure financing because infrastructure accounts for a major portion of the cost of land development. Developers must understand how their development will affect the revenues and costs of the local jurisdiction where they want to build. Increasingly, development approvals are tied to whether or not a new development has a positive impact on local finances, and the calculation of fiscal effect can be subjective.

The legal test for impact fees is that a *rational nexus* can be proved to exist between the fees charged and the benefits received by the future residents of the development. The developer should not be expected to pay the entire cost of facilities that benefit other residents of the community.

Ironically, growth moratoriums and building permit caps are motivated, in part, by the lack of adequate impact fees. Residents who vote for moratoriums claim that developers are not paying their full share of the cost that they impose on a community. Developers may find that it is in their own best interest to support "you pay, you play" impact fees, although a community should not expect development to pay more than its fair share.

Unfortunately, developers have been caught in the middle of a tax revolt in many parts of the country. As development fees have become popular and developers have accepted them, communities have looked to developers to provide an ever-increasing share of the costs of urban services—so much so that in many communities, new residents are subsidizing existing residents. Many cities now require developers to pay for half the cost of major arterials that abut their property.[27] Further, developers typically must pay for some or all of the new utility lines required to serve their property, although a portion of these installation costs may be recoverable once the development is occupied. These off-site requirements have a major impact on the location of subdivisions. Even for very large developments, the cost of bringing in water and sewer services from more than a mile away is prohibitive. Unless the municipality can underwrite the cost directly or through some form of special district, the amount that developers can afford to pay for off-site facilities is limited. The first developer is often required to install infrastructure—notably roads, sewers, water, and drainage—to serve a new area. Many cities require other property owners who benefit from that infrastructure to reimburse the developer later, when those owners subdivide their own property. This procedure gives the developer the potential to recoup the cost, albeit over the course of many years. Some communities, however, do not give any interest on upfront investment to the developer. Thus, the developer's current project alone must effectively support the off-site infrastructure.

AVOIDING PITFALLS. Many regulations serve vital functions—protecting the environment, reducing flooding, controlling traffic, and ensuring that adequate infrastructure is built. From the developer's point of view, however, increasing government regulation adds considerably to the time, expense, and risk of land development.

The larger the land development project, the more likely it is to be a target of special regulatory concern. One way to minimize the impact of regulation is to choose infill areas located in older jurisdictions that have more established regulations. They may present other problems, however, as infill tracts are typically surrounded by existing development and developers may have to deal with vocal homeowner groups.

In general, developers can reduce the regulatory risk by following these suggestions:

- Stay closely in touch with local planning staff, and document correspondence.
- Know and respect local representatives. Planning boards will often listen to these leaders when projects affect their constituents.
- Monitor pending ordinances and referenda.
- Join the local building industry association and participate.
- Once a concern has been identified, consult the regulatory agency's staff and, if necessary, an attorney to find out how to protect or exempt the project.
- Consider working with redevelopment agencies, which often have the power to expedite approvals.
- Consider using a development agreement, on larger projects, to protect development rights.
- Select local architects, engineers, and zoning and other consultants who have worked extensively in the community.

Maintaining Flexibility. The development value of land is tied to the number of units or square footage that can be built on a site, which shifts the approval risk, in part, from developers to sellers, because the purchase price is lower if developers cannot get permission to build a prenegotiated number of units or square feet. Most land sellers are unwilling to accept

regulatory risk after closing. The developer must either accept this risk or find a seller who is willing to defer the closing until zoning or other approvals are completed. The land price will reflect which party takes on the entitlement risk. The price should be significantly lower if the developer closes without the entitlements than it would be if entitlements are in place. Developers are advised to share the risks where possible with the seller, even if it means less profit, unless they are very confident that they can obtain zoning approval for enough units to make the project profitable.

At the same time that government approvals are becoming harder to obtain, planning commissions and city councils are requiring developers to meet specific timetables. Developers are often required to build roads and community facilities by a specific time, often in advance of selling lots. In some cases, developers must commit to building a specified number of units per year. The cyclical nature of the real estate industry, however, makes periods of boom and bust inevitable. Developers must retain the flexibility to build more units when times are good and to reduce production (and infrastructure installation) when times are bad.

Developers should also retain the flexibility, where possible, to program the mix of units for each development phase. Because of the frequent delay between approvals and construction, developers must be able to respond to current market conditions when deciding on their final unit mix. Otherwise, they may be forced to sell lots to homebuilders to meet a market that is no longer in demand and may be precluded from selling lots for houses in a price category that is in demand. For larger projects, developers should work in increments or stages that are small enough for them to vary the product mix as the market indicates. Many communities now require approval of specific plans that lock the developer into specific unit sizes and finishes, adding substantially to the developer's risk, as a change in the market requires a new series of public hearings to change the specific plan.

Working with the Community. Good relationships between a developer and neighboring homeowners are critical to a project's success. The most common objection raised by homeowner groups to a proposed subdivision is that it will reduce the quality of the neighborhood—exacerbating traffic problems or bringing in people who have lower incomes and live in smaller houses. In urban fringe development, opposition tends to focus on spillover costs and inadequate infrastructure. The developer's best counterargument is to emphasize the quality of the new development.

Most experienced developers prefer to talk to homeowner groups themselves instead of hiring someone to represent them. Developers must convince the community that they will keep their promises, and this trust is more likely to be gained in person.

The developer of a small project may not need to talk to homeowner groups if few public approvals are required. Although doing nothing and hoping that no one will notice is a temptation, this approach is seldom the best. Homeowner groups in most parts of the country are too aware of, and involved with, development for the developer to rely solely on the quiet approval of the planning commission and the city council. Such groups become particularly intransigent when they feel that they are being ignored—especially if they do not learn about proposed projects until the public hearing.

A better approach is to identify in advance the groups that may have concerns about the project and then seek them out. A developer should also be careful to identify the most influential leaders in a local community. Peiser Corporation, for example, lost a zoning case because it met with the president of the local homeowners association but not with another community leader, a minister, who came out against the project in part because he was not consulted initially.

When a public hearing is required for approval, the following approach is recommended:

- Educate the public affected by the project.
- Talk to planning departments early in the process to explore options.
- Be aware that the public hearing process is not adequate for addressing all opposition. Serious concerns need to be addressed in side meetings.
- Be proactive: talk to the city council or legislators to get in touch with citizens groups, develop contacts with them, and, possibly, form a citizens advisory committee.
- Use press relationships and a clear Web presence to communicate plans to those who are not at the public hearing.
- Be certain that all plans are clearly explained, and all numbers (density, unit count, traffic studies) are adequately illustrated.
- Allocate time for the development staff to communicate with the public.

Much of the slow-growth movement is motivated by the belief among existing homeowners that they are required to pay an unfair portion of the cost of facilities that will be used by future residents. But each new generation of residents benefits from previous generations' investment in infrastructure. Major infrastructure investment—typically, streets and utilities—is characterized by debt payments over 20- to 30-year

Charter Homes was the developer and homebuilder for Veranda, a 180-lot residential community in Lancaster, Pennsylvania. (A financial analysis for Veranda begins on page 101.)

ALLIANCE RESIDENTIAL COMPANY

periods, slow deterioration, and periodic replacement. When the financing life is shorter than the economic life of a facility and when a community's growth rate is more than 3 percent per year, the residents of that community pay for benefits faster than they receive them. When taxes to pay for growth rise faster than property values, dissension between current residents and future residents (represented by the developer) soon follows.

The main justification for impact fees and other development charges is that they will alleviate the burden that growth imposes on existing homeowners. Developers can expect more and more communities to impose impact fees, and for those fees to be, in some cases, economically prohibitive for some types of development.

Theoretically, impact fees are imposed for the developer's share of facilities from which the developer benefits, including those that have been installed and paid for earlier. In some cases, such facilities may be off site and may benefit other parties as much as they directly benefit the developer's project. Developers are advised to seek out or form homeowner groups to maintain communication within the community and if problems arise, turn first to informal contacts, then to mediators or facilitators instead of lawyers.

FINANCIAL FEASIBILITY ANALYSIS

Financial feasibility analysis for land development is performed in two stages. The first stage is a "quick and dirty" pro forma that summarizes the project's sales revenues, expenses, interest, and profit. The second is a multiperiod discounted cash flow (DCF) analysis that provides a detailed projection of cash flows, equity and loan needs, profits, and basic return measures, including internal rates of return (IRRs). Developers should perform both stages of analysis before they commit earnest money to a project. They should then update the cash flow analysis regularly during the feasibility period as they establish sales, price, and cost information with greater accuracy. The DCF analysis feeds into the investor return analysis, which provides a picture of the returns to the different parties that furnish the equity for the project—the investors and the developer—under a deal structure. The DCF analysis and the investor analysis are the developer's primary spreadsheets for evaluating a project's financial prospects, for obtaining a land development loan, and for raising equity from investors. Lenders and investors will ask the developer questions that cannot be credibly answered without having

done this exercise. Although the software tools available to small developers allow a variety of analytical techniques, the most important tool is a conceptual understanding of project cash flow.

BASIC CONCEPTS. Financial analysis for land development differs from that for other property types, and developers should be aware of some basic concepts for this type of analysis.

For-Sale versus Income Property. The fundamental difference between financial analysis for land development and other property types is that land is for-sale property, whereas apartments, offices, retail stores, and warehouses are income properties. For-sale property is analyzed over the development period, which depends on how long it takes for the market to absorb the land for homes or other property types—one or two years for a small subdivision, three to five years for a larger one, and decades for new town–scale development. For-sale projects are typically financed by a combination of equity and a land development loan, though multiple loan types may be employed. As lots are sold to homebuilders, subdevelopers, or end users, the land developer's profit is the difference between revenues from land sales and the costs of purchasing the raw land, planning the project, acquiring approvals, installing infrastructure, and marketing the land to end users, including the carrying cost of all of these expenditures. In contrast, financial feasibility of income-producing properties focuses on computing the value of the completed and fully leased property using a before-tax and after-tax analysis that includes permanent financing and, typically, a seven- or ten-year holding period. The development profit is the difference between the value of the completed property and the "all-in" cost of developing it.

FIGURE 3-2 | Approximate Residential Lot Yield per Acre

Lot Size (ft²)	LOT YIELD/ACRE	
	With Alleys	Without Alleys
10,000	3.0	3.3
8,500	3.6	3.8
7,500	4.1	4.4
6,500	4.7	5.0
6,000	5.1	5.4
5,000	6.1	6.5
4,000	7.0–8.0	7.5–8.5

Gross versus Net Developable Acreage. Developers must understand the distinction between gross acres, net developable acres, and net usable acres.[28] *Gross acreage* refers to the total acreage at the time of purchase. *Net developable acreage*, or net acreage, omits major streets, open spaces, floodplains, and major easements that are significant to the entire project. *Net usable acres* omits interior street rights-of-way, alleys, and any other areas that are not actually for sale from net developable acres. Total net usable acres should equal the total area actually sold—the aggregate total area of building lots plus multifamily, commercial, industrial, and office sites. These distinctions become important in analysis, as developers need to know their cost, sale price, and margin on any given transaction, as well as on the whole project.

Most rough calculations are performed on the basis of net developable acreage, which includes interior streets. When a developer investigates a new piece of property, it is essential to know the amount of land *not developable* because of floodplains, easements, major road rights-of-way, or dedications for schools, parks, or other community facilities. The remaining acreage is used to calculate the number of lots and the number of acres of apartments or commercial sites to be sold separately.

A reasonably good estimate can be made of the number of lots that can fit on a specified property by using yield formulas. For example, 7,500-square-foot (697 m²) lots produce a typical yield of four lots per acre (they may be called *quarter-acre* lots because of the yield, even though they are smaller than a quarter acre, which is 10,890 square feet (1,012 m²):

4 lots × 7,500 square feet per lot = 30,000 square feet
Estimated street right-of-way = 12,000 square feet

Total = 42,000 square feet (about 1 acre)

The yield may differ, depending on the standard street rights-of-way and whether alleys are required. Most planners allow for some waste because, for example, corner lots are larger and irregularly shaped sites are difficult to develop efficiently.

The developer should check with a local planner for lot yield, but the following rules of thumb may serve as starters. Deduct 25 percent of the acreage for streets (30 percent if alleys are required), and then divide the remainder by the lot size. (Representative densities for residential development are shown in figure 3-3.) It is important not to confuse the rough yield estimates shown here with the formal process

of yield calculation. Many systems of zoning require a "yield plan" to illustrate the actual buildable density under a set of zoning rules. This number is then used as the unit count under another, alternative zoning. A formal yield plan must conform strictly to the governing code, and this calculation may bear little relation to an accurate yield estimate.

Land Use Budget. The allocation of total net developable acreage into different land uses is called the *land use budget*. Including all product types, roads, open space, and community facilities, it should add up to total developable acreage. The most profitable (optimal) land use budget is determined by the marketplace, based on those product types that are being absorbed most quickly and reliably and at the highest prices. To get started, a rough estimate of cost may be obtained from other developers, civil engineers, and contractors. With this information, plus sale prices and

---

FIGURE 3-3 | Densities by Residential Type

Product Type	FAR	Net Density (units/acre)	Gross Density
Single-family detached	0.2	8	5
Zero-lot-line detached	0.3	8–10	6
Two-family detached	0.5	10–12	4
Rowhouses	0.8	16–24	4
Stacked townhomes	1.0	25–40	4
Three-story walkup apartments	1.0	40–45	4
Three-story walkup over parking	1.0	50–60	4
Six-story elevator apartments	1.4	65–75	4
13-story elevator apartments	1.8	85–100	75

Source: Kevin Lynch and Gary Hack, *Site Planning*, 3rd ed. (Cambridge, Mass.: MIT Press, 1985), p. 253.

Note: Density ranges for apartments have been adjusted upward.

FIGURE 3-4 | Land Use Budget for a 100-Acre Site

Uses	Land Use Budget (acres)	Absorption (acres/year)
Residential		
Single-family detached (7,500 ft² lots)	40	10
Single-family detached (5,000 ft² lots)	20	6
Apartments (30 units/acre)	10	5
Retail	15	5
Community facilities	2	0
Parks and open space	8	0
Subtotal	95	26
Arterial (highway dedication)	5	
Total	**100**	

marketing and tax and administrative cost estimates, a developer can produce the "quick and dirty" analysis. An example of the land use budget for a 100-acre (40 ha) site is shown in figure 3-4.

The land use budget should be roughly established before meeting with the land planner. The land use mix should be primarily an economic decision, within regulatory constraints. Planners and engineers should shape and enhance the allocations, but not invent them, because they will become the major initial input into the financial feasibility analysis. Serious planning or engineering of the project cannot be undertaken until these factors are known.

The absorption rate for the land is expressed as the number of acres that can be sold each year. In the example shown, it should take four years to sell out the 7,500-square-foot (697 m²) single-family lots, more than three years for the 5,000-square-foot (465 m²) lots, two years for the apartment land, and three years for the retail land (all selling simultaneously, which, it should be noted, is an assumption). These relatively high absorption rates for the retail component are based on the project's high-visibility location, which fronts on a new freeway.

The ideal land use budget maximizes the value of the property by allocating as much land as possible to high-value uses within the constraints of absorption. Developers often mistakenly allocate too much land to high-value uses, such as office or retail, which command higher sale prices but have slower absorption rates. In addition, land absorption for higher-density projects such as high-rise apartments takes longer, by definition, than it does for lower-density projects because more units must be sold to absorb each acre.

Another difficulty is distinguishing between land sales to builders and other developers and those to end users. In larger projects, if enough land for 20 or 30 years of absorption has been reserved for office and retail use, it is tempting simply to assume that the unsold inventory will be sold to "land investors" at the end of the development life—say, three or five years later. The developer must, however, assume a significant discount (25 to 50 percent or more) in the retail sale price of lots to end users. Investors who buy the unsold inventory will have to wait until demand from end users warrants building out the site and so will not pay retail prices. Such a large difference between retail and wholesale price points up an obvious difficulty in land use budgeting: absorption and price are not independent. As the analysis proceeds, developers should question whether the absorption could be improved by aggressive pricing.

Optimal Land Use Planning. Clearly, the relative value of high-value-per-acre land and fast absorption must be established, and some factor must be applied to recognize the time value of these sales. Figure 3-5 illustrates the computation of land value and the allocation of land uses for a 35-acre (14 ha) tract of land. Suppose that retail land can be sold for a net profit of $200,000 per acre, whereas 7,500-square-foot (697 m²) single-family lots bring $80,000 per acre ($32,400/ha) at $20,000 each. Suppose also that demand is one acre per year for retail land versus 40 lots (ten acres) per year for single-family lots. Note that retail absorption is much slower than single-family lot absorption. Figure 3-5 shows the present value of land sold for retail use each year for eight years. To compare the value of retail land sold today with that sold in seven years, the value is discounted at a hefty 15 percent per year—a discount rate that reflects both the high holding cost of land and the high risk associated with land development. A retail acre sold in seven years is worth only $75,000, compared with $200,000 today. By comparison, an acre of single-family land sold today is worth $80,000. In this example, therefore, it is more advantageous to sell single-family land today than another acre of retail land in seven years. These present values are ranked, in the table, in order of each acre's present value.

The developer should allocate land to the highest-value use as long as the present value of that year's absorption rate is greater than the next highest value use. Figure 3-6 shows the resulting allocation. The developer would allocate the first seven acres to retail use (seven years of absorption of retail land at one acre per year), because the present value is greater than that for single-family land sold today, even though it will not be consumed by the marketplace for up to six years (allocations 1 through 7, indicated in parentheses in the figure). The next ten acres would go to single-family land (allocation 8), however, because the present value ($80,000) is higher than the value of the retail land sold in seven years ($75,000). Ten acres—one year of absorption—is allocated to single-family use. The next acre would go to retail use (allocation 9). The next ten acres would go to single-family lots (allocation 10) and then one more acre to retail (allocation 11). At this point, 20 acres are assigned to residential use and nine acres to retail use. The last allocation (allocation 12) goes to residential. Because only six acres are left to bring the total to 35 acres, the third year's allocation of residential absorption is not completely used. The final budget is 26 acres of single-family lots and nine acres of retail use.

This procedure for allocating land is an application of linear programming to real estate.[29] It works for any number of uses and can be done by hand. The only information needed is net developable acreage, sale price, development cost, and absorption rate for each land use or product type. A good starting discount rate—representing opportunity cost—is 5 percent above the current interest rate for development loans. The resulting land use allocation is only a guideline for the land use budget and will probably be modified by zoning, political, or environmental constraints. Nevertheless, a market-based land use allocation is the only accurate and reliable method for determining the land use budget. It should determine the land use plan, not vice versa.

QUICK AND DIRTY ANALYSIS. The developer analyzes financial feasibility several times during the course of a project. The first analysis is performed before tying up the property; as the deal progresses, the analysis becomes successively more thorough and complex. A good financial feasibility analysis becomes the basis for managing the project once it begins construction; therefore, the categories in the analysis should coincide with the project manager's chart of accounts.

The financial analysis illustrated here is from Veranda, a project in Lancaster, Pennsylvania, by Charter Homes. The land development component of the project, now completed, consists of 180 finished lots, permitted for three for-sale housing types arranged in an amenitized, walkable community plan. Charter Homes is the developer and homebuilder and, as recommended in this chapter, analyzes the land and homebuilding businesses separately. Revenue, in this example, refers to sales of lots from developer to builder. Costs include acquisition, carrying costs, entitlement, and soft and hard costs of site development.

Quick and dirty analysis provides the initial estimate of financial performance. It summarizes projected revenues from the sale of lots, land and development costs and interest, and expected profit. All figures are aggregated for the entire project life. No time dimension for development or sales is considered. Quick and dirty analysis represents the starting point for evaluating the deal. It does not, however, give the developer all the information needed to make proper decisions.

Figure 3-7 shows the quick and dirty analysis for Veranda. Charter Homes has developed the property in four phases. Sale prices for the three lot types are $35,000 for townhomes, $45,000 for carriage houses (duplex), and $68,000 for single-family detached lots. The average lot price is $59,367 for total revenue of $10,686,000.

Land for the project cost $26,000 per developable acre, or roughly $2.3 million. Development costs include on-site land improvements with hard costs of $5.1 million, off-site road improvements of approximately $500,000 and soft costs before sale of $1.3 million. Total development costs are $5.2 million. Financing costs are estimated by assuming that

FIGURE 3-5 | Effect of Present Value Factors on Land Allocation for Multiple Uses

Project Years	Present Value Factor at 15 Percent	Profit on 1 Acre Retail Land	Rank	Profit on 1 Acre Single-Family Detached Land	Rank
0	1.000	$200,000	1	$80,000	8
1	0.869	$173,800	2	$69,520	10
2	0.756	$151,200	3	$60,480	12
3	0.657	$131,400	4		
4	0.571	$114,200	5		
5	0.497	$99,400	6		
6	0.432	$86,400	7		
7	0.375	$75,000	9		
8	0.327	$65,400	11		

Note: 15 percent represents an estimated opportunity cost. Values are computed by multiplying Year 0 value by the factor for the year in question. For example, $200,000 × 0.869 = $173,800.

FIGURE 3-6 | Allocation of Land for a 35-Acre Tract
Using Present Value Rankings from Figure 3-5

Project Years	Retail Use (acres)		Single-Family Use (acres)	
0	1	(1)	10	(8)
1	1	(2)	10	(10)
2	1	(3)	6	(12)
3	1	(4)	0	
4	1	(5)	0	
5	1	(6)	0	
6	1	(7)	0	
7	1	(9)	0	
8	1	(11)	0	
Total	**9**		**26**	

Note: Assume absorption of one acre per year retail and ten acres per year single-family land.

Charter invests $3.7 million in equity and borrows the rest at 7.5 percent. In actuality, the development loan will not reach the maximum shown in the analysis (total project costs of $7,832,000 minus equity of $3,700,000). In this "back-of-the-envelope" methodology, interest is estimated by assuming that it takes one year to develop the project with an average loan balance of $1.8 million. Profit is $2,853,652, or about 38 percent of total costs. Traditional rules of thumb suggest that these ratios should be at least 25 to 30 percent. Such rules, however, are not very meaningful because they do not provide any estimate of return on equity or take into account the holding period. In fact, the holding period is, in any project with unentitled land, an essential factor, and a limitation of this type of analysis. For example, a 30 percent return on equity in one year would be good, whereas a 30 percent return over three years would be only 10 percent per year uncompounded and 9.14 percent per year compounded.[30] Developers should keep in mind that expected returns are market determined. The risk of land development means that investors will require returns that exceed those obtainable in other, less risky investments. Over the long term, the appropriate discount rate should track, with a premium, long-term returns from stocks, bonds, and other asset classes. Developers can never assume that last year's rule of thumb will be appropriate to attract investment capital this year.

Because the time value of money is not included in the quick and dirty calculation, comparison with other investment alternatives is not possible. This analysis has other shortcomings:

- It gives no indication of how quickly lots are sold.
- It has no means of introducing inflation.
- Computation of interest on the development loan is haphazard.
- It gives no information about when funds are needed or the amount needed.
- It has no means of computing present values or internal rates of return.

The loan calculation is the weakest part of the back-of-the-envelope analysis. In the example above, the loan amount is chosen so that it covers all of the costs, including loan interest, which can usually be borrowed. The size of the loan at any moment depends on how quickly the lots are being sold, however—a factor that this analysis does not take into account. Whether or not the loan amount will cover 100 percent of the costs depends on the raw

land appraisal, the development cost, the borrower's creditworthiness, and current lending standards and business outlook in the market. Most land development projects require some form of real equity—cash investment or significant appreciation in land value above the developer's basis.

The main advantage of the back-of-the-envelope analysis is that it forces the developer to make explicit assumptions concerning land uses, site planning, sales rates, prices, costs, and financing. These assumptions can then be tested against market data. This exercise provides a rough indication of whether or not the deal makes economic sense, and it serves as the foundation for all subsequent investigation.

MULTIPERIOD DISCOUNTED CASH FLOW ANALYSIS. Multiperiod DCF analysis is an application of the capital asset pricing model to real estate. The cash flow analysis assigns revenues and expenditures from the quick and dirty analysis above to specific periods of time, tracking the resulting net cash flows through the project life. Project returns, which were simple multiples in the quick and dirty analysis, now reflect the present value of all predicted cash flows in and out of the project. Note that the cash flows in figure 3-7 reflect the funding and repayment requirements of equity investors and lenders available to land developers. (Common financing terms are discussed later in this chapter under "Financing.") The multiperiod DCF analysis for the 180-lot development at Veranda is shown in figures 3-8a through 3-8c. Its principal purpose is to compute (1) returns to the overall project (100 percent owner/developer), (2) loan requirements, and (3) returns to joint venture participants. It is a before-tax computation.

Land development financing is similar to construction financing during the development period of income property (Stage 3 analysis in chapter 4). No permanent mortgage exists as the purpose of land development is to sell developed lots to homebuilders, and apartment, shopping center, and office building developers. Another important difference from income property analysis is that the development loan is retired by the sale of lots rather than by funding of the permanent mortgage, which takes out (pays off) the construction loan. Land development DCF analysis is used to determine the building program, phasing, and expense budget that the project can support. Like Stage 2 analysis for income properties (see chapter 4), land development DCF analysis is rerun many times during the feasibility period and over the life of the

FIGURE 3-7 | Veranda Land Development
Quick and Dirty Analysis

PHASING WORKSHEET					
Lot Mix	Lot Price	Phase 1	Phases 2 & 3	Phase 4	Total
Single family (sf)	$68,000	40	52	30	
Carriage house (ch)	$45,000	24	12	-	
Townhome (th)	$35,000	22	-	-	
Total lots		86	64	30	180
Average		$53,140	$63,688	$68,000	

LAND SALES REVENUE						
	Mix	Number of Lots	Avg. Price/Lot	Revenue	Total	Per Lot
Phase 1	40 sf, 24 ch, 22 th	86	$53,140	$4,570,000		
Phases 2 & 3	52 sf, 12 ch	64	$63,688	$4,076,000		
Phase 4	30 sf	30	$68,000	$2,040,000		
Project Total Sales		180			$10,686,000	$59,367

EXPENDITURES			
		Total	Per Lot
Land Cost (87 acres @ $26,000 per acre)		$2,262,000	$12,567
Development Costs			
Grading	$210,000		
Paving	$600,000		
Storm sewer	$250,000		
Water	$200,000		
Sanitary sewer	$180,000		
Power	$85,000		
Teledata/network	$160,000		
Off-site street improvements	$506,031		
Fees & permits	$800,000		
School fees	$350,000		
Indirect land development	$300,000		
Financing costs (2.0% of max loan)	$73,815		
Pursuit/transaction costs	$156,075		
Marketing (6.0% of sales)	$641,160		
Administration & contingency (6.0% of sales)	$641,160		
Total Development Costs		$5,153,241	$28,629
Subtotal		$7,415,241	$41,196
Interest Calculation			
Equity	50.0%	$3,707,620	
Debt	50.0%	$3,707,620	
Average balance (estimate)	50%	$1,853,810	
Duration (years)	3		
Rate	7.5%		$417,107
Total Expenditures		$7,832,348	$43,513

PROFIT		
	$2,853,652	$15,854
		38.5% of total costs
		26.7% of total revenue

Source: Hempfield Valley Partnership and Charter Homes.

project. The land use budget, cost, and sales assumptions are fine-tuned as more accurate information becomes available. The cash flow analysis for land development is used for both planning the design of the project and obtaining financing.

Several key items should be noted about the methodology of the DCF analysis for land development.

Time Periods. Intervals should be selected that cover five to ten time periods of analysis. For example, for a sale of 120 lots at the rate of 30 lots per quarter, plus 12 months for development, the total time required is about two years. Quarterly time periods (three months per period) would provide eight total periods, a good starting point for analysis. For larger projects that require, say, ten years to be developed, annual periods would be appropriate for the first DCF analysis.

Level of Detail. The purpose of the early runs of the DCF analysis is to obtain a picture of the total project. Beginners often go into too much detail at first, forgetting that every item in the spreadsheet is subject to change. Because the developer has not yet done a detailed site plan and sales and cost estimates are, at best, rough approximations, a monthly cash flow analysis would be meaningless. The spreadsheet can always be enhanced by adding more periods and more line items as more information becomes available. Usually, the developer should wait to prepare a monthly cash flow forecast until the site plan has been adopted, the market study has been completed, contract bids are available, and a monthly forecast for loan approval is needed.

Construction of the Analysis. Keeping in mind the previous point, that nearly every input may be subject to change, cash flow models should, where possible, aggregate all variable inputs in one place, or in one column and one row. Where these numbers are needed in the analysis, we can refer to the input cell and adjusting the model will require changing only these cells.

Time Period Zero. Time period zero represents the starting period of analysis and can be set for any time. It should always be included in cash flow analysis. For existing projects, time period zero is recommended to be set three to six months earlier than the present date at some point where the exact amount of money spent to date and a monthly burn rate are known. In projects where money has already been spent, a line item on the spreadsheet, *costs to date*, should be added that aggregates the total money spent, including carry costs, as of time period zero. For new projects, time period zero is normally selected as the closing date on the land. Any costs incurred before closing are simply included under the land cost or cost-to-date category.

Timing of Sales. Enough time should be allocated to develop the property and investigate the effects of slower-than-anticipated sales. One computer run should assume half the expected sales pace and compute the maximum loan amount needed for this downside case.

Inflation. DCF models typically include three different inflation rates—sale price inflation, cost inflation, and the inflation rate implicit in the interest rate. These rates are correlated but not necessarily the same. A 3 percent inflation rate in sale prices, for example, indicates a development loan interest rate of 7 to 11 percent (3 percent inflation plus 2 to 3 percent real rate of return plus 2 to 5 percent risk). Higher inflation assumptions can make a project look better than it probably is. Lenders are rightfully cautious of overly high inflation assumptions and may insist on a DCF analysis run with zero inflation in sale prices. Even if inflation is included, a common mistake in DCF modeling is setting price appreciation at a higher rate than cost increases. In relatively mature markets, this assumption is seldom justifiable.

Development Loan Borrowings. The development loan provides bank financing for all borrowing needs after the equity. Once the loan has been reduced through the sale of lots, developers are usually not allowed to return to borrow additional money (as they would be able to with a revolving line of credit) because the collateral for the loan—namely, the land—has been partially sold off. In the Veranda development loan calculation, the loan balance does go up and down as successive phases are developed and then sold. In actuality, this ability to reborrow money would likely require separate loans on each phase or a revolving line of credit for improvements only, separate from the land-secured financing, or would include provisions tying new borrowings to the new phases.

Loan Repayments. Loan repayments (releases) represent the amount by which the land note and/or the development loan must be repaid as property is sold. Every time a lot is sold, the land that was pledged as collateral for the development loan must be "released" from the construction loan or land loan lien by the lender. These releases are shown as *cash out* or repayment items (development loan repayments and land note repayments, lines 85 and 86, in figure 3-8c).

Before-Tax Computation. Before-tax rates of return may be used for evaluating the economic feasibility of a land development project as long as they are compared with before-tax returns from other investment opportunities. Unlike the development of income property (see chapter 4), in which tax benefits are an important part of the return, land development offers no special tax benefits (such as deductions for depreciation and current interest). The Internal Revenue Service (IRS) treats the land developer as a "dealer in land," and, as such, the developer must pay ordinary tax on reported profits. For example, if the developer's tax rate were 33 percent, he would pay $333 in tax on each $1,000 of profit.

Return Measures. The unleveraged internal rate of return (line 114) assumes that all cash requirements are financed from cash equity. It is computed on line 77 in figure 3-8c, "profit before interest," exclusive of all financing. The unleveraged return varies from year to year but should be at least 15 to 20 percent.[31] It should exceed the cost of borrowing money so that the developer can obtain positive leverage. If, for example, the unleveraged IRR is 15 percent and the interest rate on the development loan is 12 percent, then the developer's return on equity will be higher than 15 percent. Negative leverage exists when the return is less than the loan rate. Positive leverage means that as the developer borrows more money, the return on equity increases. The unleveraged return in the figure is 28 percent per year for this project.

Return on Equity. The return on equity is also an IRR calculation. In contrast to the unleveraged IRR, the return on equity takes financing into account. The developer's cash investment, plus any in-kind equity, such as the value of land contributed to the deal, is represented as a cash outflow. "Cash flow after financing" (line 87) shows cash inflows to the developer. Sometimes, no net cash inflows occur until the development loan is fully retired, although it depends on the lender's loan release provisions. The return on equity should be higher than the unleveraged IRR because the amount of equity is usually only a fraction, say, 20 percent, of total project cost. The return on equity should always be higher than the loan interest rate because equity investors have lower priority for access to cash flows than mortgage holders and thus incur more risk. If the project is financed by 100 percent equity (no debt), the return on equity is the same as the unleveraged IRR (45.2 percent). In the figure, the IRR on $2,000,000 equity is 60.7 percent per year. The rate of return that constitutes an acceptable return on equity varies, but by any criteria, the land

component of this analysis is strong. Most developers require a return on equity that is 12 to 15 points higher than what they could obtain on risk-free government bonds. If, for example, one-year Treasury bills (T-bills) are paying 5 percent, most developers want a return on equity of 15 to 20 percent.

If no equity is invested (that is, the project is 100 percent financed), then the return on equity is infinite. An infinite return does not necessarily mean that the project is economically feasible. Even if the project equity is zero, the *unleveraged* IRR should be on the order of ten points above the T-bill rate and preferably should be around 15 points for land development.

FIGURE 3-8a | DCF Results

Profit before interest	$2,823,004	Cash flow after financing	$4,719,107
Less interest	(103,897)	Less repayment of equity	(2,000,000)
		Less unpaid loan balance	–
Profit	2,719,107	Profit	2,719,107
UNLEVERAGED RETURN[a] (CASH FLOWS BEFORE INTEREST & FINANCING)		**LEVERAGED RETURN ON EQUITY[b] (NET CASH FLOWS AFTER FINANCING)**	
Net present value @ 15%	$1,578,806	Net present value @ 15%	$1,688,177
IRR	45.2%	IRR	60.7%

Year	Net Profit	Year	Equity	Cash Inflows
0	(2,518,075)	0	2,000,000	481,925
1	(1,356,031)	1	–	(481,925)
2	(47,722)	2	–	–
3	948,822	3	–	–
4	894,698	4	–	–
5	1,174,137	5	–	991,933
6	1,892,620	6	–	1,892,620
7	888,757	7	–	888,757
8	945,798	8	–	945,798
9	–	9	–	–
10	–	10	–	–
11	–	11	–	–
12	–	12	–	–
13	–	13	–	–
14	–	14	–	–
15	–	15	–	–
16	–	16	–	–
Total	**$2,823,004**	**Total**	**$2,000,000**	**$4,719,107**
			Profit	$2,719,107

[a]The unleveraged return is computed on the cash flows before financing. Thus, it is an all-equity rate of return. The unleveraged return should be significantly greater than the interest rate on financing. Otherwise, no profit will be left over after financing costs are paid.

[b]The return on equity is computed on cash flows after financing. A leveraged rate of return gives the IRR on equity for the entire project (the owner/developer provides all necessary equity).

FIGURE 3-8b | Assumptions: Sales, Prices, Development Costs, Land Note

1	NUMBER OF TIME PERIODS PER YEAR: 4 (1=ANNUAL, 2=SEMI-ANNUAL, 4=QUARTERLY, 12=MONTHLY)					
2				Q4 2004	Q1 2005	Q2 2005	Q3 2005
3	Sales (Lots)[c]		Total	0[d]	1	2	3
4	Phase 1		86			20	36
5	Phase 2		52				
6	Phase 3		12				
7	Phase 4		30				
8	Total		180	–	–	20	36
9	Sales prices[e]	Price Escalation/Period[f]	Price/Ft²	Price/Lot	1	2	3
10	Phases 1 & 2	0.75%	–	$53,140	$53,140	$53,539	$53,940
11	Phases 3 & 4	0.75%	–	63,688	63,688	64,166	64,647
12	Phases 5 & 6	0.75%	–	63,688	63,688	64,166	64,647
13	Phases 7 & 8	0.75%	–	68,000	68,000	68,510	69,024
14	Sales Revenues[g]		Total	0	1	2	3
15	Phases 1 & 2		4,642,953	–	–	1,070,771	1,941,843
16	Phases 3 & 4		3,424,556	–	–	–	–
17	Phases 5 & 6		793,349	–	–	–	–
18	Phases 7 & 8		2,141,539	–	–	–	–
19	Total		11,002,398	–	–	1,070,771	1,941,843
20	Costs[h]		Total	0[i]	1	2	3
21	Land		2,262,000	2,262,000			
22	Grading		210,000		30,000	100,000	30,000
23	Paving		600,000		–	200,000	200,000
24	Storm sewer		250,000		50,000	100,000	50,000
25	Water		200,000		20,000	100,000	20,000
26	Sanitary sewer		180,000		60,000	60,000	30,000
27	Power		85,000		20,000	20,000	20,000
28	Teldata/network		160,000		20,000	60,000	60,000
29	Off-site street paving		506,031		506,031	–	–
30	Fees & permits		850,000		350,000	100,000	100,000
31	School fees		350,000		100,000	50,000	50,000
32	Indirect land development		1,050,000	100,000	200,000	200,000	200,000
33	Pursuit/transaction		156,075	156,075			
34	Interest per period (decimal)	0.075/year		0.0188	0.0188	0.0188	0.0188
35	Land Note[j]	Data Input	Total	0	1	2	3
36	Total land cost	2,262,000		2,262,000			
37	Lots sold—enter release price/lot	41,000	180	–	–	20	36
38	Downpayment		1,262,000	1,262,000			
39	Beginning lots released	41,000		30.8	30.8	30.8	13.2
40	Ending lots released				30.8	10.8	–
41	Lots to be released			–	–	–	22.8
42	Land note		1,000,000	1,000,000			
43	Repayment terms					10.0%	20.0%
44	Minimum land payments			–	–	100,000	200,000
45	Maximum land note balance			1,000,000	1,000,000	900,000	700,000
46	Starting balance			1,000,000	1,000,000	1,000,000	900,000
47	Land note releases	41,000	900,000	–	–	–	900,000
48	Remaining balance			1,000,000	1,000,000	1,000,000	–
49	Additional note payments			–	–	100,000	
50	Ending balance			1,000,000	1,000,000	900,000	–
51	Additional lots released	41,000				2.4	–
52	Interest for period[k]	1.5%	43,500		15,000	15,000	13,500
53	Land note total		$43,500	($1,000,000)	$15,000	$115,000	$913,500

Q4 2005	Q1 2006	Q2 2006	Q3 2006	Q4 2006
4	5	6	7	8
30				
	27	25		
		12		
			15	15
30	27	37	15	15
4	5	6	7	8
$54,345	$54,752	$55,163	$55,577	$55,993
65,132	65,620	66,112	66,608	67,108
65,132	65,620	66,112	66,608	67,108
69,542	70,063	70,589	71,118	71,651
4	5	6	7	8
1,630,339	–	–	–	–
–	1,771,747	1,652,810	–	–
–	–	793,349	–	–
–	–	–	1,066,769	1,074,770
1,630,339	1,771,747	2,446,159	1,066,769	1,074,770
4	5	6	7	8
20,000	20,000	10,000		
100,000	50,000	50,000		
20,000	20,000	10,000		
20,000	20,000	20,000		
10,000	10,000	10,000		
10,000	10,000	5,000		
10,000	5,000	5,000		
–	–	–		
100,000	100,000	50,000	50,000	
50,000	50,000	50,000	–	
200,000	100,000	50,000		
0.0188	0.0188	0.0188	0.0188	
4	5	6	7	8
30	27	37	15	15
–		–	–	
–	–	–	–	–
30.0	27.0	37	15	15
35.0%	35.0%			
350,000	350,000	–	–	–
350,000	–	–	–	–
–	–	–	–	–
–	–	–	–	–
–	–	–	–	–
–	–	–	–	–
–	–	–	–	–
–	–			
–	–	–	–	–
–	–	–	–	–

cSales by product type are entered for each period. Units of measurement do not have to be the same. Thus, residential sales may be expressed as number of lots sold per period (lines 3 through 8); office space is expressed in acres sold per period.

dEach period is a quarter (line 2). The number of periods per year should be chosen to produce five to 15 periods overall. A ten-year project is best analyzed with annual periods (ten periods), a 20-year project with two-year periods (ten periods), and a three-year project with quarterly periods (12 periods).

eSale prices are expressed in the same units as are sales. Thus, if residential sales are expressed in lots, sales prices should be expressed in price per lot (lines 9 through 13).

fLot prices may be escalated at a given rate per period (lines 9 through 13).

gSales revenue is computed from the number of acres or units sold per period times the price per period (lines 14 through 19).

hCosts are entered by category and period. Detailed cost breakdowns for individual categories, such as utilities, are best handled in supporting spreadsheets (see lines 20 through 33), since an overabundance of detail makes the analysis more difficult to follow.

iTime 0 should be treated as a separate period. Typically, Time 0 is the time of closing. Costs incurred before Time 0 should be lumped together as "startup costs."

jThe land note defines the terms, if any, of the land purchase from the land seller. The release price negotiated in the land note is $41,000 per lot (note that the release price often differs for different lots). Given a downpayment of $1,262,000, 30.8 lots (line 39) are released immediately from the note. The land note also defines the repayment terms (line 43). If sales are slower than the terms of the note, then the developer must pay additional money to satisfy the land note (line 49), which releases additional lots (line 51). If lot sales occur faster than the note repayment terms require, then additional lots must be released (line 41) in order to sell the lots. In the example, the sales pace is slower than the terms of the note. If releases from sales are slower than those required under the amortization terms of the land note, then the shortfall is covered by the development loan or additional equity (line 49).

kInterest on the development loan typically is borrowed as part of the development loan. It may, however, be funded by cash payments rather than additional borrowing (line 49).

FIGURE 3-8c | Cash Flow Summary

54	Cash Flow Summary[l]	Total	0	1	2	3
55	**Income**					
56	Sales revenue	11,002,398	–	–	1,070,771	1,941,843
57		–	–	–	–	–
58	Total income	11,002,398	–	–	1,070,771	1,941,843
59	**Expenses[m]**					
60	Land[n]	2,262,000	2,262,000	–	–	–
61		–	–	–	–	–
62	Grading	210,000	–	30,000	100,000	30,000
63	Paving	600,000	–	–	200,000	200,000
64	Storm sewer	250,000	–	50,000	100,000	50,000
65	Water	200,000	–	20,000	100,000	20,000
66	Sanitary sewer	180,000	–	60,000	60,000	30,000
67	Power	85,000	–	20,000	20,000	20,000
68	Teldata/network	160,000	–	20,000	60,000	60,000
69	Off-site street paving	506,031	–	506,031	–	–
70	Fees & permits	850,000	–	350,000	100,000	100,000
71	School fees	350,000	–	100,000	50,000	50,000
72	Indirect land development	1,050,000	100,000	200,000	200,000	200,000
73	Pursuit/transaction	156,075	156,075	–	–	–
74	Marketing[o] (6.0%)	660,144	–	–	64,246	116,511
75	Administration & contingency (6.0%)	660,144	–	–	64,246	116,511
76	Total expenses	8,179,394	2,518,075	1,356,031	1,118,493	993,021
77	**Profit before Interest[p]**	2,823,004	(2,518,075)	(1,356,031)	(47,722)	948,822
78	Less development loan interest	(60,397)	–	(8,414)	(18,528)	(20,084)
79	Less land note interest	(43,500)	–	(15,000)	(15,000)	(13,500)
80	**Net Profit**	2,719,107	(2,518,075)	(1,379,445)	(81,249)	915,238
81	**Financing**					
82	Plus Equity	2,000,000	2,000,000			
83	Plus Development Loan Borrowings	1,110,516	–	897,520	181,249	20,084
84	Plus Land Note Borrowings	1,000,000	1,000,000	–	–	–
85	Less Development Loan Repayments	(1,110,516)	–	–	–	(35,322)
86	Less Land Note Repayments	(1,000,000)	–	–	(100,000)	(900,000)
87	**Cash Flow after Financing**	4,719,107	481,925	(481,925)	–	–
88	**Cumulative Cash Position**	$4,719,107	$481,925	–	–	–

FIGURE 3-8d | Cash and Loan Calculations and IRRs

89	Cash Account and Loan Calculation					
90	**Cash Account**	Total	0	1	2	3
91		–	–	–	–	–
92	Starting cash balance		0	481,925	0	0
93	Additions to equity	2,000,000	2,000,000	0	0	0
94	Profit before interest	2,823,004	(2,518,075)	(1,356,031)	(47,722)	948,822
95	Land note	(43,500)	1,000,000	(15,000)	(115,000)	(913,500)
96	Subtotal	4,779,504	481,925	(889,106)	(162,722)	35,322
97	Amount to be financed before interest	1,051,828	0	889,106	162,722	0
98	Cash available for loan & interest		481,925	0	0	35,322
99	Loan repayments	1,110,516	0	0	0	35,322
100	Interest	1,708	0	0	0	0
101	Ending cash balance	4,719,107	481,925	0	0	0

4	5	6	7	8
1,630,339	1,771,747	2,446,159	1,066,769	1,074,770
–	–	–	–	–
1,630,339	1,771,747	2,446,159	1,066,769	1,074,770
–	–	–	–	–
–	–	–	–	–
20,000	20,000	10,000	–	–
100,000	50,000	50,000	–	–
20,000	20,000	10,000	–	–
20,000	20,000	20,000	–	–
10,000	10,000	10,000	–	–
10,000	10,000	5,000	–	–
10,000	5,000	5,000	–	–
–	–	–	–	–
100,000	100,000	50,000	50,000	–
50,000	50,000	50,000	–	–
200,000	100,000	50,000	–	–
–	–	–	–	–
97,820	106,305	146,770	64,006	64,486
97,820	106,305	146,770	64,006	64,486
735,641	597,610	553,539	178,012	128,972
(894,698)	(1,174,137)	(1,892,620)	(888,757)	(945,798)
(11,663)	(1,708)	–	–	–
–	–	–	–	–
883,036	1,172,429	1,892,620	888,757	945,798
11,663	–	–	–	–
–	–	–	–	–
(894,698)	(180,496)	–	–	–
–	–	–	–	–
–	991,933	1,892,620	888,757	945,798
–	$991,933	$2,884,553	$3,773,310	$4,719,107

[l]The cash flow summary presents the net cash flows from the land development (lines 54 through 88).

[m]Expenses summarizes the cost entries in lines 59 through 76. Figures in the summary are higher in most categories because they include inflation.

[n]Even if land is contributed to the deal, its cost should be included as an expense (lines 78 and 79).

[o]Some cost categories, such as marketing, are typically calculated as percentages of sales revenues (line 74).

[p]Profit before interest is derived from line 77, which sums the differences between total income and total expenses. This line gives the unleveraged cash flows, before financing, found in the results summary in figure 3-8a.

[q]A primary purpose of the analysis is to determine the amount and timing of development loan requirements (lines 83 through 86). Cash equity (or land equity that is considered "cash" if it is contributed to the deal) is infused into the project initially (line 82). As money becomes available from sales, it is used to retire the development loan.

[r]Development loan repayments, called "releases," are typically a negotiated ratio, usually 1.1 to 1.3 times the loan amount per lot (line 85). Release prices are usually assigned to each lot, depending on its relative value. In this analysis, all positive cash flows are assumed to go toward paying down the development loan until it is fully retired.

4	5	6	7	8
–	–	–	–	–
0	0	991,933	2,884,553	3,773,310
0	0	0	0	0
894,698	1,174,137	1,892,620	888,757	945,798
0	0	0	0	0
894,698	1,174,137	2,884,553	3,773,310	4,719,107
0	0	0	0	0
894,698	1,174,137	2,884,553	3,773,310	4,719,107
894,698	180,496	0	0	0
0	1,708	0	0	0
0	991,933	2,884,553	3,773,310	4,719,107

CONTINUED

Cash and Loan Calculations and IRRs | CONTINUED

102	Loan Account					
103	Beginning balance		0	0	897,520	1,078,769
104	Loan draws		0	889,106	162,722	0
105	Loan repayments		0	0	0	35,322
106	Trial ending balance		0	889,106	1,060,242	1,043,447
107	Average balance		0	444,553	978,881	1,061,108
108	Interest rate		0	0	0	0
109	Interest		0	8,414	18,528	20,084
110	Interest paid from cash		0	0	0	0
111	Ending balance		0	897,520	1,078,769	1,063,532
112	Borrowings after interest		0	897,520	181,249	20,084
113	NPV and IRR Calculations[s]	Quarter IRRs				
114	Unleveraged return	45.22%	2,823,004	(2,518,075)	(1,356,031)	(47,722)	948,822
115	Return on equity	60.69%	2,719,107	(1,518,075)	(481,925)	0	0
116	Cumulative return on equity			(1,518,075)	(2,000,000)	(2,000,000)	(2,000,000)

FIGURE 3-8e | Investor Return Analysis

		Data Input	Total	0	1	2	3
117							
118	Cash Flows to Investors						
119	Cash in/cash out		4,719,107	481,925	(481,925)	–	–
120	Starting equity balance				2,000,000	2,040,000	2,080,800
121	Equity investment		2,000,000	2,000,000	–	–	–
122	Subtotal			2,000,000	2,000,000	2,040,000	2,080,800
123	Cumulative preferred return[u]	2.0%		–	40,000	40,800	41,616
124	Noncumulative preferred return[v]	–		–	–	–	–
125	Preferred return paid		67,622	–	–	–	–
126	Preferred return accrued		164,864	–	40,000	40,800	41,616
127	Subtotal			2,000,000	2,040,000	2,080,800	2,122,416
128	Reduction of equity		2,164,864	–	–	–	–
129	Ending equity balance			2,000,000	2,040,000	2,080,800	2,122,416
130	Cash for distribution[w]		2,486,621	–	–	–	–
131	Equity partner	50%	1,243,310	–	–	–	–
132	Developer	50%	1,243,310	–	–	–	–
133	Rate of Return Calculation						
134	Equity partner investment		(2,000,000)	(2,000,000)	–	–	–
135	Preferred return		67,622	–	–	–	–
136	Reduction of equity		2,164,864	–	–	–	–
137	Cash distribution		1,243,310	–	–	–	–
138	Total cash flows to investor		$1,475,797	($2,000,000)	–	–	–
139	Net present value	3.0%	$875,993				
140	IRR[x]		38.1%				

1,063,532	180,496	0	0	0
0	0	0	0	0
894,698	180,496	0	0	0
168,833	0	0	0	0
616,182	90,248	0	0	0
0	0	0	0	0
11,663	1,708	0	0	0
0	1,708	0	0	0
180,496	0	0	0	0
11,663	0	0	0	0
894,698	1,174,137	1,892,620	888,757	945,798
0	991,933	1,892,620	888,757	945,798
(2,000,000)	(1,008,067)	884,553	1,773,310	2,719,107

[s]IRRs are calculated on the profit before interest (line 114) and cash flows after financing and interest (line 115). These IRRs are included in the results in figure 3-8a.

4	5	6	7	8
–	991,933	1,892,620	888,757	945,798
2,122,416	2,164,864	1,216,229	–	–
–	–	–	–	–
2,122,416	2,164,864	1,216,229	–	–
42,448	43,297	24,325	–	–
–	–	–	–	–
–	43,297	24,325	–	–
42,448	–	–	–	–
2,164,864	2,164,864	1,216,229	–	–
–	948,636	1,216,229	–	–
2,164,864	1,216,229	–	–	–
–	–	652,066	888,757	945,798
–	–	326,033	444,378	472,899
–	–	326,033	444,378	472,899
–	–	–	–	–
–	43,297	24,325	–	–
–	948,636	1,216,229	–	–
–	–	326,033	444,378	472,899
–	$991,933	$1,566,586	$444,378	$472,899

[t]The investor return analysis is a before-tax computation of cash flows to the developer and investors in a joint venture (lines 118 through 140). If the landowner contributes the land to the deal, the land value is treated as cash equity for purposes of this calculation.

[u]Preferred returns are priority returns of cash flow to the investors. Cumulative preferred returns are accumulated into succeeding periods whenever the amount of cash available is insufficient to pay the preferred return in the current period (line 123).

[v]Noncumulative preferred returns are not accumulated into future periods. If the amount of cash from the current period is insufficient to pay the noncumulative preferred return, it is forgotten (line 124).

[w]The cash distribution percentages are negotiated between the developer and the equity investors (lines 130 through 132).

[x]The investors' IRR is computed on line 140. The IRR is the discount rate for which the present value of future cash flows equals the initial investment ($4 million in Period 0). Since the periods are quarters, the IRR is multiplied by four to give an annualized rate of return. Note: Due to rounding, some totals may not add exactly.

The calculation of net present value (NPV) offers a better method of ranking projects than IRR because it provides the value in today's dollars of the wealth that a project will generate in the future. The appropriate discount rate should be the developer's opportunity cost rate—the rate that can be earned in alternative investments of similar risk. The project with the highest NPV is preferred. If only one project is being considered, then the NPV should be sufficient to justify the time and risk of development, even if the developer has no equity invested in the project. For example, suppose the NPV on a four-year project with $1 million equity, discounted at 15 percent, is $200,000. Thus, the developer would have earned the equivalent of $200,000 in today's dollars over and above a 15 percent return on the initial investment. The developer must then determine whether the project is worth the time and risk involved. If it would be necessary to work on the project full-time for four years or sign personally on a $5 million loan, it probably is not.

Developers must often extend personal guarantees on loans, even when they have no equity invested in a project. Some developers treat their guarantee as a component of equity and compute an IRR on that basis. Because the guarantee is a contingent liability (neither the necessity nor the actual size of the investment is known) rather than a cash investment, the appropriate return on the guarantee is not comparable with the IRR on equity when the equity is in the form of hard cash.

Relationship between Returns, Inflation, and Risk. All returns move with inflation. Return on equity has three components—a real rate of return (2 to 3 percent), an inflation premium, and a risk premium.[32] If expected long-run inflation (over the life of the investment) is, say, 4 percent and the risk premium is 10 percent, then the required return on equity would be 16 to 17 percent. The risk premium depends on the status of the real estate—whether it is fully leased, under construction, or in predevelopment—as well as on the amount of leverage (all equity versus 60 to 95 percent or more financing), the property type, location, and other factors that bear on the likelihood of success or failure (such as neighborhood opposition, competition, market and economic trends). The risk premium alone may range from 10 to 20 percent or more depending on the amount of perceived risk. The earlier the stage of development, the greater the risk. Unentitled property is considered the riskiest of all forms of development because there is no assurance that the developer can entitle the land to build, and failure means the land has only agricultural or conservation value, typically a fraction of the proposed development value.

Although required rates of return change quickly and are hard to generalize, some rules of thumb apply. For example, pension funds making all-equity investments in fully leased investment-grade income properties (large shopping centers, office buildings, apartments) may look for returns as low as 10 percent. Projects that have entitlements but are not yet built typically should offer at least a 15 percent unleveraged before-tax IRR or a 20 to 25 percent leveraged before-tax IRR. Because land with entitlement risk is considered the riskiest form of real estate, leveraged returns on equity have historically ranged from 15 to 30 percent or more. These figures may be appropriate for times of expected 3 to 4 percent inflation, but if inflation is higher, required return rates rise as well. The Great Recession and ensuing housing market turmoil have, in many markets, obscured these historical relationships. At this writing, with riskless rates near zero, traditional investment capital for land development is unavailable in many markets, and the discount price of existing land deals indicates that investors are seeking double or more average returns for their effort. It remains to be seen whether the land development risk premium will revert to mean, or if the result will be revised rules of thumb for the future.

One of the most common misunderstandings in real estate is the relationship between IRRs, inflation, and capitalization rates (cap rates). As noted earlier, hurdle IRRs (required returns on equity) go up with inflation. This situation occurs because inflation and risk are two components of the required rate of return. Capitalization rates, however, tend to go down as inflation goes up. Because capitalization rates are simply the ratio of current net operating income (NOI) to the purchase price for income property, buyers are willing to pay more for property as inflation is expected to increase—causing capitalization rates to go down and prices to go up for the same NOI. On the other hand, as risk goes up, cap rates go up as well because buyers are willing to pay less money for property if they perceive the risks to be greater.

Design and Site Planning

Land planning begins with target buyers or end users and a marketing concept for the buildings that will ultimately be built on the finished lots to attract these customers. The end product—the size, style, and quality of building—dictates how the land should be subdivided.

Good subdivision design involves much more than an engineer's efficient layout for streets and utilities. Historically, developers favored the most cost-efficient plan—the rectangular grid. Beginning in the mid-20th century, however, developers began to prefer curved streets and culs-de-sac that took advantage of natural features. Today, the grids of towns and cities are once again favored over the organic forms of suburbia. In the best plans, natural features are considered as well, and the grid may bend and curve to accommodate hills and valleys, streams, wooded areas, and other important features. The new urbanist movement has shown that a grid network of streets and short blocks not only is more cost-effective but can also aid in calming traffic and improving access for pedestrians.

EVOLUTION OF SUBDIVISION DESIGN

The evolution of subdivision design has been shaped primarily by three forces: the automobile, increasing housing costs, and a growing awareness of the environment, first as an antidote to urban ills and more recently as a casualty of careless development.

THE AUTOMOBILE. Automobiles have long been the most dominant influence on subdivision design. Indeed, private automobiles helped create suburban growth by allowing workers to live at some distance from public transportation lines. Without the automobile, low-density single-family housing would not have been possible. Suburban streets have always been designed to accommodate automobile circulation and parking; suburban houses have typically been designed with driveways and carports or garages—first for one car, then for two. Today, garages for three or more cars are not uncommon. Over the years, innovative methods of dealing with traffic have been tried. A three-level hierarchy of streets (local streets, collectors, and arterials) and separation of pedestrians from cars were pioneered in Radburn, New Jersey, in 1929.[33] Culs-de-sac were also first introduced in Radburn to reduce traffic on residential streets. Today, this system is being reconsidered. Because it forces all traffic onto arterials while underusing local streets, many transportation planners now realize that a hierarchical system can cause, rather than alleviate, congestion. Where traffic is focused, rather than distributed, pedestrian connections suffer. Furthermore, these systems increase infrastructure and service costs. The Com-

monwealth of Virginia recently passed legislation to severely limit the use of culs-de-sac in future subdivisions, denying maintenance services to developments that do not comply with the new rules.

INCREASING HOUSING COSTS. Housing costs have risen faster than personal incomes and national inflation rates throughout the post–World War II period. This escalation in costs has been driven in part by increasing land prices, and as a long-term trend has survived even the 2008–2009 correction. In response, developers have been building at ever-higher densities, in an effort to reduce land costs per unit. In the 1950s, a typical single-family suburban house occupied a one-acre (0.4 ha) lot; today, in many of the more expensive regions of the United States, it is common to find single-family lots as small as 4,000 square feet (370 m²). The need to achieve higher densities has stimulated new methods of subdividing land—clustering houses in planned multiuse developments (usually zoned as *planned unit developments*, or PUDs), patio or zero-lot-line homes, and a greater variety of attached housing at all price levels. Increasing interest in multifamily products has been one positive outcome of the housing crisis. Design standards have evolved slowly, following generation-long shifts

The Rainier Vista Community in Seattle, Washington, is a mixed-use development designed as a cohesive, transit-oriented neighborhood focused on a light-rail station. At completion it will be home to 875 households.

TONKIN/HOYNE

in consumer preferences and institutional incentives. Following the proven viability of some of these models, many city zoning and subdivision ordinances have been changed to accommodate density, with accompanying political debate.

Labor-intensive construction methods have also played a role in increasing costs. In many respects, construction methods have altered little since Roman times. Although many housing components (roof trusses, floor joists, and millwork, for example) are now manufactured, much is still done by hand. Cost savings of 10 to 20 percent have been achieved in manufactured housing, chiefly in the areas of time and interest, but both consumers and building officials have been slow to accept units manufactured off site. Lenders and government agencies have also been reluctant to treat manufactured housing the same way they treat conventional, stick-built housing. Construction quality has improved in many ways—energy-efficient windows, roofing, and mechanical systems; improved methods of insulating and waterproofing; and new lower-maintenance materials. Much of what has been gained by such efficiencies, however, has been lost to increasing land and labor costs and to some degree to the costs of regulations related to the environment, safety, and growth.

SUSTAINABILITY. The environmental movement has touched all aspects of the real estate development industry, including community and housing design. Environmental concerns in many communities have led to stricter open-space requirements, more comprehensive planning reviews of subdivision infrastructure design, and increasing restrictions against building in environmentally sensitive areas. The most obvious effect of these concerns has been to substantially restrict the amount of developable land and its permissible uses. Addressing these concerns is no longer optional for developers.

All development puts stress on land. Zoning and comprehensive planning give guidance, but developers must ultimately decide how they will manage these stresses. Developers should carefully consider the location of their projects. Increasing regional planning and widespread use of GIS technology mean that valuable ecologies are less and less subjective, and more likely to be well defined and documented. Developers must know from the outset which kinds of environmental assets to avoid. Parcel-scale mapping of unfragmented wildlife habitat, watersheds, and prime agricultural lands is often available from planning

offices, or from state environmental agencies. Experts like wildlife biologists can be hired to analyze data in the preliminary site search. For the beginner, choosing to work against regional plan goals by developing on an identified asset is usually not a good idea.

Once a parcel and use have been identified, developers should quickly establish a strategy for developing that parcel at a reasonable profit without violating its natural features. If the natural features are of particular value as amenities, developers should determine which development practices, if any, will complement what exists and should consider as well whether these assets can be enhanced by improved stewardship. Developers do not just react to regulatory policy; they help create it by their actions, and it is not uncommon for innovative developers to outperform regulatory requirements, which are usually a minimally acceptable standard.

Homebuyers increasingly place value on more sustainable development. Though it is seldom a primary motivation of buyers, developers must be able to address these concerns, and sales can benefit from good decisions made early. It is far more effective to be "green" in project design than to attempt to make a conventional project appear thoughtful later. Conservation can be incorporated into the projects in many ways. For example, developers can

- reserve open spaces that enhance natural characteristics, such as stands of trees or bodies of water;
- create stewardship plans for resource areas within the development;
- legally and physically protect areas of natural beauty and reserve areas for passive recreation or agriculture;
- integrate storm drainage features and water retention areas into the site plan, which, properly designed, can become amenities;
- create rich landscaping and planting areas that enhance a project's appearance and biological function;
- build and landscape to prevent erosion of steeply sloping areas;
- avoid water and air contamination and control erosion and excessive noise during construction;
- establish homeowners associations and other structures to care for open-space areas; and
- provide opportunities for residents to engage the landscape by planning for hiking, fishing, and horseback riding.

SENSITIVITY TO DESIGN ISSUES

The developer's awareness of and sensitivity to marketing issues should complement the planner's and landscape architect's skills and knowledge about layout and infrastructure design. Considerable time and effort are required to develop a critical eye and an accurate intuition about site design. Beginning developers can take the following steps to educate themselves about subdivision design:

- become familiar with classic subdivisions and with innovative new communities;
- talk to other developers and architects about the types of designs that do and do not work in their markets;
- attend planning commission meetings to hear what staff, citizens, and environmental groups find important;
- talk to brokers at competitive subdivisions because they usually hear customers' uncensored reactions; and
- attend planning-related educational sessions at meetings held by professional organizations.

A developer should also gain familiarity with classic examples of each major building type, through travel and courses in architectural history, planning, and development. Understanding architecture and urban design history is vital, because it allows a developer to examine structures that have survived both social and technological change and to understand the variety of ways in which memorable and functional places are created.

Good developers supplement their knowledge of design with the opinions and tastes of homebuyers in their market area. They conduct focus groups and interview homebuyers to discover what aspects they like or dislike about local subdivisions and how well they meet the needs of different age groups, household types, and income segments. Visual preference surveys, which gauge consumer reaction to actual design elements, can fine-tune this process and detect preferences that may be subconscious or counterintuitive to the buyers themselves. California developer Dan Kassel emphasizes the close link between good design and objective market research. "The first thing to forget is your own preconceptions and design opinions. They are no substitute for solid market research. Your target market in any given deal is more likely than not to run counter to your own preferences."[34]

CONSERVATION DEVELOPMENT, CLUSTERS, NEW URBANISM, AND PUDS

Among the key planning concepts with which a developer should be familiar are conservation development, cluster development, new urbanism, and PUDs.

"Conservation development" is an approach to exurban community development that proposes that sensitive landscapes and development can coexist. Conservation communities can range in size from a few acres to thousands, but they generally have several items in common. They usually include legal protections for some areas of the plan, such as a conservation easement. They also typically control housing design to a greater degree than comparably located subdivisions.

Clustering is the most common zoning-approved method of conservation development. In cluster development, higher densities in certain areas permit protected open space elsewhere on the site. Following traditional zoning, overall, gross density usually remains the same for cluster developments as for traditional tract housing where housing is spread more uniformly over the entire tract. Each cluster may contain homes of a similar style, and styles may vary among clusters, imparting an individual village character to each. Cluster planning requires more design skill than conventional subdivision planning; unskilled planning or exploitation of the cluster concept can easily generate an unattractive bunching of dwellings.

"New urbanism" offers another alternative to conventional subdivision design, emphasizing traditional neighborhood planning based on grid street patterns. Featuring narrower streets with sidewalks, small public squares and parks, narrower lots with rear garages to manage car traffic, and walkable town centers, this approach proposes land use patterns similar to those of traditional cities and towns. Seaside in Walton County, Florida, is among the earliest examples of the new urbanist approach, and its success has spawned hundreds of development plans that refine the core concepts. New urbanism typically relies on typological coding, rather than zoning, as its primary regulatory tool. Coding, which is more design-oriented than zoning, specifies building, street, and open space "types" for each lot in the development without dictating uses. The results are a mixed-use, mixed-housing-type community, flexible enough to accommodate many uses, but conforming more or less to a formal design for the streetscape.

Beginning developers aspiring to these characteristics should be advised: it is not as simple as it sounds.

First, the more comprehensive design vision of a community like Seaside requires substantially more attention and expense in the design phase, which can be tough for a small firm to sustain. Second, the consistent vision of a master-planned community requires legal structure, governance documents and boards, and operational funding for common area maintenance, as well as ongoing design review and builder oversight. This "software" is just as complex as the actual construction. Third, many developers have encountered trouble when shaping community plans to a formal ideal without adequate research to prove a deep market for the resulting mix of home typologies. That said, demographics clearly support more of this type of development, particularly the aging of the U.S. population and the increasing diversity of household types that are poorly served by conventional suburban houses. The Congress for New Urbanism and other professional advocacy groups offer an array of symposiums and training opportunities for individuals to learn about these ideas.

Whereas conservation and new urbanist development are design and governance concepts, PUD is a legal concept. PUDs are zoning classifications typical in many jurisdictions, under several common names, such as *planned residential development* or *planned residential unit*, but the purpose remains the same. In PUDs, traditional zoning classifications are discarded in favor of a more flexible approach that considers the project in its entirety instead of in zoning overlays. The PUD is approved as an entity and is essentially a customized rezoning for a desirable project. It may combine commercial and residential uses, include several types of residential products, and provide open space and common areas with recreational and community facilities.

In a PUD, residential areas may be outlined and a certain number of units designated, but no detail regarding the specific site plan is required for approval. Most jurisdictions require later public review of the specific site plan; some treat this review as cursory, if the plan is being followed. Developers have the right to build a certain number of units or a certain number of square feet of commercial or office space as long as they conform to the stipulations of the PUD ordinance.

PUDs usually involve negotiations between the developer, the reviewing agencies, and the public. The negotiations give the community an opportunity to tailor development proposals to meet community objectives. Often, the developer will be required to place more land in open space or to commit more land or cash to community facilities than originally planned. In return, the developer may receive permission to build more units than the regular zoning would allow.

Planning and development trends have been leaning toward greater mixing of land uses. Planners, developers, and the public have discovered that a considered mix of uses can create a more functional and pleasing environment, with benefits to local ecology, infrastructural efficiency, and public health.

SITE PLANNING PROCESSES

After the site investigation has been completed and base maps prepared, the land planner should present the developer with a site plan that describes a number of different approaches toward developing the site. The site plan, which combines information regarding the target market with the base map, must consider many different items:

- topography;
- geology and drainage;
- natural vegetation;
- vistas and sight lines;
- private and public open spaces;
- neighboring uses;
- easements and restrictions;
- roads;
- utilities;
- patterns of pedestrian and bicycle and other vehicular circulation—ingress and egress, sidewalks, and alleys;
- market information;
- sales office location, visitor parking, and other temporary operational concerns;
- buffers for noise and privacy; and
- building types.

The design process involves considerable trial and error, and it can quickly spiral out of control without a dedicated project manager. Developers must consider future users and their relationship to every aspect of the site. The site planner first produces a diagram showing constraints and opportunities with all the site's relevant features—undevelopable slopes and wetlands, neighboring uses, view corridors, arterial roads, access points, streams, forests, and special vegetation. Next, using the developer's land use budget from the market analysis, the site planner prepares alternative layouts showing roads, lots, circulation patterns, open space, amenities, and recreation areas.

Throughout the schematic planning phase, developers must ensure that the plan will meet their marketing and financial objectives. They should mentally drive down every street, examining traffic patterns, and consider such aspects as attractive vistas, landscaping, and homeowners' privacy. They should also envision the entrance to the subdivision, playgrounds, and street crossings. Sequence and the sense of arrival are key elements that the developer should always keep in mind.

A team approach usually works best, and the contractor, civil engineer, political consultant (if needed), and especially sales and marketing staff should be involved as early as possible. Rough drawings of alternative schemes should be reviewed at regular intervals. Another way to develop a plan is by holding a *charrette* in which the land planners work with the public, community leaders, and other representatives to incorporate their concerns and ideas. This model of public participation, if handled correctly, allows stakeholders to feel they had a say in shaping the proposal. If handled poorly, it is a recipe for disappointment and expense. Charettes are work sessions with the public, but decisions should never be announced in this environment. The project design team is ultimately responsible for fulfilling the development's objectives, and the desires of any other stakeholder must be considered but only adopted if they add value to the proposal.

When the developer is satisfied with the schematic plan, the planner produces the final version. The final plan also goes through several iterations. Because it will ultimately be submitted to the city for plat approval, the final plan must show the boundary lines, dimensions, and curvatures of every lot and street. Jurisdictions typically offer detailed guidelines for these submittals, but it has become common for these guidelines to include a troubling line: ". . . and anything else that may be requested for departmental review." Developers must meet with reviewers early on and obtain a clear list of what documentation, including engineering calculations, will be required for review and approvals.

Design guidelines provide an important tool for land developers in setting the tone and overall appearance for a subdivision. In master-planned communities, detailed urban design guidelines can cover all aspects of design, from the streetscape and landscaping to individual house sites, materials, setbacks, and architecture. Although guidelines that are too severe can create monotonous subdivisions where everything looks alike, well-crafted guidelines can help establish an attractive subdivision. Creating design guidelines is a skill that may not be within the capability of the project planner. There are firms specializing in coding and guidelines, but developers should coordinate such documents closely with the attorney drafting the governance documents for property owners' associations, understanding that the association, or its agent, will need the legal authority, design support, and operational budget to follow through for many years. Developers should also be sure to retain the right to modify guidelines if buyers react negatively to the initial approach. Architectural guidance should be framed positively: "How porches can create an active streetscape" rather than "all porches must be eight feet deep and painted white."

SITE INFORMATION

The design process begins with a base map that delineates the parcel's relevant physical and legal features. All subsequent design schemes are drawn on the base map. Zoning and other resource mapping and aerial photos are often available for download from planning departments or from private companies. Aerial photos are invaluable for understanding the property, as well as for marketing the project later. City halls, local libraries, utility agencies, state highway departments, and local engineering firms are sources for topographic maps, soil surveys, soil borings, percolation tests, and previous environmental assessments. Title companies and the development attorney are the sources for existing easements, rights-of-way, and subdivision restriction information.

TOPOGRAPHIC SURVEY. Site planning begins with the topographic map that shows the contours of the property, rock outcroppings, springs, marshes, wetlands, soil types, and vegetation. Although topographic maps are available for many counties, a custom-drawn topographic survey is invaluable for sites with significant grading. In tight subdivisions, or on sites with substantial vegetation, on-site surveys are often needed to obtain more accurate information in specific areas. The topographic map should show

- contours with intervals of one foot (0.3 m) where slopes average 3 percent or less, two feet (0.6 m) where slopes are between 3 and 10 percent, and five feet (1.5 m) where slopes exceed 10 percent, with the caveat that the reviewing engineer or zoning may require a specific interval for final approval;

- existing building corners, walls, fence lines, culverts and swales, bridges, and roadways;
- location and spot elevation of rock outcroppings, high points, watercourses, depressions, ponds, marsh areas, and previous flood elevations;
- location and spot elevations of any on-site utility fixtures or emergency equipment;
- floodplain boundaries (determine in advance which boundary the jurisdiction will require);
- outline of wooded areas, including location, size, variety, and caliper of all specimen trees;
- boundary lines of the property; and
- location of test pits or borings, such as for bridge locations, to determine subsoil conditions.

SITE MAP. Developers should prepare a vicinity map at a small scale that shows the surrounding neighborhood and the major roads leading to the site. The map can be later adapted for marketing, loan applications, and government approvals. In addition to location information, the map should show

- major land uses around the project;
- transportation routes and transit stops;
- comprehensive plan designations;
- existing easements;
- existing zoning of surrounding areas;
- location of airport noise zones;
- jurisdictional boundaries for cities and special districts, such as schools, police, fire, and sanitation; and
- lot sizes and dimensions of surrounding property.

BOUNDARY SURVEY. The boundary survey shows bearings, distances, curves, and angles for all outside boundaries. In addition to boundary measurements, it should show the location of all streets and utilities and any encroachments, easements, and official county benchmarks from which boundary surveys are measured or triangulation locations near the property. It is important to know which elements the lender will require—typically the American Land Title Association standard—and also to think ahead to requirements of the final plat and engineering review.

The boundary survey should include a precise calculation of the total area of the site as well as flood areas, easements, and subparcels. Calculations of area are used to

The 7,000-acre (2,800 ha) Lake Nona property in Orlando, Florida, includes 2,000 acres (800 ha) of lakes and open space. Development includes office and retail space, medical and educational facilities, and nearly 2,000 residences.

- determine the number of allowable units based on zoning information;
- determine net developable area (the size of this area serves as the basis for both site planning and economic analysis of the project);
- determine sale prices—often, sale price is calculated per square foot or per square meter (for instance, $2 per net developable or gross square foot [$21.50/m²]) rather than as a fixed total price; and
- provide a legal description of the site.

UTILITIES MAP. The utilities map is prepared at the same scale as the boundary survey. It shows the location of

- all utility easements and rights-of-way;
- existing underground and overhead utility lines for telephone, electricity, and street lighting, including pole locations;
- existing sanitary sewers, storm drains, manholes, open drainage channels, and catch basins, and the size of each;
- rail lines and rail rights-of-way;
- existing water, gas, electric, and steam mains, underground conduits, and the size of each; and
- police and fire alarm call boxes.

CONCEPT DEVELOPMENT. Once base maps have been prepared and gross and net developable acreage calculated, the true design process begins. Before the planner begins drawing, the developer should define the target market, the end product (including lot sizes), and the approximate number of units needed to make the project economically feasible.

Base maps outline developable areas as well as features such as lakes, stands of mature trees, and hills

LAKE NONA PROPERTY HOLDINGS, LLC

on the site. The developer determines which features should become focal points for the design based on the site's physical condition and specific market. For example, although a creek and its floodplain are often excluded from the developable area because of potential flooding problems, it may be the site's best feature when used as a focal point for public open space or as a private amenity for certain lots. Most likely, it also performs a vital drainage function that may be expensive and destructive to alter.

The goal of site planning is to maximize the value of the property subject to market absorption and zoning constraints. Lots with views, or that adjoin open space or water, sell at a premium. Developers may achieve high returns by placing higher-density products such as townhouses, multifamily housing, or zero-lot-line homes next to valued features. Lots that do not front on these features will sell for more if the plan provides them physical and legal access. The best plans create value by using a desirable feature as a generator of lot premiums—for example, a town square with houses fronting it. The public has access to the square and its surrounding streets, while the houses that front on it have special views. A lake, golf course, or other active or passive recreational amenity could similarly enhance value.

If the development's use is perceived as incompatible with adjacent uses, the project may be contested by local residents. For example, if single-family houses face a developer's property, any non-single-family use is likely to draw objections from the neighbors. Although different uses on adjoining properties are appropriate in many situations, the burden falls on the developer to demonstrate the reason for not maintaining consistency in use or density.

Many residential tracts border major streets. Because such commercially suitable frontage usually sells for three to five times the value of single-family land, the developer may wish to consider placing retail, office, or multifamily uses with ground-floor commercial space at these locations. The risk of reserving a large amount of commercial or multifamily frontage at the edge of the development is that, in the event of a slow market, the vacant lot serves as an unattractive front entrance to the project. If frontage is retained for future development, the entrance into the residential portion of the tract should be carefully designed and landscaped. A parkway entrance with an entrance feature and landscaping has become a common element of many subdivisions, but more urban-style options that play down the entrance and

connect seamlessly to adjacent developments are gaining favor. The key is to communicate arrival, and quality, in other ways, such as with a consistent design aesthetic, material palette, street furniture, lighting, and signage.

STREETS AND STREET HIERARCHY

In the design of street systems for a new development, a street's contribution to the neighborhood environment is as important as its role as a transportation link. The street system should be legible to visitors so that the intended function of a particular street segment is readily apparent.

Although debate over the appropriate functions and definitions of street types persists, the concept of a hierarchy of streets remains practical. The commonly used functional classification of streets includes, in ascending order, local streets, collectors (sometimes called "boulevards" or "avenues"), and arterials (including freeways).

- **Arterial Streets**—Arterial streets are seldom created as parts of new subdivisions. The primary purpose of arterial streets is mobility—movement of as much traffic as possible as fast as is reasonable—and the mobility function of arterials therefore overshadows their function of providing access to fronting properties, such as residences or commercial uses.
- **Collector Streets**—Collector streets serve as the link between arterial streets and local streets. Typically, they make up about 5 to 10 percent of total street mileage in new developments. Increasingly, new collector streets are fronted by active properties, such as neighborhood commercial centers, institutions, and multifamily residences.
- **Local Streets**—Local streets usually account for around 90 percent of the street mileage in new communities and are intended to provide access to the residential properties fronting them. As the preponderant class of streets in terms of mileage, they contribute much to the signature of their neighborhoods. They also constitute the backbone of neighborhood pedestrian and bicycle networks.

When designing streets for a new development, designers should begin with the minimum width that will reasonably satisfy traffic needs. On most local streets, a 24- to 26-foot-wide (7.3–7.9 m) pavement is appropriate. This width provides two parking lanes and a traffic lane or one parking lane and two moving lanes. For lower-volume streets with limited parking, a 22- to 24-foot-wide (6.7–7.3 m) pavement is adequate. For low-volume streets where no parking is expected, an 18-foot-wide (5.5 m) pavement is adequate. It has been found that widening access streets a few more feet does not increase capacity, but it does encourage higher driving speed. A wide access street also lacks the intimate scale that makes an attractive setting. Designers should consider the viability of bicycle traffic to evaluate whether any widening might be better used for bike lanes, which can expand the nonmotorized domain on the street.

A residential collector street should be designed for higher speed than local or access streets, permitting unrestricted automobile movements. Residential collector streets 36 feet (11 m) wide provide for traffic movement and two curb parking lanes. When parking is not needed, two moving lanes of traffic are adequate, with shoulders graded for emergency parking.[35] Designers should keep in mind that a street section, once chosen, need not remain constant for the length of the street. In fact, special moments in street design, such as expanding sidewalk area periodically to allow outdoor dining or allowing nose-in diagonal parking to alternate with traffic-calming landscape elements, are powerful signals that something of value is happening in these locations.

Residential streets should provide safe, efficient circulation for vehicles and pedestrians and should create positive aesthetic qualities. The character of a residential street is influenced to a great extent by its paving width, its horizontal and vertical alignments, and the landscape treatment of its edges. Residential streets are community spaces that should project a suitable image and scale. For example, much of the character of older neighborhoods is derived from the mature street trees that form a canopy over entire streets, whereas a neighborhood with wide streets devoid of trees conveys an entirely different image. Vertical elements, including not only trees but light posts, shading structures, bollards, and signs, can be more important than the surface of the street in communicating pedestrian safety and insulating lower-floor building programs from the effects of traffic.[36]

Straight streets with rectangular lots give a more urban ambience, whereas curvilinear streets tend to create irregularly shaped lots and provide a more pastoral feel. A minor problem for the developer is that irregular lots may have to be resurveyed when the builder is ready to start construction because the iron pins that mark lot corners tend to get moved or lost during construction of other houses.

SITE ENGINEERING

Adequate grading and the optimal provision of utility services are important elements of site design, and the cost of providing them is critical to a project's bottom line. Developers should never leave the decision about these elements to the civil engineers; the lowest-cost site engineering is rarely the most profitable subdivision design. The developer's objective is to maximize the sale value of the lots subject to efficient site engineering, but this value may also derive from a harmonious relation between built and natural landforms.

GRADING. The grading plan must contain precise details and take into consideration such factors as the amount of dirt that will be excavated, the finished heights of lots, steep areas that may require retaining walls, and graded areas that may be subject to future erosion (developers are liable for erosion even after they have sold all the lots on a site). Grading is used as an engineering tool to correct unfavorable subsoil conditions and to create

- drainage swales;
- berms and noise barriers;
- roads and driveways, plazas, and recreational spaces;
- topsoil at a proper depth for planting;
- circulation routes for roads and paths; and
- suitable subsoil conditions and ingress for facilities.

Grading is also used for aesthetic purposes to provide privacy, create sight lines, emphasize site topography or provide interest to a flat site, and connect structures to the streetscape and planting areas.

Homebuilders usually do their own fine grading of lots in addition to that done by the land developer, but they expect—and may be contractually entitled to—a buildable site with no grading required other than topsoil clearing. When the final foundation location is unknown at the time of sale, developers should be extremely careful about such promises. When homebuilders feel a site requires fill, the developer may receive a request for a rebate of fill and trucking costs, if expectations are not set appropriately at the time of sale or option.

STORM DRAINAGE AND FLOODPLAINS. Storm drainage systems carry away stormwater runoff. In low-density developments with one-acre (0.4 ha) lots or larger, natural drainage may suffice, and generally natural approaches are more cost-effective. In denser developments, however, some form of storm drainage system is always needed, and the best design may be a hybrid of conventional and low-impact techniques.

Gently rolling sites are the easiest and cheapest to drain; flat sites and steep sites are more difficult and expensive. As with other environmental issues, drainage problems can come back to haunt a developer long after the lots have been sold, and these issues can be difficult to predict.

If a property contains any hint of wetlands, a floodplain study is among the first studies a developer should commission before buying a site. Developers should understand where the property lies in relation to floodplains. They can start by obtaining the Federal Emergency Management Agency's flood hazard boundary maps (see www.fema.gov), or flood hazard GIS data from the municipality. Land that is within the 100-year floodplain—that is, the area that is expected to flood once every 100 years—is usually not developable except for uses such as golf courses, parks, or storage of nontoxic materials. Even if uses are permissible, developers should consider whether they make sense, and whether the resulting structures will be insurable.

In some localities, land within the 100-year floodplain *is* developable, albeit with restrictions, and structures can be mortgaged by federally insured institutions only if the structure carries flood insurance. To alter floodplain areas, developers must apply for a permit from the EPA, U.S. Army Corps of Engineers, or other body, such as state environmental or natural resources agencies, with authority over the

local wetlands or creek system. The Army Corps of Engineers designates floodways as well as 100-year floodplains. A floodway is that portion of a channel and floodplain of a stream designated to provide passage of the 100-year flood, as defined by the corps, without increasing elevation of the flood by more than one foot (0.3 m). Developers may not build within floodways. Floodways must retain the same or better rate of water flow after development as before it; otherwise, floodplain elevation is likely to rise upstream from the development, causing increased flooding in those areas. Developers can alter the floodway, but any changes must be engineered properly to preserve water flow and must be permitted by the appropriate authorities, including the Corps of Engineers.

Irrespective of the frequency with which they flood, areas within a property may be defined as wetlands and thus come under the jurisdiction of the EPA as well as other federal, state, and local agencies, such as the corps and the U.S. Fish and Wildlife Service, or more commonly, the state department of environmental quality. Often, all agencies must be

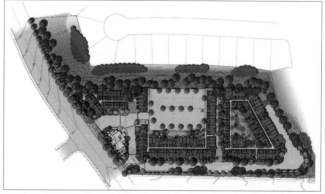

Sterling Collwood is a 260-unit student rental community in San Diego, California. More than half the site is set aside as green space, restored with native plants.

satisfied before the Corps of Engineers will issue a permit to disturb a wetland.

Wetlands come in many forms, including ephemerally wet swales, intermittent streams, hardpan vernal pools, and volcanic mud flow vernal pools. Regulatory streamlining has encouraged coordinating agencies to adopt standard definitions of these features, but delineation is, ultimately, done by an individual field biologist or hydrologist on site, and jurisdictional determination is subjective.

In evaluating a site that contains potential wetlands, developers should hire a qualified biologist to conduct a preliminary wetlands evaluation report, to map potential wetland sites on the property, and to suggest mitigation measures and alternative approaches to the design of the property.[37] Developers should be aware that some features, such as vernal pools, may be only seasonally visible, meaning that a project that is ready to go in September may be delayed by six months for a complete wetland delineation.

LOW-IMPACT DEVELOPMENT. Several aspects of land development can adversely affect site hydrology in multiple ways. Expansion of impervious surfaces and changes in vegetation can concentrate and accelerate surface stormwater flow. The introduction of vehicles, new uses, and landscape maintenance regimens can increase pollutant discharge, and the combination of increased water use and reduced permeability can impair the recharge of aquifers on which the development and surrounding uses depend. Low-impact development (LID) water quality management strategies can make up an integrated approach to improve water quality.

Integrated LID methods can result in better environmental performance while reducing development costs when compared with traditional conventional stormwater management approaches.[38] LID techniques are a simple yet effective approach to stormwater management that integrates green space, native landscaping, natural hydrologic functions, and other techniques to generate less runoff from developed land. These processes can also remove pollutants, such as nutrients, pathogens, and metals from stormwater.[39] In short, LID is used to maintain—as closely as possible—the benefits of natural site hydrology and to mitigate the adverse effects of stormwater runoff and nonpoint source pollution associated with some conventional stormwater management methods.

Common LID practices include the following:

- **Conservation Design and Impervious Surface Reduction**—Following conservation design methods, such as clustered housing, shared driveways, and narrower roadways, as well as rainwater collection systems on buildings, can reduce the overall impervious surface and decrease stormwater management costs.
- **Bioretention (Rain Gardens)**—A bioretention cell is an engineered natural treatment system consisting of a recessed landscaped area constructed with a specialized soil mixture and site-appropriate vegetation. Slightly recessed, the cell intercepts runoff, allowing the soil and plants to filter and store runoff; remove petroleum pollutants, nutrients, and sediments; and promote groundwater recharge through infiltration. These "rain gardens" can be relatively inexpensive to build and can become site amenities.
- **Temporary Erosion Control**—More ecologically sensitive approaches are not limited to permanent installations. Up to a quarter of stormwater management costs can be expended on temporary measures of erosion control during construction and landscape establishment. Filter-fabric and compost constructions have increasingly been deployed in lieu of silt fences and check dams in these applications. Typically costing more to install, these measures can be deployed so that they remain in place permanently, making the life-cycle cost comparable with conventional measures.
- **Vegetated Swales, Buffers, and Strips**—Constructed downstream of a runoff source, a vegetated or grassed swale is an area that slows and filters the first flush of runoff from an impervious surface. From both a budget and an environmental perspective, swales are nearly always preferable to culverts.
- **Permeable Pavement**—This type of pavement allows stormwater to infiltrate the soil. Materials and maintenance costs are substantially more expensive than conventional pavements, but their use can radically reduce impervious surface, a metric that is increasingly evaluated by approval authorities.
- **Low-Impact Landscaping**—Increasingly, native plants may be specified for site landscaping. These varieties are often more expensive, but they reduce operational cost and impact and require less water and maintenance.

- **Green Roofs and Rainwater Collection**—Capturing rainwater for reuse and slow discharge reduces concentrated runoff. Green roofs capture rainwater while improving buildings' thermal performance in several ways. As designers and contractors become more skilled, the typically large cost differential is falling rapidly, and historical concerns about maintenance have been addressed. Still, these are complex systems, and experienced designers and installers are the key to successful implementation.

Demonstrated by multiple EPA case studies, the use of LID practices can be both fiscally and environmentally beneficial to developers and communities. These systems can often substitute for more expensive elements like curbs and gutters, and sometimes they can reduce requirements for intensive site engineering, such as flood-control structures.[40] In case studies, capital cost savings have ranged from 15 to 80 percent when LID techniques were used.[41] Engineering departments increasingly recognize low-impact best management practices as functionally superior, or at least equivalent, to conventional stormwater measures. It is likely that virtually all developers will soon use a mix of conventional and LID techniques, and communities in very sensitive areas, or projects seeking sustainability certification, will benefit from a comprehensive LID system. The best examples of LID use functional features as landscape amenities, in ways that increase value, and studies have shown that attractive implementations of these systems can result in developments that appreciate at a higher rate than conventionally designed subdivisions.[42] Whether they are used comprehensively or à la carte, familiarity with these systems is now an absolute necessity for planners, landscape architects, and site contractors, and only an experienced team can advise a developer on the suitability of these types of techniques for a particular site.

SANITARY SEWERS. The layout of the sanitary system is determined by the topography of the site and the location of the outfall point—that is, the point of connection to the sewer main. Sewers are primarily gravity driven, so if the sewer main that connects the subdivision to the treatment plant is not located at the low point of the site, the developer may have to provide a pumping station, which brings both construction and operational expense.

Beginning developers should avoid tracts of land for which nearby sewage and water services are not available because the cost of bringing these services in from off-site locations can be prohibitive. When major off-site utility improvements are necessary, developers usually require a minimum of 200 homes to recoup their investment and risk. Creating a utility district to provide service or building a plant where none exists typically takes two or more years, as well as significant front-end investment, and can entail substantial operational and legal entanglements.

One option available to developers whose sites do not have sanitary service is to buy or lease a package treatment plant, a small self-contained sewage treatment facility, to serve the subdivision and to design the system to tie eventually into the community's system. This option can work in rural areas and in communities that are accustomed to working with package treatment technology.

Septic tank systems are usually feasible only in rural areas. Their use depends on soil conditions and, in most areas, they are allowed only on lots of at least one-half acre (0.2 ha). A minimum of one acre (0.4 ha) is typical. If a well is included on the same site as a septic tank, even larger lots are sometimes necessary to prevent contamination of the well water, and health department approvals will be contingent on an adequate physical separation of the two, usually both by distance and by extending the well casing's grouted seal.

In planning a sewer system, the developer should investigate

- sewage capacity requirements, which may vary, but 100 gallons per day (379 L/day) per person is common;
- available capacity of the treatment plant and connector lines;
- number of hookups contracted but not yet installed;
- the municipality's method of charging for sewer installation; and
- the people responsible for issuing permits and establishing requirements for discharging treated sewage into natural watercourses.

Sanitary sewer lines are normally located within street rights-of-way but not under road pavement. House connections to sewers should be at least six inches (15 cm) in diameter to avoid clogging; all lateral sewers should be at least eight inches (20 cm) in diameter. Sanitary lines and waterlines should be laid in different trenches where possible, although some cities allow a double-shelf trench that contains the sanitary sewer on the bottom and the waterline on the top shelf. Except in very high-density communities, these "wet" infrastructure elements should not be colocated with power and voice and data communications services.

WATER SYSTEM. A central water system is standard in urban communities. Like the requirements for sewage capacity, those for water supply vary, but 100 gallons per day (379 L/day) per person is common. Requirements can vary greatly in their calculation of occupant load: jurisdictions may count bedrooms, bathrooms, or habitable square footage.

Water mains should be located in street rights-of-way or in utility easements. Residential mains average six to eight inches (15–20 cm) in diameter, depending on the water pressure. Branch lines to houses are three-quarter-inch or one-inch (2 or 2.5 cm) pipe connected to a five-eighths- or three-quarter-inch (1.5 or 2 cm) water meter, respectively. Because waterlines are under pressure, their location is of less concern than that for sewer lines, which rely on gravity flow.

Developers should consult the fire department about requirements for water pressure and the placement of fire hydrants. The fire department is likely to restrict the depth and slopes of culs-de-sac and the maximum distance between fire hydrants and structures. Fire department requirements, like road requirements for emergency services, are increasingly used as "backdoor" development restrictions, and developers should be aware very early of these requirements.

Water, sewer, and drainage lines should be installed before streets are paved. If installation before paving is not possible, developers should install underground crossing sleeves where the lines will cross the streets so that the utility contractor can pull the lines through later; otherwise, streets will have to be torn up to install and maintain lines.

UTILITY SYSTEMS. Electricity, gas, telephone, and data cable services are typically installed and operated by private companies, although in the case of underground electrical service, it is not uncommon for the site contractor to act as the utility's agent. Designating the location of utility easements is an essential step in the process of land planning. If the land planner does not specify a location, the utility company may do so with little regard for aesthetic considerations. Usually, easements run with the street right-of-way, and along the back or side lot lines, within five or ten feet (1.5 or 3 m) of each lot. Most planners prefer to place all electrical power transformers underground or

FIGURE 3-9 | Typical Designs for Bioretention Basins

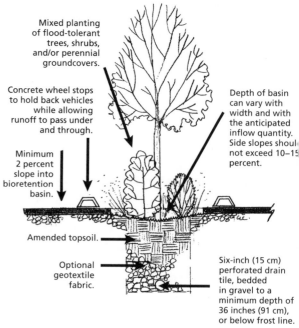

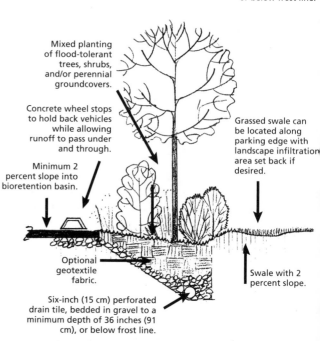

Source: Martin F. Quigley and Timothy Lawrence, 2002. Ohio State University Extension: CL-1000-01, *Multi-Functional Landscaping: Putting Your Parking Lot Design Requirements to Work for Water Quality.*

in semiexposed secure cabinets, but local custom and ordinances may dictate whether lines are above- or belowground. Local power companies often communicate their preference with prohibitively high costs for the less preferable option. The installation of transformers underground can be done at a reasonable cost and can prevent vandalism and the need for frequent maintenance. Transformers located aboveground can be hidden and protected from vandals by wooden lattices or painted metal cabinets with thorny shrubs or similar landscaping devices. Landscaping for these areas should closely follow the utility's operational guidelines, as it is almost certain that major work will occur here as homes are built in the development.

Although electricity, gas, telephone, and cable tend to play a smaller role in site design than do public utilities, such as water, sewer, and drainage, they still determine where structures can be built on each lot. Because the rapid development of data infrastructure has reshaped so many aspects of domestic and work life, many developers have made major investments in fiber-optic network installation for their communities. The value of these networks to retail lots or homebuyers over time is not known. Developers of communities must think beyond the year or two of the development period and consider not just the function of the utility service but the durability of the "deal" they have made for their customers, by committing to providers. Developers have, in some cases, saddled their communities' residents with long-term contracts in order to get affordable and high-quality service, only to find that falling costs make their packages unattractive in just a few years. The safest approach is to attempt to "future-proof" development projects by installing additional empty conduit and equipment space during development, when unit costs are low. In this way, a disruptive technology can, as long as it fits in the pipe, be accommodated at modest cost later.

The developer should talk to each utility provider as early as possible. Utilities are by nature uncompetitive, and within their concession area, providers may have little incentive to move quickly or improve service. Delays in obtaining services are common and can easily throw off the developer's schedule and hold up final sales.

PLATTING

Lot size and layout should reflect the nature of the surrounding community. It is especially important in an infill site to match the character of the new development with its surroundings. A developer should not try to suburbanize an urban community with deep setbacks, wide lots, and side garages. Alternatively, a compact development in a rural setting may not be appropriate or marketable.

Two determinants of a community's layout are lot width and garage placement. Many postwar suburban subdivisions were designed with wide lots—some up to 100 feet (30.5 m) to accommodate a house and a two-car garage and driveway. More recently, 25- to 40-foot (7.6–12.2 m) widths have become more common. The new urbanist approach embraces the concept of narrower lots, smaller frontyards, and garages at the rear of lots, typically accessed by an alley. This layout creates a better streetscape because the view is not dominated by garage doors. For developers, this approach can be desirable because it allows the placement of more houses on the same length of street, saving per-unit infrastructure costs.

In the past, attached townhouses tended to be sited in rows surrounded by parking lots. Today's townhouses often include individual garages that are tucked under the living space at the front or rear or in separate, dedicated buildings at the rear. Garage townhouses can be very cost-effective for builders and developers because they use less land and cost little more to construct.

Sidewalks, curbing, planting strips, and catchment basins must all be adjusted to the density and price point of the development. A single-family subdivision of 20,000-square-foot (1,860 m²) lots on minor streets need not be developed with the same street improvements required for a higher-density subdivision on 2,500- to 4,000-square-foot (230–370 m²) lots.

If the development adjoins a busy street, that edge must be handled with great care. Ideally, the community should not turn its back on the street but should take advantage of the traffic and activity and turn it into an asset. If the project is a mixed-use development, this location could be ideal for intensive uses, such as a retail district. Or it could be the site of neighborhood facilities, particularly if they are shared with the greater community, such as schools, libraries, or parks. If houses must be sited along a busy street, visual and sound buffering may be needed, which could take the form of service streets, landscaping, or site walls, or potentially upgrades to the building envelope. If sound isolation is required, developers are advised to retain acoustic consultants, as landscape effects on noise can be highly unpredictable.

Because lots facing busy streets may yield lower prices than interior lots, the developer should consider ways to boost their appeal or possibly use them for lower-priced units. Experienced developers, like good architects, understand which items can create value. But even experienced developers should spend time in the field investigating why people react more favorably to one design element than to another. The need for market research cannot be overemphasized. Successful developers always review the competition, use focus groups, and collect exit data from potential buyers who stop at sales offices or visit community websites or events.

Buyers react differently in different markets to both location and cost. For example, in western states, many buyers prefer single-level houses, whereas in the Northeast they are usually considered less desirable. In urban areas, buyers may like three-level townhouses, while farther from large cities, only a single-family house will do. Buyers may like certain features, such as deeper frontyards, but may not be able to afford the additional land cost. Good market research can reveal buyers' preferences in the target market.

HIGHER DENSITIES

Throughout the country, land cost as a percentage of house value has risen steadily since the 1960s, from 15 to 25 percent on average. In certain areas of major cities, land costs may exceed 50 percent of the house's value.

In response, traditional housing types are being rescaled and redesigned for modern use. Bungalows and cottages on small lots are particularly suited to move-down empty nesters, single parents, and others who make up today's smaller households. Townhouses are a popular housing type in both urban and suburban areas, offering an alternative to those who do not want the maintenance of a single-family house. Townhouses are not always lower-priced options and can be as upscale as any other housing.

Large estate houses in exclusive communities remain an American icon that appeals to certain market segments. In many areas, estate-style houses are now being rescaled to fit on quarter-acre (0.1 ha) lots. These houses (called *small-lot villas* or, pejoratively, *McMansions*) typically have highly articulated two-story facades that face the street, giving an impression of height, volume, and high quality.

ZERO-LOT-LINE OR PATIO HOMES. Traditionally, local zoning codes have established minimum side yard setbacks ranging from three feet (0.9 m) to 10 percent of the lot width. Three- or five-foot (0.9 or 1.5 m) side yards result in unusable spaces. Windows from one house often look into windows of the next house, only six feet (1.8 m) away. To make side yards more usable, zero-lot-line lots, which allow densities up to nine units per acre (3.6/ha), were created. Today, most major cities and high-growth counties have modified their zoning codes to allow them.

A zero lot line means that the house is left or right justified; that is, one side of the house is built on the lot line so that the opposite side yard can occupy the total width available (10 feet [3 m] is considered the minimum width for usable space). The side of the house on the lot line is usually a windowless, but not shared, wall. Each lot must take care of its own drainage. If builders design a roof that drains water onto the next property, they must obtain a drainage easement from the owner of that property. In addition, a maintenance agreement, which can be made before construction while the builder or developer owns all the lots, must be recorded if using the neighbor's lot is necessary to maintain the wall on the lot-line side of the house. Creative architects have mastered the challenge of designing zero-lot-line homes (also called patio homes) by making good use of the outdoor space and developing floor plans and elevations that maximize light and space (see figure 3-10 for various zero-lot-line configurations and associated densities). Small-lot, high-density housing must be carefully coordinated with scattered-lot or multiple-builder land sale programs. The land plan, in fact, should be drawn up concurrently with the house plan. The lot layout should seek to achieve a variety of goals:

- a site that does not require excessive grading or unusually deep foundation footings;
- the presence of sufficient usable area for outdoor activity (one or two larger areas are preferable to four small areas);
- adequate surface drainage away from the house, with slopes running toward the front or rear of the house; land developers should grade the lots so that they all drain toward the storm drainage system;
- minimum on-lot grading and maximum retention of specimen trees; and
- a minimum number of adjoining lots—preferably no more than three (one on each side and one along the back).

OTHER SMALL-LOT VARIATIONS. Variations of the zero-lot-line concept include Z-lots, wide-shallow lots, and zipper lots. Z-lots are shaped like a Z, with the house placed on the diagonal between its frontyard and backyard. The concept yields seven or eight units per acre (17 or 20/ha).

In wide-shallow developments, lots are 55 to 70 feet (17–21 m) wide but half as deep as conventional lots, allowing the developer to achieve densities upward of seven units per acre (17/ha). Wider lots add proportionately to street and utility costs but may yield greater curb appeal. Wide-shallow lots usually necessitate two-story houses. If the lots are less than 65 feet (20 m) deep, the back-to-back rear yards may be too small for privacy. Depths of at least 70 feet (21 m) are recommended.

Zipper lots are like wide-shallow lots except that space is borrowed from adjacent lots to avoid the problem of narrow, rectangular rear yards. Easements are used to make the rear yards of back-to-back houses abut on an angled, rather than parallel, property line. The main disadvantages of zipper lots are the complexity of the plot plan, loss of privacy from second-story windows that overlook the neighbor's backyard, and possible resistance from buyers and government jurisdictions. Nevertheless, they offer a creative solution to high-density housing in selected markets.

With careful design, densities of seven to eight units per acre (17–20/ha) can be achieved in a single-family detached setting, and densities of 10 to 12 units per acre (25–30/ha) are possible for small senior housing units or projects without garages. Even higher densities have been achieved in traditional neighborhood developments.

Creative site planning and unit design make it possible to achieve greater densities without sacrificing privacy and livability. Increased densities are one tool to be used in solving the crisis of affordable housing in areas with high land costs. Community acceptance of higher densities is more likely if developers are careful to design attractive, livable communities that enhance their surroundings.

Financing

The major difference between the development of land and the development of income property is that land is usually subdivided and sold rapidly, whereas income property is usually held and operated over a period of years. The holding period is the key to deciding the appropriate type of financing. Land

FIGURE 3-10 | Lot Yield Analysis for Different Zero-Lot-Line Configurations

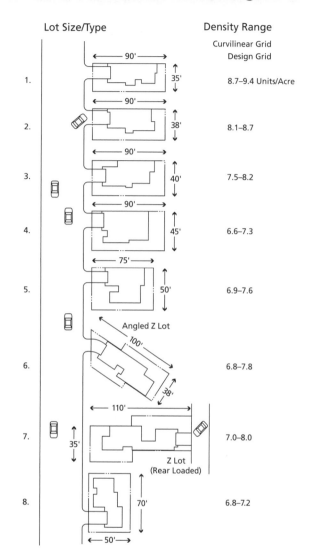

Density ranges based on:

- **Representative relatively flat ten-acre irregular site with both curvilinear and grid layouts.**
- **Comfortable, achievable densities.**
- **No recreation centers or common open space.**
- **50-foot dedicated street right-of-way.**
- **32-foot private street system—can increase density by ± one-half unit per acre.**
- **Individual characteristics and constraints of each site. Actual densities obtained will vary up and down from these generalized guidelines.**

Source: Richardson-Nagy-Martin, Newport Beach, California.

development is financed by a short-term development or construction loan, which is paid down as sales occur. Income property development is financed by both a construction loan and a permanent mortgage, the latter of which is known as a *takeout loan*. For income property development, the construction lender depends on the permanent lender to replace (take out) the construction loan with the permanent mortgage. For land development, the construction lender relies on the developer's ability to sell the finished lots within the agreed-on time frame and at the projected price.

Success in land development—and the developer's ability to repay the development loan—thus depends on the successful marketing of the lots. Because no takeout exists for construction lenders, they must be satisfied that the developer will be able to sell enough lots fast enough to pay off the loan. Often, construction lenders require other collateral, such as letters of credit, in addition to a mortgage on the property. The amount of the loan is usually limited to 30 to 50 percent of the projected sale proceeds to provide a cushion in the event that sales occur more slowly than projected. Slower sales translate into greater interest costs because the balance of the development loan is reduced more slowly than the developer initially projected.

OBTAINING FINANCING

The most difficult task for beginning developers is obtaining financing. Most developers will need to convince lenders to provide them with financing. In most situations, developers must contribute equity and sign loans personally. A developer's equity can be furnished in cash or in land. Suppose, for instance, that a developer purchased land for a project for $100,000 and the market value of that land after entitlement and planning rose to $400,000. If the total cost of the developer's proposed project is $1 million ($600,000 for development costs plus the market value of the land), the developer could probably find lenders willing to lend 70 percent of that amount. In other words, the lenders require $300,000 equity. Because the market value of the land is $300,000 greater than the original land cost, the developer should be able to use the land equity to satisfy the lender's requirement for $300,000. In fact, the loan would cover the developer's original $100,000 land cost because the $700,000 commitment exceeds the development cost of $600,000 by $100,000.

PURCHASE MONEY NOTES. The terms of the purchase money note can play a vital role in financing the project. PMNs automatically have first lien position and must be paid off before the developer can get a development loan because the development lender must hold a first lien position on the land. If the developer can get the seller to *subordinate* the PMN to the development loan, however, it is possible to reduce or eliminate the need to raise outside equity—the hardest money for any beginning developer to obtain.

It is difficult, but not impossible, to find a seller who will subordinate the PMN. Beginning developers should look for sellers who do not need cash immediately and who are willing to accept the risk of subordination in return for more money. The developer should expect to pay a higher land price, higher interest rate on the PMN, or both in exchange for subordination. Because a subordinated PMN can be crucial for covering a beginning developer's equity requirements, it may even be worth giving the seller a percentage of the profits as added incentive to subordinate. This arrangement merely recognizes what is already a reality: the seller is, by virtue of his loan, a secured partner in the deal.

Even with subordination, the developer will have to negotiate with the development lender to treat the subordinated PMN as equity. Subordinated or not, the PMN's *release provisions* are among the most important business points for negotiation with the seller. The release provisions provide for removing designated subparcels of land as collateral from the PMN so the developer can give the development lender a first lien (where the PMN is unsubordinated) or a buyer can get construction financing to build a home.

The release provisions designate which subparcels of land are to be released from the first lien of the PMN. They have two main parts: (1) initial land release concurrent with the downpayment and (2) land released by future principal payments on the PMN. On larger tracts, the downpayment on the land provides for the release of the first subparcel the developer plans to develop. The land that is to be released first must be designated specifically in the purchase contract and the PMN mortgage to avoid any conflict or confusion. The unencumbered parcel provides the initial collateral for the development loan, although the developer may have to provide additional collateral, such as a personal guarantee, letter of credit, or other assets, including real estate. The development loan can be extended to cover other subparcels as they are released from the PMN, thereby providing construction money for development.

The land development contractor will be able to build improvements on only those parcels for which the development lender has a first lien. If the contractor begins work on any part of the land before the lender has *perfected* the lien (recorded it), the lender may halt construction until possible lien conflicts are cleared. Clearing lien conflicts can take several months because all suppliers who have delivered material to the property and all subcontractors who have worked on the property must sign lien waivers indicating that they have received full payment. If anyone is unhappy for any reason (a common occurrence in building), he may use the developer's need for a signature on the lien waiver as leverage to get more money.

BUILDERS' PRECOMMITMENTS. As part of the market feasibility stage, the developer obtains from area builders indications of interest in purchasing the lots. Next, the developer must secure commitment letters from builders, which are part of the documentation the developer will have to submit to the lender to obtain a loan commitment. The commitment letter specifies the number of lots each builder will buy in the project.

Ideally, the developer will have commitments for most of the lots on a site before approaching potential lenders. Although commitments help reduce the market risk, they do not guarantee that the lots will be sold unless they are backed by letters of credit (LCs). LCs provide guarantees to the developer that the builder's unpaid balance on the lots will be paid off by the bank that issues the LC. If the developer intends to build on all the lots himself rather than selling to other builders, the financing may be more complicated. The lender would look at equity and financing needs for the entire project, including the buildings.

Builders, who are often underfinanced, are reluctant to guarantee that they will purchase the lots. The developer must convince his lender that builders' commitments are solid or must provide proof with the LCs. The developer should know the type of documentation that lenders will require before talking to builders. If the lender requires firm commitments backed by LCs, then the developer must address that requirement as part of the deal with the builders.

BUILDERS' PURCHASE TERMS. The purchase terms that builders require for lots vary according to local market conditions. Downpayments range from $100 earnest money to 10 percent—or even 20 percent—of the purchase price. Builders pay the earnest money when they reserve the lots. The balance is covered by a note that typically sets the interest rate beginning the day the developer delivers finished lots. The contract for purchasing lots usually defines *lot delivery* as the date on which the city accepts public street dedications or the engineer certifies that the project is substantially complete. The contract may actually stipulate a list of conditions that must be satisfied to convey the "finished" lot.

In slow markets and in workout situations (when the developer has defaulted on the loan), builders hold a stronger position than the developer. To generate interest from builders, developers sometimes subordinate to the construction lender some portion of the land note

Developers of Ten Fifty B used public and private financing for an affordable high-rise community in downtown San Diego.

on builders' model houses, allowing builders to reduce upfront costs, or they may provide seller financing to builders. Another approach that developers use to generate interest from builders in slow markets or workout situations is to discount the initial lots. For example, if the lots normally sell for $20,000, developers may sell the first two lots to builders for $10,000 and the next two for $15,000. Any of these concessions should be cleared well in advance with lenders and investors, and preferably presented as a marketing cost in the business plan. Unexpected sales concessions could cause the lender to review release provisions on the project, effectively revaluing the collateral value of the developed lots.

TIPS FOR DEALING WITH LENDERS. Although each deal with a land development lender is unique, several guidelines usually apply:

- The developer should borrow enough money at the beginning of the project; the developer should not think that a loan can be renegotiated later or that lots can be sold faster.
- The developer should allow enough time on the loan to complete the project or to provide for automatic rollover provisions, even though the lender will charge for the rollover option.
- If working with a lender on multiple projects, the developer should consider that terms on one project may become open to renegotiation if progress on a second project is not to the plan.
- Typical points for the land development loan are two points up front and one point per year, starting in the third year. Points are calculated on the total loan request, not on the amount drawn to date. For example, two points on a $1.5 million loan request amount to $30,000.
- The loan can be structured as a two-year construction loan with three automatic renewals.

Development loans are a form of construction loan. The amounts by which the developer pays down the loan cannot be borrowed again later. If possible, developers should structure the development loan as a revolving line of credit that allows borrowing up to the maximum limit of the credit line, regardless of repayments already made. Doing so will likely require the provision of additional collateral as the lots are sold.

The development lender holds a first mortgage on the entire property and must release its lien on individual lots so that the purchaser (the builder or end user) can obtain construction financing. The *release price* is thus a major item for negotiation between the devel-

oper and the lender. The lender wants to ensure that the loan is paid off faster than the land is released from the mortgage, which protects his security in the event that the developer defaults on the loan. The developer, on the other hand, prefers that the release price simply be a prorated share of the development loan. For example, if the development loan is $1 million for 100 lots, the sale of one lot would retire the loan by $10,000 (1 ÷ 100 × $1 million). Most lenders set the release price at 1.2 to 1.5 times the prorated share (called the *multiple*). For a multiple of 1.2, the release price is 1.2 times $10,000, or $12,000 per lot. Thus, every time a lot is sold, the developer pays down the loan by $12,000. The lender often wants a high multiple, 1.3 or greater, for releasing lots. The developer wants a multiple as low as possible, 1.2 or lower, because he needs cash flow. In return for a low multiple, the lender may require some form of credit enhancement, such as an LC or second lien on other property. Particularly in developments with widely divergent lot prices, the lender may simply set release prices as a percentage of an agreed-on lot price list, but the same acceleration of loan repayment (a higher percentage) will be the lender's goal.

JOINT VENTURES

In the cash flow analyses shown earlier in this chapter, the developer was assumed to own 100 percent of the deal, investing 100 percent of the equity and receiving 100 percent of the cash flow. The developer would also have 100 percent of the downside risk and liability. All or any part of a land development project, however, may be packaged as a variety of *joint ventures*.

The various legal forms of joint ventures are described in chapter 2. In this chapter, the business side of joint ventures is the focus. Most joint ventures involve three major points of negotiation for distributing cash flow from the venture:

1. preferred returns on equity;
2. priorities of payback of equity, fees to the developer, and cash flows from the venture; and
3. split of the profits.

In addition to dividing the spoils of the venture, the joint venture specifies how risk is shared between the parties—the timing and amount of equity contributions, fees to the developer and other parties, personal guarantees on notes, and management control of the development entity and other operating entities and associations (see chapter 6).

DEVELOPER AND LANDOWNER. One of the most common forms of joint ventures is that between a developer and a landowner. The land is put into the deal at a negotiated price; it is common that land value covers in full the equity that the developer may need to obtain development financing, although partners may demand some additional cash as "skin in the game." The landowner may hold a purchase money mortgage subordinated to the development loan or a first priority for receipt of positive cash flow. The order in which cash flows are distributed (the order of *cash distribution priorities*) might be as follows if land value equals total equity:

- **Priority 1**—The landowner is returned the equity land value allowed by the lender.
- **Priority 2**—The landowner receives a preferred return (cumulative or noncumulative) on the equity (see chapter 4).
- **Priority 3**—The developer receives a development fee, some of which may be paid during the construction and leasing periods.
- **Priority 4**—The developer and the landowner split the remaining profits; priorities and fees are subject to negotiation.

When required equity is less than land value, the landowner gets some value out of the first loan draw. If equity is greater than land value, a two-tiered partnership provides for additional equity investment.

If the landowner has a subordinated PMN on the land, that loan agreement provides for releases similar to those in the development loan agreement. Both liens must be released before homebuilders or other buyers of the lots can obtain free and clear title, which they need to obtain construction financing. For example, suppose a subdivision has both bank financing and a subordinated PMN from the seller. Suppose also that the PMN calls for repayment of $10,000 to release a lot from the note and that the development loan calls for $20,000 repayment. If the developer sells ten lots that net $35,000 each, the cash flow would be

Sales revenue:	
10 × $35,000 =	$350,000
Minus repayment of development loan:	
10 × $20,000 =	$200,000
Minus repayment of PMN:	
10 × $10,000 =	$100,000
Cash available for distribution:	$50,000

Most joint venture agreements provide for the venture to retain *cash available for distribution* as working capital until the development loan is retired. The cash provides a safety net to cover future equity needs in the event that sales slow or costs increase. Alternatively, such cash could be given to the landowner until the land equity has been fully recovered, or it could be considered profit and divided among the joint venture parties. The landowner would prefer, of course, to receive first priority on all cash flows until recovering the value of the land equity.

Sometimes, the revenue from land sales does not cover the required loan release payments for a given parcel or series of lots. In that case, the joint venture partners would be required by the partnership's operating agreement to invest new equity to cover the deficit. The development loan agreement may require the lender's approval for sales below a certain price, although the developer would prefer to have full control over pricing decisions. Such pricing approval, while common, can be a recipe for disaster if the lender withholds approval of lower prices to match current market conditions. A common middle ground is for the developer and lenders to agree on a base price, and an allowable maximum discount, which are preapproved and can be executed quickly by the sales team.

One benefit for landowners of putting their land into a joint venture is to save on taxes, especially when they have owned the land for a long time and their basis is well below the current market value. If they sell it outright, they must pay taxes immediately on the full capital gain. If they put it into a joint venture, they can defer paying taxes until the property is sold by the joint venture and capital is returned to them. A tax accountant should be brought into the negotiations early with the landowner to understand IRS requirements for "installment sales." Taxes on the gain are paid as principal payments on the PMN are made. In a joint venture with a subordinated PMN, the principal payments are usually timed to occur when lots are sold to homebuilders or according to a prenegotiated schedule (typically three to ten years), whichever comes first. For example, suppose land originally purchased for $100,000 is put into a joint venture at the current market value of $1 million, with a PMN for $750,000. One-quarter of the $900,000 gain is taxed initially because the downpayment is one-quarter of the sale price—$250,000 of $1 million. The rest of the gain is paid as the PMN is retired. Note that this structure works with any PMN, even if no joint venture is created with the land seller. Taxes are deferred longer, however, if the PMN is subordinated. If it is unsubordinated, it must be paid off as soon as the developer obtains a development loan.

DEVELOPER AND INVESTOR. Joint ventures between the developer and third-party investors are far more common than joint ventures with the landowner. The third-party investors (*third party* because they are not involved in the original transaction) furnish the cash equity needed to complete the deal. For example, in the deal shown above between developer and landowner, the developer purchases the land outright from the land seller. The investors put up the cash needed to purchase the land, which was the landowner's equity in the first deal. The developer's arrangement with the investors might closely resemble the deal with the landowner with respect to priorities for cash distribution:

- **Priority 1**—All cash available goes to investors until they have received their total cash investment (*return of equity*).
- **Priority 2**—The next cash available also goes to the investors until they have received, say, an 8 percent cumulative (or noncumulative) return on their investment (*return on equity*).
- **Priority 3**—The next cash available goes to the developer until the agreed fee is reached.
- **Priority 4**—All remaining cash available is divided between the developer and the investors based on the agreed-on terms and conditions. (With institutional investors, multitiered "waterfall" provisions are more common.)

Every term of the deal is negotiable, including the order of priorities and the amount of personal liability on the development loan. A straightforward 50/50 split between the developer and the investors, without any priorities, used to be typical and some large developers still use this format, but beginners typically must give a larger share to investors to attract their interest. In the case of a 50/50 split with no priorities, developers are able to take out profit as each acre is sold. The risk to investors is that developers may sell off the prime tracts, take the profit, and then fail to sell off the balance of the project, leaving the investors with a loss. Most investors, therefore, insist on receiving all their equity before developers participate in any profit. Until this milestone is achieved, compensation for developers may be structured as a percentage of net proceeds, and reimbursement of professional fees for work performed on the project.

DEVELOPER AND LENDER. Some lenders provide more favorable debt financing for a deal—a higher loan-to-value ratio, for example, or lower initial interest rate—in exchange for some percentage of the profits in the form of a *participating loan*. In this structure, all the deal financing might be structured as debt, but the loan is convertible at various points to a predetermined amount of equity: the "equity kicker." For the developer, this arrangement is the easiest form of joint venture because it involves only one other party. The lender can structure involvement in a variety of ways. The financing can be considered a 100 percent loan, or some portion can be considered equity. The difference between a 100 percent loan and, say, an 80 percent loan with 20 percent equity is that the equity portion usually receives a "preferred return" rather than "interest." The preferred return is paid when cash is available, whereas interest must be paid immediately. Some development loans have accrual provisions that allow interest to be accrued in a fashion similar to that for preferred returns. They allow the project to accrue unpaid interest into future periods until cash is available to pay it. The split with inexperienced developers could be 65/35 or 75/25, with the lender receiving the larger share. Joint ventures with lenders usually allow developers to receive a fee for administrative expenses. Developers may request fees of 5 to 10 percent of construction costs, but 3 to 5 percent is more common.

Construction

The construction phase of land development consists primarily of grading the land and installing drainage systems, streets, and utilities. Land development involves fewer subcontractors than building construction, but the process can be just as complicated, not least because of the role played by the public sector. The facilities built by land developers are usually dedicated to the locality to become part of its urban infrastructure. The locality maintains the streets, and the utility company, which may also be a city agency, maintains water and sewer lines. Consequently, all facilities must be built in strict accordance with utility company standards; city, state, and federal codes; and management practices.

If possible, the contractor should be part of the development team from the beginning. Even if developers select a contractor after plans and specifications are completed, they should go over preliminary plans with a construction manager who can offer money-saving advice for various aspects of the design layout.

The following tips are useful in dealing with general contractors:

- Negotiated-price contracts are usually better than competitively bid contracts. On smaller jobs, developers should negotiate with two or three qualified contractors simultaneously and take the best deal.
- A fixed fee for the contractor of, say, $5,000 to $10,000 for a $100,000 to $200,000 job (costs based on actual dollars spent, verifiable by audit) is recommended. For change orders, developers should pay the contractor the additional cost but no additional fee or markup. Equipment should be charged based on direct time in operation.
- Developers should hire a member of an engineering company for which business currently is slow to be on site to check that everything is installed properly. Developers should not rely solely on the engineer's certification and should ensure that the engineer will spend enough time on site. The engineer of record (responsible for the original drawings) should certify the work (check progress at least twice per week), but the on-site engineer should check that everything is installed properly and should be pres-

ent for deliveries and for any event that requires quantity surveying to price, such as remedial fill for inadequate subgrade. An engineer should also be present for any visits by inspectors, who should arrange their visits with the engineer.

- The standard 10 percent retention of payment for subcontractors is recommended. Subcontractors should sign lien releases and bills-paid affidavits with every request for a draw. The general contractor must obtain these affidavits and releases from the subcontractors and suppliers before paying them.
- If the contractor is not performing satisfactorily, developers should notify the contractor in writing (by registered mail), citing the specific paragraphs of the contract that are being violated and stating the possible consequences if performance does not improve by a certain date.
- When hiring a general contractor to construct for-sale housing, developers should include a clause stating that any deceptive trade practice suits that are not warranty items belong to the general contractor, not the developer.

Key Points on Contracting

Contracts are necessary for controlling costs, scheduling, and performance of those involved in a project. It is important to get everything in writing. Contracts are a commitment. Once signed, it is difficult to backtrack.

THE CONTRACTING PROCESS
- Bidding
- Assembly of bid package contents
- Prebid meetings
- Bid review and award
- Review of bidding issues and ethics
- Review of other issues

CONTRACT CONTENTS
- Details of commitments
- Behaviors agreed to that benefit and bind future managers
- Firm commitments versus general understandings (represents a meeting of the minds; words on paper must reflect intention of parties and needs involvement of principals)

- Fee structure: fixed fee, GMAX (guaranteed maximum price, with contractor sharing any savings), time and materials, or hybrid

BID PACKAGE CONTENTS
- Complete drawings
- Bid submission package terms with instructions
- Payment conditions and terms
- Schedule commitments
- Inspection and progress payments
- Incentives
- Change order provisions
- Retention provisions
- Dispute resolution language
- Basic contract terms
- Right not to award
- Right not to select low bidder

PREBID MEETINGS
- Meeting on site
- Including all personnel who will be involved (owner's rep, contractor's rep, engineers, architects)
- Achieving a meeting of the minds: all know expectations, where to get answers
- Defining who can make decisions for each party
- Conveying full understanding of site conditions
- Getting a sense of who everyone is and how they will work together

Source: H. Pike Oliver, Cornell University, Ithaca, New York.

A developer may choose to be its own general contractor, hiring various subcontractors to do the work—for example, an excavation subcontractor to move dirt, a utility subcontractor to install water, storm, and sanitary sewer drains, and so on. One deterrent to subcontracting in this manner is the difficulty in coordinating the work of the separate subcontractors and controlling the condition of the site during the transition from one subcontractor to the next. For example, the paving contractor may complain that the utility contractor left the manholes too high or that more dirt is needed. The developer/general contractor must then choose between paying a late charge to the paving contractor, who must wait until the utility contractor comes back to correct the problem, or paying the paving contractor exorbitant change fees to fix it. If the project is coordinated correctly, the utility contractor is still on site when the paving contractor arrives, allowing any apparent problems to be solved immediately. The general contractor is encouraged to withhold 10 percent of the contract price until the city accepts the utilities, or at least until the reviewing engineer has issued final approval of the installation.

A problem that developers encounter is deliberate bidding mistakes. Most contracts are bid on price per unit (not as a fixed price) calculated from the engineer's estimate of quantities. If subcontractors see an area in which the quantity of an item was underestimated, they may bid lower on other items so that they get the job. They deliberately bid high on the item for which the quantity was underestimated so that the developer ends up paying more on the total contract after the correct quantity has been determined. Engineers should not be allowed to bid *and* to supervise the site; otherwise, developers will never know whether money was lost. It is better to negotiate a price-per-unit contract and then convert the bid to a fixed-price contract as soon as quantities can be better determined, perhaps after vegetation and topsoil are cleared, making subgrade visible. The developer may pay a little more to allow for a margin of error in the quantity takeoff, but major overcharges are less likely.

During construction, it is important to remember to do the following:

- Supervise subcontractors closely. A subcontractor who needs a piece of equipment for another job is likely to remove it unless the developer is watching closely.
- Plan drainage correctly for each lot. The usual five to ten feet (1.5–3 m) of fall from one side of the

property to the other is a sufficient slope. Storm sewers are normally located in the streets, so lots should slope toward the street where possible. As many lots as possible should be higher than curb height. Excavating shallow streets may save money at the front end but may cost money in the long run.

- Work closely with the electric utility contractor to determine the location and price of transformers and other required gear. Carefully review designs to know what existing conditions the design requires: common omissions are a concrete pad or a level-graded gravel base. These conditions should be noted "NIC" or "not in contract," and the manager should know who is providing them, at what cost.
- Design and execute grading carefully. Grading is cheaper than constructing retaining walls, but a poorly executed grading job can lead to costly repairs, maintenance headaches, back-charges by builders, and even lawsuits from homeowners. Developers should employ an engineer familiar with the rapidly evolving technologies of slope retention. Compost, engineered fabrics, and various techniques may eliminate the need for retaining walls under some conditions.

If FHA financing is planned for homes in the subdivision, the developer should pay especially close attention to grading to ensure that it meets FHA's strict requirements. Although FHA and Department of Veterans Affairs (VA) financing for homebuyers can greatly aid the sales pace of a subdivision, especially for lower-priced homes, developers must understand not only standards but also the institutional process of inspection and approval.

If possible, all rights for off-site road, drainage, utility, and other easements should be obtained before buying the property. The seller should assist the developer in this effort, according to specific terms that should be negotiated in the earnest money contract. The price for obtaining off-site easements can increase dramatically after closing if the neighboring landowner knows that the easement is required for development.

Marketing

Generally, developers are not directly involved in retail sales to the general public, unless they also build homes or are engaged in condominium or recreational developments. Subdivision marketing begins before the developer closes on the land and continues until the last lot is sold. Various aspects of marketing, including public relations, advertising, staffing, and merchandising, are described in detail in chapter 4. Certain items, however, are unique to land development.

For the land developer, the primary marketing objective is selling lots to builders, but the sale of houses to consumers drives lot sales. Except for large-volume builders, who purchase large blocks of lots, most builders take down a few lots at a time. In most subdivisions, builders handle the sale of their houses themselves or use outside brokers. The developer is not involved directly with house sales but may undertake advertising and public relations for the subdivision as a whole, and it is increasingly common for the developer to market affiliated builders as an extension of the development team.

Virtually the entire development process can be viewed as a marketing exercise. Even before selecting a site, the developer should have identified the target market, and every step of the process, from lot design to selection of builders, should be consistent with the demands of that market.

The market determines

- price range for the houses;
- product type or mix of product types;
- appropriate builders for a subdivision;
- design of the lots;
- types of permanent financing for builders;
- variety and quality of amenities;
- type of public relations and advertising campaign to be conducted; and
- means by which homebuilders will market their houses to buyers.

Focus groups can provide useful feedback for understanding the preferences of prospective buyers. Larger homebuilders use them extensively to inform decisions on floor plans, styling, features, and amenities. Focus groups are also useful to land developers at the beginning of a project, providing important input on lot size, siting, pricing, amenities, and other critical market information for serving a particular clientele. A consultant with experienced focus group leaders on staff is usually assigned the task of assembling, leading, and reporting the results of focus groups.

MARKETING BUDGETS

Marketing budgets are based on the estimated cost of marketing, promotions, and sales strategies. A typical marketing budget is 5 to 7 percent of gross sales for nonrecreational projects and 10 to 12 percent for recreational projects. The budget includes 1 to 2 percent for advertising and the balance for commissions for the sales staff and cooperating brokers.

Large developers generally use their own in-house sales staff to handle direct marketing. Even if they use an outside brokerage firm, however, developers need an in-house marketing director and sufficient staff to represent their interests in day-to-day negotiations. Fee and listing negotiations with outside brokers should specify in detail exactly which responsibilities will fall to the developer and should define any deliverables by the agent. These agreements commonly specify size, frequency, and publication of choice for advertisements; they may even specify a particular agent, and his or her hours on site. Small development firms should consider using one or more local brokerage firms as sales staff or as a source of sales referrals. In larger markets, some brokerage firms specialize in new homes and have established marketing programs for builders and developers. The great majority of real estate agents have never sold a new home and are not experienced in community marketing. Experience in staffing a development sales center, touring, merchandising, and design guidance should not be assumed of even very successful local agents.

The sooner a marketing director is hired, the better. Before construction begins, the marketing director can help by getting to know the market area. The marketing director should be skilled at sales techniques and at motivating sales personnel and should have firsthand experience with the types of products being sold. If sales are handled in house, a minimum of two salespeople should be hired, with one or two more available to help during peak periods.

Some developers argue that salespeople should be paid on commission; others advocate a combination of salary and commission. A few rely on straight-salaried staff, although salaries may need to be quite high to attract top-notch brokers. Prizes, bonuses, and competitions are proven good practices. Higher commission rates may be paid for selling certain "problem" lots or homes, and bonuses should be awarded if sales personnel exceed monthly or yearly quotas.

Marketing low-priced production homes requires a different approach from that for high-priced custom houses. If sales are routine, the best method of compensation may be salary. For higher-priced housing, however, sales are seldom routine; the agent may need to deal with special financing and a wide variety of home customizations. Further, because a buyer with a substantial amount of money usually has a greater selection of houses from which to choose, salesmanship is at a premium. A cooperative broker arrangement also is more important for higher-priced houses. An effective sales program requires thorough training and constant motivation, investment in online communications and contact management, and process tracking. Salespeople need productivity support as well as incentives. Good sales programs usually include

- well-paid, well-trained, and motivated sales staff;
- a public relations strategy tuned to sales needs;
- regular sales meetings to discuss prospects and policies;
- a system for communicating with, and following up on, prospective buyers;
- a system for obtaining and apportioning leads and referrals;
- a structure for fairly and transparently splitting commissions and bonuses among responsible agents;
- a reporting system to inform management of buyers' objections, preferences, and attitudes;
- a design guidance system for handling the selection of options and upgrades; and
- a customer support protocol for closing details, move-in procedures, and postsales warranty and service issues.

MARKETING TO HOMEBUILDERS

Many different methods can be used to market a subdivision. Apartment, retail, or office sites are marketed directly to building developers. Lots in custom home subdivisions may be sold directly to homebuyers, who then hire their own custom builder or select from a list of builders approved by the developer. In some cases, a custom builder is also the developer. In most cases, however, the developer sells lots to builders who, in turn, sell to homebuyers. Developers usually operate at a distance from the customers who drive demand for their product. A close, supportive marketing relationship with builders is therefore essential.

Builders typically market their product in one of three ways:

1. Builders may offer a range of basic plans with varying degrees of options in facades, interior finishes, and lot location and type. They may build model homes from which homebuyers select their preferences or establish a design center to facilitate this process. The model home approach is used primarily by production builders for whom economies of scale can be realized by standardizing the basic units. Moreover, the costs of model homes can be amortized over a large number of lots. Depending on the market, production homebuilders typically build 25 to 100 or more houses per year in a given subdivision. Production builders may be active in many subdivisions in a region, or regions, or even nationwide. This method of building and marketing new homes is the most common and includes homes in all price ranges. It is not always essential for all these functions to occur at the development site. Particularly in the case of resorts or projects targeting a relocation market, some sales functions may be located close to buyers.

2. Builders may build houses on spec (speculation) to be sold during or after construction. The buyer contracts for the house during construction, or, in a slow market, the house may be completed before a buyer is found. Both large and small builders, in all price ranges, use this approach. The builder selects the design, which may be customized to varying degrees for the buyer, who selects interior finishes, appliances, cabinetry, and so on. Spec building is most common in strong housing markets because builders cannot afford the risk of a long sale period.

3. A custom builder may purchase lots from the developer, then sell a house to the buyer. The builder may sell a completed house or a partially completed house, giving the buyer the chance to customize it, or may contract with a buyer to build a custom home on a particular lot. Custom homebuilders typically build one to ten houses per year in a given subdivision. Most—but not all—custom builders tend to market higher-end products.

Cascade Village, a 242-unit mixed-income rental community in Akron, Ohio, offers a variety of recreational amenities and on-site resident services. It is close to public transit and employment centers.

TYSON WIRTZFELD

Market studies should indicate the types of builders for developers to target in marketing the development. Builders with a strong reputation in the market will have an edge in attracting homebuyers. Interviewed for the first edition of this book, Don Mackie of Texas-based Mill Creek Properties gave advice still useful today. Developers should not let first-tier builders control their subdivisions. "They will want ten to 15 lots at the beginning and a rolling option on the rest. They will build four models and construct six to ten specs at a time. You need to give them enough lots for models and specs, with a rolling option as they sell the specs.

"In pioneering areas, you convince builders by telling them how much you will spend on promotion: 'Here's what we will spend. If we don't do what we promise, we will take the lots back.' You get better absorption if you can keep traffic moving around in the subdivision. On small, 200-lot subdivisions, you must choose between selling all the lots to one major builder or working with small builders who take one or two lots each. Developers need 300 to 500 lots to run a cost-effective on-site marketing program. In a 300-lot subdivision, they would sell half the lots to the 'market maker' and the rest to three other builders. The market maker will attract many potential buyers. Smaller builders will use one of their spec houses as a model and an office."[43]

To obtain commitments from builders, developers should begin contacting potential builders as soon as the land is tied up. Savvy local builders are often experts on the area, and developers should solicit their advice on the target market and its preferred products.

To broaden their markets, larger subdivisions (200 houses or more) may include two to ten homebuilders that build two or three different product types in different price ranges. A 300-house subdivision may, for example, be divided into two sections, with one production builder taking down 200 lots and two or three custom builders taking down the other 100, with the mix depending on the market. The developer should retain some flexibility for allocating more lots to one builder or another as sales progress. A rolling option that allows builders to take down blocks of five, ten, or 20 lots at a time helps the developer avoid the problem of losing lot sales if one product type is not moving as quickly as another.

Developers should meet with and examine the completed projects of homebuilders who build the type and price of product market studies recommend. Beginning developers should be able to compete effectively against well-established developers by offering builders a continuing lot inventory, minimum cash up front, and seller financing. Ideally, builders should be required to put up a 10 percent downpayment, but beginning developers may have to settle for any amount that is sufficient to hold builders' interest.

After preliminary contact with prospective builders and as soon as a preliminary plat is available, the developer should prepare a marketing package. This package should include information about the site and the neighborhood (shopping, schools, daycare facilities, churches, and recreation), and data about the site, including the subdivision plan, restrictive covenants, amenities, and the marketing program.

Terms for buying lots vary depending on the market. In softer markets, builders may put down a token amount of, say, $1,000 cash per lot. When the commitments are made before site development, builders are not obligated to take down or close on the stipulated number of lots until the engineer has certified that the lots are ready for building. Before then, builders have the option only to buy the lots at the specified price. The option (or purchase contract) is not a specific performance contract. In other words, if builders fail to close, they lose only their earnest money.

Once the lots are ready for building, builders are usually liable for interest on the lots that are committed but not yet closed. If a rolling option exists, builders are committed to taking down a certain number of lots at a time. Builders may pay cash for the lots, with funds provided by the builder's construction lender, or the developer may finance the lots for builders during the period between closing and start of construction. For example, builders may commit to take down two lots immediately for model houses and have an option to purchase 30 lots every six months, beginning, say, January 1. If the builders exercise the option, the interest meter starts running on January 1 for the portion of the 30 lots not closed on that date. Six months later, if the builder does not exercise the option on the next 30 lots, they are released for sale to other builders.

If the developer wants to use the builder's credit to help secure the development loan, rolling options on lots are not sufficient. If possible, beginning developers should have a firm contract of sale for the lots covered by the development loan, either to a creditworthy builder or to a smaller builder with a letter of credit for the unpaid balance of the sale price.

MARKETING LARGER PARCELS

In addition to single-family or townhouse lots, a larger parcel may also include nonresidential sites for commercial, apartment, office, or other use. Reaching potential buyers for these sites requires an approach similar to that for marketing office park and business park sites (see chapters 5 and 6).

Two main sources of business are outside brokers and drive-by traffic. Experienced outside brokers require the payment of a generous commission, but many developers believe they are well worth the investment. Although advertising is not an especially effective technique, newsletters and broker parties do help generate and maintain brokers' interest. On-site representation—at least a place provided for brokers to come in and talk to prospects—is desirable.

Typically, the buyer of a $1 million site puts up $25,000 to $50,000 of earnest money, in cash or by way of a letter of credit. Standard closing times range from 60 to 120 days, depending on the market. Buyers almost always want the option to buy or the right of first refusal on adjoining sites. Developers should try to avoid giving these options, which can complicate a future sale, but they may be granted as part of a larger deal. Declining to give options is especially important during the initial project stages when the developer is trying to encourage absorption.

SITE MERCHANDISING

Whereas advertising is intended to reach a wide audience and to persuade people to visit a development, merchandising is designed to stimulate the desire of potential buyers once they come to the site. Developments of 500 houses or more can support a visitor center in which all builders in the subdivision can merchandise their homes. Given the reach of Internet communications, it is increasingly common for developers to market the builders in their community, often funded by a builder marketing fee or flat membership dues in the builders' guild or association. A visitor center should be equipped so that prospective purchasers can get an initial impression of all products available in the subdivision and should offer meeting spaces to allow semiprivate interviews and coordination meetings. Smaller subdivisions can generally support only a very modest visitor center, such as a trailer furnished as a sales center or an existing home furnished for temporary use.

The developer should encourage all the builders to place their models in the same area. In this way, the builders benefit from the traffic generated. Each builder builds two to four models in separate but interconnected areas. The model home "park" should be large enough to illustrate the effect of the land plan, including common spaces, street furniture, land-scape standards, and pedestrian paths. The developer is responsible for the landscaping and common area maintenance of these facilities. Dirty streets and unkempt construction areas deter potential buyers. It is also important to consider how the model home area will work as a neighborhood, since the houses will ultimately need to be sold.

The design of the sales office and arrangement of model units are central to the merchandising plan. Signage that is coordinated with other marketing materials should lead visitors directly to the sales office, the model houses, and the major amenities.

Interstate and Internet Marketing

In recreational and larger land development properties, the developer may want to market to out-of-state residents. Jo Anne Stubblefield cautions that interstate marketing of land is a legal minefield, and that even the establishment of a promotional webpage can trigger (sometimes costly) legal responsibilities for developers. "By and large, we've found that marketing consultants are clueless regarding the legal issues that surround the marketing of land. Tending toward zealous promotion, they are in a hurry to get to the grand opening and push the process of establishing a website, mailings, and other promotions." Establishing a website to market land is considered the legal equivalent of advertising in a publication with national subscribers. Like a mass mailing, it is interstate marketing. Stubblefield adds that about half the states require registration of a sale, full disclosure, or both. "Many states claim to have 'uniform acts' that are interchangeable with other states' regulations. They are almost never uniform. Each state has its own requirements for the documents to be submitted and a different schedule of fees, ranging from $250 to $500 to New York's requirement, which is calculated as a percentage of the total value of common areas of the development. To market the project in multiple states, developers should not rely on marketing consultants to negotiate this terrain, but should consult a lawyer with a national practice before even starting the marketing of the project."[44] These laws are poorly understood by most developers, but compliant practices are actually well defined for most states, if the sales and management teams are educated on the requirements.

Development Maintenance after Completion

Among the developer's most important tasks is the creation of a proper set of mechanisms to handle long-term maintenance after the project is complete. Such mechanisms protect not only the developer's investment but also the investment and living environment of the future residents of the subdivision.

A developer's stewardship of the land may take many forms. First, a developer may make express guarantees or warranties concerning the care of streets, landscaping, and amenities when selling lots to builders. Second, a developer normally creates and records a set of deed restrictions and protective covenants. The covenants enable residents to enforce maintenance and building standards when other residents violate the restrictions. Third, a developer normally creates a homeowners association that sets and modifies rules of community governance, bears the financial and management responsibility for long-term maintenance, has the power to collect and spend money on common areas, and helps to build a sense of community. Fourth, unless streets are to be made private, a developer dedicates streets, and sometimes amenities, to the city or county. The city or county then takes responsibility for various public services, such as street cleaning and repair, parkway mowing, and trash removal. Because the types of public services available differ from city to city, a developer must make sure that all public services are provided. Trash and recycling collection, for example, is a municipal service in some jurisdictions but is handled by private contractors in others.

PROTECTIVE COVENANTS

Protective covenants, which embody the agreements between the seller and purchaser covering the use of land, are private party contracts between the land subdivider and the lot or unit purchasers. Covenants are intended to create and ensure a specific living environment in the subdivision. Purchasers of lots and houses in the subdivision should perceive the covenants as assurance that the developer will proceed to develop the property as planned and that other purchasers will maintain the property as planned. Strict enforcement of suitable covenants gives each lot owner the assurance that no other lot owners can use their property in a way that will alter the character of the neighborhood or create a nuisance. Lenders and government agencies, such as the FHA and VA, often require covenants as a means of protecting the quality of the neighborhood and the condition of the houses.

Deed restrictions and covenants can augment zoning and other public land use controls by applying additional restrictions to size of lots, building massing, location of structures, setbacks, yard requirements,

architectural design, and permitted uses. Affirmative covenants can be used to ensure that certain land remains as open space and that the developer will preserve certain natural features in that space. They may also create a mechanism for assessing homeowners on the maintenance of common facilities, ranging from roads to fiber-optic networks.

If both public and private restrictions apply, the more restrictive condition is operative. Covenants should take the form of blanket provisions that apply to the whole subdivision, and they should be specifically referenced in each deed. These covenants, together with the recorded plat, legally establish a general scheme for the development. They should be made superior to any mortgage liens that may be on record before recording the covenant to ensure that everyone is bound by the restrictions, even someone buying a house through foreclosure.

Although covenants are automatically superior to any future lien, many covenants and restrictions also provide for an automatic lien for payment of homeowners association fees and assessments. The documents must provide that the lien for assessments be automatically subordinated to purchase money liens. Not all covenants are legally enforceable, however. Covenants that seek to exclude any buyer on the basis of race, religion, or ethnic background are both unconstitutional and unenforceable.

Usually, developers do not want to be the enforcers of covenants in established neighborhoods, unless a long-term building project requires them to keep control over an area. Subdividers may retain control over enforcement as long as they are active in the subdivision. Thereafter, however, the covenants should grant enforcement powers to the homeowners association and to individual owners. Some cities also require a provision that lets the city take over enforcement under certain circumstances.

The covenants should not be recorded until developers have received preliminary subdivision approvals. Covenants frequently do not have to be recorded until issuance of the first deed. Stubblefield advises, "Don't write yourself into any covenants until you have to."

Further, if developers intend to use FHA, VA, or other sources of federal financing (such as the Government National Mortgage Association [Ginnie Mae] or the Federal National Mortgage Association [Fannie Mae]), they should ensure that the proposed covenants meet with the approval of those agencies. The FHA and VA have jointly developed acceptable model legal documents.

Rock Row, Los Angeles: Compact Sustainable Living on an Infill Site

Rock Row is a successful small subdivision in the Eagle Rock neighborhood of Los Angeles. Conceived and developed by a two-person firm, with only a few small projects under its belt, this project illustrates the kind of innovative and sustainable land development that can be done by small but ambitious developers. The concept's positive reception and rapid sellout in the face of adverse market conditions and substantial regulatory delays offer several lessons to the beginning developer.

THE DEVELOPER

The Heyday partnership was founded in 2002 by the Wronske brothers: Hardy, an engineer and construction manager, and Kevin, an architect. Beginning with a four-unit apartment building, they have built an integrated design-develop-build business model to address infill opportunities in transitional neighborhoods in Los Angeles. The two principals are now supplemented by an administrative staff of two and three construction employees in the field. Like most small development firms, Heyday keeps overhead low, but even with a lean headcount, it serves as its own general contractor and designer.

THE OPPORTUNITY

The Rock Row project is a response to several simultaneous opportunities the firm identified and acted quickly to pursue. With the passage of a Small Lot Ordinance in 2006, the city of Los Angeles essentially legalized the townhome dwelling type within large sections of a market that was, and remains, dominated by single-family detached homes on conventional urban lots, and by low- and mid-rise condominium and apartment structures. A nimble developer could quickly deploy a concept that would be largely unique in the marketplace. The proposed development could offer price advantages of multifamily housing, without the legal liability and operational concerns of the

REGINA O'BRIEN

condominium structure. Meanwhile, Eagle Rock, the partnership's home and target neighborhood, was rapidly gentrifying, with a relatively old stock of single-family homes rapidly appreciating in price. Located between Pasadena and Glendale, with an easy commute to downtown Los Angeles, this neighborhood of 36,000 had benefited from a recent influx of young creative professionals who, the partners reasoned, would be open to a more contemporary and sustainable lifestyle, if such an alternative were available. Preliminary analysis showed that, with the right land price, the firm could offer a single-family product at prices roughly competitive with existing inventory, but with new construction, higher-quality finishes, and more contemporary and functional plans.

THE CONCEPT AND THE SITE

The regulatory and market opportunities came together on Yosemite Drive in Eagle Rock. The 24,700-square-foot (2,300 m²) site was surrounded by

city-owned senior housing and at the time included a single-family home, five apartments, and an incidental commercial use. Most important, the property lay within a small strip of land zoned "RD1.5" within a context of almost uniform single-family homes, some with accessory apartments. The zoning's maximum density of one dwelling unit per 1,500 square feet (139 m²) of land implied 16 potential units, although preliminary study of vehicular, service, and emergency access requirements indicated that 15 might be more realistic.

Tying up the parcel, Heyday quickly defined a concept that would split the site into two distinct phases (eight and seven units) along a double-loaded two-way access drive. Competing on price was necessary, but not sufficient, and the firm began to explore ways to differentiate its concept from available inventory. Simply by virtue of its compact site plan and location, the development would meet basic definitions of smart growth, and the partners had long been seriously interested in sustainable construction. The partners decided to take the sustainability of the project to the maximum, within the constraints of their projected pricing. They pursued certification under the relatively new criteria of Leadership in Energy and Environmental Design (LEED) for residential development, and made a modern, sustainable urban lifestyle the overarching concept that would inform all aspects of the design and construction. Their one-line description of the project became the "Lean Green Living Machine."

ACQUISITION AND SITE PREPARATION

Amid a still-frothy real estate market, the land seller had little incentive to allow an extended free-look period. The land was purchased in early 2007 for $1.2 million. Following a $100,000 downpayment, an additional $10,000 per month was applied to the purchase price during the extended due diligence period, with another $10,000 per month to replace the seller's lease income. Tenant evictions were required, and cost about $70,000. During the 18-month period before recording of the tract map, entitlements were processed, the design was completed, and construction lending was finalized. Including miscellaneous fees, the land cost at closing was just under $1.4 million ($57 per square foot [$614/m²] of land), or approximately $94,000 per unit. Considering a potential average unit price of approximately $500,000, the outlay seemed cheap as a portion—under 20 percent—of finished lot–home package cost, but with structures on the site, and utilities to pull, expenditures toward finished lots were far from over.

The entitlement process was, as expected, a bumpy ride. Rock Row was among the first development projects to proceed under the new ordinance, and both staff and applicant were at various points uncertain of the next step in the process. Heyday's small size allowed the principals total focus on dialogue with city reviewers, and ultimately the application was approved without losing additional units, or incurring uneconomical fees or off-site requirements. Since the ordinance has come into effect, Rock Row and other pioneering projects have sparked interest in this type of development; as of this writing, over 150 small subdivision applications have been made.

Immediately upon entitlement, Heyday was prepared to proceed with structure demolition and other site preparation, including rough grading, soil compaction, walls, and other improvements to the edge of the site. Including engineering, survey, and off-site work, the project's total to move from acquisition to finished site was approximately $450,000, or $30,000 per proposed unit.

DESIGN

The project includes 15 urban-style, two- and three-story houses with two-car garages. The image of the project is thoroughly distinct from surrounding and competitive buildings: a kind of warm palette modern minimalism, with extensive use of daylighting and unusual access to outdoor spaces. Five floor plans range from 1,310 to 1,605 square feet (121–149 m²); all have two or three bedrooms with two or three baths. The plans are open and feature ten-foot-high (3 m) ceilings, virtually unknown in comparably priced condominium projects.

Comparable condominium units in neighboring communities varied widely, but $350–$450 per square foot ($3,800–4,800/m²) seemed a common range, which would imply a $525,000–$675,000 price range on average 1,500-square-foot (140 m²) units. Other details not often found at this price point include high-quality contemporary finishes and materials, custom millwork, solid-core doors and superior hardware, and numerous low-maintenance composite

roof decks, balconies, and patios, as well as the project-wide emphasis on energy efficiency and indoor air quality of the finished construction.

Most significant, perhaps, is the fundamental characteristic of the new type: each home is structurally independent, separated by five inches (13 cm) of airspace, and sits on its own property, offering occupants the acoustic privacy and other benefits of single-family living at the condominium price point.

SUSTAINABILITY AND COMMUNITY OPERATION

The project is the largest LEED-rated subdivision in Los Angeles to date and the least expensive LEED-rated homes in Los Angeles. Eleven of the 15 homes are LEED Platinum and the other four are LEED Gold. Surprisingly, virtually all the "green" features of the construction were offered with the base package, rather than as options. Although including those features was necessary to achieve LEED rating, the developers also felt that sustainability would be the most important differentiator of this project, and to leave these decisions to a semicustom buildout would undermine the story of the project.

Standard elements of the construction included recycled content or renewable materials in flooring, countertops, decking, and even engineered framing materials. Operational efficiency was achieved with tankless water heaters, dual-flush toilets, and a highly efficient envelope, including a "cool roof" radiant barrier, low-E argon-filled windows, green roofs on some units, and optional solar photovoltaic (PV) installations. To maintain indoor air quality, special attention was paid to passive cooling, and mechanical heating, ventilating, and air-conditioning systems, laid out efficiently and run by SEER 14–rated air handlers, were supplemented by a whole-house fan approach and separately ventilated, sealed garages.

CONTINUED

Because the Rock Row development was conceived as a single-family alternative to the many potential pitfalls of condominium structures, the developers were cautious about burdening their buyers with legal entanglements. The developers did not charter an actual homeowners association, but instead created a deed obligation to fund third-party common area maintenance, trash removal, and other common costs. The service package was priced at sale at around $40 per month, comparing favorably with condo fees. The properties are subject to minimal covenants and restrictions, intended to preserve the design integrity of the houses, which appear to a casual passerby to be one building.

FINANCING AND DEVELOPMENT

Just as the market was beginning to turn, Heyday obtained a construction loan commitment to fund 90 percent of its roughly $6 million project cost, likely one of the last available, at 275 basis points over a LIBOR index rate, which at the time was slightly over 5 percent. This annual interest cost of just over $300,000 was reasonable, but it certainly focused the partners' attention on quickly getting the project to sales.

Construction began in June 2008 with two model homes in the first phase, completed in nine months. The rest of this phase of eight homes was completed in September 2009, and a second phase of seven homes was begun in February 2010. The project was completed in 2011. The development period coincided with the worst sustained housing downturn since the Great Depression, and California represented, with other Sunbelt states, one of the most challenging markets in the country.

SALES

The most popular unit at Rock Row was the smaller, lower-cost version of the three-bedroom house plan. These units' beginning sale price of $467,000 allowed buyers to secure conventional financing (the 2007 limit was $417,000) with 10 percent down. The maximum selling price, for larger units, was $599,000. All marketing material was designed in house with a budget of $40,000, and a publicist was used to promote the project. Neighborhood connections and the project's interesting story gave the developers an opportunity to get the message out with minimal paid advertisements, and an emphasis on free editorial content and word-of-mouth communications. A large kickoff party of about 400 people generated buzz and attracted the local news station, and numerous articles, particularly in the local alternative press, featured the new type of development and the team behind it. Despite deteriorating market conditions, all 15 homes sold within five weeks of the opening party. After three weeks, prices were increased 4 percent. No concessions were offered on the sale price.

Though very few options were offered at initial sale, the team did propose one interesting incentive: for buyers who closed without a buyer's agent, the developers would throw in a custom solar PV installation. The brokers' fee was a wash, with the installation cost, and the developers correctly assumed their buyers would rather have the hardware than the representation. The offer clearly communicated the developers' serious commitment both to sustainability and to their value proposition, and 11 of 15 buyers took the deal.

LESSONS LEARNED

The developers attribute the rapid sales pace to a hole in the market. Kevin Wronske explains that "at least in Los Angeles, there is a huge potential market of people who know what they want, who have an image in their mind, but they can't find it." The macroscale market's ample supply of homes, even distressed homes, can influence these buyers only so far because properties conforming to their idea of a suitable home are incredibly rare. This rarity was created over decades of regulatory constraint, where the only way to satisfy these buyers was with condominium products—most of the Rock Row buyers cite the single-family lot as a driver of their decision—or a conventional home at a much higher price.

At least half of the buyers were interested in the sustainable aspects of the development, and the comparables available in the market study during underwriting included no similarly conceived projects. Many developers are uncomfortable pioneering, but when obvious momentum has built behind a trend, as was clearly the case with sustainability in 2006, an innovative project may be the only one to reach a potential market. Finally, and most important, the developers credit their success at Rock Row to an excruciating attention to detail. Partially because of the firm's size and relative inexperience, and partly because of the ample time allowed during an extended entitlement, every element of the development, from architectural design and systems engineering to marketing brochures, was—if not executed entirely in house—directed and managed closely by a principal of the development firm.

DESIGN CONTROLS. Provisions for design control should reflect the tastes and attitudes of the target market. The types of design controls and degrees of constraint differ, depending on whether the target market is production builders or custom builders. For the developer who is selling finished sites, the best basic mechanism for design control is to include an "approval of plans" clause in the purchase agreements for building sites.

Even though individual designs may be attractive, incongruous styles may detract from the overall appearance of a subdivision. A design review committee should therefore be established to approve proposed designs. Such a committee also shields the developer from accusations of arbitrariness.

Encouraging good design is easier than discouraging bad design. The developer's primary tool is to specify dimensional limitations, such as yard setbacks, building heights, bulk, and signs. But size covenants may backfire. For example, the city of Highland Park, a wealthy Dallas suburb, passed severe lot coverage limitations. Builders of houses that averaged 6,000 to 7,000 square feet (560–650 m²) responded by building two-story boxes that completely filled the allowable building envelope. Similar boxes have appeared on small lots in other communities where soaring lot prices virtually guarantee that buyers will build houses as large as possible on their lots.

Covenants that are too restrictive may lead to boring uniformity and eventual rebellion among residents, leading many developers to minimize restriction by covenant. Communities have faced lawsuits over paint colors, swing sets, pickup truck bans, and other elements that were too rigidly controlled by covenants. One of the most difficult areas to control is future alterations and additions. Materials are difficult to match or become obsolete. Costs change over time. New fire codes may prohibit the use of certain materials, such as the once-popular cedar shake roofing. New technologies are developed, such as small-scale satellite dishes, and lifestyles change, as in the proliferation of home-based work. Covenants should therefore provide for a procedure to accommodate changes over time—a *variance*. The design review committee must consider not just the project under review, but the potential precedent when it approves variances from the specified restrictions.

OTHER COVENANTS. Some covenants attempt to preserve the property values of the community directly by limiting construction in several ways. Cost covenants are universally unsuccessful. A $60,000 minimum cost requirement, for example, may have built a mansion in the 1950s, but a garage in today's market. One common method for establishing quality is to set minimum square-footage standards for living areas, exclusive of garages, basements, and accessory buildings. These too can become obsolete as housing needs change. Since 2007, a leveling off of the 60-year rise in average home size has occurred, implying a possible change in the market for large homes.

In cluster home, duplex, and townhouse subdivisions where houses are attached, the long-term value of a development requires a covenant that protects other owners when one house is damaged or destroyed by fire or other causes. Such a covenant should make owners of damaged property responsible for rebuilding or restoring the property promptly. The restoration should be substantially in accordance with the architecture and engineering plans and with the specifications for the original buildings.

If a subdivision includes common open space, a covenant should be included that provides for the use, preservation, and limitation on future development of the space. Open-space easements may be used to ensure long-term protection of common open space. In some cases, the granting of open-space easements to the community may be a basis for obtaining planning approval for the development.

Boats, mobile homes, campers, and trucks all require special storage areas. The developer may include a covenant that prohibits on-site parking of these vehicles or requires visual screening. Alternatively, the covenant may limit parking to specified areas. Other restrictive covenants may prohibit keeping certain types or numbers of pets or livestock on site, cutting trees of a certain caliper, repairing automobiles, and parking inoperable vehicles.

Developers walk a fine line between introducing too little and too much restriction. Developers want to maintain the value of the subdivision without overly limiting their market. A potential homebuyer who cannot keep the family boat or camper on the property may look elsewhere for a house.

EFFECTIVE TERM AND REVISION. Although some covenants may include a definite termination date, covenants should generally be designed to renew themselves automatically and *run with the land* indefinitely. Property owners also should be able to revise the covenants with the approval of a stipulated percentage of other property owners. The developer may decide to allow some covenants to be revisable with a simple majority vote, whereas other covenants may require approval by 75 percent or even 90 percent of property owners. The developer may also want to allow homeowners to revise some covenants, such as changes in fencing, after three to five years, whereas others, such as "single-family use only," may be revised only after 25 to 40 years, or with near unanimous approval. Proposed revisions in covenants should be submitted sufficiently ahead of time to allow property owners to review them—three years for major covenants and one year for minor covenants.

Residential developers disagree about whether or not the developer should retain the power to make minor amendments to covenants. Some feel that the flexibility to adjust building lines and make modifications in design character from one phase to another is essential for the developer. Others feel that such modifications should be handled through the design review committee. Developers who frequently amend covenants risk hurting their credibility with property owners, who may doubt the developer's intentions to fulfill promises and carry out future development plans. Given the history of unintended consequences from covenants, beginning developers are advised to maintain some flexibility in "founders' rights" to change elements of governance while they still own a substantial portion of the community's lots.

ENFORCEMENT. Legally, anyone who is bound by covenants may enforce them against anyone else who is bound by them. Because doing so may set neighbor against neighbor, providing a homeowners association with the power of enforcement is the best solution. Failure to enforce a covenant in a timely fashion may render the covenant void. For example, in a Dallas subdivision, the homeowners did not enforce a covenant that restricted fencing of an open-space easement running along the back of the owners' lots. Several years later, the homeowners association attempted to enforce the covenant against several homeowners who had fenced the open space. The homeowners who had fenced in the open space successfully challenged the association on the grounds that the covenant was void for lack of previous enforcement.

COMMUNITY AND CONDOMINIUM ASSOCIATIONS

The developer must create the association and file the articles of incorporation and bylaws before selling any lots to homebuilders or individual buyers. Any sales

that predate the establishment of the association are exempted from the association. Therefore, forming the community association is a critical part of the developer's initial activities.

TYPES. Four main types of homeowners associations exist: community association with automatic membership, condominium association, funded community trust, and nonautomatic association.

Community Association with Automatic Membership. In most subdivisions in which fee simple interest in the lots is conveyed to buyers, membership in a community association occurs automatically when a buyer purchases a dwelling or improved lot. The association may hold title to real property such as open space and recreational facilities in the subdivision. It is responsible for preserving and maintaining the property. Members have perpetual access to the common property. They must pay assessments to finance the association's activities and must uphold the covenants.

Condominium Association. This approach resembles the community association, except for the form of ownership. When someone purchases a condominium, the title applies only to the interior space of the particular unit. The structure, lobbies, elevators, and surrounding land belong to all the owners as *tenants in common*. Owners are automatically members of the condominium association and have voting privileges and responsibilities for operating and maintaining the common facilities.

Funded Community Trust. This approach is an alternative to the automatic membership association. The funded community trust holds and maintains the common areas in a development. The funded trust differs from a community association in that a fiduciary organization, such as a bank, is the trustee responsible for the costs of overseeing maintenance of the property.

The funded community trust limits the ability of owners to act directly on their own behalf. The advantage of the trust is that it eliminates much of the day-to-day governance and participatory requirements of members. This form has not been used widely primarily because banks and other institutions have been reluctant to become trustees.

Nonautomatic Association. This form of association provides for the voluntary support of homeowners. It does not work, however, if the development owns common properties because if owners are not automatically members, assessments cannot be mandated. A nonautomatic association cannot participate in the enforcement of covenants and, therefore, can serve only as a focus of interest and social pressure for conformance.

LEGAL FRAMEWORK. An automatic community association includes five major legal elements: a subdivision plat, an enabling declaration, articles of incorporation, bylaws, and individual deeds for each parcel. The subdivision plat is the recorded map showing individual lots, legal descriptions, common spaces, and easements. The plat should indicate areas that will be dedicated to the association as well as those that will not be dedicated for use by the general public (often called *reserve parcels*). It should also reference and be recorded with the enabling declaration, which sets forth the management and ownership of common areas, the lien rights of the association against all lots, the amendment procedures, the enforcement procedures, and the rights of voting members.

The articles of incorporation and bylaws are the formal documents for creating a corporation with the state. The articles of incorporation set forth the initial board of directors, procedures for appointing new directors, membership and voting rights, amendment procedures, dissolution procedures, and the severability of provisions. The bylaws of the association describe the rules by which the association will conduct business. They set forth the composition and duties of the board and the indemnification of officers of the association and describe the role and composition of subordinate boards, such as the design review board.

Each individual deed conveyed by the developer should reference the declaration of the association. The developer should summarize the formation, responsibilities, and activities of the association in a brochure that homebuilders in the subdivision can give to their buyers.

THE DEVELOPER'S ROLE. Homeowners associations, protective covenants, and the common facilities managed by homeowners associations are as important to the overall success of a subdivision as the subdivision's engineering and design. If handled properly, they can serve as a major component of the developer's marketing strategy.

The developer usually donates commonly owned land and facilities to the homeowners association. The costs are covered by lot sales to builders. For the purpose of property taxes, permanently dedicated open space has no real market value and is either not assessed or taxed at all or assessed at a nominal value, with the taxes paid by the homeowners association.

During the course of development, the developer usually maintains the open space and common facilities. These responsibilities are turned over to the association when the development is completed. Control of the association passes from the developer to the residents when the residents elect the officers of the association. The developer should design the accounts and record keeping so that the transition to the association is smooth.

The developer establishes initial assessments for homeowners that must realistically reflect the number of residents of the community at any one time. Because buyers evaluate monthly association assessments the same way they do monthly mortgage payments, the assessments cannot be too high. Although developers would like to place as much of the burden as possible on the association, they should keep the assessment competitive with that of other subdivisions.

Residents appear to be somewhat more tolerant of association dues than they are of general taxes because the results of dues are more directly apparent. The upper limit to place on dues depends on local conditions. In Orange County, California, for example, before Proposition 13 limited property taxes to 1 percent of the house purchase price, homeowners tolerated a combined tax bill (property taxes plus special district assessments) of up to 2 percent of the house value. Homeowners may tolerate as much as an additional half percentage point per year in association dues in areas where the association owns and operates substantial common open space and recreation facilities.

In the past, homeowners associations gave boards the feeling that they must be extremely restrictive toward members; today, however, the emphasis is much more on empowerment than enforcement. Wayne Hyatt of Atlanta-based Hyatt and Stubblefield notes that developers are using covenants to improve quality of life, meaning that rather than simply restricting nuisances and design choices, the homeowners association can be used to establish community goals—activities, charities, voluntarism, and other enhancements of the way the community lives.

According to Hyatt, "There's been a sea change in the sophistication of the law and of many private developers with regard to covenant development. The emphasis today is much more on empowerment of the owner-members than on enforcement. The law has become much more precisely defined, and as the fear of uncertainty [with regard to fiduciary duties and conflict of interest] wanes, the focus of litigation has changed dramatically. Where ten years ago disputes were typically developer versus board, now they are primarily owner versus members versus board. But the reputation for disputes among members is really a reflection of society, magnified through these private governmental bodies."[45]

Conclusion

Beginning developers will find many opportunities in land development. Particularly for individuals with expertise in legal, urban design, and entitlement issues, the higher risk of land development can be mitigated by thorough knowledge and good management. Although land development may be combined with building development, in general, it should be considered a separate business to be evaluated on its own merits.

Land development is one of the riskier forms of development because it is so dependent on the public sector for approvals and infrastructure support, involves a long investment period with no positive cash flow, and, especially in large projects, requires the ability to change direction to meet changing markets and economic situations. Beginning developers should concentrate on smaller, less complex deals. Problem sites, such as those containing environmentally sensitive areas, can offer attractive opportunities, but developers should be wary of getting bogged down for several years in litigation and entitlement disputes.

Beginning land developers will find that obtaining financing without significant cash equity and strong financial statements is a difficult process. Nevertheless, land development offers the opportunity to use commitments from builders as collateral for securing financing. Those starting out will find that seller financing and joint ventures with landowners and financial institutions can enable them to build a track record and successfully launch a development career.

Although opportunities are always present, so are pitfalls. Cities are holding land developers responsible for an ever-higher share of the cost of providing public facilities and solving environmental problems. In many cases, developers are becoming the de facto agents of cities in building arterial streets, libraries, fire stations, and sewer and drainage facilities and in cleaning up toxic waste and restoring environmentally sensitive land. The liability of developers for construction standards, especially streets, utilities, and drainage, extends for many years after developers have sold out of the subdivision.

Dos and Don'ts for Homeowners Associations

GENERAL ADVICE

- The senior person on the development team responsible for the project should not serve on the board. Many developers ignore this advice, but understand that doing so opens the developer and the association to conflict of interest claims.

- The developer should not try to do everything alone. The developer should document whatever it or the association does, and should never underestimate the role of the association manager. The developer should budget for these tasks, even if they'll be done by development staff for the foreseeable future.

DO:

- Observe the required corporate formalities, such as holding regular meetings, keeping a corporate minutes book, and properly authorizing and documenting all board actions.

- Purchase or renew adequate insurance.

- Collect assessments and increase assessments as necessary.

- Enforce architectural control.

- Review the association's budget and produce quarterly and annual reports.

- Always remember to protect members' interests.

- Use due care in hiring personnel, including compliance with nondiscrimination laws.

- File tax returns and other required IRS forms.

- Require the developer to complete and convey the common areas in a timely manner.

- Order an impartial inspection of the common areas by the association.

- Maintain common areas adequately.

DON'T:

- Enter into long-term contracts, such as maintenance, against the bylaws of the association. If it turns out not to be in the best interest of the association, you could be liable.

- Enter a dwelling unit without authorization.

- File a lawsuit after the statute of limitations expires.

Source: Wayne Hyatt, *Protecting Your Assets: Strategies for Successful Business Operation in a Litigious Society* (Washington, D.C.: ULI–the Urban Land Institute, 1997).

Cities and land developers have always formed a kind of partnership because land development has been the primary vehicle by which cities grow. As the burdens of responsibility shift more toward developers, developers must come to understand not only how to build financially successful subdivisions but also how to ensure the fiscal health of their cities.

NOTES

1. Sometimes called "super pads." The buyer is responsible for installing local streets and utilities. Lots are often subject to design guidelines imposed by the master developer.

2. H. James Brown, R.S. Phillips, and N.A. Roberts, "Land Markets at the Urban Fringe," *Journal of the American Planning Association* (April 1981): 131–144.

3. Smart growth is defined in different ways, but at its core, it is about accommodating growth in ways that are economically sound, that are environmentally responsible, and that enhance the quality of life.

4. Most communities require public hearings for subdivision approval but not for building plans, which are approved by the building department only. Public hearings are political by definition and involve much more risk—of disapproval, reduction in density, or increase in exaction cost. Building department approvals are essentially administrative: as long as one satisfies the regulations, approval is automatic.

5. For further discussion, see Charles Long, *Finance for Real Estate Development* (Washington, D.C.: ULI–the Urban Land Institute, 2011), chapter 3.

6. The lender's release price from the loan may be higher than $16,000; thus, the developers would have to make up the difference.

7. Interview with Harlan Doliner, partner, Nixon Peabody, LLP, Boston, Massachusetts, 2000.

8. Ibid.

9. Interview with Jack Willome, former CEO, Rayco, Ltd., San Antonio, Texas, 1987.

10. Interview with Don Mackie, partner, Mill Creek Properties, Salado, Texas, 1987.

11. Title insurance companies do not survey property and therefore do not insure against encroachments and boundary disputes that would be disclosed by a proper survey. A correct survey, however, corresponds to the description in the deed, and if the description in the deed is wrong, the title insurance company is liable. The company insures the accuracy of the documents.

12. Interview with Dan Kassel, president, Granite Homes, Irvine, California, 2002.

13. This paragraph and the next two are from an interview with Steve MacMillan, chief operating officer, Campbell Estate, Kapolei, Hawaii, 2002.

14. See Mike Davidson and Fay Dolnick, "A Glossary of Zoning, Development, and Planning Terms," *Planning Advisory Service Report*, no. 491/492 (Chicago: American Planning Association, 1999).

15. Interview with Jo Anne Stubblefield, president, Hyatt and Stubblefield, Atlanta, Georgia, 2000.

16. Interview with Scott Smith, La Plata Investments, Colorado Springs, Colorado, 2000.

17. Interview with Al Neely, executive vice president and chief investment officer, Charles E. Smith Co., Arlington, Virginia, 2000.

18. Interview with Tim Edmond, president, St. Joe/Arvida, Tallahassee, Florida, 2000.

19. Interview with Roger Galatas, president, Roger Galatas Interests, the Woodlands, Texas, 2001.

20. *Golden v. Planning Board of the Town of Ramapo*, 285 N.E.2d 291 (N.Y. Ct. App., 1972). This case upheld regulations for timing, phasing, and quotas in development, making development permits contingent on the availability of adequate public facilities.

21. *Construction Industry Association v. City of Petaluma*, 522 F.2d 897 (9th Cir. 1975). The U.S. Supreme Court let Petaluma's residential control system stand after lengthy court battles initiated when the city was sued by homebuilders.

22. Kevin Lynch and Gary Hack, *Site Planning*, 3rd ed. (Cambridge, Mass.: MIT Press, 1985), p. 124.

23. Interview with Roger Galatas, 2001.

24. "Brownfield Redevelopment: One Highly Successful Approach," *Leavitt Communications: An International Public Relations Agency*, Leavitt Communications, 2006; and June 29, 2011, www.leavcom.com/mactec_1006.htm.

25. Interview with Roger Galatas, 2001.

26. Interview. Matthew Kiefer, attorney, Gouston and Storrs, Boston, Massachusetts, 2010.

27. The city might require the developer to pay for, say, the first one or two lanes of paving, with the city paying the rest. Alternatively, it might require the developer to pay for or install the entire arterial, with subsequent reimbursement by other developers whose subdivisions front the arterial.

28. Although the terms *gross acres* and *net acres* are commonly used and understood, *net usable acres* is far less popular.

29. Richard B. Peiser, "Optimizing Profits from Land Use Planning," *Urban Land*, September 1982, pp. 6–10; and Ehud Mouchly and Richard Peiser, "Optimizing Land Use in Multiuse Projects," *Real Estate Review*, Summer 1993, pp. 79–85.

30. The compound return is $(1 + 0.3)1/3 - 1 = 0.09139$, or 9.139 percent. The general formula is $(1 + r)1/n - 1$, where r equals the total rate of return and n equals the holding period.

31. All return figures presented here are IRRs. They give the annual return on equity per year that should be made on an alternative investment (with annual compounding) to accumulate the same total amount of money by the end of the life of the project.

32. The rate of return on equity is the same as the discount rate used for determining the present value of a stream of future cash flows. It is also the same as the target IRR that an investor would use as the hurdle rate for making an investment.

33. Radburn was established by the City Housing Corporation, led by Henry Wright and Clarence Stein. See Eugenie Ladner Birch, "Radburn and the American Planning Movement," *Journal of the American Planning Association* (October 1980): 424–439.

34. Interview with Dan Kassel, 2002.

35. See Walter Kulash, *Residential Streets*, 3rd ed. (Washington, D.C.: ULI–the Urban Land Institute, 2001).

36. Ibid.

37. See Jeanne Christie, "Wetlands Protection after the *SWANCC* Decision," *Planning Advisory Service Memo* (Chicago: American Planning Association, 2002), pp. 1–4.

38. *Reducing Stormwater Costs through Low Impact Development (LID) Strategies and Practices* (Washington, D.C.: U.S. Environmental Protection Agency, Nonpoint Source Control Branch, 2007).

39. Ibid.

40. Ibid., p. 9.

41. Ibid., p. 34.

42. *Economic Benefits of Runoff Controls* (Washington, D.C.: U.S. Environmental Protection Agency, Office of Water, 1995).

43. Interview with Donald Mackie, 1987.

44. Interview with Jo Anne Stubblefield, 2000.

45. Interview with Wayne Hyatt, principal, Hyatt and Stubblefield, Atlanta, Georgia, 2001.

Multifamily Residential Development

Overview

This chapter focuses on multifamily residential development, primarily rental income property, but it also covers topics common to all forms of development. Rather than presenting separate generic discussions of the development process throughout the book, this chapter begins with a discussion of income property development and incorporates a detailed discussion of each step of the development process into its treatment of rental and condominium apartment development. This chapter primarily addresses rental housing. Condominium development (for-sale multifamily housing) is similar in many respects to apartment development (rental multifamily housing) except for the financial analysis. (Several fundamental subject areas, such as site acquisition, the regulatory process, site engineering, and financial analysis of for-sale condos, are covered in detail in chapter 3.)

Despite the apparent preference of U.S. households for owning single-family dwellings, multifamily housing continues to be an essential housing type for a broad range of the population. Apartments house the young and old alike, whether they are aspiring homeowners, residents who cannot afford to own a home, or renters by choice—those who choose to rent apartments even though they could afford to buy a single-family house. To its residents, multifamily housing offers convenience, affordability, and flexibility.

Like other real estate, multifamily residential development is highly cyclical. Typically, in times of low interest rates, multifamily units are built by the thousands. Conversely, when interest rates are high (10 percent or above), multifamily construction slows considerably. However, low interest rates also make houses more affordable, which reduces demand for apartments. And in times following deep recessions, rents are often too low to make new apartments economically viable.

Major demographic trends also exert substantial influence on multifamily construction. As local growth rates influence the overall demand for units, the composition of the population influences the demand for particular types of multifamily housing. The aging of the baby boomer generation will continue to play a leading role in the demand for housing, but also echo boomers will have even larger numbers than their baby boom parents. As the leading edge of the baby boom generation reaches 65 years old, demand for retirement housing will increase, as well as other housing types geared for the active adult market, assisted living and continuing care. Between 2010 and 2020, the number of echo boomers will reverse the declines in younger households of the last decade and feed demand for apartments. Even with only modest immigration, minorities will fuel 73 percent of

Pacific Station is a mixed-use infill development in downtown Encinitas, California. The project replaces an old warehouse and railroad shed with a Whole Foods grocer, residential condominiums, and 248 underground parking spaces.

household growth, with Hispanics leading the way at 36 percent of total household growth.[1] Unlike white household growth where the majority will be single-person households, minority growth will add demand for all housing types, especially family apartments. Studies show that aging baby boomers and generation X (those born from 1961 to 1981) are increasingly interested in urban living. Demand for apartments and condominiums in cities and redeveloping suburbs will increase, presenting opportunities for infill development, rehabilitation of older structures, and new types of medium- and higher-density housing.

RECENT HISTORY

In the early 1980s, syndicators brought huge inflows of equity to finance apartment development in tax-driven deals offering little or no cash flow. Sale prices of apartment projects rose to uneconomic levels, often with zero and even negative cash-on-cash returns. The Tax Reform Act of 1986 effectively eliminated the market for these types of investments by limiting the ability of investors to write off tax losses against other income, and project values were accordingly adjusted downward. Developers of multifamily housing were hit hard when they discovered, too late, that they had built more units than the market could absorb. After the real estate crash in the early 1990s, real estate investment trusts (REITs) became the dominant buyers of larger apartment properties. At that time, other institutional investors, such as pension funds and insurance companies, also began to upgrade apartments to institutional status, giving them the same place in institutional property portfolios previously reserved for office and larger retail properties. The competition from institutional investors to buy apartment properties that were performing well resulted in higher sale prices and lower capitalization rates, making new apartment development more profitable.

Until the market crash in 2008 in the wake of the subprime mortgage crisis, apartments remained the most attractive property type. Then, low mortgage interest rates and lax documentation requirements made for-sale housing increasingly affordable. At the same time, government programs that assist low- and moderate-income apartment development were substantially cut back, considerably reducing the construction rate of affordable apartments. However, low-income housing tax credits (LIHTCs), which are the major supply-side subsidy program, produced an average of 103,000 units per year from 1995 to 2006, of which 60 percent were new construction.[2] From

1993 to 2000, some 300,000 public housing units were torn down, but the LIHTC program compensated for the decline in the public housing stock during this period.[3] Both market-rate apartments and affordable apartments offer development and repositioning opportunities for beginning developers. Even when new construction is at a low point, LIHTC projects will continue to be built, although developers should be aware of the extreme complexity and the need to partner with a nonprofit organization in many states.

The recovery from the recession of the late 2000s is occurring slowly, hampered by low job recovery. ULI's *Emerging Trends in Real Estate 2010* projects that pent-up demand will assist the recovery for apartments. The generation now in their 20s want to move out of their parents' homes as soon as they find jobs. The growth in echo boomers combined with delay in marriage and children to build careers, lack of available mortgage financing, and larger downpayment requirements for homes will contribute to apartment demand in the 2010s. Access to Freddie Mac and Fannie Mae financing has cushioned apartment owners from precipitous drops in prices during the recession.

PRODUCT TYPES

Residential building development includes everything from single-family houses to high-rise apartment buildings and condominiums. The market can be segmented in a variety of ways, either by ownership or building type:

- **Rental Products**—Rental apartments, such as garden, low-rise, mid-rise, and high-rise units, and rental houses. Tenants in rental apartments are lessees of the landlord. Their interest may range from a verbal agreement with the landlord for a month-to-month lease to a lease term ranging from six months to one year. Leases longer than one year are rare.
- **For-Sale Products**—Condominiums, cooperatives, and timeshares. *Condominiums* are arrangements whereby the household has individual ownership of its unit (defined as the space enclosed by the unit's interior walls) plus an undivided ownership interest in the property's common elements. In a *cooperative*, the residents of the building do not own their unit, but own shares in the corporation. The corporation actually holds the title to the building, and residents lease their units from the corporation. Since the passage of condominium legislation in 1961, cooperative forms of ownership are rare except in New York

City, Washington, D.C., Chicago, and parts of Florida. *Timeshare ownership* is the right to use, or the fee simple ownership of, real estate for a specified period each year, usually in one-week increments. Many multifamily buildings in vacation destinations around the world use this form of ownership.

- **Design**—Number of stories, walkup or elevator, and parking arrangement. Parking requirements often determine the type of residential building constructed.
- **Type of Construction**—Wood frame versus concrete or steel. Wood frame is nearly always used for single-family and townhome construction. It can be used for multifamily buildings up to four or five stories. It is cheaper than concrete or steel construction.

Within each general product category, further distinctions can be made based on the segmentation of the target market—by income, family composition, and age. Each segment demands different floor plans, room sizes, finish details, and amenities.

Product types are often confused with forms of ownership. *Apartment*, for example, is often used as a generic term covering both multifamily rental and for-sale (condominium) products. Although the form of ownership greatly influences product design, marketing, and financing, it may refer to any physical product type. Technically, any rental property can be designed for, or converted to, for-sale condominiums. Similarly, any for-sale product can be operated as rental property if condominium covenants permit it. This chapter focuses on multifamily residential development—rental and condominium apartments. No standard definition of multifamily or apartment types exists, but there are four major categories:

- **Garden Apartments**—One- to three-story walkup buildings built of wood frame on slab, with repeated floor plans. Garden apartments are typically designed with stairways serving two to four apartments on each stairway landing. Parking is at grade or tucked under part of the building. Densities range from 16 to 40 units per acre (40–100/ha), although densities higher than 30 units per acre (85/ha) stretch the limits of surface-only parking.
- **Low-Rise Apartments**—Three- and four-story walkup or elevator buildings with repeated floor plans that are constructed of wood frame on top of a slab or concrete deck with one or two levels of parking above grade but below the deck. Densities range from 40 to 90 units per acre (100–220/ha).
- **Mid-Rise Apartments**—Five to eight stories, with elevators and central halls for apartment access on each floor. Densities range from 60 to 120 units per acre (150–300/ha).
- **High-Rise Apartments**—Above eight stories, with densities ranging from 80 to 200 units per acre (200–500/ha). Both mid-rise and high-rise apartments are constructed of steel frame or reinforced concrete. Depending on the location of the development, parking for these buildings may be in surface lots surrounding the building, at grade but below the first floor of the building (which may sit on a podium), in a full-fledged parking structure, or in a below-grade parking garage.

The construction cost for each of these product types determines the rent that must be charged. Lower-density wood-frame garden apartments with surface parking cost less than one-third as much to build (on a per-square-foot basis) as high-rise apartments with elevators, a steel or concrete frame, and structured parking. Underground parking can add another $40,000 per parking space.

Randolph Hawthorne of RGH Ventures observes that "people have segmented the residential market like many other industries—for example, the way Fidelity Investments segmented the mutual funds business with specific target markets. Clearly, what has happened in multifamily units now is that developers tend toward the very high rental market (renters by choice) or work on affordable housing (much of it fueled by low-income housing tax credits). So, very little new development is occurring of what would be called 'bread-and-butter' apartment complexes aimed at the typical mid-range renter."[4]

Residential Product Types

SINGLE-FAMILY PRODUCTS

- Single-family houses (one unit per lot)
- Patio houses (or zero-lot-line)
- Duplexes (two attached units, either side by side or upper and lower floors)
- Townhouses (attached units on separate lots)

MULTIFAMILY PRODUCTS[a]

- Garden or low-rise apartments (typically one to three stories)
- Mid-rise apartments (four to eight stories)
- High-rise apartments (more than eight stories)

[a]For more detail, see feature box on page 194.

FIGURE 4-1 | Time Line of Events

Ideally, the developer does not close on the land until he is ready to start construction. In most cases, however, the land seller will not wait that long.

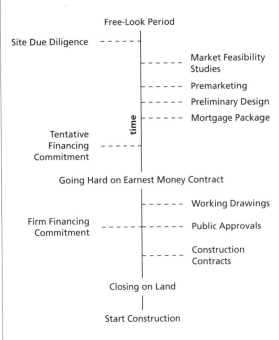

Two trends currently affecting apartments are a movement by aging baby boomers back to the city and an increasing demand for high-end luxury apartments. "In general, a lot of people who would move into houses are now renting high-end apartments in the cities, basically for lifestyle and convenience. According to Randolph Hawthorne, "There seems to be a demand in the high end for apartments. People find it almost easier to finance a high-end project because it's not a big increase in rent to add amenities (and in fact the cost of amenities is less than the increase in rent and generates better financial feasibility). That means you can get your development off the ground when financing is not available for other types of apartments."[5] With respect to the years following the financial crisis of 2008–2009, Hawthorne adds, "Only the strongest financially and most experienced developer sponsors can get construction financing in this environment. There will be the inevitable trend to consider downsizing square footage in an attempt to keep absolute rent levels more affordable while at the same time achieving high rent per square foot. Most costs for newly built apartments are inelastic (land

cost, financing, architectural and engineering fees, and basic construction) so the marginal extra costs for high-end finishes, for example, stone countertops, are easily recovered by premium rents."[6]

GETTING STARTED

Developer Edward Zuker states, "No one can start on their own without a track record and relationships. It is essential to develop the knowledge and contacts while working for someone else before starting your own ventures. This can be accomplished by working in a larger corporate setting, or starting with smaller deals and working your way up.

"Developers often start as local homebuilders and then use the profits from one project in order to branch out into other property types because they already have an established base and the experience of building. In addition, they have income coming in that can sustain them during downturns and make them more attractive borrowers to lenders.

"Some of the larger developers in the Boston area started off small as homebuilders and graduated into larger and larger projects. The ones that have been successful have done so by focusing on income-producing larger projects rather than for-sale properties, thereby ensuring a continued income stream during downturns."[7]

Methods of construction and issues regarding marketing and design are similar, whether a developer is building single-family or multifamily units. The differences are often ones of scale and whether the units are for rent or for sale.

Most homebuilders (that is, builders of single-family houses) act as their own general contractors, and much of their profit in homebuilding is derived from construction. Profit margins, which typically range from 10 to 15 percent (over hard and soft costs), must cover construction risk.

Many multifamily developers also do their own construction, but others hire third-party general contractors. Unless they already own a construction company, beginning developers should probably start with a third-party general contractor. Once they have developed a track record, they can consider establishing a construction division in house. The general contractor absorbs the construction risk and earns the construction profit, which typically runs from 6 to 8 percent of hard construction costs. The development profit, which typically runs from 8 to 15 percent of total cost, is in addition to the contractor's profit. The development profit represents the difference between the capitalized value—the market value—of the property at stabilized occupancy and the total development cost to reach that point.

In general, developers bring a wide variety of backgrounds, approaches, and concepts to their first projects. The key to success, however, is skillfully executing the steps in the development process and paying attention to every detail. Jerome Rappaport, Jr., states, "The first requirement is for developers to have the skill set to cover all of the tasks necessary to implement the project, either through their own past experience or expertise on their team. Development is a lot more than site control. It also entails construction implementation, financial controls, budget compliance, government relations, neighborhood relations, marketing, and sales."[8]

Project Feasibility

Project feasibility encompasses the full range of analyses that a developer must perform before committing to a given project. As feasibility analysis progresses, the developer must acquire more information that will indicate whether it makes sense to proceed further.

During the feasibility period, the project may be canceled at any time, usually limiting losses to the costs of the feasibility study plus the cost of tying up the land. Positive information, however, usually justifies making the next increment of expenditure to acquire additional information. Project feasibility includes four major activities:

- market analysis;
- site selection/engineering feasibility;
- regulatory approvals; and
- financial feasibility.

In some cases, these activities are performed sequentially; more often, they overlap. Developers must be satisfied, however, that all four activities have been completed satisfactorily before making a final go/no-go decision. Moreover, developers must treat the findings of their research objectively and not become enamored with their site or concept.

Developers rarely close on a site (finalize the acquisition) until they are certain that the project will go ahead; in practice, that means when all financing commitments are in place for both debt and equity, and major public approvals have been received. For beginning developers, most of the steps taken during the feasibility period are aimed at securing financing and ensuring that no unexpected surprises show up later during construction or lease-up.

MARKET ANALYSIS

Market analysis occurs both before site selection and after site selection. The choice of sites depends on the market that the developer wants to target. High-quality market information is essential to determine accurately what to build, whom to build for, and how much to build.

No matter how familiar a developer is with the local submarket, an up-to-date market study is indispensable, both to support loan applications and to verify current rents and unit types that are most in demand (number of bedrooms, amenities, configurations, and quality, for example). The primary benefit of analyzing the market before selecting a site is that such an analysis will help identify the niches in the market.

The more clearly a developer defines the target market, the more specific the requirements are for a site. For example, when a developer knows who the prospective homebuyers or tenants are—their preferences, their income level, their family situation—then the developer has the facts needed to make careful decisions. Particular market needs imply particular site

---

Advice on Market Analysis

Experienced residential developers offer the following pointers for obtaining the most useful market data:

- **The results of market analysis should be balanced with a developer's assessment of his ability to deliver a particular project.**

- **The determination of how much market share can be captured is critical. Capturing more than 2.5 percent of any market that absorbs more than 15,000 housing units per year is an ambitious undertaking. Although a developer in a small town may capture 50 percent of a market, the same developer in a large metropolitan area probably would not capture more than 5 percent.**

- **In an unfamiliar market, a new developer may estimate his potential market share by studying what success other developers have had in the area with a similar type of product and sales promotion program.**

- **It is extremely important to identify the idiosyncrasies of an unfamiliar market. The proposed project will likely need to be modified somewhat to meet local tastes.**

- **A developer should not rely on the architect to do the market research. Decisions on project features, such as unit mix, unit sizes, and amenities, should be based on solid market research and on the tastes and preferences of the target market.**

MARKET ANALYSIS: Jefferson Pointe

Following is a short summary of a market study conducted for Jefferson Pointe, a multifamily development in eastern Pennsylvania. The full study can be found online at www.uli.org/PRED.

M|PF Research analyzed the development potential for a 234-unit luxury apartment community in West Chester, Pennsylvania, a Philadelphia suburb. The study was completed in 2006 for the developer, JPI East, a division of JPI Multifamily, Inc. (The developer is now called Jefferson Apartment Group after a buyout completed in 2009.) The subject property consists of an 11-acre (4.5 ha) site with an existing 50,000-square-foot (4,600 m²) warehouse building to be demolished. The developer projected having the first units delivered in late 2009 and completed in 2010. However, the project was delayed both by a lengthy approval process and by the difficulty of obtaining financing during the recession. The project began construction in 2010 with first deliveries in late 2011. At the time of the market study, the proposed unit mix consisted of 34 percent one bedroom/one bath; 16 percent one bedroom/one bath/den; 43 percent two bedroom/two bath; and 6 percent three bedrooms, with sizes ranging from 658 to 1,523 square feet (61–141 m²) and averaging 1,003 square feet (93 m²). The intended market is high-end young professionals and empty nesters. The development is a four-story, wood-frame building with an above-grade parking garage that provides all residents with direct access to their apartment's floor. Project features will include a resident lounge, movie theater, fitness center, business center, outdoor pool, dog park, and landscaped courtyards.

M|PF examined market fundamentals, potential absorption, resident profile, proposed program, and rental rates (base and all-in). Although the Philadelphia metro area experienced minimal rent growth from 2001 to 2005, it was expected to improve over the next five years (see figure B). Following the 2001 recession, apartment absorption in the Philadelphia metro area failed to keep up with new supply; however, supply and demand were forecast to be close from 2006 to 2010 (see figure C).

West Chester is a high-occupancy apartment market area and M|PF's forecast indicated that demand should outpace new supply from 2006 to 2010. Like the metro area, West Chester experienced minimal or negative rent growth from 2001 to 2005 but was expected to see both strengthening rent growth and occupancy from 2006 to 2010. Based on current market absorption and new supply, the study predicted an absorption period of ten months with a lease-up rate of 22 units per month. For

FIGURE A | Jefferson Pointe Site Plan

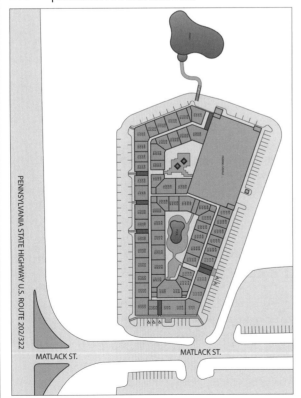

FIGURE B | Apartment Occupancy and Rent Growth

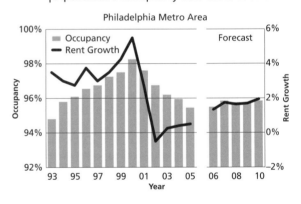

FIGURE C | Apartment Supply/Demand Trends

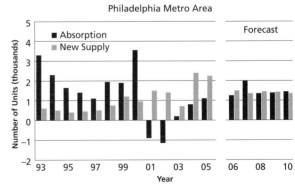

2009, when the project was originally planned to be delivered, 425 units of new supply were forecast to come online in the West Chester market area, meaning that the subject property's 234 units would account for 55 percent of the new supply. Absorption for 2009, meanwhile, was forecast at 471 units, or 39 per month. If the site were to capture its fair share, then the units would be absorbed at 22 per month. Stabilized occupancy (95 percent) was projected to take ten months:

234 subject units ÷ 425 total units of new supply = 55% subject share
471 units absorbed ÷ 12 months = 39 units per month
39 units per month × 55% subject capture = 22 units per month
234 subject units × 95% stabilized occupancy = 222 units
222 units ÷ 22 units per month = 10 months

To evaluate demand for the project, M|PF designed a resident survey, mailed to competitive communities regarding the project's desirability. The survey asked residents to evaluate the site's location, unit types, and amenities. The subject location was viewed as desirable or acceptable by 66 percent of all respondents, making it the second most preferred site overall. Based on the data collected, M|PF arrived at pricing recommendations versus the competitors. The survey also looked at resident preferences for unit types. Based on the survey of residents and the current unit mix in competitors, M|PF determined that JPI's proposed program met the needs of the market (see figure D).

M|PF examined the current competition in the market to arrive at recommended rental rates. It surveyed nine stabilized properties and one in lease-up, totaling more than 2,300 units. The projects averaged 97 percent occupancy. Base rents averaged $1.33 per square foot ($14.32/m²), while quoted all-in rates were $1.37 per square foot ($14.75/m²). On average, the competitive properties offered base amenity packages valued at $224 per month. Figure E shows M|PF's recommended rents in relation to the competition. M|PF determined rents for the property by adjusting rents at competitive properties for age and amenities to derive a "stripped rent." These age-adjusted amenity-stripped rents theoretically factor out the measurable factors influencing rent performance, suggesting that the remaining differences relate to intangible factors, such as location, appearance, and management. M|PF then ran a regression to determine a trend line for the stripped rents. Based on the survey regarding the project's desirability, M|PF determined a premium of 6 percent on top of the stripped rent trend line for the subject property.

M|PF recommended base monthly rents averaging $1.49 per square foot ($16.04/m²), and an all-in rent with premium amenities and parking of $1.62 per square foot ($17.44/m²). Base amenities at the subject property were valued at $273 and would position its rent, including amenities, near the top of the existing market. Premium features on top of the base rent at the subject property included computer desks ($25 value), entry

hall closets ($3), kitchen islands ($20), patios/balconies ($5), and parking spaces (first space $100). According to the resident survey conducted by M|PF, there are relatively few features for which more than half of those surveyed would be willing to spend extra. On average, those surveyed were willing to spend $154 extra for their preferred package of amenities.

M|PF's conclusion was that the proposed development would be appropriate for the market, given feedback from the resident survey, the performance of existing supply, and projections for future supply and absorption.

Source: Greg Willett and Janine Steiner at Real Page, Inc., authored this market study. The synopsis was prepared by Lily Gray, student at Harvard Graduate School of Design, November 2011.

FIGURE D | Proposed Program versus Resident Survey and Competitors

	UNIT TYPE (BED-BATH)			
	1-1	1-den, 2-1	2-2	3-2, 3-2-den
Target Market Survey Data				
Presently occupied (%)	29	17	41	13
Preferred (%)	28	12	48	12
Income qualified for preferred floor plan (%)	28	11	50	11
Stabilized Competitors				
Mix (%)	37	17	39	7
Rent/ft²	$1.473	$1.184	$1.298	$1.264
Unit size (ft²)	873	1,045	1,140	1,387
Occupancy (%)	98	99	97	92
Lease-Up Competitor				
Mix (%)	44	6	45	5
Rent/ft²	$1.348	$1.300	$1.168	$1.261
Unit size (ft²)	844	977	1,203	1,340
Proposed by JPI				
Mix (%)	34	16	43	7
Unit size (ft²)	790	906	1,154	1,361

FIGURE E | Rent Recommendations

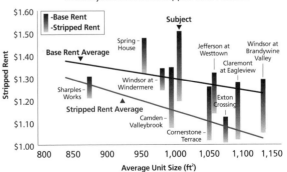

The Subject's Base and Stripped Rent Position

Multifamily Residential Development

requirements. If a need for high-end apartments is identified, for example, a developer should be willing to pay more for a superior site with special amenities, such as views, trees, water features, or recreational opportunities.

Developer Marvin Finger's niche is the high-end rental market in major cities around the country. The Finger Companies concentrate on developing inner-city sites in the affluent parts of town, focusing on upscale residential communities. "We identify the employment base and the retail locations where affluent renters would likely spend time. Further, we bracket the price of the land to what we can afford based on the final product appropriate to that market."[9]

The market study in the early stages does not need to be as comprehensive as it will have to be in the future. Market information is not only time-consuming but also expensive to obtain, and a developer should concentrate on specific issues:

- What geographic submarkets have the greatest need for apartments/condominiums?
- What product type is in greatest need?
- What product types are attractive to renters/buyers and why?
- Who is the target market? What are the demographic characteristics (age, income, household size) of potential renters/buyers who have the greatest need for apartments?
- What types of units or unit sizes are expected in this market? What is the appropriate rent/price range?
- What types of features, amenities, and services do renters/buyers expect?

The focus should be on *greatest need* rather than on vacancy rates or hottest areas, but a low vacancy rate points to a need. Need is measured by the relationship between demand (the absorption rate for new units) and supply of units (existing and anticipated) for a particular submarket. The submarket is identified not only by geographic area but also by product type and renter profile.

Developers often confuse existing supply with need. Certainly, historic absorption rates of existing supply are an important source of information for predicting future absorption, but because a particular product type is absent from an area does not necessarily mean that demand exists for that product type. Often a product type is not there because there is no demand for it.

In summary, the goals of the preliminary market analysis before site selection are to

- identify holes in the market—market niches where demand exceeds supply and locations and circumstances that offer special opportunities to build a project serving a particular market;
- define the target market for the project as narrowly as possible—number of units needed with particular designs, amenities, unit characteristics (number of rooms, size, and mix of units), and rent range; and
- develop a market strategy—whether to compete directly with other projects or to look for market niches.

Once a site is selected, the submarket should be analyzed in much greater detail. By collecting submarket information on rents, unit sizes, types of renters, levels of activity, and vacancies for each unit type, a developer will be able to determine how best to position a project. A project-by-project catalog of existing multifamily developments in the submarket should be created and used to decide whether to engage in direct competition with other local properties or to cater to a market niche that shows need and little competition.

Developer Marvin Finger says that once a site is placed under contract, "market analysis goes right to the top of the list of due diligence. In my firm, we send in-house staff people to interview property managers and analyze the current needs of tenants in properties that we consider to be in the same market and price range. Often we follow that up with a professional management company to confirm our findings."[10]

Location, site, and market potential determine the appropriate product to be developed. An urban locale demands a different type of residential development from a suburban one. The typically higher price of urban infill land requires higher densities. Greater automobile dependency in suburban communities necessitates more parking. A historic neighborhood might have specific height and architectural controls that dictate development parameters for a particular site. A waterfront site with panoramic views is better used for luxury condominiums than for entry-level housing.

The identified market segment should suggest special types of development. If the research detects strong demand from young families with small children, then the project should be planned with this market segment in mind, and the greatest percentage of units should be large enough for such households. If the target market is young, first-time renters, a moderately priced project with few amenities and maximum unit space for the dollar might fit the bill. A growing elderly population might suggest a need for a retirement community and elder care facilities. Amenities, features, design, and unit size should reflect residents' needs and should be determined through market research.

Although it is frequently easy to continue developing and marketing rental products that have leased well in the past, it can be rewarding, both financially and in terms of serving a public need, to develop a new type of product. However, in times of economic stress, it may be harder to finance innovative product types. Comparable residential projects might not currently exist in the immediate market area, but if the demand analysis shows a need, the analyst should explore the possibilities. In an overbuilt market, consideration of less standard types of development may lead to better opportunities but will require looking beyond the immediate market area for examples of successful comparable projects.

Traditionally, the largest multifamily housing markets have been those at both ends of the housing cycle: young singles and couples, and older empty nesters. In addition to these age-related cohorts, lifestyle niches provide further market potential. They include people in all income and age brackets who traditionally would purchase a single-family home but for any number of reasons choose multifamily living instead. In many instances, they make up target markets for more innovative product types.

DEMAND AND SUPPLY. A formal market analysis increases in importance as developers move farther away from familiar locations and product types. Beginning developers are unlikely to have the firsthand knowledge of local market conditions required to compete successfully and therefore need to make an extra effort to collect reliable market information before making even basic decisions about site selection.

Market Area. The developer's first task is to define the geographic study area. The study should start with the metropolitan area (data are available for metropolitan statistical areas [MSAs]) and then proceed to the locality where the project is to be located. Ultimately, it will focus on the narrow submarket area where the project will compete directly with other similar projects.

The narrow submarket is defined as the area of generally comparable population characteristics and is usually limited to one or two surrounding neighborhoods. Although the employment center or corridor

that the project serves generally defines the broader market, the *primary market area* is usually restricted to a radius of two or three miles (3–5 km) around the project and may even be smaller, especially if freeways, railroads, or other physical barriers exist between neighborhoods. It may, however, be larger if the proposed product is very specialized, or if the market area contains few direct comparables. An understanding of local renters and competitive projects is essential for determining the market area.

A *secondary market area* should also be defined. This area includes apartment projects that may not be directly competitive but offer an alternative to renters who are less sensitive about location.

The importance of defining the correct market area cannot be overemphasized. All too often, beginning developers omit competing projects or include an area so large that absorption rates are overestimated. In addition, many market areas are hard to define because they have no particular identity in the marketplace. This lack of identity poses problems not only for market definition but also for future lease-up and sales because projects perform better in areas that have distinctive identities. Creating a market identity where none exists can be quite a challenge.

Various factors are considered in delineating the target market area for a proposed development:

- **Travel Time from Major Employment Centers—** With traffic congestion a serious problem in most metropolitan areas, housing decisions are usually based on proximity to employment. By identifying major employment centers and making assumptions regarding acceptable commuting time, market analysis defines a target market area.
- **Mass Transportation Facilities and Highway Links—**Commuting patterns and times are based largely on ease of access; thus, the target market's geographic size is influenced by the availability of mass transit, the location of transportation corridors, and the speed at which they operate at peak travel times. Convenience of transportation and availability of public transit are especially important considerations for multifamily development.
- **Existing and Anticipated Patterns of Development—**Most urban settings contain areas of both growth and decline. Growth areas might be distinguished by desirable attributes, such as proximity to employment, availability of affordable housing, physical attractiveness, and/or outstanding community facilities.

- **Socioeconomic Composition**—An area's income, age, household characteristics, and other demographic characteristics influence housing choice and location (but note that it is illegal in the United States to target market segments based on race, religion, or ethnicity).
- **Physical Barriers**—Natural features like rivers, bluffs, and parklands, as well as constructed features like highways or intensive development, can sometimes form a wall through which the market's boundaries do not penetrate.
- **Political Subdivisions**—Municipal boundaries can be especially important when adjoining jurisdictions differ markedly in political climate, tax policies, or status, or hold different attitudes about growth. School district boundaries are important if households with school-age children represent a target market segment. For easier data collection, it is sometimes necessary to manipulate a target market area to conform to a political jurisdiction, such as a county or planning district in a county or city.

Demand Factors. On the demand side, the market study measures the number of households with particular age, size, and income characteristics. Market research firms employ many statistical techniques to refine their estimates of the number of households, but their basic approach is the same and takes into account the following factors:

- employment growth in *basic* industries (manufacturing and other industries that generate sales outside the city);
- employment growth in *service* industries (retail, local government, real estate, professionals, and others whose activities support the local community);
- percentage of growth expected to occur in employment in the city and submarket;
- socioeconomic characteristics, such as population, age, education, income distribution, and household size and characteristics—families with children, couples without children, singles, divorcees with children, and so on; and
- in- and out-migration.

Each factor must be carefully analyzed so that the developer understands the characteristics of the target population groups. From these statistics and other market surveys, the market analyst estimates the number of new households moving into an area or being created by marriage or divorce from within the area (by income, family composition, and age). From the total and year-over-year change in the number of households, the number of those who will need apartments or condominiums is computed based on historic ratios combined with new information about income and preferences. This estimate of annual demand represents the *absorption* or *take-up* of units in the submarket for the year. *Absorption* is the most important number in the market analysis because it provides the total quantity of units that will likely be rented in the submarket for the year. These aggregate *absorption rates* (units absorbed per year) are then broken down into absorption rates for individual product types and unit types. For example, a study that indicates demand for 500 apartments per year for a given market area is incomplete. It should subdivide that number according to product type: say, 350 adult units, 100 of which are luxury units, and 150 family units, 50 of which are luxury units.

Supply Factors. The supply of housing includes the existing housing stock, the units currently under construction, and the units planned for the future. The vacancy rate is usually considered the most important indicator of market need, but it can be very misleading. For example, vacancies may be 40 percent in older buildings without central air conditioning but as low as 5 percent in newer buildings. Equally important, a 15 percent vacancy rate in a submarket with only 100 total units may be quickly absorbed, especially if a new company is planning to move into the area; elsewhere, however, 15 percent may indicate a very soft market. A more meaningful measure is *total number of months it will take to absorb the existing and planned inventory*. This number is based on the estimated demand as measured by the absorption rate expressed in units per month. The computation is illustrated in the next subsection.

Information about the existing housing stock and vacancy rates can best be determined by personal inspection and interviews with managers of surrounding apartment complexes. Even though such information may be proprietary, most managers are willing to cooperate, especially if the developer promises to reciprocate when the project is completed. Neighboring property managers are usually willing to share information because they realize that in the future it will be important to cooperate with one another about bad tenants, break-ins, and other issues of mutual concern. Other sources of information include local real estate boards, local homeowners and apartment associations, public utility companies, mortgage companies, lending institutions, and the Federal Housing Administration (FHA).

The most common mistake that developers make in estimating supply is to ignore units on the drawing board—that is, projects that have not been announced and do not yet appear on any standard sources, such as city building permits. Often, local brokers, bankers, and architects are the best-informed sources concerning planned units. Of course, many such units may never be built and some planned projects may never get off the ground, but the most likely estimate of the number of units that will be built should be included in the projections of future supply.

Capture Rates. The percentage of total demand in the submarket that a project absorbs (units leased or sold per month) is the *capture rate*. A fundamental principle of market analysis is that, in the long run, a project will capture its pro rata share of total supply. If a project has 200 units and total supply currently available for leasing is 2,000 units, the developer's expected capture rate is 10 percent of the total supply. This capture rate is multiplied by the demand. In the example above, if demand is 100 units per month, the developer's pro rata capture rate would be ten units per month. At this rate, it should take 20 months to lease up 200 units.

The most common mistake in market analysis is to assume that one's project is better than the competition's and will achieve a higher capture rate than that indicated by the pro rata share. The fallacy here is that competitors faced with losing market share will eventually cut prices to attract more tenants. In the long run, projects are unlikely to capture more than their pro rata share, no matter how much better they are than the competition because of competitors' reducing their prices to a level where they recapture their share of the market. This situation is exactly what happened in the recession of the late 1980s and early 1990s. Although it took longer than expected for owners to slash rental rates—often because their loan agreements stipulated that rents be at a given rate or higher for loan funding—eventually (often after foreclosure) rents were sliced by half or more to lease up properties with high vacancies. Although a superior project may beat the competition even if its rents are 10 to 20 percent more, at a 30 to 50 percent discount, competitors will take away tenants. Therefore, no matter how superior one's property is to the competition's, the market study should compute absorption based on a pro rata capture rate. It is acceptable to include higher capture rates as well, but among financial scenarios should be one that shows lease-up based on the more conservative pro rata capture rate for estimating absorption.

Net Market Absorption and Months to Absorb Current and Projected Inventory. The decision concerning whether the market is strong enough to proceed with project development depends on one of the key outputs of the market analysis—the number of months required to absorb the current and projected inventory of units in that submarket. This figure should be broken down according to the different unit types planned for development. For example, the market study may show a short six-month inventory of one-bedroom units but a long 24-month inventory of three-bedroom units. The number of months to absorb the inventory should preferably be 12 or fewer for apartments. Twelve to 18 months is considered soft but not impossible; longer than 18 months should be avoided unless the developer has truly strong reasons to believe that his product will be absorbed significantly faster than the competition's.

To illustrate, suppose that the market analysis indicates demand for 1,200 middle-income adult apartments per year in the developer's submarket. Suppose further that the current inventory of existing vacant units is 500 apartments with another 500 units under construction and that the developer is aware of 400 units on the drawing board. Suppose the developer

Wolff Waters Place in La Quinta, California, is an apartment complex affordable to low-income families. The 218 units are arranged so as to create an attractive streetscape and safe places for children to play.

MARK DAVIDSON PHOTOGRAPHY

Multifamily Residential Development

estimates that he has learned of only half of all units planned (for a total of 800), but of the planned units, perhaps only 60 percent (480) will likely be built. Thus, the total supply of units is an estimated 1,480 and the estimated absorption period will be 14.8 months:

Vacant units	500
Units under construction	500
Planned units estimated to be built	480
Total estimated supply	1,480
Total estimated annual demand	1,200
Total estimated monthly demand	100

Number of months to absorb projected inventory =
Total estimated supply ÷ Total estimated demand =

$$\frac{1,480}{100} = 14.8 \text{ months}$$

In this example, if the developer plans to begin construction immediately and to be open for occupancy in 12 months, the current and projected supply will be only about three months of inventory when the developer's units come onstream.

What is a reasonable number of months of absorption of inventory? The lease-up period is derived from the projected number of units absorbed each month by unit type. A soft market is usually one with 18 months or more of projected inventory (including vacant, under-construction, and planned units). The period required to lease up the project is a critical component of the budget since it determines the line item for "interest carry during lease-up." Although no widely accepted guidelines exist, it is customary to include a 12-month leasing reserve plus some cushion in the form of a contingency reserve in case leasing takes 16 to 18 months. Although a larger reserve gives both the developer and the lender additional protection in case the market turns sour, too large a reserve will make the project appear more costly than the competition, which will scare off investors and lenders. Although reserves should be as large as possible, they cannot be too generous or the construction budget will be too high relative to the competition.

MARKET STUDY GUIDELINES. Market studies serve two purposes: they facilitate internal decision making and they provide documentation for lenders and investors. Lenders and investors are suspicious of market analyses because developers often perform them as ex post facto justifications of decisions already made. Lenders and investors also know it is easy to find someone to write a market study showing that an

area has a strong market. G.U. Krueger states, "The 'term sheet market research' trap uses market analysis to justify predetermined development decisions rather than using market analysis as an integral component of the feasibility analysis. There had been enormous pressure to proceed with deals, but now that this is no longer the case, there is an opportunity for meaningful research."[11] He also cautions about relying just on demographics: "Demographics by themselves may not be wrong, but they are driven by mechanical calculations and historical precedents and therefore don't say anything about behavior. The fact that baby boomers were supposed to have played such a big role in the bubble of the 2000s turned out to be faulty because it was a misinterpretation of their behavior, which wasn't caused by the fact that there were so many of them and that so many of them were affluent. It was driven by the financing and leveraging bubble that caused them to behave in a certain way."[12]

The following guidelines should be observed for the market study to be most useful to lenders, investors, and developers:

1. Give specific directions to the market research firm concerning boundaries of both primary and secondary areas to be researched and the types of products to be researched. The larger the boundaries and the greater the number of product types, the more expensive the study will be.
2. Be aware that general statistical information is by itself inadequate for making market decisions. Critical differences exist between market studies that collect general statistics on the market and those that gather data on specific projects. The latter type is significantly more expensive but is essential unless developers are *certain* that the market is good and the competition is weak. General statistics—housing inventory, vacancies, average rents, average unit sizes, number of housing starts in the past five years, number and dollar volume of permits, number of completions—are a useful starting point, but they must be supplemented with current survey data from projects in the specific market area. Even if the market research firm has a data bank with project-by-project information, the data should be updated to reflect the latest market conditions.
3. Although vacancy rates may be helpful indicators of market demand in areas where rates are very low, in general, do not rely on vacancy rates alone. The preferred indicator is the number of months of inventory in the marketplace—the time it will take at projected absorption rates to consume the exist-

ing supply of units, units under construction, and units on the drawing board. The number of months of inventory correlates directly with the amount of interest reserve that developers will need.

4. Hire the best firm available to undertake the market study. Firms that specialize in rental apartments and condominiums for particular market areas have information at their fingertips that other firms charge thousands of dollars to replicate. Developers certainly do not want to pay a firm to collect raw data from scratch. They should evaluate firms on the basis of their information sources and track records: How accurate have they been in their projections? Which banks and other financial institutions rely on their studies?

A good study of the market for multifamily residential development should include the following:

1. Figures for the total yearly demand for the metropolitan area, the city, and the submarket where the project is located. *Demand* refers to the number of multifamily units the marketplace will absorb during the period in which the project will be under construction and leasing.

2. Figures for total supply on a project-by-project basis. The data on each project should include
   • target market, location, developer, completion date;
   • number of units by type (one bedroom, two bedroom, and so on);
   • square footage of each unit type;
   • rent or sale price for each unit, along with premiums and concessions;
   • vacancies (if possible, by unit type);
   • amenities of complexes; and
   • amenities of individual units (appliances, fireplaces, and so on).

3. An assessment of how many units (for rent or for sale) the market will absorb each month by unit type. Developers should guard against anticipating unreasonably large capture rates and should run stress tests (scenarios) on cash flows assuming they capture only their pro rata share of the market.

Data from geographic information systems make market analysis today much more sophisticated than it was in the past. Also, market analysis today relies much more on focus groups and interviews to determine tenants' needs although focus groups are a limited sample and one does not know the quality of input one will get. G.U. Krueger offers the following advice from the Great Recession:

• In the current economic environment, it is more important to think about what the behavioral characteristics will be moving forward. The tools for identifying behavioral patterns are not that well developed.

• Once you have examined long-term prospects, look at the local economies in which you are operating. A national developer can look at the MSAs where there will be more growth than others. How well connected is the local economy in which you are operating to the global economy and how well can it serve the global economy? Is it being driven by the manufacturing sector producing goods the rest of the world needs or value-added design (as in Silicon Valley)? Stick with metropolitan areas and their hinterlands that service and are connected to the global economy.

• If an area is not part of the global system, it will be hard for it to achieve any sort of meaningful economic development unless there is massive government investment.

• Leverage was the primary driver in the past cycle. That may now be changing, and the source of income is more important in determining the need for rental housing.

• You cannot rely on demographic research for small-scale projections. One approach is to talk to Realtors in the field and visit projects that are similar to your concept. You need to know what you are looking for and get away from the notion that this exercise is to justify the decision to your boss or the lender. Talk to sales agents and try to get a current buyer profile and then look at the demographic models.

• Lenders should scrutinize the content and methodology of market analysis as a major component of their investment decisions.

• Even market research cannot help you if you do not have a strategy to use that information to maximize the asset value.[13]

SITE SELECTION

According to an old real estate adage, the worst reason for developing a parcel is that you already own it. Although owning a plot of land may not by itself be a good reason for developing it, a site should not be eliminated from consideration just because a developer owns it. Almost every site is developable for some purpose. The developer's challenge is to identify the *highest and best use*—the use that maximizes the property's land value.

During the acquisition process (see the guidelines in chapter 3), the ability to buy more time can be crucial for beginning developers. For example, when Peiser Corporation and Jerome Frank Investments purchased a site in Dallas for a 160-unit apartment project, they had what seemed to be a comfortable 120-day period during which to close. The project was economically attractive only if the partnership could obtain permission to issue tax-exempt housing revenue bonds available for low- and moderate-income housing. Approval from the city council was needed to issue the bonds. Because housing revenue bonds were a new program for the city of Dallas, the city council kept postponing the hearing date to allow more time to work out the details of the bond program. Fortunately, the partnership had negotiated the right to extend the closing by up to three months at a cost of $5,000 per month, and the extra time allowed the partners to receive the necessary approvals. Options to extend the closing are especially important in hot markets where the seller may receive a higher offer from another buyer.

LOCATION AND NEIGHBORHOOD. It has often been said that the success of a real estate project depends on three factors: location, location, location. David Farmer of Keystone Development Advisors always asks some basic questions when looking at property: (1) How far is my child's school? (2) How far is my place of employment? (3) How far to get a cup of coffee? (4) How far to get a tank of gas? Location can be categorized by macrolocation factors and microlocation factors.[14] *Macrolocation* refers to a property's proximity to major urban nodes, *microlocation* to a property's immediate environs. A property's long-term value depends not only on its current macrolocation and microlocation but also on how they are changing over time.

Both macrolocation and microlocation influence multifamily residential development. Macrolocation determines what part of the city offers the best long-term potential to preserve and enhance value—proximity to downtown and suburban employment centers, major growth corridors, medical centers, regional shopping and entertainment, regional parks, and recreation. Microlocation determines how well a site is situated in its immediate neighborhood—access to freeways and arterial roads, quality of schools, parks, shopping, daycare, and health care facilities. Ideally, a site is visible from a major road yet situated to ensure privacy, a sense of security, and a low noise level.

The ability to foresee changes in the urban fabric before others is one of the hallmarks of the most successful developers. Whether their predictions are based on careful research, intuition, luck, or some combination of all three, successful developers understand the dynamics of location well enough to survive over the long term.

An important component of their success is tied to the fiscal health of the cities or suburbs where they build. If the level of public services in a city declines, real estate values decline as well. Successful developers understand how much they depend on the physical and financial health of the communities where they build—which is why so many of them are active in community affairs.

It takes a lifetime of practice to fully understand all the dimensions of location that affect real estate value over time. Trends in public investment, private investment, design, demographics, and personal

The Value of Focus Groups

For their first project in Barcelona, Jay Wyper, head of the London office for Hines, had heard that local residents refused to buy apartments above the 12th or 13th floor. Indeed, there were virtually no towers taller than this height. This negative viewpoint was a serious concern as Hines was planning to build new towers in its Diagonal Mar waterfront project that would be 22 stories. Through a series of focus groups, the firm discovered that the resistance to taller buildings resulted primarily from one issue: traditional building elevators were small and inadequate and frequently broke down, resulting in long stairway climbs. Hines, of course, knew how to provide proper elevator systems to towers, but the team was concerned that perceptions about taller buildings among older residents would be hard to change.

They therefore decided to completely alter the target market for the project by appealing to a younger, more active demographic group that would be less affected by the traditional bias. They also decided to challenge the tradition in Barcelona of having three-foot-wide (0.9 m) balconies. Wyper thought that larger balconies with enough room for people to eat outside would prove to be very popular. The subsequent success of Diagonal Mar is testimony to the value of the focus groups and the company's willingness to challenge traditional standards where it had reliable data to support the change.

Source: Gerald Hines, Jay Wyper, and Gregg Jones (Pelli Clarke Pelli Architects), presentation to the joint real estate clubs at Harvard Business School and Harvard Design School, Cambridge, Mass., November 29, 2011.

preferences are critical components of location. The rate of change in most American neighborhoods is very slow—often 30 to 50 years from peak to trough. It is much faster in poorly designed or poorly built neighborhoods, however, which often cycle downward within 15 to 20 years after they are built. On the other hand, some neighborhoods seem only to increase in value, often for reasons having to do with not only location but also the availability of shopping, open space, and other amenities, and ongoing investment by private owners to renovate and improve their properties.

The character of adjacent areas also affects the use of an undeveloped parcel. If adjoining areas are compatible, they can enhance the desirability of a proposed multifamily project. When they are deleterious or conflicting, developers should proceed very cautiously.

In recent decades, it has been common practice to locate higher-density multifamily projects closest to commercial and industrial districts. Doing so serves as a buffer to single-family areas and allows the multifamily residential areas to benefit from proximity to the higher-capacity streets and more intensive commercial and employment centers that help support higher population densities. In turn, cluster and attached housing is often located as a buffer between multifamily housing and lower-density single-family development.

More recently, however, these planning practices have come into question. Local governments are increasingly willing to view development proposals in terms of integrating rather than separating different uses, a point illustrated by the increasing flexibility of land use controls through the widespread acceptance of mixed-use zoning and concepts that have long been associated with good planning but popularized by the new urbanists. Such development plans permit the mixing of previously separated uses, provided they are properly designed. The result is often a more varied, efficient, and attractive development.

A good site for multifamily development is one that has positive synergy with surrounding land uses. For example, a multifamily site in an established or emerging suburban business core offers residents the convenience of employment and commercial services within easy driving or walking distances. A site in an area with several other successful apartment projects may also be more desirable than one that stands alone because of amenities, shopping, and mass transit that are attracted to concentrations of apartments. The

Alterra and Pravada at Grossmont Transit Center in La Mesa, California, take advantage of an excellent location. The projects together comprise 527 units, 80 of which are designated as affordable.

best locations are naturally costlier than those with detrimental surroundings but are usually worth the additional expense, particularly for high-end development. When selecting sites for multifamily uses, developers should look for sites with positive synergy with surrounding uses and avoid those where uses are not as compatible.

In considering compatibility, developers should be aware of potential liabilities that could be incurred from building residential units too close to conflicting uses. Proximity to large storage tanks of gas, oil, and other flammable material should be avoided. Fire protection must be considered in heavily wooded or fire-prone areas. Generally, protecting the public from such hazards rests with the municipality through its police powers (including zoning), but developers also need to protect themselves against possible liability by examining the potential conflicting uses near a given site.

SIZE AND SHAPE. The best size for a site varies according to local market conditions, including lease-up rates, acceptable unit densities, and preferred amenity packages. For example, suppose a developer wants to build a project that can be leased within 12 months from its completion. If 15 units can be leased per month (180 units per year) and the product being built has an average density of 24 units per acre (60/ha), then the ideal site would be 7.5 acres (3 ha), that is, 180 divided by 24. The size of a site is also influenced by property management considerations.

Multifamily Residential Development

Although the optimum number of units varies with each project, many developers consider 150 or 200 units the minimum number necessary to support a full-time on-site maintenance staff, and they look for sites that are large enough to accommodate that many units. In Los Angeles, where the availability and cost of land make it very difficult to assemble sites large enough for 200 units, developers often build several smaller complexes in a neighborhood that are run as a single project with shared property management and maintenance staffs.

Design options increase as the size of the site increases. A site that is too narrow prevents the inclusion of double-loaded parking or back-to-back units, which may increase efficiency and reduce costs.[15] A site that is too deep, however, may require a loop road or a turnaround for fire trucks. One should always draw a preliminary site plan to see how a site can be laid out before going hard on an earnest money contract.

Beginning developers should look for individual tracts that are large enough to accommodate the type of product they want to build. They should avoid tracts that require assembling several parcels under different ownership. The process of land assembly is virtually a development business in itself, offering its own risks and rewards. Problems in assembling tracts include multiple closings, extra legal costs, multiple lenders, and the possibility that key parcels will not close. Incomplete assembly carries costly penalties for developers, who may have to pay exorbitant prices for outparcels or spend extra money on design and construction to squeeze as many units as possible on a less than ideal site.

ACCESSIBILITY AND VISIBILITY. In evaluating a multifamily site's accessibility, a developer should ask several questions:

- How will prospective tenants approach the property? What will they see as they drive to the site that may make it more or less desirable? (In brochures and advertisements, developers often select the most attractive, although not necessarily the shortest, route to a project from the major roads.)
- How will visitors enter the property? Will they be able to turn left across traffic? Can approval for curb cuts and/or multiple entrances be obtained?
- Will the current roadway network support the additional traffic generated by a new development?
- Will it be difficult for residents to exit the project?

- How long will it take residents to travel to work, schools, shops, and recreational facilities?
- Is the site served by public transportation?
- Is road construction planned? If so, rentals will be severely impaired during the construction period.
- Are existing roads adequate for the type of development planned? (In general, high-density development requires collector and/or arterial street access, whereas lower-density development can be undertaken on smaller local streets.)

Visibility is critical for marketing and leasing. Prospective residents must be able to see a project to know that it is there. A developer can enhance a project's visibility in several ways, including using special design elements, special landscaping features, striking colors, off-site signage, flags, and nighttime lighting, especially of the frontage. The aim should be the creation of an appealing, distinctive project.

SITE CONDITIONS. Apartment and condominium development offers somewhat more latitude with respect to the physical characteristics of a site than do other types of development. A developer of multifamily residential projects is less constrained by slopes and by the size and shape of parcels because residential building pads tend to be smaller and more flexible than pads for office or industrial buildings. Residential building layouts can be manipulated to fit odd-shaped parcels. Nonetheless, a developer must still carefully evaluate every potential aspect of a site, including its slope, geology, soils, vegetation, and hydrology.

The Alexan Midtown is a 275-unit transit-oriented infill development in Sacramento, California. Parking is provided in a six-level, 414-space garage—a parking ratio of one space per bedroom.

DENNY BAILLY

Slope and Topography. Developers have always been attracted to hilltops and other places offering views. Moderately sloping sites are preferable to steep or flat land. Slopes create opportunities for more interesting design, such as split-level units and varied rooflines. They also help reduce the amount of excavation needed to provide structured parking in denser developments (densities greater than 35 units per acre [85/ha] usually require some form of parking structure).

Improvement costs, on the other hand, rise sharply on slopes greater than 10 percent. Retaining walls, special piers, and other foundations can add to the time and cost of construction. Further, some cities—San Diego, for example—have adopted hillside development ordinances that restrict development of steeply sloping sites. Allowable densities are reduced on slopes greater than 15 percent, and development is forbidden on slopes greater than 25 percent.[16] Flat land may also create additional expense. Sewers must slope downward to create flow; thus, pumping stations may be required if a site is entirely flat or if part of the site lies below the connection point to the city sewer line.

Geology, Hydrology, and Soils. In earthquake-prone areas, a geologic survey is essential. If a site is crossed by fault lines, it may be unbuildable. The same is true of a site in an area with abandoned subterranean mines. Even though building around the fault line or mine may be possible, obtaining insurance may be impossible. Moreover, proximity to a fault line creates an intractable marketing problem.

If a site contains, or borders on, a creek or wetlands area, a floodplain study must be conducted. Areas that are wet only part of the year may be considered vernal pools, which may be protected under the North American Wetlands Conservation Act of 1989.[17] Standing water on a site may also indicate the presence of an underground stream, which must be located because some portion of the site will almost certainly be unbuildable. A developer should be able to obtain a rough approximation of how much land lies in the floodplain or wetlands area by hiring a civil engineer and ecologist/biologist who has done work in the area.

Like floodplains, soil conditions are problematic. Even if a site looks clean, a developer should always hire a geologist to take soil samples of a site before purchasing it. Geologists usually take at least one core sample near each corner of a property and one or more in the center to determine what type of soil is present, its viscosity, its plasticity, its bearing capacity, and the depth of the water table and underlying bedrock. Good soil like sandy loam is moderately pervious to water. Clay soils, however, expand and contract with water, which may cause foundations to crack. Impervious soils cause increased water runoff. If rock is located near the surface of a site, excavation may cost significantly more than for a site with deep soil.

Vegetation. Plant cover provides useful information about soil and weather conditions. Red maple, alder, hemlock, and willow indicate wet ground that is poorly drained, whereas pitch pine and scrub oak are signs of dry land and of good drainage.

Efforts should be made to preserve mature trees. Large, healthy trees face several dangers. Construction activity under a tree can compact the soil and may kill the tree. Builders often do not like saving trees because it makes their work more time-consuming and costly. Trees often die during construction because of chemical poisoning. Even if they survive construction, they often die later because their root systems have been disturbed or because the amount of water they receive has been altered. A developer should consult a tree surgeon about saving trees and should clearly mark and place a protective barrier around trees that are to be preserved.

Other forms of vegetation may also require special handling. Grasslands, particularly in coastal areas, are a crucial component of erosion control. Many kinds of grasses, vines, shrubs, and wildflowers provide wildlife habitats or are included on the endangered species lists, and their preservation becomes a legal issue.

Stormwater. In the past, stormwater runoff has been handled by the most convenient method possible: the rapid disposal of surface water through closed, manmade systems. Stormwater runoff has often been mismanaged under this philosophy, aggravating the velocity and volume of runoff problems downstream and increasing the pollution of local streams. Potential legal issues concerning the effects of stormwater management on adjacent properties during and after construction have led many jurisdictions to adopt stormwater management standards restricting the runoff's quantity and velocity after development to no more than predevelopment levels. Many areas also require filtration or treatment of stormwater before its release. Detention and filtration ponds are common in stormwater management systems, the former designed to slow down stormwater runoff and the latter designed to filter stormwater through layers of materials, such as sand and gravel to remove pollutants.

The preparation of a functional and aesthetic stormwater runoff plan requires coordination among the project's architects, engineers, planners, and landscape architects. Much of the runoff can be handled through passive design elements, including proper grading, swales, and landscaping materials, rather than engineering systems. Such considerations need to be part of the early design plan. Recent trends in stormwater management encourage eliminating large stormwater ponds in favor of smaller "rain gardens" located throughout the development. Local stormwater management regulations may vary by state or locality.

Existing Buildings. In most cities, developers must receive approval to demolish any structures on a site. Historic structures are protected, but even nonhistoric buildings usually require demolition permits. Before purchasing a site for major renovation or redevelopment, developers should make certain that they can evict the current tenants. Eviction can take a long time—often four to six months or more—and can be expensive, especially if relocation assistance is required from the developer. In extreme cases, the developer may be required to find or build the tenant a comparable unit.

ENVIRONMENTAL ISSUES. Environmental due diligence is required now for every development site (see chapter 3). A preliminary Phase I environmental site assessment (ESA), performed for as little as $1,000 to $3,000, gives the developer a history of the property and indicates the need for any further investigation. Every potential lender requires at least a Phase I ESA report, so a standard part of purchase contracts is that the offer is subject to the buyer's determination that no significant environmental problems exist.

Many urban infill sites have at least one environmental issue. In most cases, no remediation is necessary, but if dirt must be removed or, in the worst case, groundwater is contaminated, cleanup costs can be enormous. The seller is responsible for cleanup, but once the buyer has closed, he becomes part of the chain of title and may be liable in the future. In any case, the cleanup must be completed before lenders will finance new construction. Because environmental problems are so prevalent, lenders seek environmental insurance policies and guarantees from companies to indemnify them from problems. The insurance can be costly, but it has made many sites developable that were not so before.[18]

EASEMENTS AND COVENANTS. An easement is one party's right to use the property of another. The land for whose benefit the easement is created is called the *dominant tenement*. The land that is burdened or used is called the *servient tenement*. Generally, unless easements are created with a specific termination date, they survive indefinitely. Only the beneficiary of the easement—the dominant tenement—can extinguish them. Subsequent owners of property that have existing easements may have to purchase the easement back from the current beneficiaries.

Protective covenants, also called *deed restrictions*, are private restrictions that *run with the land*; that is, once created, they remain in force for all future buyers or heirs. Deed restrictions may be created by a property owner at any time. Once created, however, they remain in force unless all parties subject to the covenants agree to remove them. Developers usually establish deed restrictions at the time they subdivide, or *plat*, a property. Some covenants expire automatically after a number of years under state statute as in Texas and Florida, but others never expire. To be enforceable, covenants must usually be filed with the county recorder and thus will appear in a title search.

Developers must carefully review any and all deed restrictions, for deed restrictions can kill a project even after developers have invested many months of time and money. In Dallas, for example, one case involved a subdivision that still had single-family-only restrictions in place despite the presence of many nonresidential uses. A developer bought property in that subdivision, assuming that the existing nonresidential uses effectively voided the restrictions. Although the developer may have been able to overturn the restrictions in court, he found that no bank would lend him money on a site that had restrictions against the intended use.

UTILITIES. Water, sanitary and storm sewers, electricity, gas, and other services are critical factors in site selection. Before purchasing a site, a developer should always confirm that services not only are nearby but also have available capacity. It is not unusual, for instance, for a major waterline to run adjacent to a property but be unavailable to that property because the line's capacity is already committed or because the city is concerned about a loss in water pressure. To verify that service is available, a developer should never simply take the word of the land seller and should instead visit the appropriate city departments or retain a civil engineer to do so.

Water and sanitary sewer services are the most costly utilities to bring in from off site. When water and sanitary lines must be brought in, the developer should undertake the work rather than wait for the city or utility company to do it to ensure that the work is performed concurrently with the project. Electricity, gas, and telephone services are usually provided by private utility companies. Except for remote sites, those utility companies usually provide service to the site at no cost to the developer since they recover their investment through charges to the end user. Each locality has its own fee structure and method of handling utility services.

A developer should ask several questions about utilities:

- How long will it take to obtain service?
- How much will it cost?
- When is payment due?
- When does one have to apply for service?
- Are public hearings involved (they may cause delays and increase the political risk)?
- Is the provision of service subject to any potential moratoriums?
- Are easements needed from any other property owners before services can be obtained?
- Is the capacity of the service adequate?

Some municipalities with scarce water have responded by imposing high water hookup fees on residential building permits. Others have imposed strict requirements for conserving water, flow-restricting devices on plumbing features, installation of drought-tolerant landscaping, and, in some extreme circumstances, partial or total moratoriums on development until new water supplies are available. Developers should check the availability of water at a site and, if it appears that supplies are limited, understand fully what will be required before a supply can be hooked up to a site.

REGULATORY ISSUES. The regulatory process has become increasingly difficult, and the ability to secure the necessary regulatory approvals has become the developer's primary concern in many communities. The increasing complexity of development regulation has created a whole new field of development—developers who bear the risk of obtaining necessary approvals and entitlements (see chapter 3) and then sell the fully entitled land to another developer to build out the property. Developers often receive the highest return on their investment from successfully obtaining entitlements because they incur the highest risk.

Even where land is appropriately zoned, no guarantee exists that developers will be able to build what they want to build. In some jurisdictions, additional hurdles must be overcome, such as approvals from design review boards and neighborhood planning committees. Setback, parking, environmental, air quality, and fire code regulations affect the density that developers can achieve on a parcel, irrespective of the allowable density under the zoning.

The regulatory process is described more fully in chapter 3. The following issues arise frequently with multifamily development.

Zoning. Zoning determines the building envelope and the density for a site. Specific issues that are usually covered in the zoning code include the number of units allowed, parking requirements, height limitations, setback restrictions, floor/area ratios, and unit size requirements. Some zoning codes give actual density constraints, for instance, up to 24 units per acre (60/ha), whereas others stipulate minimum land area per unit, such as 1,500 square feet (140 m²) of land per unit. The other major zoning constraint for apartments is parking. A common requirement is one parking space per bedroom (up to two spaces for a three-bedroom apartment) plus spaces for visitors. A developer may petition to change the zoning or obtain a variance, but it is often a long and arduous process, especially if higher densities are involved.

Many suburbs are very hostile to multifamily housing, and NIMBYism (the not-in-my-backyard syndrome) tends to focus more on multifamily development than on any other product type. Jerome Frank, Jr., advises, "For a beginning developer, it's very difficult—unless the land is already zoned—to find and develop a piece of property that needs rezoning. Find land that's already zoned and pay for the zoning."[19] Marvin Finger adds, "Even extremely low-density upscale developments represent nothing but evil to the surrounding single-family owners. To overcome this perception, you have to employ the premier professional, who would probably be an attorney, to negotiate your case in that neighborhood. It cannot be done in house."[20]

Developer Ken Hughes advises beginning developers to avoid landmarks commissions for historic structures: "In Texas, if you go through a landmarks commission review process, there is no opportunity for appeal. It is not territory for the inexperienced developer." He adds, "We do not like to build replicative architecture on infill lots in historic districts. If we are interested in building a more contemporary structure,

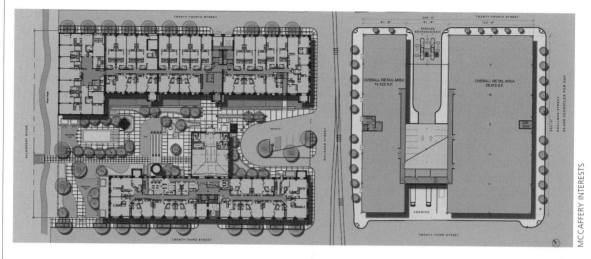

MCCAFFERY INTERESTS

The Cork Factory is a renovation of an abandoned factory in downtown Pittsburgh. The redevelopment includes 297 apartments, ground-level retail space, and 427 parking spaces.

we can avoid the landmarks commission by going directly to the planning and zoning board."[21]

Mixed-Use and Transit-Oriented Development. Two areas where cities tend to be more favorably inclined toward higher-density development are near transit stations and close-in neighborhoods where they are favoring mixed-use development. Many cities have *transit-oriented development (TOD) overlay districts* where they encourage apartments and higher-density development. The California Department of Transportation recommends that communities establish minimum zoning densities in TODs that are equal to the maximum density the market will support.[22] Projects within TODs typically have lower parking requirements (maximum one per unit) and receive preferential treatment for public approvals. Ken Hughes cautions, however, "Most transit authorities do not know how to acquire land or develop it; therefore, most stations are not amenable to higher-density development. Between 30 and 40 stations will be opening in the Dallas area, but only about five or six of those are appropriate for high-density development." Hughes adds, "People view no change as preferable to better change if they do not know how to define 'better.' The developer must clearly know what makes projects work; people recognize this even if they don't know why they work. The developer is the 'imagineer' who must understand what people respond to emotionally even if they cannot identify it."[23]

Fire Codes. Fire codes have particular importance for residential construction because residential buildings

are usually wood frame and therefore especially prone to the risk of fire. Fire codes determine the number of stairways each unit requires as well as the maximum distance each unit must be from a fire hydrant. The codes directly affect the number of units that can be placed on a site as well as the cost of building them.

Many communities encourage developers to install fire sprinklers in their apartment projects by imposing stringent requirements on wood-frame construction without sprinkler systems. Beginning developers should consult architects who are familiar with local fire codes and the type of product under consideration to determine the best way to meet fire regulations. Even if fire sprinklers are not required by code, it is advisable to install them. The complex will be more competitive when it comes time to sell it and insurance costs will likely be lower.

Rent Control. Developers considering multifamily rental housing projects must consider the degree of rent control prevailing in the area and local politicians' general attitudes about rent control. Rent control ordinances often restrict potential developers' and

166

Professional Real Estate Development

investors' ability to obtain the rent required to make the project feasible.

Apart from the obvious economic disadvantages of rent control that restricts rent increases, developers find financing harder to obtain for projects in communities with rent control. Rent control laws differ dramatically from community to community. Most rent control laws exempt new projects. Many laws also allow the landlord to raise rents to market rates when a tenant moves out (called *vacancy decontrol*). Cities that prohibit vacancy decontrol also typically prohibit (or make it very onerous to remove) any rental units from the housing stock for conversion to condominiums. The threat of rent control can hurt developers almost as much as its enactment. Even if existing rent control regulations exempt new buildings, the possibility of a future referendum or a vote by the city council to place new buildings under rent control creates uncertainty about one's ability to raise rents. This uncertainty makes it more difficult for developers to raise the necessary equity and debt financing at favorable rates.

Building Codes. Building codes are legal documents that set minimum requirements for sanitary facilities, electrical work, lighting, ventilation, construction, building materials, fire safety, plumbing, and energy conservation. They are local laws that vary from city to city. The United States has no uniform building code, but one of four separate model codes is generally used as the basis for a municipality's set of regulations. Although the trend is toward greater uniformity, developers must still deal with a diverse set of codes that is often applied inconsistently.

A major problem for developers is that governments do not accept responsibility for review of the plans. Although one department may review and stamp a plan *approved*, the local government's field inspectors, who exercise considerable control over a project, often interpret the codes differently and do not advance an opinion before construction. To make the process of obtaining permits as smooth as possible, developers should work with local development professionals and consultants. Any questions about interpreting the local building code should be addressed as early as possible in meetings with those in the building department who check plans. During construction, it is helpful for the developer to build a strong working relationship with code enforcement officials—in particular, building inspectors.

Condominium Conversions. Condominium conversions—the conversion of rental units to for-sale units—provide an attractive entry point for beginning developers because seller financing is often available. The development process is shorter and less risky than in other types of multifamily residential development, and the amount of money developers must raise is also usually smaller. The major risk involves the inability to handle interest-carry during an extended sales period and cost overruns for renovation expenses to upgrade the units. Condo conversions tend to occur in waves. Beginning developers should be wary of the high number of units available for conversion to condominiums from apartments built during the period leading up to the financial crisis.

Conversions are subject to special regulations in many communities. Concerns about preserving their rental housing stock have caused cities such as New York and San Francisco to pass laws that limit or complicate condominium conversion. Before entering the conversion business, developers should carefully investigate local procedures, which can be time-consuming and intricate. The advice of a local attorney who specializes in condominium conversion is critical and should be sought before developers commit to a project.

Developers should be wary of litigation over construction defects. Such litigation resulted in frenzied activity in California in the 1990s among attorneys who organized condominium associations to sue their developers before a ten-year time limit on construction lawsuits expired, resulting in a dramatic decrease in new condominium construction. Changes in liability laws combined with tighter construction supervision have restored condominium construction activity somewhat, but concerns about litigation still overshadow the market. Savvy developers employ an inspector to photograph the project in great detail during construction. Not only does this documentation help protect the developer against construction defect litigation but it also makes the contractor more conscientious, knowing that his work will be inspected before it is covered up.

Exactions and Impact Fees. To recover what is perceived as the public cost of new development, local ordinances often require developers to dedicate land, improvements, or fees as a condition of approval. In the past, such dedications were primarily for the basic infrastructure necessary to serve the development site, such as on-site roads and utilities. Now, however, dedications or exactions are often required for off-site improvements above and beyond the immediate infrastructure needed for a development site, including improvements to arterial streets, flood-control facilities, sewage treatment plants, schools and parks, fire and police stations, open space, or almost any other public necessity.[24] Despite many alternatives for financing capital improvements, including taxes, general obligation bonds, revenue bonds, tax increment financing, user charges, special assessments, and special districts, the trend has been toward more widespread use of exactions by local governments.[25]

Some local governments have adopted standards for exactions, whereas others determine exactions project by project, thereby complicating a developer's ability to predetermine a project's feasibility. When no standards exist to measure exactions, developers can use exactions levied on similar developments in the area to estimate exactions for a feasibility analysis.

In small developments, which characterize the lion's share of multifamily housing developments, exactions will more likely be made through impact fees rather than dedication of land and infrastructure improvements. A requirement for dedication of parks, schools, and other public facilities would be too great a burden for a small site. Instead, fees are combined with those obtained from other small developments to provide the necessary public improvements at some off-site location. A 2008 national survey found that for apartments, impact fees averaged $7,092 per unit, about $4,200 lower than for single-family units. The largest fees were for roads, water, wastewater, parks, and schools. Other impact fee categories included drainage, library, fire, police, and general government.[26]

FINANCIAL FEASIBILITY ANALYSIS

The next important step in feasibility analysis is financial feasibility. In essence, this analysis is the one lenders require to ensure that the project will live up to its performance expectations. How one analyzes the financial feasibility of apartments is similar to the process used for all income property. The steps of financial analysis begin with a simple back-of-the-envelope capitalization and end with a multiyear discounted cash flow analysis that includes returns to investors or joint venture partners.

Evaluating financial feasibility for all income property development involves several stages of analysis, each more detailed than the previous one, from land purchase to a final go/no-go decision on a property. How much analysis is necessary before purchasing land? Experienced developers working in their own area know from experience what they can spend. They know the local market and therefore know when they see a good deal.

Beginning developers, however, must overcome several handicaps:

- lack of experience in determining a workable price;
- lack of visibility in the brokerage community, hence hearing about deals only after larger players have rejected them; and
- less staying power, so they must be more careful about which deals to pursue.

Sophisticated developers perform a sequence of financial analyses for income properties, starting with simple capitalization analysis and ending with monthly cash flow analysis of the development period. The main difficulty in terms of financial feasibility studies is understanding what type of analysis is appropriate at what stage. Too much detail too early is a waste of time and money. Too little detail gives insufficient information on which to base informed decisions. Analysis of any *income property* (as distinct from *for-sale property* discussed in chapter 3) involves five stages:

- **Stage 1** (the pro forma statement)—Simple capitalization of pro forma net operating income (NOI) when it reaches stabilization;
- **Stage 2**—Discounted cash flow (DCF) analysis of annual cash flows during stabilized cash flows of the operating period;
- **Stage 3**—Combined analysis of the development and operating periods;
- **Stage 4**—Monthly cash flows during the development period; and
- **Stage 5**—DCF analysis for investors.

FIGURE 4-2 | The Development Period and the Operating Period

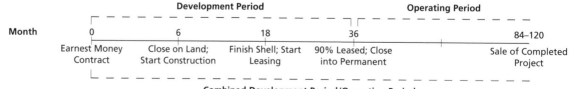

This chapter concentrates on Stages 1, 2, and 3, and a before-tax version of Stage 5.[27] The spreadsheets used as examples are from West River Commons in Minneapolis, Minnesota. A narrative describing this project appears at the end of this chapter. Of all the stages of analysis, Stage 2 is the most important. It is known by various names, including *discounted cash flow analysis*, *multiperiod cash flow analysis*, and *justified investment price analysis*. Appraisers do a form of Stage 2 analysis when they compute the unleveraged returns on a building from the time of stabilized occupancy to final sale in seven or ten years.[28]

It is helpful to distinguish the development period from the operating period (figure 4-2). The development period runs from the time the developer purchases the land through lease-up of the property. Although the operating period begins when the property is put into service, appraisers and lenders typically evaluate the property from the time it reaches stabilized occupancy, normally 90 or 95 percent (5–10 percent vacant). This period is the time that the permanent mortgage is typically funded (although in some cases, the permanent mortgage may be funded in stages). The operating period ends when the property is sold. Stage 2 analysis is used to evaluate this operating period. It is the developer's version of

the architect's sketch pad. Just as the architect draws many versions of a building before settling on the final design, the developer goes through many iterations of Stage 2 analysis as he obtains better information. For the first iteration, rents, expenses, costs, and other assumptions are crude estimates based on cursory evaluation. By the time developers are ready to commit to the earnest money contract (that is, remove any contingencies that may allow them to get back the full purchase deposit on the land), they should have the best information possible about the property's expected performance. This information forms the basis for computing expected returns to the developer and investors—assuming the property is purchased at the given price. If the property is to be built, then the total estimated project cost from inception to stabilized occupancy is used instead of the purchase price.

The stages of analysis correspond to major hurdles in the course of financing a project. Stage 1 is the developer's first cursory analysis based on simple pro forma income and cost estimates. Stage 2 justifies the overall value of the investment as an operating real estate venture and is given to mortgage brokers and lenders who will provide permanent financing. Stage 3 gives the developer a picture of the overall development, from inception through final sale. Stage

FIGURE 4-3a | STAGE 1a: Rental and Sales Revenue Summary

Apartment Unit Types	No. of Units	Rent/Ft²	Area/ Unit (ft²)	Total Ft²	Rent/ Month/Unit	Total Annual Rent
1 Bedroom, 1 Bath	10	$1.13	800	8,000	$900	$108,000
1 Bedroom, 1.5 Bath	27	$1.10	956	25,800	$1,053	$341,100
2 Bedroom, 1 Bath	8	$1.03	1,138	9,100	$1,169	$112,200
2 Bedroom, 2 Bath	6	$1.21	1,450	8,700	$1,750	$126,000
2 Bedroom, 2 Bath, Den	2	$1.02	2,450	4,900	$2,495	$59,880
Total Apartment Rental Revenue	53	$1.10	1,066	56,500	$1,175	$747,180
Total Retail Rental Revenue	4	$1.31	1,981	7,925	$2,592	$124,437
Other Rental Revenue[a]						$18,300
Other Miscellaneous Revenue[b]						$2,400
Total Apartment Rental Revenue	57	$1.15	1,130	64,425	$3,767	$892,317
Retail Tenants						
Restaurant	3	$1.25	2,333	6,998	$2,916	$104,970
Dry Cleaners	1	$1.75	927	927	$1,622	$19,467
Total Retail Rental Revenue	4	$1.31	1,981	7,925	$2,592	$124,437
Condominium Homes						
Condominium Homes	3	$162.50	2,000	6,000	$325,000	$975,000
Total Sales Revenue	3	$162.50	2,000	6,000	$325,000	$975,000

[a]Other Rental Revenue includes additional revenue derived from leasing space at the property. Examples of Other Rental Revenue include leases for parking, rooftop telecommunication devices, storage space, and billboards.
[b]Other Miscellaneous Revenue includes additional revenue as a result of conducting daily business activities. Examples of Other Miscellaneous Revenue include late fees and penalties, forfeiture of deposits, and lost-key fees. Specific to this case, miscellaneous revenue from participation in the tax increment financing program accounts for the majority of the line item amount.

4 is given to the construction lender in support of the estimated construction loan required and interest reserves during construction and lease-up. Stage 5 is given to potential investors in support of the returns they will receive if they invest in the property under a specific deal structure.

STAGE 1—SIMPLE CAPITALIZATION. Figures 4-3 to 4-9 illustrate the stages of analysis for West River Commons, a new 75,000-square-foot (7,000 m²) mixed-use project by the Lander Group in Minneapolis. The project has 53 rental apartments, three for-sale townhouses, and 8,000 square feet (743 m²) of retail space. (See the West River Commons case study at the end of this chapter.) It should be noted that a mixed-use project involving both income-producing uses (rental apartments and retail) and for-sale uses (townhouses) significantly complicates the analysis compared with an apartment analysis by itself. The Stage 1 analysis consists of five subparts beginning with the rental summary, loan computation, and development cost, and ending with the simple return computations.

Stage 1a—Rental and Sales Revenue Summary. Stage 1 analysis is used to develop the two simple return measures common to all income properties—overall capitalization rates and cash-on-cash returns. To compute these ratios, begin by projecting NOI, project development costs, and leverage (maximum mortgage amount) for the proposed project. Figure 4-3a shows the rental and sales revenue summary. For West River Commons, the 53 apartment units range in rent from $900 to $2,500. Rents per square foot typically fall as unit size increases, although in this case the two bedroom/two bath units have the highest rents per square foot. Rent on retail space is $1.31 per square foot ($14/m²) per month. The three condominium units sell for $325,000 each, or $162.50 per square foot ($1,750/m²) for 2,000 square feet (186 m²).

FIGURE 4-3b | STAGE 1b: Pro Forma NOI

	Factor		Annual Revenue/Cost
Revenue			
Gross Potential Revenue[a]			$892,317
Less: Vacancy	5.00%		($44,616)
Less: Bad Debt	0.50%		($4,462)
Effective Gross Revenue			**$843,240**
Expenses[b]			
Property Management	3.00%	of Effective Gross Revenue	$25,297
Controllable Costs[c]	$1,950	per unit	$103,350
Real Estate Taxes	1.36%	of estimated total project cost	$135,000
Insurance	$400	per unit	$21,200
Utilities	$500	per unit	$26,500
Replacement Reserve	$150	per unit	$7,950
Total Expenses			**$319,297**
Net Operating Income			**$523,942**

[a]Gross Potential Revenue is provided by the prior Rental and Sales Revenue Summary exhibit. Vacancy and Bad Debt are customary charges against gross revenue.

[b]Customary expense items have been shown. In the pro forma, per-unit expense items are applied against 53 units. For expenses based on project cost, the total project cost used to estimate expenses is $9,900,000, which accounts for the apartment and retail portions only before application of any subsidies.

[c]Controllable Costs typically include salary, administrative, marketing, and maintenance expenses.

FIGURE 4-3c | STAGE 1c: Maximum Debt Calculation

Pro Forma Net Operating Income (NOI) and Value	
Pro Forma NOI[a]	$523,942
Capitalization Rate	6.00%
Value of Income Property Only (NOI/Cap Rate)	$8,732,373
Loan Terms	
Interest Rate[b]	5.75%
Amortization (years)	30
Debt Based on Loan to Value (LTV)	
Maximum LTV Ratio[b]	75.00%
Maximum Loan Based on LTV for Income Property	$6,549,280
Using Debt Coverage Ratio (DCR)	
Monthly NOI	$43,662
Maximum DCR	1.20
Maximum Monthly Payment (NOI/DCR/12)	$36,385
Maximum Loan Based on DCR for Income Property	$6,234,849
Maximum Loan (Lesser of LTV or DCR Result)	
Maximum Loan for Income Property[c]	$6,234,849
Add: Loan for For-Sale Property[d]	$682,500
Total Initial Project Debt	$6,917,349

[a]The pro forma NOI figure is provided by the prior eponymous exhibit and does not include any revenues from the condominiums.

[b]The assumed interest rate and loan-to-value reflect the availability of financing that was current at the time of the project.

[c]In the typical valuation of pure income properties, the maximum debt calculation ends with selecting the lesser of two loan values, based on LTV or DCR.

[d]It is assumed that an additional loan in the amount equal to 70 percent of the condominium sales revenue is provided by the construction loan lender.

FIGURE 4-3d | STAGE 1d: Development Costs

		Gross	Total Usable	Apartments and Retail	For-Sale Condominiums
1	Number of Units	60	60	57	3
2	Square Footage	75,696	70,425	64,425	6,000
3	Percentage of Total Square Footage		100	91	9
4	**Development Costs**[a]				
5	Land	$16.53 per gross ft^2	$1,251,500	$1,144,876	$106,624
6	Land Carry[b]	3.65% rate for 12 months	27,418	25,082	2,336
7	Approval Fees	$1.17 per gross ft^2	88,800	81,235	7,565
8	Environmental Remediation	$1.46 per gross ft^2	110,574	101,153	9,421
9	Construction Hard Cost	$98.77 per gross ft^2	7,476,741	6,839,745	636,996
10	Soft Costs:				
11	Architecture & Engineering	5.06% of hard cost	378,000	345,796	32,204
12	Legal & Other Fees	$228,910 (estimate)	228,910	209,408	19,502
13	Appraisal & Title	$10,883 (estimate)	10,883	9,956	927
14	Marketing	$1,225 per total units	73,500	67,238	6,262
15	Taxes during Construction	$50,000 (estimate)	50,000	45,740	4,260
16	Insurance during Construction	$19,800 (estimate)	19,800	18,113	1,687
17	Total Soft Costs		761,093	696,250	64,843
18	Contingency	2.82% of hard cost	210,825	192,864	17,962
19	**Total Development Cost before Interest and Operating Reserve**		**$9,926,951**	**$9,081,205**	**$845,747**
20	**Estimate of Construction Interest**[c]				
21	Construction Loan	$6,917,349			
22	Construction Interest	12.00%			
23	Construction Period (months)	12			
24	Average Draw	65.00%			
25	Estimated Construction Loan Interest		539,553	493,585	45,968
26	**Total Project Cost before Operating Reserve**		**$10,466,505**	**$9,574,790**	**$891,715**
27	**Estimate of Operating Reserve**[d]				
28	Gross Potential Rent (monthly)	$74,360			
29	Lease-Up Period (months until stabilization)	6.0			
30	Average Occupancy during Lease-Up	65%			
31	Estimated Rent during Lease-Up		$290,003		
32	Estimated Operating Expenses during Lease-Up		159,649		
33	NOI during Lease-Up		130,354		
34	Construction Interest during Lease-Up		415,041		
35	First-Year Operating Reserve Required		284,687	260,432	24,254
36	**Total Project Costs**		**$10,751,191**	**$9,835,222**	**$915,969**
37	Less: Development Cost Subsidies[e]		(2,476,984)	(2,415,812)	(61,171)
38	**Total Project Costs after Subsidies**		**$8,274,208**	**$7,419,410**	**$854,798**

[a]The following outline of development costs include customary expenses.

[b]Land Carry refers to interest paid to the land seller as part of the land purchase contract. The interest rate is applied to the negotiated purchase price less any upfront paid amounts. Specific to this case, $500,000 was paid to the seller as part of the initial deposit.

[c]This calculation is a preliminary estimate of interest during construction and reflects the availability of then-current market rate construction financing. A more accurate estimate will be made as part of the Stage 3 analysis and an even more accurate estimate would be appropriate for a Stage 4 analysis (not shown).

[d]Operating Reserve represents the amount that will be required to cover operating costs and debt service before the project reaches break-even occupancy. Customarily, the Operating Reserve is based on the average occupancy during the term in which the property leases up to full occupancy. Specific to this case, 30 percent of the units were preleased, hence the average occupancy is 65 percent ((30%+100%)/2). Additionally, based on the details of the case, the project was expected to be fully leased within six months and in fact did achieve that goal.

[e]Specific to this case, several local and federal subsidies were procured to finance the development of the project. Subsidies include the tax increment financing (TIF) subsidy, low-income housing tax credit (LIHTC) funds, a brownfield grant, a HUD Home grant, and a community development block grant (CDBG). The present value of these subsidies has been deducted from the total project cost as a means to simplify the overall setup of the analysis since project financing is outside the scope of this chapter. Also, due to the varying nature of the subsidies, the subsidies are prorated based on the applicable portion of the project and not by square footage of the project as previously done for other development costs.

Stage 1b—Pro Forma NOI. The first step is to create a pro forma statement that estimates rents and expenses for the stabilized project. Inputs include the types and sizes of apartments to be built and market rents for the apartments (see figure 4-3b). The other needed inputs are estimated vacancy rate and operating expenses. Both income and expense estimates should reflect local conditions and any specific features of the project. Income and expenses should reflect conditions as they will be at the time that leasing begins; for example, if the project is expected to require a year to design and build, rents and expenses should be projected as of a year from now. For West River Commons, the pro forma indicates total income of $843,240 and NOI of $523,942 (see figure 4-3b).

Stage 1c—Maximum Debt Calculation. The project's pro forma NOI is the basis for determining the size of the permanent mortgage for the project. Lenders use two common criteria to determine the maximum loan amount: debt coverage ratio (DCR) and loan-to-value (LTV) ratio. The maximum loan amount is the lesser of the resulting amounts computed by the two methods.

The debt coverage ratio is a tool used to measure the financial risk of an investment. It is calculated by dividing NOI by the debt service for the project. A DCR of 1.0 means that NOI equals the debt service for the project. For income-producing properties, most lenders require a DCR of at least 1.2. The DCR represents the cushion by which the NOI could fall before the property had insufficient cash flow to pay the debt service on the mortgage. The greater the cushion, the less risk of default. Lenders prefer as much cushion as they can get. Developers prefer more leverage (to obtain as large a mortgage as they can get) because it reduces the requirement for equity.

The NOI can be divided directly by the DCR to determine the maximum monthly mortgage payment that can be assumed for the loan. Given the lender's requirements for amortization and interest, it is then possible to calculate the maximum loan that could be serviced by the project's income, less the extra coverage. In this case, a DCR of 1.2 would allow monthly payments of $36,385 (monthly NOI divided by 1.2). Assuming an interest rate of 5.75 percent and 30-year amortization, $6,234,849 is the maximum loan a lender would allow (the present value of $36,385 for the given rate of interest and term (months):

$$PV\ (PMT = 36{,}385,\ i = 5.75/12,\ n = 30 \times 12)$$

To establish the maximum loan available using the LTV ratio, it is necessary to first determine the project's value, which is calculated by applying a capitalization rate to the pro forma NOI. The capitalization rate is determined by the market and by the recent selling price of similar properties. It reflects the relationship between a property's income and its value. The lender ultimately requires an appraisal to verify the income and assumptions about the capitalization rate used to establish the value. The value is then multiplied by the LTV ratio to determine the maximum loan amount. In this case, a capitalization rate of 6 percent yields a value of $8,732,373. With an assumed maximum LTV ratio of 75 percent, the most the lender will lend under the LTV constraint is $6,549,280.

Lenders typically look at both criteria when underwriting a loan and use the more restrictive one. When interest rates are low, LTV tends to be more restrictive, and when interest rates are high, DCR tends to be more restrictive. In this example, DCR is more restrictive because the LTV ratio at 75 percent is generous (LTVs of 60–70 percent are common in times of tighter money), so the maximum loan on the property would be $6,234,849 (see figure 4-3c).

Stage 1d—Development Costs. Development costs are the other part of the equation needed to evaluate a project's feasibility. An overall cost estimate for the project must be calculated. It should include the cost of acquiring the site, construction costs, and soft costs, such as legal and accounting fees, architecture and engineering, and contingencies. In addition, it should include financing costs during construction as well as interest and operating losses until the property reaches stabilized occupancy and the permanent mortgage is funded (taking out

FIGURE 4-3d(a) | Calculating the Average Occupancy Rate

If lease-up is expected to take 16 months to reach 95 percent occupancy, then the average occupancy rate for each year is computed thus:

Year 1: $\frac{12\ months}{16\ months} \times 95\% \div 2 = 35.6\%$

Year 2: $\frac{(71.25\% + 95\%)}{2} = 83.1\% \times \frac{4\ months}{12\ months} = 27.7\%$

$95\% \times \frac{8\ months}{12\ months} = 63.3\%$

Average occupancy for Year 2 = 91%

the construction loan). Eventually, the developer will have firm cost bids for building the project. The initial financial feasibility analysis, however, relies on the developer's experience from other similar projects and information provided by contractors and consultants.

The costs should also include the developer's overhead and costs associated with the initial marketing and lease-up of the project. As an initial rough estimate, interest costs can be approximated by assuming an average draw and length of the loan. The operating reserve during lease-up can be approximated by assuming a lease-up period and computing the rent lost from vacancies during that time. Figure 4-3d shows total development costs for West River Commons before interest and lease-up of $9,926,951. With estimated interest during construction of $539,553 and an operating reserve during lease-up of $284,687, project costs total $10,751,191. West River Commons receives a number of subsidies, including tax increment financing and low-income housing tax credits (see figure 4-3d, footnote e).

If the lease-up is expected to take more than one year, figure 4-3d(a) shows how to estimate average occupancy for Years 1 and 2. If, for example, a 16-month lease-up is anticipated for the project to reach 95 percent occupancy, then the average occupancy rate would be 35.6 percent during the first year and 91 percent during the second year. Thereafter, it would be 95 percent. Subtracting the average occupancy rate for each year from 100 percent produces the average vacancy rate—in this case, 64.4 percent (100 minus 35.6) and 8.96 percent (100 minus 91.04) for the first and second years, respectively.

Stage 1e—Simple Ratios. Stage 1 analysis is sometimes called a *back-of-the-envelope analysis* because the simple returns can literally be computed on the back of an envelope. Still, the overall return (NOI divided by total project cost) and cash-on-cash return (cash flow after debt service divided by equity) are the two most commonly cited measures of return in the industry for income property. For an apartment project, cash-on-cash returns in excess of 10 percent are desirable although initial cash-on-cash returns are often in the 7 percent range. As inflation picks up, the initial cash-on-cash return may go down even lower as developers look to the future for higher cash flows and profit from sale of the complex. It is important to separate the income property from the for-sale condominiums. Consequently, we deduct the cost of the condominiums to determine the net cost of the rental apartments. For West River Commons, the overall return is 7.1 percent ($523,942 ÷ $7,419,410). The cash-on-cash return is 7.4 percent ($87,324 ÷ $1,184,560; see figure 4-3e). Both of these returns are on the low side, but the combination of the subsidies and the for-sale condominiums makes the project more attractive. Figure 4-3e also shows development profit of $1,312,963, which represents the difference in the market value of the apartments at stabilized occupancy minus total project costs to reach that point.

In summary:

Total Apartment Project Cost (figure 4-3d)	$7,419,410
Less: Mortgage (figure 4-3c)	6,234,849
Equity	1,184,560
NOI (figure 4-3b)	523,942
Less: Debt Service (figure 4-3e)	436,619
Cash Flow after Debt Service	87,324

FIGURE 4-3e | STAGE 1e: Summary Analysis & Simple Ratios

Net Operating Income (NOI)	$523,942
Total Project Cost	10,751,191
Less: Development Subsidies	(2,476,984)
Project Cost after Subsidies	8,274,208
Less: Development Cost of For-Sale Condominiums	(854,798)
Total Adjusted Cost for Income Property Only	7,419,410
Overall Return, Overall Cap Rate (NOI/Total Adjusted Cost)	7.1%
Net Operating Income	523,942
Annual Debt Service[a]	436,619
Cash Throw-Off (CTO or BTCF)	87,324
Total Adjusted Cost	7,419,410
Permanent Mortgage[b]	6,234,849
Equity	1,184,560
Cash-on-Cash Return (CTO/Equity)	7.4%
Development Profit for Apartments	
Net Operating Income	523,942
Overall Cap Rate at Sale	6.0%
Capitalized Value (NOI/Cap Rate)	8,732,373
Less: Total Adjusted Cost	(7,419,410)
Development Profit	$1,312,963

[a]Annual Debt Service reflects the total mortgage principal amount of $6,234,849, which excludes financing the For-Sale Condominiums.

[b]Mortgage excludes financing of the For-Sale Condominiums. Also, if applicable, the Mortgage amount is capped so as to not exceed the Total Project Cost after Subsidies.

Multifamily Residential Development

FIGURE 4-4a | STAGE 2a: Analysis

		Total	Apartments	Condominium
1	**Project Costs**			
2	Total Project Cost	$10,751,191	$9,835,222	$915,96◆
3	Operating Reserves	284,687	260,432	24,25◆
4	Total Project Cost before Operating Reserve	$10,466,505	9,574,790	891,71◆
5	Total Project Cost after Subsidies	$8,274,208	7,419,410	854,79◆
6	Total Project Cost after Subsidies before Operating Reserve	7,989,521	7,158,978	830,54◆
7	Land Cost	1,251,500	1,144,876	106,62◆
8	**Financing Assumptions**			
9	Equity	1,356,858	1,222,984	133,87◆
10	Mortgage Principal[a]	6,917,349	6,234,849	682,50◆
11	Interest Rate		5.75%	12.00%
12	Amortization (years)		30	N/A
13	Annual Debt Service	$482,587	$436,619	$45,96◆
14	**Depreciation Assumptions**			
15	Building Basis[b]	$7,022,708	$6,274,534	$748,17◆
16	Life (years)	27.5		
17	Acceleration Factor	1.0		
18	Straight Line (calculated)	$255,371	$228,165	$27,20◆
19	**Alternate Project Cost Assumptions for Vacancy Override[c]**			
20	Total Project Cost after Subsidies before Operating Reserve	7,989,521	7,158,978	830,54◆
21	Equity	1,072,172		
22	Building Basis	6,738,021	6,014,102	723,91◆
23	Straight Line	$245,019	$218,695	$26,32◆

	Mortgage Calculation for Apartments & Retail	Year 1	Year 2	Year 3	Year 4	Year 5	Year 6	Year 7	Year 8
24									
25									
26	Beginning Balance	6,234,849	6,154,642	6,069,700	5,979,743	5,884,475	5,783,582	5,676,733	5,563,575
27	Ending Balance	6,154,642	6,069,700	5,979,743	5,884,475	5,783,582	5,676,733	5,563,575	5,443,737
28	Amortization of Principal	80,207	84,942	89,957	95,268	100,893	106,849	113,158	119,839
29	Interest	356,412	351,677	346,662	341,351	335,726	329,769	323,461	316,780
30	**Depreciation Calculation for Apartments & Retail**								
31	Beginning Balance	6,274,534	6,046,369	5,818,204	5,590,039	5,361,874	5,133,709	4,905,545	4,677,380
32	Less: Annual Depreciation	(228,165)	(228,165)	(228,165)	(228,165)	(228,165)	(228,165)	(228,165)	(228,165)
33	Ending Balance	6,046,369	5,818,204	5,590,039	5,361,874	5,133,709	4,905,545	4,677,380	4,449,215
34	Cumulative Depreciation Taken	228,165	456,330	684,495	912,659	1,140,824	1,368,989	1,597,154	1,825,319
35	Cumulative Straight Line	228,165	456,330	684,495	912,659	1,140,824	1,368,989	1,597,154	1,825,319
36	Remaining Book Value	7,191,245	6,963,080	6,734,915	6,506,750	6,278,585	6,050,420	5,822,256	5,594,091
37	**Annual Cash Flows for Apartments & Retail**								
38	Override Vacancy Rates[c]	0.0%							
39	Gross Potential Revenue (3.00% inflation)	892,317	919,087	946,659	975,059	1,004,311	1,034,440	1,065,473	1,097,437
40	Less: Vacancy (5.00% vacancy)	(44,616)	(45,954)	(47,333)	(48,753)	(50,216)	(51,722)	(53,274)	(54,872)
41	Less: Bad Debt (0.50% bad debt)	(4,462)	(4,595)	(4,733)	(4,875)	(5,022)	(5,172)	(5,327)	(5,487)
42	Effective Gross Revenue	843,240	868,537	894,593	921,431	949,074	977,546	1,006,872	1,037,078
43	Total Operating Expenses (3.00% inflation)	319,297	328,876	338,742	348,905	359,372	370,153	381,258	392,695
44	Net Operating Income	523,942	539,661	555,850	572,526	589,702	607,393	625,615	644,383
45	Annual Debt Service	(436,619)	(436,619)	(436,619)	(436,619)	(436,619)	(436,619)	(436,619)	
46	Before-Tax Operating Cash Flow	87,324	103,042	119,232	135,907	153,083	170,774	188,996	
47	Taxes (see below)	–	–	–	–	–	(2,776)	(23,375)	
48	After-Tax Operating Cash Flow	87,324	103,042	119,232	135,907	153,083	167,999	165,621	

49 Income Tax Calcuation for Apartments & Retail	Year 1	Year 2	Year 3	Year 4	Year 5	Year 6	Year 7
50 Net Operating Income	$523,942	$539,661	$555,850	$572,526	$589,702	$607,393	$625,615
51 Add: Replacement/Capital Reserve	7,950	8,189	8,434	8,687	8,948	9,216	9,493
52 Deduct: Interest	(356,412)	(351,677)	(346,662)	(341,351)	(335,726)	(329,769)	(323,461)
53 Deduct: Depreciation	(228,165)	(228,165)	(228,165)	(228,165)	(228,165)	(228,165)	(228,165)
54 Taxable Income/(Loss)	(52,684)	(31,992)	(10,542)	11,698	34,759	58,675	83,482
55 Passive Loss Offset[d]	–	–	–	(11,698)	(34,759)	(48,762)	–
56 Taxable Income	–	–	–	–	–	9,913	83,482
57 Passive Loss Carryforward[d]	(52,684)	(84,677)	(95,218)	(83,521)	(48,762)	–	–
58 Annual Income Taxes (28.00% rate)	–	–	–	–	–	2,776	23,375
59 Sale Calculation of Apartments & Retail (Including tax)							
60 Cash Flow from Sale							
61 Sale Price (cap rate applied to following year NOI) (7.5% cap rate)							8,591,774
62 Less: Commission (2.50% rate)							(214,794)
63 Adjusted Sales Price							8,376,980
64 Less: Remaining Mortgage Balance							(5,563,575)
65 Before-Tax Cash Flow from Sale							2,813,404
66 Total Tax at Sale (recapture & capital gain, see below)							(533,787)
67 After-Tax Cash Flow from Sale							2,279,618
68 Tax Calculation from Sale							
69 Adjusted Sales Price							8,376,980
70 Remaining Book Value							(5,822,256)
71 Total Taxable Gain							2,554,724
72 Passive Loss Carryforward[d]							–
73 Total Net Taxable Gain							2,554,724
74 Total Depreciation Taken							1,597,154
75 Recapture Tax @ 25% (25.00% rate)							399,289
76 Capital Gain							957,570
77 Deduct: Capital Reserves[e]							(60,917)
78 Net Capital Gain							896,653
79 Tax on Capital Gain (15.00% rate)							134,498
80 Total Tax at Sale							533,787
81							

CONTINUED

STAGE 2a: Analysis | CONTINUED

82	Return Measures	Investment	Year 1	Year 2	Year 3	Year 4	Year 5	Year 6	Year 7
83	**Unleveraged IRR**								
84	Project Cost	(8,274,208)							
85	For-Sale Revenues[f]		975,000						
86	Net Operating Income		523,942	539,661	555,850	572,526	589,702	607,393	625,615
87	Adjusted Sales Price								8,376,980
88	Unleveraged Cash Flow	(8,274,208)	1,498,942	539,661	555,850	572,526	589,702	607,393	9,002,594
89	Unleveraged IRR	9.15%							
90	Net Present Value @ 8.00%[g]	475,479							
91	**Before-Tax IRR**								
92	Equity	(1,356,858)							
93	Before-Tax Cash Flow from Condominiums[f]		246,532						
94	Before-Tax Operating Cash Flow		87,324	103,042	119,232	135,907	153,083	170,774	188,996
95	Before-Tax Cash Flow from Sale								2,813,404
96	Total Before-Tax Cash Flow	(1,356,858)	333,855	103,042	119,232	135,907	153,083	170,774	3,002,400
97	Before-Tax IRR	21.42%							
98	Net Present Value @ 15.00%	446,121							
99	**After-Tax IRR**								
100	Equity	(1,356,858)							
101	After-Tax Cash Flow from Condominiums[f]		204,461						
102	After-Tax Operating Cash Flow		87,324	103,042	119,232	135,907	153,083	167,999	165,621
103	After-Tax Cash Flow from Sale								2,279,618
104	Total After-Tax Cash Flow	($1,356,858)	$291,785	$103,042	$119,232	$135,907	$153,083	$167,999	$2,445,239
105	After-Tax IRR	18.07%							
106	Net Present Value @ 15.00%	198,880							
107	**Simple Return Measures**								
108	NOI/Adjusted Project Cost Excluding For-Sale Condos		7.1%	7.3%	7.5%	7.7%	7.9%	8.2%	8.4%
109	Before-Tax Cash Flow/Equity		6.4%	7.6%	8.8%	10.0%	11.3%	12.6%	13.9%
110	Tax Shelter/Equity		0.0%	0.0%	0.0%	0.9%	2.6%	3.6%	0.0%

Note: N/A = not applicable.

[a]The Mortgage Principal is determined based on value and cash flow as shown in figure 4-3c, but is capped so as not to exceed development costs. Note that the annual debt service for the For-Sale Condominiums reflects the interest-only construction loan shown on figure 4-3d, which is based on interest payments during the construction period only.

[b]Customarily, the building basis is the difference between the total project cost and the land value. For this analysis, however, the building basis has also been adjusted to subtract the cost of the condominiums and the development cost subsidies based on the allocated development cost from figure 4-3d.

[c]If the user wants to incorporate vacancy rates during lease-up directly into this spreadsheet, the user may do so by entering the vacancy rates on line 38. If left as zero, then the Total Project Costs and Equity are taken from lines 1–7. If they are not zero, then Total Project Cost, Building Basis, and Equity are taken from lines 19–23.

[d]Current tax regulations treat real estate investments as a passive activity for non–real estate investors. As a result, tax losses in real estate are considered passive income losses and can only be taken against other passive income (with minor adjustments for small investors). In the event that an investor does not have any passive income, the passive losses are carried forward until they can be used against future passive income. See William B. Brueggeman and Jeffrey Fisher, *Real Estate Finance and Investments*, 13th ed. (New York: McGraw-Hill, 2010) for more information.

[e]Specific to this model, a simplifying assumption has been made that the yearly replacement reserves (shown as being included in the net operating income in figure 4-3b) are accumulated during the hold period and spent on capital needs immediately before the sale of the Property. Consequently, the replacement reserve amount spent on capital needs is not depreciated. As a result, the amount is deducted from the estimated capital gains from sale of the Property.

[f]Cash flows related to the sales and profit of the For-Sale Condominiums are calculated separately and shown in figure 4-4b.

[g]Net Present Value equals the present value of future cash flows, less the initial investment. Note that Stage 2 analysis assumes all equity is invested at the beginning of the project. Also note that the unleveraged NPV represents the development profit.

STAGE 2—DISCOUNTED CASH FLOW ANALYSIS.
Discounted cash flow analysis of the operating period is the most important of the five stages. It is used by lenders, appraisers, and investors to project returns of the proposed development. Even if the developer plans to sell the project as soon as it reaches stabilized occupancy, Stage 2 analysis is the most widely used methodology to evaluate an income property investment or development (see figure 4-4a).

To calculate operating cash flows, the pro forma NOI is projected over time, usually seven or ten years, showing growth in both rents and expenses. In this case, both rents and expenses are assumed to increase at a rate of 3 percent per year.

At the end of Stage 2, three internal rates of return (IRRs) are computed—the unleveraged before-tax IRR, the leveraged before-tax IRR, and the leveraged after-tax IRR. These three IRRs, in addition to the two simple return measures for overall cap-rate and cash-on-cash return, constitute the five most important measures of project performance. Many investors also like to see the equity multiplier—the ratio of total undiscounted cash received divided by the equity.

Appraisers and many institutional investors focus on the unleveraged before-tax returns because those numbers give the "pure" real estate value of the property (without financing or income tax considerations). Pension fund retirement accounts do not pay taxes and often buy properties on an all-cash (unleveraged) basis. Both leveraged and unleveraged analysis can be done on the same spreadsheet simply by changing the assumptions about the mortgage and income taxes.

Developers use Stage 2 analysis to determine whether the proposed project offers an attractive rate of return. The DCF analysis is performed many times as more detailed and accurate information becomes available about design, development costs, and anticipated rents. The initial runs of Stage 2 analysis may focus on the unleveraged returns for the project—the internal rate of return on all-equity financing of total project cost, annual cash flows representing the full NOI (with no mortgage or debt service), and the adjusted sale price at the end of the seven-year holding period. The IRR represents the relationship between the present value of the cash flows from operations and sale, and the capital invested. Technically, it is the annual rate of return (discount rate) that equates the present value of the future cash flows with the initial investment. This return should range from about 10 to 15 percent, depending on the type of property, its location, and interest and inflation rates. (The higher

the inflation rate, the higher the overall return.) The unleveraged rate of return is computed on NOI for each year of ownership, starting from the time the building is fully occupied and ending with the sale of the project. The unleveraged (before-tax) return for West River Commons is 9.15 percent. Although this figure is unusually low for a to-be-developed deal, the low interest rates in 2004 generate extremely favorable leverage and very attractive cash-on-cash returns.

Note that in the example, Stage 2 analysis begins *after* the building reaches stabilized occupancy. All the interest subsidies during lease-up are included in the total investment cost. Alternatively, one could assume that Year 0 figures include only development costs through the end of construction—up to the certificate of occupancy—and Year 1 (and 2 if needed) are the lease-up years. In this case, the project does not reach stabilized income until Year 2 or 3 (see figure 4-3d[a]). Vacancy rates are one minus the occupancy rates and would be inserted into the Stage 2 analysis for Years 1 and 2. The resulting negative cash flows are included in the Development Cost spreadsheet (see figure 4-3d) under the heading Estimate of Operating Reserve.

Including lease-up in Stage 2 rather than in the total development costs lowers the apparent IRRs but makes it easier to see how different lease-up rates affect the cash flows during the lease-up period and the total development costs.[29] These nuances are incorporated explicitly into the more detailed analysis of Stage 3. In summary, one has the choice of estimating operating reserves during lease-up as part of the total development costs (figure 4-3d) or in Years 1 and 2 of the Stage 2 analysis through the vacancy rates.

Appraisers calculate the present value of the future cash flow stream at a discount rate determined by the market. The discount rate is used to convert future cash flows to a present value. It also represents the investor's required rate of return. The resulting present value represents the value today of the building once it is fully leased. The difference between the present value of future cash flows and the development cost is the developer's profit, also known as net present value (NPV). Using the NPV method of DCF analysis, a prospective investment must show a positive NPV to justify the investment. The unleveraged NPV at 8 percent is $475,479. This amount is the development profit for West River Commons, assuming that the unleveraged rate of return in the marketplace is 8 percent. If it is lower, the development profit will be higher.

The unleveraged IRR in figure 4-4a is 9.15 percent, which is lower than historic unleveraged IRRs for a project yet to be developed. IRR requirements change directly with changes in interest rates and inflation.[30]

Although the unleveraged IRR is important, developers are primarily interested in their return on equity. The return on equity is also expressed as an IRR and takes into account the financing (leverage) and personal income taxes of the owner/developer. Stage 2 analysis focuses on the returns on the project as a single, undivided investment where one individual (the owner/developer) puts up all the equity and receives all the cash flows.

Figure 4-4a shows the leveraged analysis of the project with mortgage financing. Developers focus on the leveraged before-tax and after-tax returns on equity because investment in the project must compete with returns available from other investments, such as stocks and bonds. West River Commons' before-tax IRR is 21.42 percent, and the after-tax IRR is 18.07 percent. With low-risk money market accounts paying 2 to 4 percent in 2004, West River Commons' return more than adequately compensates for the risk of to-be-developed real estate.

INCLUSION OF FOR-SALE UNITS IN STAGE 2 OF THE INCOME PROPERTY SPREADSHEETS. Combining for-sale units with income property units significantly complicates the Stage 2 analysis. The combination is included here because such developments are increasingly common. The advantage of including for-sale units is that the sales bring in early cash flows that can significantly raise IRRs. The condominiums appear in several spreadsheets, including Rental and Sales Revenue (figure 4-3a), Maximum Debt Calculation (figure 4-3c), Development Costs (figure 4-3d), Stage 2 (figure 4-4a), and Stage 2—For-Sale Condominium Cash Flow (figure 4-4b).

Stage 2 uses the cost allocation from Development Costs for tax purposes. Only the apartment cost is used for the depreciable basis. The cash flows from sale of the condominiums are incorporated at the bottom Stage 2 in the return calculations. Figures for For-Sale Revenues, Before-Tax Cash Flow from Condominiums, and After-Tax Cash Flow from Condominiums are included in the three IRR calculations. These figures are taken from the spreadsheet shown in figure 4-4b. As noted, West River Commons would not be a good investment if the for-sale condominiums were omitted.

WHEN TO DO STAGE 2 ANALYSIS. The DCF analysis of a project should be updated at each of the following times:

1. Before a developer submits the earnest money contract—By setting up the DCF model at this stage, subsequent updates will be easy to accomplish. The purpose of the analysis at this stage is to reconfirm that the project is worth the time and investment required to proceed with the feasibility studies.

In addition to the information used for Stage 1, the developer will need estimates of soft costs for financing points, interest, and legal, marketing, administrative, architecture, and engineering costs; and estimated time to lease-up the project and vacancy

---

FIGURE 4-4b | STAGE 2b Analysis
For-Sale Condominium Cash Flow

Revenue and Expense for Condominiums	
Sales Revenue	$975,000
Development Costs & Expenses[a]	(854,798)
Profit	120,202
Tax Determination for Condominiums	
Profit	120,202
Tax Rate	35.0%
Tax Liability	42,071
Mortgage Calculation for Condominiums[b]	
Beginning Balance	0
Borrowings	682,500
Releases	(682,500)
Trial Ending Balance	0
Average Balance	341,250
Interest Owed	45,968
Interest Paid	(45,968)
Ending Balance	0
Cash Flow Determination for Condominiums	
Revenues	975,000
Less: Condominium Releases to Lender	(682,500)
Less: Interest Paid[b]	(45,968)
Before-Tax Cash Flow	246,532
Less: Taxes	(42,071)
After-Tax Cash Flow	$204,461

[a]Specific to this case and Stage 2 analysis, operational expenses pertaining to the marketing and sales of the condominiums have been accounted for as a development cost.

[b]Specific to this case and Stage 2 analysis, it is assumed that the condominiums are effectively presold such that the construction loan is immediately repaid at the completion of the construction. The interest owed is the amount of interest that accrued while the project was being constructed. Note that this amount had previously been accounted for in determining the total development costs and initial equity required. As a result, the interest owed amount is not shown to affect the ultimate cash flows for the condominiums.

---

rates for the initial operating years during the lease-up period.

2. After a developer signs the earnest money contract but before going hard on the contract— By this time, the developer should have formed a firm concept of the proposed project, including a site plan and building program that defines the number of units obtainable, the mix of units, and average unit sizes. Equipped with information from market studies, the developer can arrive at detailed projections of rental income based on a breakdown of unit types and more accurate rents per unit.

The decision to go hard on the earnest money contract usually hinges on the findings of consultants' studies, especially those regarding soils, floodplains, utilities, easements, and zoning, which should uncover any factors that may affect what can be built and how much it will cost. This information is critical before the developer's at-risk investment is increased through nonrefundable earnest money.

3. After a developer goes hard on the land purchase contract but before closing on the land—The developer wants to accomplish as much as possible before having to close on the land. At the very least, the developer wants to have a tentative financing commitment. To produce both the mortgage brochure and the next iteration of the DCF, the following information is needed:

- market studies that define unit mix, unit size, amenities, and rent per unit;
- conceptual design drawings that have sufficient detail to be used to obtain construction cost estimates within 5 percent of the final bid; and
- construction cost estimates from two or three general contractors (unless the developer has an in-house construction staff or a contractor as part of the team). For purposes of comparison, the contractors' bids should follow the 16 categories laid out on the standard form issued by the American Institute of Architects. The developer should be especially careful to specify what the bid will and will not include.

STAGE 3—COMBINED ANALYSIS OF THE DEVELOPMENT AND OPERATING PERIODS. Before the developer makes a firm commitment on the earnest money, he should compute a more refined estimate of cash flows during the development period and the operating period. Stage 3 analysis provides measures of return for the entire life of the proposed project and is therefore more accurate than Stage 2.

Stage 2 assumes that equity is invested at the time of stabilized occupancy, whereas in fact it must be invested before construction begins. Because the time frame is extended one to two years before Stage 2 analysis and the initial years produce little if any cash flow, the IRRs for Stage 3 are necessarily lower than for Stage 2. Nevertheless, they represent the most accurate picture of how the project will perform.

Stage 3 evaluates cash flows quarterly during the development period, taking into account the anticipated construction schedule and projected monthly lease-up rate. It also shows when equity and debt funds will be needed and how long they will accrue interest before the project's cash flow can support the debt service. In this example, costs are projected quarter by quarter.

Stage 3 is the most complicated of the spreadsheets presented here. It has three parts. Figure 4-5 shows the quarterly cash flows during the development period (construction and lease-up). Figure 4-6 shows the sources and uses of cash accumulated by year for the development period. It summarizes project costs and separates the capitalized costs from the first-year operating losses. Both are project costs that need to be funded but are treated differently when calculating income taxes because operating losses after the certificate of occupancy is received are deductible, while capital costs are not. Total project cost, total capital cost, depreciable basis, operating reserves, and cash resulting from the permanent loan takeout are inputs to figure 4-7. Figure 4-7 combines the development period cash flows and the operating period cash flows in a single overall spreadsheet. The quarterly figures from figure 4-5 are summed to obtain annual numbers in figure 4-6 and are brought forward to figure 4-7. This analysis resembles Stage 2 analysis except that the construction and lease-up years (1 and 2) are included, whereas Stage 2 analysis assumed that the first year already had stabilized occupancy. Note that the cash flow for Year 1 is zero because all the equity is invested before Year 1 and all costs are covered by construction draws.

Stage 3 provides a much more refined estimate of construction interest and operating reserves during lease-up than Stages 1 and 2. In Stage 3, the estimate for construction interest is $401,313, compared with $539,553 in Stage 1 (Development Costs, figure 4-3d). Stage 3 operating losses in Year 2 are $309,738 (figure 4-6) compared with $284,687 in the operating reserve estimate for Development Costs (figure 4-3d). The resulting total capital cost, including the operating

FIGURE 4-5 | STAGE 3a: Analysis
Cash Flows during Development Period, Including Initial Lease-Up Activities

		Data	Total	Time Zero	Year 1 Total	Year 2 Total	DEVELOPMENT Quarter 1	Quarter 2
	Development Costs							
1	Land	$1,251,500	$1,251,500	$1,251,500	$0	$0		
2	Land Carry	$27,418	27,418	$27,418	0	0		
3	Approval Fees	$88,800	88,800	$88,800	0	0		
4	Environmental Remediation	110,574	110,574	110,574	0	0		
5	Construction Hard Cost	7,476,741	7,476,741		7,476,741	0	1,869,185	1,869,185
6	**Soft Costs:**							
7	Architecture & Engineering	378,000	378,000		378,000	0	378,000	
8	Legal	228,910	228,910	228,910	0	0		
9	Appraisal & Title	10,883	10,883	10,883	0	0		
10	Marketing	73,500	73,500		36,750	36,750	9,188	9,188
11	Taxes during Construction	50,000	50,000		25,000	25,000	6,250	6,250
12	Insurance during Construction	19,800	19,800		9,900	9,900	2,475	2,475
13	Contingency	210,825	210,825		105,413	105,413	26,353	26,353
14	Development Subsidies	(2,476,984)	(2,476,984)		(2,476,984)	-	(619,246)	(619,246)
15	Total Development Cost, Excluding Construction Loan Interest & Operating Reserves	7,449,968	7,449,968	1,718,085	5,554,820	177,063	1,672,205	1,294,205
16	**Condominium Sales Schedule**							
17	Units Sold		3		3	0		
18	Cumulative Units Sold				3	3		
19	Revenue per Unit		650,000		325,000	325,000		
20	Condominium Sales Revenue		975,000		975,000	0		
21	Expenses[a]		0		0	0		
22	Condominium Net Revenues		975,000		975,000	0		
23	**Operating Income/(Loss) during Lease-Up**							
24	Initial Occupancy upon Opening	30%						
25	Months to Reach Stabilized Occupancy	6.00						
26	Apartments Leased per Quarter				16	37		
27	Cumulative Number of Apartments Leased				16	53		
28	Vacancy Due to Lease-Up (% of gross potential)[b]				85	18		
29	Stabilized Vacancy (% of gross potential)	5			0	5		
30	Overall Vacancy Rate (%)				85	20		
31	Gross Potential Revenue (3%)[c]	223,079	892,317			892,317		
32	Vacancy Loss[d]		(178,463)			(178,463)		
33	Bad Debt[c]	0.50%	(4,462)			(4,462)		
34	Effective Gross Revenue		709,392			709,392		
35	Operating Expenses (3%)[c]		(319,297)			(319,297)		
36	Net Operating Income		390,095			390,095		
37	**Net Cash Flow before Debt during First Three Years**		(6,084,873)	(1,718,085)	(4,579,820)	213,032	(1,672,205)	(1,294,205)
38	**Equity Contribution Account**							
39	Total Development Costs[e]	8,274,208						
40	Maximum Loan Balance[e]	6,917,349						
41	Equity Required	1,356,858	1,356,858	1,356,858	0	0	0	0
42	Equity Account Ending Balance[f]		1,356,858	1,356,858	1,356,858	1,356,858	1,356,858	1,356,858

DEVELOPMENT		LEASE-UP				FIRST STABILIZED YEAR				
Quarter 3	Quarter 4	Quarter 5	Quarter 6	Quarter 7	Quarter 8	Quarter 9	Quarter 10	Quarter 11	Quarter 12	Year 3 Total
										$0
										0
										0
										0
1,869,185	1,869,185									0
										0
										0
										0
										0
9,188	9,188	9,188	9,188	9,188	9,188					0
6,250	6,250	6,250	6,250	6,250	6,250					0
2,475	2,475	2,475	2,475	2,475	2,475					0
26,353	26,353	26,353	26,353	26,353	26,353					0
(619,246)	(619,246)									
1,294,205	1,294,205	44,266	44,266	44,266	44,266	0	0	0	0	0
	3									
	3	3	3	3	3	3	3	3	3	3
	325,000	325,000	325,000	325,000	325,000	325,000	325,000	325,000	325,000	0
	975,000	0	0	0	0	0	0	0	0	0
	0	0	0	0	0	0	0	0	0	0
	975,000	0	0	0	0	0	0	0	0	0
	16	19	19	0	0	0	0	0	0	0
	16	34	53	53	53	53	53	53	53	53
	85.00	52.50	17.50	0.00	0.00	0.00	0.00	0.00	0.00	0
	0.00	0.00	0.00	5.00	5.00	5.00	5.00	5.00	5.00	5
	85.00	52.50	17.50	5.00	5.00	5.00	5.00	5.00	5.00	5
	223,079	223,079	223,079	223,079	223,079	229,772	229,772	229,772	229,772	919,087
	(117,117)	(39,039)	(11,154)	(11,154)	(11,154)	(11,489)	(11,489)	(11,489)	(11,489)	(45,954)
	(1,115)	(1,115)	(1,115)	(1,115)	(1,115)	(1,149)	(1,149)	(1,149)	(1,149)	(4,595)
	104,847	182,925	210,810	210,810	210,810	217,134	217,134	217,134	217,134	868,537
	(79,824)	(79,824)	(79,824)	(79,824)	(79,824)	(82,219)	(82,219)	(82,219)	(82,219)	(328,876)
	25,023	103,101	130,986	130,986	130,986	134,915	134,915	134,915	134,915	539,661
1,294,205)	(319,205)	(19,243)	58,835	86,720	86,720	134,915	134,915	134,915	134,915	539,661
0	0	0	0	0	0					
1,356,858	1,356,858	1,356,858	1,356,858	1,356,858	1,356,858					

CONTINUED

		Data	Total	Time Zero	Year 1 Total	Year 2 Total	DEVELOPMENT Quarter 1	Quarter
43	**Construction Loan Account and Interest Calculation**							
44	Beginning Balance				366,645	5,588,891	366,645	2,074,9.
45	Loan Draw & Releases							
46	Construction Draw—Initial Request[g]		6,093,109	361,227	5,554,820	177,063	1,672,205	1,294,2(
47	Construction Releases[h]	70%	(682,500)	0	(682,500)	0	0	
48	Operating Deficit		0	0	0	0	0	
49	Trial Balance		6,026,545	361,227	5,479,646	6,026,545	2,038,850	3,369,1:
50	Additional Equity Required		0	0	0	0	0	
51	Construction Draw—Net Funded[g]		6,093,109	361,227	5,554,820	177,063	1,672,205	1,294,2(
52	Ending Balance before Interest			361,227	5,479,646	6,026,545	2,038,850	3,369,1:
53	Average Loan Balance before Interest			180,613	2,923,145	5,807,718	1,202,748	2,722,0.
54	Total Construction Loan Interest	12.0%	1,101,145	5,418	395,894	699,833	36,082	81,6(
55	Interest Accrued during Construction Period		401,313	5,418	395,894	0	36,082	81,6(
56	Interest Accrued during Operating Period		699,833	0	0	699,833	0	
57	Interest Paid from Operations		(390,095)	0	0	(390,095)	0	
58	Interest Paid from Condominium Sales[h]		(45,968)	0	(45,968)	0	0	
59	Trial Ending Balance		6,075,692	366,645	5,588,891	6,075,692	2,074,932	3,450,7!
60	Additional Equity Required		0	0	0	0	0	
61	Interest Accrued—Net[i]		665,082	5,418	349,926	309,738	36,082	81,6(
62	**Ending Balance**		6,075,692	366,645	5,588,891	6,075,692	2,074,932	3,450,7!
63	**Total Additional Equity Required**		0	0	0	0	0	
64	Net Cash Flow after Debt[j]		$246,532	$0	$246,532	$0	$0	$

DEVELOPMENT		LEASE-UP				FIRST STABILIZED YEAR				
Quarter 3	Quarter 4	Quarter 5	Quarter 6	Quarter 7	Quarter 8	Quarter 9	Quarter 10	Quarter 11	Quarter 12	Year 3 Total
3,450,799	4,867,941	5,588,891	5,776,465	5,891,587	5,982,279					
1,294,205	1,294,205	44,266	44,266	44,266	44,266					
0	(682,500)	0	0	0	0					
0	0	0	0	0	0					
4,745,004	5,479,646	5,633,157	5,820,730	5,935,853	6,026,545					
0	0	0	0	0	0					
1,294,205	1,294,205	44,266	44,266	44,266	44,266					
4,745,004	5,479,646	5,633,157	5,820,730	5,935,853	6,026,545					
4,097,901	5,173,793	5,611,024	5,798,597	5,913,720	6,004,412					
122,937	155,214	168,331	173,958	177,412	180,132					
122,937	155,214	0	0	0	0					
0	0	168,331	173,958	177,412	180,132					
0	0	(25,023)	(103,101)	(130,986)	(130,986)					
0	(45,968)	0	0	0	0					
4,867,941	5,588,891	5,776,465	5,891,587	5,982,279	6,075,692					
0	0	0	0	0	0					
122,937	109,245	143,308	70,857	46,426	49,147					
4,867,941	5,588,891	5,776,465	5,891,587	5,982,279	6,075,692					
0	0	0	0	0	0					
$0	$246,532	$0	$0	$0	$0					

[a]Expenses related to the selling of condominium units have already been included as part of the development costs.

[b]The Vacancy calculation assumes that the units leased in the present quarter are economically realized in the middle of the quarter. Hence, the Vacancy for the quarter is an average of the vacancy from the prior quarter and present quarter.

[c]The following estimates pertaining to the revenue and expenses of the apartment and office portions of the project are taken from the pro forma, figure 4-3b. Gross potential revenue and operating expenses are inflated 3 percent in the second year.

[d]Vacancy Loss is a product of the Overall Vacancy Rate, which was determined by the absorption schedule in the preceding section.

[e]The Total Development Costs after Subsidies was previously provided in the Development Costs worksheet, Figure 4-3d, and includes interest and operating reserves. The Maximum Loan Balance was previously provided by the Maximum Debt Calculation worksheet, Figure 4-3c, and is capped so as to not exceed the Development Costs.

[f]Banks want to ensure that developers have sufficient equity up front so they require that all the equity be committed first, before draws from the construction loan are allowed. Construction draws cover any remaining shortfall in funding.

[g]Construction Draws are provided by the lender as construction progresses. In the event that the draw request, together with the carried balance of the construction loan, exceeds the maximum draw limit, then additional equity is required to maintain the construction loan balance at the maximum draw limit. The net construction draw amount is the amount borrowed after additional equity is contributed, if any. Also note that any operating deficits that need to be funded by the lender are requested and included as part of the draw.

[h]Construction releases are provided by sales of condominium units. Specific to this case, it is assumed that releases are scheduled as 70 percent of the revenues. Additionally, the portion of the interest accrued during the development period is paid as condominiums are sold. Refer to figure 4-4b for revenue, expense, and tax calculations for the condominiums.

[i]Accrued interest is added to the overall balance of the construction loan. In the event that the accrued interest, together with the carried balance of the construction loan, exceeds the maximum draw limit, then additional equity is required to maintain the construction loan balance at the maximum draw limit. The net accrued interest amount is the amount accrued after additional equity is contributed, if any.

[j]Positive Net Cash Flow in Quarter 4 results from selling three condominiums: Condominium Net Revenues ($975,000) – Loan Draw & Releases ($682,500) – interest paid from condominium sales ($45,968) = $246,532.

FIGURE 4-6 | STAGE 3b: Analysis
Development Cost Summary

	Uses	Total	0	1	2
1	Total Development Costs	$7,449,968	$1,718,085	$5,554,820	$177,063
2	Construction Loan: Capitalized Interest	401,313	5,418	395,894	0
3	Total Capital Costs	7,851,281	1,723,503	5,950,714	177,063
4	**Cash Flow from Operations**				
5	Net Sales Revenue of Condominiums	975,000	0	975,000	0
6	Net Operating Income of Apartments	390,095	0	0	390,095
7	Less: Construction Loan Interest during Operations	(699,833)	0	0	(699,833)
8	Less: Construction Loan Releases	(682,500)	0	(682,500)	0
9	Cash Flow from Operations after Interest	(17,238)	0	292,500	(309,738)
10	Construction Loan Balance to Be Refinanced	0			0
11	**Total Uses**	7,868,518	1,723,503	5,658,214	486,801
12	**Sources**				
13	**Construction Loan Funding**				
14	Construction Loan: Net Draws	6,093,109	361,227	5,554,820	177,063
15	Construction Loan: Net Accrued Interest	665,082	5,418	349,926	309,738
16	Net Construction Loan Funding	6,758,192	366,645	5,904,746	486,801
17	Equity Sources	1,356,858	1,356,858	–	–
18	Additional Equity Required	–	–	–	–
19	Permanent Mortgage Refinancing	–			–
20	Less: Positive Cash Flow after Interest—Distributed	(246,532)	–	(246,532)	–
21	Less: Cash Proceeds from Construction Loan Takeout	–			–
22	**Total Sources**	$7,868,518	$1,723,503	$5,658,214	$486,801
23	Equity for Capital Investment (equity sources + cash flow from operations—positive cash flow after interest)[a]	1,093,089	1,356,858	45,968	(309,738)
24	Equity for Capital Investment (total capital costs—loan sources)	1,093,089	1,356,858	45,968	(309,738)

[a]Equity for Capital Investment provides a helpful check for Stage 3. One must be careful not to double-count this equity since it comes not only from new equity but also from positive operating cash flows during lease-up. Line 23 and line 24 should be equal for each year.

FIGURE 4-7 | STAGE 3c: Analysis
Combined Annual Before- and After-Tax Cash Flows during Development and Operating Period

		DEVELOPMENT PERIOD		INVESTMENT PERIOD					
		Year 1	Year 2	Year 3	Year 4	Year 5	Year 6	Year 7	Year 8
1	**Mortgage Calculation**								
2	Beginning Balance[a]			6,075,692	5,997,532	5,914,759	5,827,098	5,734,262	5,635,944
3	Ending Balance			5,997,532	5,914,759	5,827,098	5,734,262	5,635,944	5,531,823
4	Amortization of Principal			78,159	82,774	87,661	92,836	98,317	104,122
5	Interest/Annual Payment (5.75%)			347,314	342,699	337,812	332,637	327,156	321,351
6	**Depreciation Calculation**								
7	Beginning Balance[b]		6,599,781	6,359,788	6,119,796	5,879,804	5,639,812	5,399,820	5,159,828
8	Less: Annual Depreciation		(239,992)	(239,992)	(239,992)	(239,992)	(239,992)	(239,992)	(239,992)
9	Ending Balance		6,359,788	6,119,796	5,879,804	5,639,812	5,399,820	5,159,828	4,919,836
10	Cumulative Depreciation Taken		239,992	479,984	719,976	959,968	1,199,960	1,439,952	1,679,944
11	Cumulative Straight Line		239,992	479,984	719,976	959,968	1,199,960	1,439,952	1,679,944
12	Recapture		239,992	479,984	719,976	959,968	1,199,960	1,439,952	1,679,944
13	Remaining Book Value		6,359,788	6,119,796	5,879,804	5,639,812	5,399,820	5,159,828	4,919,836

CONTINUED

		DEVELOPMENT PERIOD		INVESTMENT PERIOD					
		Year 1	Year 2	Year 3	Year 4	Year 5	Year 6	Year 7	Year 8
14	**Annual Cash Flows**								
15	Gross Rent (3.00%)	0	892,317	919,087	1,004,311	1,034,440	1,065,473	1,097,437	1,130,360
16	Vacancy Rate (5.00%)	85.00%	20.00%	5.00%	5.00%	5.00%	5.00%	5.00%	5.00%
17	Vacancy ($)	0	(178,463)	(45,954)	(50,216)	(51,722)	(53,274)	(54,872)	(56,518)
18	Bad Debt (0.50%)	0	(4,462)	(4,595)	(5,022)	(5,172)	(5,327)	(5,487)	(5,652)
19	Effective Gross Revenue	0	709,392	868,537	949,074	977,546	1,006,872	1,037,078	1,068,191
20	Operating Expenses (3.00%)	0	(319,297)	(328,876)	(338,742)	(348,905)	(359,372)	(370,153)	(381,258)
21	Net Operating Income	0	390,095	539,661	610,331	628,641	647,500	666,925	686,933
22	Less: Construction Loan Interest during Operating[c]	0	(390,095)						
23	Less: Annual Debt Service			(425,473)	(425,473)	(425,473)	(425,473)	(425,473)	(425,473)
24	Plus: Operating Reserve Funded by Construction Loan[d]		0						
25	Before-Tax Cash Flow		0	114,188	184,858	203,168	222,027	241,452	261,460
26	Taxes (see below)		0	0	0	0	0	4,735	37,823
27	After-Tax Cash Flow		0	114,188	184,858	203,168	222,027	236,717	223,637
28	**Income Tax Calcuation for Apartments & Retail**								
29	Net Operating Income	–	390,095	539,661	610,331	628,641	647,500	666,925	686,933
30	Add: Replacement/Capital Reserve		7,950	8,189	8,434	8,687	8,948	9,216	9,493
31	Deduct: Interest	–	(390,095)	(347,314)	(342,699)	(337,812)	(332,637)	(327,156)	(321,351)
32	Deduct: Depreciation	–	(239,992)	(239,992)	(239,992)	(239,992)	(239,992)	(239,992)	(239,992)
33	Taxable Income/(Loss)	–	(232,042)	(39,457)	36,074	59,524	83,819	108,994	135,083
34	Passive Loss Offset	–	–	–	(36,074)	(59,524)	(83,819)	(92,081)	–
35	Taxable Income	–	–	–	–	–	–	16,912	135,083
36	Passive Loss Carryforward	–	(232,042)	(271,499)	(235,425)	(175,901)	(92,081)	–	–
37	Annual Income Taxes (28.00% rate)	–	–	–	–	–	–	4,735	37,823
38	**Sale Calculation of Apartments & Retail (including tax)**								
39	Cash Flow from Sale								
40	Sale Price (cap rate applied to next year NOI) (7.5% cap rate)							9,159,108	
41	Less: Commission (2.50% rate)							(228,978)	
42	Adjusted Sales Price							8,930,130	
43	Less: Remaining Mortgage Balance							(5,635,944)	
44	Before-Tax Cash Flow from Sale							3,294,186	
45	Total Tax at Sale (recapture & capital gain, see below)							(701,827)	
46	After-Tax Cash Flow from Sale							2,592,359	
47	Tax Calculation at Sale								
48	Adjusted Sales Price							8,930,130	
49	Remaining Book Value							(5,159,828)	
50	Total Taxable Gain							3,770,302	
51	Passive Loss Carryforward							–	
52	Total Net Taxable Gain							3,770,302	
53	Total Depreciation Taken							1,439,952	
54	Recapture Tax (25.00% rate)							359,988	
55	Capital Gain							2,330,350	
56	Deduct: Capital Reserves[e]							(51,424)	
57	Net Capital Gain							2,278,926	
58	Tax on Capital Gain (15.00% rate)							341,839	
59	Total Tax at Sale							701,827	

CONTINUED

		DEVELOPMENT PERIOD			INVESTMENT PERIOD			
60	Return Measures	Year 0	Year 1	Year 2	Year 3	Year 4	Year 5	Year 6	Year 7
61	Unleveraged IRR								
62	Project Cost	(7,449,968)							
63	For-Sale Revenues[f]		975,000						
64	Net Operating Income		–	390,095	539,661	610,331	628,641	647,500	666,925
65	Adjusted Sales Price								8,930,130
66	Unleveraged Cash Flow	(7,449,968)	975,000	390,095	539,661	610,331	628,641	647,500	9,597,056
67	Unleveraged IRR	10.68%							
68	Net Present Value @ 8.00%[g]	1,099,933							
69	Before-Tax IRR								
70	Initial & Additional Equity Required	(1,356,858)	0	0					
71	Before-Tax Cash Flow from Condominiums[f]		246,532						
72	Before-Tax Operating Cash Flow		–	0	114,188	184,858	203,168	222,027	241,452
73	Before-Tax Cash Flow from Refinancings			–					
74	Before-Tax Cash Flow from Sale								3,294,186
75	Total Before-Tax Cash Flow	(1,356,858)	246,532	0	114,188	184,858	203,168	222,027	3,535,638
76	Before-Tax IRR	22.21%							
77	Net Present Value @ 15.00%	564,467							
78	After-Tax IRR								
79	Initial & Additional Equity Required	(1,356,858)	0	0					
80	After-Tax Cash Flow from Condominiums[f]		204,461						
81	After-Tax Operating Cash Flow		–	0	114,188	184,858	203,168	222,027	236,717
82	After-Tax Cash Flow from Refinancings			–					
83	After-Tax Cash Flow from Sale								2,592,359
84	Total After-Tax Cash Flow	($1,356,858)	$204,461	$0	$114,188	$184,858	$203,168	$222,027	$2,829,076
85	After-Tax IRR	18.61%							
86	Net Present Value @ 15.00%	$262,261							

[a]The permanent mortgage balance was determined based on value and cash flow from the retail and apartment portion of the project. The permanent mortgage would replace the outstanding construction loan upon stabilization of the project. Moreover, the portion of the loan amount pertaining to the condominiums would not be included since it would be paid off upon sale of the condominium units and before stabilization of the project. Note that the construction loan is interest only, whereas the permanent mortgage is amortizing.

[b]The depreciable basis is the total project cost, excluding land costs and operating losses during the lease-up period. The remaining book value includes the land cost. Personal property is included in the depreciable basis here for simplicity. It can be tracked separately. Also, apartment buildings may be brought onstream at different successive months as construction is completed. A separate depreciation spreadsheet may be added to account for these nuances. That level of accuracy, however, is inappropriate for Stage 3 analysis since other assumptions are at best good approximations.

[c]Construction Interest during Operating represents the amount of interest charged during the operating period that was paid from operating revenues. Note that since condominium sales and profits have been consolidated and shown separately, the amount of interest paid from condominium sales are not shown. See figure 4-4b for specific detail regarding the revenues, expenses, and taxes pertaining to the condominiums.

[d]The Operating Reserve includes funds needed to cover operating costs and debt service during the lease-up period.

[e]Specific to this model, a simplifying assumption has been made that the yearly replacement reserves (shown as being included in the net operating income in figure 4-3b) are accumulated during the hold period and spent on capital needs immediately before the sale of the Property. Consequently, the replacement reserve amount spent on capital needs is not depreciated. As a result, the amount is deducted from the estimated capital gains from sale of the Property.

[f]Cash flows related to the sales and profit of the For-Sale Condominiums are calculated separately and shown in figure 4-4b.

[g]Net Present Value equals the present value of future cash flows, less the initial investment. Note that the analysis assumes all equity is invested at the beginning of the project. Also note that the unleveraged NPV represents the development profit.

reserve, is $8,161,018 (from Stage 3b; see summary below). This result compares with $8,274,208 in Stage 1d (figure 4-3d).

	Stage 1d (fig. 4-3d)	Stage 3 (fig. 4-6)	Difference
Construction interest	$539,553	$401,313	$138,240
Operating reserve	284,687	309,738	–25,051
Total	824,240	711,051	113,189

The construction period interest is lower in Stage 3 analysis primarily because equity is assumed to be used to pay for initial construction before the construction lender starts to fund the construction loan. Lenders usually require that the entire equity be invested before funding the construction loan. With equity funding the initial phases of construction, the average construction loan balance is usually less than the 65 percent required by the bank and assumed in Stage 1d (figure 4-3d, line 24). Less conservative is the assumption that units pay rent from the beginning of the quarter in which they are leased because many of those leases will start in the second or third month of the quarter. The reason that operating losses are higher in Stage 3b is the assumption that the permanent loan does not fund until the beginning of Year 3 so that the project is carrying the 12 percent construction loan interest for 12 months of operations versus six months in Stage 1d. Note that the permanent loan interest rate is dramatically lower (5.75 percent) than the construction loan (12 percent).[31] The capital costs and operating deficits from Stage 3d are summarized in figure 4-8. Several numbers are key inputs to the combined annual DCF analysis in Stage 3c, such as the Depreciable Basis and the Total Operating Reserve Funded by Construction Loan. Note that the Construction Loan Interest paid during the operating period ($390,095) appears in figure 4-7, Year 2, line 22. This funding makes the cash flow in Year 2 zero. Otherwise, additional equity would be needed to pay for operating deficits in Year 2.

The more precise figures for construction interest and operating reserves in Stage 3 give the developer ammunition to discuss with the construction lender the amount of reserves actually needed. The lender wants to be as conservative as possible, ensuring that sufficient interest reserves are available to protect the developer in the event of construction delays or slower lease-up. The developer must have these resources available but would prefer not to have to set them aside if they are not needed. An estimate that is too conservative raises the total project cost unnecessarily and may make the project uncompetitive.

The IRRs shown in figure 4-7 for Stage 3c analysis indicate that the before-tax IRR is 22.21 percent and the after-tax IRR is 18.61 percent. These figures are more accurate estimates of the project's performance than Stage 2 analysis—where the before-tax IRR was 21.42 percent and the after-tax IRR was 18.07 percent—because they take into account quarterly construction draws and projected lease-up. Normally, IRRs for Stage 3 analysis would be lower than in Stage 2 because the positive cash flows from stabilized performance occur in Year 3 rather than in Year 1. They are almost the same in this illustration, however, because the more accurate estimates of construction interest and operating reserve during lease-up produce lower overall development costs.

STAGE 4—MONTHLY CASH FLOWS DURING THE DEVELOPMENT PERIOD. Stage 4 analysis is not shown. It focuses on just the development period and refines the cash flow projections to support the request for the construction loan. Stage 4 analysis resembles the quarterly analysis shown in figure 4-5 except that projections are made monthly rather than quarterly. The schedule in figure 4-5 assumes that the project will be built during the first four quarters and that it will be leased over the next four quarters. The estimated lease-up time (12 months) was calculated

FIGURE 4-8 | Summary of Stage 3 Costs

Capital Costs	
Total Development Cost Excluding Interest	$7,449,968
Interest Accrued during Construction (figure 4-5, line 55)	401,313
Total Capital Costs	7,851,281
Depreciable Basis	
Total Capital Costs	7,851,281
Land Cost	1,251,500
Depreciable Basis (Capital Cost, minus Land)	6,599,781
Operating Reserve	
Operating Loss during Lease-Up (figure 4-5, line 35)	0
Interest Accrued during Operating Period (figure 4-5, line 56)	699,833
Interest Paid during Operating Period (figure 4-5, line 57)	(390,095)
Total Operating Reserve Funded by Construction Loan	309,738
Total Net Project Costs	
Total Project Cost (Capital Costs plus Operating Reserve)	8,161,018
Positive Cash Flow after Interest	(246,532)
Interest Paid from Condominium Sale	(45,968)
Total Project Cost after First-Year Operations (Year 2)	7,868,518
Construction Loan Takeout at Stabilization	
Permanent Mortgage Amount for Income Property (Year 2)	6,075,692
Construction Loan Ending Balance for Income Property	6,075,692
Cash Proceeds from Construction Loan Takeout	0

Sources and Uses, End of Year 2

Uses	
Total capital costs	$7,851,281
Apartment cash flow after interest	309,738
Condominium cash flow after release	(292,500)
Total investment end of Year 2	**7,868,518**
Sources	
Permanent mortgage	6,075,692
Equity	1,356,858
Construction loan paid off by condominium sale	682,500
Condominium cash flow distributed	(292,500)
Interest paid from condominium sale	45,968
	$7,868,518

from the anticipated absorption of apartments based on the market study. The project reaches stabilized occupancy after the second year.[32] A primary purpose of the monthly analysis of the development phase is to estimate the amount of the loan that needs to be set aside to cover interest expenses and operating losses during construction and startup. Based on the quarterly cash flow computation in figure 4-8, the total project capital cost is $7,851,281 (also figure 4-6, line 3). Total project costs including operating reserves funded by the construction loan are $8,161,018. With positive cash flows after interest of $246,532 and interest paid from the condominium sale of $45,968, total project cost after the first year of operations is $7,868,518 (figure 4-8 and figure 4-6, line 11). Project costs at the end of Year 2 are the same.

A monthly Stage 4 analysis would provide an even more accurate estimate of these figures. It is not uncommon for developers to do only a Stage 3, presuming that quarterly cash flow analysis will provide a sufficiently accurate picture of their funding needs. But monthly projections are recommended because they give both the developer and the lender the most accurate picture of funding needs and serve as a useful tool for monitoring cash flows once construction begins.

STAGE 5—DISCOUNTED CASH FLOW ANALYSIS FOR INVESTORS: JOINT VENTURE–SYNDICATION ANALYSIS. Stages 1, 2, and 3 examine the real estate project in its entirety. We assume that all equity and all subsequent cash flows are invested or received by a single owner or developer entity. The final step in the analysis is to divide the cash flows for the whole project into the investor's and developer's shares.

Stage 5 is the joint venture–syndication analysis. It is used to structure the deal between the developer and the equity investors. The developer uses Stage 5 to determine the best combination of preferred returns and profit splits he must offer investors to attract the required equity for the project. He will likely experiment with a number of different deal combinations before making a final selection. Because different types of equity investors are accustomed to different deal structures, the final structure depends on whom the developer is approaching for equity.

Although the final version of Stage 5 for the offering package is usually prepared by an accountant on an *after-tax* basis, the developer's analysis typically focuses on *before-tax* cash flows and IRRs to the investor. The project's viability hinges on attracting sufficient equity capital so the investor's IRR is one of the key measures of return.

Stage 5 analysis should be done before a firm commitment for the earnest money is made for the land. If the investor's IRR is below 15 percent (18–20 percent or higher is common), the land price or purchase price is too high to offer investors attractive returns. Alternatively, investors can be given a greater share of the profits, but if too little money is left over for the developer, the deal is not worth doing.

Figure 4-9 shows the before-tax Stage 5 analysis. The cash flows in figure 4-9, line 8, are taken from the Stage 3c combined analysis in figure 4-7, line 75. Note that although Stage 5 analysis illustrated here uses cash flows from Stage 3, it can just as easily be tied to Stage 2 analysis. In that case, before-tax cash flows from Stage 2 (figure 4-4a, line 96) are substituted in Stage 5 (figure 4-9, line 8).

The investor who puts up the equity typically requires a preferred return. The preferred return is most often cumulative, which is to say that if funds are not sufficient to pay the preferred return, the deferred return is added to the equity balance and accrues interest. In this case, the investor receives an 8 percent cumulative preferred return and takes 70 percent of the remaining cash flow after the equity and cumulative preferred return are paid back.

The investor puts up 95 percent of the equity and the developer 5 percent. The investor receives 95 percent of all cash flows until he or she has received back all of the equity and cumulative preferred returns. Any remaining cash flow is split 70/30 between the investor and the developer. The investor's IRR is 19.41 percent; the developer's IRR is 47.25 percent, which is much higher because his or her equity investment

FIGURE 4-9 | STAGE 5: Analysis

FIGURE 4-9 | STAGE 5: Analysis
Investor Return

1	Initial & Additional Equity[a]			$1,356,858				
2	Investor Equity Contribution[b]			95%				
3	Cumulative Preferred Return			8%				
4	Investor Proportionate Payback of Equity[b]			95%				
5	Investor Share of Remaining Cash Flow			70%				

6		DEVELOPMENT PERIOD		OPERATING PERIOD				
7		Initial Investment	Year 1	Year 2	Year 3	Year 4	Year 5	Year 6	Year 7
8	Before-Tax Cash Flow	($1,356,858)	$246,532	$0	$114,188	$184,858	$203,168	$222,027	$3,535,638
9	**Preferred Return[b]**								
10	Beginning Equity Account Balance		1,356,858	1,218,875	1,218,875	1,218,875	1,212,360	1,106,180	972,648
11	Preferred Return Earned		108,549	97,510	97,510	97,510	96,989	88,494	77,812
12	Preferred Return Paid Currently		108,549	0	97,510	97,510	96,989	88,494	77,812
13	**Unpaid Return Account[b]**								
14	Beginning Balance		0	0	97,510	80,832	0	0	0
15	Deferred Preferred Return		0	97,510	0	0	0	0	0
16	Deferred Preferred Return Paid		0	0	16,678	80,832	0	0	0
17	Ending Balance		0	97,510	80,832	0	0	0	0
18	**Equity Account Balance[b]**								
19	Beginning Equity Account Balance		1,356,858	1,218,875	1,218,875	1,218,875	1,212,360	1,106,180	972,648
20	Equity Payback		137,983	0	0	6,516	106,179	133,533	972,648
21	Ending Balance		1,218,875	1,218,875	1,218,875	1,212,360	1,106,180	972,648	0
22	**Equity Payments Recap[b]**								
23	Preferred Return Paid Currently		108,549	0	97,510	97,510	96,989	88,494	77,812
24	Deferred Preferred Return Paid		0	0	16,678	80,832	0	0	0
25	Equity Payback		137,983	0	0	6,516	106,179	133,533	972,648
26	Total Payments on Equity		246,532	0	114,188	184,858	203,168	222,027	1,050,459
27	**Remaining Cash Flow**								
28	Before-Tax Cash Flow		246,532	0	114,188	184,858	203,168	222,027	3,535,638
29	Total Payments on Equity		246,532	0	114,188	184,858	203,168	222,027	1,050,459
30	Remaining Cash Flow		0	0	0	0	0	0	2,485,179
31	**Investor Share of Equity & Remaining Cash Flow (based on terms above)**								
32	Investor Share of Equity Payments		234,205	0	108,478	175,615	193,010	210,926	997,936
33	Investor Share of Remaining Cash Flow		0	0	0	0	0	0	1,739,625
34	Total Share to Investor		234,205	0	108,478	175,615	193,010	210,926	2,737,562
35	**Developer Share of Equity & Remaining Cash Flow**								
36	Developer Share of Equity Payments		12,327	0	5,709	9,243	10,158	11,101	52,523
37	Developer Share of Remaining Cash Flow		0	0	0	0	0	0	745,554
38	Total Share to Investor		12,327	0	5,709	9,243	10,158	11,101	798,077
39	**Investor Cash Flows**								
40	Before-Tax Cash Flow to Investor	(1,289,015)	234,205	0	108,478	175,615	193,010	210,926	2,737,562
41	Investor Before-Tax IRR	19.41%							
42	Net Present Value, at 15.0%	302,676							
43	**Developer Cash Flows**								
44	Before-Tax Cash Flow to Developer	($67,843)	$12,327	$0	$5,709	$9,243	$10,158	$11,101	$798,077
45	Developer Before-Tax IRR	47.25%							
46	Net Present Value, at 15.0%	$261,791							

[a]In this simplified investor return analysis, it is assumed that all equity, or committed capital by the investors, is invested in the initial year into an escrow account.

[b]In this analysis, it is assumed that the investor and the developer have equal priority to the preferred return and that the payback of their respective equity is proportional to their contributed amount. Hence, the preferred return and equity balance calculations are performed for both the investor and the developer and later individually proportioned according to their proportionate share.

is only 5 percent. Note that in this deal structure, the developer's equity and the investor's equity are "pari passu"—treated equally. An alternative structure would subordinate the developer's equity payback to the investor's, in which case the developer would not receive any cash flow until the investor had received back all of his or her equity. No deal structure is "typical." It is up to the developer to devise a structure that will attract the necessary equity.

When a single large investor is involved, the deal is negotiated directly between the developer and the investor. Institutional equity investors typically require 75 to 80 percent of the profits. Developers can often raise money more cheaply from private individuals.

WHAT TO WATCH FOR. Financial analysis is often misused. Experienced developers sometimes scoff at the latest DCF and IRR techniques because the old rules of thumb (such as capitalized value should exceed cost by a comfortable margin, say, 15 to 20 percent, or cash-on-cash return should be 10 to 11 percent) work just as well when a project is obviously a good investment. Stage 2 analysis can easily be misused to overestimate a project's returns. Beginning developers especially should be aware of the major pitfalls:

- underestimating costs;
- overestimating rents;
- underestimating operating expenses, especially after five years;
- underestimating or omitting a reserve for replacements;
- underestimating or omitting expenses for tenant turnover, such as repainting and replacing carpets, draperies, and appliances;
- overestimating rent escalation;
- assuming a sale-year capitalization rate that is too low (which increases sale value); and
- not allowing a sufficient interest reserve during lease-up or assuming an insufficient lease-up time.

Errors in analysis are compounded by developers' natural optimism. Making one optimistic assumption, such as too short a lease-up period, may not alter the results too much, but when two or three such assumptions are made, the resulting returns may represent a *very* optimistic and unrealistic case. Thus, one must be very careful about selecting assumptions for the variables that represent *average* or *most likely* values.

The other common mistake is going into too much detail too early in the analysis. A basic rule is that the level of detail should be no greater than the accuracy of the information analyzed. It is inappropriate to analyze monthly cash flows when first looking at a project because the data for costs and rents are so crude that the extra detail does not help; in fact, it may make it harder to see what is going on. Therefore, Stage 4 monthly cash flow analysis is appropriate only after considerable time and money have been spent collecting the best possible information about operations and development costs.

Last, one should always use common sense. The various measures of return should correlate with standard rules of thumb. Good projects typically meet the following measures of return, although they vary according to the degree of risk and current interest and inflation rates:

Measure of Return	New Development	Stabilized Property
Cash-on-cash return (Cash throw-off/equity)	7–10%	6–9%
Overall return (overall cap rate: NOI/total cost)	10–11%	8–10%
Unleveraged IRR	12–15%	9–11%
Before-tax leveraged IRR	20–25%	13–18%
After-tax leveraged IRR	15–20%	9–14%
Investor's before-tax IRR	16–20%	12–16%

These rules of thumb are rough guidelines. Returns may be higher or lower, depending on the risk associated with a particular deal and the general economic environment and geographic location. The returns also vary with inflation and interest rates. The above returns have trended downward significantly since the 1990s, resulting from the enormous influx of cash into real estate during the economic expansion of the 2000s. The economic crisis of 2008–2009 caused the rates to jump from their low point in 2007; but for apartments, they still remain lower than their historic averages.

The status of the property is a critical component in determining which cap rates and rates of return are appropriate. "New development" refers to apartment projects that have already received full entitlements and are ready to start construction. The return expectations include construction and lease-up risk, but if zoning approvals are required, the return expectations would be even higher. "Stabilized property" refers to apartment projects that are fully leased (90 to 95 percent occupancy) and that have funded into their permanent mortgages. These returns are in line with those that private investors would expect. Institutional returns for investment-grade apartments would be lower—between 1 and 3 percent for IRRs. "Investment-grade apartments" refer to projects that are attractive to institutional investors—typically new projects or well-seasoned projects of 150 or more units in prime locations, or somewhat smaller projects in high-priced cities like New York, San Francisco, Los Angeles, and Washington, D.C. The size requirement is tied to the number of units necessary to support professional on-site management.

Financial analysis is an iterative process. Stage 2 analysis is performed many times in the course of collecting increasingly better information about a project. Fortunately, once the model is set up, it is a ten-minute exercise to input new information and rerun it. But one must double-check that the assumptions and results make sense. Simple measures of return for cash-on-cash returns and capitalization rates still apply. Avoid the trap of creating so complicated a spreadsheet that key numbers become lost in pages and pages of analysis.

THE GO/NO-GO DECISION. Each stage of project feasibility requires a go/no-go decision. A decision to go forward does not commit the developer to construction but takes the developer to the next level of investment and risk. Each level may involve substantial or very little additional commitment. For example, some projects may have all necessary regulatory approvals already in place, thereby allowing the developer to apply directly for a building permit as soon as construction drawings and financing have been obtained. Other projects may require little investment in feasibility studies, because the physical aspects of the site are already known, the lender does its own appraisal, the market has been proved through past experience, preliminary engineering is unnecessary, or the architect provides preliminary design drawings on spec.

The importance of holding down front-end costs cannot be overemphasized. It is pure risk money because the odds are still heavily against a project's proceeding, even after a developer has decided to go hard on the land. The key to success is knowing what information is required and obtaining it at the lowest cost. A developer must walk that fine line between spending money unnecessarily and doing sufficient investigation to evaluate the property properly.

The two most important decisions—especially for developers with limited resources—involve purchase of the land and the beginning of construction, both of which usually require the largest financial commitments.

The DCF analysis provides data that influence the go/no-go decision to purchase the site:

- expected dollar profit;
- IRR;
- amount of total money needed;
- amount of equity and debt needed; and
- length of the commitment.

The decision to purchase is not made solely on the basis of the DCF analysis, however. The developer must also weigh other available investment alternatives, the amount of risk involved in the project, and a host of other considerations, including the following:

- Does the developer have the personnel and capital resources to carry through the project?
- Is this really the project that the developer wants to spend the next three years or so working on?
- Is the project worth the developer's time, effort, and risk?
- Is the project of such a scale that the developer can survive major delays and unforeseen difficulties? If not, is this project worth risking the loss of all the developer's assets?

Design

The developer's conceptualization should be based entirely on the target market—not his personal preferences. The rental apartment and for-sale condominium markets are segmented into many submarkets, with each niche demanding specific elements. Submarkets vary enormously by demographics, level of competition, and preferences related to unit mix, unit finishes, parking arrangements, and amenities. Design standards and preferences vary enormously from one geographic region to another. No matter how good the pro forma for a project might look, if the product does not satisfy the market's needs at a price that customers can afford, the project will not succeed.

Each building type, from suburban garden apartments to downtown lofts, offers a different set of problems and opportunities for design to meet the needs of the submarket. Luxury garden apartments, for example, typically include some or all of the following features: generously sized rooms, kitchens with deluxe appliances and cabinetry, ceramic tile or marble bathrooms, vaulted and/or nine-foot-high (2.7 m) ceilings, fireplaces, balconies, in-unit laundry facilities, and community recreational facilities, such

Bijou Square Condo Rescue

Philip Kuchma's experience in salvaging the financing for an 84-unit half-finished condominium project in Bridgeport, Connecticut, illustrates the difficult steps a developer often has to go through to save a project caught in the middle of an economic crisis. Kuchma headed a 30-year-old construction firm that also did development for its own account. Construction activities make up around 85 percent of the firm's billings and development activities make up about 20 to 25 percent. Kuchma sees these two businesses as complementary; he thinks that doing both adds value to the company and to its clients—and therefore they work synergistically. When his firm works with developer clients on construction jobs, it can understand the client's interests more clearly. Often, its clients have a good understanding of construction; they are easier to work with and end up with better results because of that understanding.

The high-profile Bridgeport condo project was half finished when the firm lost its financing in the midst of the 2008 financial crisis. The condos anchored a high-profile mixed-use redevelopment project that city officials considered key to the successful renovation of downtown Bridgeport—the poorest city

in the wealthiest county in Connecticut, less than a one-hour commute from New York City and adjacent to Stamford, Connecticut, where several Fortune 500 companies are based. The project included 84 luxury residential condominiums and seven retail units at street level. Scheduled to open in late 2008, the one- and two-bedroom units ranged from 815 to 1,300 square feet (76–121 m²). It was designed to resemble a row of buildings, in keeping with prevailing architecture in the area. The new development is adjacent to a group of buildings Kuchma owns, which are collectively known as "Bijou Square," a renovation that turned vacant storefronts into restaurants, industrial space into commercial and living spaces, and vacant apartments into renovated, occupied units. A vintage movie theater has also been renovated.

Kuchma states, "The city did not come to grips with the need to change perceptions of the city in order to lure people downtown. As a result, the city stagnated for 25 years." Until Kuchma's most recent project, little new construction had occurred since two new buildings were completed more than 20 years earlier. "There has been a significant change in the city economic development administration in the last five years that has

resulted in greater emphasis on housing. The previous administration believed that increases in housing would be accompanied by an increased need for services that would not be offset by the tax revenue generated. It has become popular to convert the upper floors in mixed-use buildings from office to residential above retail. There is some adaptive reuse in Bridgeport now, though it has slowed in the economic downturn.

"Mixed-use developments in cities the size of Bridgeport have to be carefully planned. Having a dead zone of even a few blocks interrupts the rhythm of the city, diminishing its pedestrian appeal."

Two lenders were vying to provide construction financing for the project: a major New York–based commercial bank and a New York–based nonprofit bank that specializes in projects that conventional commercial banks did not feel comfortable funding. The nonprofit lender was reaching out to developers in cities like Bridgeport to take the place of conventional lenders.

The project commenced while Kuchma was still in the process of obtaining construction financing. The New York–based commercial bank granted a loan commitment in 2008. But as 2008 wore on, the

---

as exercise rooms, swimming pools, and tennis courts. Other features might include extra sound-proofing, security systems, elevators, and attached garages with direct access for residents. Property management services might include grocery shopping, pet sitting, dry-cleaning delivery, and trash pickup.

Luxury urban apartments typically include many of the features of the garden apartments mentioned above. It is typical to see concierge services, security/doorman services, underground or structured parking, modern appliances, high-end kitchen and bathroom finishes, in-unit laundry, fitness and business centers, club rooms, and other community amenities. Luxury urban apartment communities compete with a very

high level of resident services and lifestyle advantages. Rents often include floor and view premiums. Special design features, like loft-style units, also command premiums. Although each of these features and services increases development costs, renters of the highest-end apartments will pay for all of them, and the increased rent should justify the additional cost. In fact, competition may make it difficult to rent the project if it does not have these features and services.

In comparison, renters of lower-end apartments are unwilling to pay for many such features. Even so, in some areas (Texas, for example), even the lowest-end garden apartments feature club rooms and swimming pools, private balconies, cable television, and high-speed Internet.

bank was having overall difficulties in its organization and told Kuchma it would have to delay releasing the funds until early 2009. In early 2009, the bank withdrew the loan commitment. Kuchma subsequently secured funding through the nonprofit lender but has not yet closed on the loan—hence, the project has been delayed. The interest rates being offered by the nonprofit lender were not substantially different, but the terms of the loan changed dramatically as a result of the economic shift that occurred between the origination of the prior loan commitment and the current debt financing.

The interest rate on the construction loan offered by the nonprofit lender was comparable to that previously offered by the commercial bank, but the original loan amount of $20 million was lowered to $18.5 million, requiring an additional $1.5 million in equity, which was agreed to. As they worked to finalize the deal, the nonprofit lender could offer only $14 million, so subsidies were needed to close that gap. The amount offered was reduced because the lender could only underwrite the project based on its performance as a rental property. The nonprofit lender also offered a permanent takeout commitment along with the construction financing.

The nonprofit lender required repositioning the project as rental units rather than condominium units. The approval was also conditioned on Kuchma's securing state and city subsidies because the high-quality building already underway would exceed the rents people would be willing to pay for the space. The city and state provided the necessary subsidies on the condition that a percentage of the units (11 of 84) be dedicated to workforce housing (not deed restricted but reserved for workforce housing for a ten-year period). The city believes that the building should eventually become condominiums since so few ownership units are located downtown. Therefore, the arrangement allows for later conversion of the units, with the city's agreeing to subsidize the difference between market value of the units and the affordable sale price.

GE Capital bought $25 million of Connecticut Finance Authority bonds with the stipulation that the money must be used for downtown Bridgeport projects. Kuchma's project qualified for $13 million of those funds at 4 percent interest. Of the construction cost, $3.2 million was covered by subsidies at 0 percent interest and no principal payback, which effectively added to equity contribution. The city contributed $1.2

million from HOME funds the city had in hand, and $2 million was provided by the state's Department of Economic and Community Development. Kuchma originally had not planned to ask for a PILOT (Payment in Lieu of Taxes) grant or for city or state subsidies, but once the firm started building and had to stop, everyone saw that the new economic conditions could not be overcome, so subsidies had to be used to prevent a building's sitting half completed in such a visible area in the city.

Kuchma would not have begun the project had he known it would require subsidies. He had always felt that the market could carry the projects he had done before. The only subsidies previously used were tax credits (new market and historic preservation tax credits). Kuchma served as a city councilor for three years and had been a longtime business leader in Bridgeport, so not only was he keenly aware of the need to conserve scarce financial resources, but he also did not want to risk the appearance of conflict of interest that might result from his civic involvement.

Sources: Interview with Philip Kuchma, president, Kuchma Corporation, Bridgeport, Connecticut, 2009; and www.bijousquare.com.

The developer is responsible for establishing the development program within which the architect will work. The developer should choose an architect experienced with the particular product being planned but should not let the architect dictate unit mix, unit sizes, and amenities; these decisions should be made jointly and on the basis of the results of the market analysis for the geographic subarea where the developer is building. Design decisions should take costs and ease of maintenance into consideration. Although the architect's mission is to design the project, the developer must also have sufficient design skills to give the architect the required guidance. The developer's ability to mentally visualize the design and floor plans is vital to success. Fortunately, computer-aided design

(CAD) helps developers visualize the drawings through 3-D computer renderings. CAD is also very helpful for marketing because it allows potential customers to visualize the new development as it is being built. CAD enables viewers to "walk through" a proposed project, looking at every room from any number of viewpoints.

Time spent scrutinizing the plans during design is among the most important the developer will spend on the entire project. The developer should mentally walk through every unit, look out every window, and envisage every view inside and outside the apartment. What does a guest first see when opening the front door? That view is the same first impression that renters or buyers will receive when they open the door to

Multifamily Residential Development

see model units. It is less expensive and easier to fix something with the architect during design than it is out in the field or, worse, after the building is built.

Multifamily residential buildings are among the most complex buildings to design. They must accommodate all the functional needs of a large number of people at a relatively high density while protecting their privacy. At the same time, they must provide a sense of owner-ship and sense of place and community. Multifamily residential design is often the result of a series of com-promises between notions of ideal living conditions and the economic realities of higher-density dwelling.

UNIT MIX

The mix of units by size and type should be based on the results of the market study. Unit types most often range from studio apartments through two- and three-bedroom units with two baths; some include extras, such as sunrooms, dens, and lofts. In many markets, apartment developers are seeing increased demand for luxury units for downsizing empty nesters. In projects designed for lower-income renters, family-sized units should predominate. If the target market is young singles just starting out, demand will likely be strongest for a mix of split two-master-bedroom

Multifamily Housing Forms

Since the 1970s, traditional forms of multifamily housing have yielded to a variety of configurations, making room for greater flexibility and creativity for both residents and developers. The forms discussed below appeal to renters from diverse market segments, many of whom perceive multifamily housing as the optimal lifestyle, offer-ing more freedom and convenience.

TOWNHOUSE FORMS

Buildings with townhouse-like exteriors can contain multiple types of units, in-cluding a mix of stacked flats and two- or three-level units, each with private outdoor spaces. Achievable densities are greater than those of traditional townhouses. Communal or individual garages underneath the buildings decrease the acreage dedicated to park-ing, allowing for better, more attractive site design.

Mews with buildings back-to-back or facing each other can be clustered more tightly than traditional townhouses. Piggyback units—for example, a flat on the first level facing front and a two-story unit above it—also allow increased densities. Such designs work well on small infill parcels and intro-duce the possibility of multiple unit types in a single structure.

FOUR- AND SIX-PLEXES

Garden apartments may consist of small buildings designed to look like a large single-family house, each containing four to six flats. Elevations incorporate traditional residential design elements, and site plans resemble those of single-family neighborhoods. Surface parking is minimized by the use of attached garages, and the parking that remains is in landscape-screened groups of three or four spaces—not the concrete sea found at earlier garden apartments. Such projects can successfully overcome difficulties in rezoning because of their single-family look.

COURTYARD BUILDINGS

Buildings oriented around courtyards provide desirable private outdoor space and views for residents, away from noise and traffic. Courtyards and build-ings erected over structured parking or with aboveground structured parking are a more efficient use of expensive land and result in higher densities than typical garden "breezeway" apart-ments. Designs of up to four stories in wood-frame construction include internal corridors and elevators.

MID RISES

Buildings of five to eight stories may provide the density that an expensive urban site requires. The design of mid rises is following a trend toward fit-

ting in the urban fabric of downtown districts, many of which have design guidelines requiring new construc-tion to incorporate a mix of uses, to be oriented toward the street, and to use traditional masonry elements in the exterior facade. Parking is usually structured, at grade or below.

HIGH RISES

Like mid-rise buildings, high rises vary in height and shape, allowing for more corner units, private terraces, and more diverse streetscapes. In the largest cities, high-rise apartments are viewed as the most desirable housing because of their security and on-site services. Responding to a very discriminating market, new buildings imitate the graciousness of pre–World War II luxury high-rise apartment buildings with their high ceilings, large, well-defined rooms, and high-quality finishes.

SCATTERED-SITE LOW-INCOME HOUSING

Massive, old-style public housing projects isolated from the larger com-munity are turning into human-scale projects integrated into mixed-income neighborhoods. Local housing authori-ties are involved in projects that scatter low-income housing on small—usually infill—sites throughout the community. Some public and private developers have combined low-income units with market-rent units in the same project.

roommate units and one-bedroom units for singles. In very high rent urban locales, studio units are popular, but in suburban areas, demand is almost nonexistent for such small units.

Nationally, the median size of new multifamily units peaked in 2007 at 1,197 square feet (111 m²). This value has since declined to 1,110 square feet (103 m²) in 2010; however, this size is up from its value of 1,039 square feet (97 m²) in 2000 and is significantly larger than the median of 955 square feet (90 m²) in 1990 and only 882 square feet (80 m²) in 1985. The percentage of new units constructed with three or more bedrooms has increased substantially over the last 25 years, peaking in 2006 at 24 percent of new units. In comparison, in 1985, three-bedroom units accounted for only 7 percent of new multifamily units. However, after rising consistently and peaking, this share declined to 13 percent in 2010, which is the lowest this share has been since 1992.[33]

Certain niche markets play a role in determining unit types. For example, apartments housing students require special floor plans that include three- and four-bedroom units, because typically the majority of students share a unit. More difficulty in getting approvals because of neighborhood opposition to higher density and increasing land and permitting costs also contribute to larger units as developers are forced to pursue higher-income tenants.

SITE DESIGN

A good site plan respects the natural characteristics of the site and its surroundings. The primary determinants of the site plan are the desired and permitted density, parking layout, and requirements for emergency access. The density of the project in turn is determined by zoning and the market. Generally, one-story apartments or townhouses yield seven to 12 units per acre (17–30/ha); two-story garden apartments with surface parking comfortably yield 12 to 18 units per acre (30–45/ha); and three-story garden apartments with surface parking yield up to 30 units per acre (75/ha). Structured parking, usually accommodated in one or two levels under the apartments or in a separate structure, is required to achieve densities greater than 40 units per acre (100/ha).

Fire codes typically permit a maximum distance of 150 feet (45 m) between a fire road or hydrant and a building. Local fire officials should be consulted early in the design process to determine requirements.

There is a conflict between neighbors who want lower apartment densities and the goal of promoting smart growth—walkable communities that are less dependent on the automobile and will better support mass transit. Typically, a minimum density of seven dwelling units per acre (17/ha) is needed to support a mass public transit system and densities greater than 30 units per acre (75/ha) are needed to support both bus and rail.[34]

PARKING. Parking—its dimensions, arrangement, and location—is more important than building coverage in the design of a project. One parking space per bedroom is standard. Typically, 1.75 to 1.8 parking spaces per unit is a recommended standard, and two spaces per unit are mandatory with for-sale condominiums in most areas. One-bedroom condominiums generally do not sell as well as two-bedroom condominiums except in dense urban areas, where parking standards may be lower. Even where standards are lower, however, the availability of parking may be necessary for units to sell well.

If possible, pedestrian circulation should be kept separate from vehicular access, although walking distances between parking and units should be as short as possible.

Concrete parking areas and driveways are cost-effective in the long run. Although they cost more initially, they look better and are cheaper to maintain than asphalt parking. Parking costs vary widely due to regional differences in construction costs, soil conditions, permitting, and codes. Scott Simpson estimates $3,000 to $5,000 per space for surface parking (asphalt on grade). For structured parking framed in steel or precast concrete, the cost would be $15,000 to $20,000 per space, depending on the economies of scale—the fewer spaces, the higher cost per space. Underground parking can easily skyrocket. The deeper the excavation, the higher the cost. Underground parking can cost from $20,000 per space to about $100,000 per space for high-cost structures, such as underground parking on waterfront sites that require significant waterproofing.[35]

Recovering the full cost of parking can be challenging. Using the 1 percent rule for the monthly rent needed to cover each $1 of additional capital cost, an owner would need to receive $500 per month in rent to cover the cost of a $50,000 underground parking space.

Underground garages and hillside cutouts for parking are especially expensive to build because fireproofing, waterproofing, air handlers, and drainage or sump pumps are required. Carports are rarely built today, but they may be a cost-effective type of

Multifamily Residential Development

covered parking, especially in areas with intense sun or severe climates. Care should be taken to make them structurally sound because flimsy carports have collapsed in heavy winds, rains, and snow, damaging the cars below.

AMENITIES AND LANDSCAPING. The selection of amenities begins with the market analysis. A good market analysis answers several questions: What are comparable properties in the market area offering? Do projects with certain amenities have an edge in marketing, or do lower-priced projects with fewer amenities attract more residents? And perhaps the most important: Will residents pay for the amenities?

Amenities help sell the product. What some communities consider essential, others view as luxurious. Generally, if amenities are wanted and used, residents will pay a reasonable price for them—unless operating costs do not correspond with residents' income levels. Therefore, the developer should design not only what the residents like but also what they can afford.

Swimming pools and outdoor Jacuzzis are standard amenities in many suburban areas, and attractively landscaped pools can add much to the marketability of a complex. In complexes designed for families, a wading pool for children separate from the adult pool should be provided. Complexes targeted toward young singles might feature dog parks and "soft" programming, like social activities.

Landscaping should be as maintenance free as possible. Focal planting areas with seasonal color should be located near the project's entrance, the leasing office, the pool, and courtyards. The landscaping plan and sprinkler system should be designed as an integral part of the site plan. Detailed plant design may be left until later, but the general plan should be completed before construction begins. Indeed, many local governments require a landscaping plan before they issue a building permit.

Depending on the particular market niche, a play area for children or even a daycare center may be a valuable amenity to include. Most projects should allow some space for play areas even if the development is geared largely to a singles market, as some of the residents will likely be part-time parents.

Landscaped areas can serve as buffers, are usually visually attractive, add to the project's overall market appeal, and serve as passive recreational areas. A six-foot-wide (1.8 m²) walking trail surrounding the property can be used for walking, running, biking, or skating and costs little to construct and maintain. Some new developments include community gardens, as well as private outdoor space adjacent to units. Integrating landscaped areas with active recreational facilities, such as pools and children's play areas, yields the most attractive site plan.

Landscape design must consider the climate, terrain, and cultural influences of the region where the

Tips for Successful Multifamily Residential Design

- Be flexible when targeting a market. In the event that the market for a project turns out to be very different from the developer's initial expectation, the presence of basic features with a broad market appeal will help sales or rentals.

- Ensure that common areas for stairs, elevators, corridors, lobbies, laundries, and so forth do not occupy more than 18 to 20 percent of total heated rentable areas.

- Property managers can make many useful contributions to the design process. Include them in all design review meetings.

- Do not put family units on the third floor.

- Renters look primarily at total rent, not rent per square foot. Design units to meet the affordability requirements of the target market.

- Condominiums often end up as rental units because of changing market conditions. Make sure that a project will not bring financial ruin if units must be rented rather than sold.

- Where possible, enclose a project's open space with buildings, creating courtyards free of cars. Views of cars detract from the courtyard environment and may reduce attainable rents.

- Avoid creating canyon-like areas and barracks-like buildings.

- Avoid placing air-conditioner condensing units in areas where children will play.

- Plan ahead for trash disposal. Make containers easy to reach, easy to clean around, and screened if possible.

- The U.S. Postal Service requires that mailboxes be grouped together. Place mailboxes near the manager's office so that the manager can see tenants as they come and go.

- Provide storage facilities near the pool for outdoor furniture during the winter.

- Ensure that the leasing office is visible from the street, is easy to find, and has reserved parking close by.

project is located. Sustainable landscape designers effectively use hardy indigenous plants that provide interest during all seasons. Xeriscaping, a method of landscaping that relies on proper plant selection and planning to conserve water, minimizes the use of chemicals and reduces the amount of labor-intensive maintenance by carefully considering the site's climate, soil, existing vegetation, and topography. Such methods can be applied to any kind of climate or site. A sustainable landscape will reduce labor inputs, making it less expensive to implement and maintain. Plant selection, implementation, and maintenance build on the design process, each having sustainability as a major consideration.

On-site business centers continue to be a popular amenity, in some ways serving a social function in addition to business functions. If the project incorporates a clubhouse, it should be centrally located, usually at one of the edges of a courtyard. Where possible, the leasing office is best situated near the clubhouse and should be visible to passing street traffic; studies have shown that up to 70 percent of rentals are the result of drive-by traffic. Some projects separate the leasing office from the clubhouse so that the business of running the development does not infringe on the sense of community provided residents. In some larger properties, developers even separate the marketing function from resident services for existing tenants.

Adam Barzilay restores historic buildings in Philadelphia. He adds contemporary details that will appeal to young professionals: doorman, lobby furniture, fitness center, yoga room, and flat-screen TVs in the laundry room. He makes cosmetic improvements to the hallways and upgrades kitchens and baths as units turn over.[36] Ken Hughes has been successful in tailoring amenities and services in luxury urban projects to draw people away from suburban alternatives. "The urban developer must be a keen observer of behavior to determine which features are likely to be more appealing to prospective customers. Parking for downtown projects in Texas must include the same number of spaces per bedroom (typically one per bedroom) as suburban projects in order to be competitive; in addition, residents want closets that are equivalent in size to what would be considered bedrooms elsewhere."[37]

EXTERIOR DESIGN

The choice of exterior materials and architectural designs should closely relate to the target market's preferences and the character of the local community. The style and materials of a new project should be

CETRA/CRI ARCHITECTURE PLLC

Third Square in Cambridge, Massachusetts, is a residential complex of two eight-story buildings that include both rental and for-sale units.

compatible with existing development in the surrounding area. A project in a new developing area should aspire to set the tone for future development.

Regional traditions and climate play very important roles in the exterior design of apartment buildings. Brick is a common material throughout the South and along the East Coast. Stucco is popular in the Southwest, whereas wood or composite siding is most common in the northern United States.

Economies of scale can be achieved by minimizing and repeating building types. The fewer the number of building types, the greater the potential for minimizing costs. Wall segments and roof trusses can be prefabricated in groups, and labor costs fall when more work can be done by semiskilled workers. At the same time, however, marketability may require considerable variety in appearance. Long, straight walls and rooflines should be avoided. Individual buildings should not extend more than 200 feet (60 m).

Marvin Finger states that his development company never goes to the architect with a generic design. "We go to the neighborhood and select the prominent features of the building elevations of that upscale community and then we take that to the architect to enhance and work into the proposed facade."[38]

The building's exterior should express the individuality of the apartment units within. Useful as private outdoor space, balconies are often instrumental design elements in denoting individual apartments. Six feet (1.8 m) is usually considered the optimal depth for a usable balcony—anything larger may cause excessive shading of windows below and anything smaller may be useful only for storage, which is unsightly. Inset balconies are visually more attractive and can be useful in establishing privacy. Such balconies in combination with an L-shaped plan allow two rooms to open onto one balcony.

The roof should help establish a residential character as well as shed rain and snow. The silhouettes of various roof forms can create a friendly, village-like impression. Like the rest of the exterior of the building, roof design is determined partly by regional traditions and styles.

Utility meters, transformers, and trash bins, always potentially unsightly, should not be overlooked during design. A bank of meters, for example, can be quite obtrusive. Utility companies prefer that meters be grouped together and usually have a say in their placement. Submetering also allows for optimal placement of meters away from visible areas.

INTERIOR DESIGN

One objective in designing an apartment interior is to make a relatively small space seem larger than it is. Large windows and angled walls that lead the eye around corners can help in this regard. L-shaped units offer greater design opportunities than do square or rectangular units. Higher ceilings can be an effective means of increasing the impression of space. A cost analysis should be done, however, to determine the cost of an increase in the exterior building envelope. The traditional eight-foot (2.4 m) ceiling height has been replaced with nine or even ten feet (2.7 or 3 m) as the current standard, especially in luxury apartments and condominiums. Windows are important not only for the views they offer but also for the light and ventilation they permit. Natural ventilation of an apartment requires that windows be placed on at least two exposures, not necessarily in the same room and preferably on opposite walls. In any room, natural lighting is improved when light comes from more than one direction.

Most markets today demand laundry facilities in the units and fully equipped kitchens with dishwashers, garbage disposals, wood cabinetry, and built-in microwave ovens. Adequate kitchen and storage areas make apartments more livable. The kitchen for a one-bedroom apartment should provide a minimum of 16 linear feet (5 m) for counters and appliances. Each bedroom should offer a minimum of 12 linear feet

(3.6 m) of closet space, and guest and linen closets should provide another four linear feet (1.2 m) of storage. These standards can be met in a floor plan of 700 square feet (65 m²) in a one-bedroom apartment and 1,000 square feet (95 m²) in a two-bedroom apartment. In smaller units, some compromises may be necessary.

In most markets, two-bedroom units should have two baths, with one bathroom for guests' use accessible from the hall, without walking through a bedroom. In higher-priced developments, master baths often include soaking tubs, separate showers, and double vanities. Quality at the lower end has risen correspondingly.

Successful developers worry about every detail. In small apartments, for example, circulation is critical. One should pay careful attention to how the doors will open so as to minimize conflicts and obstructions. In large developments, full-scale mock-ups of prototypical units are a good idea. The cost is modest, and the savings can be huge. It is possible to simulate the *appearance* of the units very closely in computer renderings, but not the actual construction aspects. Such mock-ups serve two main purposes: (1) they reveal problems in the design and (2) subcontractors can use the mock-ups to familiarize themselves with the plan; make decisions about the placement of wiring, plumbing, and ductwork; and correct potential conflicts between subcontractors. For example, a plumbing pipe may interfere with the best route for an air-conditioning duct. Such conflicts often do not become apparent until the construction stage.

Finish materials in an apartment should be chosen for ease of maintenance and also to reflect the tastes of the market. Vinyl tile is commonly used in kitchens, baths, and entries, although ceramic tile or stone may be used in higher-end apartments. Other rooms are typically carpeted, with the quality of the carpet varying with the market. Or flooring may be hardwood or simulated wood.

Certain optional features can add value to the unit in terms of additional monthly rents. Bookcases, decorative moldings, ceiling fans, and undercabinet lighting can all increase a unit's sense of quality but are desirable only if they are supported by the market. Fireplaces, for instance, take up space, and many tenants of smaller apartments are reluctant to pay the increased rent charged for such amenities. The appropriateness of amenities such as washer/dryers also depends on the market. To recover amenity costs, the developer should be able to increase an apartment's monthly rent by at least 1 percent of the construction cost of any amenities. For example, units with a $1,000 fireplace should be able to command rents at least $10 per month higher than those without fireplaces. Separate heating, ventilating, and air-conditioning (HVAC) systems for each unit are typical for most garden and mid-rise developments. Mechanical systems can be contained in the walls, ceilings, or roof spaces of the unit but require an outside compressor. The compressor can be located on the roof, where it must be screened and integrated with the roof design, or on the ground outside the unit, where its noise is more noticeable and where it may create an obstruction. In high-rise projects, "VAV [variable air volume] is common. However, chilled beams have recently caught on, and raised floors are gaining traction as well. The location, climate, orientation, and local market all play a roll in system selection. Also, if the building is slated for LEED certification, then heat recovery wheels are often added. Some lower-end apartment buildings use through-wall unit ventilators, so it is definitely not a question of one size fits all."[39]

Up-to-date wiring systems are essential. Units should be prewired for cable television, security systems, Internet connections, and multiple telephone lines, with outlets in all rooms. Retrofitting wiring in a completed building is very expensive and difficult, but more and more developers see the wisdom of building smart buildings, with all systems integrated and controlled by computer. Such technology is essential in luxury apartments and before long will be an expected feature in lower-end projects as well. John Porta buys and upgrades existing apartment projects. He observes, "Laundry is a critical factor that remodeling can't always easily accommodate. Latino residents require bigger kitchens. Gen-Y residents want a nice-looking kitchen, but it does not have to be particularly functional." He adds that kitchens vary somewhat from market to market, as do amenities and exteriors, but interior layouts are largely consistent. "Parking can be a revenue center in certain cities and in others, it is a standard amenity for which you cannot charge an additional fee."[40]

DESIGN ISSUES

PRIVACY AND SECURITY. The layout of apartment buildings needs to provide privacy for each apartment, regardless of the project's density. Many of the techniques employed in the design of the site, units, and building exteriors are devices for creating visual separation between units. Building codes also provide useful criteria: for example, a code might stipulate that a wall with windows should be separated from a facing wall with windows by at least 30 feet (9 m), that a wall with windows should be separated from a facing wall without windows by at least 20 feet (6 m), and that two outside walls without windows should be separated by a minimum of 10 feet (3 m). Vertical and horizontal projections, such as walls and balconies, should be placed to help screen views into bedrooms from other apartments or from common spaces.

Security is an important consideration in site design. A plan that minimizes the number of entries to a project provides greater control of traffic and therefore better security. Entries to units should not be hidden from view, and walkways and breezeways should be visible from several points. Exterior lighting can do much to create a feeling of security. At the same time, exterior lighting should be designed so that light does not shine directly into apartment units or adjacent properties or cause glare for passing motorists.

Electronic security systems for individual units as well as project entrances are common in some parts of the country, most notably in California, Florida, and Texas. Gated community entrances are another growing and somewhat controversial trend. Although the gate lends an air of security as well as prestige to some communities, research does not indicate that crime rates are lower in gated communities. Jerome Frank, Jr., notes, "People are very concerned about covered parking or garage parking and related issues of security. People like to see a security gate. They are a maintenance hell and don't provide much security, but it works psychologically." He adds, "Many higher-density apartments deal with this issue by putting parking in the middle. How traffic is handled—vehicular and pedestrian—has to be worked out in terms of planning for overall circulation (proximity of parking to housing and the length of walk to one's unit, for example)."[41]

Design elements can be used to create a sense of ownership. Studies of successful subsidized housing projects have shown that tenants take better care of their apartments when a "semiprivate" transition area is provided between the outdoor public space and their private apartment. Tenants like to be able to assume ownership of this transition space and so this concept can also work well for luxury apartments. The semiprivate space may range from an inset doorway to a fenced-in front patio.

RENTAL APARTMENTS VERSUS CONDOMINI-UMS. Rental housing and for-sale (condominium) housing differ in their design in a number of respects. Security and privacy are even more important issues in condominiums than apartments. If rental and for-sale units are combined in the same complex, they should be physically separated because rentals' proximity hurts the sale of condominiums. Renters are not confronted with the long-term investment of a mortgage and are less likely to be critical of a less desirable location within the complex as a whole. Many condominium complexes forbid investor-owned units because owner-occupants do not want to live next to renters.

Some condominium developers recommend higher bedroom counts in the unit mix. In general, there should be a smaller number but a greater variety of dwelling units per building in a condominium, compared with a rental project. Kitchens need additional countertop space and cabinets. Baths must have better appointments. Closets and general storage areas must also be larger.

One-quarter to one-half more parking space per condominium unit is often required, compared with rental units. Moreover, condominium parking spaces should be identified and separated from rental unit spaces. Assigned spaces can, however, create management problems as a result of the misuse of those spaces.

DESIGNING TO SAVE COSTS. Developers must make many tradeoffs between construction costs and operating costs. For example, the use of exterior wood siding may save construction costs, but because it needs frequent repainting, its use may increase maintenance costs over a more costly but permanent material like brick. High-maintenance materials also depress the sale value of a rental project because proper accounting for operating expenses indicates the extent to which replacement reserves and maintenance expenses reduce net operating income.

APPROVALS

Some developers believe that the safest way to deal with local government officials is to tell them very little until documents are submitted for project approval. This policy is not, however, wise. If any public review is required, the developer should meet with an official of the reviewing agency before drawing up preliminary plans. A preapplication conference is a useful means of meeting the planning staff and learning their interests and concerns. In turn, the planning staff can inform the developer of requirement factors to consider during the planning stage. The conference also gives the developer the chance to involve the staff in the project, thereby encouraging a sense of cooperation that is likely to make the entire project proceed more smoothly.

Even in cases when the developer can apply directly for a building permit, it is possible to obtain valuable information from members of the planning department before starting to draw up design plans. For example, the fire inspector at one building department informed Peiser Corporation and Jerome Frank Investments of proposed changes that their architect had not heard of regarding the regulations governing fire walls. The changes made it more economical to use sprinklers than floor-to-rafter fire-rated partitions. Six months later, when they returned for plan approval, the proposed changes had taken effect. Thus, the fire inspector's forewarning saved Peiser and Frank the time and money that would otherwise have been necessary to redraw the plans.

A developer should not spend too much money on preliminary plans in case, as often happens, the

Ten Fifty B is the first LEED-certified affordable high rise on the West Coast. Located in downtown San Diego, it is designated for families earning 20 to 60 percent of area median income.

AFFIRMED HOUSING GROUP

project does not proceed. But sufficient care should be taken so that the plans satisfy government agencies and financial backers. Further, the most creative part of the design process often occurs in drawing preliminary plans. The preliminary plan phase is sometimes divided into a rough concept planning phase and a refined schematic phase. Rough concept plans consist of floor plans and elevations that may be prepared for testing the market for financing and for tenants, whereas refined schematic drawings represent the last opportunity for major design decisions. Refined schematic drawings are also used to solicit lenders and tenants. Once the plans are approved, most major features of a project cannot be changed.

A collaborative design process is important for ensuring that the design is as functional and marketable as possible. Regular meetings should be held with property managers, construction superintendents, and leasing managers to obtain their input and to have them critique the latest plans. Beginning developers should ask mentors and other developers to review the plans as well. They may see problems in the design that others do not.

Many communities hold design review hearings that are open to the public. The developer should meet with design review board members (often local architects) as soon as possible to learn about their primary concerns. Neighbors usually have strong opinions about the design, including facades, ingress, egress, parking, materials, landscaping, elevations, open space, and views. Developers should be prepared to answer their criticisms. It is advisable to meet with them sooner rather than later in the design process. The meetings can help establish a rapport if the neighbors feel that their concerns are being addressed. In addition, the neighbors may understand the compromises and tradeoffs better if they are part of the process rather than being asked to react to final plans.

Final plans and specifications become part of the official contract package used by the contractor and submitted to the lender and the city building department. They include the construction drawings and material specifications required to build the project.

Unless a developer is certain that the project will go ahead, final plans and specifications should not be ordered until all feasibility studies are completed, all predevelopment approvals—such as zoning changes—are in place, and a tentative financing commitment is received. Final plans and specifications, which typically cost three or four times as much as the preliminary plans, represent a major increase in at-risk investment.

They must be completed in their entirety before plans can be submitted to the city for a building permit. In some cities, the building permit process is so lengthy that a developer cannot afford to make any major changes to the plans once they have been submitted.

Because the drawings and specifications become contract documents, the more precise and well coordinated they are, the better. At the same time, items such as air-conditioning equipment should not be specified too exactly in case the contractor can make a cost-saving substitution. Change orders during construction are the single-largest source of construction cost overruns. Unfortunately, they are unavoidable, and prudent developers carry a 3 to 5 percent construction contingency for these unexpected events. The fewer changes that are made, the fewer opportunities the contractor or subcontractor has to raise the contract price. If the developer has done his homework properly during preliminary plans, the

Tips for Working with Architects

- **Keep a direct line of communication open with the design architect. Intermediaries are a liability in the initial phases of design.**

- **Establish team milestones to ensure that the project stays on schedule.**

- **Use an initial design workshop to streamline the concept design phase.**

- **Always use a qualified contractor who has experience and legitimate references and involve him from the very beginning of the design process.**

- **Pay very careful attention to the circulation of the building and site plan. Sometimes, the investment in a computer simulation helps clarify unresolved issues about circulation.**

- **Invest in design that creates a particular ambience and sense of identity, but keep cost considerations in mind.**

- **Identify the norms for the region when choosing amenities and functional systems.**

- **Always have a furniture plan drawn up for each apartment type proposed by the architect. Sometimes, the design may seem very good, but the configuration and dimensions of the rooms will not allow for even the most typical furniture, like couches and larger beds, to be located well in the unit.**

Sources: Jan Van Tilberg, Van Tilberg, Banvard & Soderbergh, Santa Monica, California; and Paige Close, Looney Ricks Kiss Architects, Memphis, Tennessee.

process of obtaining final drawings should be routine. The contractor should be involved as early as possible in reviewing the drawings so as to minimize problems in the field and provide cost-to-value assistance to the entire development team.

Financing

Rental apartment projects, like other income property developments, have traditionally relied primarily on three types of financing: construction loans, permanent loans, and equity. For-sale condominium projects, like land development, usually involve only equity and a construction loan, the latter covering the construction and sales period. Buyers of individual condominium units obtain their own permanent loans. By contrast, in rental apartment projects, the developer uses the permanent loan to *take out* the construction loan as soon as the project reaches a specified level of income or occupancy. The amount of the construction loan usually equals that of the permanent loan because the construction lender will lend up to, but no more than, the amount that the permanent lender will fund. The construction lender looks to the permanent lender's mortgage to retire the construction loan.

Equity makes up the difference between total project cost and the amount of the construction and permanent loans. At one time, construction and permanent loans often covered 100 percent of project costs, and developers were not required to contribute additional equity. After real estate crashes in the late 1980s and again in the late 2000s, however, rigid loan coverage requirements usually demand that equity cover 20 to 40 percent of the project's value at completion. This value is the capitalized value of the stabilized NOI after all construction and lease-up risk is over. Because the completed project value usually exceeds the total all-in development cost (the difference is development profit), the permanent lender's loan-to-value (L/V) ratio as a percentage of completed project value should result in a higher L/V ratio as a percentage of development cost. For example, if completed capitalized value of a project is $12 million, and total all-in development costs are $10 million, then a 60 percent L/V requirement by the lender will result in a $7.2 million permanent loan, or 72 percent of total development cost.

Equity is the most expensive source of funding because equity investors receive returns only after other lenders have been repaid. Equity investors therefore have the riskiest position, and they require much higher rates of return to compensate for the risk. Con-struction lenders usually require developers to invest most or all of the needed equity in a project before they begin to fund the construction loan to ensure that the developer has enough money to complete the project. Even after the construction loan has been retired by the permanent mortgage, equity investors receive cash flow only to the extent that the property produces cash flow over and above the annual mortgage debt service. If a shortfall occurs, developers (or their investors) are responsible for injecting additional equity to cover the shortfall so that the bank always receives its full monthly debt service payment when it is due. Otherwise, the permanent mortgage goes into default, and lenders can begin foreclosure proceedings on the project.

For beginning developers, the task of finding lenders is perhaps the hardest job after finding equity investors. Lenders look chiefly at track record, credit, and the project itself. By definition, beginning developers lack a track record, and they rarely have the financial net worth of more experienced developers. Thus, the project must be well above average in terms of its market feasibility, design, and economic appeal to capture a lender's interest. Beginning developers can improve their chances of securing loans by joint-venturing with experienced developers and/or wealthy individuals. Beginning developers should also bear in mind that smaller localized lenders are more likely than large banks to consider their requests. Many developers begin as homebuilders, which allows them to build relationships with lenders that carry over to subsequent larger projects. Lenders are just as concerned about the way developers handle their business (meet deadlines, handle draw requests, build within budget, and so forth) as they are about the size of developers' previous projects, although they must be satisfied that the developer has the competency to complete larger, more complicated projects. (See chapter 2 for a review of the various financial institutions that provide construction and permanent financing for real estate.)

CONSTRUCTION LOANS

Traditionally, developers obtained a permanent loan commitment before obtaining a construction loan commitment, even though construction financing occurs before permanent financing. The construction lender approves the construction loan on the basis of the promise that the loan would be retired by the permanent loan at some specified date. In the early 1980s, however, when interest rates soared, open-ended construction loans without permanent takeouts became common. Floating rate *miniperms*—three- to five-year construction loans that carried over into the operating period—were granted on the expectation that permanent rates would come down. The provision of open-ended loans, however, generally depends on the track records and financial statements of developers.

The construction loan is characterized by its short term, installment draws, variable interest rate, and single repayment when the project is completed and the construction loan is taken out by the permanent loan.[42] The developer files draw requests with the construction lender each month as work progresses on the project. The lender's inspectors check the property each month to confirm that the work was done, and the lender then funds the request by transferring money into the developer's project account. This money is available for the developer to pay the contractor (see figure 4-10). The amount, term, and interest rate of the construction loan are defined by the loan agreement. Interest payments are added to the loan balance at the end of each month so that the developer does not have to make out-of-pocket payments for interest. If the project is not fully leased and the permanent loan is not funded within the stated term limit, the construction lender is technically able to *call the loan*—that is, demand immediate payment from the developer. In practice, however, the con-

struction lender does not want to have to foreclose on a bad construction loan as long as a reasonable likelihood exists that the project can be completed successfully. If the developer has kept the construction lender regularly informed about the project's progress and reasons for delay, the lender will probably be willing to extend the construction loan term by six or 12 months. Such extensions almost always require the payment of an additional one or two points. In times of economic crisis, lenders may be under regulatory pressure to reduce real estate exposure and may be unwilling to extend loans. At such times, the developer stands to lose the project if he cannot come up with substantially more equity or bring in a replacement lender.

Construction loans suffer from a high degree of uncertainty: delays caused by weather, labor troubles, and material shortages; cost overruns; bankruptcies by contractors and subcontractors; and leasing risk (lease-up rates and rents that fall below expectations). Consequently, lenders providing construction funding take special precautions to ensure that they are protected.

Moreover, construction lenders have become increasingly suspicious of the viability of permanent commitments. Permanent loans sometimes contain such stringent covenants that developers must meet before funding is provided that the takeout loan funding is questionable. In negotiating permanent takeouts, developers must take care that they have bankable commitments—that is, commitments that construction lenders will lend against.

The lender's security comes from two sources: the project itself and the developer's credit. The developer is typically required to sign personally on the construction loan and must show a net worth at least equal to the loan. During economic downturns, the credit requirements may become even more stringent, and the developer may have to prove a *liquid* net worth (cash, stocks, and bonds) equal to the amount of the loan.

CALCULATING INTEREST FOR A CONSTRUCTION LOAN

Suppose a developer has a $1 million construction loan with two points ($20,000) paid up front (out of loan proceeds). Assuming 10 percent annual interest, interest on the construction loan and the draw schedule are shown in figure 4-10. The bank will accrue interest monthly. The loan must be repaid at the end of the 12th month.

For apartments, the construction loan usually has a term of one to three years, which must cover both

FIGURE 4-10 | Calculating Interest for a Construction Loan

Month	Beginning Balance	Interest Charges	Current Draws	Ending Balance
0			$20,000	$20,000
1	$20,000	$167	40,000	60,167
2	60,167	501	80,000	140,668
3	140,668	1,172	80,000	221,840
4	221,840	1,849	100,000	323,689
5	323,689	2,697	100,000	426,386
6	426,386	3,553	100,000	529,939
7	529,939	4,416	100,000	634,355
8	634,355	5,286	100,000	739,641
9	739,641	6,164	100,000	845,805
10	845,805	7,048	100,000	952,853
11	952,853	7,940	80,000	1,040,793
12	1,040,793	8,673	0	1,049,466
Total		$49,466	$1,000,000	
Total amount to be repaid to the bank:				$1,049,466
Effective yield to the bank:				14.49%

the construction and lease-up periods. Interest rates depend on the developer's credit and typically range from 1 to 3 percent over prime with one or two points up front.[43]

Construction lenders usually require the developer to put the total required equity into the project on the front end, before the developer can draw down on the construction loan. Any necessary equity must therefore be raised before construction can begin.

Interest is calculated each month on the average daily balance. Developers can make precise calculations of their interest requirements (as illustrated in figure 4-10), but banks have their own method for estimating interest during construction and lease-up. For example, if the total construction loan amount is $10 million with a one-year term at 10 percent interest, the bank may apply a standard factor as high as 0.75 to determine the average loan balance, even though the developer may show the average loan balance to be 0.5 percent of the final amount. This factor is used to determine the interest reserve, or $750,000 in the example above ($10,000,000 × 0.75 average balance × 10 percent interest × 1 year).

Construction and permanent lenders require a first lien on the property.[44] Existing loans automatically have a superior position to subsequent loans under the rule of *first in time, first in priority*. Thus, any prior loans, such as seller financing or land development loans, must be paid off, releasing the senior liens, at the time of the first construction draw. This rule means that seller financing *must* be subordinated (the seller agrees to accept a second lien position) in order for a construction or permanent lender to fund the mortgage. Construction loan draws are tied to stages in the construction process, called *percent completion*, based on an appraisal of the work completed to date. The appraisal is conducted by an inspector hired by the lender. If the value as measured by the preagreed formula for percent completion is lower, additional draws will not be permitted, irrespective of the dollar amount expended by the developer. The developer makes a detailed line item budget of off-site expenses, such as street improvements and traffic signals; on-site expenses, such as asphalt and landscaping; and direct construction expenses for the whole project. For example, he may tell the lender that he is 50 percent done with concrete and wants 50 percent funding of the line item for concrete. The lender's inspector may check and say that only 40 percent of the work has been done. The developer may attempt to convince the inspector that more work has been done, but the

inspector's opinion will prevail for monthly construction loan draws. Construction loans have traditionally been made by *institutional* lenders, namely, commercial banks and sometimes insurance companies and pension funds. Institutional lenders are subject to close scrutiny by the Federal Reserve, which carefully monitors loan balances and reserves. If a loan is not repaid on time or if interest payments are not made, the loan is placed into a separate category that requires significantly higher *loan reserves* (cash balances held by the bank to offset potential losses).

The Financial Institutions Reform, Recovery, and Enforcement Act (FIRREA) was enacted in 1989. Among other things, it regulates the amount of bank reserves required to cover high-risk real estate loans. The average equity reserve was raised to 6 percent to minimize defaults. The rates are variable and depend on whether the loan is standard, development, or speculative. Many law firms specialize in compliance with FIRREA.[45]

Banks are eager to avoid any construction loans that involve unnecessary risk, meaning it is especially difficult for new developers to obtain financing. The difficulty notwithstanding, community banks are likely to be the most willing construction lenders to beginning developers.

Loan reserves are established internally based on the perceived risk of each particular loan. Banks often hold appraisals to be valid for a year or more depending on the property, stability of tenant, and stability of the market. Under unstable market conditions and periods of declining property values, banks may require appraisal updates more frequently than one per year.

The task of finding a construction lender is much simpler if a developer has a takeout loan commitment for the permanent loan. Jerome Frank, Jr., emphasizes that finding the lowest loan rate is less important than establishing a relationship with a good banker: "A quarter to a half point in interest is not going to make or break the deal. The most important thing for the developer is not going to be the rate but the time—making sure that he negotiates enough time for himself to get it done." Frank adds that developers should watch out for future balloon payments that might require refinancing. "Try to build in the ability to renew or extend the loan at the beginning and buy yourself time."[46]

Randolph Hawthorne observes that tension always remains between the construction lender and the permanent lender about who is going to finance the lease-up risk. "People are pretty skilled at building competently without significant time overruns. The real risks are what the demand is and how quickly the property will lease-up initially, which have a huge effect on the pro forma. In times of optimism, you see a lot of open-ended construction loans, the so-called miniperms without a forward commitment for permanent financing. When markets get soft or when people get concerned about regulatory pressures, they do not seek open-ended construction loans but look for forward commitments and permanent financing instead."[47]

Karl Zavitkovsky says it is important to distinguish between loans provided by small banks and loans provided by big banks. Smaller regional banks originate loans that they plan to keep on their own balance sheets, whereas large banks syndicate the loans to other banks and get them off their books as soon as possible. Large developers like JPI and Trammell Crow Company depend on banks with high-volume credit facilities—those that deal in $15 million to $20 million and larger syndicated transactions. "Smaller banks tend to underprice the big institutions, because they do not have the portfolio exposure limitations of big banks. Big banks issue loans with flexible pricing language that reserves the right to ratchet up the interest rate, say, from LIBOR [London Interbank Offered Rate] plus 200 to LIBOR plus 225 to syndicate it.[48] Even with these types of tools, it is almost impossible to syndicate loans on spec buildings because of current attitudes in large financial institutions."[49] Beginning developers who must find a third party to guarantee the loan should look for an experienced developer or investor who knows how to manage the construction loan from start to finish. Someone with deep experience in the industry will give the lender confidence that the loan will be repaid even if problems arise during construction.

PERMANENT FINANCING

Permanent financing—a long-term mortgage on the completed project—is a critical ingredient, especially for projects undertaken by beginning developers who are unlikely to receive construction financing without a permanent loan takeout. Permanent loans take many forms. In addition to bullet loans and the standard fixed-rate, adjustable-rate, and variable-rate mortgages, lenders make participating loans and convertible loans.[50] Participating loans give lenders a participation in cash flows after debt service and sometimes a participation in residual cash flows from sale. These participations, called kickers, raise

lenders' IRRs above the loan rate by an additional 2 or 3 percent—an amount sufficient for lenders to consider funding 80 to 95 percent of a project's costs. A comparison of a standard bullet loan with two lender participation loans is shown in figure 4-11, showing how these different approaches change the loan terms, cash flows, and yields. The best approach depends on the developer's situation and preferences. The summary statistics indicate that the participating loan with owner priorities gives the highest return to the developer, as measured by net present value— $427,000 in this example. The participating loan with lender priorities gives the highest return to the lender—12.52 percent.

Another popular variation on standard mortgages provides a note rate, which is higher than the pay rate. The note rate is the nominal interest rate on the mortgage, say, for illustration purposes, 12 percent. The pay rate (used to determine the monthly debt service) is lower, at, say, 10 percent, because the initial cash flow from the property will not cover mortgage payments at the note rate. The difference in interest payments between the 12 percent note rate and the 10 percent pay rate is accrued until the property is sold. The advantage of a lower pay rate is that the borrower can obtain a larger loan than if the mortgage payment were calculated from the note rate because the lower interest rate reduces the mortgage payment (see figure 4-12 for an illustration of the calculation). Conduit loans (so called because the loan originator in effect has a conduit through Wall Street directly to investors) have significantly increased the amount of mortgage money in recent years. Mortgage brokers, banks, and other lenders prenegotiate the sale of a package of mortgages, say $100 million, to a Wall Street underwriter under certain terms. They then proceed to originate the mortgages to borrowers or to buy existing mortgages from other originators. The Wall Street underwriter sells the package of mortgages to investors, using the proceeds to reimburse the originator. Sales of commercial mortgages in the secondary market, of which conduit loans represent one form, are a relatively new phenomenon. They follow years of evolution of single-family residential mortgage sales in the secondary market through quasi-governmental organizations like Fannie Mae and Ginnie Mae.

In the case of a conduit loan, the original borrower is known as the sponsor. Typically, this individual is the owner of a completed project, a large-scale building, and is seeking new sources of capital. The owned

FIGURE 4-11 | Comparison of Bullet and Participating Loans for a Prototypical Income-Producing Development

Bullet loans are standard fixed-rate mortgages, amortizable over 30 years but with a five-, seven-, or ten-year call (repayment) provision. Participating loans, commonly made by pension funds, give the lender a participation in annual cash flows and proceeds from sale. The developer or the lender may receive a priority cash flow before the participation is calculated.

Assumptions (000)

Project Cost	$11,000
Net Rentable Square Feet	93
Depreciable Basis of Building	$9,500
Depreciation Method	31½ years SL
Initial Gross Potential Income	$1,674
Income Appreciation Rate	4%
Vacancy Rate	5%
Initial Operating Expenses	$419
Expense Inflation Rate	4%
Ordinary Tax Rate	28%
Costs of Sale	4%
Holding Period	5 years

Loan Terms (000)	Bullet Loan	Participating Loan with Developer Priorities	Participating Loan with Lender Priorities
Required Debt Coverage Ratios	1.2	1.15	1.15
Maximum Loan-to-Value Ratio	75%	90%	90%
Loan Amount	$8,788	$10,546	$10,546
Note Rate	9.60%	8.75%	8.75%
Loan Fee	0%	0%	0%
Loan Amortization (years)	30	30	30
Cash Flow Kicker to Lender	–	50%	50%
Owner's Threshold Cash Flow	–	$20	–
Lender's Threshold	–	–	$20
Reversion Kicker to Lender	–	50%	50%
Owner's Threshold Reversion	–	$200	–
Lender's Threshold Reversion	–	–	$200
Land Sale Price	–	–	–
Land Lease Payment Rate	–	–	–
Land Repurchase Price	–	–	–

After-Tax Cash Flows from First Year of Operations (000)

Annual Tax Liabilities

	Bullet Loan	Participating Loan with Developer Priorities	Participating Loan with Lender Priorities
Net Operating Income	$1,172	$1,172	$1,172
Less: Interest	(844)	(920)	(920)
Less: Depreciation	(302)	(302)	(302)
Less: Land Lease	–	–	–
Less: Lender Participation	–	(78)[a]	(98)
Taxable Income	26	(128)	(148)
Taxes Paid (saved)	7	(36)	(41)

Annual After-Tax Cash Flow

	Bullet Loan	Participating Loan with Developer Priorities	Participating Loan with Lender Priorities
Net Operating Income	1,172	1,172	1,172
Less: Land Lease	–	–	–
Less: Mortgage Payment	(896)	(996)	(996)
Less: Threshold Amount Paid to Developer	–	(20)	–
Less: Threshold Amount Paid to Lender	–	–	(20)
Cash Flow Subject to Participation	275	156	156
Less: Lender Participation	–	(78)[a]	(78)
Before-Tax Cash Flow	275	98[b]	78[c]
Less: Taxes Paid (saved)	7	(36)	(41)
After-Tax Cash Flow	268	134	119

	Bullet Loan	Participating Loan with Developer Priorities	Participating Loan with Lender Priorities
After-Tax Cash Flows from Sale (000)			
Tax Liability upon Sale			
Net Sale Price	$13,160	$13,160	$13,160
Less: Adjusted Tax Basis	(9,492)	(9,492)	(9,492)
Taxable Capital Gain	3,668	3,668	3,668
Tax on Capital Gain	1,027	1,027	1,027
Tax Savings from Lender Payments	–	402	458
Total Tax Liability	1,027	625	569
After-Tax Cash Flows upon Sale			
Net Sale Price	13,160	13,160	13,160
Less: Land Purchase Price	–	–	–
Mortgage Balance	8,466	10,092	10,092
Threshold Amount Paid to Owner	–	200	–
Threshold Amount Paid to Lender	–	–	200
Cash Flow Subject to Participation	4,694	2,868	2,868
Less: Lender Participation	–	(1,434)	(1,434)
Threshold Amount Paid to Owner	–	200	–
Before-Tax Cash Flow	4,694	1,634	1,434
Less: Tax Liability	(1,027)	(625)	(569)
After-Tax Cash Flow from Sale	$3,667	$1,009	$865
Summary Statistics for Developer and Lender (000)			
Developer:			
Sale at End of Year	5	5	5
Owner's Equity Contribution	$2,211	$454	$454
Undiscounted Before-Tax Net Cash Flows	4,348	1,915	1,615
Net Present Value of Cash Flows Discounted at 20%	227	427	327
Lender:			
Loan Amount	$8,788	$10,546	$10,546
LTV Ratio	75%	90%	90%
Effective DCR	1.31	1.18	1.18
Lender Yield	9.59%	12.05%	12.52%

aCalculated below.
bIncludes threshold amount paid to owner.
cIncludes threshold amount paid to lender.

Multifamily Residential Development

building is put up as collateral for the loan. The *originator* is the institution that loans the money against the building at a discounted rate to the sponsor. The *issuer* could be that lending institution or another institution that securitizes and issues a bond against the collateral.

The popularity of different types of permanent mortgages changes frequently, sometimes every few months. The basic alternatives for permanent loans, however, remain the same—a fixed-rate or adjustable-rate mortgage for 65 to 80 percent of value, or some form of participating mortgage for 80 to 95 percent of value that gives the lender higher returns to cover the additional risk associated with higher leverage.

Mezzanine loans are second loans that reduce the amount of equity a developer needs. Because they increase the leverage and therefore the risk of default in a project, primary mortgages typically have covenants that preclude a mezzanine loan without express permission of the primary lender. Mezzanine loan interest rates range from 12 to 20 percent. The interest may be accrued and paid later or when the project is sold or refinanced.

Lessons of the 2008–2009 Financial Crisis

Inadequate bank regulation was a major cause of subprime lending and securitization that led to the financial crisis of 2008–2009. In 1991, the United States implemented the Basel Accords that linked required bank capital to the default risk of the asset held, ranging from zero capital for government bonds to 8 percent for commercial loans. The requirement for mortgages was 4 percent, but for GSE (government-sponsored enterprise) securities from Fannie Mae and Freddie Mac, the requirement was only 1.6 percent.[a] Many institutional investors purchased the investment-grade tranches of the securitized bonds sold by Wall Street. The sale of securities was further aided by structured investment vehicles (SIVs), which purchased the below-investment-grade tranches left over from institutional investors. In the event of default, the SIVs obtained commercial bank credit lines to pay off holders of commercial paper that the SIVs issued to finance their purchases of the low-rated high-risk tranches. This line of credit did not appear on the bank's balance sheet and did not require any bank capital. "In effect, the commercial bank was taking all the risk of decline in the value of the tranches, removing incentives of the SIV to limit the risk of the tranches it purchased."[b]

Investors may also have underestimated the risk of the investment-grade tranches. Rating agencies systematically underrated the risk associated with higher-rated tranches in the securitized pools. This underrating occurred because the rating agencies thought that cash flows above certain thresholds of default would be safe, overlooking the fact that the entire mortgage pools of many commercial mortgage–backed security (CMBS) bonds consisted of higher-risk and subprime mortgages. When the housing bubble burst in 2008, defaults by borrowers caused massive calls on commercial bank lines of credit to pay off SIV paper holders, endangering many banks. Rating agencies also downgraded many higher CMBS tranches. The loss on junk mortgages led to the collapse of Bear Stearns, a large investor in unrated private-label asset-backed security tranches. In September 2008, Fannie Mae and Freddie Mac were placed in receivership by the U.S. government. Within a few weeks, "two of the four remaining independent investment banks, a global insurance company (AIG), and two of the six largest U.S. banks succumbed to the mortgage crisis."[c] The United States entered its worst economic recession since the Great Depression as credit markets froze up and CMBS issuance went to zero, making it impossible to refinance many CMBS loans to major

real estate developers as they came due, forcing some of the biggest names in real estate, such as General Growth Properties, to declare bankruptcy.[d] The lesson for beginning real estate developers is that whenever the market seems too good to be true, there will inevitably be a correction. The bigger the bubble, the bigger the correction and the longer it will take for the market to return to normal. After a collapse, debt markets often freeze up, making it impossible for even large and experienced developers to obtain bank loans. During such periods, any project that is undercapitalized is in jeopardy of default. The only remedy for developers, both beginning and more experienced, is cash that they can draw on. One of the ironies of the 2008–2009 recession was that commercial real estate was not overbuilt as it usually is in economic downturns. However, it was still hit very hard as consumer spending dropped precipitously and vacancies soared due to failing and downsizing companies.

[a]Patric Hendershott, Robert Hendershott, and James Shilling, "The Mortgage Finance Bubble: Causes and Corrections," *Journal of Housing Research* 19, no. 1 (2010): 16.

[b]Ibid., p. 8.

[c]Ibid., p. 11.

[d]General Growth was able to restructure and extend the great majority of its CMBS debt, allowing it to emerge from bankruptcy largely intact.

FINANCING ISSUES

Developers should be aware of a number of issues related to financing.

PERSONAL GUARANTEES AND LOAN FUNDING.

Although standard practices may vary, most developers must personally guarantee their construction loans. On occasion, they may also be required to guarantee some part of their permanent loans (such as the top 25 percent),[51] at least until their projects reach some threshold level of debt coverage or occupancy.

When times are good, lenders have more money available than good projects to lend on, so they ease their requirements in order to compete for business from experienced developers. When times are tough, loan requirements become more restrictive. Loan-to-value ratios are lowered and debt service coverage ratios are raised. Personal guarantees also become much more prevalent. Beginning developers, however, should be prepared to sign personally on their construction and development loans. They should be able to avoid personal liability on standard permanent loans for fully leased properties.

No developer wants to be a perpetual guarantor of the loan. Many developers refuse to agree to unconditional liability and will negotiate for some performance criteria that release them from personal liability. The following are some alternative compromises:

- Lenders cannot call on the guarantor directly in the event of default. They must instead foreclose on the defaulting property and obtain a legal decision against the guarantor. Because judicial foreclosures can be time-consuming and expensive, lenders may prefer to take over the property immediately in return for releasing the developer from some or all of the liability under the guarantee.
- The note limits the amount of any deficiency over time. For example, if the loan is current for three years, then the guarantor's liability reduces to, say, 50 percent of any deficiency.
- The note states that if all the land improvements have been installed within budget and if the project has been completed, the developer's (guarantor's) liability reduces to zero after three years.
- The developer places money in escrow to cover potential losses. Suppose a developer undertakes a project appraised at $12 million but it requires only $10 million in costs. The developer may borrow the full $12 million, leaving $2 million in escrow

to eliminate any personal liability. This solution, of course, involves added interest costs, which in turn add to the project's risk.

Personal liability is defined as meaning either the "top half" or "bottom half" of the loan. Suppose the developer guarantees the top half of a loan. If a project with a $10 million loan sells for $7 million, a guarantee of the top half means that the developer owes the deficient $3 million. If the developer guarantees the bottom half, then nothing is owed unless the project sells for less than $5 million. In some cases, ambiguously worded loan documents that fail to specify whether the developer is guaranteeing the top or the bottom half of a loan have caused the developer and lender to end up in court. The prospect of a long court battle to satisfy the deficiency has motivated some lenders to settle with developers.

Beginning developers find it difficult to eliminate personal liability altogether, but they can negotiate to limit it. If they can limit their liability to a specified amount, they may be able to sell pieces of that liability to their investors along with pieces of the transaction. It is hard enough, however, to raise equity without also asking investors to accept liability for potential losses. If they do accept liability, they will expect to receive more equity (a greater share of the upside).

BALANCE SHEET.

For construction loans, the developer's balance sheet must be strong enough to satisfy the lender that he will get paid back. Nicholas Lizotte worked for 18 months to secure financing on the Sagamore Residential project in Westchester County, New York. "Currently, the only entity willing to lend on multifamily product is FHA. Fannie Mae and Freddie Mac have shut down all of their bridge lending and other lenders are not interested in nonrecourse lending.

"[Consequently], debt financing is dependent on either government insurance on the loan or an equity partner with a significant balance sheet to back the project. Fannie Mae and Freddie Mac are looking for a balance sheet with assets equal to the amount of the loan and liquid assets equal to the annual debt service. The balance sheet must belong to a key principal in the project for it to fulfill this criterion."[52]

CLOSING.

Obtaining the funding for a permanent loan (closing the loan) may involve almost as much work as originally securing the lender's commitment to provide that funding. The loan commitment document specifies the requirements for permanent loan funding. Typical requirements include a certified rent roll showing the property's actual cash flow as well as all signed lease documents. Loan closing can be an exasperating process, and any issues not clearly spelled out in the original commitment can come back to haunt the developer at closing. For example, loan documents may be ambiguous as to whether a project

must be 90 percent leased, 90 percent occupied, or 90 percent occupied and paying rent. Lenders usually take the most restrictive interpretation, so developers are well advised to ensure that qualifying standards are described precisely.

Some loan commitments require that a project have attained certain rental objectives, say, 80 percent occupancy for a specified period—one month, six months, or 12 months. The shorter the period for qualification, the better for the developer. Lenders often require that releases, credit reports, or other paperwork be obtained from all tenants. Such procedures should be confirmed at the outset, thereby allowing the property manager to obtain the necessary documentation as tenants sign new leases. Obtaining such documents later can be much more difficult and costly.

Closing on condominium loans can pose a different set of problems. When markets are soft, sales may not reach targets set by permanent lenders, and developers may be obliged to give investors unsold units in lieu of a cash return. If a developer subsequently decides to consolidate ownership and to convert a project to a rental project, the price of acquiring units sold previously may be very high.

How difficult loan closings are depends on the local real estate market at the time of closing. When conditions become soft, lenders naturally become more concerned about the safety of their investments and thus more rigorous in the enforcement of the various requirements for closing.

EQUITY: JOINT VENTURES AND SYNDICATIONS.
Developers use a variety of joint venture formats to raise equity, provide loan guarantees, and secure financing. This section focuses on joint ventures with equity partners.

Syndications are a form of joint venture in which equity from a number of smaller investors is raised through a private or public offering subject to regulations of the Securities and Exchange Commission. Investors in syndications receive a security interest similar to what they own in stocks or bonds, whereas joint ventures of only a few parties typically, but not necessarily, involve direct real estate interests. Every joint venture deal is different. Nonetheless, certain formats are more common, such as those described by the following three developers.

Harry Mow, former board chair of Century West Development in Santa Monica, California, recommends keeping it simple. "If you cut too sharp a deal with your investors, you probably won't get them to invest

---

FIGURE 4-12 | Mortgage Calculation: Pay Rate versus Note Rate

Suppose a mortgage has the following terms:

Mortgage Amount	$1,000,000
Term	30 years
Note Rate	12%
Pay Rate	10%

The monthly payment under the note rate would be

PMT $(PV = \$1,000,000, i = 12/12, n = 30 \times 12)^a =$ $10,286.13

The monthly payment under the pay rate would be

PMT $(PV = \$1,000,000, i = 10/12, n = 30 \times 12) =$ 8,775.71

Difference in Monthly Payments (accrued)	**$1,510.42**

The borrower would pay the lower amount, $8,775.71, and would accrue the difference of $1,510.42 per month. Suppose the borrower wanted to retire the mortgage after five years (60 months). The borrower would calculate the mortgage balance under the note rate:

PV $(PMT = \$10,286.13, i = 12/12, n = 300)^b =$ $976,632.18

Next, the borrower would calculate the accrued interest:

FV $(PMT = \$1,510.42, i = 12/12, n = 60) =$ 123,354.71

Total Payment to Retire Mortgage	**$1,099,986.89**

To retire the mortgage, the borrower would pay the combined amount, or	$1,099,986.89

To check the calculation, the present value of the monthly payments plus the present value of the combined payment at retirement, discounted at the note rate, should equal the initial mortgage of $1,000,000:

PV $(PMT = \$8,775.71, i = 12/12, n = 60) =$ $394,512.64

PV $(FV = \$1,099,986.89, i = 12/12, n = 60) =$ $605,487.36

Total	**$1,000,000.00**

[a]PMT = the mortgage payment; PV = the mortgage amount; i = the interest rate; n = the term; all represented as monthly figures.
[b]The ending balance on a mortgage is calculated on the remaining number of payments: 30 − 5 years = 25 years × 12 months = 300 months remaining on the mortgage.

---

in another deal." Mow, whose company does its own construction, adds a 15 percent fee to the hard and soft costs (excluding land and financing costs). The fee pays the superintendent, the project manager, corporate overhead, and the costs of raising equity. If the construction loan is sufficiently large to cover the 15 percent fee, it is paid to them in installments during construction. Otherwise, it is left in as a loan to the partnership until the property is sold, when they receive it out of sale proceeds. Cash flow from operations and sale of the property is distributed in the following order:

1. The limited partners receive back their capital.
2. The limited partners receive a 6 percent cumulative return.
3. The limited partners and the general partners split the remainder equally. The developer also receives a 5 percent or 6 percent management fee and a 6 percent brokerage fee for selling the property.

Richard Gleitman, president of R.J. Investments Associates of Sherman Oaks, California, gives his equity partners—who tended initially to be friends and business associates—50 percent of the profits and an 8 percent noncumulative preferred return. He recovers all cash advances for land, entitlements, or other initial expenses for a project from the equity partners when they make their initial investment. Gleitman creates the joint venture before the close of land escrow as soon as he has reliable financial projections. Gleitman's firm charges a minimal contractor's fee—2 to 3 percent of hard costs—and a larger management fee—4 to 5 percent—that help cover the cost of using the largest, most active outside broker in an area to sell a project.

In his first deal, Paul Schultheis, president, Real Property Investment, Inc., of Arcadia, California, raised $400,000 in cash, splitting profits 50/50 with investors after they received back their capital. Because he had no previous direct experience, Schultheis brought in a builder and a broker/marketing director as general partners. He and his brother acquired the land, secured planning approvals, and performed the front-end work. The broker received 10 percent of the general partners' share of the deal; the three other partners received 30 percent each.

Jerry Rappaport, Jr., states, "Private equity firms currently take the position that 2.5 to 10 percent co-investment is insufficient to encourage a joint venture partner to remain diligent through downturns and will either push much harder for higher coinvestment or profit participation that happens at a much higher threshold and may represent a development fee rather

Contents of a Mortgage Application Package

Applications for both construction and permanent financing should be accompanied by a mortgage package—usually a notebook or file—that includes many of the following items as appropriate:

INTRODUCTION
- Letter of transmittal
- Loan application (supplied by lending institution and filled out by ownership entity and each major principal)
- Good-faith deposit
- Mortgage loan submission sheet summarizing the major aspects of the project and terms of the loan request

PROPERTY DESCRIPTION AND RATIONALE
- Description of the physical aspects of the property
- Acquisition, title, and zoning

- Environmental reports
- Attachments, including location maps, aerial photographs, surveys, floodplain maps, and so forth
- Community profile

ECONOMICS
- Financial forecasts or historical operating statements for the project
- Projected or current rent roll
- Survey of competitive projects
- Supply and demand information
- Information about market rents and comparable sales
- Market vacancy rates

DEVELOPMENT PLAN
- Land comparables showing sale prices of similar tracts of land in the area
- Overall development plan

- Complete engineering data covering soils tests, bearing strength, grading, road specifications, drainage, floodplain surveys, and so forth
- A copy of the purchase option

BUILDINGS
- Plans and specifications of proposed buildings
- Architectural drawings

CREDIT INFORMATION
- Credit report on entity and principals
- Financial statements of borrower and principals
- Copy of the purchase money mortgage from seller (if any)
- Financial statement of the landowner

Source: Steven M. Bram, president, George Smith Partners, Inc., Los Angeles, California.

than complicating the ownership structure. Ten to 40 percent is now expected. The private equity market has evolved such that senior management are coinvested and senior management own more of the company and of the upside, so that senior management decisions are directly aligned with performance."

Rappaport observes that the sponsors of one of the deals in which the New Boston Fund invested—Vincent G. Norton's Schoolhouse at Lower Mills project—"could have taken the construction cost savings achieved and put it toward their equity contribution, or they could have reduced its basis to make it easier to carry. Instead, the developers used the savings to fund upgraded interior finishes and amenities."[53]

In structuring joint ventures with investors, the priorities of payback and cash distributions are even more important than the final split of profits. As indicated in the previous examples, it is common for investors to receive back their investment before the developer shares in any profit. When both the investor and the developer have money invested in a project, the investor may receive, say, the first $100,000 as a priority payback before the developer receives the next $100,000 of cash flow. Priorities become a way of dealing with risk—the person who bears the most risk receives money back last. Risk is higher because, if a loss occurs, there may be no money left to pay back lower priorities.

Preferred returns are similar to interest on money invested in a savings account. The difference is that they are paid only if cash flow is available—like dividends—whereas interest must be paid currently whether cash flow from a project is available or not (if not, then the general partner must cover the interest from other sources or default on the loan). The basic concept behind preferred returns is that the investors will be paid back as a top priority at least the equivalent interest on their investments that they would earn in an interest-bearing account. Although many deals have no preferred returns, beginning developers are advised to include them because they make raising equity a little easier. Investors like the notion that they will receive back their initial equity plus a preferred return before the developer receives any profit. It is customary for the developer to receive a "development fee"—3 to 5 percent of total costs (sometimes excluding land) during construction to cover overhead. But any significant profit to the developer carries a lower priority than the investor's return of capital and preferred return.

One of the simpler and more common deal structures has four priorities (similar to Harry Mow's structure described above):

1. Investors receive a current preferred return.
2. Investors receive unpaid but accrued preferred returns.
3. Investors receive back their equity.
4. Investors and the developer split the remainder according to a *profit split* ranging from 80/20 (80 percent to the investors) to 50/50.

The payment of preferred returns can be structured as *cumulative* or *noncumulative*. In the case of a cumulative preferred return, any unpaid preferred return in one period is accumulated until funds are available to pay it in a later period. A noncumulative preferred return does not accumulate in this fashion, and if cash flow in a given year is insufficient to cover all or part of the preferred return, the unpaid balance is forgotten and left unpaid.

The *current* preferred return is that amount owed each year, found by multiplying the preferred return rate by the equity. For example, if the preferred return rate is 8 percent and the equity is $1 million, the current preferred return is $80,000. Figure 4-13 shows how the cash flows and IRRs would differ for the same deal under the two different preferred return structures. Both deals illustrate a 10 percent preferred return with a 50/50 split of the remaining profits. Note that the cumulative preferred return is accrued in Years 1 and 2 because the cash flows of $5,000 and $8,000 are insufficient to cover the 10 percent preferred return of $10,000. The outstanding sum is finally paid off in Year 5. Because of the accumulation provision, the total cash flow to the investor is $104,000, compared with $100,500 in the noncumulative case. The investor's IRR is 17.02 percent, compared with 16.6 percent. The developer's total cash flow is less in the cumulative case, $54,000 as opposed to $57,500, because the investor receives more from the same total project cash flows.

In some deals involving cumulative preferred returns, the *accrued return balance* earns interest. Many developers, however, prefer not to pay such interest because it further reduces their share of the proceeds without enhancing the marketability of their deals. Another variation gives accrued but unpaid preferred returns a lower priority, and they are paid *after* the investor's equity is paid back. This twist further helps the developer because current preferred returns are reduced as investors' equity is paid back (from annual cash flows that exceed the *current* preferred return).

DEVELOPER FEES. One of the most delicate issues in raising equity is when and how much the developer will receive. Both investors and lenders want assurances that their positions are ahead of the developer's—and that they get back their money as well as a reasonable return on their money *before* the developer receives significant profit. They want assurances that the developer has strong incentives to work hard on their behalf throughout the development process.

This situation creates potential conflicts of interest, which are generally resolved in favor of the investors. When Peiser Corporation raised its first equity, a popular refrain (uttered mainly to themselves) was "developers have to eat too." Lenders and investors unfortunately like to see very thin developers. They believe that the more money the developer receives on the front end of a deal, the less incentive there is to work hard on their behalf. Therefore, they want to see virtually all the developer's compensation, both in fees and profit share, deferred until the end (final sale of the project). The developer, on the other hand, needs to cover at least the out-of-pocket costs for managing the deal and for performing all the functions necessary to complete it properly. As a rule, lenders allow the developer to take out 3 to 5 percent of the construction cost to cover direct overhead costs—in addition to any on-site construction superintendents.

Developers can receive fees from a number of different activities in the course of a deal. The fees fall into two main categories: (1) compensation for specific achievements and (2) share in the upside profits. Even when fees are earned, their timing of payment to the developer is subject to priorities as described above. The developer, for example, may earn fees totaling 10 percent of the development cost during construction and lease-up of the project. He may be allowed to receive (or take out) only half of those fees during the construction and lease-up period. The other 5 percent may be subordinated to the investors' receiving back all their equity plus any preferred return.

The developer's share of upside profits is, by definition, something that is paid on the back end of a deal, usually when it is sold. Most joint venture agreements also allow the developer to take out cash if a project is refinanced, although even here, the cash is often subordinated to return of capital and preferred return to the investors. Refinancing often occurs when a project achieves certain rental objectives, such as major lease rollovers at higher rents. If, for example, the developer refinances a project for $5 million that previously had a $4 million mortgage, $1 million in cash is left over after paying off the old mortgage. This cash from refinancing is especially attractive because it does not create any immediate tax consequences and therefore is available in its entirety for distribution. The joint venture agreement specifies how the money is to be distributed. It may call for splitting the entire proceeds of refinancing 50/50 between the developer and the investors, or after the investors receive, say, $500,000, or only after the investors receive back all their equity.

An infinite number of deal structures are possible. Joint ventures with institutional investors (firms that invest money on behalf of their own clients, such as pension fund advisers) are described in detail in chapter 6.

Beginning developers cannot usually attract institutional investors. The advantage of starting with smaller deals is that it is much easier to raise $100,000 or $200,000 in equity than $1 million or more. The developer usually raises money from family or friends, who will want a fair deal and the developer must decide what to offer them. Because of his inexperience, the investors, however supportive personally, want the developer to defer as much compensation as possible.

Simple deal structures are recommended, primarily because they are easier to explain to potential investors. For tax reasons, it is advantageous to set fees that can be expensed immediately rather than being amortized over five years or, in some cases, never expensed at all. An experienced real estate tax accountant is an essential member of the developer's team,

Tips on Joint Ventures and Deal Packaging

- **In drawing up the partnership agreement, be very clear as to the rights and duties of each partner. Use arbitration to solve disputes.**

- **Beware of "dilution squeeze-down" provisions that allow investors to squeeze the developer out if a project does not generate a given level of current return.**

- **Consider overborrowing. Some developers recommend overborrowing if possible because it allows them to withdraw money from a project without tax. Overborrowing increases the risk of default, however.**

- **Make sure that investors have no right to tell the developer how to run the project.**

- **If investors commit money to be paid in the future, make sure that the money is available by persuading investors to post letters of credit.**

even before the process of raising equity begins.[54] In addition to the developer's fee, other common fees include those shown in the box below.

INVESTORS' PRIMARY CONCERNS. Investors are most concerned with the following five aspects of joint venture deals:

1. **Preferred Return Yields**—These yields tend to approximate the interest rate on money market accounts plus 1 to 3 percent. In 2010 and 2011, preferred returns typically ranged from 6 to 10 percent multiplied by the equity account balance at the beginning of each year.

2. **Share of Residual Profits** (also called "carried interest" or "promote")—In deals sold privately and in joint ventures with financial institutions or large investors, profit splits range from 80/20 (80 percent to investors) to 50/50. In public syndications, the profit split is usually 80/20 or at best 70/30. The percentage to investors is higher because stockbrokers and financial planners who sell the deals claim that investors are reluctant to buy into projects that offer lower profit shares.

3. **Downside Liabilities**—Most syndications and joint ventures are structured as limited partnerships that restrict investors' downside liabilities. Unless investors sign notes for more than their direct equity investment, their downside risk is limited to the loss of their equity.

4. **Cash Calls**—Cash calls occur when a partnership requires additional equity from the investors to meet its obligations. Sophisticated investors tend to be more concerned about the handling of cash calls. Most partnership agreements have provisions that penalize partners for not making cash calls that dilute their interest. For example, consider a partner, Smith, who has invested $50,000 out of total equity of $100,000 for a 50 percent interest. Suppose each partner makes a $10,000 cash call. Smith fails to come up with his $10,000, so the other partner, Jones, must come up with $20,000. In a prorated dilution arrangement, Jones would have invested $70,000 out of $120,000, reducing Smith's interest to $50,000 out of $120,000, or 41.67 percent. A penalty clause might reduce Smith's ownership by, say, 1 percent for each $1,000 he fails to produce, giving him a 31.67 percent interest. In the extreme, although not uncommon, case, Smith could lose his entire interest.

5. **Developer Fees**—The treatment of front-end fees differs considerably between private offerings and public syndications (including Regulation D private offerings to 35 or fewer "nonqualified" investors).[55] Stockbrokers and financial planners selling public syndications and Regulation D private offerings focus on the ratio of front-end fees to total equity raised and frequently will not offer a deal where front-end fees account for more than 25 percent of total equity. By comparison, in private joint ventures, front-end fees often exceed 25 percent of total equity, especially for new apartment projects in which the developer is also the contractor. The construction fee alone may exceed 25 percent of the equity, as it is based on total construction costs. For example, an 8 percent construction fee on a $1 million construction cost is $80,000. If $200,000 in equity were needed, this fee alone would be 40 percent of the equity raised.

Front-End Fees

Front-End Fees	
Acquisition fee	1–2 percent of acquisition cost
Organization fee for partnership	1–3 percent of equity raised
Financing fee	1–2 percent of financing raised (usually shared with outside mortgage brokers, if used)
Fees Paid during Construction or Lease-Up	
Development fee	3–5 percent of hard costs or total cost; may include or exclude land
Construction fee	4–8 percent of construction cost (usually paid to contractor)
Leasing fees	4–6 percent commissions on leases (shared with outside brokers)
Fees Paid upon Sale of the Project	
Sales fee	4–6 percent commission on sale price (shared with outside brokers)
Profit	
Preferred return	Same as investors (6–10 percent) on equity invested[a]
Profit share	20–50 percent of profit (usually after investor receives back all equity plus preferred return)

[a]Many investors require the developer to make some sort of equity investment in the form of cash or a contribution such as land that has appreciated in value over and above its cost. The developer's equity can be treated in one of two ways: (1) identical to the investor's equity, so that priorities of preferred return, repayment, and profit are identical to the investor's (called pari passu), with all distributions based on one's prorated share of total equity; or (2) subordinated to the investor's equity, in which case the investor receives priorities ahead of the developer (see chapter 5 for an illustration).

FIGURE 4-13 | Cumulative versus Noncumulative Preferred Returns

	Project's Cash Flows	Year 0	Year 1	Year 2	Year 3	Year 4	Year 5	Total
1	Equity Investment	($100,000)						($100,000)
2	Cash Flows from Operations		5,000	8,000	10,000	15,000	20,000	58,000
3	Cash Flows from Sale						200,000	200,000
4								
5	Total	($100,000)	$5,000	$8,000	$10,000	$15,000	$220,000	$158,000
6								
7	Cumulative Preferred Return							
8	Preferred Return Owed	10.00%	10,000	10,000	10,000	10,000	10,000	50,000
9	Preferred Return Paid		5,000	8,000	10,000	10,000	10,000	43,000
10	Unpaid Preferred Return		5,000	2,000	0	0	0	7,000
11								
12	Preferred Return Accrued		5,000	7,000	7,000	7,000	2,000	
13	Accrued Return Paid		0	0	0	5,000	2,000	7,000
14	Accrued Return Balance		5,000	7,000	7,000	2,000	0	0
15								
16	Return of Equity		0	0	0	0	100,000	100,000
17	Equity Balance	100,000	100,000	100,000	100,000	100,000	0	0
18								
19	Cash Flow for Distribution		0	0	0	0	108,000	108,000
20	50% to Investor		0	0	0	0	54,000	54,000
21	50% to Developer		0	0	0	0	54,000	54,000
22								
23	Net Cash Flow to Investor	($100,000)	$5,000	$8,000	$10,000	$15,000	$166,000	$104,000
24	Investor's IRR	17.02%						
25								
26	Noncumulative Preferred Return							
27	Preferred Return Owed	10.00%	10,000	10,000	10,000	10,000	10,000	50,000
28	Preferred Return Paid		5,000	8,000	10,000	10,000	10,000	43,000
29	Unpaid Preferred Return		5,000	2,000	0	0	0	7,000
30								
31	Preferred Return Accrued		0	0	0	0	0	
32	Accrued Return Paid		0	0	0	0	0	0
33	Accrued Return Balance		0	0	0	0	0	0
34								
35	Return of Equity		0	0	0	5,000	95,000	100,000
36	Equity Balance	100,000	100,000	100,000	100,000	95,000	0	0
37								
38	Cash Flow for Distribution		0	0	0	0	115,000	115,000
39	50% to Investor		0	0	0	0	57,500	57,500
40	50% to Developer		0	0	0	0	57,500	57,500
41								
42	Net Cash Flow to Investor	($100,000)	$5,000	$8,000	$10,000	$15,000	$162,500	$100,500
43	Investor's IRR	16.60%						

How the Bascom Group Raises Apartment Equity

Derek M.D. Chen, Jerome A. Fink, and David S. Kim formed the Bascom Group in 1996 to purchase value-added real estate in southern California. Bascom's primary objectives were to (1) capitalize on the recovering southern California economy by investing in multifamily rental properties with a three- to five-year turnaround; (2) diversify its portfolio in southern California by location and industry; and (3) provide investors with attractive current *cash-on-cash yields* and total investment returns.

Bascom seeks "the worst property on the best block." The firm targets multi-family properties located in infill areas with high barriers to entry that offer value-added opportunities. Targeted properties need renovation or suffer from poor resident profiles relative to the competing trade area, below-market rents, high expenses, high vacancies, poor management and marketing, and undercapitalization. Although these myriad problems may seem overwhelming and tend to scare away traditionally conservative investors, they can be overcome with a good strategy and effective implementation.

Bascom creates single-purpose limited liability companies (LLCs) to own and operate each property to protect its entire portfolio in the event that any single property defaults or has issues that could affect other properties in the portfolio. These LLCs are capitalized from several sources, including (1) private and institutional investors contributing pari passu (equally) or preferred equity and subordinated debt (for example, second mortgage loans and mezzanine financing) and (2) traditional institutional lenders funding senior mortgage debt (for example, a primary mortgage loan). A typical structure requires 5 to 10 percent Bascom-sponsored equity, 10 to 15 percent institutional coventure partner equity or mezzanine financing, and 80 percent senior mortgage debt. The equity typically requires a minimum preferred return of 9 to 12 percent and allows for Bascom to participate in the profits after the preferred returns are paid currently. This equity structure aligns Bascom's interest with that of the passive investor by creating an incentive for Bascom to maximize the total return to the investor. The senior mortgage debt is typically a three-year bridge loan based on total cost (property plus renovation cost) with a LIBOR-based interest rate, which is similar to a construction loan. The lender retains funds for renovation (lender holdback) and releases it to the sponsor as work is completed, allowing Bascom to purchase and renovate the property with much less equity.

During the Great Recession, the firm benefited from the fact that it did not cross collateralize its equity (pledge one project as a guarantee for other projects). Bascom's longtime equity partner, Chenco Holdings based in Taipei, raised equity in relatively small increments of $10 million per fund from a handful of related investors. Each fund had a duration of three to five years compared with a more common eight to ten years.

THE ADVANTAGES OF PRIVATE OFFERINGS. Public offerings and Regulation D syndications may appear to be better deals for the investor but they tend not to be, for three reasons. First, developers dislike giving away more profits than necessary and so prefer to engage in private ventures. The deals sold by outside brokers are therefore often those for which a developer could not raise private money and may consequently be a lower preference for the developer. Second, Regulation D offerings and public offerings involve much greater expense for legal work, due diligence, and broker commissions. Third, developers must make a certain level of profit or they will not stay in business. If they must take lower front-end fees and a lower share of residual profits, they usually compensate by "selling" the project to the syndication at a higher price.

For example, Harry Mow's company, Century West, packaged deals in which the front-end load on a $1 million deal with 80 percent financing was 45 percent of the equity rather than the 25 percent syndicators prefer. However, the price to the partnership was his actual direct cost. A public syndication offering has a lower ratio of fees to equity but a higher total project price to the partnership, and therefore higher risks to the investors.

In addition to the higher front-end load in private offerings, Century West received 50 percent of the residual profits after the investor received a 6 percent preferred return. Despite the seemingly higher fees, Century West's deals were very well received by investors who appreciated the opportunity to buy into projects at cost rather than at a higher price that included development profit.

Economically, the ratio of front-end fees to total equity raised is much less important than the investor's expected returns. Unfortunately, brokers, financial planners, and others who sell real estate securities focus on such ratios rather than on the likelihood that investors will achieve certain levels of return. For public offerings through securities brokers and financial planners, developers must conform their deals to

Chenco deployed capital quickly so that in the end, it lost money only in its 11th fund. Chenco provides its funds "sponsor" capital—Bascom's share required by its institutional partners, such as GE Capital, Lehman Brothers, Warburg Pincus, and Rockwood. Bascom's deal with the institutional funds at the peak of the market in the mid-2000s was a 90/10 equity split (90 percent institution and 10 percent Bascom) with a 10 percent preference and a 50/50 profit split over 10 percent. When Bascom first started doing institutional deals and was unproven, the investment split was 80/20 with a 60/40 profit split after a 14 percent preference to the investors.

Kim observes, "The environment in 2010 is not that different from the 1990s. The only difference now is that private individuals have more incentive for fixed dividends in property as a hedge against inflation. In the mid-1990s, we did not have the global financial problem."

In a deal in 2010, Bascom raised $4 million in equity in two weeks from private investors who put in an average of $25,000 each for a project in Colorado. "We can sell investors on an eight- to ten-year play. When we know we are bouncing around the bottom with a shaky recovery, real unemployment in the 15 to 20 percent range, budget deficits, and inflation concerns, we don't see stabilization until 2015." The Colorado deal is a 10.5 cap at stabilization with midteens (14 percent) pretax returns. The deal has an 8 percent preferred return, 90/10 equity contributions (90 percent from investors and 10 percent from Bascom). Distributions are pari passu up to 8 percent and then a 70/30 upside split (70 percent to investors and 30 percent to Bascom) after 8 percent. Bascom receives a 1.5 percent acquisition fee on the total basis and a 1 percent annual asset management fee. The firm uses third-party property management and receives no other fees for construction, refinancing, leasing, or disposition.

Bascom's value-added deals involve a certain amount of risk. At each step in the process—from purchasing to renovating to operating to disposition—Bascom's principals have learned that surprises will happen and risk cannot be totally eliminated. The tenant profile may be worse than anticipated and higher-than-expected turnover may result. The cost of renovation may increase because of labor shortages or increases in materials' costs or simply because of conditions discovered after work begins. Although the use of high leverage can magnify a deal's potential total returns, it can also hurt cash flow if interest rates rise more than expected. Clear roles, goals, and expectations for investors, lenders, property managers, and even residents are paramount to ensure that each investment meets the mutually agreed-on pro forma. Most important, it is clear that frequent reporting and the open disclosure of any issue or surprise are critical to maintaining a trustworthy relationship between investors and lenders.

Source: Interviews with David S. Kim, managing director, the Bascom Group, Irvine, California, September 2002; June 2010.

syndication standards in the marketplace at the time. Jerry Rappaport, Jr., points out, "There is an ever-growing pool of high-net-worth individuals focused on retirement with burgeoning amounts of money for whom real estate will be an important part of their portfolios." He says, "Two strategies for securing private equity funding are (1) sell the team's track record and capacity to a local private equity real estate fund, or one that is known to have funded private developers, and understand its underwriting criteria as you identify, seed, and execute predevelopment activities; or (2) go to the Urban Land Institute annual conference to learn the rules, tie up the project, and then hire a consultant to help you source the private equity so that you will create a small sense of competition."[56]

Developers will find that private syndications to small groups of investors remain a mainstay for raising equity. Developers must always be careful to observe legal requirements for private syndications, such as registering the offerings in each state where they plan to solicit investors.

GOVERNMENT PROGRAMS AND WORKING WITH NONPROFIT ORGANIZATIONS

Government programs are no longer as fruitful a source of financing for subsidized housing as they once were, but they still can provide helpful financing to new developers. Over the years, numerous government programs have been created to generate low- and moderate-income housing and housing support programs remain available from federal, state, and local sources.

Housing revenue bonds are issued to finance construction of housing in which a specified proportion of the units will be rented to low-income households. These securities may provide financing either directly or through a loans-to-lenders program, and may be secured in whole or in part by federal agency guarantees or subsidies. To qualify for issuing tax-exempt bonds, developers must set aside 20 percent of the units to renters with incomes below 50 percent of the area median income, or, alternatively, 40 percent of the units may be rented to individuals with incomes below 60 percent of the area median income.

The Tax Reform Act of 1986 created low-income housing tax credits as an alternate method of funding housing for low- and moderate-income households. Tax credits are granted to each state on a per-capita basis and are administered competitively through the states' housing agencies. Developers may use the credits for new construction, rehabilitation, or acquisition of residential properties that meet the following minimum requirements:

- Twenty percent or more of the residential units in the project are both rent restricted and occupied by individuals whose income is 50 percent or less of the area median gross income, *or* 40 percent or more of the residential units in the project are both rent restricted and occupied by individuals whose income is 60 percent or less of area median gross income.
- Properties receiving tax credits must stay eligible for 15 years.

Developers who receive the credits may use them or sell them to private investors to generate equity.

Building under government programs can be time-consuming and frustrating. Government financing programs involve more paperwork and other hurdles than private financing. The programs often contain vague guidelines that cause differences in interpretation. Associated legal costs can also be onerous. Bond deals, for example, involve as many as nine different parties, each represented by its own attorney. The developer pays everyone's fees, and because most of the attorneys do not work directly for the developer, monitoring their time and fees is difficult.

Yet despite the added costs, bond programs generated many thousands of housing units throughout the United States. The sale of tax credits for low-income housing remains an important source of funds for apartments, although it must be supplemented by other forms of subsidies (that development agencies and the U.S. Department of Housing and Urban Development [HUD] may provide) to make these apartments financially feasible. Beginning developers who are interested in low- and moderate-income housing development should investigate the financing programs available by contacting local housing departments, redevelopment agencies, state housing finance agencies, HUD, and Fannie Mae. A number of low-income housing programs, including LIHTCs, give nonprofit organizations an advantage in obtaining

money, the result of government policies to encourage the growth of community-based nonprofits.

The nonprofits often lack development expertise and are eager to form joint ventures with private developers to build housing. Although financing for low-income housing limits the amount of profit a developer can earn, the limits are high enough to make such housing development attractive. The financing programs provide beginning developers a source of money that may be easier to qualify for than private banking sources. Moreover, tax credits, once obtained, are easily sold to investors (because of the virtually guaranteed tax write-offs) and effectively take care of equity requirements, the hardest money for beginning developers to raise. Although nonprofit partnerships offer special opportunities for financing, they also bring much greater complexity, paperwork, time, and the need to apply for multiple loans. Experienced nonprofit organizations can greatly assist beginning developers in the process, while inexperienced nonprofits may make their lives impossible. As with any partnership, success depends on the personalities of the people involved.

Randolph Hawthorne observes, "Demand for LIHTC units is pretty constant. There is a limited amount of upfront profit you can generate, so you generally need some soft money. The tax credit business became robust enough that it is just a matter of pricing. The business model is viable."[57] The amount of the tax credit is based on the percentage of units reserved for low-income tenants and the cost of purchase and rehabilitation excluding land. For example, suppose a project costs $100,000 for the land, $400,000 for an existing building, and $1,000,000 for rehabilitation. Suppose also that 80 percent of the units are low income, that there are no tax-exempt bonds, and that the state agency awarded $70,000 per year of credits. The credits are computed as follows: The building purchase credit is $400,000 × 80% × 3.5%, or $11,200; the rehabilitation credit is $1,000,000 × 80% × 9%, or $72,000. The total maximum credit is $83,200, but it is more than the award by the state, so the deduction is limited to $70,000 per year. If the market value of the credits was $0.85, then the developer could sell them for $70,000 × 10 years × 85%, or $595,000. With total costs of $1.5 million, this amount of equity would give a 39.6 percent equity-to-cost ratio, which should be large enough to cover the developer's entire equity requirement.

Tax credits for historic rehabilitation may be attractive vehicles for beginning developers. To qualify for the 20 percent rehabilitation credits, a building must be a "certified historic structure," that is, listed individually in the National Register of Historic Places or located in a registered historic district and certified by the secretary of the interior as being of historical significance to the district. To illustrate how it works, suppose that a historic building costs $1 million to acquire and requires rehabilitation work that costs $500,000 plus architecture fees of $50,000. The allowable deduction would be $550,000 × 20%, or $110,000. State historic tax credit deductions of a similar amount may also be available, bringing the total to $220,000. The deduction can be taken in full the year the building is placed in service. Any unused write-off can be carried forward 15 years or back three years.

Randolph Hawthorne states, "The very best historic preservation opportunities were seized years ago. . . . Most of the properties that would still qualify for historic preservation tax credits will be more marginal locations, will be difficult projects, and will involve more complex construction issues. Developers of rehabilitation projects typically have availed themselves of both LIHTCs and historic preservation tax credits to fill the equity gap." He adds, "You will occasionally still see historic preservation deals being done and there is a developed market for those tax credits. There are funds available for that purpose as well."[58]

A third tax credit opportunity is the New Markets Tax Credit Program for investments in designated Community Development Entities (CDEs) to stimulate private investment and facilitate economic and community development in Low-Income Communities. CDEs must be certified by the Community Development Financial Institutions Fund of the U.S. Department of the Treasury. The credit allows investors to receive tax credits equal to 39 percent of the cost of the investment. The credit is taken over a seven-year period: 5 percent for each of the first three years and 6 percent for each of the last four years.[59]

Construction

General contracting is distinct from development (see chapter 2 for a general discussion of construction contractors). Many general contractors engage in development, and many developers, especially of residential products, engage in construction; nonetheless, they are two different businesses, each with its own set of risks and rewards. In general, if a project makes economic sense only if the developer can earn a contractor's profit, then it is not worth pursuing.

Many projects undertaken by developers to keep their contracting arms busy have led those developers into bankruptcy.

Most major difficulties faced by developers who perform their own construction arise from the fact that they must run another business—a labor- and detail-intensive business—that leaves them insufficient time to pay adequate attention to their development activities. Most of the major benefits of an in-house construction company stem from the developer's ability to take care of construction problems rapidly and to exercise control over costs of change orders. Construction does offer a relatively easy entry into development, and many homebuilders draw effectively on their construction background to make the transition into apartment development.

Residential construction differs from nonresidential construction in many ways. Typically, residential construction involves smaller subcontractors, a smaller scale of construction, and a less skilled, nonunion workforce. The architect's role is also more limited in residential than in nonresidential development. Usually, the architect is not involved in the residential bidding process and does not manage subcontractors' work for compliance with plans and specs. Any time that the architect does spend is usually priced on an hourly basis instead of a fixed-fee basis, thus raising costs for developers who keep changing their minds.

John Porta, owner of MLP Investments in St. Louis, has never looked at his property management or construction arms as revenue centers. "We focus solely on managing our own assets in order to protect our interests. The same is true for our construction entity." He adds, "A typical general contractor, who is not accustomed to doing wood-frame construction, cannot function as efficiently as our own in-house arm." MLP sources many fixtures from overseas. The firm also favors panelized apartment construction since it replicates the same model in each market.[60]

MANAGING AND SCHEDULING THE JOB

In construction, one quickly learns that delays are the norm rather than the exception. Most problems occur around scheduling different subcontractors or material deliveries—hence, the importance of employing a good construction manager who can monitor the work of subcontractors as well as deal with architects, engineers, and city inspectors. A job superintendent—ideally, one with at least five or more years of experience on comparable projects—should always be on site to monitor subcontractors. This person handles the purchases from major suppliers and manages the contracts with all subcontractors who do the labor, giving the developer full control of construction while minimizing the number of direct employees.

One benefit of developing multifamily residential projects containing several buildings rather than one large building is that, with proper scheduling, the first units can be occupied and producing income well before the last units are completed. The contractor can facilitate early completions by paying subcontractors on the basis of buildings completed rather than on percentage of contract completed. The subcontractors, on the other hand, may prefer to run their crews from building to building. For example, a framing contractor may prefer to frame the first story of all buildings before starting the second story. Therefore, the developer may need to negotiate a rolling completion schedule as part of the subcontractor's contract.

One way to ensure cooperation between the construction and property management teams is to have both belong to the same entity and under one roof rather than hiring them on a fee basis. There should be good communication with the superintendent who handles site inspections, and the developer should have a business relationship with building department officials.

The developer should be personally involved in negotiating contracts and working with each subcontractor. Preconstruction meetings are the time when the superintendent talks directly to the people who head the different trades—both bosses and foremen who will actually be on the job. The meeting allows people to meet and get to know one another, leading to a smoother operation. While construction is in progress, the developer should convey orders through the superintendent.

Building mock-ups of each of the major unit types may save time and money during construction. Bringing all the subcontractors together to review the mock-ups helps them identify potential sources of conflict during construction. For example, the air-conditioning subcontractor may find joists that he needs to cut in order to run ventilation ducts or pipes or wires that are in his way. By identifying these problems in advance, the subs can find solutions before they have replicated the same problem in 50 units. When such problems arise, even though the subcontractors are responsible for fixing them, the developer almost always ends up having to pay more money.

The biggest source of cost overruns is change orders. A contractor can almost always find discrepan-

cies in the plans and specs that he can claim were not part of his original bid. The question of who should bear unanticipated costs is a constant source of conflict between the developer and the contractor, or if the developer is his own general contractor, between the GC and the subcontractor. For example, when Peiser Corporation and Frank Construction were building August Park Apartments in Dallas, they discovered that a pony wall (half-height) in one of the units had mistakenly been built to the ceiling. It blocked the view across the apartment when one entered the unit, making it seem smaller and less inviting. They had every right to require the subcontractor at his expense to tear down the wall and rebuild it in the 20 units that had already been framed. Recognizing that if they did so, the sub would find other ways to get back the cost of rebuilding the wall, they decided to live with the problem in the units that were already framed as long as the rest of the units were done correctly. This decision paid off later when the subcontractor did not charge extra for a change order that was not on the plan. In small construction, there is constant give-and-take between the developer and the subcontractors. Rigidly enforcing every construction plan detail usually comes back to haunt the developer.[61]

INSPECTIONS

Construction involves numerous inspections, all of which must be correctly performed if the developer/contractor is to guard against liability. In addition to city building inspectors, the construction lender usually requires an outside inspector to verify that work is completed in conformance with plans and specs. The developer should ask the lender for recommendations for an inspector and then consult with other builders on that inspector's reputation. Most lenders will cooperate with a developer to find a mutually agreeable inspector.

Developers should hire an outside inspector on any project above $2 million, even if the bank does not require it. Inspectors not only protect developers and the bank from lawsuits by independently verifying that work is correctly performed but also help ensure that subcontractors' work conforms to plans. Moreover, developers should undertake several inspections to protect themselves, including an independent engineering inspection of all foundations (to check that they are level and correctly located and elevated and to test the strength of cable tendons and concrete) and a verification that soil has been properly compacted. On government-funded projects, a government inspector may work on the site. When changes or additional requirements are made in the middle of a job, work should not proceed without a change order approved by the proper authorities to ensure that it is paid for. Dan Kassel, copresident of Granite Homes in Irvine, California, hires an inspector to videotape homes during construction. This record of the quality of work underneath the wallboard is available in case the firm later gets sued for construction defects. The inspector also helps ensure that the work—especially that which is eventually covered up—is performed properly. The developer's liability, as well as the contractor's, can extend for ten years or more after the completion of a building.

SUBCONTRACTORS AND DRAWS

Typically, apartment subcontractors are smaller than nonresidential subcontractors and are not bonded. To be competitive, most builders rely on nonunion subcontractors but also appreciate that they will sometimes go out of business or fail to complete a job. Developers should not automatically avoid working with a financially weak subcontractor. They should, however, check on the subcontractor's clients, suppliers, banks, and record and make sure that the subcontractor pays social security taxes. "Just be careful," cautions Jerome Frank, Jr. "Check his insurance coverage. If he doesn't have liability insurance, then you arrange for him to get it and charge him for it."

Every time a subcontractor makes a draw, the developer/contractor should have the subcontractor sign a *lien waiver* and an affidavit showing that suppliers, taxes, insurance, and other bills have been paid and then attach the lien waiver to the check stub and file it in the job's folder.

The purpose of the lien waiver is to prevent subcontractors from subsequently claiming nonpayment or one of their suppliers from filing a lien. Liens, even completely unwarranted, can delay loan closings and sales. If a lien is filed, a developer can post a bond for the amount of the lien or leave money in escrow to cover the potential liability.

One of the most difficult problems in construction is removing a subcontractor whose work is substandard. To reduce the associated delays, some developers require subcontractors to sign a stringent subcontract that provides for their removal for slow work or nonperformance.

INSURANCE

A good insurance agent who specializes in construction is invaluable to a contractor. Developers/contractors must be familiar with many different types of insurance: workers' compensation insurance, subcontractor's general liability insurance, builder's risk insurance, completed operations insurance, and contractor's equipment floater. Like the general

Cascade Village in Akron, Ohio, is a 242-unit mixed-income rental community that replaced a public housing project. About 100 units are reserved as replacement housing for former public housing residents.

THE COMMUNITY BUILDERS INC.

contractor, subcontractors must each have their own builder's risk insurance that covers, say, the theft of material from a site. It is important to get a copy of their insurance and check copies of their workers' compensation, general liability, and builder's risk insurance before they begin work. It is the superintendent's responsibility to make sure that documents are in. It is also advisable to take out completed operations insurance, which protects builders from claims for injury or damage caused by building collapse or structure failure after its completion. It does not, however, cover faulty workmanship.

Marketing

Marketing begins while a project is still on the drawing board and does not end until a project is sold. In the residential development business, developers cannot create a market where one does not already exist. On the contrary, their foremost objective is to identify the specific market segment for which more housing is needed and then to design the best possible product to serve that need. Marketing is the process of finding the renters or buyers and then attracting them to the property at a time when they are in a position to make a decision. Marketing serves a number of objectives:

- analyzing what market to pursue and what product to build;
- persuading—through careful presentation—buyers and renters that the product meets their specific needs;
- packaging the product and offering assistance to enable those people to buy or rent it; and
- ensuring afterward that the product meets their expectations.

Insufficient predevelopment market research can result in a product that has been built for a certain market but does not appeal to that market. In such cases, developers must determine which market the product does appeal to and then repackage it to attract that market. Although almost any product will sell or rent at a low enough price, its developer is unlikely to turn a profit if prices must be discounted.

Jerome Frank, Jr., says that developers can do two things for marketing and public relations: "You can market your company's history—for example, if you are Lincoln Properties or a similarly large company, you talk about the 'Lincoln style.' But what you're really selling is the company's management style." Alternatively, developers can sell the personality of the property, promoting the uniqueness of the development. "Find something in every development that you like and get excited about, for example, beveled mirrors over the fireplace or an abundance of closets, so that your manager gets really excited about it also. Some developers spend a lot of money on club rooms and swimming pools and in many ways waste money, especially in markets where low- to moderate-income tenants are targeted. Potential residents might be attracted to these amenities at first but find that interior features in the units are more important in the long run. In luxury markets, however, it is the sense of community that residents find in an apartment complex that attracts and holds tenants. Luxury apartment complexes feature their clubhouses, exercise rooms, game rooms, and paneled gathering places near the main entrance. The integrity of the management company is very important for dealing with clients. The developer has to exhibit a continued commitment to constantly train the property's managers."[62]

Market analysis is vital not only for predevelopment feasibility studies but also throughout the life of a project. Ongoing market analysis assesses the accuracy of the original analysis of the target market and identifies any important changes in market projections, rents, prices, and even the target market itself. Typically, 12 to 24 months elapse from completion of the first market study to the leasing of a project, and, in the interim, major changes may have occurred in the market. The developer must constantly monitor the market, especially by watching neighboring projects, to remain up-to-date on current rental activity, pricing, concessions, and preferred physical characteristics and amenities. Changing market strategy in midstream can substantially increase construction and operating costs, but failing to respond to market changes can be fatal.

DEVELOPING A MARKETING STRATEGY

A marketing strategy is the philosophy the team supports and consistently follows throughout the life of the project. The strategy focuses on what is to be done, why, and the projected outcome. The cornerstone of any market strategy is its target submarket. Once it has been identified through market analysis, every aspect of development—from design through property management—should reinforce the appeal of the project to that submarket.

After the development program and marketing strategy are established, preparation of project objectives can help the marketing team understand the strategy as well as the basic facts about the product and the market. The property's advantages should be clearly defined. What makes the property different, better, or more marketable than its competitors? In short, what makes it special from the point of view of marketing? A project's distinctiveness may be its affordability, location, aesthetics, units, lifestyle, or other characteristics that make it outshine the competition.

The marketing plan ties into the established marketing strategy and can be thought of as a blueprint for the advertising campaign, public relations efforts, and leasing activities, including hiring and managing the leasing staff and preparing budgets and schedules for each component.

The plan also specifies the design of all elements to create a coordinated image for the project. Based on the target market's profile and the project's distinctive selling points, it defines an overall theme to be carried out in all community design elements, including the name, logo, signage, sales displays, interior design, brochures, and other print and media materials.

THE MARKETING AND LEASING BUDGET

The marketing and leasing budget should cover all aspects of marketing. It should include appropriate amounts for exterior and interior marketing-related features, preleasing activities, general marketing, and promotional materials and events. A typical marketing budget includes

- **Exterior Marketing**—Directional signs, identification signs, banners, and flags;
- **Interior Marketing**—Model apartments, sales displays;
- **Preleasing**—A website, flyers, voice mail setup, staff, signs for construction and leasing, advertisements in appropriate websites and publications;
- **Recognition Marketing**—Advertising campaign, staff, promotion materials, public relations, press releases and other print media, community involvement in charitable events, memberships in community organizations; and
- **Other**—Nominations for awards, move-in gifts, goodwill gestures to outside leasing agents and contractors.

For leasing up new projects, the rule of thumb for the budget is the following:[63]

- **Suburban Garden Apartments**—$400–$600 per unit (for 200 units at $500 per unit, the budget would be $100,000 over 12 months, or $8,000 per month);

- **Urban Mid Rise**—$800–$1,000 per unit; and
- **Urban High Rise**—$1,500–$2,500 per unit (leasing is done by floor, and rental prices are higher than other types of apartments and conversion rates [converting leads to leases] are lower).

About 60 to 70 percent of the total budget should go to Internet marketing. Marketing in newspapers, magazines, radio, and television should receive approximately 20 percent. The remainder goes for temporary signage, banners, and outdoor signage, such as subways, billboards (one billboard can cost $20,000), advertising dioramas in shopping malls, and so forth. These figures are for the period of active lease-up. Marketing costs decline substantially when the property is stabilized, to just a fraction of the lease-up numbers. For example, with a suburban apartment community, marketing during the lease-up period may be $500 per unit annually, whereas at stabilization, it may be $500 to $1,000 per month for the entire apartment complex.

LEASING AND SELLING. Prospective residents are sophisticated home shoppers, and the leasing staff should be chosen accordingly. Staff should comprise well-trained professional sales personnel experienced in dealing with clients.

The old rule of one leasing agent for every 100 units in a new project is considered inadequate today. With staffing at that level today, agents do not have time to give prospective residents the service and attention they need. If the leasing center is understaffed, sales are lost. Using additional personnel is cost-effective when compared with the cost of losing leases.

Even the best leasing team can convert only a percentage of leads to leases. The purpose of advertising is to generate the prospects. AvalonBay, a multifamily REIT with properties nationwide, converts 25 to 30 percent of its appointments—prospects who walk in the door—to leases. The firm experiences a 30 to 35 percent no-show rate. Its conversion rate of leads to appointments is 8 percent for e-mail and 35 to 40 percent for telephone. Therefore, each lease requires 67 e-mail leads and 14 phone leads.

Because apartments turn over regularly, marketing is a continuous and long-term effort. Therefore, a well-trained, professional sales staff contributes a great deal to the project's marketability. Some developers use in-house teams of leasing and sales agents, providing them with greater control over the leasing and sales process—but also entailing greater management responsibilities. Another alternative is to use leasing companies that specialize in grand openings and initial lease-up. Because they are rewarded according to the number of leases signed rather than the long-term performance of the project, the developer should monitor tenants' creditworthiness very carefully. Another solution is to engage the services of an outside agency to take ongoing responsibility for marketing and leasing the project.

PRICING. Pricing, the most important tool for influencing leasing in the short run, cannot be based on pro forma projections. Rents must reflect current market conditions at the time the property is being leased, especially the prices charged by neighboring projects. Pricing should be monitored weekly, or even daily. Conditions change quickly, and a vacant unit costs a developer much more than a slight reduction in rent.

Funding requirements for permanent mortgages usually specify a target NOI that must be met for the mortgage to be fully funded. This target implies an average rent level. In declining markets, the developer may be obliged to obtain rents that are above market rate.[64] In such cases, the developer must find other incentives to make the *effective* rental rate (including all concessions) in line with the current market. To make a project more competitive in a soft market, a developer can

- give concessions, such as a half to a full month's free rent;
- reduce the amount of the deposit required;
- offer accruing deposits, where tenants make little or no initial deposit and earn deposit credits at the rate of $20 or $30 per month, which they receive at the end of six months or so (this incentive also helps improve the punctuality of payments);

Public Relations Tasks

A developer who hires a public relations firm to work on behalf of his organization should expect that firm to undertake the following tasks. A designated individual on the developer's marketing staff could also undertake these tasks.

- Develop a program.

- Compile fact sheets and biographies for the developer's company, projects, product(s), and principals. Assist in developing a company website.

- Identify potential story lines: announcements of new products and openings, for example, personnel appointments, awards, design features.

- Write simple, concise releases that include all pertinent facts and affix a dollar value if at all possible. Post on the website.

- Develop a local, regional, and national press list for print, broadcast, and the Internet. Identify reporters who wish to receive news via e-mail, fax, or mail.

- Make personal contact with news media representatives on the press list.

- Establish contacts with national trade publications and consumer magazines and newspapers.

- Try to place interview articles for the development company's principals.

- Obtain media kits and editorial calendars from all appropriate national and trade publications.

- Plan regular visits to local, regional, and national media as appropriate. Invite media representatives to visit the developer's offices and projects.

- Obtain dates of awards competitions; coordinate design and marketing awards.

- Try to place the company's principals as speakers for local, regional, and national conferences.

- Develop a photograph file of people and projects and a graphics file of renderings, logos, and so on. Scan images and save on computer or disk to accompany e-mail distribution of articles.

- Develop a mailing list of the developer's old, present, and potential clients for promotional mailings (if not handled by the marketing director).

- Reprint articles about the developer's projects that appear in magazines and newspapers. Use them, accompanied

by a letter, for direct mailings to client list. Post articles on the company website.

- Develop a company newsletter. Post newsletter on the company website.

- Establish contact with the public relations directors of all the developer's clients and coordinate projects to secure mention for the developer's projects in client news releases and advertisements.

- Call, e-mail, or send thank-you notes to press who feature the developer's projects.

- Plan special events to attract people and attention to the developer's projects.

- Encourage the developer's participation in professional organizations and community organizations and activities.

- Personally participate in organizations and attend programs, seminars, and conferences that affect or support the developer's activities.

Source: Patty Doyle, president, Patty Doyle Public Relations, Inc., Fort Lauderdale, Florida.

- provide free cable television or other services that normally carry a monthly charge;
- install additional appliances, such as microwave ovens, ceiling fans, and washer/dryers (such appliances represent a permanent capital improvement to the unit);
- offer decorating allowances for carpet, wallpaper, window coverings, or light fixtures;
- offer privileges at health or other clubs; or
- offer giveaways, such as TVs, vacations, or iPhones (this strategy may work for new hot items, but prospects and residents up for renewal prefer cash in hand).

Point-of-sale incentives are also invaluable tools for selling condominiums. The amount and type of sales incentives depend largely on local market conditions. Kevin Thompson of AvalonBay says that his company tries to maintain occupancy at the 96–97 percent level at all times. "We do what we have to in order to achieve this. During the 2008–2009 recession, rental rates dropped 5 to 10 percent below previous peak levels and we used pricing and other concessions to attract prospects."

PUBLIC RELATIONS

The purpose of public relations is to create a favorable public image. The result of good public relations is free advertising. Proactive public relations include housekeeping functions (day-to-day communications with residents and the public) and crisis communications and management (dealing with on-site incidents where residents must be notified and that might generate negative media coverage).

Public relations play an important role on site and off site. Developers who enjoy good off-site public relations are active in their communities with civic groups, the local chamber of commerce, churches, and other organizations. Developers who promote on-site public relations ensure that visitors to their sites receive a positive general impression—a neat and orderly site and sales office and polite staff, among other things.

Public relations experts are particularly useful to developers by virtue of their relations with local news media. Through their contacts, they should be able to obtain coverage for announcements and news releases about a new property. Potentially newsworthy events include purchasing the land, obtaining financing, closing loans, ground breaking, the grand opening, the first families to move in, attaining certain

HUMPHREYS & PARTNERS ARCHITECTS, L.P.

The leasing center at 660 Apartments in Atlanta.

lease hurdles, human interest stories about tenants (especially stories that highlight a special feature of the project, such as units for the handicapped), and special events. Other stories may be crafted about the product itself, featuring such elements as the design of the interior or exterior.

Public relations firms may also stage special events for a developer. Useful events include press parties, previews of a complex for community leaders and media representatives, and sponsored community events aimed at fundraising. Awards competitions are another fruitful source of favorable publicity and provide third-party endorsement for a project.

Newsletters are a particularly effective public relations tool. Their frequency depends on the size of and the level of activity in an individual project. Newsletters, through e-mail and occasionally by direct mail, should be sent to residents, area employers, brokers, prospects, neighborhood stores, and community facilities. They are helpful for attracting prospective buyers and tenants and for informing current residents about what is going on in the community. Most important, newsletters suggest to residents that the management cares about them. Usually, an advertising agency designs the newsletter and a public relations firm writes the copy, though many public relations firms handle the whole process.

A public relations campaign waged by a large development firm should target different publics with different messages:

- **Land Sellers**—Building faith in the developer's ability to perform;

- **Lenders**—Building faith in the developer's capacity to deliver what he promises and to repay loans;
- **Government**—Announcing that the company takes care of consumer complaints and is a good citizen in its dealings with the public sector;
- **Future Employees**—Creating the impression that the company is a fun and profitable place to work;
- **Competitors**—Conveying a sense of mutual respect and a shared readiness to work together in industry and civic organizations to address common problems;
- **Customers**—Establishing the developer's preoccupation with satisfying the demands of customers; and
- **Media**—Conveying respect and a willingness to share information.

ADVERTISING

The primary purpose of advertising is to motivate potential tenants and buyers to visit a project. Advertising is vital but can be very expensive. Discussions with other local developers, property managers, and advertising agencies can help identify the best media for advertising the project. Advertising agencies typically recommend that the advertising budget equal about 1 percent of the developer's hard costs. This amount is variable, however, depending on market conditions and the property's size, nature, and visibility.

The most prestigious advertising agency may not necessarily be the best for a beginning developer who requires considerable personal attention. A developer should interview at least three firms, obtain recommendations from their clients, and then select a firm that is genuinely interested in the developer's account. Advertising agencies provide various services, including developing a long-range advertising strategy, planning individual programs, selecting the best media for presentation, preparing copy and design layouts, and monitoring the performance of their efforts.

Advertising for a project typically employs a common logo, theme, and style. A well-crafted logo can be used in advertising, on signage, brochures, and stationery, and even as a design motif. A project's name likewise plays an important role in creating an image for a project. New developers should promote a project's name first, with the developer's name of secondary importance. Names should be descriptive, not misleading. A complex should not be named "Forest Hills" if it sits on a Kansas-like prairie.

The most cost-effective media for advertising vary by project and location. Some typical outlets include websites, neighborhood newspapers, metropolitan newspapers, radio and television, and temporary signs.

WEBSITES. A good website is essential to advertise a property. The Internet is the dominant marketing tool to reach potential renters and buyers. Smaller developers may wish to have their properties linked to websites and Internet apartment rental services that provide information on a variety of properties. In this way, individual properties that might not be able to attract any attention on their own can piggyback on the larger service to gain visibility in the Internet marketplace. Websites dedicated to one property or a group of related properties involve much more than making an initial investment and waiting for customers to access the information. Websites require ongoing maintenance to ensure that information is up-to-date and accurate. Websites make it possible to customize the information and provide details for prospects, such as floor plans, photographs, virtual tours, and neighborhood amenities.

CALL CENTERS. Call centers are an important extension of the industry. They are open 24/7 and will answer calls and respond to e-mails 24/7. Kevin Thompson states that 21 percent of AvalonBay's appointments are made after hours. It gets bilingual help from the call centers and finds their service and phone skills to be excellent. The call centers answer 100 percent of e-mails within two hours and 70 percent within one hour. Each AvalonBay community has its own 800 number. The call center service costs approximately $500 per month. "It pays," says Thompson. "We see it as customer service."

BROCHURES. Developers should ensure that advertising brochures are begun at least two months before they will be needed. The brochures should be ready for mailing to local employers, brokers, community leaders, and apartment locators during construction as part of premarketing. Despite the need for early preparation, brochures should not tie developers to specific figures; therefore, they should not contain prices (which change continually) or bound floor plans (people always want the floor plan that has already been rented or sold out). Prices should be listed on a separate page that can be easily changed. The square footage of a unit should be omitted from a floor plan unless its inclusion is a very competitive advantage. Special features and amenities, however, should be emphasized.

Many developers opt for a folder with a high-quality printed cover and pockets inside for inserts. The jacket is the major printing expense; inserts can be changed and updated as needed. Brochures can be of all shapes and colors. When people are shopping for apartments, they pick up a number of materials and are more likely to notice distinctive brochures. Brochures that fold into the shape of, say, a door key or a house may cost extra to print but are more memorable. "Professional high-quality photography is the key to success for both brochures and websites," according to Kevin Thompson. AvalonBay invests extra money in a beautiful shoot. High resolution is very important. The photographs emphasize lifestyle with people actively enjoying the amenities in a project. "Be cognizant of fair housing. Photos should feature people of every shape, color, size, and disability."[65]

NEWSPAPER ADVERTISING. Layout and copy for newspaper advertisements should be simple and specific and should not exaggerate the project's attributes. The name of the developer and clear directions to the project should be included; in this respect, maps are helpful and allow prospective tenants to be directed along the route that creates the most favorable impression as they approach the project.

Classified advertisements, the least expensive form of newspaper advertising, are helpful in certain markets.

Larger newspaper ads are much less prevalent than they were a few years ago. A display ad can

Internet Marketing

Internet marketing has changed dramatically since the 1990s. In the early 2000s, it primarily consisted of secondary listings—banner ads and featured listing on Internet listing services (ILSs). The incremental leads and bumps in traffic from ILSs encouraged traditional media and print people to use the Internet more. Major newspapers started having online listings. Search engine marketing (SEM) emerged around 2005. SEM uses keyword search (pay-per-click) campaigns to boost traffic. The more you want to pay, the more people you will lead to your website. AvalonBay hires a third-party agency to handle its SEM and spends approximately the same amount as it does on ILSs. It has 300,000–400,000 key words. Success of search engine marketing is very specific to each locale. For example, if a prospect wants a two-bedroom apartment in Arlington, Virginia, the SEM key words need to include "Arlington, Virginia."

Of AvalonBay's traffic, 63 percent comes from Internet sources and 45 percent of the total traffic is direct to its website; an equal amount is generated from the ILSs. Craigslist, which the firm has used since its inception, generates 7 percent of the Internet leads. For its own website, AvalonBay has hired a consultant for search engine optimization (SEO). SEO considers how search engines work and what people search for. Optimizing a website primarily involves editing its content HTML and associated coding both to increase its relevance to specific keywords and to remove barriers to the indexing activities of search engines. One should start with SEO before spending any money on SEM.

AvalonBay is the first large apartment company to hire an Internet marketing manager. It has seen its numbers swing from 36 percent of Internet traffic in 2005 to 63 percent in 2010. During this period, apartment guides in grocery and other stores fell from 10 to 1 percent. Kevin Thompson says the company is very surgical in what it does. It still finds print guides critical for Class B or C properties and around colleges.

Social networking sites like Facebook, MySpace, Bebo, and Friendster are invaluable for enhancing customer service and neighbor connectivity, but they are not good lead-generation tools. Avalon Fort Green in Brooklyn, New York, has 330 residents but 500 fans. Many fans who are not residents enjoy the site's referrals for concerts, restaurants, and other neighborhood activities. Thompson observes, "Many apartments jump right into social networking. They forget ILSs and SEM, and that is a big mistake. You manage the social sites on site with daily or weekly posts. If the site is not kept up-to-date, it will *upset* residents. A third party can manage the site for $500 per month or more per community. Don't do it unless you are going to keep it up."

Mobile sites like Google, Twitter, Dodgeball, and Flickr are designed specifically for use on mobile devices. They have fewer buttons and are much simpler than regular websites. Searches done on mobile sites are now at 3 percent but growing. Thompson advises, "Leave off pictures and other memory hogs. Give quick simple facts like a location map, prices, and phone numbers."

AvalonBay's budget for print publications is very small, with the vast majority (80 to 90 percent) devoted to Internet marketing, of which the bulk goes to aggregators like Apartments.com, Move.com, and Rent.com. All AvalonBay's ads are directed toward prospective tenants, so it does not advertise in trade publications, which would target competitors.

Source: Interview with Kevin Thompson, vice president of marketing for AvalonBay Communities, Inc., June 2010.

Multifamily Residential Development

cost $10,000–$20,000 for one issue. AvalonBay may occasionally run an ad to announce a major new property in Boston or New York City. However, it currently spends less than 1 percent of its advertising budget on newspaper ads and is not currently pursuing the classified sections of newspapers' websites.

RADIO AND TELEVISION. Radio advertising is useful for drawing attention to grand openings of larger projects and groups of projects by one developer. To select a station, first check listener profiles and pick a station whose general programming is similar to the tastes of the target market. In addition to spot advertisements, live remote broadcasts work well during times when many people are out driving. Radio advertisements may generate considerable traffic on site. If a developer is not prepared to handle a large number of people on site, the advertisements may do more harm than good.

Television is the most expensive medium. It is probably not cost-effective in large metropolitan areas, but it may be effective in smaller markets for grand openings.

SIGNS. Billboards help establish name identity and may be useful as directional signs near a project. Transit advertising—such as bus banners, bus benches, and commuter station posters—can also be an effective way of keeping the developer's name in the public eye. Direction signs are probably the most effective signs of all. Removable "bootleg" signs are an inexpensive and efficient means of bringing people to the project from major arterials within a two-mile (3.2 km) radius for special events.

MERCHANDISING. Whereas advertising is intended to tell people about a project and entice them to visit it, merchandising is concerned with on-site displays and practices. Visitors' first impressions are critical to a project's success. Particular attention should be paid to the condition of entrances, signs, landscaping, and buildings. A pleasant environment should be created as soon as possible, even while construction is still in progress. A well-designed and carefully located entrance not only helps merchandising but also bolsters a project's future identification in the neighborhood. Entrance signs and nameplates should be modest, designed to blend with the character of the community. Generous landscaping may be expensive, but it is also cost-effective—as a visit to any successful project demonstrates. Restrictive signs (prohibiting, say, walking on the grass) should be pleasant and inoffensive

and should be designed, where possible, to relate to other merchandising features.

SALES OR LEASING OFFICE. The sales or leasing office should be easy to find and should open up to attractive views of interior courtyards or other features of the project. Colors and furnishings should be consistent with the project's theme and should be chosen with the target market in mind. In the sales office, brochures, models, and maps should be placed so that visitors can view them at their leisure. Drawings of the apartment site plan and unit plans make attractive and informative wall hangings. Graphics give visitors an impression of what an uncompleted project will eventually look like. Perspective drawings are important. Visualizing a project from two-dimensional plans is difficult for most people. Small models of the project, although expensive, make attractive focal points and can help renters and buyers see how their apartments are located with respect to major amenities, access, security, and views. Aerial photographs also help show a project's relationship to off-site facilities, such as schools, churches, libraries, daycare centers, shops, and parks.

MODEL UNITS. Model units play an important part in selling and leasing by giving customers a sense of what the unit will look like and what they can do to personalize it. Model units should be close to the sales office, offer pleasant views of either the project or the surrounding area, and benefit from afternoon sunlight (afternoon is the most popular time for visitors).

Although decorating a sample of every unit type is unnecessary, those units that are decorated are likely to lease or sell more quickly. Decor for the models should be selected to appeal to the target market. Decorating should emphasize making units look brighter and larger. Doors may be removed to add to a sense of spaciousness. Nonstandard built-ins should be avoided because they may mislead customers and because the model units may be moved to different locations in the complex once the project is leased. Moods may be enhanced through the use of background music, colors, and lighting. AvalonBay increasingly relies on virtual models, which are much easier to manage and much less costly (about half of the traditional model budget).[66]

CONDOMINIUM SALES. Marketing for condominiums is similar to that for single-family houses. Despite their desire to sell units during construction, developers have found that few buyers will commit themselves before they have seen the completed lobbies and amenities.

For smaller projects, an in-house sales staff is often uneconomical, and many developers use outside brokers, who are paid on commission. Developers who own other apartment houses or condominiums find that word-of-mouth advertising can be very effective. Some developers send out announcements to tenants or owners at their previous projects every time they open a new project. Paying a referral fee of, say, $50 to tenants or owners in other projects often helps generate sales, although in some states this practice violates real estate license laws.

John Math recommends that to sell 50 to 100 condominium units, a developer should hire a sales manager plus one salesperson. For projects of 100 to 200 units, two salespeople should be hired. Their total compensation should amount to 1.5 to 3 percent of gross sales. Many successful salespeople prefer to work totally on commission. If a developer expects them to be in the office during certain hours of the day, they should receive a salary plus commission or draw against commission.[67]

Many condominium developers and lenders restrict non-owner-occupied units under the assumption that absentee owners take less care of their property and thereby depress sales to owner-occupants, who will pay the highest prices. At the same time, developers need to be flexible and prepared to respond to changing market conditions. When condominium sales are slow, some companies decide to operate the projects as rental units. Paul Schulthe, a developer in Arcadia, California, undertook a condominium project during a downturn in the market: "We set up an intensive marketing budget with an all-out push for 90 days. Only three of the 16 units were sold. We decided to change direction and set the building up as apartments. Now we own a deluxe-deluxe apartment house." In many cases, however, projects conceived as condominiums do not work financially as apartments and subsequently lose money or go through foreclosure.

Operations and Management

No matter how well it is designed and built, an apartment project will be profitable only if it is well managed. Further, management must be competent at many levels for a project to succeed:

- initial marketing and lease-up (often assigned to an outside source);

- ongoing marketing and leasing;
- collecting rents, handling accounts, and keeping records;
- making ongoing reports to owners;
- maintaining and repairing units, readying them for new tenants;
- maintaining and repairing building systems and common areas;
- maintaining landscaping and building exteriors;
- hiring and training new staff;
- keeping residents informed about apartment policies and operating activities of interest to them;
- initiating services for residents;
- dealing with residents' complaints;
- maintaining good relations with brokers, community organizations, and local government;
- maintaining good relations with managers of neighboring apartments to share information and work together on security and other common problems; and
- developing budgets and operating plans.

The nature of the relationship between the developer and the property manager depends, in part, on the property's size, the extent of the developer's property portfolio, and the nature and structure of the businesses. The manager can be the developer, the developer's employee, a subsidiary or in-house department of the development/property company, or an individual or third-party management company under contract. Most large apartment property companies, including REITs, manage their own properties through an in-house department or owned subsidiary company.

For most apartment projects, the decision on whether or not to use an outside property manager is based on the developer's willingness to invest time in the project. Properly addressing residents' needs and maintaining the property are extremely time-consuming. Most developers prefer to delegate these responsibilities to a qualified property manager.

Although the operation and management of condominiums are the responsibility of unit owners through their condominium association, the legal framework for the condominium association must be established by the developer (see chapter 3).

Even though most developers would prefer not to be in the management business, many feel that only by managing their own projects can they get the service they need. Beginning developers usually do not have an organization in place, however, and must

Plus Flats in Istanbul, Turkey, is a 27-unit residential development. The building is earthquake resistant and includes green features such as solar panels and a green roof over the garage.

therefore rely on outside managers. Greg Vilkin, a California developer, notes that property management fees have dropped as larger management companies compete for business. "You are not going to make money if you do management, as you can hire someone at a 3 percent fee. They consider 3 to 3.5 percent of gross rent what it costs them to do it."[68]

In selecting outside managers, beginning developers should look for companies with a good reputation for managing a particular type of property in terms of size, design, and tenant characteristics. It is also useful to investigate on-site procedures for accounting and collecting rents. An audit should be performed at least twice a year, preferably quarterly. The auditor, who should appear unannounced, reviews collection reports, rent rolls, and individual leases and inspects vacant units to ensure that no "skimming" is occurring.

The management company should prepare monthly reports that show gross potential income, actual income, and line-by-line expenses. The reports should also detail which units are vacant and which are not producing revenue. Cash receipts should be deposited daily. Monthly cash collection reports should be reviewed and approved by off-site staff.

The larger the property and its operating budget, the more likely it can accommodate specialists on staff, such as equipment engineers, gardeners, painters, or security guards. Many developers consider 150 or 200 units the minimum number necessary to support a full-time maintenance staff consisting of a property manager, assistant manager, maintenance worker, and porter. Management of smaller properties can be a more formal undertaking at the beginning, possibly by employing a resident manager, which may be less expensive in the short run but mostly inadequate for today's markets. In many urban areas, however, assembling a site that will support 150 units is very difficult, so developers have learned how to cope with smaller complexes.

The developer should endeavor to have as much good information as possible on future operations and maintenance, including but not limited to costs, to make informed design decisions. Property managers can make many useful contributions to the design process and should be included in all design review meetings. The increasing importance of residents' personal and property security can be addressed in part by improving design. Property managers' perspectives, based on experience with defensible space, can be valuable in this effort.

HIRING STAFF

Property management is one of the fastest-growing specializations in the real estate profession, "emerging as a managerial science. Today, [property managers] must have at their fingertips the knowledge, communication skills, and technical expertise needed to be dynamic decision makers. They also must be versatile, because they may be called on to act as market analysts, advertising executives, salespeople, accountants, diplomats, or even maintenance engineers. Interpersonal skills are needed to deal effectively with owners, prospects, tenants, employees, outside contractors, and others in the real estate business."[69]

Jim Perley summarizes his property management strategy: "Empower property managers as small business managers. Allow them to respond to market conditions by offering concessions to maintain occupancy. We want our managers to be comfortable enough with the owners to propose solutions. Owners should function as coaching staff: it is critical that they listen to input from personnel in the field." He adds, "Managers like having a relationship with the owner. Delegation helps managers feel good, and helps him grow the business by freeing his energies to focus on business development."[70]

Beyond hiring and training, a third component of effective customer service is feedback and reward. Leading apartment management companies tend to stress the bottom-up "culture of service" in their organizations, based on closely monitoring residents' satisfaction and compensation schemes that reward employees for keeping residents satisfied.

TURNOVER

The most volatile element in net operating income is usually the turnover rate. Although turnover sometimes offers a good opportunity to raise rents for units renting near the market rate, turnover can be costly in terms of rent lost during vacancies and of the renovations and cleanup required to prepare an apartment to rent again. In general, after a property has reached stabilized occupancy, the focus turns to keeping the property stable.

"It's good to raise rents, but the more important key number you should watch is turnover. Reward your management for renewing leases of existing tenants. Make sure that there is not a lot of turnover. That's a key thing to watch; stabilization, during the long run, keeps turnover and maintenance costs down."[71] Every turnover entails a minimum loss of two weeks of rent plus up to $500 for cleaning and carpet shampooing. In garden apartments, for example, turnover rates average 55 percent per year and can reach as high as 70 percent. In soft markets, turnover can exceed 100 percent.

Turnover occurs for many reasons, some of which— a tenant's changing jobs, for example—lie outside the developer's control. But the developer can reduce turnover caused by poor construction, design, maintenance, or management. Residents become disenchanted if their refrigerator leaks, if their unit is too noisy, or if they cannot find parking.

Property management experts stress the importance of communication to reduce turnover. Owners should communicate often and regularly with managers and staff so that all parties understand their goals and concerns. On-site managers should communicate regularly with residents, answering questions and reducing uncertainty among tenants. For example, if a swimming pool must be emptied to make repairs, tenants should know when they will be able to use it again.

Problem tenants can create difficulties for an entire complex. Controlling noise and other irritants among neighboring tenants is critical for maintaining low turnover. The property manager can set the stage for tenants from the beginning by going over a written list of rules and regulations for the property before tenants move in, and asking tenants to sign the rules signifying that they understand them. When problems arise between tenants, the manager should first try to reach an amicable solution with both parties. Moving a tenant to a different unit sometimes solves the problem. If one party is at fault and an amicable solution does not work, the lease should be used to enforce the rules of the property, up to and including eviction. Timely response and firm enforcement of rules are vital for maintaining good tenant relations.

Jim Mattingly at LumaCorp in Dallas emphasizes property maintenance and customer service. "We believe that you have to have good, solid product. Even if it is older, it has to be attractive." On-site personnel training emphasizes people skills. To stimulate a culture of customer service, LumaCorp has concentrated on improving ratings on online apartment-rating services. This real-time feedback helps staff focus on customer service. He adds that the relationship between your property managers and residents is the key to success. Mattingly advises spending more money on marketing, resident functions, and communication.[72]

REFINANCING AND SELLING THE PROPERTY

One of the great advantages of owning property is the ability to refinance it and take out the additional financing proceeds tax free. As the NOI increases over time, savvy owners will refinance their properties regularly to take advantage of the tax-free cash they receive by obtaining larger mortgages. Jim Mattingly advises beginning developers to design flexibility into their financing. For LumaCorp, this flexibility has meant looking for longer, open-ended payment periods so the company is not obligated to refinance a property in any given year. Mattingly recommends trying to negotiate a two-year window in which to refinance so that one can choose the year.[73]

The life cycle of property management has three stages: leasing up the property, stabilizing income, and positioning the property for sale. The third stage usually involves a different management approach from the first two.

When the time comes to sell a project, on-site staff should be informed about the developer's goals and should be given some financial incentive to motivate them to help put the apartment in the best possible physical and financial condition for sale. It is an intense period when rents are raised and vacancies are filled. Experienced developers recommend that residents not be informed of a pending sale, but each tenant should receive a letter immediately *after* the sale. In Texas, for example, the law requires that tenants be notified within 48 hours of a sale about the status of their security deposits, which are transferred with the asset.

Cash flow is generally the most important consideration for buyers. Some steps will increase short-term cash flow at the expense of long-term profitability. For example, some developers become less selective about tenants to increase their occupancy and the rent roll when they get ready to sell a property. Other owners cut back on operating expenses and capital expenditures. Sophisticated buyers will use their own experience with respect to operating costs so that sellers' attempts to artificially reduce costs will have little effect on the sale price. Short-term efforts to raise cash flows are not advised, but many sellers do it. If a sale does not go through, the owner will have to deal with the consequences of the short-term strategy, such as getting rid of unreliable or troublesome tenants.

Conclusion

Beginning developers will find multifamily residential development one of the easier points of entry into the development industry, especially if they have some background in homebuilding. Like other types of development, multifamily housing is rapidly evolving. The process begins and ends with market analysis. If the depth, characteristics, and preferences of the target market are not correctly identified, delivering a product that best serves the market's needs is impossible.

Jim Perley notes that a beginning developer has to adapt to new situations and to try to predict the flow of situations. "You are trying not only to make money but also to develop a good product. It is also important to build equity and develop a good staff to make a difference."[74] Marvin Finger also emphasizes the people side of the business. "The three components of multifamily development are location, product, and management. If you don't have the location, the product and the management will not make a difference and you'll never be successful. If you have the location, you can miss on the product somewhat if it is reasonably designed. But you must have the people if the product is to be sold. Renters rent from an individual when they sign the lease agreement. They have made a bond with an individual. It's very important not to have turnover in the office. You must groom and build an organization that is somewhat permanent, because people create relationships. When these relationships are not in place anymore, tenants will take their business elsewhere. People are key in the management business."[75]

To obtain financing today, new projects must demonstrate solid cash flows and produce real economic returns. This trend should offer long-term benefits to developers who face less tax-motivated competition. REITs and pension funds have helped generate more money for apartment development in recent years by buying new and existing properties and making forward commitments to buy projects under development. In many areas, rents have lagged behind other cost-of-living increases, resulting in fewer apartment starts throughout the 1990s. In the wake of the financial crisis of 2008–2009, apartments have been the favored product type. Cap rates were approaching lows before the collapse, but the market has been bifurcated. Class A (core) apartment properties in

Advice on Property Management

Stable occupancy with low turnover and high-quality tenants who pay market rate rents punctually is every property manager's goal. The following advice will help achieve it:

- If you make promises, deliver.

- Check the credit and criminal history of new tenants through credit agencies, applicant-screening services, and Web-based services.

- Make vacant units ready for occupancy quickly; ready units lease more quickly and reduce vacancy loss. The manager's challenge is to balance the need to respond promptly to current residents' requests for service with

the need to prepare newly vacated units for occupancy. It may be necessary to use outside contractors to ready units if a large number of units must be prepared or a large number of service requests are pending.

- The property manager can help minimize the possibility of receiving a large number of move-outs in any one month by carefully monitoring lease expiration dates and staggering expiration dates for new leases accordingly.

- Collect the first month's rent plus a security deposit from new tenants to guard against their leaving without giving notice.

- Work hard to hold on to current tenants in a slow market. For lease renewals, meet with tenants 45 days before their lease is due to expire.

- Deal with problems quickly and efficiently; unresolved problems will only grow.

- Remember that fewer callbacks by tenants on maintenance and repairs mean greater tenant satisfaction and fewer turnovers.

- Even when cash flow is low, try to minimize cutbacks on maintenance, repairs, and replacements, because they can lead to a lower standard of maintenance.

cities on the East and West Coasts, such as San Francisco, Washington, D.C., and Boston, have elicited strong buying support driving down cap rates, while properties in the Midwest and South have seen higher vacancies and weaker buying support. Institutional buyers prefer markets that are hard to build in, where future competition is less likely to increase dramatically. As the combined effects of echo boomers entering the workforce, homeowners who lost their homes in the recession of 2008–2009, and baby boomers who sell their homes for city living are felt, apartment demand is expected to go up, putting pressure on rents to rise more quickly. Developers are also finding opportunities to build apartments for new niches, such as luxury renters in upscale communities who want to stay in the same community but no longer want a large suburban home to maintain.

More stringent fire codes; energy, sustainability, and parking requirements; density restrictions; and standards for amenities are raising the cost of apartment construction. At the same time, the scarcity of land, neighborhood opposition to development, stricter environmental regulations, and growing difficulties with public approvals are raising the price of land for apartments. Historically, rents have lagged behind inflation in the general economy. Rents will have to rise more sharply than they have in the past for apartment units to remain financially attractive—a trend that is likely to increase pressures for rent control in many communities. Although new apartment construction on suburban greenfield sites remains the easiest way for beginning developers to start, smaller urban infill projects, conversions of older industrial and office buildings to apartments, and affordable housing programs, such as tax credits, offer appealing opportunities for beginning developers. Their most important goal should be to build a track record of successful projects in which tenants, investors, and lenders are pleased with their performance. There are advantages to working on smaller, simpler projects than on larger complicated ones. Completing three smaller projects over two to three years will take a beginning developer further than completing one large project over the same period.

NOTES

1. Joint Center for Housing Studies of Harvard University, *The State of the Nation's Housing, 2009*, Cambridge, Mass., 2009.

2. Office of Policy Development and Research, U.S. Department of Housing and Urban Development, *Updating the Low-Income Housing Tax Credit (LIHTC) Database: Projects Placed in Service through 2006*, Washington, D.C., January 2009. A total of 1.23 million units in 16,754 projects were built altogether from 1995 to 2006.

3. Nathaniel Baum-Snow and Justin Marion, "The Effects of Low Income Housing Tax Credit Developments on Neighborhoods," Brown University and Santa Cruz University (manuscript, December 2008).

4. Interview with Randolph Hawthorne, RGH Ventures, Brookline, Massachusetts, 2000.

5. Ibid.

6. Ibid., 2011.

7. Interview with Edward Zuker, Chestnut Hill Realty, Chestnut Hill, Massachusetts, September 2009.

8. Interview with Jerome L. Rappaport, Jr., New Boston Fund, Boston, Massachusetts, November 2009.

9. Interview with Marvin Finger, the Finger Companies, Houston, Texas, 2000.

10. Ibid.

11. Interview with Gerd-Ulf Krueger. principal economist and founder, housingEcon.com, Los Angeles, California, August 2009.

12. Ibid.

13. Ibid.

14. See Richard B. Peiser, "The Determinants of Nonresidential Urban Land Values," *Journal of Urban Economics* 22 (1987): 340–360.

15. *Double-loaded parking* has parking stalls on both sides of the driveway. *Back-to-back* apartment units adjoin the back of another unit along the rear wall. This shared wall can accommodate plumbing for both units and reduces the total amount of outside wall per unit, thereby saving money.

16. The San Diego general plan requires at least one acre (0.4 ha) for lots with an average slope of 15 percent or less, two acres (0.8 ha) for an average slope of 15 to 25 percent, and four acres (1.6 ha) for an average slope greater than 25 percent. Interview with Neal LaMontagne, County of San Diego Department of Planning and Land Use, 2000.

17. NAWCA contains no specific definition of vernal pools. The U.S. Fish and Wildlife Service uses the "Classification of Wetlands and Deepwater Habitats of the United States" (December 1979) for defining types of wetlands, which is also used for NAWCA. Typically, a vernal pool is a shallow, intermittently flooded wet meadow, generally dry for most of the summer and fall. Interview with David Buie, U.S. Fish and Wildlife Service, 2000.

18. Interview with Greg Vilkin, president, Forest City Development, Los Angeles, California, 2000.

19. Interview with Jerome J. Frank, Jr., Jerome Frank Investments, Dallas, Texas, 2000.

20. Interview with Marvin Finger, 2000.

21. Interview with Kenneth Hughes, president, Hughes Development, LP, Dallas, Texas, August 2009.

22. California Department of Transportation, *Transit-Oriented Development Compendium*, June 2005, www.dot.ca.gov/hq/MassTrans/TOD/compendium.pdf.

23. Interview with Kenneth Hughes, August 2009.

24. For an excellent discussion of exactions, see James E. Frank and Robert M. Rhodes, eds., *Development Exactions* (Washington, D.C. and Chicago: Planners Press and the American Planning Association, 1987). See also Alan Altshuler and Jose Gomez-Ibanez, *Regulation for Revenue: The Political Economy of Land Use Exactions* (Washington, D.C., and Cambridge, Mass.: Brookings Institution and Lincoln Institute of Land Policy, 1993); David L. Callies, Daniel J. Curtin, Jr., and Julie A. Tappendorf, *Bargaining for Development: A Handbook on Development Agreements, Annexation Agreements, Land Development Conditions, Vested Rights, and the Provision of Public Facilities* (Washington, D.C.: Environmental Law Institute, 2003); and Robert H. Freilich and David W. Bushek, eds., *Exactions, Impact Fees, and Dedications: Shaping Land-Use Development and Funding Infrastructure in the Dolan Era* (Chicago: State and Local Government Law Section, American Bar Association, 1995).

25. For a good overview of alternatives for financing infrastructure improvements, see Robert W. Burchell, David Listokin, et al., *Development Impact Assessment Handbook* (Washington, D.C.: ULI–the Urban Land Institute, 1994).

26. *2008 National Impact Fee Survey*, Duncan Associates, Austin, Tex., October 2008, www.impactfees.com/publications%20 pdf/2008_survey.pdf.

27. See www.uli.org/pred for electronic spreadsheets.

28. Stage 2 analysis is standard throughout the real estate industry and is taught in most real estate graduate schools and executive training courses. Most real estate finance textbooks describe DCF analysis in detail; see, for example, William B. Brueggeman and Jeffrey Fisher, *Real Estate Finance and Investments*, 13th ed. (New York: McGraw-Hill, 2010); and Charles Long, *Finance for Real Estate Development* (Washington, D.C.: ULI–the Urban Land Institute, 2011).

29. To avoid double-counting, it is important to remember to use the total development costs *before* lease-up in the Stage 2 analysis.

30. When interest rates are well below overall capitalization rates, cash-on-cash returns on equity skyrocket as leverage (debt/total project costs) increases. Because inflation is a component of the IRR (along with risk and real return rates), the IRRs required by investors are also lower.

31. Construction loan interest rates are typically higher than permanent loan rates, but the difference shown here is unusual.

32. Time period zero is typically considered to be the time when the developer closes on the land. When closing occurs a long time before start of construction, it is simpler to assign time period zero as the start of construction and to include land carrying, design, and other earlier costs as "costs to date."

33. U.S. Census Bureau, "Characteristics of New Housing," www. census.gov/construction/chars/.

34. Hank Dittmar and Gloria Ohland, eds., *The New Transit Town: Best Practices in Transit Oriented Development* (Washington, D.C.: Island Press, 2004), pp. 34–35.

35. Interview with Scott Simpson, senior director, KlingStubbins, Cambridge, Massachusetts, September 2011.

36. Interview with Adam Barzilay, general partner, Vintage Residential, Philadelphia, Pennsylvania, June 2009.

37. Interview with Kenneth Hughes, August 2009.

38. Interview with Marvin Finger, 2000.

39. Interview with Scott Simpson, September 2011.

40. Interview with John Porta, MLP Investments, Brentwood, Missouri, July 2009.

41. Interview with Jerome J. Frank, Jr., 2000.

42. Both construction and permanent loans are called *mortgages* because they are backed by the collateral of the property.

43. A *point* represents a front-end fee equal to 1 percent of the loan amount. Points are usually paid out of the loan proceeds. On a $1 million loan with two points, the lender receives $20,000 in fees, and the developer receives the net amount of $980,000. Points are a normal part of the developer's financing costs and should be included in soft costs.

44. Hard-money lenders may accept a second lien position but their interest rate will be much higher than a regular lender.

45. Interview with Richard Klein, senior vice president of corporate development, Environmental Industries, Inc., Calabasas, California, 2000.

46. Interview with Jerome J. Frank, Jr., 2000.

47. Interview with Randolph Hawthorne, 2000.

48. *LIBOR* is the interest rate offered by a specific group of London banks for U.S. dollar deposits of a stated maturity. LIBOR is used as a base index for setting rates of some adjustable-rate financial instruments.

49. Interview with Karl Zavitkovsky, managing director, Bank of America, Dallas, Texas, 2001.

50. See Brueggeman and Fisher, *Real Estate Finance*, chapters 4 and 5, for how to calculate a mortgage.

51. *Top 25 percent* means that the developer guarantees the first 25 percent of loss. For example, if the loan is for $1 million and the lender loses $300,000, the developer is responsible for the first $250,000 of the loss.

52. Interview with Nicholas Lizotte, Sagamore Residential, Port Chester, New York, October 2009.

53. Interview with Jerome L. Rappaport, Jr., November 2009.

54. Real estate tax accounting is a highly specialized area. Although all accountants are familiar with depreciation rules, the categorization of upfront fees requires a specialist with experience in the technical aspects of real estate partnership tax and law.

55. Regulation D private offerings are not subject to the intense review by public agencies that public offerings receive. Public offerings must be offered to no more than 35 "nonqualified" investors, who are defined as investors with personal net worths of less than $1 million or incomes of less than $200,000 per year. A Regulation D private offering may be offered to an unlimited number of "qualified" investors.

56. Interview with Jerome L. Rappaport, Jr., November 2009. "Sidecar" investors are large national funds that will coinvest equity in projects along with the local owner-operator syndicator/fund. The syndicator/fund's deal with the sidecar investor may provide several different forms of fees—a management fee of up to 150 basis points, or no fee and an override, or no fee or override but annual property management fees.

57. Interview with Randolph Hawthorne by Kristen Hunter, August 2009.

58. Ibid.

59. *Federal Register*, vol. 75, no. 67, April 8, 2010, Notices, p. 18017.

60. Interview with John Porta, July 2009.

61. Interview with Jerome J. Frank, Jr., 2000.

62. Ibid.

63. Interview with Kevin Thompson, corporate vice president of marketing, AvalonBay Communities, Arlington, Virginia, by Richard Peiser, June 2010.

64. Permanent lenders have been stung by artificially inflated rental rates and usually require full disclosure of all rental concessions.

65. Interview with Kevin Thompson by Richard Peiser, June 2010.

66. Interview with Kevin Thompson, August 2011.

67. Interview with John Math, president, Associated Property Management, Lake Worth, Florida, October 2001.

68. Interview with Greg Vilkin, 2000.

69. Floyd M. Baird, Marie S. Spodek, and Robert C. Kyle, *Property Management*, 6th ed. (Chicago: Dearborn Real Estate Education, 2004), p. 1.

70. Interview with Jim Perley, Western America Properties, Los Angeles, California, by Kristen Hunter, June 2009.

71. Interview with Jerome J. Frank, Jr., 2000.

72. Interview with James Mattingly, president, LumaCorp, Inc., Dallas, Texas, June 2009.

73. Ibid.

74. Interview with Jim Perley, 2000.

75. Interview with Marvin Finger, 2000.

CASE STUDY: West River Commons, Minneapolis, Minnesota

BY COREY ZEHNGEBOT

West River Commons is a 75,000-square-foot (7,000 m²) mixed-use multifamily project by the Lander Group, a Minneapolis-based development firm founded in 1984 by Michael Lander. Although the Lander Group had historically focused on smaller (two to 16 units), neighborhood infill projects, West River Commons represents the firm's first foray into larger-scale mixed-use development. With 53 market-rate rental units ranging in size from 800 to 2,450 square feet (74–228 m²), the project was attractively located on Lake Street, a main thoroughfare connecting Minneapolis to St. Paul. Targeting a "lifestyle renter," the project successfully tapped into a relatively new rental market with little competition in the area.

SAM NEWBERG, JOE URBAN INC.

Supplementing the 53 apartments were three 2,000-square-foot (186 m²) townhouses, and 8,000 square feet (743 m²) of retail space at the street level. The retail tenants include a neighborhood bistro, a coffee shop, and take-out pizza place. With its proximity to the Mississippi River and associated trail system, the ground-floor retail quickly became an important magnet for recreational users.

SITE

West River Commons is located on a 1.1-acre (0.45 ha) site on the north side of Lake Street, and immediately west of the Mississippi River, which forms the border between Minneapolis and St. Paul. With the project's adjacency to the Lake Street Bridge, which connects the Twin Cities, West River Commons provides new housing and retail for the area and serves as a gateway to the city. The project is located adjacent to the Mississippi River, allowing for river views from some apartments.

The site is near several public and private universities, including the University of Minnesota, University of St. Thomas, and Macalester College. In addition, several regional hospitals are a short drive away.

To the north and south of the site are residential zones consisting of modest single-family houses that date to the 1920s. Lake Street, which cuts directly through the neighborhood, serves as the major commercial corridor with a mix of low- and mid-rise office and commercial properties. Though the area is stable, several blighted and underused properties are located along the street corridor. Two one-story office buildings and the Rivergate Apartments are directly opposite the site on the south side of Lake Street.

West River Commons is located on the site of a former gas station, and therefore qualified for a Hennepin County brownfields grant to help alleviate the cost of soil remediation. The developer's commitment to cleaning up a contaminated site located next to the widely used river trail system provided an important amenity both at a project and at a neighborhood level. Apartment units are oriented to provide river views, and the ground-level retail serves as a natural rest stop for recreational cyclists and joggers.

The site also previously contained a parking lot and religious assembly hall. Because the hall, built in the 1930s, was historic, its demolition had to be approved by the Minneapolis Historic Preservation Commission.

DEVELOPMENT AND DESIGN

The development entity, Gateway Real Estate, LLC—consisting of Michael Lander of the Lander Group and Mike Cashill and Alan Spaulding of At Home Apartments—secured the site in fall 2001, seeking to develop and manage an apartment project. At Home Apartments is a property management company based in St. Paul that owns and manages over 3,000 rental units in the Twin Cities area. As managers for the apartments across the street from the site, At Home was already established in the area and consequently made a natural partner.

CONTINUED

Zoning irregularities, unforeseen construction setbacks, and strong involvement by the local community characterized the design and development process for West River Commons.

Design of the project was contingent on the split zoning for the site. Retail uses and housing were allowed on the eastern third, and housing only was allowed on the western two-thirds. The development team sought approval to combine the zoning for the entire site but was unable to do so, limiting retail use to a fraction of ground-level space potentially available to commercial development. A conditional use permit, site plan review, and setback variances were also required.

In partnership with Minneapolis-based DJR Architecture, the Lander Group sought to create a multifamily project consistent with new urbanist principles. Michael Lander, a member of the Congress for New Urbanism, is conscientious about blending new development into the urban context. West River Commons, as a gateway project, was designed to function as an iconic development, but also one to be thoughtfully integrated into the surrounding neighborhood.

The site was designed to be pedestrian friendly with public sidewalks that envelop the site, ample bicycle parking, and a bus shelter in the site's southwestern corner. The mixed-use apartment building, though a single entity, can be broken into three parts that reflect the different zoning requirements on the site. Retail is consolidated on the ground floor of the eastern part of the project and is oriented toward the Mississippi River and the Lake Street Bridge. Above the street-level retail are three floors of apartments. The middle third of the building contains three stories of apartments, and the western third contains three two-story 2,000-square-foot (186 m²) townhouses that are rotated to face 46th Avenue,

which intersects Lake Street. The project steps down gradually in height from four stories at its most visible frontage facing the Lake Street Bridge to the two-story townhouses, which respect the height of the single-family homes that are prevalent on the western edge of the site.

As an additional amenity, the project contains a 1,000-square-foot (93 m²) public plaza featuring sculpture by a local artist. This plaza is located in front of the retail component and is animated by the recreational users during the day, and by outdoor restaurant and coffee shop seating during both day and night. During summer evenings, the landscaped plaza functions as an outdoor waiting space with walls at an ideal height for seating and with ample room for children to play.

Creating different facades that relate to the three parts of the project helps to break up the scale of the monolithic building and relates better to the neighborhood context. A third-story setback diminishes the impact of the building height and is given a different exterior treatment to further break up the facade.

The impact of resident parking was minimized by locating the majority of parking spaces underground. Underground parking accounts for 74 stalls and is accessed through a discreet entry. Along with limited on-street parking, an additional 37 stalls are located behind the building for customers and visitors. Hiding the bulk of customer parking behind the building allows more space for landscaping and retail frontage.

With designs approved, the project broke ground in August 2002, and occupancy was scheduled for fall 2003. However, in June 2003, stormy weather caused the wood frame to catch fire as a result of electrical complications. The fire destroyed the unfinished frame of the building, delaying completion

until August 2004. Property insurance covered the cost of the damage, but the delay was costly.

The fire was not the only complication; the developers faced considerable neighborhood opposition in securing the necessary approvals. Though a formal neighborhood organization supported a mixed-use project of three to four stories, several immediate neighbors were adamant that only six single-family homes be built. Mediating between the formal and informal constituencies was a challenge.

Seeking to build support for the concept, the Lander Group held a total of 45 public meetings, mostly with neighbors in the immediate area. The developer also created a website for the project that was intended to generate public input (particularly from surrounding neighbors) on design and other development issues. This input influenced several aspects of the final plan, including the townhouses, architectural characteristics, and parking layout.

EXPERIENCE GAINED

West River Commons was a first in many ways for the development team. At Home Apartments had owned and managed numerous projects in the past but had no development experience. Combining over 50 rental units with retail space and for-sale housing on a contaminated site was a new challenge for the Lander Group, which previously had worked on smaller-scale developer projects.

Ultimately, the success of West River Commons stemmed from the precise mix of retail and residential in an underserved neighborhood. However, the amount of retail that was ultimately built was less than what the development team desired. Michael Lander believes the high-quality finishes helped distinguish his project, but he laments that the development team was unable to integrate a greater mix of retail into the ground floor of the project. The rigid, outdated zoning of the western part of the site forbade retail, which he felt was a missed opportunity. As a consolation, the ground floor was designed as convertible space if and when zoning should allow for a mixed-use opportunity.

Lander's other regret was with the architecture. He admits he "would have liked to have been more adventuresome with the design, not so timid and historicist." The low vacancy rates and demand for a more contemporary style of apartment indicate that Minneapolis and St. Paul are a market that desired more modern rental options.

Another important lesson learned was the importance of having the necessary insurance protections in place to cover the cost of the building and material. Unfortunately, soft costs were not insured, and they wound up being unavoidable additional costs.

In retrospect, the developer wished that the interaction with the neighborhood residents could have been conducted differently. Rather than holding an excessive number of public meetings, Lander believes that having someone to act as an advocate could have served them well. Finding a liaison to champion the project from within the community would have been ideal.

A significant unanticipated use was related to the project's connection to the river trail paths. Lander acknowledges that there are advantages and disadvantages to the recreation traffic that passes through the project. The public bathrooms that are shared by the ground-floor retail became a de facto rest stop for bikers and joggers. In retrospect, he would have separated the bathroom facilities and provided separate restroom accommodations for the retail and for public users. He acknowledges that this use drives up his

common area maintenance charges but believes it to be a worthwhile tradeoff for the number of users coming in from the park and for the visual effect of having people using the outdoor plaza. The project's location near several universities was an additional boon for the retail tenants. Soon after opening, the coffee shop extended its hours to accommodate the university students who keep a later schedule.

Even in a down economy, the project has continued to do quite well. Still close to full occupancy, Michael Lander points to the uniqueness of the property as the major contributor to its success. His firm plans to hold onto West River Commons as an income property, given both its high occupancy rates and the very low interest rates (2–3 percent) it was able to secure.

5

Office Development

SOFIA DERMISI

Overview

Office development is a critical component in the economic vitality of urban and suburban areas, with location and market conditions influencing the type of structure. Office users can vary widely in size, occupying spaces from 500 square feet (46.5 m²) to several million square feet.

This chapter focuses on office buildings most frequently built or retrofitted by beginning developers—costing under or around $10 million and ranging from 5,000 to 100,000 square feet (465–9,300 m²).

The increasing adoption of technology, sustainable practices, and the aftermath of the Great Recession along with its lasting effects create a new reality for all developers, especially those new in the field.

CATEGORIZING OFFICE DEVELOPMENT

Office developments are categorized by class, building type, use and ownership, and location.

CLASS. The most basic feature of office space is its quality or class. The relative quality of a building is determined by a number of considerations, including age, location, finish materials, amenities, and tenant profile (see figure 5-1). Office space is generally divided into three major classes:

1. **Class A**—New highly efficient properties in prime locations with first-rate amenities and services, as well as older significantly renovated or upgraded buildings with prestigious or landmark status. They achieve the highest possible rents and sales prices in the market. Certain office developers acknowledge an A+ class for LEED-certified properties achieving 10 to 15 percent energy efficiency versus comparable buildings.[1]
2. **Class B**—Older, somewhat deteriorated buildings in good locations with finishes, amenities, and services that are lower than Class A. Newer properties might also be designated as Class B if they offer lesser services and amenities. They achieve lower rents and sales prices compared with Class A properties.

3. **Class C**—Facilities with inferior mechanical and building systems, below-average maintenance, and very limited services compared with Class B. Rents and sales prices are the lowest in the market and are often in less attractive locations than Class A or B buildings.

BUILDING TYPE. Four major office building types are widely used for categorizing purposes:

1. **Typical Office**—Single structure located in downtowns or suburbs with office use being the main revenue stream; possibly a minor retail component;
2. **Mixed-Use Development (MXD)**—One or more structures combining at least two significant revenue streams (for example, retail, office, residential); suburban MXDs cover more than 100 acres (40 ha) with buildings of various heights;
3. **Garden Office**—Low-rise structures clustered together in office parks with extensive landscaped areas; and
4. **Flex Space**—One- or two-story buildings usually located in business parks that facilitate an office component combined with space for light industrial or warehouse use.

Comcast Center is a 58-story office and retail development in the heart of Philadelphia's downtown.

BUILDING HEIGHT. Buildings are categorized by height as follows:

- **High-Rise**—Typically higher than 12 stories;
- **Mid-Rise**—Four or five to 11 or 12 stories; and
- **Low-Rise**—One to three or four stories.

The Council of Tall Buildings and Urban Habitat suggests that better indicators of building height designation are (1) height relative to context (comparison with other structures in the area and local zoning codes), (2) proportion (slenderness of the building against low urban backgrounds), and (3) tall building technologies (for example, vertical transport technologies).

USE AND OWNERSHIP. Office buildings can also be classified by their users and owners. Buildings can be single- or multiple-occupant structures. A single-occupant building may be leased from a landlord or owned by the tenant. In the latter case, it is referred to as an *owner-occupied building*. A building designed and constructed for a particular tenant that occupies most or all of the space is called a *build-to-suit development*. A single- or multiple-occupant building designed and developed without a commitment from a tenant is considered a *speculative (spec) building*.

Medical office space is often a unique product, designed specifically for doctors' offices. It can be single-tenant or multiple-tenant space. It is often located in a campus setting near a hospital, or even on hospital grounds.

LOCATION. In most urban areas, at least four distinct types of office nodes can be found, distinguished by their location:

1. **Central Business District (CBD)**—High land costs in CBDs encourage more vertical development in the form of mid-rise and high-rise structures. Typical tenants in downtown offices include Fortune 500 companies, law firms, insurance companies, financial institutions, government, and other services that require high-quality prestigious space.[2]
2. **Suburban Locations**—Since the latter part of the 20th century, a decentralization trend has led to greater diversity in office locations outside the city center. Suburban nodes of large and small office buildings are often found in business districts, in clusters near freeway intersections, or in major suburban shopping centers. Rents are traditionally lower than the CBD and tenants include regional headquarters, high-tech and engineering firms, smaller companies, and service organizations that do not require a location in the CBD.
3. **Neighborhood Offices**—Small office buildings are frequently located away from the major nodes, where they serve the needs of local residents by providing space for service and professional businesses. Neighborhood offices can be integral parts of neighborhood shopping centers or freestanding buildings.
4. **Business Parks**—Business parks include several buildings accommodating a range of uses from light industrial to office. These developments vary from several acres to several hundred acres. Flex-space office buildings, with capabilities for laboratory space and limited warehouse space, are typically located in business parks.

In recent years, some developers and tenants have focused on dense urban transit-oriented locations rather than greenfield sites. Suburban areas are increasingly undesirable for certain companies and developers due to suburban sprawl, the resulting traffic, and the lack of public transportation. Substantial rent increases in suburban areas over the last 25 years have further increased the desirability of urban infill locations. However, companies interested in lower-cost space and labor, as well as build-to-suit facilities, will continue to find suburban locations attractive.[3]

TRENDS IN OFFICE BUILDING DEVELOPMENT

The office market is a highly cyclical business that is subject to boom and bust periods. The playing field for office development comprises many elements, and unforeseen changes in basic forces can influence office markets in unexpected ways.

MARKET TRENDS. In the 1980s, significant increases in liquidity combined with investor and developer optimism on demand and rents led to significant overbuilding, causing substantial vacancies—around 20 percent—in the early 1990s. It took ten years of economic expansion with relatively little new office construction to decrease the national vacancy rate to around 10 percent—when 5 percent is considered the "normal" rate. Development started increasing when the 2001 recession (caused by the dot.com bubble and attacks of September 11, 2001) triggered employee layoffs and corporate cost cutting, leading to higher vacancies and lower rents. The short recession of 2001 was followed by the Great Recession, creating a financially frozen market (lack of debt and equity). Although the Great Recession ended in 2009 its effects remain into 2012, with vacancies hovering around 13 percent while development continues to face challenges. The lack of corporate reinvestment, anemic job growth, tight capital, and lack of credit market liquidity marginalize development. Regardless of project type, location, or leasing activity, construction loans remain difficult to obtain. In 2007–2008, the preleasing requirement for office buildings was 40 to 50 percent; by the summer of 2010, it increased to 75 percent, with an equity requirement of 20 to 30 percent and substantial guarantees.[4]

RECENT FINANCIAL TRENDS, CREDIT FREEZE, WORKOUTS. Several factors caused the credit freeze in commercial lending from 2008 through 2010:

- significant exposure of lenders to residential defaults/capital losses;
- a major shift of commercial bank asset portfolios to real estate (37 percent in 2007 compared with 25 percent before 2000);
- poor due diligence and underwriting standards (investors and capital providers overrelied on quality ratings by rating agencies, such as Moody's, rather than in-depth due diligence, leading to significant suppression of cap rates from 2000 to 2006;

- a widespread lack of transparency in financial dealings and instruments; and
- a mismatch of duration between borrowing short and lending or investing long.

Two additional factors affected commercial property liquidity of suppliers, beyond bankers:

- perception of risk after the bust of the housing bubble and the possibility of a commercial bubble due to the continuing price increases; and
- international accounting standards (promoted by the Securities and Exchange Commission) requiring property owners/investors to identify the fair or true market values of their assets when computing their balance sheets.[5]

As a result of the Great Recession, a number of under-construction office projects required workouts. The approach used in each workout is different due to the parties involved, type of lender, problem, and reputation of the developer. Some insights are provided regarding some causes of project challenges during and after the Great Recession:

- Development participants were not conservative enough; they became increasingly greedy, in part due to market liquidity.

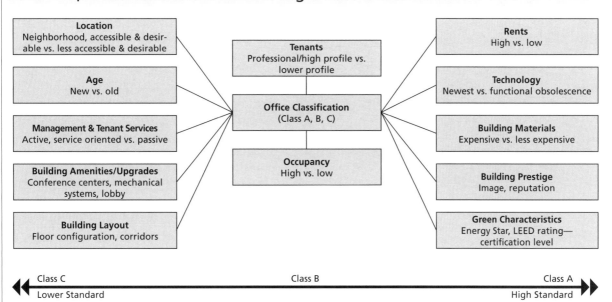

FIGURE 5-1 | Characteristics Determining Office Classification

Sources: R.B. Peiser and A.B. Frej, *Professional Real Estate Development: The ULI Guide to the Business*, 2nd ed. (Washington, D.C.: ULI–the Urban Land Institute, 2003); Sofia Dermisi; and *Office Building Management* (Chicago: Institute of Real Estate Management, 2002).

- Developers were significantly overleveraged, assuming they would refinance with improved terms or sell the asset for profit when the loan was due.
- Developers underestimated budget expenses, which were not finalized before construction.
- Developers' capital structure was problematic with significant debt, minimal equity, and not enough preleasing.
- Permits were not secured and/or were delayed by local municipalities, adding to costs.[6]

INFLUENCE OF TECHNOLOGY. Technology is the driving force behind increased efficiency and long-term cost savings. Technologies such as Building Information Modeling (BIM) can be applied in the design and construction process, as well as used in the building automation system (BAS). The BAS allows building managers and owners to monitor and create efficiencies in major building systems, such as heat exchangers, automatic dimmers, and OLEDs (organic light-emitting diodes), creating "smart" buildings with single rather than multiple network systems communicating through Internet protocol.

A developer's budget, market conditions, and the type of tenant pursued will determine the most balanced approach regarding the applied technology innovations and the rent premium tenants will be willing to pay. Developers should also review the various incentives offered by local, state, and federal governments. An excellent source on renewable energy and energy-efficiency incentives is the Database of State Incentives for Renewable Energy (www. dsireusa.org/). DSIRE was established in 1995 by the U.S. Department of Energy.

GREEN DEVELOPMENT. The two most popular green property designations are Energy Star,[7] launched by a joint effort of the U.S. Environmental Protection Agency and the Department of Energy in 1992, and LEED,[8] launched by the U.S. Green Building Council in 1998. LEED is designed around a point system, as shown in figure 5-2. The most recent LEED guidelines (Version 3.0) were released in 2009, with four relevant ratings for office buildings:

- **LEED-NC** (New Construction);
- **LEED-CI** (Commercial Interiors);
- **LEED-CS** (Core & Shell); and
- **LEED-EBOM** (Existing Buildings Operations & Maintenance).

Some developers consider Energy Star more meaningful than LEED because it emphasizes energy efficiency with a greater impact on the operating budget. LEED certification, however, can be accomplished with little or no financial premium if the building has modern systems and a curtain wall. Some driving forces behind LEED construction include a higher likelihood of obtaining bank financing with lower interest rates for construction and permanent loans; pension fund investment interest; and increasing preference among Fortune 500 and other companies with green mission statements.[9]

Developers and managers of both new and existing sustainable properties face certain financial challenges. From an operating budget standpoint, the upfront capital required for LEED certification might take more than three years to recapture, which can exceed the developer's holding period. Further, the cost savings cannot be easily determined yet because of (1) the small number of LEED buildings with historical information, (2) a lack of documentation on the cost savings received separately by the tenants and the building, (3) minimal documentation on changes in employee satisfaction and health patterns, and (4) the disparity between who pays for most of the LEED certification and who reaps the benefits, with tenant participation in the cost still lagging.[10] However, new and revised building codes are increasing the energy-efficiency requirements, thereby reducing the cost premiums to achieve LEED certification.

Research on the effect of sustainability on real estate is expanding. Eichholtz, Kok, and Quigley's[11] study of a group of green and nongreen comparable properties identifies a premium of 3 percent in rents and 16 percent in prices for the green properties. Fuerst and McAllister,[12] as well as Miller, Spivey, and Florance,[13] also found premiums among the green versus the nongreen group of properties. A study by Dermisi[14] of the spatial distribution patterns of LEED ratings and certification levels across the United States suggests aggregations in certain areas with certification levels affecting the total assessed values of office properties.

SUBURBAN VERSUS URBAN. The dispersed and low-density nature of most suburban offices causes transportation challenges. Despite certain large companies (such as Apple and Cisco) continuing to locate in sprawling suburban areas, developers are also noticing that companies targeting a young, highly compensated and/or specialized workforce are more likely to be located downtown or close to a transit line. Beginning developers should consider opportunities in urban infill developments that are ripe for redevelopment, assuming they are financially feasible and the complex permitting and approval processes and codes are understood.

CORPORATE CAMPUSES. A countertrend to the move back to the city has been the move of major corporations into corporate campuses. During the 1990s, for example, Sears vacated its namesake tower in Chicago and relocated to a suburban campus. In Kansas City, Sprint has created a new 240-acre (97 ha) headquarters campus in the suburb of Overland Park. USAToday's headquarters moved from a high-rise tower close to downtown Washington, D.C., to a campus in suburban Virginia.

Some technology companies are embracing green corporate campuses, such as Google's headquarters in Mountain View, California. Google's facilities are built with sustainable materials and are designed to maximize fresh air ventilation and daylight penetration. All rooftops are covered with solar panels, while biodiesel shuttle service is available to all employees from the Bay Area. Points for charitable donations are provided to those who use other green transportation means, such as biking or walking. The campus also has plug-in vehicles and multiple bikes for intercampus movement.[15]

Project Feasibility

MARKET ANALYSIS

The first task for developers is to conduct a market analysis, a critical assessment tool for any successful project, to determine whether a market exists for additional office space. It also provides direction for site selection and design by indicating the type of space and amenities that office users are looking for. The market analysis also provides critical input for the financial analysis, which will ultimately be used to demonstrate the feasibility of the project and to provide investors and lenders with the information they need to fund the project (see figure 5-3).

Market analysis requires a combination of data sources and usually the assistance of a market research firm, although the developer should be sufficiently familiar with the market to make an initial determination of whether the project is likely to be feasible. Brokerage firms can be a source of major tenant information, leasing activity, and overall market trends. These firms also know what the current trends

in the market are and what segments of the market have the largest unmet demand.

The market analysis is a study of demand and supply, which ultimately determine vacancy rates, rents, cap rates, and property values. It should survey the economic base of the local metropolitan area, including existing employers and industries and their potential for growth. It should also identify whether the market contains headquarters, regional, or branch offices. The type of tenant to be targeted will affect the design with respect to office depths, parking, amenities, and level of finish.

Developers should keep in mind that companies seek new space for several primary reasons:

- to accommodate additional employees or a new subsidiary;
- to expand an existing business;
- to improve the quality of their office environment;
- to consolidate dispersed activities into a single space; and
- to improve their corporate image (thereby improving both sales and customer contacts and enhancing employees' morale).

FIGURE 5-2 | Office-Related LEED Ratings and Certification Levels for Office Buildings

	LEED-NC (Max Points)	LEED-CI (Max Points)	LEED-CS (Max Points)	LEED-EBOM (Max Points)
Sustainable sites	26	21	28	26
Water efficiency	10	11	10	14
Energy and atmosphere	35	37	37	35
Materials and resources	14	14	13	10
Indoor environmental quality	15	17	12	15
Innovation and design process	6	6	6	6
Regional priority credits	4	4	4	4
Total possible points	**110**	**110**	**110**	**110**

TYPE OF CERTIFICATION	POINTS
Certified	40–49
Silver	50–59
Gold	60–79
Platinum	80–110

Sources: U.S. Green Building Council; and Sofia Dermisi.

DEMAND. The first step in any market study is to define the area of competition in the submarkets and in the region. For regional employment, a step-down approach can be used to allocate employment growth from the region to the local market. Office buildings compete most closely with other buildings in the immediate vicinity. Rents, amenities, parking, and services can vary considerably among submarkets, though regional conditions affect all submarkets. It is therefore important to understand how a particular development will address its competitive environment. The analysis of the metropolitan economic base involves studying existing employers and industries in the market and their growth potential, with particular focus on the sectors of the economy that generate demand for office space.

Projected employment growth is the key driver of office space demand. It includes new and expanding firms in the area, broken down by industry, ultimately yielding office-based employment growth projections for the local economy. Local employment projections are available from commercial brokerage companies as well as local governments and chambers of commerce. When an area's projected office employment is available, the following equation can be used to estimate the total square footage demanded:

Projected office space demand =
Number of projected office employees
× Gross space per employee

If area employment projections are not available, the following formula can be applied to determine the annual demand in square feet (see figure 5-4):

Office employment demand of industry$_i$ =
Change in employment of industry$_i$ in the last two years
× Office share of industry$_i$

Annual office demand in square feet for industry$_i$ =
Office employment demand of industry$_i$
× Area's gross space per employee

where i represents a specific industry
that drives office demand.

FIGURE 5-3 | Market Analysis Data and Sources

Data Input	Source
Space trends	
Existing, under construction: planned square footage, occupancy, vacancy, absorption, rents, tenant information (square feet leased, lease length, etc.)	CoStar Group; Loopnet; and reports from Studley, CBRE, Jones Lang LaSalle, Grubb & Ellis, etc.
Competitive development	CoStar Group; FW Dodge; local building, planning, and zoning departments; architects, and brokers/developers
Financial feasibility	
Land costs	Key person interviews, recent transactions
Construction costs	Dodge construction reports by McGraw-Hill
Operating expenses	Property managers and reports: Institute of Real Estate Management or Building Owners & Managers Association International *Experience Exchange Report*
Easy to do business with	
Zoning and ease of local permitting	City/county planning department, state environmental protection agency
Attractive tax position	
Area tax structure and incentives	City, county, and state departments of revenue, assessor, and economic development; media
Nontax incentives	
Various types of new construction or adaptive reuse incentives	City, county, and state departments of economic development; business retention, etc.
Workforce demographics	
Public	U.S. Census, Bureau of Labor Statistics/Bureau of Economic Analysis; local and regional economic development and planning agencies
Private	CoStar Group, Economy.com, FreeLunch.com
Transportation infrastructure	
Road, transit, access	Local transportation agencies

Sources: Jon DeVries and Sofia Dermisi.

The annual office demand in past years is then used to project future trends of more than ten years.

Two good resources for the amount of space required per employee are Building Owners and Managers Association (BOMA) International's *Experience Exchange Report* and the Institute of Real Estate Management's (IREM's) *Income/Expense Analysis: Office Buildings Report*.

The demand for space is also affected by market rents and tenants overleasing when space is readily available and rents are relatively low. Over time, office space per employee has tended to decline.

Users' space requirements inevitably affect the design and type of facility, including average floor area, number of entrances, and the location of hallways and elevator cores. The bay depth—the distance between the glass line and the building core—is particularly important. Large users frequently desire large bay depths, but small users require smaller bay depths to increase the proportion of window offices. Space requirements are influenced by a potential tenant's mix; 200 to 250 square feet (18.5–23 m²) per employee is now considered the norm due to the elimination of file cabinets and improved space efficiency, but space requirements per employee can vary greatly. Office cubicles can range from 6 by 6 feet (1.8 by 1.8 m) to 8 by 8 feet (2.4 by 2.4 m), while the physical office room space in most offices is 10 by 12 feet (3 by 3.6 m) or 10 by 15 feet (3 by 4.5 m). Although spaces are tight, they can become tighter if workers lack individual privacy, with more conference and phone rooms.[16]

Other critical components of the demand analysis include the determination of the annual net absorption, the obsolete space, and the net rentable square footage demanded per year. Net absorption represents the net change in the amount of occupied space in the market. Obsolete space could be replaced by new Class A space. All Class C space older than 50 years

will likely be replaced within the next 20 years at a rate of 5 percent per year.

SUPPLY. After establishing market demand, the analysis should focus on the competitive supply within the market. The supply information gathered provides the basis for estimating rents, concessions, design features, desired amenities, and finishes. The key elements of the supply analysis are an inventory of existing competitive buildings within the market area and projects under construction and in planning stages. An inventory of competitive buildings should include the following information:

- location;
- gross and net building area;
- scheduled rent per square foot per month;
- lease terms;
- tenant finish allowances;
- building services;
- amount of parking provided and parking charges (if applicable);
- building and surrounding area amenities (restaurants, conference facilities, health clubs, and so forth); and
- list of tenants and contact people.

This information provides the basis for estimating rents, concessions, design features, and desired amenities. The market area for supply should take into account regional and metropolitan supply. The submarket definition—areas that include the primary competitors for the subject project—is especially important. All competitive buildings in this area should be carefully documented.

The analyst should determine total existing supply plus the future supply of office space. By subtracting the expected supply from the expected demand for office space, the deficit or surplus of office space for a particular period can be determined. This knowledge

FIGURE 5-4 | Use of the Annual Office Space Demand Formula by Industry

	Change in Employment from 2009–2010	Office Share (%)	Office Employment	Square Footage/ Employee	Annual Office Demand (ft²)
Construction	−5,000	5	−250	250	−62,000
FIRE (finance, insurance, and real estate)	2,000	80	1600	250	400,000
Services	5,000	10	500	250	125,000
Government	3,000	5	150	250	37,500
Total		**100**			**500,500**

Source: Jon DeVries.

allows the developer to estimate the market conditions that will prevail when the proposed building comes online. Vacancy levels are an important part of the supply calculation and vacancy trends can indicate changes in demand. If demand is increasing faster than supply, vacancy rates should be falling, creating a more favorable market for the developer. Alternatively, if supply is increasing faster than demand, vacancy rates should be increasing. The vacancy rate resulting from turnover, sometimes referred to as the *natural* or *stabilized* vacancy, is inevitable.

The absorption time, in months, of all the vacant space can be calculated as

$$(\text{vacant space})_t = (\text{vacant space})_{t-1}$$
$$+ (\text{net construction})_t - (\text{net absorption})_t$$

$$AT = \frac{(\text{vacant space} + \text{new construction})}{\text{net absorption}/12}$$

where *t* represents the quarter or year the estimates takes place and *t*-1 the previous period.[17]

For an application of the AT equation, assume that the area of interest has 600,000 square feet (55,700 m²) under construction, with a vacancy of 1.5 million square feet (139,000 m²) and a net absorption of 1 million square feet (93,000 m²), and will require a 25-month absorption period. The AT equation assumes that the rate of new demand growth continues as indicated by the net absorption rate and that there is no new construction in the market other than what has already been started. No firm guidelines exist for determining what constitutes a soft market, although a market with fewer than 12 months of inventory is considered a strong market, 12 to 24 months a normal market, and more than 24 months (18 months in slower-growing areas) a soft market.

A common mistake is to assume that a proposed project will capture an unrealistically large share of the entire market. Developers should have sufficient cash available to cover situations in which leasing takes longer than expected, which can be influenced by such factors as timing of the project delivery, amenities, rent levels, and especially market conditions.

SUBLEASED SPACE. It is important to recognize subleased space in assessing supply because, although technically leased, it is often available, formally or informally, and is thus part of the market competition.

In the late 1990s, some firms engaged in defensive leasing to ensure their future ability to expand in prime locations. But when their growth plans did not materialize, they were forced to sublet the space.[18] In markets where vacancy rates are low, if unanticipated subleased space and new product come online simultaneously vacancy rates can soar. Recent economic downturns have led to the availability of large blocks of subleased space.

SHADOW SPACE. Vicky Noonan of Tishman Speyer defines shadow space as "a leased space for which a tenant pays rent but it is vacant or not fully occupied and it is not yet available for sublease."[19] It is a potential threat to a building's rental stability and market recovery during a down cycle because an increase indicates tenant contraction, which can eventually increase vacancy if the trend continues. The presence of shadow space is inefficient for a landlord because it cannot be considered stable income and the space could be offered on the market with a better return. Unfortunately, none of the published data sources track shadow space, and developers can only assess it by talking to area property managers. A rule of thumb in estimating the extent of the shadow space in suburban properties is to look at the building's parking lot. If a building occupancy rate is more than 90 percent, but there are consistently plenty of available parking spots, it is an indication of possible shadow space.

EFFECTIVE RENTAL RATES. An important distinction in office market analysis is the difference between quoted (*face*) rents and *effective* rents. Property owners sometimes use incentives to maintain the appearance of certain rent levels while effectively reducing rent for certain times or tenants. Typically, lenders determine a specific rent and preleasing threshold as a condition of funding or for releasing of the developers' personal guarantee on the construction loan. To meet these conditions in a soft market, developers may offer tenants concessions in the form of free rent for a specified period, an extra allowance for tenant improvements (TIs), or moving expenses, as long as the rent meets the lender's requirements. The extent of the TIs is always market driven, with tenants pressuring landlords for more during periods of increased construction costs. Today, TIs are on average $5 to $6 per square foot ($54–$65/m²) per year of lease-term for Class A (for a ten-year deal, it is $50 to $60 per square foot [$540–$650/m²]) properties, while TIs for downtown new Class A buildings are $70 per square foot ($753/m²) and for Class B properties $30 to $50 per square foot ($323–$538/m²) for a seven-year lease. TIs for suburban office buildings are about $20 per square foot ($215/m²).[20]

Rental concessions are harder for market analysts to identify than asking rents because brokers tend to understate concessions due to the negative influence on their commission. Factors influencing the number and amount of concessions include tenant size, lease term, and tenant rating. Concessions remain common practice across markets, especially during economic down cycles, and lenders generally use effective rents in their analyses before funding a loan. In strong markets, building owners do not offer free rent, except perhaps during an initial period when tenant improvements are being completed.

The Studley Effective Rent Index provides in-depth analysis of major real estate markets for Class A office properties, including effective rental rates, concessions, and a breakdown of rent components (net rent, operating expenses, real estate taxes, and electricity).

Scheduled rental rate increases change the effective rent. For example, a lease with flat rent for ten years has a lower effective rate than a lease with annual 2 percent increases. A lease with annual 2 percent increases is likely to have a lower effective rate than a lease with annual increases tied to the consumer price index, because the CPI historically has increased more than 2 percent per year.

GENERAL ADVICE ON OFFICE MARKET RE-SEARCH. When conducting office market research, developers should keep the following trends in mind:

- Tenants will continue to downsize and consolidate their office space in an effort to minimize their costs and improve their efficiency while reducing redundancy.
- Buildings with flexible floor plates are becoming increasingly attractive to tenants.
- Green, energy-saving, and energy-producing buildings are increasingly important for perspective tenants.

Allan Kotin of Kotin & Associates and the University of Southern California offers additional comments:

- The larger the tenant, the more difficult it is to determine what the tenant is actually paying in rent after taking into account rent concessions, such as free rent, expense caps, free parking, and extra tenant improvements.
- A problem with assessing the effect of larger tenants is their susceptibility to consolidations or changes in business plans from swings in the economy. Such actions can result in their putting large amounts of space on the sublease market.
- Major markets are stratified by scale as well as by quality, rent, and location. A 10 percent vacancy rate may be very misleading if the largest space available is only 20,000 square feet (1,860 m²). The market for 50,000-square-foot (4,650 m²) tenants is very different from that for 100,000-square-foot (9,300 m²) tenants.
- For major buildings, control of a single large tenant is far more important than generic measures of space.
- Despite the sophistication of market analysis, the fact remains that many small and medium firms decide where to rent space on such distinctly unscientific grounds as "where the boss lives."[21]

SITE SELECTION

Site selection is a crucial step in the project feasibility analysis because it directly affects the rent and occupancy levels. Developers should compare location, access, physical attributes, zoning, development potential, and rents and occupancy of comparable buildings and sites to identify potential opportunities and obstacles.

Calculation of Effective Office Rent

Suppose a developer has an office space of 1,000 square feet (93 m²) with a nominal rent of $24 per square foot ($258/m²) for five years. Concessions include six months of free rent and $3 per square foot ($32/m²) in extra tenant improvements. The developer's discount rate is 12 percent. To find the effective rent, the developer must convert the lease and the free rent to present value, which can be computed per square foot.

Present value (*PV*) of lease per square foot: *PV* ($2/month, 1%/month interest, 60 months	$89.91
Less:	
Present value of free rent per square foot: *PV* ($2/month, 1%/month interest, 60 months)	$11.59
Extra tenant improvements (already stated as present value)	$3.00
Present value of effective rent	$75.32
Convert present value to equivalent monthly rent: *PMT* ($75.32 *PV*, 1%/month interest, 60 months)	$1.67
×12 months	
Effective annual rent per square foot	$20.04

In general, office use can support the highest rents of any land use type and thus is often located on the highest-priced land. This factor should not deter developers because a high price is usually indicative of site desirability. Similarly, developers choosing sites based on a lower price can find themselves unable to compete in the market, even at lower rents.

The site should be able to accommodate an efficient building design. Office buildings are less flexible in size and shape than are most other development types. Floor plates (area per floor) are a key factor in a building's suitability for a tenant. Those deviating significantly from 25,000 square feet (2,322 m²) require more than one building core due to the travel distance required of individuals. A second core substantially increases building costs because it requires additional stairwells, restrooms, and elevators).[22] Developers should make sure that a larger structure will be in demand in the area. Small office users prefer buildings with floor sizes ranging from 16,000 to 20,000 square feet (1,500–1,860 m²), although smaller floor plates are not uncommon. The most efficient buildings are 100 feet wide and 200 feet long (30 by 60 m). Such a shape allows a core of about 20 by 100 feet (6 by 30 m) and a typical depth of around 40 feet (12 m) between the core and the exterior wall. Such plain rectangular boxes might be the most cost-effective, but prospective tenants may respond negatively depending on their type of business. For example, major law firms seek buildings that make a statement with their exterior facade and interior amenities, while call centers do not.

When land values are high, the cost of parking structures is often warranted, and parking structures are less flexible than buildings in their layout. Structured parking modules with efficient layouts should be designed in bays that are 60 to 65 feet (18–20 m) wide, with a minimum of two bays; therefore, a parking structure needs to be at least 180 feet (16.5 m) long to efficiently accommodate internal ramps.[23]

Topography can play an important role in site selection. Hilly sites may require extensive grading, which will increase construction costs, but they may also provide excellent opportunities for tuck-under parking that requires less excavation than a flat site.

Access is a primary consideration in site selection. Sites should have convenient access to the regional transportation system. Public transit options are important in urban locations. Developers should check the site's highway and transit access with transportation authorities before proceeding, as well as the need for a traffic study.

Jim Goodell of Goodell Associates recommends that office buildings be located in areas with a sense of place. "A synergy exists between office buildings and activities such as restaurants, shopping, entertainment, hotels, and residential uses. A mixed-use environment generates benefits that translate into higher rents and better leasing."[24]

REGULATORY ISSUES

Historically, office developers were concerned only with local zoning and building codes. Floor/area ratios (FARs), height limitations, building setbacks, and parking requirements were the primary determinants of how much space could be built on a particular site.

Today, communities often have wide discretion in reviewing projects not only for compliance with zoning but also for environmental and community impacts that are difficult to quantify. In some cases, specific impacts, such as increased traffic at a particular intersection, can be addressed by constructing off-site improvements, such as traffic signals or turn lanes. Others, such as increased regional congestion or lack of affordable housing, may be mitigated through the payment of impact fees.

Office developments generally have a positive fiscal effect by generating more in tax revenues than they require in public services. Shrinking local tax revenues from other sources have led many cities to look toward office development as a way to fund public projects and affordable housing, which has backfired in some cases, particularly when the economy weakens. For a time, San Francisco experienced an exodus of businesses from the city's core when it instituted a combination of very high impact fees, exactions, and housing linkage programs.

Certain cities are in such distinctive and attractive locations that they can exact above-average concessions from developers, but even these cities have suffered a slowdown of new business development when the cost of their exactions made development unprofitable. Developers pass on the regulatory costs to future tenants in the form of rent or operating expenses and depending on the market conditions, tenants might seek space elsewhere.

Government bodies continuously revise local building codes covering building safety and public health, spurred in some cases by litigation or the threat of litigation. Many government agencies have also enacted stringent energy codes. This trend toward stricter building codes will likely continue.

ZONING AND LAND USE CONTROLS. In addition to the typical zoning restrictions on building setbacks, height, and site coverage, the regulations specifically affecting office development include FARs, building massing, solar shadows, and parking requirements. FAR is obtained by dividing the gross floor area of a building by the total site area. Some cities—Los Angeles, for example—have dramatically reduced allowable FARs, giving cities unusual leverage in negotiating with developers for facilities or services the city wants.

Some cities, including New York and Chicago, award FAR bonuses to developers that embrace sustainable development practices or provide public amenities in high-density commercial districts. For example, the FAR of One South Dearborn in Chicago, completed in 2005, increased from 16 to 21.27. The combination of a park in front of the building, the ground-floor retail, and the setback, which reveals the north elevation of the Inland Steel Building—a Chicago landmark—allowed for the additional credit.[25]

Most zoning ordinances include provisions that carefully define allowable building envelopes and shapes to stop buildings from casting permanent shadows, to prevent streets from becoming canyons, and to prevent the glass on buildings from reflecting excessive heat onto other structures. In addition, some government agencies regulate the types of materials, styles of architecture, locations of entries, and various other design aspects of office projects. Developers must recognize and work within these restrictions to determine the maximum envelope that their buildings can occupy.

One special regulatory device that has been used with urban office development is transferable development rights (TDRs). Although not widely adopted, TDRs allow for the sale of development rights on a property from one owner to another. If one owner wants to retain a two-story building on a site zoned for ten stories, that owner may sell the right to build the additional square footage to another landowner. Once sold, however, the original owner cannot build any more square footage than that for which zoning rights were retained. A number of obstacles exist in establishing a TDR (for example, allocating higher-density development, calibrating values for development rights, and creating a program that is simple to understand and administer but also fair). TDRs work well with historic landmark buildings because

they might not take the fullest advantage of a site's development potential. In addition, designation of older buildings as historic landmarks can complicate and even prevent major changes to their structure and exterior facade.

Parking requirements vary by location and building type, but they typically stipulate a minimum of three to four spaces per 1,000 square feet (95 m²) of rentable floor area. Developers often find that they must provide more spaces than required in order to secure financing. Communities wishing to encourage use of mass transit may however restrict the amount of parking. Some cities have also proposed mandatory off-site parking for some portion of the parking requirement for buildings in congested downtown areas. One concept that can satisfy local government's desire to limit parking while providing the ability to meet tenants' future needs is *deferred parking*. Deferred parking is shown on the approved development plan but need not be built until demand for parking is proved.

Local communities have also become increasingly concerned about the aesthetics of office developments. Although developers and their architects do not always appreciate the opinions of regulators, local planning staffs and officials are not shy about expressing their preferences about building massing and shape, exterior materials, and finishes.

JAS Worldwide International Headquarters is a renovation of three vacant, obsolete buildings in Atlanta. The amount of green space was increased through removal of unnecessary parking.

MIDCITY REAL ESTATE PARTNERS

TRANSPORTATION. A development's traffic impact is a politically sensitive issue with congestion increasing beyond the central cities into the suburbs.

An increasing number of office developments are now required to provide a traffic impact study during the approval process due to the increased traffic loads in peak hours. Traffic mitigation measures can range from widening the streets in front of a building to adding a traffic signal or widening streets and intersections surrounding a site. Satisfying off-site infrastructure requirements can be extremely costly and time-consuming, not least because of the need to work with public agencies and other property owners.

An office developer may be required to undertake any of the following actions:

- restripe existing streets;
- add deceleration and acceleration lanes to a project; construct a median to control access;
- install signals at entrances to a project or at intersections affected by the project;
- widen streets in front of a project or between a project and major highways or freeways;
- build a new street between a project and a major highway; or
- contribute to construction of highway or freeway interchanges.

Instead of requiring certain improvements through exactions, some areas have created impact fee programs (assessed per peak trip generated or a fee per square foot) to cover traffic improvements. The number of expected peak trips generated by the project becomes a critical factor in the cost of the project because fees can be as high as several thousand dollars per peak trip generated. Peak traffic trips can be reduced by (1) adding a minor retail component to a project (a major retail component can possibly increase the traffic impact), (2) providing residential facilities on or adjacent to the site, and (3) providing links with public transportation systems.

Transportation demand management (TDM) programs (or *transportation system management*) have become a popular mechanism for reducing traffic. A number of cities require large projects to implement ride-sharing programs, such as car- or vanpools; to include reduced-price passes for public transit; and to provide preferential parking spaces for individuals who carpool. The developer is often responsible for ensuring the implementation of TDM programs because they are often a condition of approval. Commuting by bicycle or foot is another strategy some cities encourage while properties receive LEED points. In Boulder, Colorado, for instance, bicycle storage and showers for employees are a requirement for any office development, and good connections to the city's network of bike trails are important for approval and marketing.

FINANCIAL FEASIBILITY

The financial feasibility process involves gathering market data from the market study, cost data for various alternatives, and financing costs and entering these data into the financial pro forma. Developers should also consult local mortgage brokers and lenders to determine current appraisal and underwriting criteria before considering a project.

Two useful sources for estimating local operating costs for office buildings are the *Experience Exchange Report* published by BOMA International and the *Income/Expense Analysis for Office Buildings* published by IREM. Both reports are published annually with a detailed breakdown of operating costs and revenues for different types and sizes of office buildings across the United States. The Studley Effective Rent Index report is another source of aggregate operating cost information for Class A office properties in selected downtown and suburban areas.

The key to accurately estimating revenues for office projects is to make *realistic* projections regarding lease-up time, vacancy rates, and achievable rents. Developers can apply the SFFS (simple financial feasibility analysis) methodology outlined by Geltner and colleagues[26] as an assessment tool for their go/no-go decision. *Financing for Real Estate Development*[27] is also a good reference on financial feasibility.

Capitalization rates (cap rate = net operating income/property value) are very important in underwriting because a project's debt capacity is a function of its value. Cap rates reflect variable market conditions over time, with low levels indicating a strong market versus high levels that indicate weak markets.

Developers should always be prepared for possible cap rate increases during construction and until stabilized occupancy is achieved for two reasons: (1) If the cap rates increase, the value of the property decreases and the lender can request the value difference from the developer, which can be substantial depending on the equity structure. If the developer cannot infuse equity or negotiate a deal, the lender can foreclose (worst case scenario). (2) Refinancing an asset in a period of increasing cap rates is difficult because of the additional equity infusion required by lenders.

DESIGN AND CONSTRUCTION

The key to any successful design is to address the area market and building codes and offer an efficient building at an appropriate price. Among the major design decisions are the shape of the building, design modules, bay depths, type of exterior, and lobby design, all of which create an image and identity for the structure.

Office buildings also need to be adaptable and flexible to meet the shifting demands of tenants for periods spanning more than 50 years. Flexibility is especially important as tenants expand or contract. Tenants are very sensitive to the amount of common areas (for example, lobbies) in a building because they are typically charged for their prorated share of common space in addition to their *usable space*.

The market analysis should help provide the design parameters for the project, although some design elements, such as the placement of corridors, restrooms, stairwells, and fire walls, are usually dictated by local building and fire codes.

As a general rule, total project costs are broken down into the following percentages:

Building shell and interior	45%
Environmental and service systems	25%
Land and site improvements	18%
Fees, interest, and contingencies	12%
Total	100%

A few comments can be made on the preceding project cost breakdown:

- The percentages differ depending on the project location (downtown versus suburbs), regional requirements, construction methods, and special fees required by local government bodies.
- There is pressure to improve environmental and service systems across the country while decreasing fees and contingencies.
- A rule of thumb is that in urban areas, the site improvements usually do not exceed 10 to 15 percent of total cost.[28]
- In high-rent districts, land is likely to represent a larger portion of the costs, as much of the increased rent can be attributed to the property's locational advantages.
- In addition to the project costs above, developers usually expect a profit of between 20 and 25 percent. A profit of around 12 percent for developers will only cover operating costs without any overhead profit.

SHAPE. A square is the most cost-efficient building shape because it provides the most interior space for each foot of perimeter wall. But it often generates the lowest average revenue per square foot because tenants pay for floor area and windows. Rectangular and elongated shapes tend to offer higher rents per square foot but cost more to build because they provide more perimeter window space and shallower bays. Developers prefer rectangular buildings for multitenant speculative space because the interior and perimeter spaces can be more balanced.

Although nonrectangular shapes may be less efficient, they often create more interesting office shapes, more corner offices, and higher rents. Beyond the developer's and architect's vision, building shape is influenced by market conditions, environment, land uses, and zoning. In Asia, for example, there is a requirement that buildings avoid casting shadows, which leads to unique shapes and orientations.[29]

DESIGN MODULES AND BAY DEPTHS. Office buildings are designed using multiple modules, which allow for the repetition of structural and exterior skin materials. Although the design module is most visible on the exterior of the building, it should evolve from the types of interior spaces planned. The market study should suggest the types of interior design (for example, open-plan or executive offices) that are in the greatest demand in the target market.

The most common design module is the structural bay. Defined by the placement of the building's structural columns, the structural bay is generally subdivided into modules of four or five feet (1.2 or 1.5 m) with the most common module being 4.5 to 5 feet (1.3–1.5 m), which provide a grid for coordinating interior partitions and window panels for the exterior curtain wall.[30] In Europe and Asia, 3 feet 11 inches (1.2 m) and 5 feet (1.5 m) are the most common.[31] The structural bay determines the spacing of windows, which in turn determine the possible locations of office partitions, ascertaining whether interior space can be easily partitioned into offices of eight, nine, ten, 12, or 15 feet (2.4, 2.7, 3, 3.6, or 4.6 m) (see figure 5-5).

Office width tends to respond to local market conditions, with the market analysis providing some guidelines. Typically, offices are 10 to 14 feet (3–4.3 m) deep, and hallways are five to six feet (1.5–1.8 m) wide. For example, private office space in Chicago is 10–15 feet (3–4.6 m) wide, whereas in Atlanta it is only 8–12 (2.4–3.6 m).[32]

The bay depth is typically 40 to 45 feet (12–13.7 m).[33] Multitenant buildings with many small tenants require smaller bay depths—36 feet (11 m)—to permit a larger number of window offices. Institutional users, on the other hand, prefer 40- to 50-foot (12–15 m) bay depths, which are more efficient to build and tend to cost less. One alternative is an asymmetrical design, with the core offset to allow flexibility in marketing and layout. The bay might be 40 feet (12 m) deep on one side of the core and 50 to 60 feet (15–18 m) on the other.

Institutional users are more likely to prefer open-space plans, while design and media firms prefer exposed mechanical systems, open ceilings, and partition-free floor-to-ceiling spaces. Large bay depths offer an advantage in such a layout while providing greater flexibility in laying out workstations, whereas a few, if any, private offices require prime perimeter locations.

Developers should keep in mind that at least 12 percent of the floor plate will be occupied by mechanical equipment. And depending on the type of tenant and zoning allowances, the floor plate may increase to 20 percent.[34]

CEILING HEIGHTS. Floor-to-floor heights are typically between 11 and 14 feet (3.6–4.2 m). In areas where the height of the building is not constrained by zoning or other codes, Class A properties' floor-to-floor heights may be 14.5 feet (4.4 m). In Asia, the most common heights are between 13 and 13.6 feet (3.9–4.1 m), while smaller concrete buildings—especially in Europe—are 12.4 feet (3.7 m).[35]

SITE PLANNING

A building's curb appeal is significantly influenced by its location on its site. Generally, a building should enjoy maximum exposure to major streets, and signage should be visible from those streets. Good site planning provides a logical progression from the street to the parking to the building's entrance. The trip from the car to the entrance of the building gives visitors and prospective tenants their first impression of the building.

PARKING. In theory, an office building in which each employee occupies an average of 250 square feet (23 m²) needs four parking spaces per 1,000 square feet (95 m²), assuming that all employees drive separate cars. The typical area required for each car is 300 square feet (27.8 m²) for surface parking (which includes parking space and driveway) and up to 400 square feet (37 m²) for structured parking to include allowances for ramps.[36] When workers carpool or take public transportation, the parking requirement is reduced. Specialty space, such as medical offices, generates more visitors and may increase the need for parking.

Lenders prefer at least four parking spaces per 1,000 square feet (95 m²) of rentable space, even though local zoning may require less. According to John Thomas of Ware Malcomb Architects, many developers reduce the parking ratio as a project becomes

---

FIGURE 5-5 | Relationship of Module to Interior Office Size

Module Size	Interior Office Width
3-foot	9, 12, and 15 feet
4-foot	8, 12, and 16 feet
5-foot	10 and 15 feet
5½-foot	11 and 16½ feet

Examples of Structural Bay Modules

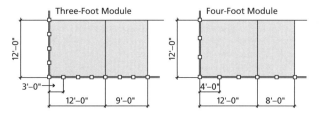

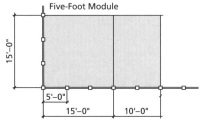

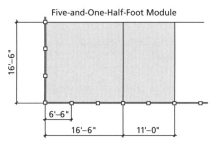

Note: Multiples of the module size determine where interior walls are joined to the exterior window wall system.

larger.[37] For example, developers commonly provide four parking spaces per 1,000 square feet for the first 250,000 square feet (23,235 m²) but then provide only two parking spaces for each additional 1,000 square feet (95/m²). Experienced developers, however, cite inadequate parking as one of the most common flaws in attracting and holding tenants.

For Gabe Reisner of WMA Engineers, the cost differential between below- and above-grade parking is not always substantial because parts of the below-grade structure can include mechanical systems, which will free a portion of leasable aboveground space. The cost of below-grade parking depends on the number of below-grade levels, water table elevation, and foundations for adjacent structures. According to Mike Sullivan of Cannon Design, the first level of a below-grade parking structure costs on average $30,000 per parking spot, but the cost doubles for each level below that.[38]

Some developers have presold their garage structures, raising a significant portion of the construction cost, while the cost to the tenants is a function of the market.

LANDSCAPING. Landscaping is critical to a project's overall appearance and value. Landscape design can tie diverse buildings together, define spaces, and form walls, canopies, and floors. Concealing, revealing, modulating, directing, containing, and completing are all architectural uses for plants. Landscaping elements not only include vegetation—trees, shrubbery, ground covers, and seasonal color—but also rocks, streams, retaining walls, trellises, and paving materials. Landscaping may be used to control soil erosion, mitigate sound, remove air pollutants, control glare and reflection, and serve as a wind barrier.

Landscape costs must be assessed with the landscape architect during design. A reasonable landscape budget accounts for 1 to 2.5 percent of total project costs, although the cost might be much less in urban areas.

Preserving existing trees can improve a project's image, assist with marketing efforts, and increase the project's long-term value. Mature trees can easily be destroyed, however, if precautions are not taken during construction.

EXTERIOR DESIGN

Exterior design concerns such aspects as exterior building materials, signs, and lighting. A building's exterior design can be an invaluable marketing tool.

BUILDING MATERIALS. The building materials used are generally part of two distinct systems: the structural system and the skin system. The structural system supports the building, and the skin protects the interior space from the weather. An office building can be built using one of six structural systems:

- **Metal Stud Frame**—Generally used for one- to five-story buildings;
- **Concrete Tilt-Up**—Generally used on one- to three-story buildings and typically employed in flex buildings;
- **Steel Frame with Precast Concrete** (hollow-core planks)—Typically used for low-rise buildings;
- **Reinforced Concrete**—Used for both low- and high-rise buildings;
- **Steel**—Used for both low- and high-rise buildings; and
- **Composite Structures** (steel gravity framing with concrete core)—Used in high-rises and superstructures.[39]

The exterior of an office building can be covered with any number of materials:

- **Exterior Insulation Finish System**—Synthetic stucco formed in many shapes;
- **Precast Concrete**—Usually cast off site and shipped to the site and usually not part of the structural system;
- **Tilt-Up Concrete Panels**—Cast on site and used as part of the structural system, limited to three stories (most common in the suburbs, although panels have very limited utility in office buildings due to glazing limitations);
- **Glass Curtain Wall System**—A combination of vision and spandrel glass hung in front of the building frame (always used on Class A properties);
- **Storefront System** (two-story height limit);
- **Metal Panels**—Aluminum or steel finished in a factory;
- **Stone**—Granite, marble, or slate in large panels or small tiles; and
- **Residential Materials**—Including stucco and brick, used as exterior cladding materials and not as a wall system.[40]

Each structural system can be combined with another to produce economical hybrids, such as a masonry building with metal trusses or prestressed concrete floor units. Concrete tilt-up construction offers an advantage in that the concrete panels serve as both the structural system and the skin (see figure 5-6). Exterior materials can also be combined; for example, a tilt-up building might incorporate a storefront system or precast elements for architectural variety.

SIGNAGE. Signs identify a building and its tenants while creating an overall impression for visitors. Although tenants will negotiate for sign privileges, developers should retain sign approval as a condition in their tenants' leases. Restrictions should stipulate the size, shape, color, height, materials, content, number, and location of all signs.

The developer's architect should work with graphic and interior designers to create a signage program for individual tenants and for interior and exterior common areas. The best approach is to develop a comprehensive signage program that includes designs, materials, and color schemes for the following purposes:

- project identification at the entry to the development;
- building identification;
- directory of major occupants;
- directional signs for vehicular and pedestrian traffic;
- building location directories; and
- interior building service signs.

Some developers hire a single sign maker to coordinate the signs for an entire project allowing for expedited replacements and changes. The system for doorplates should allow for easy replacement of old signs when tenants change. Coordinating the installation of signs is the responsibility of the on-site building manager.

EXTERIOR LIGHTING. Exterior lighting can enhance the security of building entrances and parking lots and can highlight architectural and landscaping features. Inadequately illuminated areas may pose a liability problem. The developer should work with an electrical engineer and architect to design exterior lighting that will accomplish the desired effects while being energy efficient and easy to maintain. Mercury- or sodium-vapor, quartz, LED (light-emitting diode), and fluorescent lights are energy efficient and may be used in exterior lighting fixtures. Many jurisdictions have become concerned about light pollution, and they require the use of high-cutoff lights and limit the use of architectural illumination that lights the sky.

Lighting standards for parking lots should be placed around the perimeter of the lot or on the centerline of double rows of car stalls. The Illumination Engineering Society recommends a minimum illumination level of 0.5 to two foot-candles for outdoor parking areas and five foot-candles for structured parking.

INTERIOR DESIGN

The interior design must accommodate all the various systems—elevators; plumbing; heating, ventilation, and air conditioning (HVAC); lighting; wiring; and life safety—and provide a flexible core and shell, which are very important in attracting tenants. The use of modular systems (flexible walls or partitions) is increasing because of their flexibility to meet tenants' changing needs.

Another boon to flexibility is the use of raised floors, which are typically four to six inches (100–150 mm) above the concrete slab,[41] allowing data cabling, mechanical systems, and power to be configured easily. Even though they have an upfront cost, the operating cost savings over time, human comfort, and sustainability can outweigh the cost.

MEASURING SPACE. Multiple local and national measurement standards of office buildings exist (gross, rentable, and usable square feet), with BOMA International standards being widely used. There are three key measurements:

- **Gross area** is measured from the exterior walls of the building without any exclusion (basements, mechanical equipment floors, and penthouses).
- **Rentable area** is measured from the inside finish of the permanent outer walls of a building except vertical penetrations (elevators, stairs, equipment, shafts, and atriums). According to local definitions, it may also include elevator lobbies, toilet areas, and janitorial and equipment rooms.
- **Usable area** is measured from the inside finish of the outer walls to the inside finished surface of the office side of the public corridor. Usable area for full-floor tenants is measured to the building core and includes corridor space. An individual tenant's usable area is measured to the center of partitions separating the tenant's office from adjoining offices. Usable area excludes public hallways, elevator lobbies, and toilet facilities that open onto public hallways.

The tenant's rentable area is derived by multiplying the usable area by the rentable/usable ratio (R/U ratio). The R/U ratio is the percentage of space that is not usable plus a pro rata share of the common area. For example, if a tenant rents 1,000 square feet of usable space in a building with a 1.15 R/U ratio, the tenant pays rent for 1,150 square feet:

Usable square feet × R/U = Rentable square feet

1,000 usable square feet × 1.15 = 1,150 rentable square feet

Tenants are very sensitive to the R/U ratio, often referred to as the building *efficiency ratio*, *core factor*, or *load factor*. The average R/U ratio for high-rise space is about 1.15. Low-rise space averages around 1.12. Developers with inefficient buildings (with R/U ratios greater than 1.2) sometimes arbitrarily reduce the ratio to make their buildings appear competitive. Developers should be careful to calculate pro forma project rental income on the actual rentable area and not on the gross building area, which is more appropriately used to estimate construction costs.

FIGURE 5-6 | Exterior Skin Materials

Material	Cost/Ft² of Building Area	Characteristics/Comments	Aesthetics	Long-Term Maintenance	Energy Efficiency
Plaster (decorative lime plaster)	$30–$50	Used on highly articulated surfaces. Can create optical illusions. Limited installers.	Excellent	Good	Fair
EIFS (exterior insulation and finish systems)	$20	Used to add architectural details at minimal cost. Fails under certain conditions; water penetration has led to lawsuits.	Very good	Very poor	Good
Flexrock	$16	More textured than stucco; looks more like concrete.	Good, depending on installation	Good, depending on installation	Fair
GFRC (glass fiber-reinforced concrete)	$36–$38	Best for mid-/high-rise office buildings. Can be used to achieve substantial design articulation with integral color.	Very good	Excellent	Good
Thin-shell GFRC	$28		Good		
Precast concrete panels	$35–$40	Heavier than GFRC but can achieve same detail.	Very good	Excellent	Good
Concrete tilt-up walls	$20	Combines structure and skin—no studs in perimeter wall. Usually limited to three stories. Paint, leave natural, or sandblast.	Very good, depending on design	Excellent	Good
Metal panels (Alucobond)	$25–$35	Used for high-tech, precise look. Can be finished in wide range of standard or custom finishes.	Excellent	Good (may corrode)	Poor if installed without foam backing
Plaster system (basic)	$17–$20	Most economical surface system. Quality depends on installer.	Fair, depending on design	Fair—surface cracking will appear; needs maintenance	Fair
Masonry (decorative)	Masonry backup = $15/ft² + brick veneer = $25 = $40/ft² for complete system	Combines structure and skin. Substantial variety to achieve various looks. Height limitations.	Very good, depending on design	Excellent	Good
Storefront (basic)	$50–$60	Used for retail stores and low-rise office buildings where large glass areas are not present.	Fair (very utilitarian)	Excellent	Depends on glass: high-performance glass excellent; tinted or clear glass poor
Glass curtain wall	$65–$80	Used for large expanses of glass in combination with various mullion systems and glass colors. Interesting geometry can be achieved.	Good to excellent, depending on design of glass mullion geometry	Excellent	Depends on glass: high-performance glass excellent; tinted or clear glass poor
Stone veneer (granite and marble)	$60–$90	Used to give building a sense of elegance and permanence. Minimum long-term maintenance.	Excellent	Excellent	Fair, depending on thickness

Sources: Initial table provided by John Thomas, Ware Malcomb Architects. Updated by Scott Peterson, Turner Construction.

SPACE PLANNING. Effective space planning involves five basic components: the space itself, the users, their activities, future uses, and energy efficiency.

The amount of space and its functionality are controlled by a building's exterior walls, floors, ceiling heights, column spacing and size, and the building core.

In a single-tenant building or a floor tenant, the tenant is responsible for improving the lobby and interior hallways. In a multitenant building, however, the developer improves the lobby, restrooms, and hallways that serve each suite, and individual tenants are responsible for their own suites.

Many modern office layouts use the open-space planning approach, which helps reduce the cost of initial construction and design changes. Partitions in open-space plans are movable, and a variety of furniture and wall systems are available that are attractive and use space efficiently.

An inviting lobby with an identity is critical in attracting perspective tenants even if it comes with a premium for the developer. Restrooms likewise can help recover high-quality decoration costs because both tenants and visitors use them.

ELEVATORS. Tenants' and visitors' initial impressions are shaped by a building's lobby and the quality of the interior finish of elevator cabs. Finish materials used in the lobby—such as carpet, granite, marble, brass, and steel—can also be used effectively inside the elevator.

Elevator capacity depends on the kinds of tenants occupying the building. Buildings occupied by larger companies tend to need high-capacity elevators to accommodate peak-hour demand. Buildings with smaller companies tend to have lower peak-period demand because more tenants keep irregular hours; but professional tenants are more conscious of time lost waiting for elevators. Waiting time for elevators should average no more than 20 to 30 seconds; longer waits can affect a tenant's lease renewal decision.

The following rules of thumb are useful for gauging elevator capacity:

- One elevator is needed per 40,000 square feet (3,700 m²).
- One elevator is needed for every 200 to 250 building occupants (for two- to three-story buildings the demand will be lower).[42]
- Buildings with two floors require one or two elevators, depending on the nature of the local market and the size of the floors.

- Buildings with three to five floors require two elevators.
- Ten-story buildings need four elevators.
- Twenty-story buildings need two banks of four elevators.
- Thirty-story buildings need two banks of eight elevators.
- Forty-story buildings need 20 elevators in three banks.

Many elevator control innovations are being used in high rises, such as kiosks where riders indicate the floor of preference and the system directs them to the faster elevator (grouping riders to various floors), significantly increasing the speed and capacity of the system.

Some very large office buildings—especially in downtowns of major cities—feature escalators in their main lobbies.

LIGHTING. Lighting plays a critical role in how users and visitors perceive the building. The 2007 adoption of the Energy Independence and Security Act meant the phasing out of incandescent bulbs between 2012 and 2014. Owners of existing buildings or developers retrofitting a property can benefit from the energy-efficient commercial buildings tax deduction, which can also be used to write off the indoor lighting retrofit cost.

Several types of artificial light are available for interior applications:

- **Fluorescent**—Fluorescent fixtures are expensive but have the advantage of long bulb life (18,000 to 20,000 hours) and reduced energy consumption. Under the 2007 energy legislation, T12 lamps will be replaced by more efficient T8 or T5 lamps.
- **Light-Emitting Diode**—LED fixtures are becoming increasingly common. LED bulbs have a long life (25,000 to 100,000 hours) and vastly reduced energy consumption.
- **Incandescent**—Incandescent fixtures are less costly than fluorescent fixtures but are more expensive to operate. They provide superior color rendering but a short bulb life (750 to 2,000 hours). They are scheduled to be phased out beginning in 2012.
- **High-Intensity Discharge**—High-intensity discharge lighting includes mercury-vapor (frequently used outdoors), metal-halide, and high- and low-pressure sodium lamps. Although they are excellent for illuminating outdoor spaces and are very energy efficient, high-intensity discharge lights offer poor color-rendering properties.

- **High-Intensity Quartz**—Sometimes called *precise lighting*, high-intensity quartz lighting is a new product that is often used in upscale environments. Multifaceted, mirrored backs reflect the light onto specific objects or areas, making high-intensity quartz fixtures appropriate for task-oriented lighting.

Office buildings use mainly direct lighting. Installed in a grid pattern across a dropped ceiling, this solution offers equal levels of illumination across large spaces. Direct lighting is available in integrated ceiling packages, including lighting, sprinklers, sound masking, and air distribution. Indirect lighting uses walls, ceilings, and room furnishings to reflect light from other surfaces. In recent years, indirect lighting has become common for general office lighting as a way to reduce glare on computer monitors. Indirect lighting generally requires higher ceilings to reduce "hot spots" on ceilings and to improve the overall efficiency of the lighting layout.

The electrical engineer, interior designer, and architect all play important roles in designing the lighting system to suit each tenant's needs.

HEATING, VENTILATION, AND AIR CONDITIONING. A building's HVAC system is one of the major line items in its construction and operation budget. Several different types of HVAC systems are available:

- **Package Forced-Air Systems**—These electrical heat pumps, usually located on the roof, heat and cool the air in the package unit, then deliver it through ducts to the appropriate areas of the building. The units are inexpensive to install and work well on one- and two-story buildings.
- **Variable Air Volume Systems**—A large unit on the roof cools the air and delivers it through large supply ducts to individual floors. Mixing units control the distribution of the air in each zone. This system offers great flexibility as many mixing units can be installed to create zones as small as an office, but it is more expensive to install than forced-air systems. The system allows for balance loads and automatically adjusts airflow. Rooms are heated by a heating element in the mixing units or by radiant heater panels in the ceiling.
- **Hot- and Cold-Water Systems**—A combination chiller and water heater is centrally located to provide hot and cold water to the various mixing units in the building. The air is heated or cooled in these mixing units and delivered to the local areas.

RBC Centre is a 43-story office tower in Toronto's financial district. The development earned LEED Gold status and will produce an estimated 50 percent energy savings relative to the Canadian National Energy Code.

TOM ARBAN

The architect and mechanical engineer will provide guidance in the selection of the HVAC system. For a development of about 100,000 square feet (9,300 m²)—four to five stories of 25,000 square feet (2,300 m²) of floor plate—the most economical system is a rooftop variable air volume system, but in some markets heat-up systems are more common. LEED can be achieved with either. The capacity of the system will be determined by several factors, including climate, building design, and types of tenants.

The American Society of Heating, Refrigerating and Air-Conditioning Engineers (ASHRAE) publishes standards on the minimum ventilation rate for different occupancy and building types, relative humidity, and maximum allowable air velocity. Poor humidity control and leaks in a building can cause sick building syndrome, which exposes building owners to possible lawsuits. ASHRAE's *Humidity Control Design Guide for Commercial and Institutional Buildings*[43] provides guidance on humidity control to the entire building team. The final authority on building ventilation is the local code authority, which may or may not have adopted ASHRAE standards. Standards for air movement and air conditioning depend on building design, climate, glazing, lighting, and building orientation.

Computer-controlled systems manage energy use of medium-sized or large buildings. A well-designed HVAC system divides the building into zones, each controlled by a thermostat. These zones should cover areas with similar characteristics, such as orientation to the sun, types of uses, and intensity of uses. A standard rule of thumb is one thermostat zone per 1,200 square feet (110 m²). Usually, each zone has one mixing damper that controls temperature by mixing hot and cold air.

TECHNOLOGY. Technology is changing the economics of office buildings in a variety of ways:

- **Design**—Building Integrated Modeling/Revit (BIM/Revit) is in the forefront of virtual coordination by facilitating complex design among mechanical, electrical, and plumbing systems. BIM allows the construction phasing to be better coordinated while providing a comprehensive data record for the operations management phase.
- **Energy Sustainability**—Buildings are consuming less energy with the help of low-E glass, external shading, automatic dimmers, and motion sensors. Some buildings are even producing energy with smart grid system and solar panels.

- **Water Conservation and Reuse**—Water system controls are becoming more sophisticated. Automatic faucets, low-flow toilets, rainwater harvesting, waterless urinals, and use of graywater for flushing toilets, landscape watering, and other nonpotable uses are increasingly part of the conservation effort.
- **"Smart" Buildings**—All building systems are integrated into one network, which allows the efficient control of life safety and security, building management, elevators, office telecommunication, and HVAC systems on site or remotely.
- **New Revenue Sources**—Every part of the office building is being examined for the potential to generate revenue. For example, income can be generated from communications towers mounted on roofs, from signage in highly visible locations, and from recycling waste materials, such as office paper.
- **Maintenance Costs**—Mechanical rooms are kept cleaner, with filters changed more often and air monitored. Recycling chutes in high-rise buildings eliminate the need for recycling bins on every floor.

ENERGY EFFICIENCY. A building's energy efficiency depends on its site orientation, skin materials, window design, and types of mechanical equipment and energy control systems. Energy costs can decrease by investing up front in continuous building envelopes that do not provide thermal bridges. The energy efficiency of the exterior facade can be improved with active and passive shading systems and other thermal technologies, while harvesting rainwater and daylight. For example, a rain-screen wall is a pressure-equalized system with minimum operational maintenance cost, although there is an upfront cost.[44]

A popular way to measure energy efficiency is the *U-value*, which measure the rate of heat loss expressed in Btus per hour per square foot per degree difference between the interior and exterior temperatures. The U-value is the reciprocal of the total resistance of construction multiplied by a temperature or solar factor. As a general rule, U-values should be a minimum of 0.09 for insulated exterior walls and 0.05 for insulated roofs. The architect and mechanical engineer can provide recommendations for insulation.

Glass reflection plays an important role in determining energy use and is measured as the *shading coefficient*, which equals the amount of solar energy passing through glass divided by the total amount of solar rays hitting the glass. The lower the coefficient, the larger the amount of heat reflected away from the building's interior. Lower shading coefficients tend to be more expensive to obtain and adversely affect the quality of light for building occupants. Many state and local government agencies have their own energy-efficiency requirements.

Numerous energy-related incentives are offered by government and nongovernment organizations. Two relatively new initiatives are the application of demand response mechanisms on buildings, which help manage energy use based on electricity grid supply conditions, and smart grid systems, which allow for two-way communication between consumers and utility companies. For Mike Munson of Metropolitan Energy, the smart grid system is simply a tool to transfer information.[45] Smart grid systems enable building owners and managers/engineers to make better decisions about their building's energy use. Munson notes that for new construction, the ability to optimize a building's operational flexibility and to maximize the control of building systems with precision enables greater certainty and increases asset value by building control capabilities from the ground up. For existing buildings, the ability to acquire, process, and implement solutions using information provides for more discerning capital and efficiency improvement analyses.

GREEN BUILDING DESIGN. Green buildings can be defined in a variety of ways, but the U.S. Green Building Council's LEED rating system has become the accepted standard. Green buildings accomplish reduced energy consumption by improving natural light penetration, using more efficient HVAC systems, and relying on more sustainable building materials.

Certain LEED points can be achieved inexpensively (for example, bicycle racks, showers, and transit subsidies), but long-term savings require the use of additional base building systems controls, such as heat exchangers, displacement air systems, double-wall systems, active shading systems, and so forth, which have an upfront premium. By adopting multilayered energy systems, the building can circulate air more effectively based on different situations and can synchronize electric lighting with daylight using lighting controls.

In cases where structures need to be demolished or rehabbed, disposing of the old materials in an environmentally friendly way can be difficult and costly. According to Tom McCaslin and John Wong of Tishman Construction Corporation, which built Four Times Square, New York City's first green office tower, green buildings generally cost more to construct, although the initial cost can be recovered later through energy savings. A green building can also generate good publicity and promote the firm as environmentally friendly with some tenants willing to pay rental premiums.[46] Four Time Square used several energy conservation features, including photovoltaic panels, fuel cells, gas-fired absorption units, and low-noise air handlers.[47]

SECURITY AND LIFE SAFETY. Life safety and security have become increasingly important in the design and marketing of an office building. The terrorist attacks of September 11, 2001, in the United States led to changes in access control and communications of major downtown office buildings. Protecting the building, its occupants, and its contents requires multiple security layers. A building has seven rings of defense:

- site perimeter;
- building standoff;
- building exterior;
- inner perimeter;
- building systems;
- screening and access control zones; and
- safe interior areas for valuable assets or personnel safe havens.[48]

The ability to control access in and out of a building is essential and can be accomplished by several methods, depending on such factors as the building's location and setting, potential threats, tenant requirements, and so forth. During construction, developers need to consider the following:

- perimeter security measures;
- lobby security controls, including electronic monitors and security guards;
- access control card readers on parking and lobby entrances and elevators;
- an intercom system to a 24-hour remote operator;
- surveillance cameras in parking lots and in all egress and ingress points; and
- a lobby entrance for parking users, which might require installation of separate elevators.[49]

Life safety features include sprinkler systems, smoke detectors, fire hoses and extinguishers, and automatic shutoffs for the HVAC and public address systems. Developers should check with local authorities on fire codes because they differ by jurisdiction. Developers should keep in mind that adoption of various life safety systems (mandated or not by area building codes) can lower fire insurance rates.

TENANT LEASEHOLD IMPROVEMENTS

As part of the lease, the developer usually provides a set allowance for tenant improvements that covers the buildout of the interior space. The allowance provides a minimum level of improvements, with the tenant financing the remaining space renovation. Because leases typically do not require the tenant to pay rent during the improvement phase, it is incumbent on the developer to ensure that work is done on schedule. Typically, TIs are $5 to $6 per square foot ($54–$65/m²) per year of term for downtown Class A space (for a ten-year deal that would total $50 to $60 per square foot [$540–$650/m²]), but it can reach $70 per square foot ($753/m²).[50]

TENANT IMPROVEMENT PROCESS. Steps in the process of completing tenant improvements in a small office building parallel the steps involved in constructing the building itself: budgeting; preliminary planning, including design and construction drawings; approvals and permits; contractor selection and bidding; and construction.

- **Step 1: Establish a Budget**—The budget is determined by the quality the tenant wants and the resources available.
- **Step 2: Prepare a Space Plan and Design for the Improvements**—The space planner/interior designer may be under contract to the developer or to the tenant. If the designer is under contract to the developer, the developer maintains greater control but will be liable for all costs if the tenant backs out of the lease. The design firm is usually selected in one of two ways: (1) the developer selects a design firm and then recommends it to all tenants, or (2) the developer approves three or four firms and then allows tenants to select from the approved list.
- **Step 3: Have Plans Approved**—Plans are submitted to the local building department for approval and permits. Whenever improvements involve safety or require electrical work or partitions, building permits are required.
- **Step 4: Select a Contractor**—Generally, the developer selects a single contractor to do all the tenant improvements in the building, but some developers prefer to approve three or four contractors and then submit the drawings to each for bids. The developer usually works with the contractor to see that the bids are within the tenant's budget.

- **Step 5: Oversee Construction**—The developer maintains close contact with the contractor during construction to ensure on-time and budget delivery. The developer should carefully monitor any claims for change orders so that the project remains within the tenant's budget. All the parties will agree on the payment format before the construction begins.

WORK LETTERS. Work letters serve as the formal agreements between the developer and the tenant concerning the amount and quality of improvements that the landlord will provide. They specify the work the landlord will do before the lease commencement date, as well as the schedule of costs.

Building standard installation (the *building standard*) includes the list of items installed in every tenant suite: partitions; doors and hardware; size and pattern of acoustical ceiling tiles; floor coverings; size, shape, and location of lighting fixtures; electrical receptacles; switches; telephone and data outlets; plumbing connections; HVAC; painting and wall coverings; and window coverings or venetian blinds. If the tenant wants items above the building standard, the work letter also specifies them, their cost, and method of payment.

A standard tenant improvement work letter is created for improvements throughout the building. This document lays out the minimum improvements that will be constructed in every tenant space.

The lease usually provides a set allowance for tenant improvements. Corus Quay, Toronto, Canada.

ELIZABETH GYDE

LEVEL OF TENANT IMPROVEMENTS. The quality of tenant improvements and the improvement allowances have a definite bearing on the success of marketing the building. Typical items specified in a tenant improvement work letter include the following:

- size and type of ceiling tiles used;
- number of linear feet (meters) of wall and doors for every 100 square feet (10 m²) of rentable space;
- type of wall coverings and color of standard paint;
- quality and type of floor covering;
- number of HVAC registers, mixing units, and thermostats per 100 square feet (10 m²) of rentable space;
- specifications for the telephone system, including the installation of conduit and boxes and the provision of equipment rooms (this item is negotiable, and many businesses have their own systems and installers); and
- type and extent of computer wiring and of alarm and security systems.

Developers should avoid stating the tenant improvement allowance in dollars; instead, they should establish the basic quality and style of improvements for every space. Compatible colors and materials will make individual tenant spaces easier to re-lease when tenants move out.

The following are some common upgrades in tenant spaces:

- kitchen bar consisting of a microwave, small refrigerator, and sink;
- full kitchen and lunchroom with a sink, disposal, microwave, refrigerator, and dishwasher;
- executive bar in office with a refrigerator and sink;
- executive bathroom containing a sink, vanity, toilet, and sometimes a shower;
- climate-controlled computer room;
- fireproof safes or fireproof file rooms; and
- built-in fixtures, such as shelves, cabinets, worktables, bookshelves, counters, and other cabinetry.

PITFALLS AND SUGGESTIONS

The architect and interior designer may want to carry exterior and lobby finishes into each tenant's suite or create a series of coordinating colors that will harmonize with the materials used in the lobby and common areas yet allow each tenant to choose a particular color for its own suite.

The spacing of columns and window mullions can lead to many problems in the design of interior spacing. Columns in the middle of a window or in the center of an office can cause challenges during buildout and leasing. When a wall must be built between mullions, one alternative is to end the wall 6 to 12 inches (15–30.5 cm) from the window. The wall is turned parallel to the window until it can be fastened to the mullion in a perpendicular joint. This solution produces oddly shaped spaces, but it does provide a soundproof seal between offices. A flexible scheme for spacing window mullions and columns is essential for meeting the particular needs of each tenant.

Availability of plumbing is also important to the flexibility of the design. Any suite larger than 3,000 square feet (280 m²) should have plumbing available for installation of a sink.

When existing spaces are remodeled, building parts, such as light fixtures, ceiling tiles, metal studs, and air-conditioning components, can be reused, thereby reducing expenses.

Financing

Office development requires significant capital. For beginning developers, the financing process is difficult because of their lack of a track record. Typically, beginning developers solicit wealthy individuals as coinvestors; after a sufficiently large portion of the total equity has been accumulated, a local bank is approached for a construction loan. At the same time, the developer would secure long-term permanent financing that would be funded after the building is completed and fully leased.

For developers with some experience, the local equity investment partnerships are overshadowed by commercial mortgage–backed securities (CMBSs), national and global real estate investment trusts (REITs), pension funds, foreign investors, municipal bonds, and property trust companies. The most common form of securitized commercial real estate debt is CMBSs put together by banks, mortgage companies, insurance companies, and investment banks.

The Great Recession continues its negative effect on capital from a debt and equity perspective. In the last ten years, the financial equation used by developers on new office construction was about 65 percent construction loan, 20 percent mezzanine, and 15 percent equity.[51] Currently, mezzanine loans are not readily available and developers might receive construction loans of between 50 and 60 percent, leaving them with 40 percent leverage, which requires 20 to 25 percent return to the equity investor, therefore significantly limiting the return for developers.[52] Some mezzanine financing might be available as part of a

In Ballantyne Corporate Park in Charlotte, North Carolina, the Boyle and Harris Buildings are twin ten-story office buildings that achieved LEED Gold certification.

package covering the cost (for example, similar to an equity investor's structure or straight subordinated loan on the project) if the developer and preleasing are strong.[53] The lack of financial conduits and the limited interest among equity investors leave a financing void that banks are not inclined to fill without significant risk-limiting guarantees. Therefore, office development is expected to be mainly need based for a number of years, with lenders and equity partners allowing very little speculation while requiring strong security.

The Great Recession caused a number of changes in lender practices:

- higher equity requirements—the equity required for the acquisitions is 30 to 45 percent, possibly increasing to a 50 percent L/V ratio due to credit or other risk;

- recourse—the importance of guarantees, depending on the strength of the guarantor and leasing the project can have less than 100 percent recourse;
- stricter loan covenants;
- constraint of future tenant improvements and commission funding; importance of tenant credit even for landlords (landlords focus on a tenant's operation in their building and evaluate the possibility of dismantling if a tenant has multiple branches); as well as who guarantees the lease;
- significant preleasing (from 40 to 50 percent in 2008 to 75 percent or more depending on the developer, recourse, and equity in the building); and
- developer's overall profile (banks are now looking at both the proposal for new construction and the financial health of the other projects the developer is involved in).[54]

CONSTRUCTION LOANS

Office construction lenders are concerned with leasing, and they typically require from inexperienced developers that 40 to 50 percent of space be preleased in normal markets, 50 to 70 percent in soft markets, and more than 70 percent, along with personal guarantees, in the aftermath of the Great Recession. The due diligence performed for construction loans is detailed, and lenders require concrete proof of rent expectation. The equity requirement can increase from 25 to 50 percent, or greater, depending on such factors as preleasing and a developer's experience.[55]

The terms of construction loans range from six months to four years with higher interest rates than permanent loans due to the higher risk. Construction loan rates are based on LIBOR for major lenders, while smaller community banks offer rates based on the prime rate. The final construction rate depends on market conditions and the bank's assessment of the credit risk posed by the project and developer. Upfront loan fees (*points*) are common on most construction loans. Most construction loan agreements call for interest to accrue through the construction period. When construction is complete and the building is leased up, the developer obtains a permanent loan or sells the project and pays off the total loan amount, which includes the accrued interest and the principal balance. Major problems that may be encountered by developers include

- the failure to leave enough cushion for cost overruns and slower-than-expected leasing;
- a lack of understanding of the covenants in the loan documents that may allow the lender to increase reserve requirements and adjust the terms accordingly; and
- an exit strategy; will there be buyers for the asset if the developer does not want to hold it after construction?

Some pitfalls can occur between the construction and permanent loans:

- **Debt Coverage Ratio (DCR)**—Typically, the construction loan has a three- to four-year initial term and a one- to two-year renewal option.
- **Valuation**—Valuation is very difficult in the aftermath of the Great Recession, with increasing cap rates, limited sale comps, and lenders expecting some equity infusion to renew the loan.
- **Recourse**—Now, every loan has recourse of 30 to100 percent.[56]

PERMANENT LOANS

The permanent mortgage is funded once the building reaches a negotiated level of occupancy—usually, about 70 to 80 percent, a level sufficient to cover debt service on the mortgage. When the loan commitment provides for funding the mortgage before the building is fully leased, usually the developer must post a letter of credit for the difference between the amount that the leases will carry and the full loan amount. Alternatively, the permanent lender may fund the mortgage in stages as the building is leased. Lenders will focus on the effective rather than the market rent, using the lower of the two to underwrite the permanent loan, and they may deduct amounts from the cash flow to cover capital costs and leasing reserves (in case of tenant defaults).

Some office buildings constructed before the Great Recession, during periods of low cap rates, are facing financial challenges with both the loan covenants and the L/V ratio because the exit assumptions are not materializing. For example, even up to 2008, L/V ratios were 65 to 70 percent, with value decreases of at least 25 to 30 percent due to cap rate increases. A shortfall is created for developers and their lenders can request that they cover the difference. If developers cannot infuse equity or a deal is not reached with the lenders, there is expectation of dispositions driven either by banks or by landlords who are trying to reduce the erosion in their equity. A strategy developers can employ to mitigate this problem is to try to coach the appraiser.[57]

LEASE REQUIREMENTS. Developers must execute leases that satisfy the construction and permanent lenders' requirements with experienced attorneys while avoiding standard lease forms. Proper building maintenance and tenant services are essential to protect the interests of lenders. Lenders require assignable leases allowing them to take assignment of the rents in the event of default. They prefer clauses that require tenants to pay rent even if the building is destroyed from a natural or other disaster. Sophisticated tenants, however, will not agree to such clauses, even though insurance is available to cover rent when calamities occur. In the event of a calamity, lenders want to receive condemnation and insurance awards first and only then pay the developer. Owners, on the other hand, usually want the insurance money to restore the building.

Lenders tend to dislike rental rates being offset against increases in pass-through expenses. For example, most leases require tenants to pay increases in operating costs over some base figure. They also object to exclusions for increases in management fees and similar items because they reduce the ability of owners to cover these increased costs.

FIGURE 5-7 | Purchase Price Calculation

Gross rent (100,000 ft² at $28/ft²)	$2,800,000
Vacancy (5%)	− $140,000
Adjusted gross income	$2,660,000
Expenses ($5/ft²)	− $500,000
NOI	$2,160,000

$$\frac{NOI}{k} = \frac{\$2,160,000}{0.085} = \$25,412,000$$

$$\frac{\text{Adjusted gross income}}{k} = \frac{\$2,660,000}{0.10467} = \$25,412,000$$

MORTGAGE OPTIONS

Bullet loans (standard 30-year self-amortizing mortgages with a ten- to 15-year call) are a common form of permanent financing for office projects. Interest rates are usually lower for short-term mortgages because of the lower interest-rate risk to the lender over time. Occasionally, when inflation and long-term interest rates are expected to fall, interest rates are higher for shorter-term mortgages than for longer-term ones. Other common forms of financing are participating mortgages, convertible mortgages, and sale-leasebacks, all of which are forms of joint ventures with lenders.

STANDBY AND FORWARD COMMITMENTS

Although experienced developers can generally obtain open-ended construction financing without a permanent takeout, beginning developers usually cannot. Standby commitments are one alternative. They represent permanent loan commitments from credit companies and REITs that are sufficient to secure construction financing but are very expensive if they are actually used. Standby loans may run three or more points above prime, thus increasing the default risk during recessions. Ideally, the standby commitment is never funded because it is replaced by a bullet loan or another type of mortgage.

Another alternative to a permanent mortgage is a presale or forward commitment by a purchaser with the developer borrowing against proceeds from the sale for the construction loan. The presale price is determined based on the market capitalization rate. A forward commitment often includes an earnout provision whereby the developer is paid part of the purchase price and the balance is paid as the leasing is completed.

For example, the purchase price of a 100,000-square-foot building with per-square-foot rent of $28 and expenses of $5 can be determined by capitalizing the gross rent from executed leases on 95 percent of the building's rentable area at 10.467 percent, which equates to approximately an 8.5 percent cap rate on the NOI (figure 5-7, with k representing the overall cap rate):

An earnout would provide for the purchaser's paying the capitalized value on that portion of the building that is leased at the time of closing and paying the balance later as leases are signed on the remainder of the building. For example, if 50 percent of the building is leased, the purchaser would pay $13,375,000 ($28 × 50,000 square feet ÷ 0.10467) at closing. The balance would be paid as the developer leases the rest of the building. If the remaining 45,000 square feet is leased at $26 per square foot, the developer would receive $11,178,000, for a total of $24,553,000. Therefore, the developer would have failed to "earn out" the full projected amount of $25,412,000.

EQUITY

Lenders normally require 20 to 30 percent of the development cost to be funded by equity sources, although it could be higher depending on the strength of the development team, the difference between the project cost and return, the strength of the market, preleasing, and the overall health of the lending industry. Lender competition to fund new construction during the market peak and before the Great Recession led to significant overleverage, with equity requirements far lower than 20 percent, therefore disincentivizing developers from salvaging their properties.

Joint ventures with lenders and tenants offer one of the easiest methods for covering a developer's equity requirement. Lenders have preferred participating loans, which give them a share of the cash flows during operations and profits from sale while shielding them from liability and downside risk.

LOAN WORKOUTS. All mortgages include lender-imposed loan covenants. One of the major covenants is a predetermined DCR requirement (currently 1.3 to 1.4). Some banks also require a debt yield ratio (DYR) (NOI divided by the loan amount), which does not account for the interest rate.

The loan covenants will outline the following:

- DCR and DYR testing frequency—usually once or twice a year;

- completion benchmarks and repercussions in case of cost overruns or other noncompliance—for example, if the building is expected to be completed in 12 months the lender provides a cushion of up to four months with monitored checkpoints on the schedule and budget; if the building is not completed after the cushion period, the lender can call for a loan default although all options will first be exhausted to avoid foreclosing on properties under construction as long as the developer is truthful and honest; and
- the time frame in which the loan will be repaid.

A developer facing monetary default must take the following steps:[58]

- Contact his attorney, who is qualified to review the legal documentation.
- Prepare a solution for the lender. The developer should analyze the causes of the cash flow shortfall and offer short- and longer-term solutions. For an interest-rate problem, refinancing with a lower rate and a comprehensive exit strategy might be the solution. Another possibility can be a request for interest-only payments, reducing payments for a while on a negatively amortized loan.
- Contact the lender and present a solution before receiving the default letter. Developer honesty is critical in resolving any type of problem.

It is important to understand the type of lender the developer is using and what that lender's guidelines allow. For example, a CMBS lender has less flexible guidelines on additional funding and fewer time extensions than other types of lenders. With a regular lender, such as a bank, the lender should know the bank's profile. Is it healthy? Is it on the FDIC's watch list? Is it going to be liquidated? The response can dictate possible outcomes. Assuming the lender is a healthy bank, the next issue for a developer is the types of commitments the bank cannot service.

The strategy for resolving the problem will depend on the type of issue (equity, developer's financial strength, property status, and so forth) the developer faces. Whether the loan is recourse or nonrecourse is very important. If the loan is nonrecourse, the developer is in a stronger negotiating position, with the only exception being a "bad-boy" guarantee where the loan automatically becomes full recourse if the developer engages in certain actions (not paying taxes, fraud, intentional illegal action, and so forth). In a nonrecourse loan, the developer can return the keys to the lender and negotiate a minimal cost exit (in a minimum equity situation) in lieu of foreclosure. If,

The Campus at Playa Vista in Los Angeles was planned as an indoor/outdoor work environment. The development is part of a large reuse of an industrial brownfield.

however, there are intervening liens (such as mechanic's liens), a no-cost transfer to the lender will be impossible. But a friendly foreclosure through bankruptcy can save money, as long as the developer agrees and has not committed fraud.

Another option might be for the developer to buy back the loan from the bank, for example, if the property is now worth less than the original loan. If the developer wants to salvage the property, avoiding default status is essential because the loan becomes classified and the bank has to report it differently to its examiners. Even if the developer makes regular payments later, the bank might need to treat the loan differently due to its default status.

In any default situation, whether a construction or permanent loan is out of balance, the lender will take the following steps:

- **Default notice**—The notice is sent to the borrower, outlining the problem and inviting the developer to discuss possible options while reserving the right to foreclose.
- **Lender's architect's inspection**—The lender's architect will visit the site to reevaluate the budget and assess the issue. Sometimes, the problem can be resolved easily, such as addressing an unpaid impact fee the developer was unaware of or a subcontractor that went out of business. The developer should have a contingency built into the budget to deal with these types of issues.
- **Title**—The lender will search for any liens against the property because they are paid ahead of the mortgage in certain states. They will also make sure that the money expended until this point has been allocated to the proper contractors and the scheduled work has been completed.
- **New underwriting**—The lender starts from zero, by examining the loan budget and the current equity and identifying any gap between them. If a gap exists, either the lender or the borrower will need to cover it.
- **Negotiations with developer**—The lender meets with the developer, who is expected to have a plan to facilitate a nonforeclosure resolution.
- **Resolution without foreclosure**—If a nondefault agreement has been reached between the lender and the developer, the shortfall will be covered by one of the following options: (1) the developer fully funds the shortfall; (2) the lender funds the shortfall because of the developer's lack of funds; or (3) the developer and the lender fund the short-

fall. If the borrower is honest and cooperative, the bank will consider extending the terminal loan and modifying it.
- **Foreclosure resolution**—The lender forecloses and a receiver is appointed for the day-to-day operations. Five key factors can lead to foreclosure: (1) the property is worth less at the time of completion compared with the initial lender investment and the developer cannot provide cash infusion; (2) developer dishonesty; (3) developer-tenant deals, with developers requesting funding for space built out without truthfully disclosing their involvement in the deal; (4) lack of developer interest in salvaging the property (key to the developer's effort to salvage the project is the amount of equity); and (5) the developer does not have any funds and cannot raise any funds to hold the property.[59]

Marketing and Leasing

Marketing an office building begins in the initial planning phases and continues through the stages of attracting prospective tenants or buyers and successfully completing negotiations with them. The crux of a marketing plan is to identify the target market segment (discussed earlier under "Market Analysis") and to convince that segment of the building's desirability.

The key to successful marketing is to focus on the criteria that are important to the target market and to emphasize the provision of these features to prospective tenants. Important features include

- exceptional location and access;
- competitive rental rates;
- efficient floor configuration;
- amenities and services (conference and fitness centers, restaurants);
- distinctive design;
- landlord stability;
- a high standard of tenant improvements; and
- Energy Star label or LEED certification, natural lighting, and air temperature control, which are among the pivotal features in an office building for tenants.[60]

MARKETING STRATEGY

Guided by the market analysis and controlled by a strategic marketing plan and budget, the developer should undertake a variety of initiatives to attract and satisfy the needs of prospective tenants with a systematic approach.

The marketing strategy lays out a basic plan for publicizing the project and defines the roles of members of the marketing team. It should include a description of the project and its target market and a realistic analysis of the project's relative position in the marketplace. It must also include a statement of the developer's financial goals and investment strategy, including exit strategies. A leasing plan with guidelines for rental rates and potential concessions is also essential.

Developers usually start marketing space when the building is still in the design phase to reduce their risk, although tenants are reluctant to lease preconstruction space. The larger the building and the longer the construction schedule, the more difficult preleasing becomes.

A good location often attracts a build-to-suit tenant. The developer must be willing to adapt the building to the tenant's distinctive requirements, which may later pose problems if the building must be leased to another tenant. Nonetheless, the advantages of build-to-suit projects—especially the advantage of a committed tenant—outweigh their disadvantages.

ADVERTISING. Advertising is a key element of the marketing strategy that promotes the project's image while trying to attract perspective tenants. The advertising must be well conceived and designed to convey the appropriate image of the project. Advertising should be unified by a theme and a style. A name, logo, and identity design—to be used in all materials, including ads, websites, and printed matter—can be developed early during the project's conceptual planning phases to ensure continuity in image from design to marketing.

Property advertising has changed by virtue of technology and client needs in recent years. Beyond listing the property information on brokerage websites, a property website can be set up and maintained easily. Features should include a project overview, building data, typical floor plans, a summary of technical specifications, and a location map. Photos illustrating construction progress and leasing updates can also help sell the project to prospective tenants before its completion. E-mails and progress newsletters are other effective advertising techniques for brokers.

On-site signboards should announce the amount of available space, a contact person, and a telephone number. Signs should be perpendicular to the road, and the letters should be large enough to be read easily by passengers inside a vehicle driving by the site.

PUBLIC RELATIONS. Public relations firms assist the developer with news releases, promotional ads, and special ceremonies covered by the press. Newsworthy items include groundbreaking, land closing, signing of leases with major tenants, securing of public approvals, construction progress, building completion, first move-ins, and human interest stories on individual tenants. Public relations events should be limited because they can be costly and not particularly effective in reaching the target market.

MERCHANDISING. The developer must ensure that the site is free from construction trash, the completed building has a high-quality image, and the lobby creates an inviting atmosphere.

Ideally, the leasing office should overlook the construction site. At the very least, the leasing office should include an executive office, a staff office, an open area for support staff, and a conference room. In terms of decoration, the office should contain the standard tenant improvements to show prospects how attractive their space will be without added expense for extras or upgrades.

Models, pictures, and other graphic aids should be displayed to generate interest and to facilitate movement throughout the sales office. Scale models are useful in obtaining financing and gaining public approvals, as well as in helping prospective tenants visualize the space. Floor plans and computerized presentations incorporating virtual reality tours of the offices can also be quite helpful.

BROKERS

Brokers are used in nearly all office-leasing transactions. Existing tenants, however, are increasingly approaching their landlords directly for renewals and extensions to benefit from the lack of the brokerage commission. Leasing can be done by an in-house team or outside brokers. An in-house team allows the developer greater control, but the cost may be prohibitive for a small or beginner developer. Arrangements with real estate brokerage firms can provide market experience and access to a professional sales force, but it does mean that the developer has less control over marketing and leasing.

WORKING WITH OUTSIDE BROKERS. A brokerage firm can bring an in-depth knowledge of major competitors and tenants looking for space. Brokers also spread the word about a new development through their network of development agencies, chambers of commerce, business organizations, and so forth. In hiring outside brokers, developers should consider certain points:

- the size and competence of the broker's leasing staff; and
- the number of competitive buildings the broker is working on (brokers with many clients may not be able to devote sufficient time or interest to a new developer's project; a younger or smaller agency with fewer clients may offer better service but may have fewer contacts).

Brokers may have a contract with the developer that ensures them the exclusive right to negotiate all deals. Alternatively, the developer may opt for an *open listing*, which allows any broker to act as the primary broker on a deal. Developers should keep brokers informed about their project through presentations and monthly news releases. Traditionally, a broker brings a prospective tenant to the developer and assists in negotiating the terms of the lease. In some situations, developers may prefer to negotiate the lease themselves or with the use of legal counsel.

Commission rates for brokers are typically a percentage of rental income determined by market conditions. As a rough guide, a beginning developer could expect a broker to request a 6 percent commission rate in the first year of the lease with a declining percentage for the later years. The typical payment schedule for brokers' commissions is half upon lease signing and half upon occupancy or at the time rental payments begin. In cases in which a substantial period of free rent is offered at the beginning of a lease, it is common for a developer to pay one-third of the commission at the signing of the lease, one-third at occupancy, and one-third at the commencement of rent.

USING IN-HOUSE BROKERS. Some developers prefer to employ an in-house staff of leasing agents. Although salaries are costly, an in-house staff can substantially reduce the cost of leasing space because of their lower commissions (typically, 3 to 4 percent of the full value of the lease).

An effective in-house brokerage department offers its employees many of the same training programs used in outside brokerage firms. For example, some companies have weekly education sessions for salespeople covering self-motivation, product presentation, and negotiation techniques. Whether to use in-house brokers or outside brokers depends largely on market conditions and the size and expertise of a developer's staff.

TYPES OF LEASES. Three types of leases are used in office projects: gross leases, net leases, and expense stop leases. Each has its advantages and disadvantages.

Gross Leases. The landlord pays all operating expenses, absorbing the risk of rising expenses. A typical rent breakdown is shown in figure 5-8.

Net Leases. Three variations of net leases are common, although definitions can vary by market. Under a net lease, the tenant typically pays a base rent plus its share of certain building operating expenses, such as utilities. Under a net-net lease, the tenant pays everything under a net lease plus ordinary repairs and maintenance. Under a triple-net (commonly referred to as NNN) lease, the tenant pays all the building's ongoing operating expenses, including capital improvements. Ultimately, the lease itself, which is a product of negotiation between owner and tenants, defines which expenses fall under the responsibility of the tenant and the owner.

Expense Stop Leases. Expense stop leases involve sharing expenses between the tenant and the landlord. The landlord pays a stated dollar amount for expenses, and the tenant pays any expenses above that amount. Normally, the expense "stop" is determined by an estimate of expenses for the first operating year. Thus, the tenant pays any increases in expenses above the stop over the term of the lease after the second year of the lease term. An expense stop shifts the responsibility for increased expenses

FIGURE 5-8 | Typical Breakdown of Gross Rent for Office Space

Base rent	$15.00
Energy	1.10
Cleaning	1.08
Management	1.00
Administrative	0.45
Grounds and general maintenance	1.20
Elevators	0.15
Security	0.05
Insurance	0.40
Property taxes[a]	2.00
Total expenses	7.43
Total gross rent	$22.43

Source: Ken Beck, senior vice president, ASW Realty Partners, Woodland Hills, California.

[a]Property taxes vary considerably, and may run as high as $12 in some markets.

to the tenant in much the same way a net lease does. A lease may also be structured so that the tenant is responsible for the increase in utility costs but not other expenses.

LEASE RATES AND TERMS

The lease document sets forth the terms and conditions under which the tenant's rights to use the space are granted. Both developers and corporate tenants have their own leasing forms, and the initial negotiations determine which form will be used as the starting point. Lease negotiations focus on four major issues: rent, term, tenant improvements, and concessions, such as free rent or moving expenses. Anchor tenants (those occupying a significant portion of the building) have lease terms running ten or more years, with rent escalations every year. The rest of the tenants usually have three- to five-year leases; the shorter term allows the landlord to renegotiate the terms of the lease to match inflation and gives tenants greater flexibility.

The base rent depends on market conditions. If local vacancy rates exceed 15 percent, tenants enjoy a strong bargaining position, and the base rent could be lowered accordingly. Provisions such as *dollar stop* or *full stop* clauses are created to allow for rent adjustments for long-term leases. An estimated dollar amount (the dollar stop) for real estate taxes and another amount for other operating expenses and insurance are determined at the beginning of the lease. Under consumer price index clauses, rent is adjusted annually based on the CPI or the wholesale price index, which is tied to the cost of living in the United States. During inflationary periods, developers tend to prefer CPI leases. In softer markets, CPI leases are harder to negotiate. In periods of low inflation, fixed increases may be more common. Tenants are often willing to accept 3 percent annual increases, which in recent years provided larger rent increases than a straight CPI adjustment.

The key to successful lease negotiations is being able to respond to the tenant's needs while negotiating for everything. Does a tenant require free rent for certain periods, low initial rent with later escalations, or above-standard tenant improvements? Generally, smaller tenants prefer higher tenant improvement allowances because they often lack the liquidity for improvements in advance; larger tenants often prefer free rent for certain periods.

Every lease should specify the following information:

- location of the space in the building;
- size and method of measuring the space;
- options for expansion, if any;
- duration of lease term, renewal options, and termination privileges;
- rent per square foot (per m²);
- services included in the lease and costs associated with those services;
- interior work to be performed by the developer under the base rent;
- operating hours of the building;
- the landlord's obligations for maintenance and services;
- the tenant's obligations for maintenance and services;
- escalation provisions during the lease term;
- number of parking spaces, their location, and terms of their use (for example, whether designated or undesignated);
- allowable use of the leased space permitted by local zoning ordinances and building rules;
- date of possession and date that rental payments are due; and
- sublease and assignment privileges, if any.

Operations and Management

Office building management requires regular maintenance, efficient operation, and enhancement of the property's value. Larger buildings have property managers on site, while smaller buildings may share a property manager. The agreement between the developer and the property manager should identify the duties and responsibilities of each party, including the authority to sign leases and other documents, incur expenses, advertise, and arrange bank/trust agreements. Also included are provisions on record keeping, insurance, indemnification, and management fees. Most management fees are quoted as a percentage (ranging from 1 to 6 percent) of effective gross income. Smaller developers might manage their buildings for the fees they generate and to maintain close ties with tenants.

The functions of a property manager include maintaining the building, developing and maintaining good tenant relations, collecting rent, establishing an operating plan, creating a budget, maintaining accounting and operating records, hiring contractors or vendors servicing the building, paying bills, overseeing leasing, developing and managing maintenance schedules, supervising building personnel, providing security, addressing issues related to risk management,

ENRICO CANO

Perseo, on the outskirts of Milan, Italy, is a 177,000-square-foot (16,000 m²) sustainable development of two office buildings connected by a slender four-story bridge.

coordinating insurance requirements, and generally preserving and attempting to increase the building's value.

The management team can significantly affect a property's value either positively or negatively. The projections of income and expenditures that are updated monthly are among a property manager's top priorities. The income side includes rents as though the project were fully occupied, along with any other income from the property. The gross income is adjusted for anticipated losses (for example, vacancies and turnovers). The three major operating expenses are taxes, utilities, and cleaning, with the management staff having better control over the latter two. A number of strategies can be applied to reduce operating expenses, such as renegotiating service contracts, making staffing changes (on-site personnel can be decreased if the facility has smart systems that allow remote supervision), reducing energy usage, setting back temperature controls, and minimizing downtime and landscaping. Operating expenses of portfolio properties can decrease if electricity is bought in bulk and the same cleaning staff is used for the entire portfolio.[61]

Key issues toward ensuring tenant satisfaction are the coordination of tenant improvements and property maintenance. Many developers have an in-house

project manager for construction oversight while maintenance is routine—preventative and corrective on the building's mechanical and structural systems. If the lease gives the tenant responsibility for maintenance or landscaping, the developer should retain the right to order the work if the tenant fails to do so and charge the tenant for the cost.

One of the most important management tools is the lease agreement. Developers should ensure that leases contain clauses stipulating that

- tenants must not alter the building without the landlord's consent;
- tenants must not do anything that might increase the costs of fire insurance or create noise or nuisance;
- tenants must not use the building for immoral or illegal purposes; and
- if tenants remove floor, wall, or ceiling coverings, they must restore the surfaces to the condition that existed when they first took possession of the space.

The management team needs to provide high-level service to the tenants and build a relationship through scheduled meetings and independent surveys. The team members should also make sure they satisfy the tenant decision makers, not only the employees.[62] Some companies also have tenant portals that include announcements, forms, life/safety training videos, and so forth.

ZOMBIE BUILDINGS

The recent recession has led to zombie buildings, which are currently worth significantly less than what their owners owe and where refinancing is not a viable option. The developer/owner might have bought a building at the height of the market; although the loan might be serviced, the market value decreased and neither the owner nor the lender is willing to provide funds for buildouts or broker commissions when space becomes vacant. This situation is less of a problem for bigger tenants because they can afford the built-out costs and take free or reduced rent incentives. But attracting medium-sized or smaller tenants that need a built-out space allowance up front while being unable to use existing space is difficult.

ENERGY STAR AND LEED

Landlords across the United States see energy efficiency, water volume control, and use of sustainable products as core sustainability factors. The main challenge is faced by older office buildings, which will eventually need to pursue Energy Star and/or LEED certification to remain competitive in the market. Many landlords of Class A and Class B buildings have tried to evaluate their buildings for LEED certification, but the retrofitting costs can be prohibitive even in a good market. The first steps in pursuing Energy Star or LEED designation are[63]

1. auditing the performance of the building's system over a 12–18 month period, including energy temperatures, water volumes, and so on; and
2. assessing the equipment changes needed to improve energy and water performance. Some landlords (especially of Class B and B- buildings) stop at this step due to the significant cost associated with the retrofit of outdated mechanical systems, regardless of the available energy incentives.

If the building receives a LEED-EBOM certification, staff will require training on new policies, while vendors and partners should abide by the new protocols established, which will be continuously monitored by management staff. Properties pursuing LEED certification see an initial hike in their operating budget for repairs and maintenance, due to the installation of filters for air quality, timers, sensors, and other equipment, while significant operating savings might take three to four years.[64]

SELLING THE COMPLETED PROJECT

The decision to sell depends on the needs of the equity partners, the term of the construction or permanent loan, market conditions, and the developer's analysis of alternative investment opportunities.

Office buildings are commonly sold at (1) stabilized occupancy, (2) after the first full year of occupancy (when the first CPI or fixed adjustments occur), or (3) after the leases are renewed. Usually, the highest internal rate of return is achieved if the building is sold as soon as it reaches stabilized occupancy. In competitive markets, however, most developers prefer to wait until just after the leases first roll over or until the first rent escalations have occurred. At this point, the highest net present value (at a discount rate of 12 to 15 percent) is often reached. On the other hand, long-term investors usually plan to hold buildings for at least seven years.

Developers can take several actions to position a building for sale:

- hire a building inspection team to thoroughly inspect a building's mechanical and other systems and to prepare a report that can be shown to prospective buyers;
- prepare summaries of a project's income and expenses and ensure that accounting records are in order;
- make sure that a building is clean and has a well-landscaped and well-maintained appearance or curb appeal;
- prepare a summary of all outstanding leases on a building; and
- create a marketing brochure that describes a project's noteworthy qualities—its tenants, management, location, and position in the market.

Conclusion

Office development is challenging but straightforward for a beginning developer. Avi Lothan notes that the marketplace for new office construction is becoming increasingly tenant specific and opportunistic based on the signing of a major lease.[65] Tenants of significant size or those consolidating multiple area operations require contiguous space, which is not always readily available in the market, triggering new construction of either buildings with big floor plates or small build-to-suit buildings. Even when space is designed carefully for specific tenants, the space needs to remain flexible and accommodate changes.

Development of flexible and sustainable space is almost a must for new development, while the addition of smart building systems is more frequently seen among existing downtown office buildings. Given the progression of technology and the resulting innovative approaches to energy management, the adoption of smart grid systems in some form seems inevitable among all new office construction in the future, according to Mike Munson of Metropolitan Energy.[66]

The Great Recession has led to a higher propensity of short-term leases (three to five years instead of a ten-year commitment) and a higher ratio of renewals compared with new tenant deals, says Vicky Noonan. Tenants with leases expiring in one to two years tend to extend them for four years, effectively reducing their rent (the cost to move can be as high as $30 per square foot [$323/m²], according to Eric Sorensen). The Great Recession and the decrease in property values have led even Class A properties in some areas to deny tenant improvements and broker commissions, even for existing tenants that renew their leases.[67]

Rents are highly dependent on location and the amenity package, with sustainability becoming an increasingly important factor. Although offices can be built almost anywhere, firms want to be located where their employees want to work. Tenants are willing to pay a premium for the right location, which attracts and retains key employees. In prime locations, office space can generate higher land values than any other use.

Central business districts no longer have the preeminence they once had (with the exception of 24/7 cities), and office buildings are widely dispersed throughout metropolitan regions, although suburban rents and property values are usually significantly less than those in the downtown area. A large concentration of office space defines today's *edge cities* that lie at major highway intersections at the periphery of every major American city, although transit-oriented development is becoming increasingly attractive among major developers compared with edgeless cities.

Office development is relatively compact and uses less land per employee than industrial or retail development. But office buildings do generate high peak traffic volumes. Office buildings constitute a primary use in redevelopment areas and local officials often embrace this use as an economic development tool.

Office buildings typically take at least two years to build and lease up, and market conditions might change dramatically during this time. During the Great Recession, a number of office developers were caught at various stages of development with their projects

requiring lender workouts to mitigate the financial shortfalls in the short and longer run. With a lot of the capital instruments used by developers on the sidelines and a weak job growth, speculative development is not expected to commence for a number of years, while need-based development is expected to gradually increase.

This chapter concludes with two case studies of LEED-certified office buildings, reflecting the increasing pervasiveness of sustainable development. The first, 17th and Larimer, is a redevelopment in downtown Denver. The second is 11000 Equity Drive, a new corporate headquarters in suburban Houston.

NOTES

1. Interview with Bill Rolander, principal at the John Buck Company, Chicago, Illinois, summer 2009.

2. Interview with Cathy Stephenson, senior vice president, national director of operations, Grubb & Ellis, Chicago, Illinois, summer 2009.

3. Interviews with Greg Van Schaak, Hines, Chicago, Illinois; Rafael Carreira, Eric Sorensen, and Bill Rolander, the John Buck Company, Chicago, Illinois, 2009; and Dennis Harder, Joseph Freed & Associates, Chicago, Illinois, 2009.

4. Interviews with Bill Rolander and Greg Van Schaak, 2009; and Milda Roszkiewicz, senior vice president, Wells Fargo, Chicago, Illinois, 2010.

5. Anthony Downs, *Real Estate and the Financial Crisis: How Turmoil in the Capital Markets Is Restructuring Real Estate Finance* (Washington, D.C.: ULI–the Urban Land Institute, 2009).

6. Interviews with Milda Roszkiewicz, 2010; and Anthony Frink, partner, Holland & Knight, Chicago, Illinois, 2010.

7. U.S. Environmental Protection Agency, Energy Star website, www.energystar.gov.

8. U.S. Green Building Council website, www.usgbc.org.

9. Interviews with Greg Van Schaak, Rafael Carreira, Eric Sorensen, Bill Rolander, and Dennis Harder, 2009.

10. Interviews with Bill Rolander, Rafael Carreira, and Greg Van Schaak, 2009.

11. Piet Eichholtz, Nils Kok, and John M. Quigley, "Doing Well by Doing Good? Green Office Buildings," *American Economic Review* 100, no. 5 (2010): 2492–2509.

12. Franz Fuerst and Patrick McAllister, "Green Noise or Green Value? Measuring the Effects of Environmental Certification on Office Values," *Real Estate Economics* 39, no. 1 (2010): 45–69.

13. Norm Miller, Jay Spivey, and Andy Florance, "Does Green Pay Off?" *Journal of Real Estate Portfolio Management* 14, no. 4 (2008): 385–399.

14. Sofia Dermisi, "Effect of LEED Ratings and Levels on Office Property Assessed and Market Values," *Journal of Sustainable Real Estate* 1, no. 1 (2009): 23–47.

15. "A Green Tour of the Google Campus," *The Official Google Blog*, http://googleblog.blogspot.com/2009/10/green-tour-of-google-campus.html.

16. Interviews with Vicky Noonan, managing director, Tishman Speyer, Chicago, Illinois, 2009; Eric Sorensen, 2009; Jon DeVries, director, Strategic Development Planning, URS Corporation, Chicago, Illinois, 2010; and Avi Lothan, principal at DeStefano Partners, Chicago, Illinois, 2010.

17. Interview with Jon DeVries, 2010.

18. D. Anderson, "The Race for Office Space," *Industry Standard*, January 11, 2000; and Joe Gose, "How Dot.Coms Pushed Office Markets to New Heights," *Barron's*, June 5, 2000.

19. Interview with Vicky Noonan, 2009.

20. Interviews with Greg Van Schaak, Rafael Carreira, Eric Sorensen, Bill Rolander, and Dennis Harder, 2009.

21. Interview with Allan Kotin, adjunct professor, School of Policy Planning and Development, University of Southern California, and Allan D. Kotin & Associates, Los Angeles, June 2002.

22. Interview with Gabe Reisner, president and CEO, WMA Consulting Engineers, Chicago, Illinois, summer 2010.

23. Full-sized parking spaces range from 8.5 feet wide by 16 feet long (2.5 by 4.9 m) to 10 feet wide by 18 feet long (3 by 5.5 m). Compact spaces are somewhat narrower and/or shorter, while spaces for the handicapped are wider. Two-way aisles for perpendicular parking vary from 24 to 27 feet (7.3–8.2 m) wide. A double-loaded parking module requires a 60- to 63-foot (18.3–19.2 m) cross section for two parking places and an aisle, plus the space required for the structure itself. The simplest design requires a minimum of two modules with continuously ramped floors that provide circulation between levels. With circulation and parking along the ends of the structure, the minimum dimension for the entire structure is about 130 feet by 190 feet (36.5 by 57.9 m). Local parking requirements should be consulted.

24. Interview with Jim Goodell, Goodell Associates, Los Angeles, California, June 1989.

25. Interview with Avi Lothan, 2010.

26. David M. Geltner, Norman G. Miller, Jim Clayton, and Piet Eichholtz, *Commercial Real Estate: Analysis and Investment*, 2nd ed. (Cincinnati, Ohio: South-Western Educational Publishing, 2007), pp. 771, 773.

27. Charles Long, *Finance for Real Estate Development* (Washington, D.C.: ULI–the Urban Land Institute, 2011).

28. Interview with Michael Sullivan, principal at Cannon Design, Chicago, Illinois, summer 2010.

29. Interview with Avi Lothan, 2010.

30. Interviews with Avi Lothan, 2010; and David Eckmann, principal at Magnusson Klemencic Associates, Chicago, Illinois, 2010.

31. Paul Katz, "The Office Building Type: A Pragmatic Approach," in *Building Type Basics for Office Buildings*, by A. Eugene Kohn and Paul Katz (New York: John Wiley, 2002).

32. Interview with Gabe Reisner, summer 2010.

33. Interviews with Avi Lothan and Michael Sullivan, 2010.

34. Katz, "The Office Building Type."

35. Ibid.

36. Ibid.

37. Interview with Gabe Reisner, summer 2010.

38. Interviews with Gabe Reisner and Mike Sullivan, summer 2010.

39. Interview with David Eckmann, 2010.

40. Interview with Michael Sullivan, 2010.

41. Norman D. Kurtz, "Mechanical/Electrical/Plumbing Systems," in Kohn and Katz, *Building Type Basics for Office Buildings*.

42. John Van Deusen, "Vertical Transportation," in Kohn and Katz, *Building Type Basics for Office Buildings*.

43. Lew Harriman, Geoff Brundrett, and Reinhold Kittler, *Humidity Control Design Guide for Commercial and Institutional Buildings* (Atlanta, Ga.: American Society of Heating, Refrigerating and Air-Conditioning Engineers, 2001).

44. Interview with Avi Lothan, 2010.

45. Interview with Michael Munson, Metropolitan Energy, Chicago, Illinois, 2010.

46. Interview with Tom McCaslin and John Wong, Tishman Construction Corporation, New York, New York, September 2000.

47. David S. Chartock, "4 Times Square: New York's First Green Office Building," *Construction News*, June 1998.

48. David V. Thompson and Bill McCarthy, "Security Master Planning," in *Building Security Handbook for Architectural Planning and Design*, by Barbara A. Nadel (New York: McGraw-Hill, 2004), pp. 2.1–2.30.

49. Interview with Carlos Villarreal, senior vice president, Whelan Security, Chicago, Illinois, 2010.

50. Interviews with Rafael Carreira, Greg Van Schaak, Eric Sorensen, and Bill Rolander, 2009.

51. Ibid.

52. Ibid.

53. Interview with John Newman, former president of the Commercial Banking group of LaSalle Bank N.A. and ABN AMRO North America, Chicago, Illinois, summer 2009.

54. Interviews with Bill Rolander, Greg Van Schaak, Dennis Harder, Rafael Carreira, and John Newman, 2009.

55. Interviews with Bill Rolander, Dennis Harder, and Rafael Carreira, 2009.

56. Interviews with Greg Van Schaak, Rafael Carreira, Eric Sorensen, and Bill Rolander, 2009.

57. Ibid.

58. Interviews with Milda Roszkiewicz and Anthony Frink, Chicago, Illinois, 2010.

59. Interview with Dennis Harder, 2009.

60. Interviews with Lenny Sciascia, director, Tishman Speyer, Chicago, Illinois, 2009; Cathy Stephenson, 2009; and Vicky Noonan, 2009.

61. Interview with Cathy Stephenson, 2009.

62. Interview with Karen Krackov, executive managing director–GEMS, Grubb & Ellis, Chicago, Illinois, 2009.

63. ibid.

64. Interviews with Cathy Stephenson and Lenny Sciascia, 2009.

65. Interview with Avi Lothan, 2010.

66. Interview with Mike Munson, 2010.

67. Interviews with Vicky Noonan and Eric Sorensen, 2009.

CASE STUDY: 17th and Larimer, Denver, Colorado

Located in downtown Denver, 17th and Larimer is a multitenant, LEED New Construction, adaptive-use office property owned by Seventeenth & Larimer LLC. The company representing the owners was formed by Kenneth Gillis, president of Centennial Realty Advisors; Randy Nichols of Nichols Partnership; and other equity partners. Nichols Partnership conducted the property renovation during 2008 and 2009. According to Gillis, the main motivation for the property acquisition was "the excellent location, which, combined with the building improvements, would raise rents, lower the cap rate, and thus increase the property value."

LOCATION

The building occupies a 0.45-acre (0.18 ha) site formerly known as the "Larimer Corporate Plaza." The current owners changed the property name to "17th and Larimer," as part of a rebranding. The property is adjacent to the Lower Downtown historic district, which is popular for its many restaurants, bars, clubs, and amenities. Larimer Square retail district is two blocks away at 15th and Larimer and the 16th Street pedestrian mall is one block away. The property is one block from the Regional Transportation District's lower downtown hub and adjacent to the 16th Street Mall bus connections. Rail and road transportation networks are also close, with Union Railway Station located three blocks away, light rail five blocks away, and the North Valley

Highway (I-25) nine blocks away. Also within walking distance are the Denver Performing Arts Complex, the University of Colorado–Denver, the Colorado Convention Center, and Coors Field baseball stadium.

PROPERTY DESCRIPTION

Originally named the Barclay Building, the property was constructed in 1979 and opened in 1982, later becoming Larimer Corporate Plaza. The current rentable building area is 118,263 square feet (10,986 m²), with 93 percent allocated to office use and the remainder occupied by five ground-level retail tenants. Underground and structured parking provide 55 parking spaces. The roof of the side parking structure is landscaped as an outdoor patio. Since 1996, the building sold three times. The most recent transaction occurred in 2007 when the property sold to Seventeenth & Larimer, LLC, for $16,825,000. Kenneth Gillis, president of Centennial Realty Advisors, LLC, selected the property and performed the financial analysis, which indicated that an extensive renovation of the asset and the improvement of the classification from B to A with a LEED certification would be a profitable venture. Vacancy was at 8.3 percent; it increased to 15 percent as a result of the owners' schedule of remodeling of both the interior and exterior. Although vacancy increased because of the renovations and economic recession, the property's repositioning lets it compete directly with the few LEED-certified Class A office properties in the area.

The interior includes a grid of columns with 20-foot (6 m) spacing, which reduces column interruption for small tenants. The building core includes an emergency stairwell and three elevators, one used for freight. The building has a classic corner office design with a sawtooth setback on both Larimer and 17th Streets, permitting multiple corner offices.

Glass and granite cladding are used for the building's exterior at the retail level, and concrete panels with stucco-clad cornices cover the upper levels. The first substantial renovation took place in 1996 and included recoloring of the concrete panels, elevator redecoration, a new signage system, and granite cladding for the retail level. This renovation improved the building's classification from C to B and attracted new tenants.

The second substantial building renovation, the focus of this case study, commenced after the latest property acquisition in 2007. The owners determined that the building was underused based on its location and the strength of the office lease market. A significant makeover was necessary to upgrade

the building from a Class B to a Class A property. The extensive renovation was completed in May 2009 and included the redesign of the facade, relocation of the main lobby to the corner of 17th and Larimer Streets, a complete remodel of all the building's common areas, and extensive upgrades to the structure's mechanical systems.

ADAPTIVE USE AND LEED

The remodeling goal was twofold: (1) to create a new identity for the property and (2) to adopt a green approach for a large-scale project with short- and long-term benefits for the owners, tenants, and those looking to lease space in LEED-certified buildings. The LEED-NC 2.2 designation was pursued based on the U.S. Green Building Council's recommendation, and construction was completed within nine months. The renovation included the replacement and reconstruction of the ground-level facade with new porcelain tile and a curtain wall window system on the corner of 17th and Larimer. The second-floor parking garage was faced with new aluminum grating panels. Metal wall panels were installed over the existing precast exterior on floors three through eight.

All windows in the building were replaced with new low-E glazing. Common areas were completely remodeled, including all new bathrooms with low-water-use plumbing fixtures; energy-efficient light fixtures; new floor, wall, and ceiling finishes; and remodeled elevator cabs. The ground-floor lobby was relocated to allow for a main entrance at the corner of 17th and Larimer. The new lobby features a 30-foot-long (9 m) backlit glass "glow wall."

A new 2,400-square-foot (223 m²) retail space was created adjacent to the new lobby and entrance. Exterior patio space on the building's third level was enclosed and recaptured as additional

leasable interior space for the building. The cost of recapturing this space was a fraction of the cost of other office space in the building, so it was beneficial to the overall project pro forma returns.

The upgrades that enabled the project to qualify for LEED certification included the following:

- WATER EFFICIENCY—All landscaping is water efficient. Potable water consumption for landscaping is reduced by 50 percent over a calculated midsummer baseline. All plumbing fixtures were replaced with low-water-use fixtures.

- ENERGY AND ATMOSPHERE—The energy performance of the mechanical systems and building envelope was optimized. Energy-efficient lighting was used throughout all building common areas. New energy-efficient windows and an energy-efficient chiller replaced old ones.

- MATERIALS AND RESOURCES—The renovation used 95 percent of the existing walls, floors, and roof, and 50 percent of the interior nonstructural elements. Forest Stewardship Council–certified wood was used where replacement was required.

- INDOOR ENVIRONMENTAL QUALITY—A construction indoor air quality (IAQ) plan was developed and implemented, as was an IAQ management plan for the construction and preoccupancy phases of the building. Low-emitting materials were selected for all adhesives, sealants, primers, paints, carpets, woods, and agrifiber products.

- BUILDING THERMAL COMFORT SYSTEMS were designed to meet the standards of ASHRAE 55-2004.

- INNOVATION AND DESIGN—The developers implemented and mandated a building-wide recycling program, as well as a sustainable operations and maintenance policy.

CONTINUED

CASE STUDY: 17th and Larimer, Denver, Colorado | CONTINUED

MARKETING AND TENANTS

Currently, 22 tenants occupy almost 74 percent of the building. A challenge during the extensive renovation was the owner's goal of high occupancy during construction. The strategies applied to accomplish this mandate required that the majority of disruptive work be completed during off-hours and that tenants be continuously updated on the construction progress. Careful scheduling and timing of potentially disruptive activities were crucial.

FINANCING

The property was acquired by Seventeenth & Larimer, LLC, in 2007 for $16.8 million. Capmark Bank provided the redevelopment loan at an initial amount of $14.2 million and the ability to increase it by $5.5 million for the redevelopment, tenant improvements, and commissions. The total loan was $19,700,294 with a floating interest rate that averages at about 6.5 percent. Seventeenth & Larimer, LLC, acquired the property with an equity amount of $3 million. The only lender requirement was to recapture the 6,877 square feet (638 m²) of leasable space on the building's third floor as part of the renovations. The final cost of the renovation was almost $11 million.

EXPERIENCE GAINED

The renovations cost the developer about $70 per square foot ($753/m²). They increased the property value for both the owner and the tenants. The key elements from the owner's perspective were the upgrading from Class B to Class A. The LEED certification was also critical to enable the building to capture that increasing niche of tenants seeking a green building. The small supply of such buildings in downtown Denver gives the property a competitive advantage over all non-LEED properties. The recapturing of

almost 7,000 rentable square feet (650 m²) by enclosing an exterior patio on the third floor added valuable leasable space. The direct benefit for the owner was the rent increase because of the property's reclassification, which allows it to compete with Class A rather than B properties. Because of the improvements, the majority of the existing tenants remained throughout renovation and rent escalation.

The tenants' perspective on the added value from the renovations was captured through a survey titled "Thermal Comfort Study" and informal comments made by the tenants to the property manager. The vast majority of tenants

were pleased with the heat load in their workplace. Before the renovations, the building's HVAC system was unable to handle the heat load especially on the south side of the building. After the renovations, the tenants throughout the building indicated that they were far more comfortable. In addition to the survey, a number of tenants approached the property manager indicating that all the interior improvements made their workspace more productive.

During construction, the project manager, Dan Schuetz of Nichols Partnership, was faced with some unexpected problems, which were time-consuming and costly to resolve:

- Construction vibration problems in the cast-in-place concrete structure echoed throughout the building and could not be isolated, requiring all hammer drilling to be performed during tenant off-hours, which increased projected costs.

- The existing exterior curtain wall glass was failing. Even if exterior renovations were not scheduled to take place immediately, the glass curtain wall would need to be resecured to the structure within the next ten years.

- The city of Denver required the new exterior wall fire rating to be brought up to code.

- To qualify for LEED credits, the existing HVAC mechanical systems needed substantial retrofitting to draw an adequate amount of external fresh air. This retrofitting was technically challenging and costly.

- The LEED "Construction Waste Management" credit can be earned by recycling a certain percentage of materials removed from the building. The team planned to divert 50 percent of the construction waste from the disposal of glass but was unable to find a company that would recycle all the removed glass even though it was being given away free.

Three key lessons were learned from the renovation process:

1. IMPACT ON THE TENANTS—The process affected the tenants, although every possible effort was made to minimize disruptions. Keeping an open dialogue between tenants, property management, and construction team was the key to the success of this project.

2. FLOOR ADDITION—The construction team spent time, money, and effort in exploring the possibility of adding one more floor, but it was not pursued because of cost and time constraints.

3. CONTINGENCY BUDGET—In this project, the contingency was 8 percent, which was totally spent on exterior wall fireproofing improvements, HVAC upgrade, exterior glazing, and so on. In hindsight, the contingency of a property renovation should have been a minimum at 8 percent and at best 10 percent of the hard cost, allowing the construction team to deal with substantial unforeseen challenges.

FINANCIAL PROJECTIONS

The project feasibility was evaluated through a pro forma examining postconstruction expected cash flows and expected postconstruction cap rates to arrive at reversion value (see figure B).

FIGURE A | Project Data

Owner	Seventeenth & Larimer, LLC
Adaptive reuse developer	Nichols Partnership
Architect	Klipp, Inc.
Contractors	JE Dunn Construction (exterior); Ponderosa Construction (interior)
Site area	0.45 acres (0.18 ha)
Rentable building area	118,263 square feet (10,986 m²)
Parking	55 spaces
Total project cost	$27,801,228

Note: Dan Schuetz, project manager with the Nichols Partnership, provided substantial help in developing this case study. Kenneth Gillis of Centennial Realty and Randy Nichols of Nichols Partnership reviewed the case study.

FIGURE B | Project Cost Summary and Pro Forma

	Rentable	Gross
Office	109,800	115,510
Retail	8,463	8,903
Total:	118,263	124,413

	Rentable Ft²	Gross Ft²	Cost ($)	$/Gross Ft²	Loan ($)	Equity ($)
DEVELOPMENT PRO FORMA						
Total Acquisition Cost			16,825,000	135.24	13,825,000	3,000,000
Hard Costs						
Building cost ($63.73/ft²)[a]		124,413	7,928,290	63.73	4,453,290	3,475,000
Contingency and escalation[b]			263,051	2.11	263,051	
Total building cost			8,191,341	65.84		
Total hard costs			8,191,341	65.84		

CONTINUED

Tenant Work	Rentable Ft²	Gross Ft²	Cost ($)	$/Gross Ft²	Loan ($)	Equity ($)
Office TIs for first two years			895,605	7.20	770,605	125,000
Total tenant work			895,605	7.20		
Soft Costs						
Architecture, design, engineering			566,982	4.56	566,982	
LEED consultant			41,750	0.34		41,750
Real estate commission (first two years only)			324,366	2.61	324,366	
Development fee (3%)			329,250	2.65	–	329,250
Construction loan fee (1.0% of loan amount)			197,000	1.58	197,000	
Contingency			429,934	3.46	–	429,934
Total soft costs			1,889,282	15.19		
TOTAL PROJECT COST			**27,801,228**	**223.46**	**20,400,294**	**7,400,934**

CASH FLOW PRO FORMA

Income						
All retail ($34.00 NNN)	8,463				287,742	
Office, floors 3–8 ($33.00 gross)	109,800				3,623,400	
						3,911,142
Parking garage: (55 spaces, $195.00/month)					10,725	
Less vacancy (10%)					(1,073)	
Total parking						9,653
Total income						3,920,795
Expenses						
Operating expenses ($8.94/ft²)					1,112,249	
Nonoperating expenses ($0.28/ft²)					34,836	
Total expenses						(1,147,085)
Reserve ($0.21/ft²)						26,127
Net Operating Income						**$2,747,583**
Return on cost						9.88%

	Cap	Value ($)	$/Ft²

BUILDING VALUE

	Cap	Value ($)	$/Ft²
Cap NOI @	7.50%	**36,634,440**	310
Profit	Value	36,634,440	
	Cost	(27,801,228)	
	Profit	8,833,212	
Cash flow	NOI	2,747,583	
	Debt service	1,547,325	
	Income per year	1,200,258	

LOAN CRITERIA

Permanent loan	$20,400,294
Interest rate	6.50%

		NOI	Debt Service	DCR	Actual LTC	LTV	Return on Value
Target DCR =1.15		2,747,583	1,547,325	1.776	73.4%	55.7%	24.10%
Target LTV =75%							

[a]Cost of renovations—hard cost contracts with JE Dunn and Ponderosa Construction.

[b]Same as building cost.

CASE STUDY: 11000 Equity Drive, Houston, Texas

This case study focuses on a multitenant, LEED Gold building in Houston, Texas, that is the corporate headquarters of Satterfield & Pontikes. The goal was to develop a cutting-edge property to house the company's headquarters and to showcase the innovative mind-set of the owner. The innovative technologies applied in the property design and development and the team structure were recognized with multiple awards from the national, state, and local chapters of the American Institute of Architects and the Associated General Contractors of America.

LOCATION
The building is located at 11000 Equity Drive in the Northwest Far Submarket on a four-acre (1.62 ha) site. It is part of the Westway Park development in Techway, which is adjacent to Beltway 8. The vision of the initial developer,

Wolff Companies, included the adoption of green strategies in its business park design, which would eventually become a green oasis in Houston. Westway Park is an area of 150 extensively landscaped acres (61 ha) with thousands of trees. Among them are more than 83 native Texas hardwood trees protected by a permanent conservation easement.

George A. Pontikes, Jr., the CEO of Satterfield & Pontikes, took this vision further with the use of technology and developed a building that became the eighth LEED-certified or -registered building in the park.

SITE SELECTION AND ACQUISITION
Pontikes's goal was to develop a green building in an energy corridor. The site is located in an energy corridor and is also in proximity to a major highway interchange (Beltway 8 and I-10). The

innovations applied in the construction process expedited the building's occupancy (only ten months from the land acquisition) and generated development cost savings of 20 percent.

APPROVALS, CONSTRUCTION
The property was developed in a business park that was already zoned for office use, and it only required the typical building permits. No restrictions were imposed by the business park, and no additional approvals were required for the development of the green building.

Pontikes's goal was the cost-efficient and expedited design-build of his new and innovative corporate headquarters. All members of the project team used 3-D modeling to improve efficiency by facilitating faster review of multiple design options and effective conflict resolution throughout the construction phase. Satterfield & Pontikes reported a 20 percent cost savings compared with traditional design methods as a result of the sharing of 3-D modeling among all project participants.

Another innovation in the preconstruction and construction phases was the adoption of building information modeling (BIM) by all the project team participants. BIM is usually applied in large-scale projects, but using it in the development of this small-scale building led to a cost saving of 10 to 15 percent and eliminated all change orders at the job site. The use of BIM facilitated the fast information dissemination of different design scenarios and material costs among the project participants. It increased the project efficiency, allowing for task completion in days instead of weeks, eventually leading to completion in only ten months. A side benefit was the reduction of paper waste because of the electronic information sharing.

The project comprises two three-story office buildings, constructed in 2006

JUD HAGGARD

CONTINUED

Office Development

JUD HAGGARD

FIGURE A | Project Data

Owner	Seligman & Associates
Architect	Kirksey Architects
Contractor	Satterfield & Pontikes Construction, Inc.
Site area	4 acres (1.62 ha)
Gross building area	65,000 square feet (6,038 m²)
Rentable building area	65,000 square feet (6,038 m²)
Parking ratio	4/1,000 square feet (93 m²)
Total project cost	$12,211,256

FIGURE B | LEED Certification Points

Category	Points (max)	Category	Points (max)
Sustainable Sites	7 (15)	Materials & Resources	6 (11)
Water Efficiency	3 (5)	Indoor Environmental Quality	10 (12)
Energy & Atmosphere	4 (13)	Innovation & Design	4 (5)

FIGURE C | Project Cost Summary

	Itemized Cost	Total	Cost/Ft²	% of Total
Land Acquisition Costs		$1,208,085	$18.59	9.89
Purchase price	$1,133,119		17.43	
Closing costs	2,112		0.03	
Survey	2,342		0.04	
Environmental survey	32,007		0.49	
Geotechnical studies	31,821		0.49	
Association fees	6,684		0.10	
Design Costs		513,022	7.89	4.20
Architectural design	486,145		7.48	
Permitting	14,964		0.23	
LEED commissioning	11,913		0.18	
Construction Costs		9,224,316	141.91	75.54
Off-site utilities	17,050		0.26	
Preconstruction costs	22,472		0.35	
Building construction costs	6,418,613		98.75	
Owner & tenant finish construction costs	2,766,181		42.56	
Legal Costs		46,144	0.71	0.38
Lease negotiations	43,259		0.67	
Other miscellaneous legal costs	2,885		0.04	
Financing Costs		1,582,434	24.35	12.96
Interim commitment fees	86,649		1.33	
Appraisal	5,417		0.08	
Construction interest	1,353,722		20.83	
Permanent loan fees	102,059		1.57	
Mortgage title insurance	34,588		0.53	
Marketing Costs		239,919	3.69	1.96
Leasing commissions	239,919		3.69	
Advertising	0			
Net Operations through Construction/ Lease-Up		(602,664)	(9.27)	(4.94)
Total Development Cost		$12,211,256	$187.87	100.00

with a rentable building area of 65,000 square feet (6,038 m²) and an FAR of 0.37. In 2008, it was acquired by Seligman & Associates for $14,675,000. The two rectangular buildings are slightly shifted and perpendicular to each other, with the second box hosting the main entrance and protecting the interior from the eastern and southern sun. The intention for the structure's interior was to accomplish a high-quality, occupant-friendly environment. This goal was accomplished with ample corridors with transparent walls, allowing for significant exterior light penetration into the building's interior. Flexible circulation space allows for tenant expansion or contraction capabilities. Corner space serves as conference areas and lunchrooms.

Each building has one elevator and one emergency stairwell. The structure's exterior is enhanced with a sunshade system that increases thermal efficiency while providing glare-free views for all the occupants. The structure is made of cast-in-place concrete with the first box being wrapped in curtain wall bays and an exterior facade mullion cap that allows interesting light reflections. The facade of the second box is capped with a thin cornice overhang that completes the trabeated design while providing sun protection.

Both boxes reduce the heat-island effect with membrane roofs. The buildings and parking lot are well landscaped. The site's perimeter includes 82 trees, which are a noise and aesthetic buffer from the roads. A central park leads to the building entrance and has benches, a walkway, and a variety of trees, creating a relaxing oasis just steps from the offices.

LEED CERTIFICATION

The property was awarded LEED Gold Core and Shell Certification in 2007, making it the first LEED Gold building in Houston. The point breakdown is contained in figure B.

During construction, more than 75 percent of the construction waste was recycled. About 96 percent of the interior space has exterior views and the combination of efficient light fixtures, window-shading devices, and fritted glazing decreases the overall energy usage by more than 12 percent. Water-efficient fixtures decrease interior water use by 30 percent. The structure's heat-island effect was minimized with cool roofing materials and landscaping. The use of a highly efficient irrigation system combined with the selection of native grasses and plants (which are more resilient and require less watering) resulted in a 50 percent reduction in exterior water use. The developer's embrace of green strategies continued after construction with the continuing purchase of more than 70 percent of its energy needs coming from a sustainable source.

MARKETING AND TENANTS

The property was completed in just over ten months after purchasing the land. Currently, it is fully leased, with 50 percent of the space occupied by Satterfield & Pontikes, 41 percent by another anchor tenant, and the rest by two small tenants. All leases are long term with expiration dates in 2012 and 2015. The property credits its desirability to a combination of location, high-quality design, and environmentally friendly construction and landscaping, all making the building an appealing place to work and to conserve energy. The cost savings generated by the property's green approach attracted tenants that pay rents exceeding the original pro forma expectations.

FINANCING

The property was financed by Amegy Bank of Texas. The total development cost was $12.2 million, including tenant finishes (see figure C). The land cost was $1.2 million. The equity for the project construction was $1,059,000. The financial feasibility was determined with a simple pro forma/capital budgeting model (see figure D).

EXPERIENCE GAINED

George Pontikes's vision for an innovative green property with an expedited construction schedule and a small budget was realized and the property reached full occupancy within a year after completion. Kirksey Architects found that the application of the BIM process was pivotal in the project's success because it expedited communication, reduced the construction schedule, streamlined documentation, identified potential conflicts and mistakes early, allowed the efficient evaluation of different materials and their effect on energy efficiency and overall appearance, and allowed for an accurate cost analysis.

Note: Satterfield & Pontikes staff members Jess Arnold and Debbie Moore and former staff member Natasha Dasher assisted in developing this case study.

FIGURE D | Operating Pro Forma

	Ft²	Gross Rent/ Ft²/Year	Total
Gross rent	63,693	$23.15	$1,474,450
Parking revenue		$0.00	$0
Vacancy			$0
Effective gross income			$1,474,450
Expenses	**Per Ft²**		
Operating expenses	$8.97		$571,502
Nonoperating expenses	$0.00		$0
Reserve	$0.00		$0
Total expenses			$571,502
Net Operating Income	**$14.18**		**$902,948**
Project costs	$191.72		12,211,256
Return costs			7.39%

Cap Rate	6.5% (0% vacancy)	6.5% (5% vacancy)	6.75% (0% vacancy)	6.75% (5% vacancy)
Valuation ($)	13,891,508	12,757,315	13,377,007	12,284,822
Value/ft² ($)	218.10	200.29	210.02	192.88
Value created ($)	1,680,252	546,060	1,165,752	73,567

	DCR	Interest	Amortization (years)	Amount	
Debt service	1.14	6.75%	30	$10,205,854	$794,340
Cash flow after debt service					$108,608
Equity required					$1,059,000
Return on equity					10.26%

6

Industrial Development

ALEX DUVAL

In addition to design and construction of buildings, industrial development involves site planning, subdivision design and platting, and the construction of utilities and internal streets. Consideration must be given to access, parking, building design, and landscaping. In recent years, green building practices have become increasingly important in the development, design, and construction of industrial facilities, and understanding this process is becoming a prerequisite for a successful project.

Beginning developers may start out with a building for lease or a site that is suitable for one or more industrial users. If a build-to-suit tenant or buyer has not been pinned down, they might proceed with a speculative building that can be leased or sold in the future. Depending on market conditions, more profit can potentially be made on a speculative building than on a build-to-suit project because negotiations over lease terms with a potential major tenant can be tough. Speculative buildings are much harder to get financed, however. Construction lenders typically will not proceed unless the developer has deep pockets, with other collateral available, and is willing to sign personally on the loan. The economic difficulties generated by the Great Recession have made it more difficult for the small independent industrial developer to get access to capital.

Consolidation of small industrial developers has been occurring, along with a higher degree of specialization, and small developers are occupying niches that large companies are unable or unwilling to fill, in some cases, playing a support or supplementary role to larger firms. Beginning industrial developers should be wary of some possible pitfalls:

- paying too much for land or capital;
- underestimating the amount of competition;
- building the wrong product for the market, which can usually be avoided by involving the right consultants in the development process from the beginning;
- using an architect who has no experience in the type of product being designed; developers should find someone who knows the local market; can provide a market-oriented, functional design; and knows how to maximize its flexibility; and

Franke Corporate Headquarters and Distribution Center, Smyrna, Tennessee.

- not properly engaging local stakeholders in the entitlement process.

Business parks offer developers the flexibility to sell unimproved land parcels or completed buildings. Generally, they are completed in phases, which helps minimize risks associated with changing market conditions. Today's business parks are the product of an evolutionary process that had its antecedents in the manufacturing-oriented industrial estates and parks of the late 19th and early 20th centuries.

The first business parks appeared in the 1950s and were focused on office rather than industrial uses. The 1960s saw the advent of specialized R&D parks that benefited from links between universities and business. These settings combined a variety of functions, from offices to laboratory research to light manufacturing. Light industrial uses, such as manufacturing and warehouse/distribution facilities, are still integral parts of many business parks today, but the proportion of office space and such newer uses as call centers is growing. Heavy industry, once a significant element of planned industrial districts, is seldom included. Economies have shifted away from heavy manufacturing, and communities concerned about environmental impacts prefer lighter, higher-tech businesses as employment generators. Zoning often restricts the location of heavy industry in business parks and closer-in areas, whereas at the same time, large manufacturing companies generally prefer to locate at stand-alone sites farther outside the city where land is cheaper.

Today, business park locations tend to be in suburban areas with freeway and airport access. Proximity to housing, shopping, cultural amenities, and educational facilities is sometimes important, depending on the types of uses being targeted. Older inner-city industrial sites with good freeway access are becoming attractive again because of the availability of existing buildings and infrastructure at infill locations.

Product Types

An *industrial building* is defined by the National Association of Industrial and Office Properties as "a facility in which the space is used primarily for research, development, service, production, storage, or distribution of goods and which may also include some office space."

BUILDING CATEGORIES

All types of industrial properties have common characteristics despite variations in functions and use. Three primary categories of buildings are typically used to categorize industrial real estate: manufacturing, warehouse, and flex. Within these categories are a variety of subcategories that have distinctive physical characteristics to accommodate specialized functions.[1] These buildings may be located in industrial areas or master-planned business parks, or they may be stand-

FIGURE 6-1 | Typical Industrial Building Characteristics by Type

MANUFACTURING: A facility used for the conversion, fabrication, and/or assembly of raw or partly wrought materials into products/goods.

WAREHOUSE: A facility primarily used for the storage and/or distribution of materials, goods, and merchandise.

FLEX: An industrial building designed to allow its occupants flexibility in alternative uses of the space, usually in an industrial park setting.

TRUCK TURNING RADIUS: The tightest turn a truck can make depending on several variables of truck configuration, trailer size, and location of adjacent objects that obstruct the inner turn radius.

PRIMARY TYPE	MANUFACTURING		WAREHOUSE		FLEX	
	GENERAL PURPOSE	GENERAL-PURPOSE WAREHOUSE	GENERAL-PURPOSE DISTRIBUTION	TRUCK TERMINAL	GENERAL-PURPOSE FLEX	SERVICE CENTER/ SHOWROOM
Primary Use	Manufacturing	Storage, Distribution	Distribution	Truck Transshipment	R&D, storage, office, lab, light mfg, high-tech uses, data/call center	Retail showroom, storage
Subsets	Heavy, Light Mfg	Bulk Warehouse, Cold/Refrigerator Storage, Freezer Storage, High Cube, Bonded	Overnight Delivery Services, Air Cargo			
Size (ft²)	Any	Any	Any	Any	Any	Any
Clear Height (ft)	16+	18+	16 to 32	16+	10 to 24	Any
Loading Docks/Doors	Yes	Yes	Yes	Cross-dock	Yes	Yes
Door-to-Square-Foot Ratio	Varies	1:5k–15k	1:3k–10k	1:500–5k	1:15k+	1:10k
Office Percentage	<20	<15	<20	<10	30–100	30+
Vehicle Parking Ratio	Varies	Low	Low	Varies	High	High
Truck Turning Radius (ft)	130	130	120–130	130	110	110

Sources: NAIOP Research Foundation, 2011; ULI.

Note: This matrix is intended to aid in classifying properties among the principal types. Actual characteristics may vary considerably from those shown; the most important characteristics of each type are highlighted.

alone structures. The typical building characteristics of the three primary industrial building types are shown in figure 6-1. This matrix illustrates the spatial configurations of the various industrial building types and the relationship of the subcategories to each primary category.

More specialized subsets exist within the categories. For example, within "manufacturing" is a further breakdown of "heavy and light" classes. Within "general-purpose warehouse" exists "bulk warehouse, cold/refrigerator storage, freezer storage, high cube, self-storage, and bonded."

MANUFACTURING. Manufacturing structures are large facilities designed to accommodate the equipment for manufacturing processes. Light manufacturing buildings can be up to 300,000 square feet (27,880 m^2); heavy manufacturing buildings are more than 1 million square feet (93,000 m^2).

Floor-to-ceiling heights range from 10 to 60 feet (3–18.3 m) and average 20 to 24 feet (6–7.3 m). Large bay doors with at-grade or dock-high parking for large trucks and ample room for trucks to maneuver are usually a necessity. With the exception of assembly-related facilities, parking ratios vary—as low as 1.5 parking spaces per 1,000 square feet (95 m^2) of building area, depending on the planned number of employees. Because of their minimal parking requirements, traditional industrial buildings frequently cover 25 to 45 percent of a site (FAR).

The development of heavy manufacturing facilities has slowed considerably since the mid-20th century, their place taken by clean light manufacturing industries that have contributed significant demand for new industrial space. Because they focus on technology-based activities, these industries typically produce fewer of the undesirable side effects that limited the location of the older heavy industries.

Manufacturing facilities are often designed specifically for a company's manufacturing process. Consequently, few tenants are interested in taking over another company's manufacturing facility. Nevertheless, these manufacturing plants often have special equipment, such as heavy-duty cranes, that some companies find very valuable. Once a new tenant is found, it will likely stay there longer because of the specialized design and equipment.

WAREHOUSE. Warehouse buildings focus on the storage and distribution of goods. Within the category are three major subtypes of facilities: general-purpose

warehouse, general-purpose distribution, and truck terminal. Some differences exist in these types in their size, ceiling heights, and loading requirements, but in general, they have similar requirements: large, flat sites with space for maneuvering trucks and access to transportation facilities.

Warehouse buildings have low employee-to-area ratios—typically one or two employees per 1,000 square feet (95 m^2). As a result, only a small amount of employee parking is needed. Most warehouses have a minimal amount of office space—5 to 10 percent of total floor area. In some buildings, however, as much as 10 to 20 percent of the area may be allotted to office uses, chiefly to accommodate the purchasing, accounting, and marketing staff of a distribution or manufacturing company. Typically, these buildings have an attractive front elevation with ample windows for the office portion of the building and provide good truck access to the rear or side of the building. Dock-high and/or drive-in doors are provided to serve the warehouse functions.

In recent years, clear height, also referred to as "clear headway," which is the distance from the floor to the lowest hanging ceiling member, of warehouse buildings has increased from 26 to 28 feet (8–8.5 m) clear to 32 feet (9.7 m) or more clear at the first perimeter bay where stacking does not usually occur. The clear height then increases as the roof slopes upward toward the center of the building to a clear height of 40 feet (12 m) at its highest point. The extra clearance provides room for higher stacking. Plentiful truck bays, preferably on opposite sides of the warehouse, are critical for moving merchandise in and out, as the added value for bulk warehouses is the ability to move goods faster with minimal storage time.

Warehouse/distribution buildings have become substantially larger than they were two or three decades ago. Previously, buildings of 400,000 square feet (37,175 m^2) were considered large. In the early 2000s, spaces from 750,000 to 800,000 square feet (70,000–74,350 m^2) are being occupied by single tenants. One reason behind the demand for larger spaces is the consolidation of distribution businesses. Many sophisticated third-party logistics companies now handle transport of merchandise and parts for other companies.[2]

Some communities oppose the development of warehouses because they bring lower tax benefits and more truck traffic than other types of industries. On the other hand, such buildings generate relatively little daily automobile traffic and can be attractively landscaped.

FLEX. As its name suggests, flex space is industrial space designed to allow its occupants flexibility of alternative uses of the space, usually in an industrial park setting. Flex buildings are typically one- or two-story structures ranging from 20,000 to 100,000 square feet (1,860–9,295 m²). The pattern for internal uses has been about 25 percent office space and 75 percent warehouse space, but this proportion is changing in favor of more office space in many markets. External designs are generally clean, rectangular shapes with an abundance of glass on the front facade. Building depths vary, so developers need to understand the market to determine the best configuration.

Specialized R&D flex buildings fall into two distinct categories. One category includes facilities in which research is the primary, or only, activity. Design of the interior spaces is frequently unique to the specific research that will be carried out there. The other type of R&D building is intended to serve multiple uses. This type of structure, which may have one or two floors, often has office and administrative functions in the front of the building and R&D or other high-tech uses in the rear.

Offices in R&D buildings typically have open floor plans to promote teamwork and collaboration, and to facilitate easy rearrangement of spaces and furniture for rapidly changing work groups. Many tenants are small startup companies; others are subsidiaries of major corporations. Activities range from the creation and development of new technologies and products to the development, testing, and manufacture of products from existing technology.

The design of tenant improvements is more important for R&D uses than for other industrial uses and is usually tailored to the needs of specific tenants. The percentage of space allocated to laboratories, research offices, service areas, assembly, and storage varies widely. Hard-to-rent space in the center of buildings is well suited for laboratories and computer rooms where environmental control is critical.

MULTITENANT. Multitenant buildings cater to customer-oriented smaller tenants, such as office, showroom, and service businesses, that require spaces of 800 to 5,000 square feet (75–465 m²). The buildings are generally one story, with parking in the front and roll-up doors in the rear for truck loading. They provide parking ratios of two to three spaces per 1,000 square feet (95 m²) and turning radii in loading areas that are large enough for small trucks. Leased spaces are built so that they can be divided into modules as small as 800 square feet (75 m²). Frequently, 25 to 50 percent of the interior is improved, leaving the balance of the building as manufacturing, assembly, or warehouse space.

Some developers build all the tenant improvements for a project along with the base building, whereas others initially build just the shell and wait to build tenant improvements as space is leased. The first method limits flexibility and increases upfront costs; the second can be expensive if materials for tenant improvements cannot be bought at bulk prices. Methods for building tenant improvements frequently depend on a project's marketing scheme and anticipated absorption rate.

Exterior designs vary. Some markets require an upscale look that can be supported only by higher rents. In other markets, multitenant buildings are considered economy space so the most cost-effective combination of construction materials is used.

OFFICE/TECH. Office/tech buildings are used primarily for office space. They may provide limited truck access and warehouse facilities. Users of such buildings generally look for large volumes of space to house employees and have only limited interest in space for laboratories or computer facilities. Large paper

The LEED Silver–certified Franke Corporate Headquarters and Distribution Center occupies about 40 acres (16 ha) near the Smyrna, Tennessee, airport. The site includes a warehouse and a two-story corporate office and research center.

©2009 JIM ROOF CREATIVE, INC.

processors, such as insurance companies and banks, require large office spaces and desire low rental costs for their back-office functions; hence, they prefer the cost advantage and efficiency of office/tech industrial buildings. High parking ratios—such as three and one-half to four spaces per 1,000 square feet (95 m²) of net rentable area—are important to office/tech users.

FREIGHT. Freight facilities are not always included as a category of industrial real estate, but they are increasingly important in supply chain management. The freight-forwarding processes involving the transfer of goods from trucks to trucks and from planes to trucks require specialized buildings, each of which has special requirements for loading capabilities, building configurations, and space buildout.

TELECOMMUNICATIONS. Two types of telecommunications facilities have emerged since the late 1990s: data warehouses and switch centers. These types of buildings can be developed through the conversion of an older building that has access to fiber-optic cable or the construction of a new building solely for telecommunications use.

CATEGORIES OF BUSINESS PARKS

Business parks are multibuilding developments planned to accommodate a range of uses, from light industrial to office space, in an integrated park-like setting with supporting uses and amenities for the people who work there. They can range in size from several acres to facilities of several hundred acres or more.

Most business parks offer a conventional mix of warehouses, flex space, and offices to meet the needs of a range of occupants. Over the past 25 years, however, more specialized types of business parks have emerged. Although each of them can be categorized by a distinctive function and design characteristics, product types and their users overlap considerably. The primary categories include the following:

- **Industrial Park**—Modern industrial parks contain large-scale manufacturing and warehouse facilities and a limited amount of or no office space. The term *industrial park* connotes a setting for heavy industry and manufacturing, but it is still sometimes used interchangeably with *business park*.
- **Warehouse/Distribution Park**—Warehouse and distribution parks contain large, often low-rise storage facilities with ample provisions for truck loading

and parking. A small portion of office space may be included, either as finished space built into the storage areas or housed in separate office structures. Landscaping and parking areas are included, but because of the relatively low ratio of employees to building area, on-site amenities for employees tend to be minimal.
- **Logistics Park**—Such business parks focus on the value-added services of logistics and processing goods rather than warehousing and storage. As centers for wholesale activity, they may also provide showrooms and demonstration areas to highlight products assembled or distributed there.
- **Research Park**—Also known as R&D and science parks, research parks are designed to take advantage of a relationship with a university or government agency to foster innovation and the transfer and commercialization of technology. Facilities are typically multifunctional, with a combination of wet and dry laboratories, offices, and sometimes light manufacturing and storage space. Biomedical parks are a specialized version.
- **Technology Park**—Technology parks cater to high-tech companies that require a setting conducive to innovation. They rely on proximity to similar or related companies rather than a university to create a synergistic atmosphere for business development.
- **Incubator Park**—Incubator parks or designated incubator sections of research or technology parks meet the needs of small startup businesses. Often supported by local communities through their economic development agencies or colleges, they provide flexibly configured and economically priced space and opportunities for shared services and business counseling.
- **Corporate Park**—Corporate parks are the latest step in the evolution of business parks. Often located at high-profile sites, they may look like office parks, but often the activities and uses housed there go beyond traditional office space to include research labs and even light manufacturing. Supporting uses, such as service-oriented shopping centers, recreational facilities, and hotel/conference centers, are provided as a focus rather than an afterthought.

Rehabilitation and Adaptive Use

Older industrial districts offer opportunities to beginning developers, especially underused buildings suitable for rehabilitation and small infill sites. Many communities have established programs to encourage redevelopment of older industrial areas.

Redevelopment agencies and economic development agencies may offer incentives such as tax abatement and financing to developers who build in designated redevelopment areas. Renovation of older industrial areas offers many development opportunities:

- upgrading low-tech, light industrial buildings to be competitive with newer facilities;
- redeveloping low-tech, light industrial buildings for higher-tech R&D and office uses;
- rehabilitating major plants, such as outmoded automobile plants, into multitenant warehouses and office/tech buildings;
- removing heavy industrial facilities and reusing the land for business parks; and
- adapting obsolete urban warehouses to commercial, office, and residential uses, which have become increasingly prevalent.

The strong economy of the late 1990s and early 2000s motivated many developers to look at underperforming older industrial buildings for their potential reuse. Many of the more easily resolved problem properties have been taken, leaving properties that are likely to have more serious difficulties. Despite these issues, developers have access to a large pool of bargain-priced properties by performing suitable due diligence before buying industrial property.

Some of the potential issues surrounding the rehabilitation of older buildings include cost overruns, title problems, building code problems, poor street and utility infrastructure, and unforeseen construction problems. A major concern that must be addressed is the cleanup of contaminated sites. The answer to which party in the ownership chain is responsible for environmental remediation and what constitutes a suitable cleanup for various planned uses is still evolving.

Reengineering older industrial buildings with historic character is a special challenge. Architectural features should be retained as much as possible, and additions and improvements should be sympathetic with the existing design. New roofing and insulation, new windows with energy-efficient double- or triple-pane glass, the repair and cleaning of exterior wall surfaces, and painting and other cosmetic improvements are common exterior changes. A significant portion of the budget for internal redesign may be required to bring a building up to current fire and safety codes: enclosing stairways, adding sprinklers and fire alarm systems, installing or upgrading new wiring and plumbing, and upgrading or installing the heating, ventilating, and air-conditioning (HVAC) system.

Project Feasibility

MARKET ANALYSIS BEFORE SITE SELECTION

The market analysis that precedes site selection for industrial development serves three purposes: to identify the types of users that will be served, to identify the type of product to be built and thus the parameters of the site to be purchased, and to identify where the product should be located. Just as for office development, the developer should be familiar with basic data about the local economy and its relation to the regional and national picture. The items that should be checked include

- national, regional, and local economic trends;
- growth in employment and changes in the number of people engaged in job categories (as measured by Standardized Industrial Classification codes);
- socioeconomic characteristics of the metropolitan area, including rates of population growth and employment patterns;
- local growth policies and attitudes toward office and industrial development;
- forecasted demand for various types of office and industrial facilities;
- current inventory by industrial subtype;
- historic absorption trends and current leasing activity; and
- historic vacancy rates and current space available.

This information is available from a host of sources, including government and commercial websites, local universities, market analysts, data service firms, chambers of commerce, and major real estate brokerage firms. In addition to evaluating statistics, the developer should consult local brokers, tenants, and other developers to verify the accuracy of the information obtained. A developer who is unfamiliar with the local area should hire a market research firm with experience in industrial real estate.

Few market data sources segment industrial space beyond the categories *warehouse/distribution*, *manufacturing*, and *flex*, and in many cases, secondary market data are lumped into a single category labeled *industrial*, making it difficult to assess the performance of individual subtypes. One method of obtaining a rough idea of the various property types when the information is not broken down is to segment properties by size categories, such as "under 5,000 square feet" or "larger than 25,000 square feet" (or "under 1,000 m²" or "larger than 2,500 m²").

Before searching for specific sites, a developer must become thoroughly familiar with industrial development patterns throughout the metropolitan area. During this investigation, the developer wants to learn as much as possible about local market conditions and which types of industrial tenants are expanding or contracting. A developer or industrial company looking for a large, single site is concerned with a number of issues:

- availability and cost of land;
- transportation infrastructure/highway access;
- labor quality and cost;
- tax structure and tax incentives;
- utilities and waste disposal;
- energy rates; and
- comparative transportation rates.

Market preferences, land costs, labor costs, utility costs, and transportation costs can differ dramatically within the same city or region. Companies with markets outside the city have different criteria for site selection from those with markets primarily inside the city. The developer's market analysis before site selection should assess the target market's preferences regarding such factors as access to transportation and location.

LOCAL LINKS. Local links are critical to many companies. Firms that have frequent contacts with suppliers, distributors, customers, consultants, or government agencies consider the following in choosing a location:

- accessibility to firms with which they do regular business;
- the number of trips to be made to and from their business inside the metropolitan area;
- congestion in and around the site;
- commuting time for employees and public transportation available; and
- vehicle cost, including taxes, maintenance, and fuel per mile traveled.

CLUSTERING AND AGGLOMERATION. A number of industries—food distribution, garment manufacturing, printing, wholesale flower marts, machinery parts and repair, commercial groceries and kitchen supplies, for example—tend to cluster together. The clustering, known as *agglomeration* or *colocation*, often relates to time-sensitive products (such as perishable foods) or to the interdependency of firms in a particular industry. High-tech firms tend to congregate in research

parks near major universities, where they can take advantage of resources such as laboratories, libraries, professors and graduate students, and large pools of highly educated and skilled labor. Venture capital is also attracted to universities because of the commercially valuable discoveries they generate.

ACCESS. Access to transportation is fundamental to all types of industrial properties, although requirements vary by type of use. Virtually all industrial uses depend on trucking, so connections to major interstate highway systems are essential. In recent years, the growing "need for speed" in distribution, particularly of high-value goods, has made proximity to highways and airports more important than ever. Although rail service has remained an important factor for some manufacturing and industrial processes, smaller and lighter industrial users depend less on rail accessibility.

Airports exert a strong attraction for industrial users. In many cases, businesses locating near an airport use cargo and passenger services regularly. In other instances, this "airport effect" is the result of good highway access, available land, and favorable zoning.

FOREIGN TRADE ZONES. A foreign trade zone is a site in the United States in or near a U.S. Customs port of entry where foreign and domestic merchandise is generally considered to be in international commerce. Firms located in foreign trade zones can bring in, store, and assemble parts from abroad and export the finished product without paying customs duties until the goods leave the zone. Many foreign manufacturing firms transport their products to a warehouse in the trade zone, store the products until they are ordered by a customer or distributor, and pay the import duties when the product leaves the warehouse to be delivered to the customer. Thus, the firms can have readily available stock without having to pay the associated import fees until the product is actually needed.[3]

QUALITY OF LIFE. The more intangible factors surrounding quality of life should not be forgotten in site evaluation. Livability is an increasingly important aspect of business location decisions. The presence of affordable housing, quality schools, and recreational and cultural resources strongly influences a company's ability to attract skilled workers.

Sample Market Analysis for a Multitenant Warehouse

This sample market analysis for warehouse space in Dallas indicates the steps to be taken in a market analysis for industrial properties. In this example, the analysis focuses on the Valwood submarket, a prime location for industrial space in the Dallas, Texas, metropolitan area.

A space inventory for Dallas and the Valwood submarket (figure A) provided a historical sketch of how the submarket has evolved in recent years. At the time of the survey, vacancy rates remained comparatively low, 6 to 7 per-cent, although some upward movement was obvious in Valwood.

Characterization of submarket rents and lease terms was obtained through a survey of brokers and a review of leasing comparables (figure B). Discussions with brokers also permitted a breakdown to be made of industrial tenants in Valwood by industry group (figure C). The breakdown indicated that rents were at attractive levels and unencumbered by concessions or high tenant improvement allowances.

Projections of warehouse space absorption in the Dallas metropolitan area were based on changes in gross metropolitan product and population. Total employment growth was also considered an indicator of demand in the market. These projections were then used to model metropolitan area warehouse absorption in Dallas. *Fair-share capture* was used to estimate what share of metropolitan absorption could be captured by the Valwood submarket. The area's locational advantages suggested a capture rate of 10 to 15 percent in the near term and 15 to 20 percent in the long term. Net absorption in Valwood was estimated to be 9 million to 10 million square feet (836,400–929,400 m²) over the next ten years.

Warehouse space construction in Dallas was found to be occurring in a number of submarkets, including Valwood. Six projects totaling approximately 1.5 million square feet (139,400 m²) were anticipated to be completed in 1998, and another 2 million to 3 million square feet (185,900–278,800 m²) was expected to enter the market in 1999 to 2001 (figure D).

FIGURE A | Space Inventory for Dallas and Valwood

Type	VALWOOD Square Feet (Millions)	VALWOOD Percent Vacant	DALLAS Square Feet (Millions)	DALLAS Percent Vacant
Flex	9.1	5.6	37,464	9.0
Warehouse	42.6	7.6	202,185	7.2
All	51.7	7.1	239,650	7.5
Year				
1989	39.6	12.1	NA	NA
1990	39.3	10.0	192,391	13.0
1991	39.5	11.0	192,952	12.0
1992	39.3	9.4	192,648	11.0
1993	39.5	6.0	192,949	10.0
1994	39.8	4.5	192,180	8.0
1995	41.1	5.0	192,548	7.0
1996	41.6	7.6	202,186	7.2
1997	44.3	6.8	213,248	6.4

Sources: M/PF Research and RREEF Research.

NA = Not available.

FIGURE B | Warehouse Rents and Lease Terms for Valwood

	Multitenant Less than 20,000 Square Feet	Multitenant 20,000–40,000 Square Feet	Single Tenant 100,000 Square Feet or More
Annual rents per square foot (double net)	$3.50–4.25	$3.25–3.50	$3.00–3.25
Term	3–5 years	3–5 years	5–10 years
Escalations	Flat for 3–5 years; midterm increase for longer terms		
Free rent	1–2 months/lease term		
Tenant improvements	$0.50–1.00 per square foot overall $2.00–3.00 per square foot office		
Expenses	$0.85–1.05 per square foot		

Source: RREEF Research.

Note: Rents and terms are for "new" warehouse properties with minimum 24-foot clear heights and office buildout of 10 to 15 percent (under 10 percent for single tenant).

FIGURE C | Industrial Tenants by Industry in the Valwood Submarket

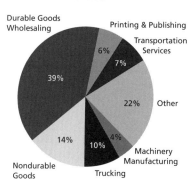

Durable Goods Wholesaling — 39%
Printing & Publishing — 6%
Transportation Services — 7%
Other — 22%
Machinery Manufacturing — 4%
Trucking — 10%
Nondurable Goods — 14%

Sources: Cognetics Real Estate, Inc., and RREEF Research.

A final step in the analysis was to present an outlook and a projection of rents for the submarket. To accomplish these tasks, warehouse space absorption and construction volume were compared and measured by projected vacancy rates. These projections showed an upward trend in submarket vacancy through 2001. It was concluded that warehouse construction in Valwood would outpace absorption, even though the Dallas economy was expected to expand at a healthy rate. The imbalance in supply was expected to correct itself by 2002 as development activity eased and absorption remained positive, but the threat of continued additions to supply remained a long-term concern.

In light of these trends, submarket rents in Valwood were expected to experience only modest growth (figure F). Larger properties of 100,000 square feet (9,300 m²) or more were not anticipated to realize any increase in rents, because much of the increase in supply was occurring in this property segment. The near-term prognosis for warehouse space in the under 25,000- and 25,000- to 40,000-square-foot (2,325– and 2,325–3,720 m²) category was more positive because of a lack of supply in these segments (figure E).

Source: Adapted from a case study by Marvin F. Christensen, RREEF Funds, San Francisco, California, in *Real Estate Market Analysis: A Case Study Approach* (Washington, D.C.: ULI– the Urban Land Institute, 2001).

FIGURE D | Warehouse Construction Pipeline in the Valwood Submarket

Building Name	Square Feet	Developer	Completion
COMPLETED EARLY 1998			
2515 Tarpley Road	36,000	Group R.E.	3/1998
1808 Monetary Lane	67,200	Industrial Prop.	3/1998
Speculative	75,000	Off Valwest Parkway	3/1998
	178,200		
UNDER CONSTRUCTION			
Frankford Trade Center #6	709,920	Argent/Meridian	7/1998
Luna Distribution Center III	260,000	Billingsley Co.	8/1998
Luna Distribution Center IV	260,000	Billingsley Co.	8/1998
	1,229,920		
PLANNED			
Frankford Trade Center 1–14	2,433,774	Argent/Meridian	
Luna Distribution Center II	250,000	Billingsley Co.	
	2,683,774		

Source: RREEF Research.

FIGURE E | Projected Change in Warehouse Rents in the Valwood Submarket, 1999 to 2007

	100,000 SQUARE FEET AND MORE		MULTITENANT 25,000–40,000 SQUARE FEET		MULTITENANT 25,000 SQUARE FEET AND LESS	
	Rent Range	Percent Change	Rent Range	Percent Change	Rent Range	Percent Change
Current	$3.00–3.25		$3.25–3.50		$3.50–4.25	
2Q 1999	3.00–3.25	0	3.25–3.50	0	3.65–4.40	3–5
2Q 2000	3.05–3.30	0–2	3.30–3.55	0–2	3.80–4.60	3–5
2Q 2001	3.15–3.40	2–4	3.45–3.70	3–5	3.90–4.75	2–4
2Q 2002	3.30–3.55	3–5	3.60–3.85	3–5	4.00–4.90	2–4
2Q 2003	3.45–3.70	3–5	3.75–4.00	3–5	4.10–5.05	2–4
2003–2007	Changes in rent will depend on future levels of construction and absorption.					

Source: RREEF Research.

Note: Rents are calculated using the midpoint of the forecast range.

FIGURE F | Completions, Absorption, and Vacancy in the Valwood Submarket, 1990 to 2007

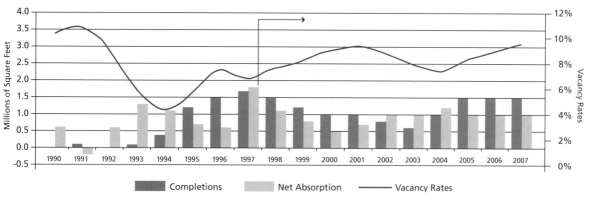

Sources: M/PF Research and RREEF Research.

SITE SELECTION

Selecting the correct site is crucial to the success of an industrial development, and it is important to ensure that as many criteria as possible are satisfied. Location directly influences a development's marketability, the rate at which space can be absorbed during leasing, the rents that can be achieved, and the eventual exit strategy.

EVALUATING SPECIFIC LAND PARCELS. Because they lack the staying power necessary to survive the many unpredictable delays of the approval process, beginning developers should avoid buying land that is not ready for immediate development. Obtaining zoning changes or variances and conditional use permits, installing major off-site infrastructure improvements, or waiting for the completion of planned transportation improvements tends to require more time and capital than most beginning developers have.

It is especially important that water, gas, electricity, telephone, and sewer services with appropriate capacities be available at competitive rates in a site for industrial use. The site should be flat to accommodate the large pads that are needed for industrial buildings and should have a minimal amount of ledge rock, groundwater, or peat with soft ground.

The presence of oil wells, natural gas, contaminated soils, high water tables, or tanks, pipes, or similar facilities can cause major problems and should be carefully studied to determine present and potential dangers. When searching for sites for office and high-tech uses, developers should also consider the following criteria:

- distinctive terrain and vegetation, such as a water feature, that can help market the project;
- the standards of development in the surrounding area and the level of commitment among neighbors to maintain high standards;
- proximity to residential and commercial areas;
- proximity to recreational and cultural amenities;
- availability of shopping, hotels, restaurants, daycare facilities, and fitness centers;
- proximity to mass transit and availability of active transportation management associations and carpools;
- proximity to educational and technical training facilities, such as universities, community colleges, or technical schools; and
- accessibility from freeways, arterials, or mass transit routes.

Despite the desirability of proximity to amenities such as shopping and recreation, industrial tenants who use trucks frequently prefer to be located in exclusively industrial areas rather than in mixed-use areas.

FINDING AND ACQUIRING THE SITE. Public agencies, such as local planning departments, redevelopment agencies, and economic development agencies, possess a considerable amount of information useful to developers in the search for potential sites. Most communities have comprehensive plans or master plans that indicate the areas favored for industrial development.

Real estate brokers specializing in industrial properties are another good source for information about potential sites. Developers should first narrow down their target area and then work with brokers familiar with it to obtain information on sites that may not currently be on the market.

Remaining sites in business parks that are approaching buildout should be considered as potential sites. Extra land around existing industrial buildings, often used for storage, may also present opportunities to expand a building for current tenants or to build another one. Owners of such properties may be interested in becoming a partner for the addition or may prefer to sell the land outright. If the land is in the back of the property, care must be taken with respect to access and visibility to ensure that the new building is leasable.

Infill sites offer developers the advantages of readily available streets, sewer, water, and other public services. But existing streets may be too narrow and space may be too constricted to allow for the creation of the high standards that tenants now expect of business parks. The developer should consult with local neighborhood groups and property managers of neighboring industrial and other properties to learn about potential problems in advance.

Site acquisition for industrial property follows the same four steps as for other forms of development: investigation before the offer is made, the offer, due diligence, and closing (see chapters 3 and 4).

During due diligence, developers should pay attention to hazardous wastes, especially if existing industrial uses are present nearby. Waste spilled locally may be spread by the water table to an otherwise clean site: a small amount of solvent or gasoline can show up as hazardous waste two or three years after it was spilled. Appropriately licensed engineers should perform water and soils tests; if necessary, developers should ensure that enough time is allowed to verify that no toxic waste is present by paying for an extension to the option. Sellers typically give buyers 60 days to perform due diligence for soils and toxic waste and 30 to 60 days for everything else.

Most developers face a standard dilemma during site acquisition. They need time to execute thorough due diligence, while the seller wants to close as quickly as possible. Both desires are perfectly reasonable, but protracted periods of time before closing are usually not met well by an eager seller and they can kill a deal. At the same time, rushing into a purchase to find out later that the site requires major environmental cleanup or going ahead without financing fully in place may be too high a price to pay to win the property.

As described in detail in chapter 3, site acquisition generally takes place in three stages: (1) a free-look period, (2) a period during which earnest money is forfeitable, and (3) closing. The agreed-on terms depend on market conditions. In a hot market, acquisition can be difficult for most developers and nearly impossible for those with financing contingencies.

Howard Schwimmer, executive vice president for Daum Commercial Real Estate Services, faced one of the hottest markets ever experienced in Commerce, California, but following a few basic tenets, he was able to successfully negotiate the purchase of a 240,000-square-foot (22,300 m²) industrial property that had fallen into foreclosure. Recognizing that complicated contracts and legalese in the first stage

of an acquisition are usually not well received by a seller, Schwimmer submitted a letter of intent stating his ability to close the deal in three weeks with cash. A week or two after the seller accepted the first letter of intent, the parties agreed to a purchase and sale agreement that included an environmental review contingent on the transfer of the deed. The property was located on a parcel adjacent to contaminated ground, and lead had migrated onto the seller's property. The lead was discovered during the environmental inspection; further testing and abatement extended the closing date by two months.

During this time, the buyer was able to conduct thorough due diligence and to leverage the project more favorably. The property was successfully acquired at a price considerably below the market rate.[4]

ENGINEERING FEASIBILITY. Preliminary engineering investigations are an integral part of due diligence. In the case of purchasing existing industrial buildings, engineering studies are among the first steps of feasibility analysis. A civil engineer usually leads the site investigation under the developer's direction. Chapter 3 provides a comprehensive review of the site evaluation process for all types of development. For industrial development, the two most significant aspects of this process are utilities and environmental regulations.

Page Business Center in St. Louis is a three-building complex that combines new construction and renovation. Each building meets a different level of LEED certification.

GREEN STREET DEVELOPMENT GROUP, LLC

Utilities. Many manufacturing and some R&D facilities use enormous amounts of water and electricity. Because most water is discharged eventually into the sewer system, both water and sewage services are affected. The capacity to service such customers can be a good draw, especially in areas where the availability of water is limited.

A developer should meet with the local water company as early as possible to discuss plans and to learn about the utility company's current capabilities and limitations. The developer's engineer can obtain preliminary information on flow and pressure from the utility company. Fire departments usually require that the water system and fire hydrants be installed and activated before construction can start on individual buildings.

Some local agencies require the installation of lines to reclaim water for irrigation and some industrial purposes. Some localities require that two parallel systems, domestic and reclaimed, be installed on every lot. The developer should meet with the sewer company to determine the following information:

- capacity of sewage treatment facilities;
- capacity of sewer mains;
- whether gravity flow for sewage and drainage is sufficient or if pumps are necessary;
- the party responsible for paying for off-site sewer extension;
- the due dates for payments and impact fees;
- quality restrictions on sewage effluent: some sewage treatment plants impose severe restrictions on the type and quantity of chemicals that firms can discharge into the general sewage system;
- discharge capacity for sewage effluent;
- flow standards; and
- periodic service charges: although the rate structure for service charges does not directly affect the developer, it will influence prospective purchasers of property, especially heavy users, such as bottling plants.

Cities that use water consumption as the basis for sewer system service charges may penalize projects that consume a large quantity of water to irrigate landscaping. In such cases, the developer may attempt to negotiate treatment costs based on anticipated discharge rather than on water consumption.

Industrial land developers usually must front the costs for water and sewage lines and for treatment plants and then recover those costs as part of the sale price or rental income. They may also be reimbursed by developers of other subdivisions and owners of other properties that subsequently tie into the water and sewage mains. Most cities that provide for reimbursement by subsequent developers, however, do not permit the original developer to recover carrying costs. Moreover, because of the unpredictable timing of such reimbursements, developers cannot rely on them to help meet cash flow requirements.

For business parks with multiple buildings, developers should provide the local utility companies with information about the types and sizes of buildings in their plans so that they can project the estimated demand from the project. Electricity can be a big issue, especially for manufacturing and R&D users. The projected demand is used to design the local distribution system as well as the systems that will feed the local systems.

The frequency of power outages and gas curtailments during the winter should be investigated because this factor can deter potential tenants and buyers. Frequent outages also may influence the developer's choice of target market or may change his decision to purchase the site altogether.

Environmental Regulations. Many federal environmental statutes can affect industrial development:

- The *National Environmental Policy Act* requires projects that use federal funds to produce an environmental impact statement for approval.
- The *Clean Air Act* requires the provision of information on anticipated traffic flow and indirect vehicle use.
- The *Clean Water Act* severely restricts discharge of any pollutant into navigable and certain nonnavigable waters.
- The *Occupational Safety and Health Act* requires employers to provide safe working conditions for employees.
- The *National Flood Insurance Act* limits development in flood-prone areas and requires developers who build in flood-prone areas to meet standards concerning height, slope, and interference with water flow. The act requires that a project not impede the water flow speed and volume that exist before development in any floodway traversed by the project.
- The *Comprehensive Environmental Response, Compensation, and Liability Act*, also known as *Superfund*, addresses issues concerning toxic waste.

In addition, each state and local municipality may have its own environmental laws that affect industrial development.

Concerns about toxic waste, water supply, sewage treatment constraints, and sensitive environmental areas are forcing developers to perform very careful site investigation before closing on a tract. Although laws in most states give developers some recourse against prior owners in the chain of title for problems such as toxic waste, such protections are of little use if developers cannot proceed with their plans.

States continue to work to ease the liability put on developers when they engage in projects that come with environmental wildcards and potentially massive costs. This trend began in the 1990s in Massachusetts, when the attorney general's office successfully negotiated a number of covenants not to sue with developers reclaiming brownfields. According to Raymond Bhumgara, the state recognized that future owners of sites should not be held liable for contamination that they did not cause.[5] These covenants protect developers from being financially responsible for cleanups after taking ownership of a parcel and then having to pull out of the project. These types of covenants were more recently used in Atlanta, Georgia, in the development of Atlantic Station, a massive mixed-use project that was built on a site formerly occupied by a steel mill.

Urban adaptive use and the conversion of industrial properties to residential or live/work spaces generate new concerns for industrial developers. These conversions can have a positive effect on economic development in underperforming neighborhoods but can simultaneously cause incompatible uses in a single zone. Consequently, developers must create environmental impact reports to show, among other things, traffic and noise effects on adjacent properties. The gradual infiltration of residential uses into industrial zones is increasing the sensitivity of environmental requirements in these newly created mixed-use areas.

MARKET ANALYSIS AFTER SITE SELECTION

Once a site has been secured with a signed earnest money contract, the second, more detailed phase of the market analysis begins. The purpose at this stage is to investigate the immediate market area for information about rental rates, occupancy, new supply, and features of competing projects.

An important step before beginning this stage of market analysis is to define the property type or types most likely to be developed at the site to focus the research and determine which other properties constitute potential competition. This often overlooked step can help narrow the amount of research and reduce unnecessary effort.

INDUSTRIAL SUPPLY ANALYSIS. The first task in identifying future supply is to identify properties that are currently under development or construction. A drive through the submarket and follow-up calls to brokers and active developers can yield information on project sizes, completion dates, costs, and rents. Information on proposed projects that have not yet broken ground can be obtained from local planning and building departments.

Estimating the amount of additional space to the industrial supply beyond two or three years is difficult. Industrial buildings take a relatively short time to build, and when vacancy rates are low, the amount of construction can increase quickly. It is useful to look at factors such as the amount of land available for industrial development in the submarket and estimate the number of years before the available land supply is absorbed, given the likely pace of development. Some market analysts and data providers use econometric models to forecast new construction. Those numbers may not be entirely accurate, but they provide an approximation of future conditions.

Developers should keep in mind that the public sector may influence future supply. Cities and redevelopment agencies offer incentives to industrial tenants. If developers are not offered the same benefits as those available to others, they are at a competitive disadvantage.

An analysis of potential competitors helps assess the strengths of the proposed project compared with its competition. Again, a good place to start to collect this detailed data is from real estate brokers or management companies involved in the marketing of industrial developments who may be willing to provide plans or brochures and marketing materials on individual properties.

The developer should collect information on competing projects for the following items:

- overall site area and the size of individual lots and buildings if it is a multibuilding development;
- schedule, including date when marketing was initiated;
- occupancy levels at the date of the survey (acres sold, total square feet leased for each type of facility, percentage of space occupied);

- estimated annual land absorption;
- estimated annual space absorption by property type;
- initial and current sale prices and lease rates per square foot (land and buildings);
- lease terms and concessions;
- tenant allowances to finish interior space;
- building characteristics and the quality of architectural and landscape design, level of finish, quality of materials, signage, overall park appearance, and maintenance;
- development cost per acre;
- major highway access, rail availability, and utilities;
- amenities such as retail services, restaurants, open space, recreation, daycare, and health and conference facilities; and
- developer or current owner.

INDUSTRIAL SPACE DEMAND ANALYSIS.
Demand models for industrial space often emulate office demand models, where a change in employment is a prime determinant of potential space absorption. However, industrial absorption often lags office demand. Multiplying the estimated number of new employees in a metropolitan area by the space allocated per employee provides an estimate of future space requirements. (It is important to keep in mind that space ratios are different for different types of industrial space.)

Analysts should also review other measures of metropolitan growth, such as gross metropolitan product or changes in total population or households. Growth in gross metropolitan product is a good indicator of absorption of warehouse or distribution space because it is a measure of the output of a local economy. Another indicator is manufacturing output as measured by the Federal Reserve Board's Index of Manufacturing Output.[6] Sometimes, demand is tied to growth in another nearby city. Warehouse space along the U.S. border in southern California is correlated with the growth of warehouse space in Mexican cities just south of the border.

After space demand is calculated for a metropolitan area, a final step is to estimate what share of the area's absorption will be captured by the submarket where the property is located. Often, the concept of fair share is used. For example, if a submarket holds 8 percent of a metropolitan area's industrial space inventory, then its fair share is 8 percent. Another method is to examine the historical share of net absorption in the submarket in relation to the metropolitan area's net absorption over time. This information should

The Perris Ridge Commerce Center in Perris, California, is a 1.3 million-square-foot (121,000 m²) build-to-suit facility. When completed in 2009 it became the world's largest LEED-certified warehouse.

provide an overview of how well the area stacks up against other locations. If a submarket is overbuilt, a developer may choose to sit on the land for months before beginning construction.

Allan Kotin, of Los Angeles–based Allan D. Kotin & Associates, observes that market analysis for industrial space has more pitfalls than for other types of development. Industrial zoning is far more permissive with respect to land use than is commercial, office, or residential zoning. Industrial zoning often allows any of the other uses except, perhaps, residential and may therefore lead to overestimation of the size of the market. "There is a blurring of key distinctions in the general category that can lead to such errors," notes Kotin. "Nominally industrial space that is half finished as office space and rents for about $1 per square foot [$10/m²] per month cannot be averaged with traditional industrial space that is 10 percent finished and rents for $0.45 per square foot [$4.85/m²]."[7] Developers must look at the type of use and the degree of finish to determine rents accurately.

Industrial development provides a back door into both office and retail development, and market analysts sometimes mistakenly include absorption figures for office and retail users in their estimates of demand by industrial users. The distinction between product types can be made primarily by the amount of tenant improvements. Care must be taken to isolate the percentage of nonindustrial users. Office users in industrial buildings are often tempted to move back into higher-image office buildings, especially if office markets are soft.

Another concern is incubator industrial space, a frequently abused concept. Originally, incubator space was intended to house small firms that have the potential to grow into large ones. In practice, however, users are often marginal firms. Those firms in incubator space that actually grow and prosper are in the minority; thus, potential tenants should be carefully scrutinized. The different ways of measuring rents must be accounted for in the analysis. Some tenants have full-service leases, in which the landlord pays all expenses, while others have triple net (NNN) leases, in which the landlord pays no expenses. Some tenants have modified industrial gross leases in which the tenant pays direct utility costs, internal janitorial costs, and insurance, but the landlord pays for common area maintenance.

REGULATORY ISSUES

The approval process for industrial parks is similar to that described in chapter 3. Although the basic procedures for platting industrial subdivisions depend on the local area, most communities begin with some form of tentative approval, such as the tentative tract map in California. After appropriate review by the public, the developer is eligible to obtain a final tract map, also called the subdivision plat. The final tract map indicates the lot lines, setback requirements, allowable floor/area ratios (FARs), and other restrictions that determine the developer's buildable site and its density.

The approval process for individual buildings may be as simple as obtaining a building permit or as complicated as the process for a full-scale business park. Normally, if the developer is building within the envelope of the existing zoning and subdivision restrictions, the approval process is similar to that for individual commercial and office buildings. If variances or changes in the zoning are sought, however, the approval process may be lengthy and expensive. Planning commissions and city councils tend to be especially concerned about truck traffic, as well as noise, fumes, and other negative effects of the planned development. Some communities are eager to attract the employment opportunities that industrial development generates, while many others are more concerned about keeping out truck traffic and preserving the character of business districts and residential neighborhoods.

ZONING. Several basic types of zoning districts are commonly used for industrial and business park development. Most common are the *by-right districts*, *planned unit developments (PUDs)* or *floating districts*, and *special districts*.

- By-right districts are the most traditional type of zoning district. Uses permitted by zoning regulations can be built by right without requiring further approvals.
- PUDs are known as floating districts because they can be applied anywhere the locality approves them. PUDs have flexible land use controls that can increase site coverage and provide for a mixture of uses. However, they usually require a long, drawn-out approval process.
- Special districts are approved by the local jurisdiction for a specific tract of land. The special district is then adopted as part of the local zoning ordinance. Provisions of the district are site specific and address issues such as land use, design, transportation, and landscaping.[8]

Zoning restrictions determine the size and placement of the structures that can be built on a given site. Typical zoning regulations for industrial buildings include

- front, side, and rear setbacks;
- height restrictions and FARs;
- access requirements;
- parking ratios;
- parking and loading design; and
- landscape requirements and screening regulations.

Most communities have maximum FARs for their industrial zones. In addition, landscape coverage ratios may be predetermined for the entire site or for the parking areas.

Although zoning ordinances have traditionally separated land uses from one another and limited the mix of uses in business parks, greater commingling of different land uses has occurred in recent years. The recognition that business parks often end up as sterile work settings without basic services or amenities for employees has led some communities to allow plans that include shopping facilities, restaurants, hotels, and even residential uses.

COVENANTS, CONDITIONS, AND RESTRICTIONS. Covenants, conditions, and restrictions (CC&Rs) are private land use controls and standards commonly used for business parks. CC&Rs take the form of a legally enforceable instrument filed with the plat or deed of individual buildings. They supplement municipal regulations, such as zoning and subdivision controls, and apply to virtually every aspect of a business park's development, including site coverage, architectural design, building materials, parking requirements, signage, and landscaping.

Design guidelines can be included as part of the CC&Rs or as a separate document. They establish very specific uniform guidelines and criteria regarding bulk, height, types of materials, fenestration, and overall aesthetic design of the building. Subdivision restrictions sometimes require facilities for employees, such as outdoor lunch areas, recreation areas, and open space.

PUBLIC/PRIVATE NEGOTIATIONS. Increasingly, developers are required to negotiate agreements with local municipalities to secure approval for proposed projects. These agreements are especially helpful in volatile political climates in which pressures for no growth may cause city councils to change development entitlements unexpectedly. Public/private negotiations are also required when a developer seeks to work with a public agency on publicly owned land or in redevelopment areas.

In California, public/private contracts take the form of development agreements that usually take considerable time to negotiate.[9] The agreements protect developers from later changes in zoning or other regulations that affect development entitlements and lend an air of certainty to the regulatory process by delineating most rights, requirements, and procedures in advance. Once adopted, no surprises related to approval should occur. Most agencies, however, require something in return, such as special amenities, fees, or exactions.

The use of public/private negotiations to shape the form of industrial developments is widespread, though not routine. In high-growth areas, public displeasure with the negative impacts of development has led to direct public involvement in negotiations with developers over specific projects. Many municipalities and counties have realized that well-planned industrial facilities such as business parks can provide significant revenues from property taxes. Some communities have therefore established redevelopment agencies to supervise negotiations with private developers and to represent the community's interests as development proceeds.

The public sector's role can include

- sharing risks with the developer through land price writedowns and participation in cash flows;
- creating utility districts and contributing toward off-site infrastructure;
- participating in loan commitments and mortgages;
- sharing operating and capital costs;
- reducing administrative red tape; and
- providing favorable tax treatment.

The role played by private developers is also expanding. Their functions may include paying for major off-site infrastructure and building freeway interchanges.

DEVELOPMENT AND IMPACT FEES. Some stages of the regulatory process require public hearings, and virtually all require some form of fee. The developer should understand the full range and scope of charges before closing on the land. Some of the more common fees that are assessed on industrial development projects include

- **Approval and Variance Fees**—Either a lump sum or a charge for the actual time spent by government personnel on processing an application;
- **Plan Check Fees**—Generally, a percentage of valuation;
- **Building Permit Fees**—Generally, a percentage of valuation;
- **Water System Fees**—Possibly based on amount of water used, meter size, frontage on waterlines, or a combination;
- **Sewer System Fees**—Usually based on expected discharge;
- **Storm Drainage Fees**—Usually based on runoff generated or on acreage;
- **Transportation Fees**—Based on trips generated or on square footage (some areas have freeway fees, county fees, and local transportation improvement fees);
- **School Fees**—Even industrial buildings are charged school fees per square foot in some areas;
- **Fire and Police Fees**—Usually based on square footage; and
- **Library, Daycare, and Various Other Fees**.

The types and amounts of fees vary drastically from one city to another. The developer must learn each city's and each agency's particular system of imposing fees. Because the fees can be imposed by a multitude of agencies, the developer should check with every

agency that could possibly set fees. In many jurisdictions, the building department handles a majority of the fees and can be a good source of preliminary information.

STATE AND LOCAL INCENTIVES. State and local governments have developed a variety of incentive mechanisms to encourage industrial development:

- Publicly owned business incubator parks are designed to accommodate small startup companies; publicly owned research-oriented parks cater to high-tech companies.
- Enterprise zones, created by many states to encourage new industry in economically depressed urban areas, offer incentives to companies that locate in the zones. These incentives include various combinations of property tax abatements, industrial development bonds, exemptions from income and sales taxes, low-interest venture capital, infrastructure improvements, and special public services.
- State and local grants offer revolving commercial loans, loan and development bond guarantees, infrastructure projects that aid particular industries, and even venture capital funds.
- Tax increment financing is useful in areas with low tax bases. The difference between new taxes generated by development and the original taxes

Main entrance, Franke Corporate Headquarters in Smyrna, Tennessee.

is reserved for infrastructure improvements for the designated area. Redevelopment agencies frequently use tax increment financing as a source of revenue for their projects.

Industrial development bonds were very popular in the late 1970s and early 1980s, but the 1986 Tax Reform Act severely restricted the types of projects that could qualify for tax-exempt financing. Originally intended to bring manufacturing to depressed areas, bonds were used instead to provide tax-exempt financing for a number of activities, in both industrial and commercial development. Some communities abused industrial development bonds by using them to finance activities such as fast-food restaurants and other businesses in areas in which conventionally financed development was already occurring. Businesses complained that the bonds gave certain firms an unfair cost advantage and questioned the contention that industrial development bonds actually stimulated much development that would not otherwise have occurred. Despite these problems, a number of cities have used industrial development bonds effectively to generate development in once-stagnant areas.

Financial Feasibility

As with other product types, financial analysis for industrial development is performed several times during the feasibility period. At the very least, it should be updated three times before closing on the land: (1) before submitting the earnest money contract, (2) before approaching lenders, and (3) before going hard on the land purchase.

At each stage of development, more information is known with greater certainty and accuracy. Data from the market study, design data, and cost estimates are incorporated into the financial pro forma as the information becomes available. Developers should not wait until these studies are done, however, before performing financial analysis; cruder information based on secondary sources may be used at earlier stages. For example, as soon as the size of the building to be built is estimated, the construction cost can be estimated from average costs per square foot for similar projects. Contractors and other developers will usually share this cost information.

The method of analysis for business park development is different from that for industrial building development:

- *Business park development* is a form of land development and follows the approach for analyzing for-sale property described in chapter 3.

- The stages of analysis for *industrial building development* are similar to the five stages of discounted cash flow (DCF) analysis for income-producing property described in chapter 4.

For building development, the major decision tool is the DCF analysis, a five- to ten-year pro forma showing the property's operations from the completion of construction to sale. It incorporates rental rates, rent concessions, lease-up time, and expected bumps in rents over the holding period.

Internal rates of return are computed on the before- and after-tax cash flows. Industrial developers like to see IRRs on total project cost of 13 to 15 percent for an all-equity (unleveraged) case in which zero mortgage is assumed. A 15 percent unleveraged IRR typically produces a leveraged IRR (with a 70 to 75 percent LTV ratio) on equity in the high 20s. Leveraged IRRs on equity need to be 20 to 30 percent to entice investors.

The developer should use the financial pro forma to perform sensitivity analysis to test the impact of various assumptions on the results:

- For industrial building development, what effect do leasing schedules have on the IRR?
- How sensitive is the IRR to changes in assumptions with respect to rental rates and concessions, construction costs, financing costs, interest rates, release assumptions, and inflation assumptions?
- For industrial park development, what effect does lowering land prices to sell the land faster have on the IRR?
- What is the effect on the IRR if more money is spent up front on such items as amenities, roads, utilities, and entrances to permit faster sales or higher prices?

Because in-depth examples of multiperiod cash flow analyses for both land development and building development are included in chapters 3 and 4, none are included here.

Design and Construction

This section deals first with design considerations for business parks and second with building design for the major industrial building types.

SITE DESIGN

Site design is the biggest unknown variable in the design and construction of industrial building projects. Therefore, it carries with it the most risk. Jay Puckhaber

---

Hints for Dealing with Regulatory Agencies

Industrial developers offer some advice for dealing with agencies during the regulatory process:

- Industrially zoned areas have the fewest restrictions of all development types, but many areas prohibit certain industrial uses.

- Check the city's general plan to make sure that the property is intended for industrial uses. Problems are more likely to occur if developers want to change zoning.

- Subdividing a lot and selling it as raw land or with buildings requires a platting process that will take at least six months.

- Be sensitive to all community activity that may lead a city to restrict or delay development by means of emergency ordinances such as water moratoriums.

Sources: Donald S. Grant, the O'Donnell Group; and Timothy L. Strader, Starpointe Ventures.

of Panattoni, a large industrial developer, notes that "the science of industrial building design has reduced the structure to a highly refined assembly with few variables; this is why across the world, the buildings are so similar. On the other hand, sites are highly variable from location to location. Soil, site hydrology, and other local conditions can greatly affect the suitability of a property for an industrial project, and therefore a good local civil engineer who understands the local conditions is an important member of the project team."

Industrial building projects require large tracts of flat land as a precondition. They are unable to adapt to significant topographical changes that a residential or office project might.

Site design for a business park must also consider a variety of interrelated variables, from lot layout to street systems to landscaping plans. Flexibility is a key issue. The site plan should easily accommodate new buildings, changes in traffic flow, and division into smaller parcels.

The planning process generally follows three general stages: concept planning, preliminary planning, and final planning. Each stage involves the collection and analysis of information about the site and the identification and evaluation of alternatives. Throughout the entire process, the developer and project planning team should maintain a meaningful dialogue with relevant public agency representatives because they can assist in compliance and in facilitating public support.

PLATTING AND LOT SIZE. Lots 200 to 300 feet (60–90 m) deep are popular for a variety of industrial uses. Large single users may require deeper lots of 500 feet (150 m), which can be subdivided if necessary. Lot width is variable and depends on the needs of the user. If parking requirements are minimal, building coverage may range from 50 to 70 percent of the total lot area. For example, a 20,000-square-foot (1,860 m²) building in an area limited to 50 percent coverage would occupy a 40,000-square-foot (3,720 m²) site. If the remaining 20,000 square feet (1,860 m²) were all used for parking, at 350 square feet (32.5 m²) per parking space on average, then approximately 57 spaces would be possible, for a parking ratio of 2.9 spaces per 1,000 square feet (95 m²).[10]

PARKING. The amount of parking required for individual buildings in a business park is dictated by zoning requirements and users' needs, although frequent-

ly these two requirements differ. Most jurisdictions' zoning and building codes require a minimum number of parking spaces based on the square footage of different uses being built, expressed as a ratio of spaces to 1,000 square feet (95 m²) of leasable space. Ratios have been increasing in recent years, and they now range from one to two spaces per 1,000 square feet (95 m²) for warehouse uses to three, four, or more spaces for R&D flex buildings and other predominantly office uses.

STREET DESIGN AND TRAFFIC. The location of external roads provides the basis for internal street systems in business parks. The ideal street layout for a business park provides easy access to the nearest major highway or freeway and discourages unrelated traffic. A public highway that runs through the middle of a park reduces the developer's expenditure on internal roads and enhances the value of frontage sites, but it also tends to divide rather than unify the development, to bring heavy unrelated traffic through the middle of the park, and to increase the possibilities of accidents.

The more points of ingress and egress in a development, the better. For instance, assume that a 160-acre (65 ha) business park is being developed with an employment density of 20 persons per acre (50/ha). With 3,200 employees at 1.1 per car, approximately 2,900 cars would be in circulation. Three planned access points could probably accommodate that volume in just over an hour. If, however, a half-hour traffic jam occurs at the park nightly and the competing industrial park down the road does not have a traffic jam, the owner of the first park faces a serious marketing problem.

Within the site, roads must be designed to permit maximum flexibility in shaping development parcels because changes in demand could require modifications in site design at some point in the future. Contemporary business parks are most often designed using simple grids common to earlier parks while also taking into consideration topographical and site-constraining conditions.

Because traffic is a chief concern of most communities, developers should understand the impact that their proposed developments will have on traffic. One lane of pavement typically handles 800 to 1,200 trips per hour, depending on the street layout and traffic control at intersections. For purposes of design, developers should estimate the percentage and directional distribution of truck traffic. Overdesigning the traffic system is better than underdesigning it, as the intensity of future uses is unknown.

Design considerations also include road thickness, pavement type (concrete or asphalt), road curvatures, and sight distances for stopping, passing, and corners. Standard drawings of the following items are available in most agencies:

- typical street sections;
- commercial entrances and private driveways;
- culs-de-sac and turnarounds;
- intersections, interchanges, and medians;
- guardrails, bridges, and bridge approaches;
- signalization, signage, and lighting;
- drainage, curbs, and gutters;
- erosion control features;
- sidewalks, paved approaches, and pavement joints;
- safety features; and
- earthwork grading.

Standards are subject to constant revision. The developer usually relies on the civil engineer to ensure that street and utility designs conform to the latest standards.

Culs-de-sac need a paved turnaround of 100 feet (30 m) in diameter to allow trucks with 45-foot (13.7 m) trailers to turn around without backing up. Roadway widths depend on the amount of traffic the roadways handle, median design, and the absence or presence

of parking. Some designers prefer that the major roads leading into a project have no parking and that interior access roads allow limited parking. Street parking can be advantageous to some businesses because it can provide space for overflow visitor parking.

WALKS AND LANDSCAPING. A carefully designed pedestrian system can be an attractive selling feature, particularly if it is connected to a nearby retail or recreation area. If the business park includes significant open space, then a pathway system (perhaps including a jogging path) through the space, away from heavy traffic, is also an attractive amenity.

In designing aesthetic features such as berms and slopes, developers should be aware that mowing equipment cannot handle slopes steeper than three to one (three feet horizontal to one foot vertical). Care must also be taken to avoid interfering with drivers' visibility by landscaping and berms at road intersections. Where industrial uses adjoin residential uses, deep lots, berms, fences, landscaping, or open space can help to create a buffer.

TRUCK AND RAIL ACCESS. Well-designed truck access, docks, and doors are critical to the operation of most industrial facilities. The distance of the truck apron from the truck dock affects the on-site maneuverability of trucks. The current maximum length for a

---

Project Landscaping Checklist

The following basic criteria must be considered when designing the landscape for a business park:

1. STREETSCAPE—Whether dealing with one parcel or a multitenant park, the objective is for the project to look good from the street, for the street to look good from the project, and for the street to serve pedestrians as well as vehicular traffic. Design elements include berming, pedestrian paths, sidewalks, and trails.

2. ENTRY LANDSCAPE—Monumental signage clearly marks and identifies a business park site. For an individual parcel, a site sign might be included in addition to exterior building signs. Standards set for the park dictate the type and placement of signs.

3. CIRCULATION—Site circulation, whether vehicular or pedestrian, should be direct and clearly marked. Wayfinding devices include signage, berming, tree planting, seasonal planting, site furnishings, and artwork.

4. FRONT DOOR—Landscape architecture can reinforce the significance of a main entrance through paving materials and patterns, plantings, fountains, and plazas. Each choice comes with a cost; when projects are subjected to cutbacks, the last thing to go is usually the identity at the front door.

5. SERVICE AREAS—Service areas include truck docks, loading areas, Dumpsters, recycling areas, and outdoor mechanical, electrical, and communications equipment. When

building orientation does not permit complete screening, other methods can be employed, such as commercial and evergreen fences, walls, and berming. Certain plant materials work better for this type of screening, and the landscape architect can recommend what is most appropriate for the site.

6. STORMWATER MANAGEMENT—Local codes contain requirements for stormwater management that typically state water must be retained on site for a period of time before it can be released. Various retention methods can be used, from wet ponds to dry ponds to underground storage. The site's size, topography, and budget help determine which is the most practical and cost-effective choice.

tractor and semitrailer can be somewhat longer than 70 feet (21.3 m). Therefore, the current recommended standard for a truck apron is 135 feet (41.1 m) minimum from the truck dock; some developers provide as much as 150 feet (45.7 m).

The path from the truck areas to the street should be scrutinized to ensure adequate turning radii for truck maneuverability. Developers should separate truck loading areas from passenger car areas to improve safety and to ensure that noise from loading and operating trucks does not interfere with R&D or office tenants.

According to David Hasbrouck, industrial buildings now have truck courts to fit 53- to 55-foot (16.1–16.8 m) trailers, compared with 43- to 48-foot (13.1–14.6 m) trailers ten years ago. Truck yards have increased from 120 feet to 135 feet (36.5–41.1 m) in depth.[11]

Most tenants do not require access to rail. If such access is contemplated, however, railroad officials should be contacted early in the design process to determine design requirements, reciprocal switching limits, frequency of switching service, and general rates. Some business park designs allow rail spurs to be installed later if a new tenant desires rail access. Developers must obtain the necessary easements and rights-of-way initially. It is extremely difficult if not impossible to do so later.

AMENITIES. Support services are an important amenity for tenants of business parks. In smaller parks, service kiosks can be installed. For example, a kiosk containing automatic teller machines, a Federal Express station, and post office services might be provided. In larger parks, a retail service center may be warranted. Specific uses vary widely; popular amenities include delicatessens, cafeterias, or full-service restaurants. Larger business parks can support small retail centers that cater to their industrial tenants and provide services such as printing, office supplies, computer supplies, and food services. Availability of hotel and restaurant facilities is also important to large-scale industrial parks, if permitted by zoning. Car repair shops and gas stations can also provide useful services to tenants.

BUILDING DESIGN AND CONSTRUCTION

The design of industrial buildings aims to combine functionality, economy of construction, and easy long-term maintenance. Beginning developers should study the design and construction of other buildings that serve the same market. They should speak to tenants

to learn which features they require and to contractors about ways to save money. Finally, they should choose an architect who specializes in the particular industrial building type that they are planning, and they should talk to contractors and other developers who have previously worked with that architect. An architect who is an expert designer of office/warehouse space is not necessarily also an expert in R&D space. As with other product types, a team approach to design and construction is the most effective, and, ideally, the contractor and the leasing agent should be part of the design team and work with the architect to obtain a design that is both functional and marketable.

Designers of industrial buildings have pioneered many construction techniques that have been gradually adopted by other product types. Tilt-up wall construction, for example, was developed for the low-cost construction of large expanses of wall. The technology has been adapted successfully to both retail and office development.

BAY DEPTHS AND CEILING HEIGHTS. Bay depths of a building depend on two elements: the stacking plan of the proposed buyer or tenant and the construction system used. With wooden roof systems, bay depths are based on a four- by eight-foot (1.2 by 2.4 m) roof system. Thus, the structural system and design of the building should be based on multiples of four feet (1.2 m). Bay depths between columns are commonly 24 by 48 feet (7.3 by 14.6 m). Increasingly, large users look for bay spacing in excess of 48 by 48 feet (14.6 by 14.6 m) to accommodate more efficient racking and storage systems. Concrete block buildings are designed with the same system—three 16-inch (40 cm) concrete blocks equal four feet (1.2 m). Preengineered metal systems frequently feature multiples of four feet (1.2 m) or five feet (1.5 m).

The developer must assess the efficiency of a building's design from the perspective of the buyer or tenant. A minimal number of columns are very important to tenants. The difference between two and three rows of columns can substantially affect the efficiency of stacking systems. The height of the building likewise depends on prospective tenants. Smaller industrial buildings and small multitenant buildings are frequently 16 to 24 feet (4.8–7.3 m) from floor to ceiling. The floor-to-ceiling height is measured as the minimum distance between the lowest structural member in the roof and the finished floor. Today, large industrial buildings and warehouse buildings are typically 30 to 32 feet (9.1–9.7 m) or higher from floor to ceiling. Because the roof must slope to allow rainwater to run off, the ceiling may be several feet higher. Clear heights above 30 feet (9.1 m) present more expensive structural issues and should be constructed only if the costs can be justified by demand. Although some taller warehouses are being constructed, most tenants cannot use the higher cubic footage.[12]

Older buildings near international airports are attractive to tenants who are part of the *just-in-time* delivery chain, which has led to the conversion of cheap older airfreight buildings. Warehouse tenants in the vicinity of Los Angeles International Airport look for a minimum of 22-foot (6.7 m) clear buildings and wide turning radii for trucks.

FOUNDATIONS AND FLOOR LOADING. Foundation design depends on the dead and live loads of each part of the building. If tilt-up wall construction is used, a concrete beam with steel reinforcement, called a *spread footing* or *continuous beam*, is poured along the line of the wall. The beam may be one foot to four feet (0.3–1.2 m) wide, depending on the load, and 12 to 24 inches (0.3–0.6 m) deep.

In areas with good soil and no earthquake risk, *spot footings* may be poured under each point where panels join. Spot footings are typically four feet (1.2 m) square and range in depth from 12 inches (30.5 cm) in good soil to 18 inches (45 cm) or more.

Where freezing weather is likely, the beam, or footing, must extend below the frost line because soil tends to expand when frozen. In Michigan, for example, footings are three to four feet (0.9–1.2 m) deep, and in Alaska they may go down five feet (1.5 m) or more, depending on the depth of the frost line. Areas with permafrost require special construction.

In areas with poor soils, a grade beam is used rather than a continuous beam to distribute the load over a greater area and to prevent cracking. Steel reinforcement is an integral part of the grade beam design, whereas a continuous beam requires fewer reinforcing bars (*rebar*) and is tied together only to the extent necessary to prevent movement during the concrete pour. The beams may be formed with plywood or by the dirt itself.

The slab is poured separately from the foundation beam, leaving a three- to five-foot (0.9–1.5 m) *pour strip* around the perimeter. The pour strip slab is poured before the walls are formed. In earthquake-prone areas, the pour strip ties the foundation and walls together into a monolithic unit through steel rebar that comes out of the footings, tilt panels, and slab.

Floor slabs that will support 250 pounds per square foot (1,222 kg/m²) provide flexibility for buildings with changing tenants and unpredictable floor loading requirements. This level of floor loading capability can accommodate different weight loads and a wide variety of users over time. Floor flatness is also an important factor so that high lift equipment can operate properly. So-called superflat floors have minimal variations in elevation from point to point and are primarily found in automated warehouses with picking machinery. Superflat floors are specified according to the F-number system that is governed by the American Concrete Institute (ACI 117).

WALL SYSTEMS. Three basic wall systems are in use today: concrete tilt-up, masonry, and preengineered metal panelized construction. Tilt-up wall construction now dominates industrial building construction in most parts of the country, although masonry is still popular for smaller buildings and in parts of the Northeast.

Concrete tilt-up buildings are constructed of large concrete panels poured on top of the slab, tilted up, and fastened together to create the exterior walls. Each panel is engineered with rebar and various steel fasteners to connect it with the adjacent panels and roof structure. These panels, which can contain windows and doors, are generally six to eight inches (15–20 cm) thick, 16 to 24 feet (4.8–7.3 m) wide, and as tall as the building (20 to 40 feet [6–12 m]). This type of construction is very economical because the panels act as the structural support system, the interior wall, and the exterior wall. To prepare for tenants, paint is applied to inside walls, and the outside face of the wall is painted, sandblasted, or finished with gravel to provide a textured appearance. Concrete tilt-up construction is one of the fastest methods of building industrial buildings because the walls are all poured at once, and, as soon as they are dry, they can all be put in place in one or two days.

After the walls are lifted into place, they may be welded or bolted (bolting requires considerable accuracy) to small steel plates that are cast into both the wall and the foundation before the concrete is poured. Temporary steel braces are used to support the walls immediately after they are lifted into place and before roof braces are installed.

Panels often break during lifting so they are sometimes braced with *strongbacks*—steel braces applied to the panels while they are being lifted and later removed. In masonry construction, heavy concrete

Comparison of Industrial Building Types

WAREHOUSE/DISTRIBUTION BUILDINGS

- Clear heights of 30 feet (9.1 m), but moving toward 32 feet (9.7 m) and higher.
- Large interior column spacing of 40 by 40 feet (12.1 by 12.1 m).
- Docks that are 4 feet (1.2 m) above ground level (truck bed heights vary from 3 feet 8 inches to 4 feet 8 inches [1.1–1.4 m]).
- Dock-high doors that are 9 or 10 feet (2.7 or 3 m) wide and 10 feet (3 m) high and double doors that are 20 feet (6 m) wide and 10 feet (3 m) high.
- Grade-level doors of 10 feet (3 m) wide by 12 or 14 feet (3.6 or 4.2 m) high if trucks are to drive into the warehouse.
- A minimum of 135 feet (41.1 m) of space in front of the dock for truck movements. Some developers prefer to make this distance 125 to 130 feet (38.1–39.6 m) to allow for a double row of parking in the space if the building is later converted into a more intense use.
- On average, one dock for every 10,000 square feet (930 m²) for warehouse buildings and one for every 5,000 square feet (465 m²) for heavy distribution buildings.
- Trailer storage, an attribute often overlooked, should provide one to two spaces per door.
- Truck ramps that optimally slope no more than 5 percent.
- Screening for loading docks and truck parking areas.
- Security features, such as fencing, gates, and guard facilities.
- A parking ratio of one space per 1,000 square feet (95 m²) is generous, though the parking ratio depends greatly on the user requirement.

MANUFACTURING FACILITIES

- Clear height rarely exceeding 30 feet (9.1 m).
- Separate entrances for cars and trucks, separate employee and public parking, overhead doors, and loading facilities. A mixture of dock-high doors and at-grade doors is usually an advantage.
- Parking ratios of two to four spaces per 1,000 square feet (95 m²) with an average of about three and one-half spaces per 1,000 square feet (95 m²).
- Emphasis on landscaping features for visitors and employees.
- Emphasis on security for employees.
- Interior column spacing conforming to manufacturing equipment requirements.
- Gas for processing.

FLEX FACILITIES

- One- or two-story buildings designed for maximum flexibility.
- Office space of 12 to 14 feet (3.6–4.2 m) slab to slab for cabling and other building systems.
- Clear height of 10 to 24 feet (3–7.3 m) in warehouse area.
- Parking ratio of four to five spaces per 1,000 square feet (95 m²).
- Curb appeal in building design.
- Campus setting, preferably.

R&D/FLEX BUILDINGS

- A combination of offices and laboratories.
- Smaller bay depths and lower clear heights (14 to 16 feet [4.2–4.8 m]) than for typical industrial buildings.
- One- to two-story buildings with 25 to 75 percent office space.
- Specialized rooms and systems.
- Higher employee density than warehouse or manufacturing/assembly space.
- A parking ratio of four spaces per 1,000 square feet (95 m²).
- High curb appeal.
- Design features such as the extensive use of glass.
- Loading capability, including drive-in doors or docks.

MULTITENANT/SHOWROOM BUILDINGS

- Customer access in the front and truck access in the rear or intermixed traffic when units are back-to-back.
- Ample visitor parking and provisions for pedestrian access.
- Generous use of glass and architectural features.
- Easily divided space.
- Clear height of 16 to 18 feet (4.9–5.5 m).
- Parking at two to three spaces per 1,000 square feet (95 m²).
- Truck access at grade.
- A comprehensive signage program and unified entrance design.

blocks serve as both walls and support for the roof. Sometimes, a layer of face brick is added on the outside of the concrete block. High-quality blocks with sufficient steel reinforcement should be used to support the ceiling joists and roof. Longer expanses of wall should contain expansion joints to prevent cracking, and weep holes should be provided at regular intervals along the bottom course of bricks to allow the brick cavities to breathe and drain properly.

Generally, a block eight inches deep by 16 inches wide by eight inches high (20.5 by 41 by 20.5 cm) is the basic unit of construction. Rebar can be laid in the hollow cavities of the blocks to provide additional strength. Windows and doors can be constructed using metal or wood headers. Many styles of concrete blocks are available in different textures and colors.

The preengineered metal panelized system is fabricated in a factory and shipped to the site to be erected. It consists of a steel post-and-frame structural system and a metal, panelized skin attached to the structural frame. The panels can be manufactured with a variety of surfaces, ranging from steel or aluminum skin to an aggregate or enamelized paint finish. Panelized systems offer speedy construction and low costs.

Prefabricated metal buildings are more attractive than they used to be. They can be designed to the developer's specifications and delivered directly to the site. Metal panelized systems are less costly than other types of systems in buildings where the roof beams must support more than just the roof and in which clerestory spans exceed 40 by 80 feet (12 by 24 m). They are especially popular for traditional manufacturing facilities in which equipment is suspended from the roof.

ROOF SYSTEMS. Historically, the standard industrial roof consisted of three layers of tar paper and hot tar topped with a fine aggregate, commonly referred to as a "BUR" or "built-up roof." In recent years, the industry has moved increasingly to specialized elastic plastics and EPDM rubber, "torch down" membranes that provide a single-ply application. These systems offer greater speed of installation as well as simplified maintenance. In some cases, these materials also qualify for sustainable building credits for their reduction of solar gain and heat-island effect. Roofs made of these materials have become competitive in cost and last longer than the five- to seven-year life span of a three-ply roof.

Different types of roof framing systems are popular in different parts of the country. Wood structure systems, for example, dominate industrial construc-

tion on the West Coast and throughout much of the Midwest, whereas metal truss systems are more popular in Texas, in the South, and on the East Coast. The preferred system is usually the one that is the cheapest in the area.

A wood structure roof system consists of laminated wood beams and girders that support the roof, with four- by eight-foot (1.2 by 2.4 m) wood and plywood panels. Two- by four-foot (0.6 by 1.2 m) or larger wood purloins are nailed to four- by eight-foot (1.2 by 2.4 m) plywood panels on the site and are lifted into place after the wood beam and girders are in place. This system is fast and economical and requires the least amount of materials.

Metal truss systems can be used to span the space between beams and walls. Plywood panels or metal panels form the roof deck. This system can provide larger bay spans than a wood structure. A metal panelized system can span the space between steel beams and girders. Manufactured metal panels are often used with preengineered wall and structure systems.

The connection between the roof and the parapet (the part of the wall that extends above the roof) is also critical. If the parapet is no taller than three feet (0.9 m), the roofing plies should wrap over the top of the parapet to prevent leaks. An alternative (though less recommended) method is to cast a *reglet* (the female part of a two-part sheet metal flashing that seals the roof to the building wall) into the wall about 18 inches (0.4 m) above the roof.

Skylights are becoming standard features in warehouses and can earn a project sustainability credits, such as LEED points, by reducing the need for artificial lighting. They can also save tenants enormous amounts of money on electricity. Some electrical companies give rebates or special credits to developers who install not only skylights but also photocells that turn off the electric lights when natural light is adequate to illuminate the facility. In addition to skylights, roof systems must include a roof hatch and ladder to permit roof drains to be cleaned and cleared, air conditioners to be maintained, and the roof to be inspected. Smoke hatches are also required to vent smoke from the building in case of fire. Requirements for sprinklers have also become more stringent in recent years.

BUILDING SYSTEMS. Power requirements have grown substantially for all industrial uses. Warehousing and manufacturing are becoming more automated; as a result, more machinery and high-tech equipment are needed, entailing a greater need for electrical power.

To support today's power needs and to ensure the flexibility to adapt to tomorrow's requirements, a building should be designed to accommodate both warehouse and manufacturing functions, which typically means 1,200 amps of 480/277-volt, three-phase, four-wire power. An underground conduit should be installed so that capacity can be increased if necessary to 2,000 to 2,400 amps by changing the transformer, pulling in cable, and boosting power without major construction costs. Additional power should not be installed at the beginning of construction, however, because it is expensive. The space for future expansion should be provided so that new power can be added when needed.

Increasingly, manufacturers require air conditioning or evaporative cooling, in part because today's systems are more efficient and affordable than in the past. Though most warehouse and distribution facilities still do not require air conditioning unless they are handling perishable products, the buildings that serve warehouses may need to be air conditioned.

A big change in life safety systems is the introduction of early suppression, fast response (ESFR) equipment. Although traditional fire sprinkler systems react to a fire that is already burning and are designed to contain the blaze until the fire department arrives, ESFR systems can put the fire out, quickly. ESFR sprinkler heads react when they are exposed to 150°F (66°C) for only 30 seconds and then pour up to six times more water on the fire than older types of sprinklers. Adding ESFR systems to a building is expensive because the building structure and roof must be precisely configured to accommodate the spacing of sprinkler heads and to prevent interference with the water supply. However, ESFR remains the most cost-effective method of fire suppression and is often an owner/tenant requirement. One thing to consider is that ESFR cannot be used with clear height ceilings of greater than 40 feet (12 m). This constraint is another factor that has led to 40 feet of clear height as the upward limit for most warehouse buildings.

GENERAL ADVICE
A metal building frame can be combined with tilt-up or brick-finished walls. These buildings typically involve the use of glass skins on the front and back facades and concrete panels on the sides to provide shear strength. Triple-layer insulating glass may be used to cut down noise near airports or industrial areas.

Combining steel with tilt-up walls also saves money on steel. To construct these combinations, the prefabricated building is lifted onto the finished slab; anchor bolts in the slab must be located so that the walls can be fastened to the foundation. Roofing systems vary depending on the manufacturer. The better systems, which include insulation, can be designed to drain into gutters or over the sides of the building.

Interior finishes are more important for R&D/flex buildings than for other types of industrial space. R&D tenants value climate control and comfort; indeed, the developer should treat an R&D building more like office than industrial space.

If the activities in the laboratory or warehouse space generate noise, dust, or toxic fumes, safety features are critical. Air locks may be required to protect the office area from the lab area because a shared HVAC system would distribute unwanted dust or fumes throughout the entire building. By having two separate HVAC systems, a developer has the flexibility to seal off the laboratory area should future tenants require it.

The most frequent problems encountered in constructing industrial buildings concern drainage and roof leaks. A wall that is too thin or a column that is too small could lead to a sagging roof, which, over time, leads to leaks or roof failure.

Some other common mistakes to avoid during construction include

- slabs that are not thick enough, causing a slab to be damaged by the crane;

In St. Louis, 8610 Page Avenue, a renovation of a manufacturing facility (part of the Page Business Center), achieved LEED Gold certification for its core and shell. The renovation retained more than 90 percent of the building's shell and used recycled and regional materials.

GREEN STREET DEVELOPMENT GROUP, LLC

- insufficient wall bracing, causing panels to fall over in high winds;
- failure to preplan the location of utilities under the slab;
- lack of a concrete area for truck and trailer storage;
- insufficient electrical service conduit (if the developer does not provide at least one extra conduit for future service, the slab and outside pavement may have to be torn up to install it later); and
- an undersized fire sprinkler system (if the system is inadequate, some prospective tenants may not be able to obtain fire insurance at competitive rates).

The market for the industrial space determines the type of construction and the quality of finishes. Cost-saving construction tips do not save money in the long run if they make a building less marketable. Industrial building techniques have been evolving more rapidly than those used for any other type of development. New materials and new systems technology often appear first in industrial structures. Beginning developers should avoid pioneering a new technique alone, but they should be familiar with current alternatives and should not fear innovation as long as experienced contractors and superintendents are working with them.

Financing

The considerations for financing industrial development are essentially the same as those for financing other income property (see chapter 4). Equity—from the developer or from others—is invested; interim construction money is borrowed until the project is completed and leased. When the project reaches stabilized occupancy as defined in the permanent mortgage agreement, the permanent mortgage takes out (replaces) the construction mortgage. For this last step, industrial property may have an advantage over other income property: some mortgage lenders believe that industrial development is a more stable investment because its market is less volatile than other markets.

The structure of the financing for business parks is likely to be more complex than that for individual buildings, especially if the developer plans to develop both the park and some or all of the buildings in it. Land development frequently involves more than one interim loan. Separate loans for land acquisition, land development, and building construction may be required. A building project, on the other hand, usually relies solely on a construction loan that also covers part of the land acquisition cost. Equity is required to pay for all predevelopment costs that occur before closing on the property because construction lenders will not fund construction loans before that event. After closing, equity is still required because loans rarely cover 100 percent of a project's costs.

Construction financing is usually nonamortizing. Funds are drawn monthly to cover a percentage of the current project costs, including interest on the current loan balance. The developer submits draw requests to the construction lender based on construction completed to date. The lender's inspector verifies that the work has been done, and then the lender transfers the money into the developer's project account or provides a check directly to the vendors. The construction loan agreement specifies a deadline for repayment of principal, typically from 12 to 24 months for individual industrial buildings. When conditions for funding the permanent mortgage are met (usually based on the property's producing a given amount of NOI for one or more months), proceeds from the permanent mortgage are used to pay off the construction loan.[13]

For business parks that combine land development with building development, funding of the permanent mortgage can occur after sufficient time has elapsed for lenders to evaluate a project's track record. The completed project is appraised and a loan equal to 65 to 75 percent of the value given, based on payments that can be supported by existing and projected revenue. Alternatively, when a business park is partially occupied, the developer may use the cash flow from existing tenants to develop the remaining land, thus reducing the need for loans. When a building is sufficiently leased to support the debt service, the permanent lender will fund the long-term mortgage.

CONSTRUCTION AND PERMANENT LOANS

For industrial land acquisition and land development loans, a commercial bank usually takes the first lien position. It may finance up to 60 percent of the land value and 80 percent of the land development costs, depending on the appraisal of the completed improvements and projected sales revenues.

A real estate investment trust, opportunity fund, hedge fund, or private investor may take a secondary lien position or preferred equity, providing additional funds at rates typically five to six points above prime. For a second mortgage, an intercreditor agreement will usually be required.

Construction/lease-up financing is arranged for individual buildings or for the entire business park. Commercial banks are the primary sources for construction loans, usually at prime plus one or LIBOR plus 300, at 65 to 70 percent loan to value and 75 to 80 percent loan to cost.

Developers should arrange permanent financing only if they plan to lease a building rather than sell it. If they plan to sell the building, permanent financing may hinder the sale if the mortgage has onerous prepayment conditions. Better financing may be available from the U.S. Small Business Administration or the buyer's corporate banker. Permanent lenders look for the following items in evaluating loan requests:

- existing leases on the property, including lease rates, types of leases, and terms and provisions of the leases;
- financial capabilities and history of tenants; and
- general health of the rental market and how the leases compare with others in the market (if they are above market rates, tenants may leave; if they are below market, the property will have to be held a certain amount of time until the leases expire or rise to market levels).

Typically, industrial property must be 75 to 80 percent leased before a permanent lender will fund the mortgage. Permanent mortgages are typically 65 to 75 percent of value, subject to a debt service coverage ratio (NOI divided by annual debt service) of 1.25 to 1.3. At this writing, cap rates for single-tenant triple net leases on industrial buildings range from 7.5 to 9 percent for noncredit tenants and lower for credit tenants. The cap rate for multitenant buildings tends to be slightly higher.

EQUITY STRUCTURE

Equity is always the most difficult piece of the financing puzzle to raise. Developers must use their own cash equity to fund predevelopment costs, due diligence, and other initial expenses. Beginning developers must usually look to family and friends to raise equity for their initial projects. Future tenants can also become partners in a project, an arrangement that provides equity, strength on the financial statement, and preleasing activity. Owners of private companies frequently prefer to own the property where their company operates. They may become joint venture partners, and their companies become building tenants.

Once a developer establishes a track record, institutional investors become a viable source of equity. Although some institutional investors limit their activities to prime office and retail properties, a number of them actively seek industrial properties and developers to form partnerships.

DEALING WITH INSTITUTIONAL INVESTORS

Institutional investors include pension funds, insurance companies, foundations, Wall Street funds, credit companies, and other entities that represent large pools of capital. They are distinguished from noninstitutional investors—primarily private investors—by their size and institutional character. In most cases, institutional investors act as fiduciaries for individuals, corporations, and other investors, large and small, that place their money with the institutions to invest on their behalf. Or, as in the case of insurance companies, they have funds to invest from policyholders or depositors representing many different accounts. Fund managers are likely to raise money directly or indirectly through Wall Street in public and private securities offerings.

Institutional investors play a larger role today in part due to the real estate crash of the late 1980s and the financial meltdown of 2008–2009. When money became scarce for any kind of real estate, institutional investors—especially vulture funds and investors searching for high-yield investments—were among the few buyers for the problem properties and loans.

JOINT VENTURE DEAL POINTS

Pension fund advisers like AEW Capital Management and Heitman introduced the concept of lookback returns in the 1980s as a means of protecting the rate of return they earned as the capital partner in joint ventures with developers. In their capacity as advisers, they act as investment managers on behalf of pension funds, endowment funds, and other institutional investors. The lookback return helps ensure that the developer—*the operating partner*—has an incentive to manage the property carefully and to spend money on maintaining the building because the great majority of his profit is not paid until the property is sold. A typical deal structure provides for the following priorities of cash flow distribution: (1) the return of capital, (2) a preferred return, (3) a lookback return to the capital partner, (4) an equivalent return to the operating partner, and (5) a split of the remaining profit.

At one time, it was common for operating partners to have no cash equity in the deal.[14] Today, however, they typically have to invest some amount of their own balance sheet capital along with an equity capital partner. If the operating partner is required to invest 10 percent of the total equity required, his equity is treated the same as the capital partner's equity for Priority 1, return of capital, and Priority 2, preferred return. This treatment, called *pari passu*, gives the operating partner's equity the same status as the capital partner's equity.

Tiered hurdle rates of return and *promotes* entered the developer's lexicon in the early 1990s when Wall Street became a major source of capital. The word *promote* does not have a standard definition among real estate operators, but among institutional investors, it is defined as the difference between the operating partner's capital contribution and his share of the profit.[15]

For example, if the operating partner puts up 10 percent of the capital in a 50/50 deal, then his equity is "promoted" by 40 percent. Basically, the equity is promoted to receive a disproportionate share of the returns. The promote is in essence compensation for sweat equity—putting the deal together and managing it. The amount of the promote becomes the first thing the capital partner asks (or demands)—the lower, the better.

Tiered hurdle rates of return provide a sliding scale under which the operating partner's promote goes up as successively higher hurdle rates of return are achieved. For example, the operating partner may receive 20 percent and the capital partner 80 percent of the cash flow up to the point where the capital partner realizes, say, a 15 percent IRR. Once that is achieved, the operating partner's share may go up to 30 percent and the capital partner's share 70 percent up to the point where the capital partner receives a 20 percent IRR. Above that, the split may be 40/60 or 50/50. In this way, Wall Street ensures that the capital partners achieve high target rates of return—something that they were able to achieve during the tight capital market of the early 1990s. As the real estate capital market normalized in the mid-1990s, Wall Street and other institutional capital providers were less able to demand very high tiered rates of return in excess of 20 percent, but the basic approach has endured to become a common deal structure with institutional partners.

The major deal points in joint ventures with institutional financial partners can be boiled down to nine main issues: (1) the operating partner's cash equity, (2) the preferred return, (3) profit share, (4) lookback return, (5) pari passu equity payback, (6) guarantees, (7) management control, (8) fees to the operating partner, and (9) fees to the institutional partner. Tradeoffs are possible among the different deal points, and the best choice for the operating partner depends on his needs and priorities. It is a mistake, however, to focus on the operating partner's share of the profit because his actual return depends more on the investor's preferences and lookback returns and the priorities of payback than on the profit split. The only way to calculate the partners' expected returns is to model the deal and to compute the operating partner's return and capital partner's return under different cash flow scenarios.[16]

AllianceFlorida at Cecil Commerce Center in Jacksonville, Florida, was developed by a public/private partnership to transform the NAS Cecil Field into a 6,400-acre (2,600 ha) multimodal industrial park.

WESLEY LESTER, CITY OF JACKSONVILLE

NEGOTIATING RISK

The negotiation over major deal points primarily concerns allocating risk—who takes what risk? The institutional investor tries to shift as much risk as possible to the operating partner, and vice versa.

DEAL SIZE AND FLOW. One important issue is future deal flow. Companies that generally would not consider a deal below a certain amount may consider it when the deal initiates a new relationship with an operating partner who can generate many more deals. The prospect of a steady flow of business from a major local developer makes the effort worthwhile.

CLAWBACK. Another important issue is the pooling of deals with an operating partner. Charles Wu says that Charlesbank Capital Partners insists that all deals with a single operating partner be pooled and subject to a *clawback*. A clawback gives the financial partner the ability to reclaim profits paid to the operating partner in one deal if a subsequent deal performs poorly. Without the pooling, Wu says, "the operating partner has an incentive to 'swing for the fences' every time, because he gets the promote on good deals while Charlesbank eats the losses on the bad deals."[17]

In arrangements involving pools of property with one operating partner, Charlesbank arranges an amount of money for the operating partner to invest over a two-year period called a *program*. The pool of properties subject to the clawback is determined by the size of the program. For example, the program may call for Charlesbank to fund, say, $30 million in equity over two years. If the full $30 million has not been invested within two years, the program duration may be extended or a new pool may be started. The operating partner would prefer to start a new pool immediately to limit the properties subject to the clawback.

DEAD DEAL COST. Another important deal point is the *dead deal cost*—what happens when money is spent chasing an acquisition that does not go through. Due diligence costs on a major purchase can easily run up to $100,000. Who should bear the loss? One would expect that if the financial partner puts up 75 percent of the cost, he should bear 75 percent of the loss. Charlesbank, however, requires the operating partner to pay two-thirds of any dead deal costs because it wants the operating partner to be careful with the money spent looking for deals.

CONTROL. Among the major deal points, control is perhaps the most important. Financial partners have learned that the hardest part of correcting a problem property is often getting control of the asset. The buy/sell clause is intended to deal with this risk. "Capital partners love the clause; operating partners hate it," according to Wu.[18] The operating partner is concerned that the capital partner will activate the buy/sell clause at a time when capital is scarce and will steal the deal from the operating partner. The capital partner is concerned that the operating partner has much more information than he has. He may trigger a buy/sell knowing that a major tenant has decided to leave or that one is about to be signed. The operating partner's protection that the buy/sell clause will not be used indiscriminately is the financial partner's reputation for using them rarely.

The operating partner is naturally concerned about the events that will allow the financial partner to take over control and wants to avoid a situation where the financial partner takes over merely when the property is performing poorly. John Williams says that Acacia Capital does not create economic defaults whereby a property is in default if it is less than, say, 90 percent occupied at rents of $15 per square foot per month ($161/m²/month). But it wants to be able to insist that necessary capital improvements such as a new roof are being made. In Acacia's buy/sell agreement, the party that buys the property has 60 days to close—enough time for the operating partner to raise the cash. If he cannot close at the buy/sell price, however, the other party can buy him out at 80 percent of the price.[19]

CROSS COLLATERALIZATION. Lenders like to cross collateralize properties; developers do not. If a lender is not getting paid on one property, it can foreclose on other cross collateralized properties to satisfy any deficit—which of course puts other properties at risk. Because they hold an equity position with the operating partner in their deals, institutional investors like Acacia do not like to see cross collateralization on permanent loans.

LOCKOUT AND PREPAYMENT PROVISIONS.
Lockout and prepayment provisions prevent the borrower on a mortgage from paying it off within a given time, usually the first two years. Thereafter, the loan is usually subject to a yield maintenance or defeasance prepayment. Lockouts and prepayments are particularly unpopular with operating partners because they prevent or restrict the operating partners from

Deal Structure Illustrated

Figure A presents a deal structure with a three-tier hurdle rate of return. To simplify the illustration, the investor puts up all the equity—$100,000. (If the operating partner puts up part of the equity, the total cash flow for each tier would not change, assuming that total equity remains $100,000. The cash flows to the investor would simply be divided between the capital partner and the developer in proportion to their share of the $100,000 total equity.) Out of initial cash flows, the investor receives his money back and a 10 percent cumulative preferred return on all unreturned equity. After he receives the preferred return (because it is cumulative, it is accrued if cash is unavailable in the current year to pay it), profits are split 80/20 (with the investor receiving 80 percent) up until he receives a 15 percent IRR on all cash invested. For undistributed cash above a 15 percent IRR and less than a 20 percent IRR to the investor, the profit split is 70/30. After the investor receives a 20 percent IRR, profit above that is split 50/50.

Figure B shows the computations and resulting cash flows for this deal. The overall IRR is 38.8 percent on the initial $100,000 investment. Positive cash flows total $290,000, for a net total of $190,000. Line 10 in figure B shows that after the equity and 10 percent preferred return are paid, a cash flow of $161,900 is available for distribution. The first-tier distribution (line 16) gives the investor 80 percent of the cash flow up to a 15 percent IRR, which is $17,533 ($9,520 in Year 2 and $8,013 in Year 3).

Line 29 in figure B computes the cash flows required to give the investor the Tier 2 hurdle of 20 percent IRR. Because

FIGURE A | Three-Tier Hurdle Rate of Return

Investor's equity	$100,000
Investor's preferred return	10% cumulative
TIER 1: PROFIT SHARING UNTIL INVESTOR RECEIVES A 15 PERCENT IRR	
Investor	80%
Operating partner	20%
TIER 2: PROFIT SHARING WHEN INVESTOR'S RETURN IS FROM 15 TO 20 PERCENT IRR	
Investor	70%
Operating partner	30%
TIER 3: PROFIT SHARING AFTER INVESTOR RECEIVES A 20 PERCENT IRR	
Investor	50%
Operating partner	50%

the totals for Years 1 and 2 consume all the available cash, the total to the investor for those years (line 30) does not change. The shortfall at the end of Year 3 of $25,180 plus 20 percent interest, however, gives a required payoff amount of $30,216. The investor has already been allocated $8,013 from Tier 1, leaving a balance of $22,203. The total cash flows to the investor that give him a 20 percent IRR appear in line 38.

Line 43 shows that after paying the investor $30,216 and the operating partner $11,519 in Year 4 for Tiers 1 and 2 combined, a balance of $108,265 is still available for distribution in Tier 3. Because the deal structure gives the operating partner 50 percent of the profit above 20 percent IRR, the $108,265 is divided 50/50.

The first-tier distribution gives the investor 80 percent of the cash flow up to a 15 percent IRR (line 17), which amounts to $17,533 ($9,520 in Year 2 and $8,013 in Year 3). The second tier gives the investor 70 percent of the cash flow up to a 20 percent IRR, which amounts to an additional $22,203 (the

second-tier IRR is computed in line 47). The final IRR for the investor on all three tiers of cash flow is 29.6 percent (line 49) on total cash flows of $121,969.

The operating partner's IRR is infinite. His total cash is $68,031. Note that the sum of $121,969 and $68,031 for the investor and the operating partner equals the total cash flow available (line 2) of $190,000.

In this illustration, the operating partner receives his profit share concurrently with the capital partner—a pari passu arrangement in which the operating partner's equity is treated exactly like the capital partner's equity. They thus receive the same hurdle rates of return and priority to distribution of cash flow. In a non–pari passu arrangement, the lookback return gives the investors *all* the profit up until they receive the hurdle IRR for that tier. After that occurrence, the operating partner receives his share of the profit for that tier. This construction places the financial partner ahead of the operating partner in receiving any share of the profit.

FIGURE B | Lookback Return with Sliding Profit Split

		Input	IRR	Total	Year 0	Year 1	Year 2	Year 3	Year 4
1	**Cash Flows to Investors**								
2	**Cash Flows**		38.8%	$190,000	($100,000)	$0	$50,000	$90,000	$150,000
3	Beginning Balance				0	100,000	110,000	71,000	0
4	Equity Investment			100,000	100,000	0	0	0	0
5	Preferred Return	10%		28,100	0	10,000	11,000	7,100	0
6	Subtotal				100,000	110,000	121,000	78,100	0
7	Preferred Return Paid			18,100		0	11,000	7,100	0
8	Equity Reduction			110,000		0	39,000	71,000	0
9	Ending Balance				100,000	110,000	71,000	0	0
10	**Cash Flow for Distribution**			161,900				11,900	150,000
11	**Cash Flows to Investor—Tier 1**								
12	Equity			(100,000)	(100,000)	0	0	0	0
13	Preferred Return Paid			18,100		0	11,000	7,100	0
14	Equity Repayment			110,000		0	39,000	71,000	0
15	Subtotal			128,100		0	50,000	78,100	0
16	Profit Share 1	80%		17,533		0	9,520	8,013	
17	IRR and Total Cash Flow to Investor—Tier 1		15.0%	45,633	(100,000)	0	50,000	87,620	8,013
18	Total to Developer—Tier 1	20%		4,383		0	0	2,380	2,003
19	Total			50,016	(100,000)	0	50,000	90,000	10,016
20	**Lookback Return 1**	15%			(100,000)	115,000	132,250	94,588	8,013
21	Total to Investor—Tier 1					0	50,000	87,620	8,013
22	Shortfall to Reach Lookback			204,218		115,000	82,250	6,967	0
23	**Recap Tier 1**								
24	Cash Flow for Distribution			161,900				11,900	150,000
25	Investor's Profit Share 1	80%		17,533				9,520	8,013
26	Developer's Profit Share 1	20%		4,383				2,380	2,003
27	Total for Tier 1			21,916				11,900	10,016
28	Cash Available for Tier 2			139,984			0	0	139,984
29	**Lookback Return 2**	20%		307,016	(100,000)	120,000	144,000	112,800	30,216
30	Total to Investor—Tier 1					0	50,000	87,620	8,013
31	Shortfall to Reach Lookback					120,000	94,000	25,180	22,203
32	Investor's Profit Share 2	70%		22,203			0	0	22,203
33	Developer's Profit Share 2	30%		9,516			0	0	9,516
34	Total Profit Share—Tier 2			31,719			0	0	31,719
35	**Recap to Investor—Tiers 1 & 2**								
36	Total to Investor—Tier 1						50,000	87,620	8,013
37	Total to Investor—Tier 2			22,203			0	0	22,203
38	Total Required for Tier 2 IRR		20.0%	67,836	(100,000)	0	50,000	87,620	30,216
39	**Recap Tier 2**			0					
40	Total Cash Flow			190,000	(100,000)	0	50,000	90,000	150,000
41	Total to Investor—Total Profit Shares 1 & 2			67,836	(100,000)	0	50,000	87,620	30,216
42	Total to Developer—Total Profit Shares 1 & 2			13,899			0	2,380	11,519
43	Balance for Distribution			108,265	0	0	0	0	108,265
44	Investor's Profit Share 3	50%		54,133				0	54,133
45	Developer's Profit Share 3	50%		54,133				0	54,133
46	**Summary to Investor**			0					
47	Total Paid to Investor—Total Profit Shares 1 & 2		20.0%	67,836	(100,000)	0	50,000	87,620	30,216
48	Investor's Profit Share 3			54,133					54,133
49	Total		29.6%	121,969	(100,000)	0	50,000	87,620	84,349
50	**Summary to Developer**								
51	Total Profit Shares—1 & 2			13,899			0	2,380	11,519
52	Total Profit Share—3			54,133			0	0	54,133
53	Total			68,031			0	2,380	65,651
54	**Grand Total for Investor and Developer**		38.8%	$190,000	($100,000)	$0	$50,000	$90,000	$150,000

refinancing a property to pull out some or all of their equity. Unfortunately, lockouts and prepayments are a common—almost required—provision in conduit loans from Wall Street. Conduits represent an increasingly large source of mortgage capital funds, including mortgages originated by banks and mortgage brokers. Conduits originate capital through mortgage brokers and other mortgage originators under predefined terms. The mortgages are aggregated and sold to investors in the CMBS market.

Lockout and prepayment provisions are popular for CMBS investors because they ensure that the underlying mortgages will not be paid off early, thus providing an assured period of return to the investor at the interest rate on the CMBS bond. In portfolio purchases of multiple buildings, lockout and prepayment provisions are often unacceptable to the operating partner, who may want to sell off individual buildings to finance the rest of the transaction. If the borrower were to sell the individual buildings, he would need to retire their mortgages (which by contract are not assumable)—an event prevented by the lockout.

STRATEGY AND REPLACEMENT COST. Capital partners focus on the acquisition strategy for any pool of investments. Currently, the most popular strategy is buying properties at prices well below replacement cost. Investors reason that no new product will be built until rents reach a level that supports new building construction. As long as properties are being acquired below replacement cost, those investors have an advantage compared with new building owners, as they can profit at lower rents. When the purchase price is equal to replacement cost, there is no advantage over new buildings and the higher target yields are not likely to be attainable. Strategies that work under certain market conditions are not appropriate when conditions change.

Marketing

Marketing an industrial project is a multistep process that revolves around creating an identity or niche for the development, identifying target users, convincing them that the space meets their needs, and negotiating the terms of the lease or sale.

Industrial developers should start approaching potential tenants as soon as they option a site or consider developing a site already in inventory. A low-key but directed approach that takes advantage of informal contacts often works best. Targeted firms may range from major national companies to regional

firms to local firms to any combination of the three. If a high-quality company is attracted to the site at the outset, it will help launch the development; the initial tenant's prestige sets the tone for the rest of the project. Developers usually begin the marketing campaign by exploiting their existing contacts, but they should also contact key brokers for leads on possible seed tenants. When a project is still in the conceptual stage, the developers will have to persuade initial tenants that the future building will suit their needs.

As development progresses, other aspects of the marketing program should advance, including creating a marketing plan, establishing a budget, preparing marketing materials, and creating a leasing program through in-house resources or with external real estate brokers. The strategy and the tone set in marketing materials must reflect the goals of the developers and target the types of tenants indicated by the detailed market analysis. Care must be taken to avoid excessive and unnecessary costs for advertising and promotion.

Local brokers are often the best source of market information because they know who specific tenants are likely to be. Prospective tenants seeking more space or different space often come from adjacent properties. Local chambers of commerce also may provide leads or find potential tenants for a project.

Beginning developers can sometimes turn their lack of experience into an advantage for marketing purposes. Small developers can claim more hands-on involvement and can give more personal attention to tenants. Their costs tend to be lower because they have lower overhead than large, established development firms.

MARKETING STRATEGY

A successful marketing program requires a clear strategy addressing what the developer is seeking in terms of types and sizes of tenants, rental rates, lease terms and conditions, and the length of the lease-up period. Marketing goals should be grounded in the realities of the marketplace as determined by market analysis and any subsequent changes in supply, demand, and the competition. They must also reflect the business objectives of the owners and investors. For example, depending on their exit strategy, some investors might prefer to emphasize short-term value and thus rapid lease-up, whereas others might prefer to hold out for opportunities for longer leases or institutional-quality tenants that can add prestige and value when the project is sold.

A first-year marketing budget generally ranges from 4 to 5 percent of a proposed project's anticipated gross revenues. The developer should keep in mind that the entire marketing budget must be adequate to cover the entire marketing period, not just the flurry of marketing activity that usually accompanies a project's opening.

Although the major elements of a marketing program for an industrial development are fairly straightforward, it can be difficult to come up with a hard and fast estimate of its costs early in the development process. A rough estimate can be made by compiling a comprehensive list of possible marketing activities and preparing a reasonable cost estimate for each item. The compensation scheme for marketing agents and the degree of reliance on outside brokers are important variables in marketing costs, although fees for agents and brokers are typically separate line items in the budget.

MARKETING MATERIALS

Two documents are essential to a successful marketing program: a technical services package and a sales brochure. The following discussion applies primarily to full-scale business parks, but developers of individual buildings should also have similar information available for prospective tenants.

TECHNICAL SERVICES PACKAGE. The developer gives the technical services package to brokers. The package consists of statistical data describing the project's target market and includes information relating to population growth and other demographic statistics, statutory taxes, real estate taxes, sales taxes, interstate commerce trucking zones and rates, and public services. The package should also include information about utilities, such as typical water and sewer dimensions, capacity, static pressure, and design flows, as well as information on fire protection services and requirements, electrical capacity, and the name and frequency of the rail carrier, if any. The technical services package also addresses

- details of protective covenants;
- development constraints, including setbacks, landscaping requirements, and exterior building materials;
- procedures for architectural approvals for tenant-built structures;
- locations of and requirements for parking and service areas;
- location and design of signage;

- permitted and nonpermitted uses;
- storage requirements; and
- procedures for dealing with objectionable situations, such as noise, odors, vibrations, and smoke.

All procedures should be explained in a positive manner. It should be clear to prospective tenants that the restrictions will benefit their property and the overall character of the industrial park. The information may be summarized in a small pamphlet that the broker can give to potential clients.

THE WEBSITE AND SALES BROCHURE. The website and sales brochure describe the ownership, location, and distinctive features of the project. Usually prepared with the help of a public relations or advertising firm, websites may feature short videos, animations, and other rich media in addition to standard information about the project. Brochures usually consist of a pocketed folder with single-page literature in the pockets. This design allows the contents to be updated without completely revising and reprinting the brochure. The sales brochure should include the following information:

- the developer/owner's and manager's track record, with information on previous projects;
- a list of anchor tenants;
- the overall development plan that identifies the preliminary parcel configuration and proposed road network;
- technical building information;
- relevant site data, including information on utilities and infrastructure;
- a location map showing the relationship of the project to the region, immediate community, and road and rail networks;
- a detailed map showing access to the site and the immediate neighborhood; and
- a summary of community characteristics drawn from the market studies and other sources.

The quality and thus the cost of the brochure needed for successful marketing vary from place to place. In intensely competitive markets and for projects that the developer wishes to position as first class, more expensive four-color glossy presentations are warranted. In less competitive markets, black-and-white brochures may suffice.

BROKERS

Whether the developer should sign an exclusive arrangement with a broker depends on local practice. In some communities, exclusive arrangements are essential for gaining the necessary attention of any one brokerage firm, especially for smaller projects. In other communities, such arrangements are harmful, as they encourage other brokers to steer clients away from the project. In markets where competitive brokerage activity is strong, another method may be to collaborate with the local brokerage community through an open listing. Because this system involves no formal agreements between developer and broker, it is important to keep brokers informed about the project and assure them that they will receive fair and timely financial remuneration for closing transactions.

Industrial brokers' commissions are typically calculated as a percentage of rental income. Rental income is specified in the lease and can be defined as net rent, rent plus expenses, and rent plus a portion or all of the fully amortized tenant improvements. Generally, the commission structure calls for a declining percentage of income for the later years of a lease term, usually after the fifth year. Half the amount is paid when the lease is signed and half when the tenant moves in.

Any exclusive arrangement should hold the broker accountable for promotion and sales. Inquiries from clients, direct contacts, sales presentations, and other activities should be monitored monthly.

Leads for prospects can come from a number of sources. Developers should hold regular meetings or lunches with the brokerage community to keep brokers informed of new developments, modified pricing, and current sales or leases, and they should offer regular tours. Developers should send brochures to clients, industry contacts, and brokers known to them in other communities in the region. And they should maintain close contact with local and state economic development agencies, public departments in the community, utilities and railroads, planning commissions, and redevelopment agencies. Advertising usually requires a steady, consistent marketing program to keep the project in the public's mind.

LEASING

Prospective industrial tenants focus on three major concerns: *effective* rent, location, and building design (especially loading areas) and amenities.

Tenants ultimately focus on the effective rent—their costs per square foot after all concessions have been taken into account (see chapter 5). In multitenant R&D buildings, tenants focus on the costs shared with other tenants. Leases for single-tenant buildings are typically triple net or net-net. In the case of triple net leases, the tenant takes care of everything; for net-net leases, the landlord is responsible for maintaining the structure of the building—the foundations, the walls, and the roof.[20] Leases in multitenant buildings typically provide for gross rent; they resemble those for office buildings in which the landlord is responsible for building operations.

Individual tenant spaces are generally metered separately so that each tenant pays its own utilities. In addition, each tenant pays its share of common area expenses, which are allocated based on square footage. In tight markets, the developer can usually negotiate

Holladay Properties developed Ameriplex in Nashville, Tennessee. (See case study at the end of this chapter.)

HOLLADAY PROPERTIES

annual increases in rent based on the consumer price index. Lease terms typically range from three to five years, although two-year terms are not uncommon.

Tenant improvement allowances for office space in industrial facilities vary according to building type. The allowance is usually a small amount, say, a $15 per square foot ($160/m²), which the tenant can supplement if it wants.

Industrial developers should try to avoid certain clauses in their lease agreements:

- Clauses that require developers to rebuild the building in the event of an uninsured loss are less desirable than those that provide the option to terminate the lease.
- Rights to renew leases should be limited. Every tenant wants a five-year option to renew a five-year lease with preset ceilings on increases in rental rates.
- Rights to expand into adjacent space should be limited. Small tenants may be refused such rights altogether. Developers may give a right of first refusal to large tenants when space becomes available.
- Developers should never agree to hold space vacant by giving an unqualified right to expand into new space after a certain number of years (for example, 40,000 square feet [3,720 m²] now, 20,000 square feet [1,860 m²] more in five years). If a compromise must be made, developers may agree not to lease a certain space for more than a three- or five-year term. If the parties agree to such a constraint on a particular space, however, finding a tenant for that space may be difficult. For example, if the tenant in the expansion space signs a three-year lease with a two-year option, the space may need to be held vacant for the last two years.
- Short-term leases (say, for only two years) and options to terminate a lease for any reason may make financing difficult, if not impossible. Major tenants often want a right to terminate the lease if a condemnation takes place or if access to the property is impaired.
- In California, smart lessees try to negotiate a limit on tax increases so that, if the building is sold, the tenant does not pay the increase in taxes that occurs automatically under Proposition 13. A possible compromise is to limit the number of sales in a ten-year period that can raise the tenant's property taxes.

David Hasbrouck, executive vice president of Cushman & Wakefield, Inc., in Los Angeles says that landlords have become much savvier in recent years. "They do not want to pay a broker on lease options now. It has created a lot of problems in the past, especially on long-term leases with options. A tenant representative has to be very careful. There has been a shift to NNN leases with landlord-specific forms, especially for newer buildings. A tenant has to pay for everything on a NNN lease. They may not have protection against an increase in tax and insurance bases as the result of a sale. Even on a gross lease, a tenant may have to pay an impound for a change in tax basis."[21]

Izzy Eichenstein, CEO of the Oakstone Company in Los Angeles, points out that many industrial tenants lease older buildings. One of the favorite clauses for landlords in this case is as-is condition. Tenants have to be very careful because maintenance of older buildings can be costly. "Lease forms have changed considerably over the last ten years. Both tenants and landlords take much more care about leases now—but mistakes still happen."[22]

Property Management

Industrial developers have become much more proactive in the management of their buildings and business parks in recent years. This attention is in response to increasingly complex operation of industrial real estate and greater concern about long-term value.

Management of industrial properties involves three stages. Priorities change during each stage.

STAGE 1: DEVELOPMENT

During the development phase, the developer's major tasks are to coordinate the installation of infrastructure and to attract seed tenants. Often, the local community is concerned about environmental issues, and, to promote the project, the developer also must display such concern. Restrictive covenants not only protect the project but also help to reassure the community that potential undesirable side effects will not be permitted.

Because of noise, dirt, and increased traffic during the development phase, the developer must foster the image of a good neighbor. Failure to respond to the community's concerns can result in time-consuming delays in approvals and inspections. On-site management is a necessity. Timely completion of infrastructure is vitally important to the seed tenant—the one that establishes an overall identity for the project. If seed tenants encounter delays in occupancy because of poor management, they are likely to convey their dissatisfaction to other potential tenants.

STAGE 2: LEASE-UP

Management during the lease-up stage emphasizes the selection of tenants, tenant relations, enforcement of standards, and the maintenance of the project's public image. Although the preliminary parceling of the property is the basis for marketing individual sites, the developer should still maintain flexibility. The principal concerns of the developer during this stage revolve around the compatibility of potential tenants, their locational relationships, and parceling.

The seed tenant sets the standards for the rest of the tenants. If the first tenant occupies 10,000 square feet (930 m²) of space, subsequent tenants tend to occupy the same amount of space. If the seed tenant occupies 100,000 square feet (9,300 m²), many subsequent tenants will occupy at least 50,000 square feet (4,650 m²).

Site planning and the design of individual buildings are critical elements in maintaining the project's marketing appeal. The enforcement of restrictions on architecture, outdoor storage, and loading and parking ensures the project's continuing marketability. The developer should enforce the standards equally and impartially. Close supervision of architectural standards and especially exterior yard controls facilitates the financing of the project during its mature stages.

Shell buildings and multitenant spaces in partially occupied buildings can remain empty for months. If such buildings are not properly cared for (for instance, if construction rubble is not removed and landscaping is not maintained), they can become unsightly nuisances that lower the value of neighboring property and give the impression of poor management. Developers who lease or sell land to other builders can avoid the problem of unsightly vacant buildings by requiring builders to post a performance bond to ensure conformity to CC&Rs and design controls within a specified period of time. The bond should require that

- exterior walls are finished and the installation of windows and doors is completed;
- all driveways, walks, parking lots, and truck-loading areas are paved;
- all construction debris is removed;
- the landscaping, including trees and shrubs planted in specified locations and sod installed, is completed and irrigation systems provided; and
- landscaped areas and parking areas are well maintained.

STAGE 3: STABILIZED OPERATIONS

The major objective during Stage 3 is to maximize long-term profitability. Revenues, infrastructure costs, and operating expense projections should be updated quarterly, or at least annually. Financial management tasks include cost accounting, pricing, and keeping track of new leasing and sales information, which should cover details about prospects, broker contacts, telephone inquiries, rental rates and available space of competitive projects, and current tenants' lease renewal dates.

The mature stage of a project occurs after it has been completely leased out or sold. Management of the completed development and enforcement of restrictive covenants are turned over to an occupants association, similar to a homeowners association. If

The 1.6 million-square-foot (149,000 m²) Whirlpool Distribution Center at Rickenbacker West in Columbus, Ohio, was developed by a public/private partnership involving the city of Columbus, the Pizzuti Companies, and Whirlpool.

GLAVAN FEHÉR ARCHITECTS INC.

the association is voluntary, it can be created as the developer phases out the project. If it is a mandatory association, it must be established at the beginning of the development so that all tenants and purchasers are bound by its provisions.

Associations can be a source of problems and expense for the developer if they become a means for occupants to press for services or benefits to which they are not entitled. Notwithstanding these concerns, a well-run association benefits not only the tenants and the community but also the developer's reputation by maintaining the standards of the project over time.

The main source of concern for developers during this third stage is the "residuals"—the future proceeds from the sale of buildings developed and any remaining unsold parcels. The developer plays the same role in the association as other owners: if they own buildings with triple net leases, they should inspect the property at least semiannually. These inspections are important for determining

- how well the building is maintained;
- problems of functional obsolescence;
- the existence of restricted activities, such as the storage or manufacture of items outside buildings;
- the existence of potential problems or liabilities resulting from toxic waste; and
- the health and well-being of tenants and whether their operations are growing, maturing, or diminishing.

Various new concerns also bedevil the owners of industrial properties. For instance, in earthquake-prone areas, masonry property built before 1934 must be reinforced with steel. Dealing with tax reappraisals on existing property and trying to work out mistakes on tax bills can consume enormous amounts of an owner's time. Leaking oil tanks on properties several hundred yards away can contaminate groundwater, making it difficult to refinance nearby properties. Defense contractors insist on four-month escape clauses from leases because they do not know whether their contracts with the federal government will be extended. All such concerns demand developers' increasing attention during the operating phase of a project.

Property management for an industrial development varies considerably depending on the building type and whether it is single tenant or multitenant. Covenants play an extremely important role for maintaining a high-quality appearance. Rules with respect to on-site storage, parking, and truck parking and loading areas are just as important as landscape maintenance and trash pickup. Truck parking in older industrial areas can create serious problems, especially if residences are nearby and the trucks impede traffic flow. If loading bays face the street, longer trucks may protrude into the street. This condition will cause continuing headaches for the owner who must contend with parking tickets and constant complaints from neighbors.

Many single-tenant buildings have triple net leases that have no provisions for an on-site property manager. Even though a lease provides for cleaning up the property and properly disposing of hazardous wastes and other sources of contamination, the owner should inspect the property regularly to ensure clean and safe storage practices.

SELLING THE PROJECT

The disposition of industrial properties follows a procedure similar to that for office and retail buildings. The developer can emphasize a number of features to potential buyers:

- the building's functionality;
- the building's adaptability;
- the site's locational attributes;
- tenants' reliability and financial strength;
- the project's financial characteristics; and
- the project's future prospects.

Many industrial developers prefer to sell occupied buildings with ten-year leases during the fourth year, just before the rent steps up in the fifth year. Before that time, the rent is often so low that buyers will not pay enough for the building. In competitive markets, industrial buildings often do not become profitable until after the first increase in rents. Although sales brokers ask for the scheduled commission, commissions are usually negotiable. Smaller developers will probably have to pay higher commissions to obtain the same amount of attention from brokers as that given to larger developers who can offer more business.

Mounting concerns over toxic waste and asbestos make the sale of industrial projects more and more difficult. If the project has any kind of maintenance or fueling facility where petroleum products or chemicals collect, it will probably have to be cleaned up before it can be sold. Although everyone in the chain of title has liability for cleanup, the owner is ultimately responsible. Even though the owner may be able to recover cleanup costs from the tenant, cleanup should be done expeditiously.

Conclusion

Warehouses are far from glamorous, but good reasons exist for developing and investing in industrial facilities. They generally take far less time to build than mid- or high-rise office structures, and, as a result, developers can respond quickly to economic downturns. Moreover, warehouses and flex space become attractive affordable office locations in tight markets. The flexibility of industrial space appeals to a wide range of small business, from light manufacturing to storage to office uses.

Industrial space has other advantages as well: capital expenditures are lower than for other product types, especially office space, and industrial property has a lower ratio of operating expenses to revenue—which means that it will perform better in up markets because more income drops to the bottom line.

Certain trends will influence industrial development in the coming years:

- The push toward greater efficiencies in logistics is leading to the consolidation of distribution centers into larger and more complex regional distribution and warehouse centers, and this trend is lessening each user's total square-footage requirements.
- The traditional role of landlord will change as tenants demand more services to run their businesses efficiently.
- Demand for high-speed connectivity and the ability to accommodate the latest technology will favor developers who build flexibility into their projects to allow for future wiring and other needs.
- The need to control tenants will make in-house management increasingly important to retain incubator tenants.
- Lower current yields will require developers to leave more equity in their projects.
- The entitlement process, which is becoming much more rigorous, will make the cost of improved land much higher; longer approval times will cause carrying costs to increase, and public exactions and development fees will raise the cost of obtaining entitlements.
- The use of nonunion contractors in most areas will be necessary to hold down costs and maintain competitiveness.

Beginning developers will continue to have many opportunities in the future, but they will have to choose their market niches carefully. Beginning developers will need to know the market well enough to identify those areas that are inadequately served by their experienced competitors, and they must be ready to pursue those opportunities aggressively.

NOTES

1. Johannson L. Yap and Rene Circ, *Guide to Classifying Industrial Property* (Washington, D.C.: ULI–the Urban Land Institute, 2003).

2. Interview with David Hasbrouck, executive director, Cushman & Wakefield, Los Angeles, California, May 2000.

3. National Association of Foreign Trade Zones website, www.naftz.org.

4. Interview with Howard Schwimmer, Daum Commercial Real Estate Services, Los Angeles, California, 2001.

5. Interview with Raymond Bhumgara, Gannett Fleming, Inc., Camp Hill, Pennsylvania, 2001.

6. David Twist, "Determinants of Industrial Space Demand," white paper, AMB Property Corporation, San Francisco, July 2002.

7. Interview with Allan Kotin, adjunct professor, School of Policy Planning and Development, University of Southern California, and Allan D. Kotin & Associates, Los Angeles, California, September 2002.

8. Note that the term *special district* is used here to refer to a special *zoning* district. The term *special district* more commonly refers to special funding districts that are empowered to sell bonds to support infrastructure investment, primarily for water and sewer.

9. See Douglas Porter and Lindell Marsh, eds., *Development Agreements* (Washington, D.C.: ULI–the Urban Land Institute, 1989).

10. Zoning ordinances usually require three to four spaces per 1,000 square feet of net rentable office area, although most lenders want to see at least four spaces per 1,000 square feet.

11. Interview with David Hasbrouck, May 2000.

12. Ibid.

13. The permanent lender requires that the construction loan be retired so that the permanent mortgage can assume the first lien position previously held by the construction loan.

14. Even then, they were generally required to have some equity, but the value added through appreciation since the time of purchase in land or buildings contributed to a joint venture was treated as equity.

15. The *promote* is defined mathematically as the difference between the profit percentage and the capital contribution. If the operating partner puts up 15 percent of the capital and receives 40 percent of the profits, his promote is 25 percent.

16. See Pete Gregovich, Phil Lukowski, Steve McSkimming, Don Morse, and Paul Saint-Pierre, "Going beyond the AIMR Performance Presentation Standards: Recommendations on Distributed Income Returns," *Real Estate Finance*, Fall 1996, pp. 34–92.

17. Charles Wu, managing director of real estate investments, Charlesbank Capital Partners (formerly Harvard Private Capital Group), lecture at the Harvard Graduate School of Design, December 2000.

18. Ibid.

19. Interview with John Williams, former partner, Acacia Capital, New York, New York, 1988.

20. Gregovich et al., "Going beyond the AIMR Performance Presentation Standards," pp. 34–92.

21. Interview with David Hasbrouck, May 2000.

22. Interview with Izzy Eichenstein, CEO, Oakstone Company, Los Angeles, California, June 2000.

CASE STUDY: Ameriplex, Nashville, Tennessee

The Nashville office of Holladay Properties was founded as a satellite office in 1986. Tom Gibson, the local Holladay partner, was familiar with industrial development from working as a leasing agent and developer in Holladay's Indiana office. The Elm Hill Pike industrial corridor in Nashville is located midway between downtown and the airport. Historically, this submarket was one of the stronger industrial areas in the Nashville metropolitan statistical area. Over the years, Holladay had developed several projects in this area:

- In 1986, Holladay developed the Fesslers Lane Business Park and two office flex projects in that development.

- In 2006, Holladay purchased a property along Elm Hill Pike and redeveloped the building for Gibson Guitar's custom manufacturing plant.

- In 2008, a second 171,000-square-foot (16,000 m²) building in this area was purchased and rehabilitated for a local candy company.

A U.K.-based holding company owned 35 acres (14 ha) behind the Gibson building. The same broker that represented Holladay in the Gibson transaction had listed the site. After

FIGURE A | Project Market Cycle Analysis

Overall industrial vacancy rate 5.5%

	Vacancy Rate (%)	Square Feet (millions)
Southeast	7.5	50.0
Industrial Central Business District	**4.0**	**47.3**
North	5.2	43.6
East	10.1	15.9
West	1.2	13.5
South	4.9	12.5
PRODUCT TYPES—VACANCY RATES		
A Bulk	13.1	
Other Bulk	**2.8**	
Warehouse	**4.2**	
Manufacturing	3.4	
Business Center	11.8	

much negotiation, the property was put under contract at $1,050,000 with a 90-day due diligence period, with an opportunity to extend the due diligence for an additional 60 days. Holladay had extensive knowledge of the property. The reason this site was still available was it had a number of difficult development issues. The property had severe topography; was located next to Mill Creek, which was home to the endangered Nashville crayfish; and was bordered by a gasoline pipeline. The site had a sinkhole, and areas of the site had been filled over the years with suspect material. After a good bit of back and forth, the contract was executed in April 2007.

Work immediately commenced on the due diligence process. An architect and geotechnical and environmental consultants were hired. The architect developed a preliminary site plan for two 100,000-square-foot (9,300 m²) buildings at the top of the site with a shared service court. An additional 80,000-square-foot (7,400 m²) building would be located at the bottom of the site. This site plan seemed to be fairly efficient and functional. The site had two access points: one was an easement through the Gibson Guitar property and the other was an owned access off Elm Hill Pike. The owned access was a combination of commercial and ten-unit-per-acre (R-10) residential zoning. The plat clearly stated that grading was permitted through this area for an access road.

The geotechnical consultant suggested that Holladay do a series of borings at the top and bottom of the site and dig test pits. Since the site was heavily wooded, it required heavy machinery to cut paths for the geotechnical crews. These same paths would also need to be used to verify topographic information. The city's aerial topographic maps were used for the initial studies. This information was dated and the accuracy of the data needed to be verified.

The due diligence team turned up a number of issues that were of concern:

- The test pits showed a large area on the site that had been filled. The test pits revealed that the fill was a combination of topsoil, rock, and organics, and this material was unsuitable to support a structure.

- There was a slight depression in the northwestern corner of the site that was labeled wetlands. The environmental consultant believed that this area was not wetlands but would have to get an opinion from the Tennessee Department of Environment and Conservation (TDEC) and the Army Corps of Engineers.

- A former streambed ran through the site. This stream had been cut by municipal sewer work and a gasoline pipeline. As a consequence, it was the due diligence team's opinion that it was merely site drainage and not a blue-line stream. This opinion would, however, need to be reviewed by state authorities.

- There was a sinkhole at the southeastern corner of the site that fed into Mill Creek, which was habitat for the endangered Nashville crayfish.

- The sinkhole issue was the least disturbing as this area was intended for Phase III of the development. It would, however, affect the ability to balance the site because no blasting was allowed to mine limestone for fill material. The issues that needed immediate attention were the wetlands and the blue-line stream.

The development team tried to track all these items simultaneously. These issues were also disclosed to the seller and an extension of the due diligence period was negotiated.

The site layout continued its evolution as TDEC negotiations continued. The geotechnical consultant indicated that approximately 20,000 cubic yards (15,300 m³) of bad fill material would

CONTINUED

have to be moved and replaced. A number of options were evaluated, including reconfiguring the building to a U shape, completing the original design with a floating slab and surcharging the site by adding good soil.

An updated analysis of the market was prepared that demonstrated that the project would hit a "sweet spot" in the Elm Hill Pike submarket. The overall industrial market consisted of 160 million square feet (14 million m²). Ameriplex's submarket consisted of 14 million square feet (1.3 million m²) with a 4 percent vacancy rate. Market rents for upscale office warehouse space were $4.50 per square foot ($48.50/ha) for warehouse and $11 to $11.50 ($118–124/ha) for office space. The market research indicated that there was a pent-up demand for 10,000- to 60,000-square-foot (920–5,600 m²) spaces. Market cycle analysis and submarket information demonstrates that demand, rents, and occupancy were favorable for a project of this type (see figure A).

The development team felt they could gain a market advantage if the project was the first industrial LEED project in Nashville. They believed the LEED concepts would be attractive to both local and national tenants. National tenants appreciated the PR value of being in a green building. LEED was to be marketed to local tenants on the added value achieved in total occupancy costs savings. The marketing team would demonstrate that the total occupancy costs would be lower due to the design features of the building, which would include

- solar lighting on the roadway to the project;
- programmed, dimmable, high-efficiency exterior lights;
- sustainable landscaping that does not require maintenance or mowing;

- a water retention system that captures water from the roof to use for irrigation in lieu of purchasing water from the city for this purpose;
- added insulation in the building;
- motion sensor controls on high-intensity interior lighting;
- permeable concrete paving that allows water to go directly into the groundwater, reducing the need for expensive on site detention; and
- daylighting wall panels in the warehouse that reduce the need for artificial interior lighting.

Based on the initial projections, Holladay estimated that tenants could be offered occupancy savings of $0.25 to $0.30 per square foot ($2.69–$3.23/ m²) per year by virtue of the buildings' LEED features. When this savings was combined with the other functional design features, the development team believed the project was economically sound. Other significant building features included

- 24-foot (7.3 m) minimum clear ceiling height;
- ample truck dock court; and
- abundant surface parking.

ENTITLEMENTS

The site was zoned IR (Industrial Restrictive) except for one small section, which was a part of the owned access. The plat clearly stated that no grading could be done in this area, with the exception of an access road. Holladay's consultants believed that the access road going through R-10 would not be a problem because it was not prohibited under R-10 zoning and was called out on the plat. Unfortunately, when the final building plans were submitted to the city, Holladay was informed that although roadways were permitted in R-10, a commercial drive, as a matter of policy, was not permitted in R-10 and this portion of the property would need

to be rezoned. A meeting was immediately set with a public relations consultant to strategize about how to approach this rezoning appropriately. The property bordered a lower-middle-class residential neighborhood, and Holladay wanted to be certain to approach the community in a politically correct fashion. The public relations consultant provided background information on the local councilman and developed a communications plan for presenting project information to the neighborhood.

A meeting was arranged with the councilman, and he was given an overview of similar developments that Holladay had completed elsewhere in the country. The councilman was informed that as a matter of right the secondary access and the remainder of the property could be used for a number of uses that would be far less aesthetically pleasing and would be more objectionable than a LEED-certified office warehouse. The councilman suggested that a specific use zoning be pursued, as it would assure the neighborhood residents that the rezoning would be specific to the use and plan that was submitted for approval. This suggestion proved to be very helpful. Holladay commenced writing letters to all the residents in the neighborhood that had to be notified according to statute. The letters were followed up by canvassing the neighborhood to explain the project and the proposed development. A public meeting was subsequently held at a neighborhood middle school at which the development team gave a PowerPoint presentation on Holladay's résumé and the project.

The neighborhood residents were concerned with lighting and security. The neighbors were assured that lighting would be minimal and that energy-efficient, dimmable fixtures would be installed along the roadway to further reduce the level of lighting during those times when lighting was not necessary for vehicular traffic. They also expressed concern about security and were informed that Holladay planned a card-accessed, gated development, which placated their concerns. Due to the approach taken, the rezoning went smoothly and it was approved without opposition.

PRECONSTRUCTION

After review of various plans, the development team decided to proceed with the original concept, which called for two buildings with a common service court.

Holladay still had to sort through several environmental issues on the lower portion of the site, but any developable ground in this area would not affect the feasibility of the project. The ten acres of land along Mill Creek were effectively the hidden asset.

A number of site-work contractors were interviewed and asked to review the preliminary plans and provide estimates and value engineering ideas for the grading plan. Summit Constructors was a contractor that proved to be the most creative. Summit was selected and the development team worked diligently with the firm on the final grading plan. Summit's team suggested that, in lieu of expensive footings, the bad fill could be excavated, sorted, and reused as acceptable to the geotechnical engineers, thus substantially reducing the costs associated with this issue. They also suggested that some of the bad fill material could be used on slopes and other areas to avoid the expense of hauling off surplus material. The civil engineer initially designed the site utilities with two waterlines. Summit suggested a single large waterline with a "T" would be more cost-effective. Monitoring plates were put under the topsoil and when they showed no movement, the topsoil could be removed or sold. This process prevented a very expensive footing system or the need to import shot rock fill.

The development team then proceeded to meet with several general contractors and commenced bidding the construction of the building shell. They solicited value engineering ideas from three contractors and implemented those that would reduce cost without affecting the quality of the project. One general contractor had an in-house structural engineering department that proved to be very helpful, suggesting that the steel requirements could be minimized if some of the load-bearing elements were shifted to the tilt-up walls.

During the preconstruction process, the national economy began to deteriorate, which was cause for concern. In an effort to respond to the market, a decision was made to phase the project and initially build only 90,000 square feet (8,300 m²). It was more cost-effective to mass grade on the site with the construction of the first phase. This approach would allow subsequent phases to be delivered more quickly as the economy recovered. The slowdown in the economy proved to be beneficial, as construction costs dropped almost $3 per square foot ($32/m²) below budget for the core and shell. The site work was approximately $1 million below what it would have been in a more heated economy.

FINANCING

Holladay's CEO indicated that it was important to find a joint venture partner to help fund equity for this project as Holladay had several large projects underway in its various regional offices. The CEO stressed that availability of equity capital for a project of this magnitude was limited. Initial projections showed Phase I project costs of approximately $12.5 million, with an equity requirement of approximately $2.5 million. A cost breakdown is shown in figure B.

Holladay contacted Q10 Vista, a commercial mortgage broker, in search of an equity partner, which in turn located a life insurance company that had a joint venture program. Under the joint venture program, the developer puts in 10 percent of the equity and the life insurance company puts in 90 percent. Each party receives a pari passu, 8 percent return on its equity. When the preferred return is met, cash flow and/or refinancing proceeds are split 50/50.

The life insurance company also provided a permanent loan takeout. However, the life insurance company's preference was to place the debt with a third party. The takeout, which was not contingent on leasing, allowed the developer to get construction financing in a difficult market.

The joint venture partner liked the fact that the project was industrial and was in an in-fill location between downtown and the airport in the preferred industrial corridor in Nashville. It was also impressed with Holladay's track record in developing similar projects in other markets.

LEED DESIGNATION

Very few industrial buildings had been constructed with the LEED Core and Shell designation and none had been done in Nashville before the construction of Ameriplex. To achieve LEED certification, one must have a LEED consultant to certify and commission the building. In this case, Hastings Architecture Associates, LLC, was hired as the LEED consultant. During the predesign sessions, the development team went through the preliminary questionnaire and felt that they could achieve LEED certification for the site and the building. (A LEED for Core and Shell project checklist can be found at www.uli.org/PRED.)

CONTINUED

Holladay also decided that its local corporate offices would be LEED certified and would include the following features:

- high-efficiency, motion sensor lighting controls;
- Trane variable air volume systems with a sophisticated energy management system;
- carpet tiles with recycled content;
- wood flooring with recycled content;
- recycled glass tiles in bathrooms; and
- wood products from renewable forests.

The project achieved LEED precertification with the LEED Silver designation. It was being delivered below budget as a LEED project.

CONSTRUCTION

The site work had taken longer than anticipated because of rezoning issues and other problems. The target goal was to have the pad for the first building complete and ready to start construction in May 2009. The pad was approximately 60 days late, primarily due an extremely wet spring in Nashville.

Holladay would be moving its corporate offices from a building down the street into the new construction. The existing location, a rehabilitated printing plant, had been sold to a health insurance company, and the new owner had to be in the building no later than October 15, 2009. This timeline presented serious scheduling problems, and the critical path indicated that the tenant finishes in the new Holladay suite would need to be completed in four weeks to meet it. A typical timetable for constructing 11,000 square feet (1,000 m²) of office space would be eight to nine weeks.

In an effort to further reduce costs, the development team segmented the contracts. They contracted directly for the site utilities, steel building, earthwork, and paving. A general contractor was hired to construct the building shell.

FIGURE B | Project Cost Summary

Item	Cost	Cost/Ft² of Bldg Area
LAND ACQUISITION COSTS, PHASE 1		
Purchase price	$897,600	$4.53
Closing costs (1%)	8,976	0.05
Subtotal Land Acquisition Costs	**$906,576**	**$4.58**
HARD COSTS		
Site grading & infrastructure	2,625,000	13.26
Building shell (198,000 ft²)	4,851,000	24.50
Office (20%)		
Office buildout allowance ($38.00/ft²)	1,504,800	7.60
Paving & landscaping (20,000 yd²)	390,000	1.97
Tenant improvement allowance/demising	136,000	0.69
Subtotal Hard Costs	**$9,506,800**	**$48.01**
SOFT COSTS		
Architectural costs—base building	35,640	
Architectural costs—interiors	39,600	
Building permit	25,023	
Civil engineering & planning	131,180	
Closing & recording	25,000	
Development fee	380,272	
Environmental report	7,000	
Materials testing	9,507	
Legal fees	15,000	
Liability insurance	6,500	
Marketing & advertising	25,000	
Real estate taxes—construction	17,007	
Recording fees	6,000	
Reimbursable expenses	6,000	
Survey	10,000	
Tenant improvement coordination	35,640	
Title work	30,580	
Signage	40,000	
Broker fees	223,255	
Vacancy	320,905	
Construction management	149,520	
Soft cost contingency (5%)	69,455	
Subtotal Soft Costs	**$1,608,085**	**$8.12**
FINANCING COSTS		
Appraisal	5,000	
Construction loan fees	104,134	
Construction interest reserve	269,257	
Permanent loan fee	95,068	
Lender inspection fees	6,000	
Subtotal Financing Costs	479,459	2.42
Total Costs	**$12,500,920**	**$63.14**

The interior finishes were bid by the general contractor and two interior finish contractors.

Tilt-up construction requires the slab to be poured so the wall panels can be formed on the slab. At Ameriplex, two 45,000-square-foot (4,200 m²) pours would be made. Because of the summer heat in Nashville, the pours were made at night. An unexpected storm rained on one section of the slab damaging the concrete, which required some creative repairs. That event had an adverse effect on an already-tight timeline.

The steel arrived on site in a timely manner and was priced below the original estimate. During construction, the general contractor discovered that the bar joist manufacturer had incorrectly fabricated the bar joists and field modifications had to be made. The steel supplier made the changes and agreed to fund certain overtime charges that would be required to meet the timeline for the Holladay interior finish work. The schedule lost two weeks during the refabrication of the joists.

The HVAC equipment was delivered for the Holladay space approximately three weeks before the planned occupancy. Unfortunately, Nashville Electric Service could not provide utilities for the site until approximately three days before scheduled occupancy. As a consequence, a generator had to be rented so the HVAC unit could be fired up to dehumidify the space to allow drywall and paint to cure properly. Air filters in the space were changed frequently to avoid damage to the unit and to ensure interior air quality. In the final two weeks, crews had to work weekends and nights to complete the space. Permits were obtained from the city the day before the

move. Holladay moved into its offices as work continued on the second half of the building.

LEASING AND MARKETING

The property was listed, locally with Colliers Turley Martin Tucker and with Ronnie Wenzler, who concentrated his efforts in this submarket. He had more than 20 years of industrial brokerage experience in the Nashville community. Holladay had a longstanding relationship with Wenzler and had faith in his abilities and integrity. Wenzler was brought in during the conceptual stages to provide invaluable input on the property design, layout, and amenities. Having branded several projects in other cities with the Ameriplex name, Holladay decided to name the project Ameriplex at Elm Hill.

As new construction, the development would be priced at top of the market. As a consequence, the development team had to demonstrate a value proposition. They believed the green features and the cost savings that would accrue to the tenants would provide a competitive advantage so the marketing strategy did not focus on rent rate, but rather on total occupancy costs. The tenant spaces were separately metered. The energy efficiency of the building and its sophisticated lighting package produced significant operating cost savings to the tenant. Early in preleasing efforts, the marketing team nearly secured a clothing company's research department. But just as leases were being circulated for signatures, the company elected to undergo a reorganization, killing the transaction. This loss was disheartening, but the team continued to believe in the great location and the quality of the product.

As the building neared completion, Holladay experienced an increased level of leasing activity, indicating that the economy was starting to recover. A major HVAC company wanted to relocate its R&D function from California to Nashville to be closer to its manufacturing plant. This company was impressed by the green features of the building and its central location. After several rounds of negotiation, a lease was signed for 23,000 square feet (2,100 m²) and the firm moved into the building 90 days after completion of the shell. Following this tenant's commitment, the building's remaining 55,000 square feet (5,100 m²) was fully leased to two additional tenants, in approximately six months.

FINANCIAL SUMMARY

The financial projections in figure C reflect completion of Phase I, including 90,000 square feet (8,400 m²) and 18 pad-ready acres (7 ha). Valuation is based on NOI of $552,000. This project will have a value of $9,915,000, assuming a capitalization rate of 9 percent. The equity created amounts to almost $1,000,000 for the owners. Fully developed, the value of the 300,000-square-foot (28,000 m²) project is expected to be approximately $20,500,000, at a 9 percent cap rate, at a cost of $16,000,000, creating over $4,000,000 of equity for the owners.

FIGURE C | Ameriplex Financial Projections

Building	$6,140,000
11 acres pad	$2,200,000
7 acres	$1,575,000
Total value	$9,915,000

7

Retail Development

NICK A. EGELANIAN

Retail development can range from the construction of a single store on a small parcel to the development of a superregional shopping center. It can be the remodeling of street retail shops in older urban settings or a new town center in combination with office and residential uses. Typically, beginning developers will be involved in the middle range of this spectrum, developing something larger than a single store but smaller than a major shopping center.

Retailing is an evolving business, and this is particularly true today with the challenges of Internet retailing, changing consumer behavior, antigrowth initiatives, and an identity crisis among retailers and the developments they occupy.

This chapter uses the shopping center as the basis for discussion, as shopping centers encompass all the aspects of retail development that a developer needs to consider.

A shopping center is a group of structurally unified commercial establishments built on a site that is planned, developed, owned, and managed as an operating unit related in its location, size, and types of shops to the trade area that it serves. Its primary purpose is the delivery of goods and services to end users, or consumers. The function, positioning, and even the valuation of shopping centers are governed by a largely different set of rules and practices than any other type of real estate.

Shopping centers are often classified by their size, location, or physical characteristics, with the types of products sold playing only a small role. But as retailers and the shopping center industry have evolved and stratified, the types of goods and services offered can be used to define two broad classes of shopping centers and the principles governing them: (1) those dealing in commodity goods and services and (2) those providing specialty goods and services—in simpler terms, daily needs versus discretionary purchases.

Commodity shopping centers are shopping venues whose primary purpose is the delivery of retail goods and services that are consumed on a regular basis from a household's primary funds. Commodity goods are often purchased without emotional connection but are primarily chosen based on price and convenience. Stores typically located in commodity centers include grocery stores, drugstores, fast-food outlets, and discounters.

By contrast, specialty shopping centers emphasize emotional feelings attained from the shopping experience, as delivered in a combination of product and place. Specialty retail goods and services are often optional purchases made from discretionary funds. Their purchase involves emotionally driven choices by consumers on how and where to spend discretionary time and income; and for which the shopper's experience is a central motivation for choosing the shopping venue. Stores in specialty shopping centers might include clothing boutiques, art galleries, gourmet food shops, and the like.

Some shopping centers may contain both commodity and specialty retail offerings; and there may be some uncertainty in classifying certain retailers as either "commodity" or "specialty."

The goal of every shopping center is to create a compelling environment for the delivery of goods and services to consumers. The mechanics of building shopping centers have changed little in the last two or three decades, but how retail buildings are arrayed by developers and used by retailers has fundamentally

Legacy Place in Dedham, Massachusetts.

changed. Today, developers must build centers to either efficiently deliver commodity goods and services or creatively stimulate the expenditure of discretionary time and income by creating unique specialty places and product mixes. Although it is necessary to understand the mechanics of developing shopping centers, it is equally important to understand the commodity or specialty market segment the shopping center will serve and the competitive environment in which it will operate.

The Evolution of Shopping Centers

Since the 1900s, significant changes in transportation and retail distribution systems have dramatically altered the organization and function of retail development. Each generational change in transportation systems and retailing formats has led to major revolutions in shopping center design. Likewise, how retailers display and distribute goods is critical to understanding the buildings and shopping center infrastructure they require. Today, the shopping center industry is nearing the end of its third major evolutionary shift, one that has all but ended the once-dominant position of full-line department stores and many of the regional shopping centers they have traditionally anchored.

FROM DOWNTOWNS TO BIG-BOX RETAILING

Without automobiles, there would be no shopping centers. Before mass production of automobiles, most Americans lived in cities or towns and shopped in downtowns for virtually all household goods and services. Urban centers in the United States, modeled after well-established, centuries-old European counterparts, usually featured integrated transit systems and functioned as hubs of commerce, and as social, cultural, and political centers, with general merchandise stores at the center of retailing. By the mid-1900s, most cities throughout the United States boasted their own homegrown department stores. From Macy's in New York, to Hudson's in Detroit, to Bullock's in Los Angeles, early department stores sold virtually everything a household would need. This model of retail shopping dominated well into the 20th century.

By the late 1940s, with the Great Depression and World War II behind it, the country entered an era of prosperity and personal mobility. New suburbs required facilities to support rapidly growing populations, and the stage was set for a period of unprecedented shopping center growth. Lacking established

Today, big-box retailers may be configured as a town center or in another format. At Lockwood Place Retail, big-box stores are part of a three-level urban development in downtown Baltimore's Inner Harbor.

commercial districts in which to locate, retailers, in collaboration with developers, experimented with new shopping center formats, eventually settling on the "city under a roof" regional shopping mall format, which would eventually lead to the development of nearly 3,000 enclosed regional shopping malls nationwide.

Although the *malls*, as they became known, were not the only form of shopping center developed during this period, anchored by full-line department stores, they formed the centerpiece of the retail delivery system and became the primary means by which consumers obtained the widest array of goods and services for the next 30 years. Suburbanization provoked an extended period of decline in downtown shopping districts. Further, with most relatively new suburban communities lacking well-developed social and cultural centers, malls became de facto social gathering places.

COMMODITY RETAILING

The regional mall dominated shopping center development for more than 30 years before reaching maturity in the mid-1980s. But by then, discount stores with diverse inventories, such as national chain Kmart and regional chains like Caldor, Walmart, and Target, had changed the way Americans shopped, seizing market share from full-line department stores, particularly in consumables, where discounters had a decided cost advantage.

During this time, Walmart and Target expanded nationally and developed better distribution logistics, which, along with offshore production, dramatically reduced operating costs. With widening assortments and low pricing, these retailers came to dominate commodity retailing. Soon, department store giant Dayton Hudson, then the owner of Dayton's, Hudson's, and Marshall Field's, made the strategic decision to abandon its department stores in favor of the Target discount store format, a harbinger of changing fortunes in both industries.

But it was the introduction of new *big-box* and *category-killer* retailers that most damaged department stores and thereby the regional malls. One by one, new, more efficient strip center retailers were introduced, each offering merchandise lines once exclusive to department stores, effectively killing those categories. From appliances and home furnishings to automotive services, electronics, toys, and stationery, new large-format big-box retailers like Best Buy, PetSmart, Marshalls, Staples, and Sports Authority became the preferred distribution model for the commodities they sold.

Inventing the Power Center

Power centers can be traced to 1982, when San Francisco–based Terranomics Retail Services developed 280 Metro Center in Colma, California. Combining big-box retailers in single centers, known as power centers, lowered building costs and provided consumers with greater choice and convenience. Nick Javaras, founding copartner of Terranomics, describes these beginnings: "While we were laying out the merchandising plan for 280 Metro Center, we began to insert retailer names into the various boxes. There were six or seven of us in the room at the time. As we were completing the plan, I looked at the results and casually commented, 'Look at all that power—we should call it a power center.' Merritt Sherr, cofounder of Terranomics, went on to trademark the phrase 'the Originators of the Power Center.'

"Looking back now, it was the retailers who actually started the ball rolling with all the new category-based concepts. Little did we know that together, we were reinventing the way in which commodity goods would be sold in America. Ironically, in the 1990s, we went on at Terranomics to do work for Prudential and other mall owners, often converting obsolete facilities to Power Center formats."

With power centers and large-format discount stores offering more convenient locations, lower prices, and larger assortments than department stores, thousands of these centers would be built nationwide in the ensuing decades. Consumers quickly transitioned from buying commodity goods in department stores and regional malls to buying those items at Target, Walmart, and other discount and big-box stores.

More than half of America's malls lost anchor stores and became functionally obsolete between1980 and 2000, and at the same time, massive ownership consolidation took place. It was during this period that Macy's (department stores) and Simon Property Group (shopping centers) became dominant leaders in their respective industries, by absorbing failing department stores and smaller regional mall owners nationwide. As a consequence, these two companies now own top-performing assets, but they are also left holding many underperforming stores and malls. The Macy's chain of today includes the aging remnants of more than 90 percent of the once-vibrant independent department store industry. Simon Property Group, the largest surviving mall owner, controls properties that once made up the portfolios of nearly 20 independent mall owners.

Many analysts expect Macy's, with over 800 stores, many in aging facilities with poor sales, to eventually reduce its store count by more than 50 percent, with similar scenarios predicted for other middle-market department stores like Arkansas-based Dillard's. With Sears having placed For Sale signs on virtually all of its stores, the loss of one or more of these or other similar stores in already weakened regional malls will inevitably result in extensive additional mall failures.

REGIONAL MALLS

With the demise of the department store and regional mall model, mall owners faced either declining revenues or reinvention to retain and build customer interest. For some, this situation meant offering a more exclusive and specialized shopping experience. Nowhere was this option more evident than in the ensuing competition for Seattle-based Nordstrom department stores. Nordstrom, a department store in name only, offers a carefully crafted mix of apparel, shoes, jewelry, and cosmetics, with few of the other traditional full-line department stores categories (such as housewares). By combining this product mix with a luxurious shopping environment, including live piano performances, an attractive café, and legendary customer service, Nordstrom became synonymous with "specialty retailing" by the early 1990s.

Competition for new Nordstrom stores was fierce, and the cost to secure a Nordstrom store soared as high as $25 million. A few regional shopping centers thrived by converting to specialty retail merchandising, often with Nordstrom in the anchor spot, but many more failed, unable to make the transition. Between 1980 and 2005, fewer than 100 new Nordstrom stores were opened, while nearly 2,000 malls failed, were converted to alternative uses, or both.

LIFESTYLE CENTERS

With small specialty retailers like Chico's, Williams-Sonoma, Coach, and Banana Republic expanding rapidly from 1990 to 2008, and relatively few regional malls successfully transitioning to specialty retail merchandising, the shopping center industry faced a shortage of high-quality specialty retail space at the same moment that regional mall failures were accelerating. The dominant new commodity retail and shopping center formats had, in fact, left small specialty retailers with few reliable anchors and developers with no clearly defined shopping center template to replicate, spawning the ill-defined and somewhat chaotic lifestyle center concept.

With commodity retailing representing the simple convenience/price formula, consumers now demanded better specialty shopping venues. Power centers, discount stores, and the new commodity retailing paradigm had not only permanently weakened the merchandising model employed successfully for decades by department stores and regional malls but had also exposed a key weakness in most malls—their failure to function as places conducive to social interaction and connection to community, essential components of daily life.

Early lifestyle centers, including Poag and McEwen's ground-breaking Germantown Center in Memphis, Tennessee, and independently owned Friendly Center in Greensboro, North Carolina, successfully combined desirable retail shops with appealing architecture and a variety of outdoor settings spawning the lifestyle center. Later entrants, such as Birkdale Village in Charlotte, North Carolina; Bethesda Row in Suburban Washington, D.C.; and University Village in Seattle, Washington, each added its own take on lifestyle center retailing in formats ranging from urban street grids (Bethesda Row) to suburban villages (Birkdale) and converted strip centers (University Village). The lifestyle center industry celebrated many early successes, but the development community and retailers could not agree on a replicable development formula.

This lack of formula left a legacy of confused and often disappointed retailers and consumers and, most important, uneven sales results and deficient investment returns.

Easton Town Center in Columbus, Ohio, is one of the more ambitious lifestyle center efforts. The mixed-use development successfully spawned 90 acres (36 ha) of shopping, hotel, and office uses at the center of a 1,300-acre (526 ha) master-planned community. Impressive in both concept and scope, the shopping center achieved a balance of place and product with a carefully crafted collection of retailers, restaurants, and attractions, in a setting unequaled in the market.

Roy Higgs, founder of Development Design Group, which designed Easton Town Center, describes the difference between designing commodity shopping centers and specialty centers: "For grocery-anchored or power centers, the primary design objective is superefficiency combined with pragmatic planning. The main difference between designing a grocery-anchored or power center development and a mixed-use or lifestyle center is the inherent need to create a powerful and different kind of place. This is especially true of mixed-use developments where, very often, it is the space between the buildings that requires more design attention. These spaces and places are . . . even more important than the buildings. This design focus can be often measured, in part, by the extended dwell time of visitors. The marketing phrase heard most often is 'I came here to shop and took home an experience.'"

Easton Town Center in Columbus, Ohio, was conceived by Les Wexner, founder of The Limited stores and Victoria's Secret; developed by Steiner + Associates with the Georgetown Company; and designed by Development Design Group.

STEINER + ASSOCIATES

Classifying Shopping Centers: Commodity versus Specialty Retail

Traditionally, shopping centers have been primarily characterized by markets served, general tenant characteristics, and center size. The classifications typically include the following:

- **Convenience Centers**—Typically anchored by personal/convenience stores, such as a minimarket, convenience centers provide for the sale of personal services and convenience goods similar to those of a neighborhood center, but in smaller formats, typically ranging up to only 30,000 square feet (2,800 m²).
- **Neighborhood Centers**—Built around supermarkets, neighborhood centers provide convenience goods (foods, drugs, and sundries) and personal services (dry cleaner, barbershop, shoe repair, for example) for the day-to-day needs of the immediate neighborhood in formats typically ranging from 60,000 to 100,000 square feet (5,600–9,300 m²).
- **Community Centers**—These centers generally provide many of the convenience goods and personal services offered by neighborhood centers with a wider range of soft-good lines (for example, apparel) and hard lines (for example, hardware and appliances). These centers, ranging up to 250,000 square feet (23,200 m²), offer a greater variety and selection of merchandise, adding, in addition to supermarkets, variety stores, super drugstores, and discount department stores.
- **Super Community Centers**—Identical in purpose to community centers, these centers are larger in size, ranging up to 500,000 square feet (46,500 m²), and more varied in merchandise collections than their smaller cousins. A power center is usually a type of super community center. It contains at least four category-specific off-price anchors.
- **Regional Centers**—Regional centers provide general merchandise, apparel, furniture, and home furnishings in depth and variety, as well as a range of services and recreational facilities, in formats typically ranging from 250,000 (23,200 m²) to more than 900,000 square feet (83,600 m²), including one or two full-line department stores.
- **Super Regional Centers**—These centers offer an extensive variety of general merchandise, apparel, furniture, and home furnishings, as well as a variety of services and recreational facilities. They are typically designed around three or more full-line department stores and usually range up to 1.5 million square feet (140,000 m²); some are larger.

The New Shopping Paradigms

The shopping center categories above, still largely employed in the shopping center industry today, are no longer adequate to classify today's shopping centers. In fact, they are often misleading. In many cases, no widely accepted industry definitions exist for classifications such as community, entertainment, off-price, and super regional centers. Instead, these terms have been used to refer loosely to groupings of shopping centers having certain dominant size or merchandise orientations.

Virtually all directional change in shopping center use and classification can be traced to the introduction of big-box or category-killer retailing. Aside from diminishing the role of full-line department stores, these retailers have changed the underlying way in which commodity goods and services are presented and sold to the public. With virtually all commodity products having been removed from the best-performing regional shopping centers today, the very underpinnings of today's thriving centers have been completely revamped.

Consumers are motivated by completely different considerations in selecting retail venues for commodity versus specialty goods. These goods are most often purchased on separate shopping trips; even when purchased on combined trips, shoppers are motivated differently in their shopping choices within each group. In fact, the factors that motivate consumers' preferences in commodity shopping centers are almost always opposite those that motivate selection of specialty shopping venues.

COMMODITY RETAILING—THE PRICE/CONVENIENCE EQUATION. Operating essentially as warehouses, commodity retailers function primarily as the final stop in the transmission of goods from factory to consumer. Since the consumer rarely has an emotional attachment to these kinds of goods and services, these centers, and the retailers that occupy them, are designed to deliver a combination of low operating costs (equating to lower prices) and a range of convenience.

The key variables to consider when emphasizing commodity retailing are price and convenience. As a general rule, the more convenience a commodity retailer offers, the higher the price of its goods will be, by design.

Commodity shopping centers can range from stand-alone drugstores built on small parcels of land to a large grouping of big-box or category-killer retailers presented in the power center format. The size of

The Future of the Strip?

For more than 50 years, retailers have favored the commercial strip: a linear pattern of retail businesses strung along major roadways characterized by massive parking lots, big signs, box-like buildings, and a total dependence on automobiles for access and circulation.

For years, planners have tried to contain and improve the strip. Now, they are getting help from consumers and the marketplace. The era of strip development is slowly coming to an end. Evolving consumer behavior, changing demographics, high-priced gasoline, Internet shopping, and the urbanization of the suburbs are all pointing to a new paradigm for commercial development. Commercial strips are not going to disappear overnight, but it is becoming increasingly clear that the future belongs not to strip centers, but to town centers, main streets, and mixed-use development. Here is why:

WE'RE OVERBUILT ON THE STRIP

From 1960 to 2000, U.S. retail space increased almost tenfold, from four to 38 square feet (0.4–3.5 m²) per person. For many years, retail space grew five to six times faster than retail sales. Most of that space came in the form of discount superstores on the suburban strip.

The recession proved that we have too much retail. Strip centers are now littered with vacant stores. By some estimates, more than 1 billion square feet (93 million m²) of retail space is currently vacant; much of that space has to be repurposed or demolished. One retail analyst estimates that we need to demolish 300 million square feet (28 million m²) of retail space.

RETAIL IS REDISCOVERING THE CITY

In 2010, Target announced plans to remodel the century-old Carson Pirie Scott department store in Chicago. This land-mark building, designed by architect Louis Sullivan, will be just one of many new big-box retailers planned for urban neighborhoods. Similarly, in late 2010 Walmart announced plans for its first-ever stores in Washington, D.C. To make the four new stores fit into an urban environment, the company has agreed to consider an array of new layouts, designs, and parking arrangements. The store planned for New Jersey Avenue illustrates Walmart's new approach. The company plans a store of about 80,000 square feet (7,400 m²; much smaller than usual) on the ground floor of a five-story mixed-use building featuring apartments, underground parking, and space for small retail stores. Home Depot already has a new urban store in Toronto with housing on top.

At the same time that Walmart, Target, Home Depot, and others are planning new urban stores all over America, as many as 400 former big-box stores sit vacant on commercial strips. Most analysts agree that urban neighborhoods are the new frontier for retail—the one place left with more spending power than stores to spend it in.

THE SUBURBS ARE BEING URBANIZED

As retail is rediscovering the city, the suburbs are being redesigned as well. Chris Leinberger of the Brookings Institution declared that "the largest redevelopment trend of the next generation will be the conversion of dead or dying strip commercial centers in the suburbs into walkable urban places." The conversion of car-dependent suburban development is already underway in many metropolitan areas and can be expected to increase in the years to come. One dramatic transformation has occurred in Arlington County, Virginia, where Wilson Boulevard, once a miles-long, low-density strip lined with used-car lots and fast-food joints, has been transformed into a walkable urban place. According to Leinberger,

"Arlington County now gets 60 percent of its tax revenue from 10 percent of its land mass."[a]

TRAFFIC CONGESTION, FUEL PRICES, AND AUTO-ORIENTED DESIGN ARE PROBLEMS FOR THE STRIP

Americans value convenience, but the perceived convenience of the strip has been reduced as traffic congestion has worsened. Add rising fuel prices and an overall physical environment designed for cars instead of people, and it's understandable why fewer people want to shop the strip. Suburban town centers and main streets provide a "place-making dividend" that the homogeneous blur of the strip can't match. They also provide a "park once" environment that will grow in importance as fuel prices rise.

YOUNG CONSUMERS FAVOR WALKABILITY AND PLACES WITH CHARACTER

Walking for pleasure is America's number one form of outdoor recreation. Combine walking with shopping—another one of America's favorite pastimes—and you have a winning combination. Time-constrained lifestyles and boredom with the dull sameness of most strip centers have meant a slow but steady decline in the number and length of stays at strip malls. People go to get what they want and they leave. The shopping *experience* is particularly important to generation Y. A mixed-use town center with street life, outdoor dining, and places to hang out, walk, and window-shop are much more likely to draw the affection and dollars of young shoppers than an auto-dependent strip.

THE ECONOMY IS RESTRUCTURING THE RETAIL LANDSCAPE

The recession saw the collapse of numerous big-box chains, and sent vacancy rates soaring. Consumer confidence has improved, but many analysts say we can expect a new "normal" when it comes to retail spending. Why? Because unemployment remains high, the days of unlimited credit are over, and retail analysts predict that a "new consumer frugality" will be the norm for years to come. What's more, strip centers without anchors (like grocery stores) and Class B malls are virtually unfinanceable, according to many experts.

We're also moving into an era of hybrid shopping centers. We used to have three standardized formats: the strip, the enclosed mall, and the power center. Now, all three are coming together in one place, in a hybrid format. According to commercial analysts, we will see a far greater mix of tenants than in the past. Also, many malls will more closely resemble old-fashioned main streets. Already, seven of the 13 regional malls in the Denver metropolitan area—including Belmar in Lakewood, Colorado—have been turned into mixed-use town centers.

E-COMMERCE MEANS FEWER AND SMALLER STORES

Today, the nation's "healthiest" retailer is not Walmart or Costco—it's Amazon. Amazon has exploited the ubiquitous availability of broadband and mobile technology to build a retail superpower. One of the major reasons why the strip is coming to an end is because bricks-and-mortar stores are a shrinking part of the retail landscape.

First, it was catalog shopping; now it is e-commerce, social media, and mobile apps. Retailers will seek smaller footprints as merchandise categories move to online channels. For example, the rise of Netflix and streaming video means the end of bricks-and-mortar video stores. E-books portend the end or at least the downsizing of bookstores; ditto for music stores, greeting card stores, and other merchandise categories.

None of these changes is meant to suggest that we won't still have neigh-

borhood centers with grocery stores, drugstores, and coffee shops. We will. But the endless expansion of the commercial strip—that homogeneous cluster of sign clutter and asphalt that once defined every suburb—is reaching the end of its useful life. A new paradigm is being shaped—not just by regulation but also by consumers and the marketplace. Commercial strips with no beginning or end, no center, and no way to get around except by car are becoming obsolete in an era of shrinking stores, rising gas prices, discerning consumers, walkable suburbs, and online shopping.

Adapted from Edward T. McMahon, "The Future of the Strip," *Urban Land*, March 2, 2011.

[a]Christopher Leinberger, "Walkable Urbanism," *Urban Land*, September 1, 2010.

BELOW: The old paradigm: a typical suburban strip. RIGHT: The new paradigm: mixed uses and access for both cars and pedestrians; DC USA has brought 500,000 square feet (46,000 m²) of big-box retail space to an urban neighborhood in Washington, D.C.

the development depends on the center type, market demand, and competition. Successful commodity retailers, having carefully selected the mix of price and convenience they wish to offer, develop a relationship of trust with the consumer in their price/convenience value equation. Likewise, in choosing between competing commodity shopping choices, consumers consciously or unconsciously select the mix of price and convenience that is most appropriate to the individual and shopping trip in question.

SPECIALTY RETAILING—THE PRODUCT/PLACE EQUATION. A specialty product is one that by its nature requires discretionary income and/or discretionary time to use or acquire. Unlike the relatively emotionless commodity shopping, which is based on the price/convenience equation, specialty shopping is motivated by the shopper's perception of the aesthetic of the place and the quality and mix of retailers and their products. It is about the experience and how shoppers feel about their use of limited discretionary time and dollars; it is also the behavioral contrast between shopping by necessity and shopping by aspiration. Specialty retail centers can include a wide range of sizes from a small strip of luxury boutiques to a major destination shopping mall.

Although some regional malls have successfully transitioned from all-encompassing suburban downtowns to the specialty retailing paradigm, most have not. Unlike the well-understood "city under one roof" model behind the original regional mall format or the "drive-up warehouse" principle behind most commodity retail, successful development of today's specialty centers requires mastering a more complex set of disciplines. The most successful of today's specialty retail centers did not follow a replicable physical plant format, but rather delivered a mix of product (retailers) and place (buildings, open spaces, finishes, amenities, and attractions) unique and appropriate to the markets they serve.

Because individual markets vary greatly in spending potential, tastes, and existing competition, the unique mix of product and place appropriate for any one market will rarely be replicable for another. Although examples exist throughout the industry of specialty retail venues emphasizing primarily one or the other, successful specialty retail development generally requires a compelling mix of both product and place to succeed.

Specialty shopping centers include a collection of retail shops appealing primarily to the consumer's discretionary time and income, regardless of physical format. Examples include

- unanchored strip centers with bookstores, theaters, restaurants, and/or women's boutiques;
- lifestyle centers designed in an open-air format presenting upscale national retailers, such as Chico's, Talbots, Williams-Sonoma, Crate and Barrel, and Coach;
- regional malls often anchored by upscale fashion department stores like Nordstrom, Neiman Marcus, and Bloomingdale's;
- factory outlet centers; and even
- theme parks and theme park retailing.

Development Opportunities

The United States has more retail space per capita than any other country.[1] Although many retail markets are overbuilt, opportunities exist for a range of retail development types, and in many locations. Some areas of the United States are gaining population and may need retail facilities to accommodate that growth. Other areas are redeveloping as more upscale areas and need repositioned retail centers.

Foreign markets offer additional opportunities. Asia is a growing market with enormous potential. Across Asia, retail is surging, with a 38 percent increase in retail deals from 2009 to 2010. China is expected to surpass the United States in total commercial real estate development by 2019, according to Primerica Real Estate Investors.[2] Eastern European retailing is also showing signs of expansion. In Ukraine, for example, the retail market expanded by more than 22 percent during 2011.[3]

COMMODITY RETAILING

Commodity retail development opportunities have become more limited as the industry has matured. Nevertheless, development opportunities will continue to exist in locations experiencing real population growth. Between 2000 and 2010, the U.S. population grew by 27 million. Texas gained the most people—4.3 million, with the Dallas–Fort Worth market alone adding over 1 million people. Areas experiencing such growth require new commodity shopping center development just to keep up with expanding populations. Nongrowth cities, such as those in the Rust Belt, however, may be oversupplied with commodity/grocery-anchored centers because of declining populations and spending power.

Densely populated urban areas present another opportunity. In most urban areas, high costs limited developable land parcels, and other barriers to entry have limited commodity shopping development in the past. Today, however, retailers like Walmart and Target are seeking sites in urban areas where they are developing smaller-format, urban prototypes to gain access to new market segments not yet fully served by commodity retailers. In many cities, local governments are welcoming this type of retail development because it expands the tax base and provides much needed jobs and shopping for local residents.

Dan Petrocchi, partner with the Evergreen Company, in Sacramento, California, has seen municipalities taking a more favorable stance toward Walmart because of the sales tax potential that had previously been acquiesced to the suburbs.[4] The local government in Washington D.C., for example, established a successful grocery store subsidy fund to incentivize locating new, full-sized grocery stores in previously neglected inner-city neighborhoods and to serve new residents moving back into the city.

According to Mac Chandler, managing director, west, of Los Angeles-based Regency Centers, "The affluent coastal markets are most ripe for development simply because the rents are higher in these markets and there's higher demand. In the retail sector, tenants are expanding in the infill markets, and they are actually having trouble filling the pipeline for 2012 and beyond because they are sensing a lack of quality product."[5]

SPECIALTY RETAILING

As more shopping malls close due to market failure or corporate consolidation, reducing retail supply, unmet demand may be returned to the market. With full-line department stores and the malls they occupy expected to continue their steady decline and consolidation, significant development opportunities will emerge again as supply and demand imbalances develop in the specialty retail sector. This shift will lead to development opportunities in existing and new retail centers. Among the malls that remain after the final stages of consolidation, those anchored by upscale specialty department stores will continue to see opportunities to diversify tenant mix, add dining and entertainment options, and create more compelling places. Subject to individual market conditions, some of these malls may be able to adopt mixed-use platforms by replacing aging anchors with a variety of other uses, including hotels, residential communities, public uses, and destination entertainment offerings.

In a time when no easily replicable development format has emerged in specialty retail, developers will have to produce more compelling specialty shopping centers than the often-disappointing lifestyle centers. The most successful developers of specialty retail will be those that create better places and product mixes that inspire retailers to embrace these venues for growth and that stimulate consumers to spend their discretionary time and income on an ongoing basis.

HYBRID SHOPPING CENTERS

Hybrid shopping centers seek to satisfy all of the customer's needs with one-stop shopping by delivering both commodity retailers and specialty retailers in a single shopping center. There are no doubt examples of successful hybrid shopping centers in complex urban and mixed-use environments with constrained real estate options and/or high barriers to entry. Nevertheless, hybrids are generally a risky option for a shopping center developer because the elements of price and convenience that underlie optimal commodity shopping center development generally weaken the elements of better product and place making essential to well-executed specialty retail centers. Likewise, the higher costs and place-making principles central to specialty retail degrade the price/convenience equation essential to commodity retailers. In practical terms, while these two shopping options might coexist adjacent to each other, rarely, if ever, will the cross

In Chevy Chase, Maryland, Wisconsin Place is a redevelopment of a department store site to create an urban mixed-use town center anchored by a Bloomingdale's.

merchandising of both commodity and specialty retail within a single shopping center maximize the sales opportunity of either.

CROSSOVER TENANTS

Two broad classes of retail and shopping centers—commodity and specialty—represent contrasting directions for consumers and tenancy choices for retailers. Some retailers can function effectively in either or both environments. Although there is no clear definition of these types of tenants and their ability to cross over market to market, tenants that have succeeded in multiple commodity and specialty shopping center formats include Costco, Whole Foods, Trader Joe's, Bed Bath & Beyond, Bass Pro Shops, ULTA Cosmetics, Old Navy, Books & Co., Panera Bread, and Starbucks. Although this list is not intended to be exhaustive, it does demonstrate the possibility to influence tenant mix by merchandising crossover tenants creatively. These tenants most often deliver a hybrid offering in one of two ways:

1. delivery of select upscale or specialty products within an otherwise commodity product line (for example, Costco Wholesale's offering $300-per-bottle wine and $1,000 cameras side by side with Kraft macaroni and cheese and gallon jugs of milk); or
2. delivery of *commodity* versions of a basic product line along with upscale or luxury options within the same product line (for example, Bed Bath & Beyond's offering inexpensive, everyday wine glasses along with options ranging up to Waterford and Riedel fine crystal wine glasses).

Underlying site, market, and shopping center research will help identify and validate opportunities to experiment with alternate merchandising strategies using crossover tenants. But developers should be cautioned that merchandising these tenants in one or the other format without considerable thought can significantly influence consumer perception and acceptance of the shopping center in question and should not be undertaken without careful consideration.

THE IMPACT OF E-COMMERCE

One of the most important changes affecting retail developers today is the growing prevalence of e-commerce, such as online and mobile shopping. Given recent trends, the percentage of online purchases will continue to increase, as consumers become increasingly comfortable with the various online retailing options, including Amazon, Craigslist, eBay, and the

thousands of individual retail sites. Although the double-digit annual growth of online shopping and purchases is consistently hyped in the media, online sales in 2011 were less than 5 percent of all retail spending in the United States. To some extent, this trend is generational and is likely to grow to more significant percentages as gen X and gen Y shoppers grow into dominant consumer segments.

Nevertheless, there is no evidence that online sales have had a significant effect on shopping center development. In fact, even in the current economic downturn that began in 2007, retail sales have continued to grow at a modest rate annually. Certain product lines (for example, books) are being dramatically influenced by changes in the technology by which the product itself is delivered to the customer rather than the purchase method. Similar scenarios have played out in music, photo processing, and movie rentals, where basic changes in product technology—not delivery—fundamentally altered the need for bricks-and-mortar stores.

Successful retailers today almost always have multichannel distribution strategies, which encourage customers to use a range of options when making the buying decision. And although the interplay of consumer behavior within multiple distribution channels is well beyond the scope of this publication, evidence suggests that while retailers will continue to integrate technological options into the buying experience, developers' primary role will continue to be delivery of shopping center facilities that meet the needs of retailers and consumers.

In the case of specialty centers, evidence again suggests that to date technology has had little effect on consumer preferences in where to spend discretionary time and income. Those shopping venues that provide an attractive experience will continue to thrive, not just because of the products they offer but also because they provide an attractive, safe, well-maintained place to share a communal experience. A prime example is Apple Stores. Although customers can purchase Apple products in a variety of stores, or online, the Apple Stores continue to draw crowds because of the experience they offer. Apple stores boast average sales per square foot of $5,647 ($60,650/m^2), the highest of any retailer.[6]

Predevelopment Analysis

The feasibility of every shopping center development should be reviewed through several analytical filters, each of which forms a primary basis of support for the shopping center under consideration. The four predevelopment filters are

- market assessment and competitive context;
- physical site considerations;
- regulatory requirements; and
- financial analysis.

The analytical, or filtering, process is identical for assessing development of both commodity and specialty shopping centers. However, the metrics applicable to each site analysis will vary depending on type of development planned. As such, this section will not differentiate commodity from specialty development in describing the analytical processes.

The four analytical filters are presented in the order in which they typically occur in practice. To some degree, however, all four analyses usually overlap somewhat, providing checks and balances during the predevelopment process. In day-to-day practice, the developer will often be introduced to a particular site before conducting any market analysis. Developers should be cautioned, however, that in such situations, they should resist the temptation to justify a predetermined market conclusion rather than conduct an unbiased market study. Some of the greatest mistakes in shopping center development have occurred in part because of these errors of omission.

MARKET FILTER—TRADE AREA AND SALES POTENTIAL ANALYSIS

At its heart, every evaluation of a retail location is an assessment of the demand for retail goods and services contrasted with the supply of retail facilities in the market that serves this demand. A key goal in every

analysis is to identify the differences between demand for goods and services and the available supply of retail filling those needs in a particular geographical area, known as a trade area.

THE TRADE AREA. Analysts evaluating new retail projects define trade areas through evaluation of a range of factors, including the location itself, strength of competing shopping centers, quality of access to these competing centers (expressed in time and distance), and the presence of physical (for example, rivers, expressways, and the like), cultural, or socioeconomic barriers that may affect the trade area.

Trade areas identified may be divided into two or more subareas reflecting differing socioeconomic characteristics of the customer base and levels of competition. In general, the trade area is defined so as to account for a designated share of total sales, depending on the regionality of the given location.

Time and Distance Analysis. Particularly for commodity goods, shoppers will go to the largest collection of retail facilities of a given type that fit the price/convenience equation most desirable to them. For example, a new shopping center that will compete with a strong existing shopping center that is easily accessible by a high-speed arterial will have a constrained trade area toward the direction of that shopping center. Conversely, the absence of a

Adams & Central Mixed-Use Development provides a south Los Angeles neighborhood with a much-needed supermarket. The project also includes 80 multifamily units for low-income residents and 154 parking spaces.

WAYNE THOM PHOTOGRAPHER

competing shopping center and equally good arterial access will ordinarily allow a more expansive trade area in that direction—the only limitation will be travel time.

Trade Area Barriers. Trade area barriers impede the flow of potential customers and, as such, significantly influence the size and draw of a trade area. Barriers exist in two broadly defined forms: physical and cultural/socioeconomic. Physical barriers, including rivers and mountains, reduce customer draw and sales potential even when bridges or roadways penetrate them. Physical barriers may also include constructed impediments, such as expressways, railroads, and large public facilities like airports.

In many cases, socioeconomic and/or cultural variations in population and neighborhoods can function as barriers, either when socioeconomic identification restricts movement between population groups or when the population in one area consumes differently from another because of differences in income, tastes, and/or needs.

Core Demographic Data. Shopping center analysts use demographic data on trade area population to support site selection decisions. Such data will typically include measures of density, median household income, educational attainment, ethnic composition, and occupational classifications. Research analysts have found over the years that certain levels of population density within specific demographic subgroups are necessary to provide adequate sales support for a range of retail uses. For example, in a suburban market, minimum population requirements can range from 5,000 to 10,000 within three miles (4.8 km) to support a drugstore location to over 200,000 within ten miles (16 km) for a large regional-scale discounter store. Income and other characteristics are used to further refine these measures.

Psychographics. Psychographic analysis uses a system of lifestyle clusters that represent an aggregation of demographic, income, and consumption characteristics. For example, the Nielsen PRIZM consumer segmentation system identifies population segments with names that provide a visual image of that group, such as "Blue Blood Estates," "Kids & Cul-de-Sacs," "Blue-Chip Blues," and "Bohemian Mix." Some retailers have identified certain lifestyle cluster groups as important targeting criteria. Ideally, the lifestyle cluster system should be used in conjunction with standard demographic and income information to afford the greatest screening perspective to the researcher.

STRENGTH OF COMPETITION. The character, profitability, and extent of retail competition in the area surrounding the site are a key factor in determining trade area boundaries. Where there is little competition, the trade area may extend a great distance, limited only by the time and distance a shopper is willing to spend in travel. Where competition exists, it must be carefully evaluated to determine not only its makeup and character but also its effectiveness in generating sales.

A retail location that is tenanted by recognized brands and store identities and appropriate price/value relationships for the market will have a great impact on the competitive effectiveness of a new location. The trade area boundary will have to be limited to account for the presence of this type of existing shopping center. However, if an existing shopping center is missing one or more destination retailers, it can be vulnerable to a new retail development at a well-situated location.

Intercepting Locations. Population growth in markets can take place in areas less conveniently served by existing shopping centers. Construction of new arterials can also dramatically alter traffic patterns. A competing location that is well situated at a key arterial interchange or intersection in a newly emerging area can negatively affect an existing competitive facility, perhaps even resulting in the departure of one or more anchor stores in favor of the new location. In such cases, the trade areas of both the new shopping center and the existing one will be altered, and the trade areas for the proposed center and the existing competition may actually overlap.

Daytime and Other Population Measures. In addition to evaluating the size and character of the trade area's resident population, in some cases it is equally, or more, important to assess the size and character of the daytime worker and tourist populations. In urban areas in particular, these customer groups may be contributing to, or in some cases driving, a trade area. Information on the resident population is primarily derived from Census Bureau tabulations and U.S. Postal Service postal route data, whereas information on daytime population is primarily obtained from Bureau of Labor Statistics business and employee counts by zip code. Tourist information can be obtained from data compiled by local and state convention and visitor agencies. Much of these data can be purchased from secondary sources, such as Nielsen SiteReports and DemographicsNow.

Shopper Data. Owners of retail properties can survey customers in existing shopping centers. This information affords perspective about where customers live, their socioeconomic makeup, the number of stores shopped, amount spent, and so on. These surveys do not, however, account for shoppers who may not patronize the shopping center at all, information that is critical when repositioning an existing property. In these cases, small consumer discussion groups, or focus groups, are commonly used to assist in developing these data. Telephone surveys, used frequently in the past to obtain shopping behavior information, have become increasingly unreliable since the passage of "do not call" regulations, and because younger consumers may not have home landlines, thus distorting the demographics and confusing the geography of intended shoppers.

CALCULATING SALES OPPORTUNITY AND SUPPORTABLE SQUARE FOOTAGE. The final step in qualifying the market potential of a retail location is calculating the estimated sales opportunity and supportable square footage for the proposed shopping center. These measures are calculated in a three-part process designed to assess the level of unmet spending potential in the trade area in question and the square footage of retail, if any, needed to satisfy that potential.

Spending Potential. The first step is to calculate the total spending potential available within the trade area. This potential is calculated as the product of per-capita or per-household expenditure for specific merchandise classes (for example, groceries or apparel and accessories or furniture and floor coverings) and the trade area population in a given year. Spending potentials are calculated for a number of years in a defined study period and are expressed in constant-dollar terms to negate the impact of inflation and local cost-of-living adjustments that may occur over the study period.

Whether purchased from a private data vendor or estimated by the researcher, per-capita and per-household spending potential for various goods is based on a combination of U.S. Census of Retail Trade tabulations and U.S. Bureau of Labor Statistics long-term studies of consumer expenditures by household type.

Spending Potential Capture/Leakage. After calculating spending potential, a determination must be made of how well existing shopping centers and retailers in the trade area are serving the market, as evidenced by their capture of the available spending

potential. This measure is established by comparing spending potential with actual retail sales in a given year. If the spending potential exceeds actual sales in the trade area, a condition described as sales leakage exists, indicating that a gap exists between spending potential and actual sales in the trade area, perhaps supporting a need for additional retail space of the type(s) under consideration. If the appropriate offerings are not available locally, consumer sales may "leak" into other markets.

Market Share. Forecasting the future sales opportunity of a new or redeveloped shopping center within a given trade area is usually based on more than one form of analysis in order to establish a likely market share range. The typical starting point is the identification of a group of successful and less successful centers that can function as analogs in the identification of a spectrum of types of operating environments and relative sales performance. This analog approach, which is based on proprietary owner information, can take the form of a multivariable predictive model that scores the locational and core customer factors described above. Regardless of how comprehensive the model is, most experienced researchers recognize that the model's conclusions need to be refined based on experience and field review to appropriately account for the population and competitive characteristics of the area under study.

Other approaches to market share estimation are based on a pro rata share of a given type of retail space operating in or affected by competitors outside the trade area. Judgments are also made regarding the volume of sales that can be drawn from reversing spending outflows and by taking market share from existing shopping centers that may be less affected by planned new development.

The work of developing market share analogs must be done with a high degree of care and expertise, as such information is fundamental to arriving at an accurate sales forecast.

Calculating Sales Opportunity and Supportable Square Footage. The final step in calculating sales opportunity is accomplished by contrasting market shares identified for the site with the spending potential over the study period. Non–trade area plus factors—such as the spending of daytime populations near the site, visitors to the trade area, or persons living in an area too diffuse to be studied geographically—are then added to arrive at the final sales opportunity. These factors typically range from 10 to 25 percent of total sales, depending on the type of location and retail development under study.

Village Mart Market Analysis

The following geographic and demographic issues and the market potential for the site and proposed retail center were considered:

- Village Mart is situated at a key crossroads in a growing suburban county. The road network favors this location, with its reasonably good access. Key north–south and northwest–southeast highways intersect near the site and create a natural and distinct trade area for the center.

- The trade area is characterized by an affluent and growing population that is well educated and consists primarily of families. Population in the trade area grew from 137,900 in 2000 to an estimated 154,000 in 2008, an annual rate of 1.4 percent. Average household income in the trade area was an estimated $88,400 for 2008, an increase of 3.45 percent per year from the 2000 average household income of $67,300. Forty-four percent of the trade area's population have attained at least a four-year college degree.

- Floor space directly competitive with the site is appreciably lacking; thus, Village Mart has an opportunity to establish itself as the primary provider of moderate to better apparel and specialty goods in the trade area. In terms of floor space and sales, the key competition's business is significantly skewed toward groceries and restaurants. Although groceries and restaurants have 40 percent of the space and 67 percent of the sales, typical retail uses, such as general merchandise, apparel, home furnishings, and specialty merchandise, account for only 15.3 percent of the floor space and 9.1 percent of the sales. Further, these competitive centers show relatively modest to lower sales productivity.

- The analysis projected sales of $65.7 million (plus or minus 10 percent) for Village Mart for 2008 with the center expanded to 180,000 square feet (17,000 m^2). This sales volume would produce retail sales at the rate of $365 per square foot ($3,930/m^2), adjusted for the center's 4,500 square feet (420 m^2) of office space. Of the $65.7 million in retail sales, $59.3 million in sales would be generated from within the trade area. The remaining $6.4 million in sales would be generated by shoppers from outside the trade area.

- The three merchandise groups targeted (in-line retail, grocery, and restaurants) show surplus demand. The magnitude of the surplus—$234.4 million for in-line retail, $191.2 million for grocery, and $86.5 million for restaurants—dwarfs the estimated sales for Village Mart. Thus, market support is ample for remerchandising the center.

ANALYSIS

The market analysis required an examination of the following issues:

- examination of the demographics of the shopper base for the area;
- analysis of the local retail competition;
- supply/demand analysis of existing sales and potential expenditures; and
- forecast of potential sales for an expanded and repositioned Village Mart.

SUPPLY/DEMAND FORECAST

The forecast of sales was based on the following assumptions:

- Leasing will focus on merchandising Village Mart with exciting and contemporary stores, principally leading national retailers in apparel, home furnishings, and specialty goods, including jewelry, sporting goods, and toys and hobbies.

- Leasing will achieve an occupancy rate of at least 90 percent for the opening of Village Mart.

MEASURING RETAILER SALES POTENTIAL. Individual retailers employ a methodology similar to that described above in arriving at sales estimates for new stores under consideration. National retailers with numerous establishments are, however, also privy to a wealth of additional proprietary information related to core shopper groups, levels of market capture under different competitive circumstances, and sales by zip code and/or census tract that facilitates even more accurate sales forecasting. This proprietary information permits the establishment of a range of very detailed store analogs against which to measure proposed new store performance.

Given the availability and depth of this information, retailers can readily define a trade area, allowing them to quickly determine likely market share of the available spending potential and sales opportunity with core shopper groups. From this market share estimate, they can then develop a projection and test store viability at various sales volumes by plugging in a rent number and backing into the needed level of sales to support that rent estimate. In addition to performing the trade area and sales potential analyses, shopping center developers will also benefit from evaluating the sales opportunity for specific target retailers as described above. In the case of single-tenant development, this exercise is critical to successfully underwriting project feasibility.

PHYSICAL FILTER—SITE ANALYSIS

Selecting an appropriate site for a retail development first requires definition of the general location and

- A marketing campaign in the print media, including local newspapers, will create community awareness of the mart.

- No new competitive centers—conventional, power, or off-price—were to open in the trade area before Village Mart's opening in 2010.

- The national and local economies were expected to maintain their present level of growth or to improve.

Figure A shows projected sales that should be achievable based on the market analysis and targeted retail categories. Figure B demonstrates the probable total available sales potential for the trade area and then a required capture rate for Village Mart to meet the development sales assumptions set in figure A. All sales estimates are stated in constant dollars.

FIGURE A | Development Sales Assumptions: Maximum Retail Development Potential

Tenants	Space (ft²)	Sales Productivity/Ft²	Total Sales	Sales Inflow (%)
In-line retail[a]	105,800	$275	$29,095,000	15.0
Grocery	56,000	580	32,480,000	5.0
Outparcel restaurants	13,700	300	4,110,000	10.0
Total project/retail	180,000	$365	$65,685,000	9.7
Total project/all uses	180,000	–	$65,685,000	–

Source: Carl M. Freeman Associates and Kissel Consulting Group.
[a]In-line retail space is considered to be a mix of apparel, home furnishings, and specialty merchandise.

FIGURE B | Sales Analysis: Village Mart Trade Areas

Economic Characteristic	In-Line Retail[a]	Grocery	Restaurants	Total[b]
Retail sales trade area potential	$280,972,000	$437,068,000	$144,088,000	$862,128,000
Trade area retail sales (key competition)	21,817,601	214,977,162	53,885,659	290,680,422
Net difference	$259,154,399	$222,090,838	$90,202,341	$571,447,578
Estimated sales at site	$29,095,000	$32,480,000	$4,110,000	$65,685,000
Sales inflow rate (%)	15.0	5.0	10.0	9.7
Inflow sales	$4,364,250	$1,624,000	$41 1,000	$6,399,250
Net estimated trade area sales	$24,730,750	$30,856,000	$3,699,000	$59,285,750
Required capture rate (%)	8.8	7.1	2.6	6.9
Net trade area surplus/deficit[b]	$234,423,649	$191,234,838	$86,503,341	$512,161,828

Sources: Claritas Data Systems, National Research Bureau, ULI–the Urban Land Institute, and Kissel Consulting Group.
[a]In-line retail is considered a mix of apparel, home furnishings, and specialty merchandise.
[b]A positive number is a demand surplus; a negative number is a demand deficit.

project size necessary to satisfy market demand, and a thorough vetting of specific opportunities and constraints unique to the site or sites under consideration. It goes without saying that the site(s) intended for a specific *commodity* retail use must fit the basic convenience parameters required for the specific intended uses, such as parking, loading, and site visibility. But beyond that, the additional factors described below, must be closely assessed.

Although all types of real estate development share commonalities, shopping center development differs significantly in many respects, requiring a distinct terminology and performance measurements. Perhaps most important for a new shopping center developer is recognition that retail real estate is the only type of property in which measures of property value are directly related to the volume of transactions taking place on the site. As such, success in shopping center development depends almost entirely on the success of the tenants in the project, as measured by sales per square foot and profitability.

SIZES AND SHAPES OF SITES. Shopping centers can be developed at a range of densities, but the most common configuration for small suburban centers usually involves a one-story building covering 25 percent of the site, or a floor/area ratio of 0.25. For this configuration, the site area needs to be approximately four times larger than the gross building area (GBA) of the project. A rule of thumb is to build approximately 9,000 square feet per acre (828 m²/ha). Urban infill projects, however, might allow 100 percent site coverage and include no on-site parking requirement, or they may share parking with other uses in mixed-use projects.

In suburban areas, where land availability is not highly constrained, the ideal shopping center site should be a regular and unified shape undivided by highways or dedicated streets. Although the term "strip center" connotes a long narrow site, a square site with an L-shaped center that wraps around a parking lot is often preferable. Triangular sites may also be suitable, especially if they are surrounded by major arterial streets and provide good access from numerous directions. If a triangular or irregularly shaped site is developed, the best use of odd portions of the site may be to develop freestanding facilities. In select, urban infill locations, ideal sites are often unavailable, requiring innovative design and retailer flexibility.

SITE VISIBILITY AND ACCESS. Site visibility and unimpeded vehicular access are critical considerations for retail sites. Shopping center sites should be accessible from multiple points; generally, the larger the market to be served, the more points of access that will be required. Traffic counts on roads serving the site are a key measure of the potential drive-by market, and the volume of customers who actually pass the site and proximity to major intersections are major advantages for any site. Likewise, a site's orientation to the principal roads serving it or to other adjacent uses that may generate customers is critical.

Even though traffic flow attracts retail business, a site that fronts on a thoroughfare with many competing distractions (including other retail stores and signs) can be less desirable than a site on a less heavily traveled arterial.

For retailers whose peak business is defined by the time of day, a location on a specific side of the road can be crucial. For example, doughnut or bagel shops prefer locations on the drive-to-work side, whereas gas stations prefer to be on the drive-home side.

PHYSICAL SITE CHARACTERISTICS. Because most shopping centers are constructed horizontally rather than vertically and cover a large footprint, a flat or gently sloping site is usually preferable. More steeply sloping sites can be adapted, but they may entail higher site improvement costs and lower operational efficiency.

Sites in floodplains, on solid rock, or with a high water table should be avoided if possible. When such conditions are present, the site requires considerable supplemental analysis to quantify and mitigate risk. If the area under consideration has known subsoil problems (rock, sand, high density/low moisture, or low-permeability clay), the extent of these characteristics and potential cost implications should be thoroughly assessed before going forward. Although soil borings on at least a 50- or 100-foot (15 or 30 m) grid will be taken when engineering studies are conducted, an initial assessment is necessary to avoid unanticipated development costs later. Likewise, serious subsoil conditions or an existing surface condition, such as wet soil that might trigger a wetlands designation, should be understood before the site is acquired.

Even with careful analysis, a small refuse dump, unrecorded oil or gasoline storage tanks, wellheads, septic tanks, or agricultural drainage fields in the middle of a grid might be missed. Retaining a local soil investigation company with a history of work in the area is generally advisable, as local professionals are more likely to be aware of the history of the site and latent site conditions, which may impede development.

Buyers should also be alert for environmental issues other than wetlands, including illegal dumping, groundwater contamination, floodplain encroachment, or contamination from asbestos, pesticides, or PCBs (polychlorinated biphenyls). The presence of endangered species, historic structures, or archeological remains on the site can significantly delay or, in worst cases, prevent development. All these factors can lead to costly remediation requirements and/or significant project delays, along with attendant cost overruns.[7]

SITE ACQUISITION. After a site with desirable physical characteristics has been identified, the developer should follow the general site acquisition steps outlined in chapters 3 and 4.

One site acquisition scenario that is especially common in retail development involves acquisition of an existing center needing renovation, or expansion, or the consolidation of several adjacent smaller obsolete buildings into a single parcel. The key factors to look for in acquiring centers for renovation are an outdated appearance and local market or demographics changes suggesting a possible retenanting or repositioning of the shopping center. An example is an older shopping center in an inner-ring suburb that has become more affluent, but the shopping center remains stuck in an earlier era with a low-end, obsolete tenant mix.

Redevelopment versus New Construction

A large number of existing shopping centers in the United States are obsolete, offering a wide range of redevelopment opportunities. Many possible advantages related to market conditions, public approvals, financing, and construction can support redevelopment of an existing shopping center; however, developers should be aware of the potential disadvantages associated with renovations.

ADVANTAGES:

- AVAILABILITY OF PRIME REAL ESTATE—Older shopping centers or other retail property, such as vacant or obsolete grocery or discount stores, can provide attractive opportunities for redevelopment. In some cases, neighborhoods surrounding older retail properties may have become more affluent or more populous since the original shopping center was built.

- FEWER COMPETITIVE SITES—Developed areas often have fewer opportunities for competitors to enter the market, limiting new competition, reducing uncertainty, and increasing the likelihood that the renovated center will be successful.

- SUITABLE ZONING IN PLACE—Restrictive zoning and other development controls limit the location of new shopping centers, often because of their traffic impact. Renovation projects often require no rezoning or subdivision approvals,

which can save years and translate into significant cost savings for projects. In some cases, the project's age may allow for variances from zoning and building codes, setback requirements, parking requirement, or land use restrictions. This regulatory flexibility may permit a development plan that otherwise would be impossible to build.

- PUBLIC SUPPORT—Municipal agencies and citizens groups often embrace projects that provide neighborhood improvements, particularly in older underserved neighborhoods. In some areas, the government agency can assist in condemnation if some leases are difficult to cancel or additional properties must be obtained. Some cities sponsor bond programs providing funding directly or through tax recovery incentives that allow the developer to recoup part of the development cost. In many cases, without such incentives, projects of these types would not be financially viable.

- LOWER CONSTRUCTION COST—The total cost of purchasing and renovating an underperforming shopping center is often significantly lower per square foot than building a new one; these cost savings must be balanced against potential renovation risks.

- FASTER TURNAROUND—In some cases, redevelopment will take less time than new construction. Public approvals

are often quicker, and financing can be easier for projects with established operating histories.

DISADVANTAGES:

- POTENTIAL COST OVERRUNS—Costs of renovations are more difficult to estimate than new construction, and some uncertainty often exists about structural integrity and renovation costs.

- INCREASED CONSTRUCTION PERIOD OPERATING COSTS—Construction must often be managed while the center remains open, making renovation more difficult if not more costly and less efficient than new construction. Construction working hours are often restricted to nights and early mornings, and extra safety precautions are required.

- LEASE BUYOUT COSTS—Existing tenants and leases may require terminations, buyouts, and/or physical moves, which can add costs and complicate redevelopment.

- LOSS OF GRANDFATHERING—Although renovation can often provide zoning and regulation advantages, as noted above, the redevelopment or remodeling of existing centers can also lead to the loss of grandfathered protection in zoning, parking, accessibility for handicapped individuals, sprinkler, building materials, and landscaping requirements.

REGULATORY FILTER—PUBLIC APPROVALS AND HANDLING OPPOSITION

Acquiring public approvals is an increasingly complicated and time-consuming exercise. It can take a few weeks for a straightforward subdivision approval, or many years, depending on how environmentally and politically sensitive the site is. A site may be subject to the approval of any number of agencies at the local, state, and even federal level. The developer should assess the likelihood of a drawn-out approval process and should determine how the process will affect the project's feasibility.

ZONING AND SITE PLAN APPROVALS. The zoning provisions and public approvals required to develop a retail site must be studied carefully before a site is purchased. Early on, the developer should carefully explore the attitudes of local residents, zoning staff, and the approving body generally and specifically toward the proposed shopping center. In cases where a rezoning may be necessary, the developer should initiate informal discussions with local zoning officials and retain respected local zoning counsel to assist in the process. These considerations are equally important to interpretation or perhaps amendment of provisions on several issues ranging from FARs, building height, and parking requirements to lot coverage, setbacks, and permitted uses.

Shopping center developments carry with them a number of special regulatory concerns, including the probable traffic impact's compatibility with surrounding uses, environmental effects, stormwater runoff, and, in some cases, impacts on existing retailing. Developers have often found that specific standards included in commercial zoning ordinances are either incompatible with retailers' needs or simply too difficult or impossible to satisfy without variances or special exceptions.

In many jurisdictions, regulatory considerations have resulted in strict design and use guidelines. They may be part of the comprehensive plan or part of adopted policy statements. And in some cases, they are unofficial staff policies that may direct planning staff evaluations. In addition, developers will often encounter biases and barriers in the local planning and approval processes applicable to any retail proposal for rezoning or for site plan and architectural approval for a building permit. In some communities, zoning for a planned use development district may be possible; however, while site-specific zoning may allow greater regulatory flexibility, it will likely trigger a much more thorough review of the project overall.

ENVIRONMENTAL CONSIDERATIONS. A range of environmental issues, including potential wetlands and habitats for endangered species, may affect the viability of a proposed shopping center site. It is critical to obtain as much information as possible about the present and past uses of any site under consideration, and it is always better to discover such impediments to development in the site review process.

Still, "in densely populated areas where land is scarce, redeveloping industrial sites and previous retail venues into new shopping centers is often the only opportunity for growth. In such cases, wetland preservation concerns are less likely to arise than issues relating to the problem of latent residual contamination."[8]

In addition, to the concerns described above, the presence of hazardous subsurface materials or farming contaminants may also render a site unsuitable without costly cleanup efforts and should be thoroughly vetted by qualified environmental consultants.

FINANCIAL FEASIBILITY FILTER

The financial feasibility of a shopping center can be determined only after a specific development program has been defined for a specific site, allowing the developer to properly estimate development costs, operating revenues, financing options, and expected levels of investment return. The generic aspects of the financial analysis process are discussed in greater depth in chapter 4. This section will focus on financial issues unique to shopping centers and, in particular, the more predictable subset of commodity shopping centers.

Although analyzed through the same process, specialty centers can be more difficult to understand. There are many types of specialty centers, with a diverse set of tenants—often small tenants. There may even be nonrevenue-producing tenants that must be considered. They also vary widely in their amenities and other costs.

CAPITAL COSTS. Capital costs unique to shopping center development are highlighted in the feature box on page 344. Although often different from capital costs for other commercial real estate projects, they are

---

Considerations for Repositioning a Retail Development

Repositioning existing retail properties in ways that increase their value can be a viable business model for many locations. A ULI panel of experts compiled these recommendations for those looking to reposition a retail center.

- Engage the local government and community in the planning and development process. Many repositioning projects require some sort of public/private partnership, and community input and support are essential.

- Seek win-win solutions with anchor tenants.

- Reuse existing facilities efficiently and cost-effectively.

- Differentiate your project from the competition. Make it unique.

- Consider and plan for ways the project can continue to evolve and densify in the future.

- Create authentic, high-quality places that appeal to the local community.

- Where open-air spaces are not practical, create indoor spaces that provide outdoor-like experiences.

- Incorporate leisure, recreation, dining, and entertainment elements in ways that make these projects the souls of their communities.

Source: Julie D. Stern, "Renewed Retail Opportunities," *Urban Land*, October 18, 2010.

as important in determining project feasibility as other costs, as discussed in chapter 4. One of the capital costs unique to shopping centers is the tenant buildout or tenant improvement allowance, which can vary widely from tenant to tenant.

INCOME PROJECTIONS. The initial analysis and subsequent refinements of rents and tenant reimbursements are a critical step in determining the feasibility of any shopping center development project. Shopping center income projections must be based on a leasing plan that represents the developer's estimate of square footage to be leased to specific types of tenants. As such, the allocation of space to various classes of tenants is a critical component in the financial feasibility analysis. Although the preliminary income side projections are based on well-considered assumptions, such assumptions must be validated in the market in the form of signed leases.

Although all shopping center rental rates are directly and indirectly related to sales productivity, the process of estimating shopping center revenues

Sustainability Measures

Thinking green can benefit the bottom line. Sustainable practices can save on development and operating costs and can create a positive image for customers. Following are some considerations for developers and operators of retail projects.

SITING
- Protect the natural flow of local stormwater to avoid increasing loads on the local stormwater system.
- Develop parts of the landscape to slow, filter, and absorb stormwater to reduce stormwater runoff.
- Renaturalize portions of the site perimeter with native plants to support native wildlife.
- Site buildings to maximize opportunities for active or passive solar gain where appropriate.

WILDLIFE CONSERVATION
- Select trees and plants as part of the landscaping and negotiate with local service clubs that will pick and deliver the flowers and fruit to senior centers.
- Protect endangered plant specimens of cultural significance in on-site gardens.

LIGHT/SHADE CONTROL
- Shade pedestrian areas and use highly reflective roof materials to minimize heat-island effect and to reduce disturbance to the natural environment and microclimates for wildlife.

- Control all exterior lighting to avoid light trespass onto neighboring properties and light pollution to the night sky.
- Control all exterior lighting (parking lot, pedestrian walkways, and building-supported fixtures) to avoid light that pollutes the night sky and that trespasses onto neighboring properties and to use energy most effectively.

DAYLIGHT/VIEWS/VENTILATION
- Create public space as exterior (nonconditioned) space.
- Provide daylight and views to all interior spaces.
- Use natural ventilation instead of mechanical measures, where appropriate.

WATER CONSERVATION
- Reduce consumption of potable water for landscape irrigation by using only native and adaptable plant selections and by employing water-efficient irrigation methods.
- Use low-flow fixtures to reduce interior water consumption.

ENERGY CONSERVATION
- Minimize the amount of indoor conditioned space.
- Use displacement ventilation.
- Use an economizer cycle to cool with only fresh outdoor air.
- Minimize power used for interior lighting, thereby reducing cooling loads.

- Use highly reflective roof materials to decrease solar heat gain, thereby lessening effects on the environment caused by energy production.
- Use thermal/energy-efficiency-certified windows.
- Perform an energy audit to monitor and/or identify opportunities for efficiency gains.

CONSTRUCTION MATERIALS/PROCESSES
- Use wood products only from certified forest sources to reduce deforestation and to discourage unsustainable harvest practices.
- Use certified low-VOC (volatile organic compound) products, such as paints, plastics, and carpets.
- Use materials manufactured regionally (within a 500-mile [800 km] radius) to mitigate the effects of transportation.

TRANSPORTATION
- Locate projects adjacent to stops on transit lines to decrease automobile use and its effects.
- Negotiate with the local transit authority to reroute transit lines to the site to lessen automobile use and its effects.
- Encourage alternate transportation arrivals to connect users to the outdoors and the natural environment.

Sources: Ronald A. Altoon, "Green Retail," *Urban Land*, November–December, 2002, p. 95; and Matthew Johnston, ULI.

Capital Costs for Shopping Centers

LAND AND LAND IMPROVEMENTS

LAND OR LEASEHOLD ACQUISITION
- Cost of land
- Good-faith deposit
- Broker's fee
- Escrow
- Title guarantee policy
- Standby fee
- Chattel search
- Legal fee
- Recording fee

OFF-SITE AND ON-SITE LAND IMPROVEMENTS
- Off-site streets and sidewalks
- Off-site sewers, utilities, and lights
- Relocation of power lines
- Traffic controls
- Surveys and test borings
- Utilities
  - Water connection to central system or on-site supply
  - Storm sewers
  - Sanitary sewer connection to system or on-site disposal
  - Gas distribution connection to central system
  - Primary electrical distribution
  - Telephone distribution
- Parking areas
  - Curbs and gutters
  - Paving and striping
  - Pedestrian walkways
  - Traffic controls and signs
  - Lighting
  - Service area screens and fences
- Landscaping
  - Grading
  - Plants

BUILDINGS AND EQUIPMENT

SHELL AND MALL BUILDING
- Layout
- Excavation
- Footings and foundations
- Structural frame
- Exterior walls
- Roofing and insulation
- Subfloor
- Sidewalk canopy
- Sidewalks and mall paving
- Loading docks and service courts
- Truck and service tunnels
- Equipment rooms, transformer vaults, cooling towers
- Heating and cooling—central plants or units
- Incinerator
- Community meeting rooms
- Offices for center management and merchants association
- Electric wiring, roughed in
- Plumbing, roughed in
- Fire sprinkler system
- Public toilets
- Elevators, escalators, stairways
- Contractor's overhead and profit
- Pylons
- Shopping center signs
- Mall furniture, fountains, etc.
- Maintenance equipment and tools
- Office furniture and equipment

TENANT IMPROVEMENTS (IF PAID FOR BY DEVELOPER)
- Tenant finish allowance
- Storefronts
- Window backs and fronts
- Finished ceiling and acoustical tile
- Finished walls
- Interior painting
- Floor coverings
- Interior partitioning
- Lighting fixtures
- Plumbing fixtures
- Doors, frames, and hardware
- Storefront signs
- Store fixtures

OVERHEAD AND DEVELOPMENT

ARCHITECTURE AND ENGINEERING
- Site planning
- Buildings and improvements

INTERNAL AND FINANCING
- Interest during construction
- Construction and permanent loan fees
- Loan settlement costs
- Appraisal costs
- Legal fees for financing

ADMINISTRATIVE OVERHEAD AND CONSTRUCTION SUPERVISION
- Construction supervision
- Field office expense
- Bookkeeping
- Home office expense
- Travel and entertainment
- Salaries and overhead of staff
- Printing and stationery

LEASING COSTS AND LEGAL FEES
- Leasing fees paid to brokers
- Salaries and overhead of staff
- Scale model, brochures, etc.
- Legal fees—leasing
- Legal fees—general

OTHER OVERHEAD AND DEVELOPMENT
- Market and traffic surveys
- Zoning and subdivision approvals
- Outside accounting and auditing
- Real estate taxes
- Other taxes
- Insurance
- Advertising and promotion of opening
- Landlord's share of formation and assessments of merchants associations
- Miscellaneous administrative costs

Source: Michael D. Beyard, W. Paul O'Mara, et al., *Shopping Center Development Handbook*, 3rd ed. (Washington, D.C.: ULI–the Urban Land Institute, 1999), p. 57.

Note: Items in this list are for all types of shopping centers, including enclosed regional malls.

is unlike that for other income-producing properties. Rental rates vary substantially, depending on the type of shopping center, target tenants, and market conditions. Commodity retail shopping centers tend to have more predictable rental ranges and lower operating costs. Rental rates for specialty retail shopping centers vary significantly, as do their operating costs, primarily because the costs associated with the amenities and ambience that make such centers successful vary widely. Overages are part of the return to owners, but lenders do not count them for underwriting purposes.

Design and Construction

The most important consideration in selecting a shopping center architect is determining whether the center under consideration will be a commodity or specialty shopping center. The utilitarian principles underpinning the design of most commodity retail buildings vary in fundamental ways from the place-making principles applicable to specialty shopping center design. The formulaic design approaches that create efficiency and predictability in neighborhood and power center design are not well suited to specialty centers, which value aesthetics over efficiency.

In the case of typical grocery-anchored or power centers, the particular design aesthetic, while important for public approvals and general perception, is not critical for the success of the shopping center. In creating specialty centers, some element of place making exists in every case—and in some cases, the *place* that is created is far more important to success than any other aspect of the shopping center. This discussion will focus on the basic principles applicable to commodity centers.

The initial design consideration for every shopping center is the creation of a preliminary site plan and building configuration plan. Shopping centers by their nature involve the efficient movement of customers on and off the property and in and out of retail stores on an ongoing basis. As a result, unlike other types of real estate, shopping centers must be designed to accommodate a large volume of customer flow through multiple points of access throughout the facility. The placement of buildings and parking lots, as well as the creation of efficient circulation patterns, must be designed to optimize the appeal and accessibility of every store in the center, while creating functional delivery systems for tenants. Traffic engineers and parking consultants are key members of the shopping center planning team.

SHOPPING CENTER CONFIGURATION

A variety of retail layout schemes have evolved as basic shopping center land use concepts over many years with varying degrees of success. After determining the underlying retail use of the shopping center, the first design consideration is to identify the most suitable building configuration that can be applied to a specific site.

For small centers, the primary design focus is on easy access, adequate parking, and visibility from the primary roadway system. In urban locations, effective pedestrian connections and access to streets and transit may be far more important than access to parking, which may or may not be located on site.

COMMODITY CENTERS. From a leasing agent's perspective, the ideal layout for most commodity shopping centers provides good sight lines for all storefronts, and modest variations in setbacks and elevation to provide contrasting design elements for individual tenants. Bay depths, widths, and column spacing should be designed to provide maximum flexibility for tenants of various shapes and sizes.

The ability to provide stores of varying depths—from 60 to 100 feet (18–30 m)—is an asset to any center. When stores must be of uniform depth, small stores can be carved out of deeper space, leaving rear overlap areas for the neighboring larger stores. But developers must avoid creating excessive depths for which neither they nor their tenants can obtain an adequate return.

South Campus Gateway in Columbus, Ohio, was developed through a collaboration of Ohio State University, the city of Columbus, and neighborhood stakeholders. The project creates a vibrant, pedestrian-focused neighborhood of shops, offices, structured parking, and multifamily housing.

CAMPUS PARTNERS

If ground-level storage space is needed, stores must be deeper. Less depth is appropriate if storage and services facilities are belowground and if pedestrian traffic passes only one side of the store.

The configuration of smaller neighborhood or community shopping centers depends largely on four factors: the shape of the site, the nature and intensity of surrounding roadways, and the space requirements of the intended retail tenants. The most common configurations for these types of centers are variations of one of three general shapes: linear, L-shaped, or U-shaped. These basic layouts can also feature variations using setbacks, curves, and multiple independent buildings. Among the most important considerations in determining shopping center configuration are site configuration, site use/efficiency concerns, parking constraints, length and depth of buildings, and visibility of tenants.

A linear arrangement is still the most commonly used configuration for smaller unanchored strip centers and grocery-anchored neighborhood centers. The linear layout is basically a straight line of stores sharing common architectural elements, sometimes tied together by a coordinated canopy system. In neighborhood centers, this configuration usually places two major retailers, most often a supermarket and other medium-sized anchor tenant, in the most prominent locations in the center, with adjacent spaces programmed for smaller tenants. A linear center (and its variations) is generally the least expensive structure to build and is easily adapted to most site conditions. Linear centers typically range from 500 to 1,000 feet (152.5–305 m) in length, including anchor tenants. When a center's length exceeds about 300 feet (90 m), building setbacks and architectural features should be visually distinguished to create more appealing aesthetics.

Although parking is usually placed at the front of small shopping centers to allow for easy access, some centers use different configurations. Truck parking and deliveries should be situated at the rear of the shopping center, where employee parking is also most optimally located.

Sites in urban areas invariably present a different set of challenges affecting site plan and building configuration. Most often, these sites are constrained by such factors as limited size, close architectural and pedestrian relationships to adjacent buildings, historic preservation issues, neighborhood consensus, transit access, and limitations on automobile traffic generated and/or provision of adequate parking.

The following are among the many unique concerns applicable to urban retail sites:

- **Streetscape**—Public policy and urban design considerations often favor or require the placement of buildings along the street with limited setback to enhance the city's streetscape.
- **Parking**—The placement and availability of parking may become a critical issue, driving the creation of new public and/or parking resources.
- **Loading and Deliveries**—It may be necessary to intermix truck delivery traffic and customer parking, necessitating deliveries before or after operating hours, or deliveries may occur from the street during business hours.
- **Multistory Retail Stores and Restaurants**—Although street-level retail is the most accessible and desirable design, tight urban sites may require a multilevel solution to produce enough square footage for financial feasibility. In some instances, this requirement has resulted in two-level stores that have traditionally been one level. McDonald's and Burger King among fast-food restaurants, Harris Teeter and Whole Foods among supermarkets, and Walmart and Target among general merchandise stores all operate multilevel stores in urban areas.

SPECIALTY CENTER SITES. Because specialty shopping centers are, by design, intended to influence the expenditure of discretionary time and income, sites selected for these centers must be sufficient in size, location, and orientation to establish the sense of place appropriate to both the market and the intended retail tenants. As such, the physical layouts of these facilities should seek to create special character that responds both to the targeted market and to the expectations and demands of the specialty retailers that will occupy the center. Although specialty centers may in fact be developed as a variation of linear centers, few design constants constrain site selection, and in fact, unique sites of all types and sizes may contribute to the creation of *place* essential to most specialty centers.

ACCESS, PARKING, AND CIRCULATION

Parking and on-site circulation plans are created as part of the site-planning process. In designing these aspects of any shopping center, the objective should be not just to meet the letter of the law but to design facilities that best meet the day-to-day needs of customers and retailers alike.

THE ROLE OF PARKING. Parking forms the customer's first impression of the shopping center and should be designed to allow minimum thought and effort by the customer. The lack of adequate parking can damage a center's financial feasibility. Customers will inevitably disfavor centers where they experience difficulty finding convenient parking. And in commodity centers, inadequate parking can by itself defeat the primary goal of delivering convenience.

Components of parking design—size of parking area, driveway layout, access aisles, individual stall dimensions and arrangements, pedestrian movements from the parking area to the center, grading, paving, landscaping, and lighting—are major elements of site planning. In some markets, land values and site constraints have made it possible to increase capacity by providing structured parking. This practice is not typical for commodity centers, however, and works best if the former surface parking areas are being redeveloped for expanded retail offerings or other vertical uses.

Historically, land planned for later expansion was often paved as a least-cost maintenance strategy. This approach is not recommended because such space often becomes commuter parking, which is difficult to retrieve later. Moreover, because paving is impervious, this excess paved area creates greater demand for stormwater management.

PARKING DESIGN CONCERNS. The guiding principles in planning the parking area are the number of spaces needed, as well as required by the local zoning ordinance, and their best arrangement. Parking that is well distributed helps minimize the need for customers to park more than one time per visit.

Based on a 1999 study of parking requirements for shopping centers conducted by ULI and the International Council of Shopping Centers,[9] the following base parking standards are still recommended for a typical shopping center:

Size of Shopping Center (Gross Leasable Area)	Spaces Recommended per 1,000 Ft² (93 m²)
<400,000 ft²	4.0
400,000–600,000 ft²	4.0–4.5
>600,000 ft²	4.5

Geographic location, an urban versus suburban setting, and large-city versus small-city settings do not significantly affect parking demand. Numerous other factors can affect the amount of parking required, including the availability and proximity of mass transit, shared parking situations, the amount of walk-in versus destination trade, and individual tenant requirements. The standards above are based on

having enough parking spaces available for all but the 20 busiest hours of the year, allowing surplus parking during all but 19 of the more than 3,000 hours during which a typical center is open annually.

Some parking standards use a measure different from GLA (gross leasable area), usually GBA (gross building area) or NLA (net leasable area). For example, an ordinance requiring four spaces per thousand square feet (95 m²) of GBA is more or less equal to five spaces per thousand square feet (95 m²) of GLA/NLA if GLA/NLA is calculated at 80 percent of GBA. Restaurants greatly increase parking demand at certain times of the day because restaurant patrons spend more time, and larger numbers occupy the space at one time than they do retail space.

SHARED PARKING. Shared parking is the use of a parking space to serve two or more individual land uses without conflict or encroachment.[10] The need to adopt shared parking strategies has grown as projects incorporate nonretail uses. Moreover, with increasing land and construction costs, the ability to reduce and share the total number of parking spaces becomes increasingly valuable to the developer.

Programs that work best are those where patrons' use peaks at different times of the day. For example, parking for most retail peaks by midday and stays fairly constant until about 7:00 p.m., while parking for cinemas peaks between 7:00 and 10:00 p.m.[11] The methodology for estimating the parking demand in a mixed-use development involves analyzing the type and quantity of land uses, local zoning requirements, parking pricing, transit use, and user characteristics. For more detailed information, the reader should consult *Parking Requirements for Shopping Centers*, 2nd edition.

SURFACE PARKING DESIGN. The layout of surface parking spaces may be perpendicular or diagonal. Perpendicular (90-degree) parking economizes on space, facilitates circulation, and provides two-way traffic through the aisle, the safety of better sight lines, greater parking capacity, and shorter cruising distances for drivers seeking a space. Diagonal (angular) parking spaces, with 45- or 60-degree angles, provide one-way circulation, are easier for drivers to enter and exit, and involve fewer conflicts between adjacent vehicles when occupants open car doors. Diagonal layouts also provide greater maneuverability for sports utility vehicles and minivans. Whether to choose perpendicular or diagonal parking should depend on the generally prevailing pattern in the community that can be best adapted to site conditions.

Ideally, aisles should be aligned perpendicularly to storefronts to allow shoppers to walk directly from their cars to the front of stores. The aisles themselves may be curved or angled to meet physical requirements of the site or the design. Parking aisles that run parallel with storefronts should be avoided, however, because customers are then required to cut between cars, which can be hazardous. However, if a center is L-shaped, this configuration is difficult to avoid.

For smaller, unanchored commodity shopping centers, perpendicular parking is often best placed along the storefronts. This design accommodates quick visits to the stores and fast turnover of prime spaces. It does, however, create a somewhat more hazardous situation, as shoppers can step out from between cars into moving traffic.

STRUCTURED PARKING. Parking structures are often built when surface parking is not the highest and best use of the land and land costs can justify the added expense. Structured parking should be seen as an opportunity to increase the project's possibilities. For example, the ground level of a structure can accommodate service and retail tenants in reasonable minimum depths. Single-sided residential or office uses that will further enhance a project's streetscape can also be used as a veneer on parking structures.

Parking structures can alleviate excessive walking distances between parked cars and stores and solve space problems that may be created by a shopping center's development, or its later expansion. At many centers, adjacent land for expansion is not available or has become so costly that building a parking structure or deck may be the most economical means of providing additional parking spaces or opportunities for additional development. For detailed information on structured parking, see *Dimensions of Parking*, 5th edition.[12]

AMERICANS WITH DISABILITIES ACT (ADA). Since 1992, the ADA has mandated the number and location of parking spaces accessible to handicapped individuals in public places, including shopping centers. ADA guidelines clearly state that "first priority should be given to measures that will enable individuals with disabilities to get in the front door."[13] For shopping centers with multiple "front doors," this guideline can create significant challenges both in interpretation and implementation.

For example, a shopping center with 100,000 square feet (9,300 m²) of GLA and requiring 400 parking spaces would require eight handicapped-accessible spaces under ADA guidelines. These spaces will need to be located next to curb ramps to walkways along the storefronts. In addition, they will need to be positioned in front of or near the anchor tenants and then occasionally along the remaining storefronts. Additionally, at least one handicapped-accessible space should be placed in front of a convenience store.

With all of this information in mind, it is easy to see that while a minimum of dedicated handicapped-accessible spaces may be required in the example above, a number greater than the minimum may be necessary to best serve the anticipated customer base. Although not required by the ADA, the provision of designated reserved spaces for expectant mothers is a current practice for toy stores and stores selling baby goods.

INGRESS AND EGRESS
Efficient ingress and egress are critical to shopping center success. Road improvements are often required as part of the site-planning process to provide for efficient location and number of curb cuts, and the use of entrance deceleration and exit acceleration lanes must be taken into account, as should the need for traffic signals to allow turns and to control traffic flow. It may be difficult to secure approvals for curb cuts at locations deemed most suitable for entrances. Left-turn lanes might be required and may also be difficult to obtain. All of these issues should be fully vetted and addressed during the feasibility study period.

SITE ENGINEERING
Design requirements for most shopping centers dictate that the development site be relatively level. Slope and other unusual features of a site's topography should be planned to achieve maximum compatibility between the shopping center and the site's natural characteristics. An engineering firm with local experience should be retained to assess on-site soils and to identify any other special site problems.

In very limited circumstances, if the best available site has significant slope, and this slope corresponds to the grades of surrounding roads, an opportunity may exist for a two-level arrangement of buildings and parking. For example, a sloping site with trees that must be preserved can be reshaped to accommodate a stepped but still essentially single-level center. Vehicles use a sloped access road, and pedestrians use wide steps with an adjacent ADA-approved pedestrian ramp to move from level to level. A front-to-back design is also possible, but it isolates upper and lower tenants from each other. It may be a satisfactory solution if the tenant mix can be logically divided or if the less attractive level can be leased to nonretail residential or office uses.

The ideal slope for a parking lot is 3 percent, which allows for sufficient drainage but helps prevent runaway shopping carts and difficulties with hard-to-open, heavy car doors. A slope of 7 to 8 percent is allowable in limited areas, such as entry drives. (In areas with substantial ice and snow, however, a maximum slope of 5 percent is typical.) If the site has areas of steeper slope, the parking lot can be divided into terraced pads separated by landscaped strips.[14] A sloping site may also facilitate entrances at both levels in the case of a two-level shopping center.

STORMWATER MANAGEMENT. Stormwater runoff is a major issue in shopping center design due to the large amounts of land covered by buildings and pavement in a typical retail project. Reducing or delaying this runoff may involve significant cost. Most communities have limited storm system capacities and often require methods to control stormwater runoff, such as rooftop ponding, temporary detention basins (in portions of the parking lot, for example), retention ponds, or other mechanisms for reducing the runoff rate and total runoff from a developed site. Stormwater management systems that take into account both the primary function of water storage and visual appearance should be designed as an integral part of the overall project.

LANDSCAPING. Attractive landscape features at shopping center entrances contribute to creating a positive first impression and should be coordinated with the location and design of signage and other design features. In general, landscaping for a parking area should be confined to trees and massed plantings in wells or in clearly delineated areas. Plantings should be located where they will not interfere with maintenance of the parking area or with snow removal and storage. Minimum landscaping requirements are often specified for shopping centers by code and are enforced as part of the site-planning process.

Landscaping at the perimeter of the center can effectively mask parking areas from the street and buffer the center from nearby residential areas. Regardless of the technique used, landscaping should not hide the center from public view. Hardy ground covers and shrubbery concentrated at appropriate places in

the buffers and trees that can be pruned to provide a high canopy are good solutions.

Small planting areas in the pedestrian areas of the center, next to and between buildings, and in conjunction with architectural features and landscape furniture, can provide buffers from large parking areas and create an attractive pedestrian environment. In specialty centers, fountains, pools, and seasonal plants can be used extensively to create a pleasant atmosphere and offer a series of refreshing vistas to visitors and tenants. Patios and other outdoor seating areas provide attractive space for eateries and other similar uses, as well as offer resting places for patrons.

LIGHTING. Exterior lighting is both an essential safety feature and a key design feature used to create an image and character for shopping centers. Providing a higher level of light attracts more attention to the center at night and enhances the sense of security. However, intensive lighting will often be viewed negatively by adjacent residents. Overly bright lighting could also negatively affect the center's image.

The primary objective of shopping center lighting is to provide the customer with both a real and a perceived sense of security. Lighting on buildings is also sometimes used to illuminate storefronts at night, particularly when the architecture is distinctive. Under-canopy lighting is also needed to aid pedestrians' vision, and accent lighting can be used to enhance the center's appearance. Frequently, under-canopy signage lights and lights from inside stores are sufficient if display windows are well lit.

Shopping centers must provide easy access to parking. At Legacy Place in Dedham, Massachusetts, 2,400 parking spaces are provided in a mix of structured and surface lots.

WS DEVELOPMENT

An effective lighting system requires consideration of a variety of factors, including mounting height, spacing, light control, and light sources. Lighting should be evaluated based on efficiency, durability, color of light, and light output. Lighting in parking areas should be placed on poles located in islands at the ends of parking bays or on the dividing line between bays when they are longer than the spread of the selected fixture and should usually provide a minimum of about one and one-half foot-candles at the pavement surface.

The mounting height of fixtures should equal approximately half the horizontal distance to be illuminated; as such, for a typical parking bay module of 60 feet (18.3 m), a 30-foot (9.1 m) mounting height is efficient. In some instances, a more intimate lighting design may be desirable.[15]

Lighting technology is changing dramatically, with greater energy efficiency and longer bulb life reducing long-term costs. Walmart has begun converting to LED lighting for parking lots. In addition to significant energy savings, the lighting can be better focused where needed, thus reducing nighttime glare. Developers should keep abreast of new lighting technologies and use the most cost-effective fixtures that are appropriate.

LANDSCAPING AND LIGHTING FOR SPECIALTY CENTERS. Although both landscaping and lighting play important roles in creating appealing aesthetics in shopping centers of all types, they play an even more central role in specialty shopping centers, where, in addition to safety concerns, lighting and enhanced landscaping also serve as key elements in place making and the creation of higher levels of aesthetic appeal. Large-scale specialty centers often include dedicated open spaces and public facilities well beyond those of the more utilitarian commodity shopping centers. They may emulate a traditional village setting, with shops wrapped around a town square lighted by Colonial-style lanterns, or they may take on a more contemporary flair, with colored lights highlighting fountains and other design elements.

BUILDING STRUCTURE AND SHELL

Small shopping centers are usually highly efficient in the ratio of rentable space and total floor area. The typical design is a shell encasing the most efficient and inexpensive bulk space possible, concealed behind an attractive facade. The buildings are usually constructed of a lightweight steel roof-framing structure and

In Miami Beach, Fifth and Alton is a 180,000-square-foot (17,000 m²) shopping center with a 1,000-space municipal parking garage.

tilt-up concrete walls or concrete or masonry units. Shopping center structural frames most often consist of steel-tube columns and bar joists. For main support members, joist girders offer lighter weight and more flexibility in duct locations and roof penetrations than steel or prestressed concrete T-beams.

Specialty shopping centers will make use of more expensive facade materials and a higher level of design, typically based on a theme or unifying design concept. The design of foundations for shopping center buildings varies from region to region and from site to site, depending on subsurface conditions. The structure must be attractive as well as functional. It should lend itself to future adaptation and updating. It should fit into the fabric of the neighborhood.

Except when side- and rear-facing walls are readily visible to adjacent property owners, or when upgrades are required as part of the site plan approval process, the choice of method for enclosing the side and rear walls of a shopping center is driven almost exclusively by cost. Tilt-up concrete wall panels are often favored, primarily because of low installation costs. Tilt-up walls are light and thin, but they should be strong enough to serve as load-bearing structural walls. An alternative is to use load-bearing concrete masonry units, eight or 12 inches (20.4 or 30.5 cm) thick. Both these wall systems can be painted, plastered, or bricked over.

Most insulation of retail building shells is installed as a tenant finish item; nevertheless, insulation should be installed by the developer at perimeter walls and above ceilings. A design practice that will affect the location of insulation is the trend toward higher vertical spaces achieved by eliminating a ceiling and leaving ductwork and piping exposed. The only place for insulation in this approach is on top of the roof decking or directly on its underside.

When renovating older structures, stripping the building to the shell may expose hazardous materials such as asbestos and lead paint, which will have to be dealt with by means of legally mandated processes and safety methods required to protect workers and air quality. Cement asbestos tile and sprayed asbestos insulation were common in the 1950s. Removal of these products may prove costly and will likely negatively affect the economic feasibility of a rehabilitation project, because of both incremental costs and the time delays resulting from inspections and additional required approvals.

FACADES. Creating attractive storefronts and building facades is a critically important aspect of all shopping center designs. Whether the shopping center is commodity or specialty focused, the objective is to create an appealing look and feel, without overpowering the retailers themselves. Materials should be locally available if possible, capable of being assembled and erected quickly, durable, and easily maintained. Important considerations in choosing facade materials are cost, durability, availability, the message conveyed, and the design theme or concept planned. Many developers create storefront and sign-design guidelines that are attachments to the lease and that specify that control over the final design remains with the developer whether the storefronts are provided by the developer or through tenant allowances.

Like other key building components, exterior facing materials contribute to the shopping center's image and overall perception. The image created should be one of harmony tempered by variation in selected details to create a distinct image. For example, stone (or synthetic stone) with stucco is a popular and attractive combination.

A variety of facing materials is used in designing and constructing typical shopping center facades—including masonry, metal panels, wood, tile, and stucco-like synthetic finish systems, also called exterior insulation finishing system (EIFS). Of these choices, EIFS has become a standard building material in commodity shopping centers of all types. Masonry, however, is the most durable and offers great flexibility in treatment. Its very durability, however, makes it less flexible and more unlikely than other surfaces to be easily modified during future remodeling. The choice of material also depends on the character of the community. In the Midwest and East, masonry is the standard of quality, while in the West, tile, wood, adobe brick, and stucco are commonly used.

Any of these materials may be used to build a colonnaded walk or arcade, the traditional means of sheltering customers and protecting storefronts from the weather. Canopies may be cantilevered from the building elevation or supported by freestanding columns. Their size is determined by the chosen architectural style; ten to 15 feet (3–4.5 m) is an ample width for a walkway without limiting tenant visibility.

FLOORS. The building's subfloor is usually a flat concrete slab. When floor slabs are poured in the normal sequence of building shell construction, allowances must be made for plumbing lines to serve future restrooms. Water and sanitary sewer lines should be placed parallel to, and three feet (0.9 m) away from, the rear wall of the building. It is advisable to delay pouring the rearmost five feet (1.5 m) of slab until tenants decide where to locate restrooms. Finishing techniques using a laser screed can significantly reduce variations in flatness, but the underlying soil may require treatment with lime or cement to reduce seasonal "shrink and swell" variations and maintain level floor slabs over time. Alternatively, on-site soils can be replaced with fill materials of higher quality to achieve the same objective.

Any location designated for restaurant use should be constructed without a slab during initial construction because of the heavy utility needs of restaurants and the varied nature of their layouts. In such cases, the slab should not be poured, if possible, until the space is leased and the tenant has designed a layout for utilities.

Tenants are almost always responsible for the floor coverings in their spaces, which must be in accordance with criteria established by the owner and specified in the lease. Special floor coverings are usually installed over the concrete slab in tenant sales areas and are often omitted in storage or other back-of-house areas. Floor coverings range from various vinyl tile products or carpeting to wood, tile, or stone. Floor surfaces of common areas may be of marble or granite, carpeting, tile pavers, wood, or poured-in-place material, such as terrazzo. Flooring should be commercial grade, nonslippery, durable, and easy to clean, maintain, and repair.

ROOF SYSTEMS. Shopping center roofs are often one of the most costly and difficult aspects of construction and operation for developers, and roof leaks are one of the most common complaints by shopping center tenants. A typical shopping center roof should last 12 to 15 years; but correctly installed and proactively maintained, it can last 20 years or more. In general, roofs should slope at least one-quarter inch per foot (0.6 cm/30.5 cm) to ensure good drainage. The future installation of rooftop-mounted HVAC units should be anticipated in designing the roof, with allowances made for their weight and prefabricated roof curbs provided to minimize random penetrations of the roof.

Three principal types of roofing are used for shopping centers—built-up, single-ply membrane, and modified bitumen. Single-ply roofs are the most common systems, used now in more than half of new construction. The elastomeric properties of these rubber-type membranes allow them to stretch and move with the roof deck, helping to prevent tears.

Additionally, white membrane roofing has been developed in response to concerns about energy efficiency and the environment. Although white membranes can cost twice as much as black membranes, cost savings in energy expenses over the life of the roof can offset the additional expense and may even generate significant savings, depending on the location.

The best roof system for a particular center may well depend on the local climate. Choosing the right roof should be based on the answers to the following questions, according to Bill Baley, vice president of Pegnato & Pegnato Building Systems:[16]

- What is the cost per square foot budgeted for this location?
- How cut up is the roof system? Does it have a lot of penetrations, curbs, and equipment?
- How much foot traffic is there near the building?
- What kind of weather will the roof be subject to?
- Will the roof be subject to any contaminants (jet fuel, oils, food grease, and so on)?
- What problems have been experienced with systems used in the past?
- What is the anticipated length of ownership of the center?

CEILING HEIGHTS. Although most stores require 11- to 12-foot (3.3 m) finished or open ceilings, some small stores find ceilings as low as nine feet (2.7 m) acceptable. Most big-box tenants, along with supermarkets and general merchandise stores, require finished ceilings heights of 13 feet (4 m) or higher.

The space between the finished ceiling and the roof usually contains air-conditioning ducts, electrical wires, plumbing lines, and other utility hardware; such equipment may require as much as two to three feet (0.6–0.9 m) of space between the finished ceiling and the structure. When open-web steel joists are used, much of the ductwork and other lines can be threaded between the webs. Thus, the clear distance from the floor slab to the underside of the roof varies with the structural design.

UTILITIES. To allow for flexibility in operations, structural elements such as plumbing and heating stacks, air-conditioning ducts, toilets, and stairways should be placed on end walls or on the walls least likely to be removed if the store is enlarged or the space redivided.

Keeping all utilities—including waterlines—overhead should be seriously considered. An overhead leak may cause some damage but can be more easily located and repaired. Leaks under the slab are much more damaging and expensive to repair and disrupt use of the space. If overhead waterlines are used, measures must be taken to ensure that the lines are not exposed to freezing temperatures.

Plumbing. For tenants that require large plumbing installations, such as supermarkets, restaurants, and dry cleaners, installation of the floor slab should usually be deferred until these tenant spaces are leased because formulation of the tenant's under-floor requirements will likely extend past the developer's shell construction schedule. Distribution of plumbing and other utilities is usually included as a tenant cost or a tenant allowance item, with the base building utilities stubbed off at the lease perimeter/owner's shell.

Electricity. Generally, a primary source of electricity provided by the developer is located at the rear of the building and individually metered. Each tenant is then required to provide the secondary electrical service from the meter, subject to the landlord's review and approval.

HVAC. Individual HVAC units are typically provided for each tenant in commodity centers. Once delivered, tenants are typically assigned responsibility for their individual units under their lease terms. Because energy costs and energy conservation are important considerations, the selection of the most appropriate HVAC system requires the skill of a mechanical engineer familiar with the alternative gas and electric systems available to evaluate initial, operating, and maintenance costs and to recommend the best system.

TENANT SPACES

Space leased by a tenant typically contains designated frontage, unfinished party walls (also called demising walls) separating the space from retail neighbors, an unfinished floor, and exposed joists for roof support. The rear door and utility stubs are generally located in plans for the shell but can be repositioned as part of the lease deal.

STORE SIZES. Store widths and depths vary for different types of tenants. Chain stores typically have specific prototype store dimensions and, in general, seek to avoid significant deviation. For most new shopping centers, the design of the shell usually requires wide spans between structural columns so that stores can be inserted into modules with minimal conflict with columns. When conflict occurs, columns can be disguised as part of the fixtures and can often be used as part of a store's decorative features.

In general, shallow depths are better and can accommodate a greater breadth of tenants. For neighborhood and community centers, store depths can range from 40 to 120 feet (12.2–36.6 m). A key principle in determining store depths is to rely on the proposed mix of tenants and store frontage they will likely require. To accommodate varying depths, buildings should be designed with offsets at the front and rear to vary the depth. Some tenants will be satisfied and may even welcome an L-shaped space that wraps around a small, shallow boutique space.

INTERIOR FINISHES. Most developers use an allowance for finishing tenant space beyond a designated "shell" delivery condition. In most commodity retail shopping centers, the industry standard delivery condition is referred to as a "vanilla shell." Subject to small variations, a vanilla shell delivery typically includes the following building features:
- building shell complete (with drywall taped and spackled, ready for tenant's wall treatment);
- storefront installed;
- rear door installed;
- bathroom(s) installed to code;
- standard florescent lighting installed to code;
- utilities delivered to premises;
- floors installed, level and ready for tenant floor treatment;
- base building insulation installed;
- HVAC installed (not distributed); and
- watertight roof installed.

JIM SIMMONS

Signage creates an identity and visibility for tenants and helps set the tone for a shopping center.

Note however, that depending on shopping center type and market conditions, delivery condition may vary from a "raw shell" to "turnkey" buildout. Additionally, allowances, usually expressed as dollar amounts per square foot, are provided by developers and used by tenants to pay for any upgrades to these delivery standards.

TENANT SIGNAGE. Signage for shopping center tenants is first and foremost critical to creating tenant identity and visibility. But it is also an important source of a project's color, vitality, atmosphere, and sense of place. It should be an integral part of the building design. Options for tenant signage available today are numerous and include[17]
- specially shaped box signs;
- individual internally illuminated letters with Plexiglas faces;
- open-face letters with exposed neon;
- reverse-channel letters with halo-effect lighting;
- bare neon, with or without special backgrounds;
- individual letters mounted on a common raceway, with or without a "receiver" channel;
- internally illuminated sign bands; and
- graphics screened onto canvas or "Panaflex" awnings.

Although tenants almost always pay for and install their own signs, shopping center developers should always exercise control over what tenants can display through a declaration of permitted and prohibited signage along with specific signage type and quality standards. Developers, however, may wish to be more specific about details of the signage program and limit some things that are permissible under the sign ordinance, such as temporary signs.

Although some developers insist on uniform scale, size, and placement of retail store signs, this practice, while easier to administer, has often been discredited for creating a bland, monotone sign standard, which restricts tenant identity and is believed to reduce sales of heavily promoted national tenants that rely on display of their individual "trade dress" to attract customers.

In general, the size, materials, and even colors of tenant signage are governed by each community's sign ordinance. In some communities, a developer may be able to submit a signage program that deviates from the standard and to obtain approval tied specifically to the center for which it is proposed.

Construction

Numerous factors dictate the correct time to begin construction, but the developer should make certain that it does not begin prematurely, which will likely lead to problems and higher construction costs. For example, if shell construction begins before anchor tenants are committed and their space requirements known, change orders requiring costly tearing out and redoing construction may be necessary. Some communities issue building permits for foundations before approval of complete building plans. This early start can again lead to cost increases if final building design approvals are delayed or if approvals result in unanticipated subsurface requirements.

Shopping center construction involves three principal areas of concern: preparation of the site, construction of the building shell, and completion of tenant finishes. (Contracting arrangements for the site and shell, which do not differ significantly by property type, are discussed in chapter 2.)

TENANT FINISHES

Retail tenant finishes present numerous challenges peculiar to retail development. Most important, the developer should establish and maintain close communication with every tenant. Successful coordination involves a clear understanding of the lease and each side's responsibilities, agreement on specifications, plans and procedures, ongoing communications, effective follow-through, and monitoring of progress.[18] This task is so critical that developers of larger specialty centers may retain an on-site tenant coordinator.

The responsibilities of each party and the specifications for construction are included in the tenant improvement schedule, usually an exhibit to the tenant's lease. The construction of tenant finishes usually involves variations on two methods: (1) shell and allowance and (2) build to suit. Each method has its own advantages and disadvantages.

The most common approach is shell and allowance, in which the developer constructs the building shell and allows the tenant a specified sum to complete all other permanent improvements to the store. Tenant allowance typically ranges from $5 to $25 per square foot ($54–$270/m²) or more for very high end or specialized space. The amount of the tenant allowance depends on the type and size of the shopping center, the size of the tenant, the importance of the tenant to the merchandising/leasing strategy of the shopping center, and the tenant's requirements.

In the build-to-suit approach, the developer agrees to complete the tenant finish work and the cost is divided based on the negotiated terms of the deal. This method allows the developer to control the quality and consistency of construction and provides a valuable service for small and inexperienced tenants. It is unlikely to be acceptable to an anchor or national chain tenant. A third alternative is also available in which the developer chooses to simply supply the shell and the tenant must bear the full cost of buildout.

Whatever basis is used, the developer must be sensitive to the tenant's needs if construction is to proceed smoothly. Supplying pertinent information and guidance will help coordination between the developer and the tenant. A data book prepared by the developer can provide the retailer and the architect/engineer with answers to many questions. The data book should contain[19]

- an index of all the developer's architectural and engineering plans, specifications, and details;
- sections through, and details of, the leased wall construction and of any other elements of construction that may affect the tenant's planning;
- definitions of symbols used for walls, partitions, ceilings, doors, various types of electrical outlets and switches, and panel boards; riser diagrams; and door and roof finish schedules;
- definitions of standard mechanical symbols and connections;
- local design factors or criteria available to the tenant's engineer;
- excerpts of unusual building code requirements that will be helpful to the tenant's out-of-town architect/engineer;
- work rules;
- developer contact information for questions; and
- descriptions of penalties for noncompliance.

In addition, the developer may provide an outline of the steps and procedures a tenant should follow to have plans and applications approved by government agencies and to file for a certificate of occupancy. The developer should also inform the tenant about any unusual jurisdictional situations and whether union labor is required.

Financing

Financing for shopping centers differs in many respects from other commercial real estate financing. (See chapter 4 for a thorough discussion of the various sources and methods of financing for income property.)

Commodity shopping centers, including neighborhood, grocery, community, and power centers, are generally viewed by lenders as more stable investments because they tend to be oriented toward the sale of nondurable consumer goods and services, those items bought regardless of changes in the economy. Supermarkets and drugstores can generally maintain relatively stable sales at all times because they sell products that most people need on a regular basis. Specialty centers, on the other hand, are more subject to fluctuations in the economy and are considered riskier investments. Thus, they are inherently more difficult to finance.

The rules applicable to shopping center finance have changed frequently over the life of the industry, based on periodic changes in lending practices, economic conditions, and trends within different segments of the shopping center industry. As a general rule of thumb, to obtain the best financing for a shopping center, the project must typically be at least 75 to 80 percent preleased with long-term creditworthy tenants. Preferred financing terms are given for shopping centers in which lease terms for at least 50 percent of the space are for at least 20 years, with the balance of leases for creditworthy tenants usually for ten- or 15-year initial terms.

GENERAL FINANCING CONSIDERATIONS

Shopping centers are generally financed with construction loans on a short-term basis during the acquisition, construction, and/or redevelopment phases. Once operating and stabilized, shopping centers are routinely financed with permanent loans for longer terms.

To obtain the best financing for a shopping center, a project should have as high a percentage as possible of credit tenants. As a general rule, 65 to 70 percent of the potential income should be attributable to leases with so-called credit tenants to maximize financing potential and to enhance long-term value. (Credit

tenants are generally considered the large national or regional retailers with excellent credit ratings.) Lenders want to be confident that even if a number of weaker tenants do not survive in a shopping center, there will still be ample cash flow to pay debt service, and enough strength in the remaining tenant base to attract replacement tenants to vacant spaces.

In addition to creditworthiness, longer-term leases (ten years or more for larger tenants) are preferable and create better financial potential for the center. In the event that the shopping center in question does not meet the above criteria, it will still likely be financeable, depending on overall market conditions, but the sources of financing will be fewer, generally consisting of smaller, regional banks, and the terms of financing will likely be less favorable, including higher rates and shorter amortization schedules.

CONSTRUCTION FINANCING

Shopping center developments are nearly always financed with a construction loan, also referred to as an "acquisition and development loan." Compared with permanent loans, discussed below, construction loans are considered far riskier and therefore are shorter term, generally tied to floating-rate terms, and these loans are typically "recourse" to the borrower—meaning that the developer must personally guarantee repayment of the construction loan note.

Because construction loans are recourse to the borrower, both the real estate and the underlying creditworthiness of the borrower are very important in underwriting project risk. In the event that the project is not successful, or is in the end worth less than the construction loan, the lender might look to the borrower to repay the loan from personal assets.

The collapse of commercial real estate values in 2008 resulted in many situations in which most projects still under construction loans—even those built and operating—experienced real or technical defaults, causing lenders to look to the recourse provisions of their loans for at least partial loan repayment. This situation occurred not only because of underlying weakness in tenant demand but also because of swift and radical changes in project valuations and underlying loan criteria, causing even "cash flowing" properties to be in noncompliance with loan covenants and unable to be permanently financed as the construction loans matured.

Interest rates and monthly payments on construction loans vary depending on the underlying base rate. The base rate in a construction loan is either the prime rate (used by smaller banks) or LIBOR. The interest rate paid is calculated by adding a "spread" tied to perceived risk, over these base rates.

Given historically low short-term interest rates in this most recent cycle, many banks have recently begun to impose rate floors establishing a minimum interest rate that the loan will carry if base rates fall further.

Construction loans are typically sized based on a percentage of the loan to the overall project cost. These "coverage ratios" cap borrowing at a set percentage of project cost and vary with market conditions. They are at or near historical highs at this writing.

In addition to debt coverage ratios, construction loans are subject to debt-to-equity ratios, generally requiring cash equity investments in the project at a set percentage of total project cost. A ratio of 75 percent of debt to 25 percent of equity is a good historical average; however, during the real estate boom in the mid-2000s, the amount borrowed could at times be 100 percent debt.

By 2008, market conditions had changed such that obtaining a new construction loan became virtually impossible for a time, and later only at historically low debt-to-equity ratios. This circumstance was made even more difficult as new government regulations were imposed on banks. By 2011, market conditions had marginally improved.

PERMANENT FINANCING

Typically, by the time a shopping center stabilizes its tenant base, the developer will repay the construction loan with the proceeds from a permanent loan. The basic characteristics that differentiate the permanent loan from a construction loan are that the permanent loan is typically "nonrecourse," meaning the developer no longer personally guarantees the loan, and the loan interest rate is set for the life of the loan, allowing monthly loan payments to remain constant over the entire term of the loan. The most common term for a permanent loan is ten years.

The primary providers of permanent loan financing have historically been institutions such as banks, insurance companies, and pension funds. In the early 2000s, the commercial mortgage–backed security (CMBS) type of permanent loan became more common. These exchange-traded instruments allowed a diversification of loan risk and therefore often resulted in lower borrowing costs and terms.

Beginning in 2007, the CMBS market began to collapse, taking a substantial amount of liquidity out of the market and leaving owners unable to repay most

Legacy Place in Dedham, Massachusetts, features L.L. Bean, Whole Foods Market, and a 14-screen Showcase Cinema de Lux.

outstanding construction loans or to refinance maturing permanent loans. As of early 2012, insurance companies and the CMBS lenders are returning to the market, making loans, but with tougher, more stringent terms (including higher equity requirements) than in the mid-2000s.

Interest rates on permanent loan have historically averaged 150 to 250 basis points over a government-guaranteed bond of similar duration to the permanent loan in question. That spread over government bonds widened dramatically from 2008 to 2010 but has been slowly coming back down.

Permanent loans are typically made at "par," meaning that no points are charged at closing, though this is subject to changing market conditions. Permanent loans have been traditionally sized at 65 to 70 percent of the appraised value of the shopping center in question. With aggressive CMBS underwriting in the boom years, those percentages hit a high of 85 percent in 2006, but again they have decreased significantly since then. The size of the permanent loan can also be determined based on the ratio of the property cash flow divided by the debt service—with a ratio of 1.2 to 1.3 being typical, depending on the type of asset and credit of the tenants.

The ability to successfully develop a shopping center not only depends on finding a suitable property and leasing it successfully but also depends on successfully timing the construction and permanent loans in fluctuating markets. Despite very careful planning and execution, it is sometimes very difficult to accomplish.

PUBLIC FINANCING

In some cases, public financing may be available for all or part of a new shopping center, especially in inner-city areas or in communities actively promoting economic development. Developers interested in inner-city opportunities should explore the possibility of a joint venture with nonprofit community groups, neighborhood development corporations, or churches, which might have capital resources, a suitable site under their ownership or control, or access to venture capital. To stimulate economic development and tax base enhancements, public financing has been used to cover "cost gaps" such as parking, to reduce financing costs to the developer, or to provide infrastructure enhancements to make the projects possible.

LAND SALES

One means of raising equity financing for shopping center development is to sell parcels to anchor tenants or outparcels, or "pad sites" to fast-food restaurants, banks, and similar businesses after the center plan has taken shape. The value of these outparcels should increase, often dramatically, as entitlements are finalized for the proposed shopping center, allowing the developer not only to recapture (or offset) equity capital required for the project but also to potentially realize a substantial profit. A comparison of typical loans from various financing sources is presented in figure 7-1.

Merchandising and Leasing

The most desirable tenant mix for a proposed shopping center is determined by a variety of factors, in-cluding the development concept, the size and type of center, competition in the area, the target market, and trends in consumer preferences. A shopping center's composition is ultimately determined by the developer's ability to attract and negotiate acceptable leases with desired prospective tenants. The mix should be targeted based on the market analysis, discussed earlier in this chapter, but the goals of the initial leasing plan may not be entirely met; tenants' preferences and varied requirements will inevitably result in ongoing revisions to the original leasing concept.

The tenant mix for any shopping center will depend almost entirely on the type of center under consideration. A balanced tenant mix that meets financial credit requirements should include both strong, credit-rated national firms, where appropriate, and strong local merchants. In all types of centers, the developer must be flexible in selecting tenants and negotiating leases with them. Interior arrangements and tenant leases will be adjusted numerous times as negotiations proceed. A plan that includes at least two tenant types targeted for each space provides flexibility in leasing.

In choosing tenants for a center in a newly developing area, the developer must secure stores that can provide a service to the trade area and that have the

FIGURE 7-1 | Comparison of Typical Permanent Loans from Different Types of Lenders

	Wall Street Conduit	Bank	Life Insurance Company	Credit Company
NOI	$1,000,000	$1,000,000	$1,000,000	$1,000,000
Recourse	Nonrecourse	Recourse	Nonrecourse	Nonrecourse
Term (years)	10	5	10	5
Type	Fixed	Variable	Fixed	Variable
Index type	Ten-year swap	Prime	Ten-year Treasury bill	LIBOR[a]
Note spread (%)	2.75	1.0–1.5	2.50	4.50
Note rate (%)	5.25	4.75	5.00	6.00
Amortization (years)	30	25	25	30
Constant (%)	6.63	6.84	7.02	7.19
DCR	1.25	1.30	1.30	1.25
Maximum loan amount (Test 1)	$12,072,839	$11,243,749	$10,965,388	$11,119,441
NOI	$1,000,000	$1,000,000	$1,000,000	$1,000,000
Cap rate (%)	8.00	8.00	8.00	8.00
Value	12,500,000	12,500,000	12,500,000	12,500,000
LTV ratio (%)	73	70	65	80
Maximum loan amount (Test 2)	9,125,000	8,750,000	8,125,000	10,000,000
NOI	1,000,000			1,000,000
Debt yield (%)	9.50			9.50
Maximum loan amount (Test 3)	$10,526,316			$10,526,316
Maximum loan amount	**$9,125,000**	**$8,750,000**	**$8,125,000**	**$10,000,000**

Source: Steve Bram, George Smith Partners, Los Angeles, California, 2012.
[a]LIBOR is the rate on dollar-denominated deposits, also known as Eurodollars, traded between banks in London.

financial stamina to weather a pioneering period. The developer should evaluate each tenant's credit rating, profit and loss experience, type of merchandise, type of customers, housekeeping practices, long-term operational record, and merchandising and advertising policies.

When a center is to be located on an infill or redevelopment site, the developer should identify tenant categories that are underrepresented in the market and should attract anchors that do not have a presence. In some instances, such merchants may not have considered opening a store at this location until they are approached.

The tenant mix should provide balanced interplay among the stores. The success of a shopping center's tenant mix lies not in including or excluding a specific type of tenant, but in selecting and combining a group of mutually reinforcing/complementary tenants that will serve the needs of the particular market. Some shopping center owners believe that it is important to include a mix of national tenants and local "mom and pops," particularly in urban village and town center settings. Some even go as far as subsidizing the rents of the smaller tenants to make it affordable enough for them to be part of the mix.

SHOPPING CENTER LEASING

Leasing a shopping center is more complex and demanding than leasing any other type of development; it involves creating an effective leasing plan, obtaining commitments from anchor tenants early in the process, and then leasing the smaller spaces according to the leasing plan. The leasing plan represents the center's investment potential and is fundamental to the planning process. Every leasing plan should include a space-by-space analysis with alternate proposed tenants, and a complete tenant mix strategy.

Prepared early in the development process, the leasing plan addresses the best tenant mix, the placement of tenants within the center, rent schedules, the pricing of store spaces, and lease specifications. The leasing plan is a living document that should be modified frequently, as the project evolves from concept to completion.

ORGANIZING THE LEASING PROGRAM. Agreements with leasing agents should address such issues as exclusive versus open listings, full commission structure, participation of in-house leasing staff, and leasing incentives. The leasing agent should be on the development team from start to finish and should provide guidance in the subtleties of tenant selection.

Developers must be actively involved in all stages of leasing, especially in the procurement of anchor tenants and in setting the merchandising strategy for the balance of the shopping center. Leasing is much more selective in shopping center projects than in office projects; the objective is not simply to lease space but to lease the right space to the right tenant. Thus, setting priorities for the leasing staff and maintaining those priorities are imperative.

Generally, development of a small shopping center cannot move forward without commitments from anchor tenants; thus, marketing to likely anchor tenants must begin very early in the process. In fact, key tenants, such as a supermarket, discount store, or drugstore, should be in contact with the development team at the planning stages. These tenants will want to be involved in the developer's decisions on building treatment, architectural style, parking, signage, and landscaping.

ANCHOR LEASING. Identification and procurement of anchor tenants are one of the first steps in a leasing program. Anchors are defined by their potential ability to draw visitors to a center. The expansion plans of anchor-type tenants often serve as the driving force behind center development. For example, larger discount stores such as Target, Walmart, and Kohl's are often cited as promoters of the resurgence of strip centers. New food retailers entering a market are also highly sought after.

Traditionally, anchors have been large retailers, but other models exist—especially for specialty centers. Entertainment facilities, such as cinemas or skating rinks, groupings of popular restaurants, or even a public library can serve the functions of an anchor. Victoria Gardens in southern California, for example, includes traditional department store anchors, but perhaps equally important, also boasts a cultural center with a children's library and playhouse. Its town square offers free outdoor movies and other events. The symbiosis created by all of these nonretail uses has the same drawing power as a department store.

In a superstore center, the search for nonanchor tenants can be difficult because the wide-ranging offerings of superstores can eliminate as many as ten types of tenants, which would offer a competing line of goods. Convenience stores are growing in popularity as anchor tenants in small centers and as attractive volume stores for larger strip centers, but they also may cause conflicts in leasing to other retailers: convenience stores sell a wide variety of goods and may insist on the exclusive right to sell certain items, such as beer, milk, and bread. Other items sold at convenience stores—toiletries, liquor, fast food, and ice cream, for example—can also cause clashes with other tenants that sell these items. Supermarkets, drugstores, and even gas stations usually do not want to be located in a center with a convenience store.

TENANT PLACEMENT. The placement of tenants within a shopping center is a critically important and complex issue. Tenants and leasing representatives have strong views about their desired position. A location that is advantageous for one type of business may be entirely wrong for another. Placement also depends on the size and depth of the space desired by the tenant. In deciding locations, developers should consider the following points:

- suitability of the tenant for the location, including the tenant's financial resources;
- compatible and complementary relationship with adjoining or nearby stores;
- compatibility of the tenant's merchandising practice with that of adjoining stores;
- parking needs generated by the tenant; and
- customer convenience.

Leasing Hints for Placing In-Line Users

- **When leasing less than an entire block of space, always lease from the sides to the middle so that only one predetermined space is left instead of two.**

- **Try to assign spaces so that the last space could be divided in half and still meet minimum requirements. That is, if 15 feet (4.5 m) is the minimum width, try to leave a 30-foot-wide (9.1 m) space instead of a 27- or 28-foot-wide (8.2 or 8.5 m) space.**

- **Try to lease the toughest space first, or if that is not possible, try to beat pro forma rents on easier space so that there is still rent negotiation flexibility for the toughest space.**

- **Consider what the next tenant will be left to deal with. Storefront width, column locations, signage area, rear or secondary access, and parking should all be standardized and flexible enough for most tenants.**

- **On to-be-built space, try to include a provision that allows the landlord to move a tenant within a certain area up to a certain time to allow for flexibility in lease-up.**

Source: ULI–the Urban Land Institute, *Shopping Centers: How to Build, Buy, and Redevelop*, workshop manual, Spring 2001, p. 16.

Anchors should be located so that shoppers must walk past the storefronts of supplementary tenants to reach them. They should be placed at opposite ends of a center, for example, rather than side by side. Multiple anchors should be spaced in a way that draws customers throughout the center and leaves no walkways without an anchor.

Retail spaces in any center may need to be reconfigured from time to time, and certain tenants may need to be relocated. Some tenants outgrow their original space, or need a smaller space, while others may need to be shifted to strengthen a center's overall operations. A mix of different sizes of retail space is essential to be able to adapt to tenants' changing needs.

THE SHOPPING CENTER LEASE

The center's leases function as an important management tool. Besides establishing obligations, responsibilities, and leasehold arrangements, the leases incorporate the means of preserving, over a long period, the shopping center's character and appearance as a merchandising complex. In effect, they establish a clear and permanent partnership between the management and the tenants. For example, the lease may have a buyout or cancellation clause for underperformance, that is, failing to meet a predetermined sales-per-square-foot figure. A developer without significant retail development experience should retain an attorney with experience in retail leases. The novice developer also needs to have a standard lease form to use as a starting point and to ensure that all important lease elements are addressed. Tenants should also use an attorney.

In the retail field, the percentage lease is a common kind of rental contract for both tenant and landlord. In its simplest form, the tenant agrees to pay a rent equal to a stipulated percentage of the gross dollar volume of the tenant's sales. The percentage lease balances the tenants' and the landlord's interests. It means, for example, that the landlord can agree to a lower base rent for a tenant that may be unable to pay a higher rent until its sales have grown sufficiently to afford a higher rent. For the tenant, it means that if the landlord benefits from higher sales, then the landlord has an incentive to market the center to help generate those overages and to provide the maintenance, management, and security that keep the center fully operating and attractive to customers. In shopping centers, the most common type of percentage lease is one in which the tenant agrees to pay a specified minimum rent plus a percentage of gross sales over a certain amount.

The developer needs to determine whether percentage rates will be acceptable to prospective tenants and whether they will be a useful tool in negotiating lease terms with at least some tenants. Evidence from developers indicates that more and more national tenants are refusing to negotiate percentage rents into their leases, particularly in neighborhood, community, and power centers.

Various types of percentage leases exist, but the typical lease has a natural break point. For example, the lease for a 2,000-square-foot (185 m²) space at $12 per square foot ($130/m²) per year with a percentage rent rate of 6 percent works as follows. The minimum rent would be 2,000 times $12 (185 times $130) or $24,000 per year. The break point where the percentage rent begins is calculated as $24,000 divided by 0.06, or $400,000. Thus, the tenant pays a base rent of $24,000 per year plus 6 percent of annual gross sales greater than $400,000. Gross sales of $500,000 would result in an annual rent of $30,000 ($500,000 times 0.06, or $24,000 base rent plus $6,000 percentage rent). The rate of percentage rent varies from tenant category to tenant category. In some cases, steps in the rate of percentage rent go up or down as sales increase. Again, these steps vary according to tenant category. With the recognition that percentage leases are declining in acceptance on the part of national tenants and that local nonpublic tenants are unlikely to accurately reveal their true sales, alternatives might include an annual increase based on the CPI or a fixed percentage increase of, say, 3 percent. Some leases require cash register systems that automatically document sales data for both the tenant and the developer, or that can be periodically audited by the owner to verify sales and rental payments. This arrangement is usually incorporated into the lease document.

SETTING RENTAL RATES. Retail rents generally include a fixed amount payable annually or monthly and, in many cases, an additional amount based on a percentage of the tenant's sales. Or the entire rent may be based on a straight percentage of sales.

Rental rates for any given space depend on the tenant's size, classification, location in the project, and the amount of tenant allowance provided. Rent schedules should indicate clearly the tenant's classification, square-footage allocation, minimum rent, and rate of percentage rent.

Percentage rents for most large tenants range from 1 to 3 percent, while those for in-line stores range from about 3 to 7 percent, with 6 percent most typical. In community centers, the rent for general merchandise stores might be around $15 per square foot ($161/m²), while that for jewelry stores might be more than $30 per square foot ($323/m²). Smaller in-line tenants pay percentage rents similar to those at neighborhood centers; however, larger anchor stores pay lower percentage rents, ranging from about 1 to 5 percent because of their ability to attract additional tenants. (See "The Lease" below for additional explanation of percentage rents.)

THE LEASE. Whether or not the shopping center lease includes a percentage rent clause, a net lease is almost always the preferred leasing format for small shopping centers. The preferred lease is triple net: in addition to a base rent (plus overages if included), the tenant pays its prorated share of real estate taxes, insurance, and maintenance. Many variations of lease terms are possible, including stepped base rent, free rent to achieve the desired base rent, and lower base rent combined with a higher percentage so that the landlord takes a greater risk but has a greater gain if the tenant succeeds. This latter arrangement is often used for desirable first-time tenants that provide a needed special character for a center.

The Rouse Company, when pioneering its festival market concept at Quincy Market in Boston, wrote short-term or month-to-month leases for very small pushcarts at a percentage of sales and zero base rent. The pushcarts were the feature that made the project different, and the risk to the Rouse Company was small because these tenants occupied space that would otherwise generate little or no rent income.

Exceptions to the net lease exist for some tenant categories, most commonly financial institutions, service shops, and offices. For these tenants, the developer would be wise to consider short-term leases or leases where the base rent escalates based on a series of specified steps or in step with the CPI. The exclusive rights to sell a particular category of merchandise within a shopping center are routinely given to anchor tenants in commodity centers.

USE CLAUSES. A retail lease must set out specifically permitted uses for leased space. For example, a restaurant lease should incorporate an attached menu that can be changed from time to time but sets an expected standard for the food style offered.

A retailer's permitted uses should be limited to those agreed to when it signed the lease agreement.

Reinventing Retail

Consider the following: Cirque du Soleil at the Mall of America; Forever 21 in Times Square; products at Macy's with QR Codes that customers can scan with their cell phones to get more information about the item while they're shopping; other cell phone apps that reward people just for walking into bricks-and-mortar stores.

"Reinventing retail is a daily exercise for all of us in merchandising and everything else," said Michael Townsend, president and CEO of Townsend & Associates, a retail and commercial developer whose clients include Forever 21 and United Colors of Benetton.

"It's all about changing quickly and changing with the market. Technology has made them very adaptable. It's not about quality so much as it is about newness; they want newness," he said, referring to generation Y shoppers, those born between 1980 and 2000.

Townsend and other industry experts predict casualties as well as opportunities ahead. Technology, demographics, and the recession are the main market drivers, according to Judith Taylor, a partner with Pro Forma Advisors, a land use consulting firm in Hermosa Beach, California. Growing Internet sales and tight credit are keeping the pressure on retailers to downsize store space, as baby boomers move toward retirement and out of their peak years for discretionary spending. At the same time, however, the Hispanic population—and its spending power—continues to grow. By 2050, it is expected that 29 percent of Americans will be Hispanic.[a]

"There's going to be a focus on upgrading and repositioning," Taylor said. "You're seeing other kinds of uses moving into shopping centers, such as institutional uses—libraries, schools, medical services. For both retailers and consumers, it's about making more with less. It's about getting consumers to leave their homes, exciting and enchanting them."

Retailers and retail developers are looking beyond price points to give their customers unique shopping experiences—which, in turn, is driving the trend to integrate retail and entertainment. Pedestrian-friendly mall alternatives are also on the rise, and like every other industry sector, retail brands are looking at global markets.

Rick Chancellor, western region vice president for the McDevitt Company, a retail developer with a client list that includes Urban Outfitters and Anthropologie, said the evolution of those companies has taken his firm from working on individual stores to putting together whole properties. Space 15 Twenty, a 65,000-square-foot (6,000 m²) urban rehab project in Hollywood, California, has been a pivotal project, mixing hip retail and food with a stage and interior courtyard.

Urban Outfitters master-leased the entire property to control the surrounding tenant mix and protect its brand identity. In addition to its own store, Urban Outfitters brought in other uses that click with its target market. The stage is used for concerts by local bands; the center hosts film festivals, fashion shows, and art exhibits, all done in a way that appeals to the hip local community.

Forever 21's Times Square megastore is another example of the move away from mall locations—and one of a growing number of exceptions to the old rule that stores that work at malls do not work at streetfront locations.

"Forever 21 wanted to go international; we decided Times Square was a great place to make a statement to the world," Townsend said. "That's what retail is today with technology and logistics and product. You put 100,000 square feet [9,300 m²] in Times Square, and you're going to do some business."

Attractions such as Legoland Discovery Centers, Madame Tussauds wax museums, and Cirque du Soleil's traveling shows are a growing presence in retail locations, where they can drive foot traffic and sales for traditional merchants.

"We effectively take snippets of a theme park and put them into an attraction and put them into urban centers," said Howard J. Samuels, president of Samuels & Company, a developer that works with Merlin Entertainments Group, parent company for Legoland and Madame Tussauds.

"We believe it's a perfect complement to a variety of mixed-use concepts," he said. "If you're [at a Legoland Discovery Center] for about two hours, you're going to exit hungry. You're probably going to want to do other kinds of shopping or other kinds of leisure activities, or you'll come back another time to look at an Urban Outfitters or Forever 21."

The synergies with local restaurants and retail have also been a major component for Cirque du Soleil, which, according to Maryse Charbonneau, its director of site location, in recent years has moved its traveling shows from central urban locations to sites such as the Mall of America and Santa Monica Pier. Consumers today are less interested in taking home a souvenir from the show than in having something that adds to their experience of the performance.

"They come to our show not only to see a show," Charbonneau said. "From the minute they come into the parking lot, that's when it starts. The experience is very important."

Adapted from K Kaufmann, "Reinventing Retail," *Urban Land*, November 9, 2011.

[a]Jeffrey Passel and D'Vera Cohn, "U.S. Population Projections: 2005–2050," Pew Research Center, February 11, 2008.

This clause prevents a tenant from converting its store to another use or adding new merchandise lines that may conflict with those of other tenants. At a bare minimum, a chain store tenant can agree to operate its store as all the other stores in its chain. In supermarkets, for example, such businesses as pharmacies, bakeries, flower shops, coffee shops, branch banks, and laundry/dry cleaning pickup are but a few examples of new features that, if unanticipated, can affect the viability of other tenants.

PASS-THROUGH COSTS. From management's perspective, establishing the sharing of certain costs in the lease is very important. Lease terms must include a provision for the sharing of real estate taxes, insurance, common area maintenance (CAM), and operating expenses. CAM includes the cost of such routine activities as cleaning and maintaining the parking lot and other common areas, snow removal when needed, security, landscaping, lighting, trash removal, and utilities. Operating expenses also include the general repair and maintenance of buildings and roofs, seasonal promotional activities, general administrative and management costs, and the depreciation of machinery and equipment used to maintain the premises and reasonable replacement reserves.

Marketing

Most shopping centers benefit from some type of marketing program. Commodity centers should promote key attributes of price and convenience, whereas the objective of specialty centers should be to more broadly promote the unique environment, collection of retailers, and experience associated with the center.

The developer should follow traditional guidelines for setting up a successful promotional program:[20]

- Financial participation in the center's promotional activities should be mandatory for all tenants, and a clause to this effect should be included in the lease.
- The center and its stores should be promoted as a single, cohesive unit. All advertising, including Internet, printed materials, and radio and television spots, should seek to reinforce this perception.
- The center should be involved in community affairs to build goodwill and to increase traffic to the center. For example, the center might financially support major community endeavors or plan and participate in civic events.
- The center's promotional unit and the merchants should always communicate with each other.

For smaller commodity retail shopping centers with small budgets, the marketing program must identify a select market and reach it through a precisely targeted approach. An effective marketing plan extends beyond advertising, sales promotion, and special events to seeking, through a deliberate series of actions, to maximize a center's potential volume.

Effective marketing should capitalize on the baseline created by anchor promotion and should seek to extend the reach and visibility of small tenants as well. Anchor tenants, such as large grocery stores and chain drugstores, often already have their own campaigns and may refuse to participate in a center-wide effort.

The concept of positioning lies at the foundation of a successful marketing plan. Positioning means more than creating a favorable image of a center; it consists of a careful analysis of a center's strengths and weaknesses and a close examination of the competition.

PREOPENING MARKETING

New shopping centers need to change consumer behavior patterns to be successful, and for this reason, it is critical to create awareness of the new center well before any grand opening. At a minimum, at least six months before a new center opens (or reopens in the case of renovation or expansion), an aggressive publicity program should be instituted.

Between three and six months before opening, a merchants association or a steering committee of merchants structured as a marketing fund should be operating—subject of course to successful preleasing. When an anchor tenant is in place, joint promotion with the owner and other merchants can stimulate substantial interest in the center. In the case of large specialty centers, preopening marketing will typically extend well beyond these minimal steps.

ONGOING MARKETING

The type and size of the center determines the extent to which ongoing marketing activities should be pursued; once established, small commodity centers may find little need for ongoing marketing. At the opposite extreme, large specialty centers should consider integrating multichannel marketing programs to reach a wide variety of potential customers and to establish and reinforce the unique environment offered at the center.

If a merchants association is used in promotion, it acts as a clearinghouse for suggestions and ideas and is responsible for the programming of promotional events. Lease agreements stipulate that an association will be formed, that the tenants will pay a specified rate per square foot to the association, and that the developer will pay a certain percentage of the annual costs. The developer/owner must organize and participate in the association and will also often be its guide and catalyst.

If a marketing fund, a technique begun in the 1970s and now widely used, will be created, tenants are still required to provide funds to promote the center, but the fund is totally controlled and administered by the developer/owner. The key advantage of using a marketing fund is that it allows the marketing director to concentrate on marketing and promotion rather than on details of the association.

Management and Operation

Changes in consumer preferences, improvements in retail distribution technology and formats, and changes in the products that are purchased occur at an ever-increasing pace, and retailers must perpetually evolve to stay fresh, relevant, and competitive. As a result, careful ongoing management, merchandising, and promotion of shopping centers—particularly specialty shopping centers—are all essential to maintaining and maximizing long-term value. Unlike most other types of real estate in which change is far slower, it is unusual today to find shopping centers of any size or type that are not constantly evolving. Shopping centers that are not actively managed and merchandised risk being rendered functionally obsolete by failures in these key disciplines.

Shopping center owners provide maintenance and management in one of three ways: by direct supervision, by employing a manager to supervise the process, or by engaging a third-party management firm. By acting directly as manager, the developer/owner maintains close control of the property and can more immediately influence the quality of the operation. By using an outside management firm, however, the developer may derive certain economies of scale and depth of expertise. Managers who work on a fee generally get a percentage of rental income, usually between 2 and 6 percent, depending on the size of the center and the scope of responsibility.

Effective management of shopping centers requires establishing a management approach and plan, executing day-to-day shopping center management, and maintaining accurate financial records. The objective is to provide day-to-day operational support for the shopping center, while minimizing operating costs as a percentage of revenue, both with an eye toward the property's long-term value.

Perhaps the most important responsibility of the shopping center's management, however, is to stimulate merchants to operate their stores at the highest level of professionalism. This objective can be best achieved by maintaining regular and clear communication with tenants. Property managers should be highly visible and should conduct at least a weekly review of each store in the shopping center. Senior management should check stores during periodic site visits with each tenant, and when problems arise, management should address the issues openly and directly with the respective tenant(s). In those cases where lease terms have been violated, management should initiate contact, and in those cases of uncured lease defaults, management should engage counsel to enforce the terms of the lease.

Security is one of management's responsibilities. Security has different meanings for the owner, the tenant, and the shopper. To the owner, it means preserving the buildings and maintaining peace and order so that tenants, shoppers, and staff are safe and not deterred from doing business. To the tenant, it means protecting merchandise and employees, as well as providing a secure environment for customers. To the shopper, security means a feeling of safety while in the center and its parking and surrounding areas.[21] The first step in determining security needs is to conduct a security evaluation or audit. Local police have knowledge of criminal activity in the community and can advise on the level of security needed.

FINANCIAL RECORDS AND CONTROL

Shopping center owners must establish acceptable financial accounting and reporting procedures to collect rents, account for revenues and expenses, conduct annual audits, adjust expenses and percentage rent escrows, and evaluate performance.

Rental calculations for a shopping center are more complicated than for other types of commercial real estate and require that tenants furnish sales records and financial reports. Data such as monthly information on sales figures, category performance, and productivity per square foot are critical in determining percentage rents.

In the early days of the shopping center industry, the usual practice was to call for payment of the percentage overage annually in accordance with a sales report certified by an outside auditor or a responsible officer of the tenant company. Today, leases generally provide for uncertified overage payments quarterly, sometimes monthly, with an annual reconciliation based on an audited statement provided by the tenant. Such an arrangement levels the flow of income while keeping a tight rein on less financially responsible tenants.[22]

Conclusion

As the U.S. population continues to grow, new neighborhood centers in newly developing suburban and exurban areas will have to match that growth. Moreover, many opportunities will be available for remodeling and repositioning older obsolete centers (see Bayshore Town Center case study). Growing affluence in certain communities will create demand for better-quality shopping centers with new tenant categories and adaptation of existing ones. Traditional anchor tenants will continue to reshape themselves and thus will seek to modify their present locations or find new, more suitable ones.

People's increasingly complicated lives and innovations such as e-commerce are changing the way people shop. Although most markets are saturated with regional malls, and many are failing, opportunities are available to fill in market gaps and target narrow infill audiences. Small centers are much easier to develop than regional centers, requiring fewer tenants, a simpler approval process, and less capital and lead time. But even with new opportunities for development of small centers, competition has increased and many areas are rapidly becoming overbuilt. Other potential problems loom on the horizon. Real estate development has always gone through cycles and will continue to do so. Communities also go through cycles of pro- and antigrowth, which frequently lag an economic boom, as it is the economic boom that drives the demand for new development that leads to public concerns about "rampant" growth and thus growth controls. The developer new to retail development needs to be aware of these cycles and that retail development tends to follow rather than lead.

Another potential problem that small centers face is a lack of small tenants and a proliferation of superstores that may preclude many other tenants. In many cases, a developer may not be able to find suitable small tenants to fill a center with a large anchor tenant. If a superstore insists on the exclusive right to sell certain items, leasing space in the center to other tenants will be especially difficult.

In the first years of the 21st century, small shopping center developments have become more difficult to finance, even in cases where public approvals appear likely to be ensured. When potential anchor tenants adjust their expansion plans and delay new starts, the process becomes even more difficult. But in spite of these challenges to beginning developers, emerging shopping patterns and new niche markets will continue to offer opportunities for those armed with good data and a good understanding of the market.

NOTES

1. Julie D. Stern, "Renewed Retail Opportunities," *Urban Land*, October 18, 2010.

2. Jeffrey Spivak, "Retail Investment in China," *Urban Land*, December 19, 2010.

3. Jaroslaw Frontczak and Katarzyna Twardzik, "Double-Digit Recovery of the Ukrainian Retail after the Financial Crisis," *Retail in Ukraine 2012: Market Analysis and Development Forecasts Up to 2013* (Kraków, Poland: PMR Publications, 2012).

4. Ron Nyren, "Small-Scale Development Outlook," *Urban Land*, January 13, 2011.

5. Ibid.

6. RetailSails.com, "2011 Chain Store Productivity Report," 2011.

7. ULI–the Urban Land Institute, *Shopping Centers: How to Build, Buy, and Redevelop*, workshop manual, Spring 2001, p. 83.

8. Connie Robbins Gentry, "Economy and Ecology Merge," *Chain Store Age*, January 2001, p. 158.

9. ULI–the Urban Land Institute and International Council of Shopping Centers, *Parking Requirements for Shopping Centers*, 2nd ed. (Washington, D.C.: ULI–the Urban Land Institute, 1999), p. 3.

10. Mary Smith, *Shared Parking*, 2nd ed. (Washington, D.C.: ULI–the Urban Land Institute and International Council of Shopping Centers, 2005).

11. Ibid., pp. 16–17.

12. ULI-the Urban Land Institute and National Parking Association, *Dimensions of Parking*, 5th ed. (Washington, D.C.: ULI–the Urban Land Institute, 2010).

13. "Title III Highlights," U.S. Department of Justice, Civil Rights Division, www.ada.gov/t3hilght.htm.

14. ULI–the Urban Land Institute, *Shopping Centers: How to Build, Buy, and Redevelop*, p. 33.

15. For more details on lighting for parking areas, see chapter 14 in ULI–the Urban Land Institute, *The Dimensions of Parking*.

16. "Protecting a Major Investment," *Chain Store Age*, January 2001 (adapted from "Choosing the Right Roof," p. 120).

17. ULI–the Urban Land Institute, *Shopping Centers: How to Build, Buy, and Redevelop*, p. 56.

18. Charles S. Telchin, "How to Improve Developer/Tenant Planning and Construction Coordination," *Shopping Center Report* (New York: International Council of Shopping Centers, 1977), p. 1.

19. Ibid., pp. 3–4.

20. ULI–the Urban Land Institute, *Shopping Centers II Workshop: Participant's Guide*, pp. 115–118.

21. Alan A. Alexander and Richard F. Muhlebach, *Operating Small Shopping Centers* (New York: International Council of Shopping Centers, 1997), p. 149.

22. Robert J. Flynn, ed., *Carpenter's Shopping Center Management: Principles and Practices*, 3rd ed. (New York: International Council of Shopping Center, 1984), p. 56.

CASE STUDY: Bayshore Town Center, Glendale, Wisconsin

Bayshore Town Center is a redevelopment of a 1950s-era enclosed shopping mall into a mixed-use, pedestrian-friendly town center. Located in Glendale, Wisconsin, a northern suburb of Milwaukee, Bayshore Town Center contains more than 1.2 million square feet (111,500 m²) of retail, office, and residential space arranged on a traditional street grid. Part new construction, part renovation, the project required extensive environmental remediation and faced a complicated land assembly process.

The project is an example of a successful public/private partnership, with the city of Glendale assisting with land assemblage and environmental remediation and providing significant public financing for the project. The development team remediated a polluted property and redeveloped it into a well-connected, walkable town center. The resulting development has significantly improved retail market share and has added new office and residential space

that commands premium rents in the marketplace. The developer, Steiner + Associates, is based in Columbus, Ohio, and has been developing mixed-use town centers for nearly 20 years.

DEVELOPMENT BACKGROUND AND SITE HISTORY

Bayshore Town Center traces its history to 1954, when the original shopping center at Bayshore (called Bayshore Mall) was erected in what was then a growing portion of the Milwaukee metropolitan area. Glendale was among the original suburbs on Milwaukee's north side, and Bayshore Mall was built in response to increased retail demand from new households. It was one of the first automobile-oriented shopping centers constructed in Milwaukee.

The original Bayshore Mall was built on 36 acres (15 ha) along the east side of Port Washington Road one block north of Silver Spring Drive. Anchored by a Boston Store and a Sears, the shopping center was added onto and enclosed in

the mid-1970s, reaching approximately 600,000 square feet (56,000 m²).

The remaining 16 acres (6 ha) of the present 52-acre (21 ha) site located along Silver Spring Drive contained a variety of uses, including a Kohl's department store, a grocery store, a post office, an auto repair shop, an electrical substation, three office buildings, and a greenhouse.

In the 1980s, the owners of Bayshore Mall recognized that the need for a major makeover was approaching. The mall had been extensively renovated during the 1970s, but newer retail centers that were planned and opened in the 1980s and 1990s threatened Bayshore's viability.

Beginning in the 1980s, the first of many potential redevelopment or expansion scenarios was drafted; none of them came to fruition. Meanwhile, Bayshore Mall was showing its age as other malls around the Milwaukee area were taking advantage of contemporary retail

CONTINUED

STEINER + ASSOCIATES

trends, adding attractions such as movie theaters. Both the mall's owners and municipal officials were aware that if a new retail center opened to the north along Interstate 43, it could severely affect Bayshore Mall, possibly resulting in its closing. Another mall, Northridge, in nearby Brown Deer, had met its fate by 2000, and neither the owners nor the city wanted to see the same thing happen at Bayshore.

Thus, in 2002, the owners of Bayshore Mall began discussions with Steiner + Associates about redeveloping the property. They were impressed with other town center projects Steiner had completed, particularly Easton Town Center in Columbus, Ohio. That same year, the two parties agreed to pursue a town center redevelopment at Bayshore.

The developer felt the site, at 36 acres (15 ha), was too small for appropriate development of a town center and believed that existing mall proportions could not accommodate contemporary tenant needs. But Steiner's internal market analysis showed significant retail potential, as Milwaukee's entire north-side suburbs were underserved. The developer knew Bayshore was averaging sales of just $300 per square foot ($3,229/m²), whereas Mayfair Mall in Wauwatosa, a suburb west of Milwaukee, was fetching $500 per square foot ($5,382/m²). At this point, the city indicated it would step in and assist with assembling the blighted sites to the south.

APPROVALS, FINANCING, ACQUISITION, AND REMEDIATION
Several obstacles—including city approvals, financing, acquisition of additional sites, and cleanup of polluted and unstable soils—faced the developer. The city played a key role in every aspect, beginning with rezoning the site for a planned development district, which allowed for the mix of uses proposed,

including retail, open space, restaurants, entertainment, and office and housing development.

The city also acquired 11 properties for the project and conveyed them to the developer at cost. One of the sites was acquired through eminent domain. In addition, a portion of the existing Bayshore Mall required condemnation in order to route a public street through the development. One parcel, containing a U.S. Postal Service (USPS) facility, could not be acquired. Overall, property acquisition amounted to $1.5 million per acre ($3.7 million/ha)—a significant cost that demanded a dense, high-end development to ensure the project's financial viability.

The site was entitled for a mixed-use town center with department store anchors but no big-box development. However, several major big-box retailers expressed interest in the site, including Costco, Target, Kmart, and Walmart. One offered twice the amount paid by the city to acquire the site for development. The city was interested in the offer, as it would have provided immediate payback rather than all the uncertainty that the town center brought. However, the city ultimately stuck with the vision and the town center plan.

To help finance the project, the city created a tax increment financing (TIF) district that provided $45 million toward the project's total cost of $400 million—the largest TIF ever agreed to in the state of Wisconsin. In addition, the city created an $18 million special assessment district, bringing the total public financing to $63 million.

The interchange at Interstate 43 and Silver Spring Drive was rebuilt and updated to coincide with the project, including an off-ramp from northbound Interstate 43 that provides direct access to a parking garage at Bayshore Town Center. The city and developer leveraged a $4.4 million federal transportation grant to rebuild the interchange.

The project required extensive cleanup and remediation of pollutants, including oil, gas, PCBs (polychlorinated biphenyls), and methane. The original Bayshore Mall had several tenants with their own underground heating-oil tanks, which were removed. The auto repair shop also required soil remediation due to oil infiltration. A dry cleaner had occupied one of the tenant spaces, and perchloroethylene needed to be mitigated. The electrical substation contained PCBs, which had to be removed. Furthermore, the Schlitz Brewing Company's use of the site as a dump included grain mash that had decomposed, emitting methane.

The developer made 113 soil borings to check for contamination and converted 57 of them to groundwater monitoring. Forty-seven methane-monitoring ports were also put in, and passive venting was ultimately installed under 300,000 square feet (28,000 m²) of buildings. In all, 89 tons (90,428 kg) of soil were removed from the site, and much of the existing development acts as a cap for that which was not removed. The Wisconsin Department of Natural Resources, which has fairly stringent cleanup standards, signed off on the remediation.

The original Bayshore Mall frequently suffered from soil settling due to the variety of refuse that was dumped over the years before 1954. Thus, not only did the soil need remediation, it also required reinforcing and compacting to provide adequate building foundations. Total remediation, including cleanup and stabilization, for the site cost $3 million, $500,000 of which was covered by a grant from the Wisconsin Department of Commerce.

A $235 million construction loan, provided by HSBC, was required to move the project forward. It was a very large loan for the medium-sized Milwaukee market, where even the largest office developments receive only $100 million loans. To receive the financing, 50 percent of the project had to be preleased. However, because the three department stores—Sears, Boston Store, and Kohl's—remained in place, 33 percent of the requirement was already covered. A few other tenants from Bayshore Mall remained as well, although most of them moved into new spaces. Thus, the developer needed only to lease or receive letters of intent for an additional 10 percent of the space before the loan was given.

DESIGN AND DEVELOPMENT

The master plan for Bayshore Town Center involved retaining the original Sears, Boston Store, and Kohl's while incorporating new retail, entertainment, office, and residential uses around them in a pedestrian-friendly setting. The primary focus of streets, shops, and public space is at the center of the site, with parking located around the edges. However, several of the streets at Bayshore Town Center connect directly into surrounding neighborhoods or major roadways.

The original Bayshore Mall featured 600,000 square feet (56,000 m²) of retail space. Including the Kohl's store, which was not part of the original mall but remains, the total square footage was 680,000 (63,000 m²). Essentially, the redevelopment preserved a little over half of that area, removed or renovated the remainder, and added several hundred square feet of retail space, bringing the total retail square footage to 938,000 (87,000 m²). As well, 187,000 square feet (17,400 m²) of office and more than 125,000 square feet (11,600 m²) of residential space was added, for a total leasable area of approximately 1.3 million square feet (120,800 m²).

The original Bayshore Mall was L-shaped, with Sears and Boston Store anchoring either end of the long edge of the L. The short wing was removed entirely. The middle of the long side of the L included the indoor portion of Bayshore Mall. This area was extensively renovated, with tenants on the west side being given entrances off the street. This portion of the mall, however, retains its indoor mall character, albeit with a facelift and mostly new tenants, and is aligned along two perpendicular corridors that cross at a food court.

The southern edge of the interior mall, near Boston Store, added a major entrance and rotunda off Bayshore Drive, the primary north–south street at the town center. A multiscreen theater was added to the complex on the second level adjacent to the rotunda. The Kohl's store remains, although it too was extensively renovated and reconfigured to adapt to the town center concept. Its western edge has been lined with a row of stores that face Bayshore Drive.

The remainder of the site is new construction, with a heavy emphasis on shops and restaurants with pedestrian entrances accessed from wide and well-appointed sidewalks and public spaces. Nearly all the frontage along interior streets at Bayshore Town Center is lined with retail storefronts.

Two core focal points anchor the project's design. One is the rotunda, which is the primary entrance to the indoor portion of the development. The other, more notable focal point is the town square, located between Bayshore Drive and Centerpark Way. The town square is flanked by restaurants on its northern and southern edges, the terminus of Fountainview Drive on its eastern edge, and the residential building that overlooks it from the west. It is the most accessible point in the project and hosts a variety of formal and informal events and activities year-round.

Retailers and restaurants are arranged in key locations or clusters. Larger, semi-anchor tenants like Barnes & Noble, Gap, and Brooks Brothers, as well as several restaurants, are located on high-profile corners or facing the town square. Several retailers that target women are clustered along Centerpark Way, and those targeting teens are along the northern section of Bayshore Drive.

Whereas the department stores are considered to be anchors, some other tenants are as well. The total area devoted to restaurants—40,000 square feet (3,700 m²) and expected to grow to around 80,000 square feet (7,400 m²)—is also collectively thought to be an anchor and generates significant revenue. Many of the restaurants are also the first or second of their kind in the Milwaukee area and thus draw patrons from across the metropolitan area. The multiplex and LA Fitness, both measuring more than 40,000 square feet (3,700 m²), are also regarded as anchors.

The site design is very pedestrian friendly. Building exteriors feature a variety of materials, and stores—although using their own marketing and signage—have extensive windows and consistent awnings according to design guidelines. Sidewalks are typically 11 feet (3.4 m) wide and lined with decorative lampposts, bollards, benches, kiosks, trees, and other landscaping. Streetlamps contain hidden speakers, which provide low-level ambient music. Street crosswalks and parking structure pedestrian entrances are well marked.

The six-story mixed-use building along the west side of Centerpark Way features stores on the ground level, parking on the second and third levels, and apartments on levels four through six. The two mixed-use structures on the southwestern portion of the site include retail space on the ground floors and offices above: the northern building is four stories tall, with retail on the ground floor, an LA Fitness facility occupying the second and third, and a Guaranty Bank call center on the fourth; the southern building has ground-floor retail stores facing Silver Spring Drive, with two stories of offices above.

CONTINUED

One major challenge that arose during the planning process was how to build around the existing Kohl's store. Kohl's was not previously part of Bayshore Mall, but it was integrated as part of the town center project. Keeping the store required not only allowing Kohl's to maintain ownership of the store but also negotiating with the retailer to renovate the interior and move the entrance to the southwestern side of the building to create an attractive pedestrian access from an interior street.

The original plan for Bayshore included purchasing the USPS distribution site, located immediately east of the Kohl's store, to provide surface parking for Kohl's. The plan also included retail uses lining Bayshore Drive south of Kohl's. When the city and developer were unable to come to terms with the USPS, they needed to provide additional parking for Kohl's. Consequently, they converted retail space planned for immediately south of the store to surface parking. To offset the loss of leasable space, they were forced to add additional office space and reconfigure some of the retail buildings in the project.

More than 4,400 parking spaces are provided at Bayshore Town Center. They include over 3,000 located in three parking structures, another 1,000 in perimeter surface lots, and nearly 200 on-street spaces along the interior street network. The retail, residential, and office tenants share a significant number of these spaces, and the overall parking ratio for the project is 3.6 spaces per 1,000 square feet (38/1,000 m²).

MARKETING AND MANAGEMENT

Bayshore Town Center held a grand opening in November 2006 and was completed in May 2007. It maintained a healthy occupancy rate in the 1990s, despite poor economic conditions in recent years. Moreover, it generates rent premiums over competitive product in every category.

Steiner town center projects typically perform 20 percent better than their competition in terms of achievable rents/sale prices. Bayshore Town Center is producing similar results. Retail rents vary widely from $20 to $60 per square foot ($215–$646/m²) annually.

Bayshore Town Center is highly programmed; it not only serves a mix of uses but also serves as the "downtown" for Glendale and several of the surrounding communities. In warmer months, the town square is used for concerts, movies, and other events and displays a large Christmas tree during the month of December. The developer also created the Bayshore Community Foundation, which raises money for community outreach and job training. On-street parking meters at Bayshore Town Center are one of the many sources of revenue for the foundation.

Before redevelopment, Bayshore Mall had a base value of $78 million and generated $2.4 million in taxes for the city. The redeveloped Bayshore Town Center is valued at $350 million and generates $8 million in taxes. Sales grew by 180 percent to $310 million per year, generating $17.3 million in sales tax revenue. Bayshore has also created spin-off value: in late 2007, before the recession, typical commercial property was increasing at around 5 to 6 percent annually; but around Bayshore, properties were increasing at rates of 30 to 40 percent.

SUMMARY

The Bayshore Town Center project can be considered a success in a number of ways. It is an example of successful public/private partnership. The initiative was to bring new residential, office, and retail space to Glendale and to revitalize the Bayshore Mall, which was facing increasing competition from new retailers. The development included 113 new residential units offering one, two, and three bedrooms. The cost to acquire the site was $103 million; with predevelopment and construction costs, the total figure rose to nearly $400 million. Perhaps even more impressive was the efficiency with which the project was completed. Planning began in early 2003; nearly two years later, the site was purchased and construction began in December 2004. Finally in May 2007, after three and a half years, the project was completed.

Bayshore Town Center is a financial success for the developer and city. Its design and mix of retail and entertainment options are popular in the marketplace. In addition, its mix of uses, pedestrian friendliness, and connections to surrounding neighborhoods are examples of new urbanism.

The developer emphasizes that the project would not have been possible without leadership and financial assistance from the city. The substantial TIF assistance helped offset acquisition and remediation costs, making the project feasible. Leadership and vision from the city also helped the project politically. Financing the project was difficult; in future projects, the developer would consider separating the financing among the different uses, which would reduce overall loan amounts and potentially streamline the process.

Project Data

LAND USE INFORMATION

Site area	52 acres (21 ha)
Off-street parking spaces	4,442

LEASABLE AREA

Use	Area
Office (net)	187,000 ft² (17,373 m²)
Retail (gross)	938,000 ft² (87,143 m²)
Residential	126,500 ft² (11,752 m²)

RESIDENTIAL INFORMATION

Unit Type	Floor	Initial Rental Prices
One-bedroom	604–1,150 ft² (56–107 m²)	$775–$1,525
Two-bedroom	1,150–1,379 ft² (107–128 m²)	$1,000–$1,190
Three-bedroom	1,493–1,675 ft² (139–157 m²)	$2,000–$2,140
Number of residential units		113

OFFICE INFORMATION

Average tenant size	3,000 ft² (279 m²)
Annual rents	$10–$20/ft² ($108–$215/m²)
Average length of lease	3–7 years

Office Tenant Size	Number of Tenants
Under 5,000 ft² (464 m²)	36
5,000–10,000 ft² (464–929 m²)	0
More than 10,000 ft² (929 m²)	3
Total	39

RETAIL INFORMATION

Tenant Classification	Number of Stores	Total GLA
Department stores	2	285,000 ft² (26,476 m²)
Food service	15	65,000 ft² (6,039 m²)
Clothing and accessories	41	193,000 ft² (17,930 m²)
Shoes	7	15,000 ft² (1,394 m²)
Home furnishings	5	14,000 ft² (1,301 m²)
Gift/specialty	13	54,000 ft² (5,017 m²)
Jewelry	4	7,000 ft² (650 m²)
Personal services	8	19,000 ft² (1,765 m²)
Fitness center	1	42,000 ft² (3,902 m²)
Financial	4	15,000 ft² (1,394 m²)
Cinema	2	40,000 ft² (3,716 m²)
Grocery	2	13,000 ft² (1,208 m²)
Total	104	762,000 ft² (70,792 m²)

Annual rents	$20–$60/ft² ($215–$646/m²)
Average annual sales	$297/ft² ($3,196/m²)
Average length of lease	5–10 years

DEVELOPMENT COST INFORMATION

Site Acquisition Cost	$102,398,127
Site Improvement Costs	$27,942,339
Construction Costs	**$149,428,675**
Office	17,632,219
Retail	84,306,295
Residential	47,490,161
Soft Costs	**$120,068,767**
Professional fees	15,875,739
Leasing	9,493,588
Marketing/operations	3,657,548
Legal	2,902,584
Taxes/insurance (OCIP)	2,333,031
Construction administration	3,331,221
Finance costs	24,712,453
Tenant Improvement Allowance	**$48,754,886**
Other Development Costs	**$9,007,717**
Total Development Cost	**$399,837,908**

DEVELOPMENT SCHEDULE

Planning started: February 2003

Sales/leasing started: May 2003

Site purchased: December 2004

Construction started: December 2004

Project opening: November 2006

Source: Sam Newberg (joe-urban.com), ULI Development Case Study.

Trends and Issues

This chapter explores ongoing structural changes in the real estate industry, emerging demographic and technological changes affecting developers, current planning and development issues, and the changing social responsibilities of developers. This snapshot of current issues, across many markets and product types, emphasizes the larger picture of real estate development, and its role in society. This review is intended to give beginning developers an understanding of long-term changes afoot in the field and to highlight opportunities and pitfalls developers will likely encounter over their careers. The chapter concludes with a discussion of the developer's social responsibilities to the community at large. ULI and the many contributors to this book are dedicated to the idea that the development of land represents a civic responsibility. To maintain the public's trust, developers must create products and developments that make a positive contribution to their communities and to the urban environment.

Changing Market Factors

The industry has changed dramatically since the 1970s and 1980s, when many of today's major developers started their firms. A formative experience for many developers is their first recession. Along with land use regulations, tax incentives, and demographic changes, the cycle of expansion and recession is an important driver of the development business. And for those that survive these cyclical changes, the lessons learned refine developers' approaches to their work. As Don Killoren of Celebration Associates puts it, "Each time we think we'll learn, and each time seems to be just different enough."[1]

Double-digit inflation of the late 1970s and early 1980s made real estate a preferred investment, relative to stocks or bonds, because of the perception that it provides an inflation hedge. This thinking led to an increase in investor demand for the tax advantages of real property, and development outpaced absorption often to accommodate investment rather than to follow market demand. The subsequent real estate crash of the late 1980s through the early 1990s catalyzed the most dramatic structural changes in the real estate industry since the Great Depression, some of which are still reverberating today. A number of factors led up to that crash:

- overbuilding of office and commercial space in most markets;
- a crisis in the savings and loan (S&L) industry and a record number of bank failures;
- changes in the 1986 Tax Reform Act that adversely affected real estate investments;
- mounting government regulation that increased the time and cost of the development approvals process; and
- rolling regional economic recessions that started in Texas and spread to the West and East Coasts as the national recession deepened.

In 1989, public concern about damage to the financial sector led to the creation of the Resolution Trust Corporation (RTC), a government institution established to take over bankrupt S&Ls and to recycle their assets back into the market. The RTC marks one of the great success stories of government intervention in the real estate market. Criticized at first for selling assets too cheaply, it succeeded in rechanneling

Downtown @ 700 2nd is a transit-oriented single-resident-occupancy development in Albuquerque, New Mexico. A rooftop solar array provides 30 percent of the heating and 80 percent of the water heating for the building.

nearly $400 billion in failing assets back into private possession between 1991 and 1995. The speedy sell-off allowed properties to quickly reenter the market, forced lenders to take losses early, and set the stage for recovery. New development would not occur until troubled properties were leased and prices returned to normal. As an ancillary benefit, it has also been argued that cheap commercial space assisted the economic recovery in the early to mid-1990s. In fact, prices and property values did quickly increase, as the incipient economic boom led to rapid absorption of vacant office and industrial space.

Still, there was debate over the success or necessity of the RTC's actions: Kenneth Leventhal argues that the government caused a 40 percent decline in value during the RTC sell-off, whereas the decline should have been only 10 to 15 percent. "In hindsight, if they had not been so draconian, more of the owners would have stayed in place, the losses would not have been so severe, and we would not have had this whole new breed of buyers—the vulture funds."[2] Debate over public sector involvement in real estate investment markets is far from over, as the financial crisis of 2008–2009 has renewed questions about whether banks should hold on to bad assets in hopes that prices recover or sell them off quickly.

INDUSTRY RESTRUCTURING IN THE 1990S

The early 1990s' crash and recovery led to several fundamental changes in the development industry:

- Real estate finance followed commercial banking into a thorough restructuring, with more multiproduct financial providers and an increasingly homogeneous and national menu of services.
- Real estate became more *institutionalized*. Investment-grade real estate earned the status of an asset class comparable with stocks and bonds and attracted new types of investors with different requirements.
- Financial innovation supported a dramatic expansion of secondary markets for debt instruments collateralized by real estate assets. The resulting capital inflows to real estate came with a cost: the increasing distance between lender-investors and underlying assets.
- Tax reform, which virtually dried up the infusion of money from syndicators, is believed to have helped the industry by restoring, at least temporarily, the importance of traditional cash flow criteria.

Pearl Qatar occupies an island in Doha, Qatar. The project includes single-family and multifamily residential units, industrial space, and retail and entertainment uses.

- The huge debt and equity resources required for the increasing scale of deals forced many developers to become manufacturers of products—"merchant builders"—rather than long-term owners. REITs and other institutional owners now form joint ventures with developers to build new buildings that the institution buys when completed. These kinds of ventures increasingly blur the line between roles and risk profiles of developer and financier.
- To develop a strong base of consistent cash flow, many of the largest developers focused on strengthening the service part of the business, especially brokerage, asset management, and property management. Owning or managing large portfolios on behalf of institutional owners gave companies ongoing cash flow to weather downturns. Wall Street valued this service-based income more highly than cyclical sources of income, such as development fees.

THE CRISIS OF 2008–2009

As of this writing, several competing explanations exist for the spectacular boom and bust witnessed between 2003 and 2010. Although debate over causes will no doubt continue for years, it is sufficient to say that this crisis has supplanted the S&L episode as the greatest challenge to the real estate industry since the Great Depression, and at least a few points are agreed on by nearly all observers:

- Globalization and financial innovation increased both the volume and technical complexity of investment in real estate and resulted in a substantial and sustained increase in credit availability for buyers.

- Cheap and easy credit boosted demand for almost all sectors of real estate, but particularly for-sale housing and commercial space. Following the "bubble" pattern, many financial institutions, developers, and end users failed to understand the risks associated with this dramatic expansion.
- Just as cash flow fundamentals were inadequately examined in the run-up to the S&L crisis, so assumptions of absorption and appreciation went underexamined in the boom of the early 2000s. The increasing distance between buyers and debt holders appears to have created a set of perverse incentives. Risk was assumed by bondholders without a realistic understanding of underlying asset values, and of threats to those values.
- Further, most regulators, ratings agencies, and policy makers failed to understand the increasing connection of property markets, via securitization, to other areas of the financial system—so-called systemic risk.
- These systemic connections extended what might have been a modest downturn in real estate prices into a serious financial crisis, as every investment portfolio was scoured for exposure first to "subprime" residential mortgages, then to other real estate debt instruments. The pullback in real estate thus translated into a broad and deep economic contraction, creating a vicious cycle of economic factors that further dragged down real estate values.

Much remains uncertain about the recovery of national economic growth, and of the real estate development business. Markets are far from understanding the long-term effect of this crisis's equivalents to the 1990s' RTC: TARP (Troubled Asset Relief Program), the Term Asset-Backed Securities Loan Facility program, and the Public-Private Investment Program. All these programs have allocated Treasury funds to purchase illiquid, so-called toxic assets, and in combination with easing of monetary policy and increased support for government-sponsored enterprises (GSEs) Fannie Mae and Freddie Mac have been intended to shore up the financial underpinnings of residential and commercial real estate. The enormous losses to the taxpayer from the bad debts of Fannie Mae and Freddie Mac leave the future of GSEs in grave doubt.

Buzz McCoy calls 2010 "not the beginning of the end, but the end of the beginning." McCoy points out that as commercial debt matures, a "state of high anxiety" is certain to persist in capital markets for more than a few years, with speculation about the nature of financial regulatory reform and tax changes

only adding to already bewildering market risks: "Put yourself in the investors' shoes; they haven't been able to write a business plan for two years!" These uncertainties will clearly reinforce conservatism in project finance, including modest leverage, enhanced underwriting standards, increasing recourse requirements for debt, and an implicit reduction in real returns over the next five to ten years.[3]

Although uncertainty has always been a part of this industry, real estate investors and developers have faced nearly unprecedented stresses as a result of the Great Recession. Though it is difficult to prognosticate, it is certainly possible to look back at some key lessons learned or relearned by developers in recent years:

- Maintain a lean team. Revenue can disappear quickly, and overhead can take time to wind down.
- Leverage works both ways. Understand the impact of debt service going into a deal. Know your "burn rate."
- Cash is king. As Stewart Fahmy noted in 2009, "Builders' positions in [the Bay Area] market are entirely based on their liquidity." Refinancing, hibernating, building your way out, and pursuing consulting business—all strategies for surviving a downturn—require ready cash.[4]
- As a corollary, a developer's coveted "institutional finance partnership" should not be mistaken for a guarantee. Many developers have recently learned that investment banks can, in fact, become insolvent.
- Acquisition terms can be as important as price. Paying more for entitlement contingencies, phased takedowns, or lease-up contingencies can be well worth the cost, as the seller shares risks with the buyer.
- Consider asset quality as a hedge. Flight to quality often accompanies declining demand.
- Managing inventory is managing risk. Don Killoren notes that "if you didn't learn it in 1980, and you didn't learn it in 1990, then learn it now: don't get stuck with a lot of standing inventory."[5]

The business of development will continue, but the terms of "the new normal," and the future relationships among government, banking, investors, and buyers, are far from clear. John Knott, president of the Noisette Company, suggests that developers over the next ten years will likely offer lower returns, but with more direct relationships to capital. "No more three to four layers of management, fund-of-funds. Instead, the incentive of equity investors will be to drive a hard bargain for control, direct ownership, and accountability of on-the-ground management."[6]

THE DEMISE OF SMALL DEVELOPERS?

In the wake of the 2008–2009 financial crisis, small developers are finding it even more difficult to obtain financing than after the S&L crisis of the late 1980s. Although it is generally understood that Wall Street capital is seldom the lowest-cost capital available, other economies of scale and barriers to entry increasingly favor larger developer-owners. The largest property managers can achieve substantial cost savings on supplies, utilities, and services. They can also frequently amortize overhead or spread personnel over more projects than smaller competitors. New technology has historically favored large owners who could make the sizable capital investments required for productivity-enhancing software and network upgrades for their properties. This trend appears to be reversing, though, as increasingly decentralized forms of communication, like social media (see chapter 4, "Marketing"), can level the playing field. Today, the most substantive advantages for the large firm are, generally, a lower cost of capital, giving them "first look" at deals, and, perhaps most important, the resources to withstand the uncertainty, delay, and potential legal action that can impede development projects.

Pursuing these efficiencies and economies of scale, the last ten years have seen a consolidation of large development firms. Regional homebuilders and medium-sized developers have found themselves targets for acquisition, allowing the purchasing firm the ability to grow its business and expand into new markets without a three- to five-year startup. Most of the targets have been builders of at least 100 homes per year, leaving the smaller builders alone. Developers' experience of the recent economic turmoil may be clarifying this trend, as the "survivors" of this episode appear, so far, to include both small and large firms, and some of the most spectacular failures have so far involved regional and medium-sized developers.

Although the challenges they face are real, small developers are not likely to disappear. In fact, small developers will likely benefit from future demographic changes. A world of increasing demographic and cultural diversity means more opportunity in niche markets that favor small local developers. The large organization typically requires a certain deal size to justify involvement, and the relative availability of infill sites, as well as the increasing interest in secondary and tertiary markets, preserves a landscape of opportunity for the nimble, disciplined, small firm. As long as personal relationships remain central to doing business, small developers will continue to thrive.

As Gerald Hines observes, "Real estate in the U.S. today is a mature industry. Starting today is very different from starting when I did after World War II. Then, there was no infrastructure in place, a lot of need for builders, and the whole concept of investment building was new. Today, there is a lot of competition in every field. You have to find a specialty and a niche where you can have some expertise above someone else."[7]

FINANCING

REITs, securitization, and commercial mortgage–backed securities all have revolutionized real estate finance. These changes have rested on conflicting assumptions: the historic perception of real estate as a low-volatility, inflation-hedged, steady cash flow asset class, and the perceived ability to dramatically improve returns on these assets with leverage. As *Emerging Trends in Real Estate 2010* states, "Real estate's touted attributes—low volatility and steady income—require reevaluation." Over the past 20 years, real estate has been highly volatile, and the "steady" cash flows of the underlying assets have recently become anything but.[8] Simultaneously, some of the financial structures overlaid on assets have, by their complexity, made understanding risk allocation more difficult than ever. Although financial markets are still being shaped by this crisis, a solid understanding of the players, and their roles relative to projects, will serve a developer well. There is no indication that any of the major players outlined below will not exist ten years hence, and parties involved in the financing of smaller projects are likely to remain the steadiest of all.

Although beginning developers' initial projects will probably be financed through small banks and local lenders, they should understand the bigger picture of financing real estate deals. Opportunities for cheap permanent mortgage money may come from different sources at any given time: from insurance companies or banks, or through mortgage brokers representing conduit loans (prepackaged pools of mortgages that Wall Street sells to investors).

And although they will need to find equity for their initial projects from friends and family, they should position themselves to be able to find institutional equity partners as soon as their track record permits. Robert Larson, past chair of Lazard Frères Real Estate and past vice chair of Taubman Centers, Inc., emphasized alignment of interests when Wall Street and other institutional investors work with developers. "Any investment of size needs to be made so that the

interests of the company and its management are very closely aligned with interests of the investor."[9]

Larson observed that investors would like a preferential position, but whether they can get one depends on the company's need for capital and the competitive market at the time. To the extent that the investor ends up with a preferred security, the possibility of divergent interests may increase.

When private companies deal with Wall Street investors, they naturally want any new investor of size to be a passive partner. This position, however, runs counter to the needs of the investor. Larson notes that structural problems exist when investors own more than 50 percent of a publicly traded company but do not have board control. If the company runs into problems, the investors need to be able to change the strategic direction of the company to protect their interests. Lazard Frères looks for opportunities to invest in whole businesses rather than individual properties, but other investors, out of concern for hidden liabilities, prefer strategic partnership with the developer, allowing equity investments directly into project assets. Two decades of consolidation have transformed the development industry from a game for small entrepreneurs to a sophisticated capital market favoring public companies. Larson believes this trend actually increases the opportunities for certain entrepreneurs because development is very specific to local circumstances. Large institutions in general are less flexible, have high pursuit costs, and are less able to respond to market opportunities, leaving opportu-

The Rathaus-Galerie Leverkusen is located in the heart of Leverkusen, Germany. The development includes a 120-store shopping center and a two-story town hall rotunda that houses office space for city officials.

nities for smaller players. Taking advantage of these opportunities, however, is more difficult than ever. Opportunities for leverage are more meager, and only well-capitalized entrepreneurs will succeed. To be able to compete, developers must have a strong balance sheet, a substantial track record, or a working alliance with a capital source.

PAYING FOR INFRASTRUCTURE

Fiscal problems have increasingly forced localities to rely on real estate development to balance local budgets and help pay for new infrastructure. Before 1980, most municipal services and infrastructure, such as schools, public safety, roads, and utilities, were paid for out of general revenues and general obligation bonds. Today, residents view crowded roads and schools as negative results of growth, and the costs of growth have become a contentious issue. Virtually every major city and many small cities across the country have adopted comprehensive systems that include impact fees, exactions (payments made to receive a permit to develop),[10] community facilities districts, and adequate public facilities, or "concurrency," ordinances (requirements that facilities or plans for new facilities be in place before new development is approved)[11] to address these issues. Based on the theory that development should pay its own way, communities impose impact fees—usually charged per dwelling unit or per square foot—on developers to fund roads, intersections, schools, and public safety improvements. In many jurisdictions, the rezoning process includes evaluation of "proffers," specific off-site improvements like parks or roads, which may be "voluntarily" performed by the developer, with benefit to both the development and to the larger community.

The trend toward higher impact fees and exactions is likely to continue as cities try to maximize revenue without raising taxes. Developers have turned to the legal system to resist exorbitant charges, and court rulings have limited the types and purposes of these fees, but the trend is inescapable.

Developers have much at stake when it comes to municipal finances, and they need to understand local financing sources almost as well as city officials do. Local fiscal problems affect developers in several ways. First, higher fees raise the cost of development and make new construction less cost competitive with existing stock. They often worsen the issue of affordable housing, which is already at crisis levels in some major cities. Further, these fiscal problems lead to cutbacks in local budgets for maintaining public facilities, causing deteriorating neighborhoods and falling real estate values. In predominately lower- and middle-class communities, these issues can cause a vicious cycle where inadequate infrastructure and service funding deters the investments needed to revitalize the community and renew its building stock and tax base.

On the other hand, fiscal problems often give cities stronger incentives to work with the development community. Some of the best opportunities for beginning developers lie in working with cities on government-owned land or in targeted redevelopment areas. If developers are willing to tolerate red tape and bureaucratic delays, cities and their redevelopment agencies can support, and sometimes streamline, the approvals process. These types of deals, sometimes with explicit public/private partnership, are increasingly available to smaller developers, as cities motivated by "smart growth" ideas push development toward more complicated infill sites.

REGULATORY CHANGE AND THE EROSION OF DEVELOPMENT RIGHTS

The increasing cost of approvals has been accompanied by a reevaluation of government's role in development in many jurisdictions. For most landowners, this reevaluation can be read as an erosion of development rights. As concerns about fiscal health and quality-of-life issues have become tied (in many cases unfairly) to development, pressure has built for increased regulatory control. Municipal strategies range from the blunt instrument of comprehensive downzoning (reduction of allowed density across a zoned area) to a set of more finely tuned incentives to locate and shape allowable development where political opposition will allow it, or where infrastructure better supports it.

Developers can do little to influence broad regulatory action like moratoriums, so it becomes very important to understand exactly the process by which development rights (typically outlined in zoning as a set of allowed uses and a density) become vested (the moment at which these rights cannot be taken away by regulatory change). This process determines how many years, and how many millions, a developer might be forced to spend before losing all right to develop. The moment of vesting can be radically different, and the consequences of misunderstanding are usually catastrophic. In California, for example, vesting protection from moratorium may be defined as erection of a foundation and structural frame, while in some states, density and use are arguably vested at the approval stage of the general plan, and certainly at the specific or final plan stage, before construction has even been bid. The difference in risk between these scenarios is stark.

One way for developers to hedge against the risk of losing development rights is to buy land subject to an "entitlement contingency." Developers pay for this consideration, but the higher price is often worth the reduced risk. Aside from the obvious benefit of delaying payment for the land, most developers find the alignment of sellers' and developers' interests to be advantageous, particularly because sellers of desirable tracts often have deep roots in the community, and sometimes political power. It is worth noting that, in extremely hot markets, often such contingencies will be off the table. Also, in some cases smaller developers with good local relationships feel they can make an offer without such a clause to outbid others with deeper pockets, by taking on more entitlement risk. Developers of larger projects can deal with the risks of vesting by negotiating "development agreements" that require them to build certain facilities in exchange for a city's locking in existing zoning and development rights.[12]

The pace of government involvement has quickened, and its scope expanded, as the environmental movement has gained strength since the 1980s. In addition to basic considerations such as density and setbacks, developers now must navigate a web of rules for water rights, stormwater, wildlife habitat, traffic, and other issues, some of them subjective items like "viewshed" and "neighborhood character." As society better understands the impacts of growth, new rules will necessarily follow. As of this writing, carbon emissions appear to be the new regulatory topic, and California is just beginning to implement policies that hold developers accountable for emissions tied to land use change. Still, the blanket disgust expressed by some developers toward regulation is misplaced. Zoning and other forms of regulation have historically been initiated or supported by developers as a means of protecting long-term property values. Value lies both in the protection of areas surrounding and serving a project and also in the barrier to entry that an approvals process applies to competitors. From the developer's point of view, it is sometimes better to struggle in a growth-averse jurisdiction, and to be one of the few that makes it through to market, than to compete on price in a wide-open and commodified market.

It is not regulation per se but the *uncertainty* about new regulation that can be the greatest risk to developers. With this in mind, recent trends are troubling. Matt Kiefer of Goulston & Storrs suggests, "As the public sector pulls back, financially . . . we are entering a period of regulatory experimentation. Rather than issue commands, or regulate simple metrics like density, the trend is toward setting goals and performance standards, and leaving it to the developer to figure out how to get there."[13] This trend is particularly apparent in green building, where a third-party standard, such as LEED, may be required, but the approach to meeting the standard allows an à la carte selection of construction practices. Although this approach can preserve owner flexibility, it can also lead to confusion, to poor operating performance, and to a more subjective determination of compliance. It can also lead to unanticipated costs, as the burden of proof of compliance increasingly shifts to the applicant. Still, the opportunities of market-driven growth control are considerable for the developer willing to invest the time to understand them. Tax increment financing districts have introduced essentially a new way to finance infill development, and transfer of development rights markets, which allow shifting of density to targeted growth areas, bring a whole new set of tradable real estate assets to the market. Kiefer

notes that "changes in regulation lag social change," so developers with long project timelines need to watch today's hot-button issue because it may be a condition of a building permit in a few years. Just as zoning can benefit the conscientious developer, so can new conditions serve as a bar that ultimately supports projects that contribute to a desirable shaping of the urban fabric.

THE TECHNOLOGICAL REVOLUTION

The implications of technology for real estate are dramatic, and new tools have transformed how real estate professionals conduct many areas of the business, from acquisition, design, and construction to marketing, brokerage, property management, community operations, and financing. Over the coming decade, it is nearly impossible to predict the outcome of any given technology, but it is possible to analyze some of the changes currently afoot.

ACQUISITION AND DUE DILIGENCE. The spread of GIS-based technologies, Web-based property tax databases, real estate listing services, and even free aerial mapping databases like Google Earth have revolutionized the "pursuit" phase of development. An initial investigation of a property can now be performed quickly, remotely, and with virtual anonymity using such tools. In this way, developers are able to move quickly toward the acquisition of properties (and discard unsuitable candidates) while delaying involvement of consultants like surveyors and planners. Under development today are stand-alone software packages that offer the ability to generate preliminary yield plans and criteria for valuation, from the most basic of available data sets. Already, it has become nearly as easy for a developer three states away to take a first pass at a property as it is for an in-town professional.

DESIGN AND CONSTRUCTION. Like the PC revolution before it, the Internet is changing how property is developed. Extranets—networks that facilitate the exchange of all forms of information, including plans, specifications, and financial data—are widely used in the design phase of development and are increasingly used during construction.[14] New techniques, such as BIM (Building Information Modeling), allow team members, clients, and contractors to manipulate and reference the same base drawings. Extensive use of 3-D imaging allows clients to visualize the project. Over the past decade, visualization has gone from an expensive design presentation technique to a nearly mandatory component of most public approval processes. Real-time design enables value engineering to occur concurrently with design, compressing the process. General connectivity of team members has shortened the time required to revise drawings and other documents and has greatly expanded the geographic range of participants in the development process. Local consultants are now used because they bring value by their expertise, no longer simply because of their location near the project. In fact, substantial international outsourcing is already occurring in many design firms.

In addition to changes in the development process, smart developers and landlords anticipate future technology needs and plan accordingly to install the most advanced wiring, cables, and backup generators that might "future-proof" the asset.[15] End-user demand for high-performance data infrastructure may be a simple enough request in urban areas, but for exurban sites, incumbent telecommunications providers may represent a virtual monopoly, and provision of fiber service may require substantial upfront cost or the involvement of third-party network operators with long-term service contracts.[16]

MARKETING. Great advances have been made in the use of technology for marketing and sales. Multiple Listing Service (MLS) and its commercial equivalents, such as CoStar, allow brokers, buyers, and tenants to almost instantly aggregate, sort, and virtually tour most available properties in a given market. Threatening this broker-controlled model are scores of for-sale-by-owner sites, with offers of flat-fee, discount, or free listings and search services applying tremendous pressure to agent commissions in many markets, both residential and commercial.

The Internet is now the medium for most buyers' or tenants' first experience of a property, and its importance is magnified in international sales or geographically remote sales of retirement or second-home communities. The project website—which in turn receives inbound traffic from traditional media and advertising, marketing blasts, social media, blogs, or word of mouth—has also become a central receiving point for information on potential buyers and tenants. Numerous free services exist to collect and analyze this traffic, allowing managers to more precisely understand the effectiveness of various marketing approaches and investments. Contact management software packages have evolved from simple "lead lists" to complex

platforms for managing flow of information between sales agents and individual prospects or groups. Emerging applications point toward a future where sales professionals are armed with detailed real-time information on any call.[17] Given the relative cost of digital approaches, versus printed collateral, on-site staffing, and event marketing, there is little doubt that the coming decade will offer more of these tools to developers.

Innovation in this area has its limits, though, and even a downside. As services like MLS aggregate listings, they tend to commodify noncomparable products, and buyers may browse right past an offering that does not fit standard price points or amenity packages. As Zvi Barzilay of Toll Brothers points out, "The Web is, for us, and for customers, a screening tool. There's still, and always will be, a lot of walking. The model home is where buyers make the big decision, and they must touch what they're evaluating."[18]

PROPERTY MANAGEMENT. Dozens of software packages are available to assist in increasing the productivity of individuals managing ever-larger portfolios. These software packages can be tailored for any type of property and are available for tenant records, lease management, maintenance scheduling, checks, taxes, profit and loss reports for one unit or an entire portfolio, payroll, and work orders. In addition to office tasks, innovative technology is causing rapid change in security, access control, and building-systems monitoring, any of which might now be as easily handled from Bangalore as from the boiler room. As in any business, owners should understand that technology represents an initial investment, not just in products, but in training personnel, and in replacement and maintenance of systems. Owners should understand both sides of these investments and should ensure that the "cool factor" does not supplant a real cost-benefit analysis.

FINANCING. The real estate and construction industries were notoriously slow to adopt new technology. In the 1990s, the industry watched from the sidelines as Internet startups grabbed a significant share of the mortgage origination business, and many developers were purposely late to the game, as they depended on captive mortgage originators to service their communities. Not surprisingly, the greatest penetration of technology in real estate finance has been in those areas serving the largest number of consumers—home mortgage originations and servicing. Still, with Web portals taking over substantial portions of Americans' financial lives, purely digital real estate transactions—digital transaction processing, information disclosure, financing, and closing transactions—are coming soon. The number of mortgages, equities, leases, and sales transactions is increasing dramatically, and Web-based appraisal services are edging into an important transactional role. If one lesson has been learned over the past decade, it is to avoid being the first to adopt an innovation, as many new tools fail or are supplanted as industry standards shake out. A successful developer will, however, stay abreast of technological development and will be ready to invest in appropriate tools when they offer improvement to productivity, marketing success, and profitability of the enterprise.

Trends

Opportunities abound for developers that are able to capitalize on the many changes taking place. Demographic trends, such as the aging of the American population, the influx of immigrants, and the impact of new technology on work and leisure, are creating demand for innovative types of living environments. Some developers will find success providing these new kinds of places for work, home, and leisure pursuits. Historically, though, the safest bet on the future is usually that it will look rather like the recent past. Developers must be cautious not to innovate beyond their target.

NEW DEMOGRAPHICS

Results of the 2010 Census show that demographic factors will have a profound effect on the nation's economy and population distribution over the next 50 years. The combined growth rate for both cities and suburbs in the 100 largest metropolitan areas dropped to little more than half that of the 1990s, due to an aging population and sluggish economy. As the white population continued to age, racial and ethnic minorities accounted for an astonishing 91 percent of U.S. population growth in the 2000s.[19] As the baby boom generation enters retirement, the United States is moving toward a population with a roughly equal number of people in each major age group. At the same time, Americans are becoming a substantially more diverse group. By 2042, "non-Hispanic whites" will no longer be a simple majority. As planner Elizabeth Plater-Zyberk points out, relative increases in single-parent households, blended households, and singles mean that two-parent households with their own children, the historical driving force behind U.S.

housing markets, now make up only a quarter of all households.[20] Developers must consider a variety of housing types in order to attract these diverse buyer types.

According to demographer William H. Frey, new regional demographic divisions will be created that will be as important as our current distinctions between cities and suburbs, rural and urban. These divisions will encompass entire metropolitan areas and states, distinguishing "multiple melting pot regions," "suburban-like new Sunbelts," "heartland regions," and "new minority frontiers."[21] The multiple melting pots—California, Texas, southern Florida, the Eastern Seaboard, and Chicago—will become increasingly younger, multiethnic, and culturally vibrant. Heartland regions will become older, more staid, and less ethnically diverse, encompassing growing parts of the Sunbelt, economically healthy states of the new West, and declining areas of the Farm Belt and Rust Belt.

The new immigrants and their children, primarily Latinos and Asians, will contribute 1 million people annually to the U.S. population, accounting for more than half of the 50 million additional residents during the next 25 years. As a result of current immigration laws, it is expected that incoming immigrants will choose to live in a handful of metropolitan areas spread from California to Texas to Florida. Two key constituencies continue to drive expansion in some of the fastest-growing cities: the young, particularly those professionals author Richard Florida calls "the Creative Class," and the old (empty nesters and early retirees).

CHANGING LIFESTYLES

Driving demographics since the 1950s, the aging baby boom generation continues to dominate market trends. The oldest cohort of this generation is already redefining retirement and semiretirement and making substantially different market choices from those of their parents' generation. With increased life span and good health, baby boomers expect to have an active lifestyle and to spend greater amounts on experiences rather than goods. Higher wealth accumulation and fewer children than previous generations will permit many to define retirement on new terms, allowing them to stay busy with volunteerism, second careers, and travel. Their demographics will determine where they retire and their preference for different types of housing. To cater to this market, more homes will offer accessible features such as first-floor master suites and accessible or convertible fixtures to facilitate aging in place.

Ten years ago, much was made of the potential reurbanization of baby boom retirees. Although preference surveys indicate that a portion of this cohort might be interested in a downtown area with ample amenities, so far the data show that these people largely remain in suburbs, with roughly equal proportions moving into city centers and moving out to exurban locales. Many of this generation chose to live their working lives in suburban metropolitan areas, and most can be expected to retire in those locations, or similar locations in other states. As with previous generations, their retirement choices will be influenced by the quality of nearby health care facilities, and a greater share of new housing construction will likely be nontraditional types of smaller single- and multifamily residences, following a consistently expressed preference for minimizing home maintenance and upkeep.

Continued full- or part-time involvement in the workforce and diverse lifestyles are likely to make the traditional "active adult" communities less attractive to seniors than more connected and authentic environments. Unlike in past decades, seniors are not expected to relocate in large numbers to the Sunbelt. Except for the wealthiest elderly boomers, who can search the country and select high-amenity locations, most are expected to age and retire near their families and other lifelong connections. Although many age-restricted communities remain focused on physical fitness, new ones are being developed around access to lifelong learning opportunities or outdoor amenities with an environmental theme. In an interesting shift, in recent years, survey respondents have raised "walking/hiking trails" to the top preferred amenity in new community construction, far outstripping the desire for golf or tennis.

CITIES VERSUS SUBURBS

The extent to which cities are on the rebound is entering the third decade of a fiery debate. Urban history during the last half of the 20th century was largely about the migration of people from cities to suburbs and the decentralization of residences and, later, workplaces. Census data for 2010 indicate that the draw of recent immigrants to urban cores is weakening. Preferences are shifting, as particularly Latino and Asian immigrants increasingly choose suburbs.[22] Suburbs are becoming much more like central cities, with larger nonwhite populations, higher percentages of retired residents, and greater poverty. Crime has been dropping throughout metropolitan areas since the 1990s. Ironically, crime in central cities fell more quickly than in suburbs. Affordable housing will be an important issue for all immigrant populations, especially Latino immigrants, who are projected to be drivers of growth,

White Provision is an adaptive use of a meatpacking plant as 94 condominium units, office space, shops, and restaurants on a 4.7-acre (1.9 ha) site in midtown Atlanta.

as they cluster in areas where land and housing costs are rising and developers have difficulty providing new housing at an affordable price.

Although immigrants are increasingly moving to the suburbs, urban living appears to be on the upswing, in some cities. Conversion of older downtown and near-downtown offices and warehouses to loft housing, apartments, and condominiums signals the resurgence of urban life. This trend received its first serious confirmation in an EPA-funded study of core and surrounding county building permits and population change.[23] While a statistically significant increase in building in center cities is documented for some of the nation's largest MSAs, this shift is uneven. The trend is undetectable, or even reversed, in many second-tier cities. Demand for urban living is fueled by three main groups: (1) aging baby boomers, approximately 15 percent of whom are moving back to the city in early retirement years; (2) young high-tech and creative workers who are interested in the walkability, shopping, restaurants, and entertainment of a 24-hour downtown; and (3) certain groups of immigrants. To maintain this interest in urban living, cities need successful downtown housing programs with several elements: committed public officials, aggressive marketing, creative financing, a flexible regulatory environment, a developer-friendly business climate, parking, amenities, and, most important, good product and urban design. Renting is the key for young professionals and minority householders to live in the city, as most renters continue to have annual incomes of under $50,000. More than 40 percent of householders ages 25 to 44 are renters, compared with around 20 percent of householders ages 45 to 64 and fewer than 20 percent age 65 and older.[24] The majority of center-city minority householders are renters.

Development Issues

A number of issues will continue to be of concern to developers in the coming years. More sustainable development will be a way to address environmental, economic, and social problems.

SMART GROWTH

Although growth has benefits, it is widely recognized that it can result in unintentional fiscal, environmental, health, and lifestyle consequences for the larger community, and for regional and national interests. As Matt Kiefer describes it, "The postwar view was of development as an engine of growth. The 21st-century view is of development as a generator of impacts."[25] Recent census and other data indicate strong growth will continue, and the challenge for many municipalities is how best to accommodate development while maintaining community identity and protecting the environment. Stepping into the unproductive "economic development versus no growth" debate is a powerful and simple concept: smart growth, also referred to as "sustainable growth," or "quality growth." It refers not to a single solution but to a set of principles promulgated by organizations like Smart Growth America. Smart growth has gained national attention as a framework for limiting, and in some cases reversing, sprawl.

As its ten basic principles—discussed in detail in chapter 3—have gained popularity and have been folded into many municipalities' comprehensive plans, they have received the endorsement of unlikely supporters: staunch environmentalists and downtown business associations, land use attorneys, and biologists. Unlike the rigid mechanisms used under earlier growth management strategies, smart growth strives to promote a higher quality of growth that accommodates and directs development activity in a way that supports the economy, by encouraging investment and job creation, raising property and tax values, providing incentives for a variety of housing and transportation alternatives, preserving the environment, and enhancing quality of life and a sense of place. The Smart Growth America organization, in concert with planners and architects associated with the Congress for New Urbanism and with the active support of ULI, has contributed to the dissemination of these ideas.

Policies derived from smart growth principles have been promoted by states, and recently the federal government has taken steps to promote similar goals through interagency partnerships between EPA, the Department of Transportation, and the Department of Housing and Urban Development. With this kind of support, it is likely that smart growth will continue to have a strong influence over development decisions, and developers should be able to frame their proposals in terms of these goals. Smart growth seems at times to be a movement more solidly supported than it is understood, and there remain those who are skeptical of its benefits to the environment, the building industry, housing provision, and transit policy. To help developers navigate these issues, ULI has published reports such as the annual series "Climate Change, Land Use, and Energy" and books, including *The Green Quotient: Insights from Leading Experts on Sustainability*.

Despite planners' and policy makers' efforts, the job of implementing better growth ultimately falls to developers, who introduce proposals and invest capital to do the actual place making. As such, in the hands of entrepreneurs, these models must satisfy not just civic ambition but also financial metrics, and the underlying principles must be able to survive the "sausage-making" process of public approvals and regulatory review. Public opposition to growth in general can deter even high-quality projects that incorporate smart growth principles, and the "smarter" plan often exacerbates the rancor of abutters and environmental groups, because these principles when applied to a given site typically result in higher densities and mixed uses where growth is desired, in order to minimize sprawl, impact, and infrastructure provision in other areas designated for protection. Advocates for these projects should not expect an easier ride through approvals, unless the jurisdiction offers an explicit fast track or public partnership for appropriate projects. Developers should, however, heed one of the key principles: planning should involve community stakeholders. At the mercy of local politics, developers may be loathe to admit outside voices into project planning, but when these plans succeed, they do so with coalitions behind them.[26]

Conceiving a project, developers must not conflate desires of the public at large with individual buyer decision making. A well-conceived smart growth project may put all the parts together in an innovative way, but demand for individual product types should be well established in the market.

PLACE MAKING

Nearly everyone agrees on the need to preserve a *sense of place*. A sense of place gives residents and workers in a community a feeling of belonging. It is achieved through a combination of policy, planning, design, marketing, and the evolution of a set of social structures and local organizations over time. Design plays a critical role, helping define boundaries, public spaces, places where people meet and have fun, character, and landmarks that people identify with that community. It does not happen overnight, though thoughtful development can accelerate the process, and thoughtless building can undermine it quickly. Classic examples are the town centers of Sienna, Italy, and Cambridge, England. More recent examples are found in San Antonio's River Walk and downtown Boulder, Colorado. Neisen Kasdin, mayor of Miami Beach, and developer Peter Rummell echo the importance of this ineffable quality in Miami Beach: "The challenge is to determine how to meet future demands while preserving the sense of place that currently makes it so attractive to residents and visitors."[27]

According to Tom Lee, former chair of Newhall Land and Farming Company, "places" take many forms— from old-fashioned main streets and town squares to traditional big-city downtowns to newly developed town centers. Each creates a public realm that gives a community its heart, character, identity, and, most important, a place where all kinds of people can come for a wide variety of everyday activities from early in the morning until late at night, seven days a week.[28] Even the absence of development, where it is not appropriate, contributes to a community's sense of itself.

Why should developers care about streetscapes and public places? Such concern is part of good citizenship, but it also translates into long-term value. Streets and plazas that are pleasant to experience, durable and accommodating of change, rather than requiring demolition, will appreciate more and hold their value over time more than less desirable neighborhoods. Developers, however, cannot improve streetscapes by themselves. They are often constrained by zoning and engineering standards that mandate the width of streets, setbacks, and building heights, and by lenders' impulses, such as mandating front-door rather than backdoor parking, or that require overbuilt roadways in pedestrian districts. On the other hand, early 20th-century planning principles favoring the separation of uses have recently begun to give way to new trends favoring mixed-use development. Many planning commissions now actively encourage mixed-use development with offices, shopping, and residences on the same or adjacent sites. And new mechanisms such as business improvement districts can help provide funding for urban design improvements and coordination of disparate property owners.

ENVIRONMENTAL CONCERNS

Environmental concerns are of central importance to the general public, to policy makers, and as a result to real estate developers who must work with all these parties. Increasingly, developers recognize that a sensitive approach to the environment is good not only for the community but also for business. Site contamination is a major problem for developers, but the industry has adopted methods for dealing with it. Both developers and lenders are slowly becoming more accustomed to dealing with brownfield sites, partly because the majority of urban sites—and even undeveloped farmland—have some contamination that must be mitigated, or at least suspected problems that must be investigated.

As always, new problems generate new opportunities. Some investment and development firms now specialize in rehabilitating properties contaminated, or suspected of contamination, by toxic materials. Because the properties can usually be purchased at significant discounts, careful analysis of the removal costs and appropriate actions can generate large profits. Although lenders have been extremely wary of loans on such properties, federal and state governments have established grant and loan programs to partially underwrite remediation costs, and knowledge of the intricacies of these programs can improve the profitability of a project. Nonetheless, developers that fail to perform adequate due diligence before purchasing new properties risk financial disaster.

Water availability and quality issues increasingly determine where and how much development can occur. In addition, communities are increasingly concerned about the preservation of hillsides, wetlands, canyons, forests, and other environmentally fragile areas. Developers that address these concerns in planning and designing their buildings will find communities more receptive to their projects. A related matter, habitat preservation, can touch nearly any land development project and can trigger unsustainable delays as field science is scoped and as preservation and mitigation plans are prepared and approved. Of considerable frustration to landowners is the perception that time, the enemy of the developer, often seems to hold little interest for the regulator, whose goal is to prevent a detrimental project from being developed, not just to approve good projects. As in so many other areas, the best defense against uncertainties is twofold: negotiating appropriate approval contingencies in acquisition and performing solid due diligence. Modest, early expenditures with reputable and experienced consultants can help owners foresee, if not forestall, such problems.

Stormwater management is one of the most common pitfalls facing developers, particularly in suburban and exurban settings. As environmental science has advanced understanding of nonpoint source pollution of waterways, regulatory attention has shifted from the stereotypical factory pipe discharging PCBs into a river to a focus on limiting sedimentation and the low-level but constant runoff of nutrient- and contaminant-laden stormwater. One manifestation has

been state or regional plans for impaired waterways, such as the Chesapeake Bay Act(s). Following interstate agreements forged in the 1980s, the states of Virginia, Maryland, and Pennsylvania have passed laws requiring local governments and other regulatory agencies to delineate impact areas and to enforce rules toward the preservation of a massive macroregional watershed. Compliance is overseen by state agencies, and penalties for noncompliance can be costly.

The experience of landowners over the 20 years of incremental implementation has been bewilderment and confusion over who is in charge, laced with occasional panic at what might happen if every possible interpretation of the law was enforced. These fears result from years of "mission creep" by the U.S. Army Corps of Engineers, which, though originally tasked with regulating navigable waters, has gradually established regulatory jurisdiction over quarter-acre wetlands miles from even canoe-scale rivers. Matt Kiefer describes the ongoing evolution of stormwater regulations as part of a larger regulatory regime change: "We're going from designing out nature to design with nature, and new performance criteria for stream crossings, for site permeability, and on-site retention and discharge are all of a piece."[29] The coming decade will likely resolve many of these regulatory uncertainties, and for the better, as best practices that mimic natural watershed function and other low-impact development strategies become commonplace and join the well-understood vocabulary of site development.

Over the coming decade, many land use and environmental professionals expect climate change to increasingly drive planning decisions. Greenhouse gas (GHG) emissions are clearly moving the planet toward irreversible climate change, with impacts that cannot yet be reliably predicted. European nations have begun voluntary trading of GHG credits, and in the United States, while national policy is being negotiated, California has passed a potentially revolutionary regulatory scheme to rein in emissions. This scheme, likely to become a model for other states, directly addresses GHG and energy impacts deriving from land use change, which puts developers in the driver's seat. This leadership role is appropriate, as the largest sinks and sources (forests, farms, utilities, industry, and building construction and operation) are all touched by real estate development, though few developers active today would consider themselves qualified to make decisions in the field of planetary energy balance.

Judi Schweitzer advises developers of long-timeline projects to jump into energy-related issues, with appropriate consultants to help navigate. "These constraints are coming, and they will be complex, and it will pay to be familiar with the terms and players early. . . . In addition to regulation, funding sources increasingly have portfolio requirements that will further motivate developers following capital to address these issues." Rather than recoil at the thought of accounting for carbon and methane in a land use plan, developers should delineate the constituencies that must be satisfied, and treat energy like any other approvals issue. "A checklist, or even a series of checklists, is insufficient. Rather than tick off points toward LEED or other certification, developers will, over the coming years, have to become familiar with the emissions profile of various land use decisions they make, in the aggregate, and working as a system."[30] Steve Kellenberg, principal of AECOM, states it differently: "What's happening now, and going forward, is a shift from qualitative (add bike lanes, preserve a wetland) to quantitative (carbon accounting, energy modeling) understanding of environmental impacts. This is good. It means, with the right tools, we are going to start making smarter and more informed decisions. . . . We think we can knock 25 percent off carbon emissions, just by using models and adjusting land uses accordingly."[31]

Separate from carbon and a tax on vehicle miles traveled is the trend of real estate as an energy producer. Increasingly, as the costs of renewable energy sources come down, and nonrenewables go up, real estate can have an important asset in the ground (geothermal heat) or on the roof (solar or wind power). Fortunately for the bewildered developer, many of the recommended—or legislated—land use solutions to climate change already closely follow principles of smart growth: colocation of jobs and housing, transit orientation, and compact and efficient buildings. As is often the case, developers that pay attention to areas of concern today will have a leg up on the issues of the future.

THE NEED FOR OPEN SPACE
Preservation of open space consistently ranks among the top concerns of both urban and suburban residents. The increasing interest in ecological function of even highly urbanized areas portends only greater focus on this issue in the coming decades. Open space comes in many different forms, from manicured golf courses to permanently wild forests and wetlands.

These spaces might allow a wide range of uses, from farming and passive recreation to structured facilities, such as ball fields. Ownership and protection of these spaces can range from public ownership, in the case of city parks, to quasi–public service districts within planned communities, to privately held easements across individually owned land, or public/private funding initiatives to rent or ease specific assets of ecological or cultural value. Each type of open space is critical for the enjoyment of different people who make up a community, and many of these spaces perform important—and sometimes economically valuable—ecological functions, such as filtering runoff and carbon sequestration. One trend worth watching is the attempt to monetize these "ecosystem services" and to establish markets that will pay landowners for their stewardship of these values by mechanisms like credit trading. Although municipal parks and other small-scale breaks in the dense urban fabric often generate the most intense public feeling and interest, environmental science has prioritized the protection of large, unfragmented spaces, where water and wildlife can more closely approximate their predevelopment functions.

Open space must be specifically protected, either by zoning, tax policy, or rolling rent payments on a long-term agreement or by a permanent legal reduction of development potential. If it is not, incremental urban development will eventually consume potential sites and cut up habitat areas. Since a landmark Supreme Court case in 1979, developers have been able to generate charitable tax deductions by donation of land, or by donation of an easement reducing development potential to a nonprofit easement holder. These returns can be attractive to investors and have spawned their own niche product: conservation development. States have responded to this relatively inexpensive method of conservation by offering their own suite of credits, which in some states are tradable on open markets for cash, to sweeten conservation deals. This response has greatly accelerated land conservation and has created an infrastructure of local and national land trusts qualified to accept and monitor these easements, and to develop plans that prioritize parcels for conservation.

At the national level, organizations like the Nature Conservancy and the Trust for Public Land provide mechanisms for developers and communities to set aside land for open space. The organizations serve as stewards of such land, providing various levels of access to the public while preserving natural amenities and wildlife habitats. Such organizations are needed because the timeline of preservation covenants is extremely long, often "perpetual." In some states, easements held by these groups are "backstopped" by state-chartered corporations, such as the Virginia Outdoors Foundation, which receive easements on their own, and when small land trusts can no longer serve as conservators.

For developers, a familiarity with local land trusts is critical, as they are often key stakeholders in community decision making. A working knowledge of the mechanisms of open space preservation will increasingly become part of the necessary toolkit for many developers, as municipalities respond to the contradictory challenge of constituents who want open space but cannot or will not pay for it from general funds.

TRANSPORTATION AND CONGESTION

Transportation has always been a major source of real estate value because of its effect on location, but solving the problem of overburdened roads continues to be one of the development industry's principal concerns. Congestion—or merely the perception of congestion—can undermine a property's value and motivate new and existing development to continue its move outward to more accessible locations. Traffic delays in some large cities increased by 500 percent or more between 1982 and 2007,[32] but lost time is only one measure of congestion's cost. Idling and inefficient operation waste tremendous fuel resources and contribute to GHG emissions, airborne particulates, and ozone.

The most direct method of reducing traffic congestion is to decrease the length and number of vehicle trips. Developers can assist in achieving these reductions by offering development in a dense, compact form with a mix of land uses accessible to mass transit. The inclusion of residential development, offices, retail uses, and entertainment venues in a convenient and accessible location reduces vehicle trips, spreads peak-hour flows on arterial roads, makes transit more feasible, and allows more people to live closer to employment and services. To achieve this scenario, federal and state agencies must work with the cities and counties that control land use. Developers, which will shoulder much of the burden for improving inadequate transportation in the suburbs, would be well advised to support coordinated, collective efforts to plan transportation in their communities. Otherwise, they will be forced to pay a disproportionate share of the cost, and what they do provide will be inadequate to hold congestion constant, let alone reduce it.

AYALA LAND, INC.

Greenbelt 5 is a four-level shopping center in the central business district of Manila, Philippines. It is surrounded by lush gardens, emphasizing the developer's commitment to preserving open space.

Social Responsibility

Developers hold special responsibilities because their activities involve large public commitments. In many communities, developers actually build most of the urban infrastructure, including roads, sewers, water treatment facilities, and drainage channels. They may also provide civic facilities, such as schools, hospitals, and police and fire stations. And as the public sector pulls back from financial commitments, this trend is likely to continue.

Communities have a right to expect the highest possible quality of design, construction, and implementation from developers. They should expect developers to be sensitive to community concerns, to the streetscape and landscape, traffic, and other dimensions of development that affect the civic environment. Developers should uphold their promises—delivering buildings on time and with appropriate attention to quality. Developers are also expected to be ethical citizens of the community, concerned with protecting its long-term interests.

What do developers have a right to expect from communities? They have a right to be treated fairly and consistently and for decisions to be made on the basis of merit and law. The community should honor its commitments to build promised infrastructure on time and to properly maintain public facilities and services. They have a right to expect the community to exercise foresight and good planning judgment in setting public policy—to ensure that new regulations are handled efficiently and do not impose unnecessary costs or delays on the development process.

THE DEVELOPER'S PUBLIC IMAGE

Developers as a group suffer from a negative public image. As the authors of *Suburban Nation* point out, "It was not always thus. When George Merrick built Coral Gables . . . he was regarded not as a developer, but as a town founder. A bust in his likeness still presides proudly over City Hall."[33] The public image of developers today is more often of a self-interested actor who profits from degradation of the environment and quality of life. That image is often undeserved—as when developers are mistakenly identified as causes of, rather than responders to, demographic and economic change. Sometimes, however, the image is deserved—when they build shoddy products, when they have been insensitive to community needs, or when they have imposed costs on the community for which they should have taken responsibility.

In expanding communities where economic growth is desired, developers can more easily overcome negative stereotypes. In communities with strong anti-growth sentiments, however, the distrust with which community members view developers in general makes conditions more difficult for even the best developers. Developers should understand the sources of the distrust that they will encounter. Many communities and neighborhood groups have relied on developers' promises that were never kept or on inaccurate predictions, such as a new office building that would not increase congestion. Developers are the standard-bearers for the real estate industry as a whole, even though real estate brokers, property managers, and even public planners may also be to blame for these failings. The public approval process for development provides the sole opportunity for most people to complain about the full array of urban ills.

GAINING COMMUNITY SUPPORT

Community opposition to growth can be one of the most difficult challenges developers face. Debates often begin with the question of how the land is currently used. Although vacant land choked with weeds may seem to builders like a prime opportunity for development, surrounding neighbors may consider this open space a recreational area, dog park, parking area, or view corridor. Failing to acknowledge these existing, very low intensity uses can make it difficult for a developer to reach consensus with neighbors about future land uses. The situation is different when the land is already intensively used. Then parties must explore the more complex question of whether the proposed land use is more or less desirable than the existing uses.

The analysis of citizen opposition to development proposals has spawned its own vocabulary, with terms like *NIMBY* (not in my backyard) and *LULU* (locally unwanted land use) often used interchangeably. A significant amount of opposition to development proposals is based on citizens' misperceptions, lack of information, or exaggerated fears of project impacts. Common areas of misinformation about new projects include consistency with zoning and general plan criteria; impact on property values, views, traffic, types of residents or commercial tenants; and changes in community character. The developer can minimize opposition spawned from a lack of information by providing clear, credible data about the project. Aside from misinformation, however, Matt Kiefer notes a substantial change in the etiquette of land use debates, over the past 20 years: "Opponents who are impacted by projects used to feel a need to hang their hat on an external, objective concern. Traffic maybe, or environmental concerns. Social mores have changed, in that it is now seen as acceptable to oppose a project based merely on the personal impact of the proposal."[34] An assumption that ownership connoted rights to determine use is no longer a given, and developers that do not understand this end up in litigation.

Developers and planners must address a variety of different constituencies: local residents, including disadvantaged populations; local merchants; preservation and arts groups; city officials; and public agency officials. Successful developers learn how to operate within their local, inevitably heterogeneous, communities.

According to Daniel Rose, community groups can, at their best, provide perspective and insight; at their worst, they can fall prey to a NIMBY mentality. "Residents often oppose the construction of a fire station in their neighborhood because they object to the accompanying noise. But the necessary services of an urban system must be located somewhere. Someone will have to work or live near a fire station or a garbage disposal site."[35]

Gerald Hines emphasizes the role that community acceptance plays in marketability. "We look at each city as a different culture, and if we don't know the culture, we're going to have an unsuccessful project. Conferring with community boards and neighborhood associations has become a part of a project's market analysis and its later acceptance by the market."[36]

Because the civic contribution of a development project is not always apparent, developers can benefit from regular civic involvement, such as serving on

Advice from Industry Leaders

This section presents the wisdom of seven of ULI's leading figures: Jim Chaffin, Bob Engstrom, Mike Fascitelli, Gerald Hines, Jeremy Newsum, Ron Terwilliger, and Lynn Thurber.[a] They reflect on what they have learned from the Great Recession of 2007–2009 and on major trends affecting the real estate industry over the next ten years. They offer advice to both beginning and more experienced developers.

LESSONS FROM THE GREAT RECESSION

Ron Terwilliger observes, "Each cycle is different. You won't see it coming and you won't know the depth or duration. You must operate your business with that knowledge. It will affect your ability to access capital and it will affect demand. I learned this time that . . . while you seem to have alignment with [your investor partners] on the up-cycle, you may not on the down-cycle. I closed on some land with financial partners alongside us. They just walked away from their investment. Land values fell by half or even more severely. I learned from a merchant builder's standpoint, you should not acquire land with debt. If you can't buy it with equity, you should wait to buy until you are ready to build on it."

Lynn Thurber learned to exercise more caution. "The notion that 'all ships rise with a rising tide' is no longer true. During the expansion, there was such a flood of capital on both the debt and equity side that secondary locations and asset quality were not differentiated amongst risk takers and in pricing. Today, both debt and equity investors are far more selective." This observation implies that regeneration of areas will take longer to implement. "Capital will first go to the best locations and best properties and properties that have the best renovation potential. It will be much harder for properties on the fringe."

Gerald Hines points out that real estate values can go down by as much as half. "Your liquidity needs to be more in bonds and less in stocks and [you need to] have other forms of liquidity. You don't want both real estate and your other assets to drop at the same speed and magnitude." He observes, "If the building is slightly off-location, it will have a much bigger drop in value than one with a better location. Risk in marginal buildings is very, very high. They will be rented during a shortage but not in a down market because there are too many other better buildings."

Jeremy Newsum says that sticking to the principles is more important than chasing the crowd. "The things that went wrong were utterly predictable. Timing is harder to predict, but that is no excuse." Jim Chaffin observes, "Most of what we know about our business has more to do with humility than intelligence, but we reserve the right to get smarter as we go along."

TAKING ADVANTAGE OF MAJOR TRENDS

Being prepared for the inevitable down-cycle is critical for building a long-term business. To take advantage of the next up-cycle, one must understand the implications of major trends in demographics, technology, sustainability, urban growth, finance, and globalization.

CHANGING EXPECTATIONS. Lynn Thurber states, "Demographics will impact geography and preferences in ways people my age can't figure out. In difficult economic times, people must be more flexible about where they will live and how they will work. This will impact where real estate markets recover first."

Jim Chaffin distinguishes between *demographics*, which has to do with income, age, and geography, and *psychometrics*, which has to do with psychological changes that affect the market. For second-home communities, he sees

a trend back toward smaller homes with less conspicuous consumption. People want smaller homes near their grandchildren. They also want a sense of belonging. College towns, for example, will be more and more popular because they offer stimulation and opportunities to be connected to a community.

RETURN TO THE CITY. City living is more attractive today than previously for baby boomers who no longer want a big house in the suburbs or a long commute. Ron Terwilliger says, "Both younger and older people will look for places where there is more entertainment close to their homes." Bob Engstrom says that smaller homes and smaller lots will be more in demand—1,200-square-foot (111 m²) foundations with room for expansion. The ambiance of mixed use in a walkable neighborhood appeals to both younger and older people. However, Lynn Thurber predicts that today's younger generation that grew up in the suburbs will return to the suburbs to raise their children because they will want them to have a similar experience. Ron Terwilliger believes that the return to the city will take place primarily in inner-ring suburbs. "There will be more suburban cores redeveloped to provide a walkable environment for shopping, restaurants, and entertainment. An increasing segment of the population will look for a more holistic environment where they have more walking and commuting options."

GREEN DEVELOPMENT. Gerald Hines observes that green building has always been a keystone of his company. "It made sense because you could operate for less."

"Green buildings are no longer considered a fad," says Lynn Thurber. "They are a very important part of our future. Those technologies are improving rapidly and are a part of all decision-making processes for investing and

CONTINUED

developing. . . . Companies on top of knowledge of what's available and the cost-benefit tradeoff, and companies that are able to collect the data will be more competitive."

Mike Fascitelli points out that many tenants and governments are forcing landlords to be state of the art as well as forcing improvements in older buildings. Jim Chaffin emphasizes the relationship between sustainability and building a community: "Sustainability gives people a sense of being responsible. People yearn for not just a big home in an exclusive project but being part of a community. Whatever you can do to weave social and environmental responsibility into a community, it gives people more reason to be there."

FINANCING. Ron Terwilliger advises young developers to align themselves with deep pockets. "Get an investor who can ride through the cycles with you. Avoid too much debt. In the latest cycle, Trammel Crow Residential did not borrow more than 75 percent of cost, which helped it survive the down-cycle." Trammel Crow decided to give as much of the ownership away as it had to in order to raise 25 percent equity for each project. Raising equity is always the hardest part for beginning developers. "If you build credibility, you will find the right financial partner—a wealthy family or a successful real estate player who is retired but wants to keep a hand in." Terwilliger adds that "a reasonable deal is whatever the investor is comfortable to begin with. A lot of young people forget if they are being paid a salary and have no money to put at risk, they can't expect an investor to give them a whole lot of upside. They should have some upside—around 20 percent. Over time, demonstrate you are capable, leave money in the business, and become an equal partner down the road."

Lynn Thurber predicts that both debt and equity capital will be difficult over the next few years. "Understanding what those sources are expecting from their partners through which they invest will be very important. Because there was so much capital available the last few years, people did not feel they needed to be good partners with their debt source and equity source. They were confident they could get the capital somewhere. Owner/developers will not be in the driver's seat over the next few years. Younger developers who commit to being good partners with their sources will do better than those who do not put time and effort into their capital sources."

Jeremy Newsum advises, "One should *never* guarantee any loan that he or she can't meet. It is better to share the equity than try to get all the upside and make foolhardy commitments." He asserts that financiers are being put in the backseat. "They're not in position to drive the market any more. True real estate professionals are coming back to the fore. Others are leaving [the field] because return expectations have dropped to something more reasonable. Fundamental gearing levels are falling."

Mike Fascitelli emphasizes the trend toward lower leverage. He says, "Investors want the stability of cash flow and inflation protection." He quotes Harvard Business School's Bill Fruhan's mantra: "DROOC!—Don't Run Out of Cash." He says that developers' balance sheets may not matter during boom times, but today they matter a lot.

STRATEGY AND BUILDING ORGANIZATIONS

Throughout his career, Gerald Hines's strategy has been to have the best building in the market with the best tenants. This clear strategic goal has defined his company's image and brought it many tenants and building opportunities. Hines says, "Strive for an outstanding reputation through the quality of what you build and how you deal with

people, and leave a good trail behind." For building an organization, he says, "Get outstanding people. Give them participation in the success. They also have to have something to lose. They need to have something left in the bank in case they make a bad mistake. We give more equity away to our employees than most developers."

Jim Chaffin observes that one should build his or her organization according to one's strengths and weaknesses. "If you come out of accounting or the finance side, you must have someone strong on the marketing side. If you come from planning, design, construction, or development, you must have a strong CFO and a strong marketing/salesperson. Later on, add an operations guy." There are four key areas: marketing and sales, accounting and finance, planning and design, and construction and operations. A firm should reach a certain size before bringing planning and design in house because they are easily contracted.

Lynn Thurber says the most important things for building an organization are cultural, with integrity and transparency at the top. "If you are honest about what you are committing to and follow through on your promises and willingly share accurate information about what is happening with your employees, service providers, and financial partners, that is hugely important. Those who have failed have not done this." Also important is to "avoid doing things outside of your core competency. When you go outside of it, you are much more likely to run into significant difficulties. You should add on *adjacent* to your core competency. Move gradually but recognize you are taking on great risk and run the risk of damaging your organization."

Ron Terwilliger observes that Charles Fraser, one of the 20th century's most innovative developers, "was a visionary and a dreamer who was way ahead of his time in terms of environmental sensitivity. Charles was able to attract a number of very capable young people. He was charismatic, but did not have any risk management sensitivity. Trammell Crow was a visionary and optimist and very charismatic, but also very generous. He pioneered the partner concept. He always wanted his partners to make a lot of money and do very well. A rising tide raised all boats. His spirit of partnership and generosity are two things I will always remember him for."

ADVICE TO BEGINNING DEVELOPERS

The seven ULI leaders offer the following advice to beginning developers:

LYNN THURBER:

- Do what you love. You really must enjoy it. It is long hours and tough slogging.

- Hire great people on your team. Trying to save money by hiring people with less experience or talent, or worrying that your hires may outshine you, is only setting yourself up for a struggle.

BOB ENGSTROM:

- "Smaller homes" and "infill" are buzz words today. Beginning developers should avoid attached products if they can help it. Even a 12-unit townhouse project, if it does not sell, can be overwhelming. But with single-family detached homes, there is usually a way to salvage it.

- Once the current overhang of inventory is eaten up, there will be opportunities. Keep things on a manageable scale. Recognize that you will have to give personal guarantees—experienced developers may be able to avoid these. Stick to your local market where you have the advantage of understanding the nuances of the market.

GERALD HINES:

- You have to find a specialty where you have some expertise above someone else. There are also opportunities in bigger firms like Hines but you have a lot of people in front of you.

- If the banks loosen up, there will be opportunity for smaller developers—taking over small properties that need love and attention that are not interesting to bigger players.

- There's a lot to learn in finance, construction, how to lead an architect—you can't turn them loose. You need to work for someone else for a long while to learn the business.

- How much equity and personal liability can you handle? Banks will be very restrictive as to who gets loans and how much equity is required. Go build some houses. You learn a lot from this.

- Learn what tenants want and how leases are done and deals are made. Learn about mechanical and other engineering aspects and finance; don't get caught short with major holes in your education. Leasing and marketing are good ways to get into the business; also, working for a general contractor. A combination of both is even better.

JIM CHAFFIN:

- Complexity and large scale are not the place to go right now. You can get started on distressed and infill properties. Then you can expand into the best products in existing areas. Don't pioneer.

- You can buy a 10- or 15-acre [4–6 ha] parcel in an existing resort that is coming back and do a terrific 75- to 125-unit project. There is a huge market out there, but you must be smart about where you do it, how you do it, and how you finance it.

JEREMY NEWSUM:

- Tying yourself to occupiers is the best way to achieve early success. Try to understand what occupiers want. When the market went bust, we had an empty building. We were able to relet it quickly because we listened carefully to understand how the occupation of buildings was changing—how companies needed flexible design and layout, what services they wanted, and how workers would use the building.

MIKE FASCITELLI:

- Be very focused on value added. Capitalize yourself for uncertainty. Don't take short-term financing; use less leverage.

- When things are down, that may be the best time to get in. You want to be on the early end of the cycle. Don't think that the current situation will last forever. When the turning point occurs, you want to be there already.

RON TERWILLIGER:

- Be a local sharpshooter who focuses on market niches. Good beginning projects are either rehabs or something the big guys can't afford to pursue. The country is growing, but changing. You need to get out in front of where change is and find your niche.

- Pick the product type you want to work in and the geographic area you want to work in. Try to get with a company in that location. Build credibility and experience. The more relevant your experience, the more likely you are to attract a financial backer.

[a]Interviews conducted by Richard Peiser in July and August 2010: Jim Chaffin, chair, Chaffin/Light Associates, Okatie, South Carolina; Robert Engstrom, president, Robert Engstrom Companies, Minneapolis, Minnesota; Mike Fascitelli, president, Vornado Realty Trust, New York City; Gerald D. Hines, founder and chair, the Hines real estate organization, Houston, Texas; Jeremy Newsum, executive trustee, the Grosvenor Estates, London; Ron Terwilliger, chairman emeritus, Trammell Crow Residential, and chair, Enterprise Community Partners, Atlanta, Georgia, and New York City; and Lynn Thurber, chair, LaSalle Investment Management, Chicago, Illinois.

boards and working with nonprofits and schools. The presumption by opinion leaders of good civic intentions can be a great asset to developers who will, at some point, find themselves asking for the community's trust. Community leaders should remember that most of their goals for community improvements will be attained only with the participation of developers. The delicate balance between the interests of communities and of developers must be maintained if communities are to grow sensibly and sustainably.

PERSONAL INTEGRITY

A developer's reputation is the foundation of long-term success, and for the inexperienced developer, a trustworthy character can be counted among a short list of assets. The development community is a very small world. Even in the largest cities, news travels quickly and reputations precede every player. Players who lie, cheat, or break the law find that reputable businesspeople will have nothing to do with them.

Dan Kassell advises that young developers consciously take charge of their reputation building: "When we started out, we had a rule: if you tell the planner you're going to fax it today, fax it today. That the fax is a minor permit change that won't be reviewed for four weeks is immaterial. To the recipient of that fax, we are people who do what we say we're going to do."[37] Many developers will run into cash flow difficulties at some point and will consequently have to renegotiate a loan or the terms of a deal. At such times, a record of honesty and transparency can make all the difference. No one likes bad news, but investors, lenders, and partners invariably like surprises even less. Projects rarely go bad overnight. When partners and lenders are kept informed of the problems, they are more understanding and more willing to try to work things out.

Conclusion

Our understanding of how to shape development to create better cities and neighborhoods is far from complete, but we are making progress. Among the greatest problems facing planners and public policy makers are how and where to invest scarce public funds so that the investment will do the most to enhance areas that are improving or to halt the fall of areas that are declining. Too often, massive public and private expenditures are made to rejuvenate one section of town, only to pull businesses and homebuyers away from another. Similarly, land use, building, and engineering regulations are too often imposed with

thought only of curbing the excesses of bad actors, and with insufficient understanding of unintended consequences.

Our recent performance in developing cities has been mediocre; our cities fall short of their potential. Spaces are often poorly planned; boring, repetitive designs are deployed where they are easy to accomplish, rather than where they are appropriate. Once-beautiful neighborhoods are not maintained; the fabric of much of our urban infrastructure is in an appalling state of disrepair. Developing new greenfield sites is easier and cheaper than maintaining or redeveloping older areas.

No one individual or group is to blame for this situation, but all can help remedy it. The development community must exercise stronger leadership, not only in constructing and renovating American cities but also in correcting the harmful aspects of the present development system. By looking after the interests of the community at large, developers serve their own interests.

Development offers one of the most tangible legacies that one can achieve. However, the most successful developers leave behind more than great buildings. Gerald Hines says he is most proud of the people who have worked with him—the team and the longevity of people in his firm, the built environment they have created, their success in a competitive environment where other developers have had to meet higher stan-

In Jersey City, New Jersey, Hudson Greene combines rental and owner residential units in two towers overlooking New York Harbor and Manhattan's skyline.

ALAN SCHINDLER PHOTOGRAPHY

dards, and the high quality that resulted in the cities where they have built.[38]

ULI Past President Robert Nahas summarized the attraction of development: "The great developers whom I've been privileged to know never worked for money per se. . . . I think these developers want to leave a footprint in the sand. It's their particular kind of immortality."[39] All developments must pass the test of serving current market needs or they will fail. But most developments also have a future clientele. Although individual homes and buildings may be replaced, the basic fabric of the community that developers create—street layout, parks, urban design elements—will last for hundreds of years. Indeed, one of development's greatest rewards—and the source of its greatest responsibilities—is its effect on future generations.

NOTES

1. Interview with Don Killoren, principal, Celebration Associates, LLC, Hot Springs, Virginia, 2010.

2. Interview with Kenneth Leventhal, founder of the Kenneth Leventhal accounting firm, now E&Y Kenneth Leventhal, 1998.

3. Interview with Bowen "Buzz" McCoy, former director, Morgan Stanley Real Estate, Los Angeles, California, 2010.

4. Interview with Stewart Fahmy, president of Calandev, LLC, San Jose, California, 2010.

5. Interview with Don Killoren, 2010.

6. Interview with John Knott, president, Noisette Company, LLC, Charleston, South Carolina, 2009.

7. Interview with Gerald D. Hines, founder and chair, the Hines real estate organization, Houston, Texas, conducted by Richard Peiser, August 2010.

8. Jonathan D. Miller, *Emerging Trends in Real Estate 2010* (Washington, D.C.: ULI–the Urban Land Institute and PricewaterhouseCoopers, LLP, 2009), p. 3.

9. Interview with Robert Larson, chair, Lazard Frères Real Estate, New York, New York, July 2001.

10. Harvey S. Moskowitz and Carl G. Lindbloom, *The Latest Illustrated Book of Development Definitions* (New Brunswick, N.J.: Center for Urban Policy Research, 2003).

11. Alvin L. Arnold, *The Arnold Encyclopedia of Real Estate*, 2nd ed. (New York: Wiley, 1993).

12. See Rita Fitzgerald and Richard Peiser, "Development (Dis) Agreements at Colorado Place," *Urban Land*, July 1988, pp. 2–5; and Douglas R. Porter and Lindell L. Marsh, *Development Agreements: Practice, Policy, and Prospects* (Washington, D.C.: ULI–the Urban Land Institute, 1989).

13. Interview with Matthew Kiefer, partner, Goulston & Storrs, Boston, Massachusetts, 2010.

14. See www.cdi.gsd.harvard.edu, the website for the Harvard Design School's Center for Design Informatics.

15. Elizabeth Hayes, "Radical Changes as Worlds of Tech, Real Estate Merge," *Los Angeles Business Journal*, January 24, 2000, p. 36.

16. Interview with Amy Westwood, technology consultant, Orlando, Florida, 2009.

17. Interview with Chad Rowe, director of sales, Bundoran Farm, Charlottesville, Virginia, 2010.

18. Interview with Zvi Barzilay, president and chief operating officer, Toll Brothers, Inc., Horsham, Pennsylvania, 2010.

19. Alan Berube, "The State of Metropolitan America: Suburbs and the 2010 Census," presentation to the Suburbs and the 2010 Census: National Conference, Arlington, Va., July 14, 2011.

20. Interview with Elizabeth Plater-Zyberk, founding principal, Duany Plater-Zyberk & Company, Miami, Florida, 2010.

21. William H. Frey, "Metro Magnets for Minorities and Whites: Melting Pots, the New Sunbelt, and the Heartland," PSC Research Report no. 02-496, Population Studies Center, University of Michigan, Ann Arbor, February 2002; and William H. Frey and Ross C. DeVol, "America's Demography in the New Century," Policy Brief no. 9, Milken Institute, Santa Monica, Calif., March 8, 2000.

22. Interview with Joel Kotkin, author of *The Next Hundred Million: America in 2050* (New York: Penguin Press, 2010).

23. "Residential Construction Trends in America's Metropolitan Regions," U.S. Environmental Protection Agency, Development, Community, and Environment Division, Washington, D.C., January 2010.

24. Compiled from www.nmhc.org, website of the National Multi-Housing Council, 2010.

25. Interview with Matthew Kiefer, 2010.

26. Interview with David Goldberg, communications director, Smart Growth America, Washington, D.C., 2010.

27. Peter Rummell, "Preserving a Sense of Place," *Urban Land*, April 2000, p. 18.

28. Thomas L. Lee, "Place Making in Suburbia," *Urban Land*, October 2000, pp. 72–79.

29. Interview with Matthew Kiefer, 2010.

30. Interview with Judi Schweitzer, president, Schweitzer & Associates, Inc., Lake Forest, California, 2009.

31. Interview with Steve Kellenberg, principal, AECOM (formerly EDAW), Irvine, California, 2010.

32. David Schrank et al., *The Urban Mobility Report* (College Station: Texas Transportation Institute, 2007), Congestion Summary Tables.

33. Andrès Duany, Elizabeth Plater-Zyberk, and Jeff Speck, *Suburban Nation: The Rise of Sprawl and the Decline of the American Dream* (New York: North Point Press, 2001), p.100.

34. Interview with Matthew Kiefer, 2010.

35. Daniel Rose, chair of Design and Politics conference, New York, April 1988, quoted in Maria Brisbane, "Developing in a Politicized Environment," *Urban Land*, July 1988, pp. 6–8.

36. Gerald Hines, founder and chair, the Hines real estate organization, Houston, Texas, quoted in "Developing in a Politicized Environment," *Urban Land*, July 1988, pp. 6–8.

37. Interview with Dan Kassell, president, Granite Homes, Irvine, California, 2002.

38. Interview with Gerald Hines, August 2010.

39. Robert Nahas, former general partner, Rafanelli and Nahas, Orinda, California, quoted in Ed Micken, "Future Talk: The Next Fifty Years," *Urban Land*, December 1986, p. 16.

Index

Italicized page numbers indicate figures, photos, and illustrations.

Bold page numbers indicate feature boxes.

H

Handicapped access. *See* Accessibility

Hasbrouck, David, 303, 317

Hawaii, regulatory issues in, 90

Hawthorne, Randolph, 149–50, 204–5, 218, 219

Hazardous materials, 52, 54, 288, 292–93, 295, 319, 342, 344, 353, 385–86

Heating. *See* HVAC systems

Heitman, 309

Hernandez, Tara, 18–19

Higgs, Roy, 330

Highland Park, Texas, 141

High-rise buildings, 148, 149, 194, 223, 255

High-tech firms, 240, 289, 292

Hines, Gerald, 376, 388, 389, 392

Historic preservation, 218–19, 249, 288

Historic tax credits, 218–19

Homeowners associations, 142–43, **144**

Housing and Urban Development, U.S. Department of, 218

Housing revenue bonds (HRBs), 217

Houston, Texas: 11000 Equity Drive, 272, **279–80**, **279–81**; regulatory issues in, 92

Hudson Green [Jersey City, New Jersey], *32, 392*

Hughes, Ken, 165–66, 197

Hughes, Phil, 4, 5

Humidity Control Design Guide for Commercial and Institutional Buildings (ASHRAE), 258

HVAC systems (heating, ventilation, and air conditioning): and industrial development, 288, 307; and life safety systems, 259; and multifamily residential development, 199; and office development, 242, 257–58, 259; and retail development, 354

Hyatt, Wayne, 143–44

Hybrid shopping centers, 335–36

Hydrology, 120, 163. *See also* Site conditions

Hypersupply, as part of market cycle, 15, *16*

I

Illumination Engineering Society, 254

Image of development industry, 388

Immigrants, 147–48, 381, 382–83

Impact fees, 93, 96, 377–78; for industrial development, 298–99; for multifamily residential development, 168; for office development, 248, 250

Incentives: bonuses, 56; leasing or sale of multifamily residential development, 224–25; state and local, 299. *See also* Tax credits

Income approach to appraisals, 57

Income/Expense Analysis for Office Buildings (IREM), 245, 250

Income-producing properties, 14, 96

Incubation approach in industrial development, 287, 297, 320

Industrial development, 283–325; and absorption, 288; and accessibility, 289, 302–3; advice about, 283, 307–8; and amenities, 303, 316; Ameriplex [Nashville, Tennessee],

case study, **321–25**; and approvals, 292, 297, 298, 317; and budgets, 314, 315; building types, *284*, 284–87, **305**; categorization of, *284*, 284–87, **305**; and cities, 294, 295; and clustering, 289; and construction financing, 308–9; and construction stage, 300–308; data for, 300; deal size and flow, 311; due diligence, 292–93, 311; and engineering feasibility, 293–95; and environmental issues, 294–95; and equity, 308, 309; and exterior design, 285, 286, 304, 306; and fees, 298–99; and financial feasibility, 300; and financing, 308–14; flexibility in, 286, 304, 320; in foreign trade zones, 289; and hazardous materials, 288, 292–93, 295; history, 283–84; and HVAC systems, 288, 307; and incubation approach, 287, 297, 320; and infill sites, 292; in institutional property portfolios, 309; and landscaping, 302; and leasing, 316–19; and location, 289; and maintenance, 316, 318; and management, 317, 319; and market analysis, 288–89, **290–91**, 295–97; and marketing, 314–17; multitenant, 286, **290–91**; and neighbors, 292, 297, 319; and occupancy/vacancy rates, 288; and parking, 285, 286, 287, 301, 319; and permanent financing, 308–9; product types, *284*, 284–87; and project feasibility, 288–99; and protective covenants, 295, 297–98, 315, 317, 319; and real estate brokers, 292, 314, 316; and redevelopment/rehabilitation, 287–88, 295; and regulatory issues, 297–99; and rent, 316, 317, 318, 319; and return, 309–10; and risk, 311–14, **312–13**; roofs, 306; and signs, 302; and site acquisition, 288–89, 292–93; site conditions, 292–93; and site coverage, 297; and site selection, 288–89, 292–97; and speculative development, 283; and streets/roads, 301–2; suburbanization of, 284; and supply/demand, 295–97; and target markets, 289, 314, 315; and technological development, 286–87, 320; and tenant improvements/finish-out allowances, 286, 317; and tenants, 285, 286, 316–19, 320; and traffic, 285, 294, 295, 301–2; trends in, *284*, 320; and utilities, 292, 294, 315, 316; and zoning, 292, 297, 301. *See also* Business parks; Manufacturing; R&D (research and development)

Industrial development bonds, 299

Industrial market and multifamily residential development, 156

Industrial parks: defined, 287. *See also* Business parks

Infill sites: increase in number of, 148; industrial development, 292; office development, 240, 243; retail development, 341–42, 360; Rock Row [Los Angeles, California], *138*, **138–40**

Inflation, 13; and land development, 102, 110; and retail development, 339

Infrastructure: and development industry trends, 377–78, 387; financing of, 93–94; and growth issues, 90; and industrial development, 292; and land development, 90, 93–94; and social responsibility, 387. *See also specific type of infrastructure*

Inspections, 69; industrial development, 319; multifamily residential development, 220–21; retail development, 353

Installation date vs. shipping date for warranty purposes, 49

Institute of Real Estate Management (IREM), 64, 245, 250

Institutional investors, 148, 204, 309. *See also specific type of institution*

Insurance and insurance companies, 67, 69; and construction stage, 221–22; office development, 261; and subcontractors, 221–22. *See also specific type of insurance*

Interest/interest rates: calculation of, *203*, 203–5; and construction financing, 202–5, *203*, 263; and multifamily residential development, 147, 202–5, *203*; and office development, 263, 264

Interior design: advice about, 261; and elevators, 256; and leasing, 223; and lighting, 198, 256–57; and multifamily residential development, 198–99; and office development, 254–61; and retail development, 355. *See also* Space; Tenant improvements (TIs)

Internal rate of return (IRR): industrial development, 300, 310; land development, 96, 103, *106–8*, 110; multifamily residential development, 177–78, 212

International Council of Shopping Centers, 349

International trade zones, 289

Internet: and construction stage, 379–80; and design, 379–80; and marketing, 136, 223, 226, **227**, 267, 315, 380; and retail development, 336

Investment and development, 14

Investors: concerns of, 214; as construction lenders, 68; joint venture with developer, 130; and multifamily residential development, 202, 214; types of, *74*. *See also* Financing

IRR. *See* Internal rate of return

Issuers in conduit loans, 208

J

JAS Worldwide International Headquarters [Atlanta, Georgia], *249*

Jefferson Pointe [West Chester, Pennsylvania], **152–53**

Jerome Frank Investments, 160, 200

Joinder, 84

Joint ventures: advice about, 27, **213**; with beginning developers, 31–33; as construction lenders, 68; and industrial development, 309–10; and multifamily residential development, 188, *189*, 190, 210–17; and office development, 264; and risk, 128–30; structure of, 128–30

JPI, 205

Just-in-time delivery chain, 304

K

Kansas City, Missouri, 243

Kasdin, Neisen, 384

Kassel, Dan, 85, 113, 221, 392

Kellenberg, Steve, 386

Kelo v. City of New London (2005), 88

"Kickers," 205

Kiefer, Matt, 52, 379, 383, 385, 388

Killoren, Don, 19–20, 373, 375

Market area, 155–56

Market consultants, 56–57

Marketing: advice about, 27; budgets for, 133–34, 223–25, 314, 315, 364; computer-aided design (CAD) to assist, 193; and development industry trends, 380; development team for, 41; example of, 140; and industrial development, 314–18; and land development, 132–36; larger parcels, 135–36; and leasing, 364–65; and location, 272; and market analysis, 222; and marketing plans/programs, 364–65; and marketing strategies, 222–23, 314–15; and model/spec houses, 134, 135, 136; and multifamily residential development, 222–29; and office development, 266–69; over Internet, 136, 223, 226, **227**, 267, 315, 380; positioning, 364; postconstruction, 364–65; and price, 224–25; to the public, 134–36; purpose of, 222; and retail development, 364–65; and sales, 132–33; and size of project, 133, 135–36; staffing for, 229; strategy, *63*. *See also* Leasing agents; Public relations agencies; Real estate brokers

Market research firms, 156, 159

Masonry construction, 253, 352, 353

Massachusetts: brownfields, 295; home rule state, 88; site acquisition process, 80. *See also specific cities and developments*

Materials, 253–54, *255*. *See also specific material*

Math, John, 229

Mattingly, Jim, 231

Maturity of development firm, 35

McAllister, Patrick, 242

McCarl, Brian, 10

McCaslin, Tom, 259

McCoy, Buzz, 375

McMansions, 124

Mechanical engineers, 48, 258, 354

Mechanic's liens, 48, 69

Merchandising, 136, 228, 267, 359–62

Merchant builders, 34

Metropolitan statistical areas (MSAs), 155

Mezzanine financing, 68–69, 208, 261–62

Michigan, 304

Microlocation, 160

Mid-rise buildings: apartments, 148, 149, 194, 223; office development, 240

Miller, Norm, 242

Miniperm loans, 66, 203

Minneapolis, **235**, **235–37**

Mixed-use development, 113, 384; busy streets in, 123; industrial development, 292, 295, 297; multifamily residential development, 166; office development, 239, 248

Mock-ups, 198

Model houses and rental units, 134, 135, 136, 223, 228

Mortgage bankers and brokers, 70

Mortgages: application package, **211**; industrial development, 308–9; multifamily residential development, 205–8; office development, 264. *See also* Permanent financing; *specific type of mortgage*

Motor vehicles. *See* Streets/roads; Traffic

Mow, Harry, 210–11, 212, 216

MSAs (metropolitan statistical areas), 155

Mueller, Glenn, 15

Multifamily residential development, 147–237; and absorption rates, 156, 157–58; and accessibility, 162; advice about, 151, **196**, **232**; and affordable housing, 148, 217–19; and aging population, 147, 150, 155; and amenities, 196–97; and approvals, 200–202; and closings, 209–10; and construction costs, 149–50; and construction financing, 202–5; and construction stage, 219–22; and costs, 233; cyclical nature of, 147; and design issues, 191–202; and discounted cash flow (DCF) analysis, *174–76*, 177–79, *178*; and easements, 164, 165; and environmental issues, 164; and equity, 202, 210–14; and exactions, 167–68; and exterior design, 197–98; and fees, 213–14; and financial crisis (2008–2009), 150, 167, 232–33; and financial feasibility, 168–91; and financing, 148, 202–19; and fire codes, 166, 195; and go/no-go decision, 191; and government programs, 217–19, 220–21; history, 148; and impact fees, 168; influences on, 147; and inspections, 220–21; in institutional property portfolios, 148, 205; and interest/interest rates, 147, 202–5, *203*; and interior design, 198–99; and investors, 214; and joint ventures, 188, *189*, 190, 210–17; and landscaping, 196–97; and leasing, 223–25; and liens, 204, 221; and maintenance, 193; and management, 219–20, 229–32; market analysis for, 151–59, 222; market demand for, 147; and marketing, 222–29; and model/spec units, 223, 228; and neighborhood, 160–61; and ownership, 148–49; and parking, 195–96; and permanent financing, 202–8; and pricing, 224–25; and private offerings, 214, 216–17; product types of, 148–50, **149**, **194**; and project feasibility, 151–91; and protective covenants, 141; and regulatory issues, 165–68; and rent, 233; and rent control, 166–67; and risk, 150, 209; scheduling of, 219–20; and site acquisition, 151; and site conditions, 162–64; and site planning, 195–97; and site selection, 159–68; and syndications, 210–17; and target market, 147–48; and tenants, 210; timeline for, *23, 29, 150*; and unit mix, 194–95; and visibility, 162; and zoning, 165–66

Multiple for release price, 128

Multiple jurisdictions and regulatory issues, 88

Multiple Listing Service, 77, 380

Multitenant industrial development, 286; design, 303; leasing, 316; market analysis, **290–91**

Municipal boundaries, 156

Munson, Mike, 259, 272

N

Nashville, Tennessee, **321–25**

National Asbestos Council, 54

National Association of Realtors, 64

National Environmental Policy Act, 51, 294

National Flood Insurance Act, 294

National Real Estate Compensation Survey, 2011, *37*

National Research Bureau (NRB), 341

Nature Conservancy, 386

Neely, Al, 89–90

Negotiated-price contracts, 131, 132

Negotiation of development agreements, 298

Neighborhood: and land development, 78, 80; of multifamily residential development, 160–61; preservation of sense of place, 384. *See also* Community groups/neighbors

Neighborhood revitalization. *See* Redevelopment/rehabilitation

Neighborhood shopping centers, 331, 348, 355, 357, 362; percentage rents, 362. *See also* Retail development

Net developable acreage, 97

Net leases, 268, 362

Net operating income (NOI), *170*, 172, 308; pro forma NOI, *170*, 172

Net present value, 177

Newsletters, 225, 267

Newspaper advertising, 223, 226, 227–28, 267

Newsum, Jeremy, **389–91**

New urbanist approach, 111, 113, 114, 123

New York City: condominium conversions, 167; office development, 249; regulatory issues in, 136

Niches, 17, 56, 151, 154, 314, 366

NIMBY, 388

NOI. *See* Net operating income

Noise and sound buffering, 123

Nollan v. California Coastal Commission (1987), 88

Nonprofit programs for multifamily residential development, 217–19

Noonan, Vicky, 246, 272

Nordstrom, 329–30

North American Wetlands Conservation Act, 163

Note rates, 205, *210*

"No-waste" clauses, 83

O

Occupancy/vacancy rates: calculating average occupancy rate, *172*; and discounted cash flow (DCF) analysis, 177, 178, 179; and industrial development, 288; and multifamily residential development, 156, 173, 231, 232; natural vacancy, 246; and office development, 246; stabilized vacancy, 246

Occupational Safety and Health Act, 294

O'Donnell, John, 36

Offer to purchase, 80, 81–82

Office development, 239–81; and absorption, 245, 246; and accessibility, 248; advice about, 247; approvals, 260; and budgets, 260, 269; and building codes, 242, 248–49, 259; and building shape, 249, 251; build-to-suit development, 240, 267; categorization of, 239–40, *241*; classes of, 239; and construction costs, 251; and construction financing, 262–63; corporate campuses, 243; corporate tenant with multiple location options, *24–25*; data for, 243, *244*; and design, 251–61; and elevators, 256; 11000 Equity Drive [Houston, Texas], case study, 272, **279–80**, **279–81**; and energy issues, 242, 249, 256, 258–59, 271; and equity, 264–66; exterior design, 253–54; and FAR (floor/area ratio), 248, 249; and financial crisis